The Shape of Sex

The Shape of Sex

Nonbinary Gender
from Genesis to
the Renaissance

Leah DeVun

Columbia University Press

New York

Columbia University Press wishes to express its appreciation for assistance given by the Rutgers University Research Council in the publication of this book.

Columbia University Press
Publishers Since 1893
New York   Chichester, West Sussex
cup.columbia.edu

Copyright © 2021 Columbia University Press
All rights reserved

Library of Congress Cataloging-in-Publication Data
Names: DeVun, Leah, author.
Title: The shape of sex : nonbinary gender from genesis to the renaissance / Leah DeVun.
Description: New York : Columbia University Press, [2021] |
Includes bibliographical references and index.
Identifiers: LCCN 2020030685 (print) | LCCN 2020030686 (ebook) |
ISBN 9780231195508 (hardback) | ISBN 9780231195515 (trade paperback) |
ISBN 9780231551366 (ebook)
Subjects: LCSH: Intersex people—Europe—History. | Sex—Europe—History. |
Gender nonconformity—Europe—History.
Classification: LCC HQ78.2.E85 D49 2021 (print) | LCC HQ78.2.E85 (ebook) |
DDC 306.76/85094—dc23
LC record available at https://lccn.loc.gov/2020030685
LC ebook record available at https://lccn.loc.gov/2020030686

Cover image: Alchemical "hermaphrodite." *Aurora consurgens*.
Zürich, Zentralbibliothek
Zürich, MS Rh. 172, front paste-down.
Photo: www.e-codices.ch.

For Macauley

Contents

Acknowledgments ix
List of Illustrations xiii

Introduction: Stories and Selves   1

1. The Perfect Sexes of Paradise   16

2. The Monstrous Races: Mapping the Borders of Sex   40

3. The Hyena's Unclean Sex: Beasts, Bestiaries, and Jewish Communities   70

4. Sex and Order in Natural Philosophy and Law   102

5. The Correction of Nature: Sex and the Science of Surgery   134

6. The Jesus Hermaphrodite: Alchemy in the Late Middle Ages and Early Renaissance   163

Conclusion: Tension and Tenses   201

Notes 209
Bibliography 269
Index 303

Acknowledgments

I couldn't write a book so concerned with the formation of the self in relation to a community without acknowledging my own community during these years of researching and writing. I've been fortunate enough to work in the company of wonderful colleagues all over the country, and I've benefited enormously from their teaching, scholarship, and companionship. It's a pleasure and a privilege to acknowledge in particular Rudy Bell, Alastair Bellany, Carlos Blanton, Daniel Bornstein, Walter Buenger, Lauren Clay, Anthony DiBattista, Carolyn Dinshaw, Mary Doyno, Ruth Evans, Paula Findlen, Marisa J. Fuentes, Jessica Goldberg, Karen Green, Monica H. Green, Leor Halevi, Anna Harrison, Sharon Holland, Tammy Ingram, Anna T. Jones, Jennifer Jones, Nick Jones, Katrina Karkazis, Samantha Kelly, Seth Koven, Greta LaFleur, Robert Lerner, Kathleen P. Long, Jim Masschaele, Lou Masur, Erica Milam, Pritipuspa Mishra, Robert Nye, Peggy McCracken, Robert Mills, Ramona Naddaff, Cary J. Nederman, Tara Nummedal, Robert A. Nye, Marcia Ochoa, Masha Raskolnikov, Steve Reinert, Elizabeth Reis, Matt Richardson, David Rollo, James Rosenheim, Mike Ryan, Johanna Schoen, Rebecca Schloss, Laura Smoller, Arlene Stein, Max Strassfeld, Susan Stryker, Paola Tartakoff, Marvin J. Taylor, Kyla Wazana Tompkins, Zeb Tortorici, Elly Truitt, and Laura Weigert for reading portions of this book, giving suggestions along the way, or encouraging my scholarly pursuits in general. I give special thanks to Katharine Park, Joan Cadden, Anna Kłosowska, and Asa S. Mittman for their generosity in giving me extensive feedback on earlier versions of this book (all mistakes are, of course, my own). I'd like to acknowledge all of my colleagues at both Texas A&M University and Rutgers University, and I'm grateful to have been a part of both universities while I worked on this book.

I also owe a debt to my labor union, the AAUP-AFT, and I wish to thank labor organizers and the labor movement in general, at Rutgers University and beyond.

I'd also like to acknowledge the work of the late historian John Boswell, whose *Christianity, Social Tolerance, and Homosexuality* was recommended to me when I was still an undergraduate by my professor, Robert Stacey. That book has long been an important work for me, showing how premodern history can continue to matter and move us even centuries later. I was lucky enough to study with other inspiring professors at both the University of Washington and Columbia University, including Robin Chapman Stacey, Mary O'Neil, R. Tracy McKenzie, Joel Kaye, Adam Kosto, and Robert Somerville, and I thank them for guiding me with their teaching and mentorship. Of all of my teachers over the years, I give special pride of place to Caroline Walker Bynum, a brilliant scholar who is also a generous teacher, tireless activist, and compassionate person. She's been a model for me for more than two decades, and I acknowledge her here with much gratitude and admiration.

Many institutions provided me with space, financial support, and intellectual community, and I thank the American Philosophical Society, the Texas A&M University Melbern G. Glasscock Center for Humanities Research, the Huntington Library, UCLA David Geffen School of Medicine, UCLA Center for Medieval and Renaissance Studies, USC-Huntington Early Modern Studies Institute, University of Texas Medical Branch at Galveston, the Rutgers Institute for Research on Women, Rutgers Center for Historical Analysis, and Rutgers University Research Council and Office of Research and Economic Development for their generous support. I also thank especially the Institute for Research in the Humanities at the University of Wisconsin, Madison, where I began work on this book, and where I was lucky to meet Richard Avramenko, Jill Casid, A. Finn Enke, Judy Houck, Michael Jay McClure, Katja Vehlow, Michael Velliquette, and Tehshik Yoon. I also thank the Stanford Humanities Center, where I spent a year as a faculty fellow and was able to enjoy the productive company of other fellows and faculty members, especially Georgia Cowart, Paula Findlen, Peggy Phelan, Gayle Rubin, Londa Schiebinger, Namwali Serpell, Debora L. Silverman, and Marilyn Yalom. I would also like to thank my colleagues who invited me to present my work at their universities and institutes, including Alex Baldassano, Brad Bouley, María Bullón-Fernández, Tina Chronopoulos, Sara Lipton, Glenn Burger, Steven F. Kruger, Chris Nygren, and Mary Fissell, who let me benefit from generative questions and helpful suggestions. I also thank my Rutgers University students, including my honors thesis students, and all of my graduate students, including Melissa Reynolds, Jesse Bayker, M. Dale Booth, Katy Gray, Hugo Marquez Soljancic, and Leo Valdes, and the new generation of emerging scholars at Rutgers and beyond, who've been pushing my thinking about gender, race, and sexuality, and who are the source of so many innovative and exciting ideas right now.

I give special thanks to the staffs of the libraries and archives that I visited, and I'd like to single out the staff at the New York Academy of Medicine for their helpfulness, as well as Rutgers University's Jim Niessen and Tom Glynn. I also thank Susan L'Engle, who sent me scans of an obscure manuscript from SLU's Knights of Columbus Vatican Library when I was in dire need. I thank Katie Jasper Benevento for assistance with my manuscripts and M. Dale Booth for help in securing permissions for the images published here.

I owe a huge debt to my parents, Gail and Esmond DeVun, who've given me endless love, support, and encouragement, and I give special acknowledgement to my late grandmother and great-grandmother, Lorraine Veazey and Therese Hebert, brilliant and creative women whose upbringing in rural Louisiana meant that—although their lives were long and rich—they were never able to realize the full promise of their talents. I continue to benefit from the support of my other family members, and I thank them here, especially Estelle DeVun, Stephanie Patton, Lauren DeVun Flanagan, Lindsay DeVun Pfefferle, Drew DeVun, Kendra Donald, and the Donald family. I thank my other ancestors too, both known and unknown. I also gratefully acknowledge the support of Katie Anania, Gwendolyn Beetham, Jess Bennett, Rebecca Bloom, Dante Brebner, Andy Campbell, Laura Campagna, Jasmine Cassata, Cassils, Liz Collins, Lainie Cosgrove, J Dellecave, Frank Discussion, Christine Doza, Jen and Tony Elias, Elena Favela, Aaron Flynn, Meghan Flynn, Jodi Frizzell, Greg Garry, Tamara Gayer, Erin Gentry, Aisling Hamrogue, Clarity Haynes, Karen Heagle, Kadin Henningsen, Riitta Ikonen, Liz Insogna, Tyler Lafreniere, Octavia Kohner, Isabelle Lumpkin, Sara Marcus, Derek Marks, Robert Marshall, Lynn McCabe, Tey Meadow, Bibiana Skraby Medkova, Andrea Merks, R.J. Messineo, Cristy Michel, K. Naca, Philip Nickel, Amanda Noa, M. Plaut, Shannon O'Malley, Janet Phelps, Kristin Poor, Laine Rettmer, L. J. Roberts, Nina Rubin, Nicole Russell, Sara Maria Salamone, John M. Sapp, Beth Schindler, Roy Scranton, Purvi Shah, Manjari Sharma, Bree Sharp, Lauryn Siegel, Elizabeth Steeby, Julia Steinmetz, Sarah Sudhoff, Gregg Sundin, Astria Suparak, Caitlin Rose Sweet, Anna Thomas, Vicky Tamaru, Jeanne Vaccaro, Wendy Vogel, Tobaron Waxman, Laura Leigh Williams, MW Wilson, and Megan Wright.

I'd like to express my gratitude to my editors and the team at Columbia University Press. I thank Wendy Lochner and Lowell Frye for their confidence in me and their enthusiastic nurture and promotion of my work. I also thank Marisa Lastres, Ben Kolstad, Marielle Poss, and Meredith Howard for their work on production and marketing, and David Lobenstine for additional help with editing.

I appreciate all the attention and care that the editorial, design, production, and marketing teams put into making this book a reality.

Finally, I thank my partner, Macauley DeVun, for so many things—for inspiring this work, for asking me questions, and for challenging my answers on many occasions. Our twenty-year-long relationship has made me the person that I am, and it has sharpened my conviction that history represents not only an antiquarian passion for manuscripts and illuminations (although I admit to that passion) but also an investment in creating narratives that give meaning to our identities and experiences now. Our partnership, as well as Macauley's personal experience as a trans nonbinary person, means that I have felt keenly the political and cultural challenges of our lifetimes, which have moved me to explore topics related to sex and gender in my historical work with special urgency. Our son, Saint Cyr, who was born around the time that I began this book, inspired me to think even harder about the nature of kinship and what we owe to both the past and the future.

Illustrations

Figure 0.1 Berengaria's story   2

Figure 1.1 "Hermaphrodite"   17

Figure 2.1 "Monstrous races"   41

Figure 2.2 Nonbinary-sexed figure   48

Figure 2.3 "Monstrous races"   50

Figure 2.4 Nonbinary-sexed figures   50

Figure 2.5 Blemmyes and epiphagi   51

Figure 2.6 Wild man and nonbinary-sexed figures   52

Figure 2.7 Janus and two doors   54

Figure 2.8 "Monstrous races"   60

Figure 3.1 Hyena   71

Figure 3.2 Manticore   75

Figure 3.3 Jews with burning bush and golden calf (Sermon of the Hyena)   78

Figure 3.4 Hyena   79

Figure 3.5 The Harrowing of Hell   88

Figure 3.6 Lucifer with Christ in majesty   90

Figure 3.7 Temptation of Christ   91

Figure 3.8 A devil burns Job's house   92

Figure 3.9 Allegory of the Redemption   93

Figure 3.10 Demons with *rouelle*   94

Figure 3.11 Satan with attendants   95

Figure 4.1 Copulating animals   103

Figure 4.2 Marginal figures   104

Figure 4.3 Marginal figures   105

Figure 4.4 Seven-celled uterus   114

Figure 6.1 Creation diagram   171

Figure 6.2 Alchemical "hermaphrodite"   173

Figure 6.3 Alchemical "hermaphrodite"   174

Figure 6.4 Hermaphroditus and Salmacis   176

Figure 6.5 Gemini   177

Figure 6.6 Gemini   178

Figure 6.7 Adam and Eve as Gemini   179

Figure 6.8 Creation of the world   180

Figure 6.9 Creation of Eve   181

Figure 6.10 Scenes from the creation   182

Figure 6.11 Creation of Eve   182

Figure 6.12 Hermaphroditus and Salmacis   184

Figure 6.13 Alchemical "hermaphrodite"   187

Figure 6.14 Crucifixion of Christ and creation of Eve   189

Figure 6.15 Androgynous wisdom   192

The Shape of Sex

Introduction

Stories and Selves

In the fall of 1331, in the Catalan town of Perelada, Guillem Castelló of Castelló d'Empúries petitioned a court to have his marriage annulled. His reasoning was simple: his wife, Berengaria, was unable to have sex. The result was anything but. To verify his claims, Guillem sought the expertise of a surgeon, Vesianus Pelegrini. After a thorough examination of Berengaria, the surgeon came to a startling conclusion. Berengaria, in his view, was not a woman at all. Instead, Berengaria had

> a male penis and testicles like a man, and she is so narrow that she can barely urinate through an opening that she has in a fissure that she has in the vulva, [which] lies beneath her penis. She has a flap stretched between her thighs like the wings of a bat, which covers the fissure in the vulva whenever she draws her knees toward her head. She has more the aspect of a man than a woman, and there is no way in which Guillem or any other man can lie with her, nor can she render her conjugal debt, nor conceive nor bear a child.[1]

According to Pelegrini's testimony, Berengaria possessed both traditionally masculine and feminine physical attributes. In modern language, Berengaria might now be called "sex variant" or "intersex."

Preserved in a manuscript now held in the Arxiu Històric Provincial in Girona, the summary of the case fills just one handwritten page (see fig. 0.1), yet it captures in detailed prose how an Iberian medical practitioner understood and described Berengaria's body. The record, however, betrays no interest in the

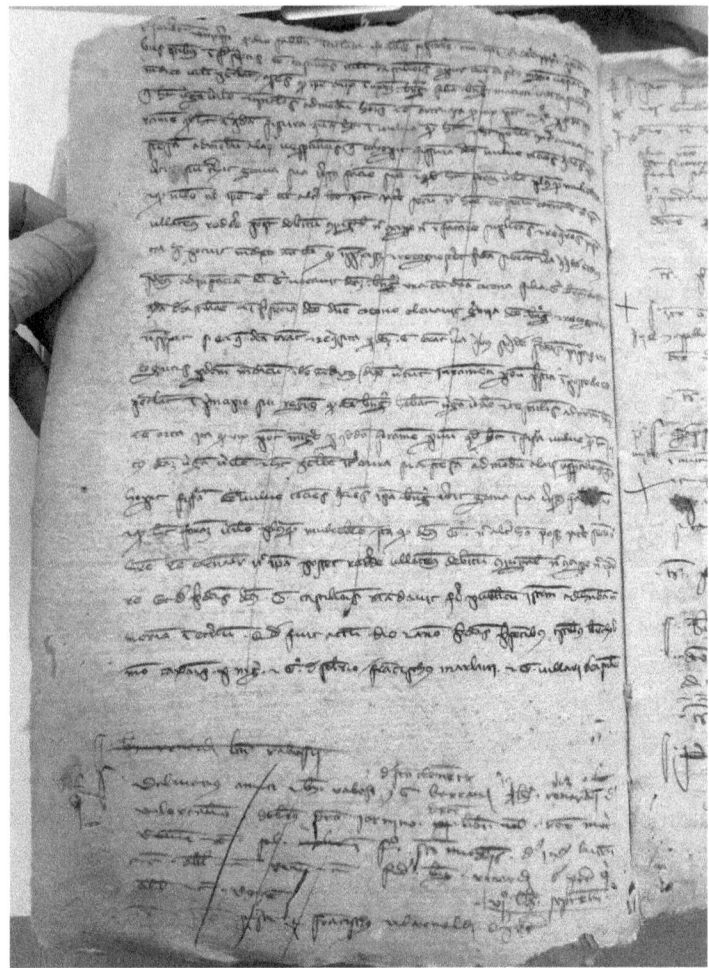

FIGURE 0.1 Berengaria's story. Girona, Arxiu Històric de Girona, Notaria de Peralada, 26 bis. *Llibre de Bernat Sunyer*, years 1331–32, fol. 52v.

consequences for the affected parties: for Berengaria and her* husband, for their extended families, or for their broader community. The brief account breaks off before we learn anything about what Berengaria had to say about her own body or about what the court ultimately ruled. We find no hint of Berengaria's

---

*. I use the pronouns she/her for Berengaria, in keeping with the only archival source in which Berengaria's story appears, and bearing in mind that we cannot know how Berengaria identified. I do not wish to impose further pronouns on Berengaria.

experiences growing up, nor anything regarding how, at a moment of crisis in her marriage, she reacted to news that her anatomy had "more the aspect of a man than a woman." The clarity of Berengaria's examination, in fact, lies in stark contrast to the opacity of the events that surrounded it. No documents have surfaced to amend these silences; we can only speculate as to what happened to Berengaria's marriage, as well as to her fate thereafter.

During the fourteenth century, marriage was a contract that required certain standards of behavior from partners. At that time, wives were responsible for familial tasks, including rendering the "conjugal debt"—that is, having sex with their husbands—and bearing and raising children.[2] Considering whether Berengaria could fulfill these duties, Pelegrini, who had practiced in the area for more than two decades, found that "[no] man can lie with her, nor can she ... conceive nor bear a child."[3] His testimony indicated that a capacity for sexual intercourse with a man, as well as an ability to bear heirs, were key to his—and the court's—definition of womanhood. During this same time period, as I explain later in this book, other surgeons went further, arguing that surgical operations could "correct" bodies like Berengaria's and return them to the "natural form" of a man or a woman.

In villages across northeastern Catalonia, lineages were closely intertwined, and residents were intimately familiar with the life stories and family histories of their neighbors.[4] Episcopal visitation records depict villagers as remarkably well-informed about the minutiae of their neighbors' private lives. In the nearby village of Vic in 1331–32, residents were sufficiently aware of one couple's marital problems to report to authorities that the pair completely lacked "carnal relations."[5] But marriage in the fourteenth century was rarely about just the two partners. It was often equally, if not more, valuable for their extended families, for whom marriage cemented alliances. In Iberian villages, a marriage was typically announced by a public ceremony, or by the reading of the banns (a formal declaration of a couple's intent to marry). As a result, Berengaria's neighbors would likely have known of her impending marriage; and just as important, they would have known of its ultimate failure.[6] We can imagine that news of Berengaria's case reached her village, providing fodder for gossip and, if Berengaria's anatomy wasn't already known, perhaps dampening her or her family's prospects.[7] While some marriages in the area were dissolved with relative ease, other breakups led to tension and animosity, with profound effects on the community. As the historian Michelle Armstrong-Partida observes, some spouses chose to leave a village after a breakup caused by infidelity or abandonment, rather than face what amounted in the fourteenth century to a "great scandal."[8] Rumors about Berengaria's case could have led to scandal, too, perhaps even causing Berengaria or her former husband to migrate, setting into motion other historical narratives that we can only imagine.

Beyond that, because Pelegrini described Berengaria's anatomy as predominantly male, it is possible that Berengaria later adopted a male legal status.[9] Chances are that Berengaria's case had momentous, and perhaps disastrous, effects.

Reading the extant record of Berengaria's life, we can see how the workings of the court—its inspections and classifications and processes—loom ever larger, while Berengaria herself shrinks, almost to the point of disappearing from view. What really happened—that is, whatever Berengaria truly felt or experienced— remains unknown. In this medieval version of what Marisa J. Fuentes calls a "palimpsest of material and meaning," we cannot find anything approximating a "voice" or a "subjectivity."[10] We can glimpse Berengaria's story only fleetingly, even as the archive limits the extent to which we can ever recover or historicize it. Though we know far more about Berengaria's anatomy than she ever likely would have wanted, we know nothing of her own perspective. We can offer little more than guesses as to what Berengaria was thinking.

The absence of Berengaria's own thoughts is especially poignant because in the Middle Ages thinking about nonbinary sex was a constant and long-lived pursuit. In discussions that ranged far beyond legal decisions and that appeared in an expansive range of texts, authors of all stripes—from judges to clerics to surgeons to poets—repeatedly embraced the idea of nonbinary-sexed figures they called "hermaphrodites" or "androgynes." During the late antique and medieval periods, such nonbinary figures appeared repeatedly as analytical tools that explained or defined the very nature of human identity. For the better part of a millennium, from 200–1400 CE, a host of thinkers—among them, theologians, cartographers, natural philosophers, lawyers, moralists, surgeons, and alchemists—identified nonbinary-sexed figures as embedded in, and able to shed light on, critical debates about sex, gender, species, and the nexus of embodied and cultural difference that we now call race. Even as actual individuals with atypical sex anatomies were rendered practically voiceless during the period, authors and artists spoke volumes about these topics through the concept of nonbinary sex. I trace their discussions across different genres of literature, looking carefully at how they explored human nature through images of hermaphrodites, androgynes, and other figures that lay outside the "binary division"—as one thirteenth-century thinker put it.[11] To be sure, such analyses took place on a different intellectual stage than did Berengaria's case before the Catalan court. And yet, these lofty considerations of sex and human nature reflected the very conditions of vulnerability that shaped Berengaria's fate.

Few of the thinkers featured in this study probably ever knowingly met what we now call an intersex person. Much of their "thinking with" hermaphroditism, androgyny, and other nonbinary ideas took place in the abstract and focused on types and concepts rather than on known individuals. But such abstract thinking had real-life consequences all the same. As I explain, when theorists used ideas about nonbinary sex to define "self" and "other"—whether to distinguish Christians from non-Christians, humans from nonhumans, or neighbors from foes—they radically shaped the fates of actual living people.[12] Speculative thinking about bodies and the ways in which those bodies are genuinely experienced cannot be entirely separated. In light of this entanglement, I shift back and forth in this book between *ideas about nonbinary sex* and *actual intersex individuals* (like Berengaria), showing how they interacted with and influenced each other.

This study bears witness to the considerable burden that sex- and gender-marginalized people shouldered in meaning-making and human-making in the history of premodern Europe. For over a thousand years, bodies that did not fit a sexual binary became a concentrated site of meaning where arguments about sex, gender, sexuality, animality, religiosity, and the nature of life on earth all played out. In such arguments, ideas about nonbinary sex provided an epistemological touchstone. Although intersex individuals were socially and textually marginalized, ideas about nonbinary sex were central to the fundamental categories that ordered the world. My book ranges widely across Christian European thought and society to explore how and why efforts to define human experience so often relied on ideas about nonbinary figures.

This book is therefore about language and fundamental ways of thinking—about how our ideas about sex and anatomy are never just about a physical act or about our physical bodies; instead, they are always ideas about what it means to be human and what it means to be a self in relation to other selves and to the world. I emphasize here the ways in which human identity in premodern Europe was wrapped up in—and worked out upon—the real or imagined properties of nonbinary sex, which gave rise to an exceptionally powerful concept. Ideas about nonbinary sex categories appeared in many areas of premodern thought because they were implicated in how thinkers imagined all kinds of diversity. And yet such ideas were also a special pressure point, allowing premodern authors—and allowing us today—to stop and think about how we think.

SEX AND SYSTEMS OF CLASSIFICATION

Classification always depends on boundaries, and boundaries always define who or what is included by deciding who or what is excluded. That is, we know what is inside a category by delineating what is outside it. Such delineations set up a binary—a pair of distinct qualities that oppose and support each other. But as soon as we imagine a binary, we tend to breach it in our thought, to imagine what lies between or beyond its contours.[13] We often, for instance, perceive black and white as a binary pair, yet once we think about their opposition, it is almost impossible not to also consider the shades of gray that exist between.

As I explain in this book, premodern thinkers embraced nonbinary sex as a part of their own classificatory systems in an effort to delineate boundaries and, often, to suggest how those boundaries might be crossed. Although "hermaphrodite" is now generally considered a derogatory term (as I explain below), in the premodern period, the word had linguistic roots that made it an especially apt tool for thinking about boundaries. "Hermaphrodite" carried with it a multilayered inheritance from classical antiquity: the term was a portmanteau of Hermes and Aphrodite, the deities who, in Greco-Roman mythology, gave birth to the bisexed god Hermaphroditus.[14] The name Hermes, moreover, derived its root from *herma*—the Latin word for boundary stone—an etymology that highlighted the boundary-marking and boundary-crossing ideas inherent in the term.[15] The concept of hermaphroditism made perhaps its most influential appearance in Ovid's first-century Latin poem *Metamorphoses*. In that text, a female water nymph named Salmacis attempts to seduce the youth Hermaphroditus at the site of her fountain. When Hermaphroditus, who is portrayed in the poem as male, rejects Salmacis's advances, she petitions the gods to join them forever. The result is a conjoined creature of both male and female parts: Hermaphroditus and Salmacis "were no longer two, nor such as to be called, one, woman, and one, man. They seemed neither, and yet both."[16] The legacy of this tale, which characterized hermaphroditism as a fusion, a negation, and a transformation of sexed categories, continued to reverberate throughout the ancient and medieval worlds, and it is a story I return to many times in this book.

In the Middle Ages, the term "hermaphrodite" gave expression to a wide variety of boundary-related notions, some of which resonate with our far more recent terms, "intersex" and "transgender" (more on those in a moment). Like those terms, "hermaphrodite" sometimes was used to describe an individual like Berengaria. But more frequently, a "hermaphrodite" was a concept that offered a highly flexible means to order the world. By drawing and crossing boundaries, the idea of a hermaphrodite enabled—and forced—communities to sort peoples, ideas, and situations into interrelated binaries and, moreover, to assign to them a positive or negative value. This idea could serve as a vector of fluidity and metamorphosis but also, at other times, as a hybrid that constricted and policed categories. These divergent paths allowed ideas about nonbinary sex to be used toward contrary ends: thinkers could emphasize the instability of premodern bodies through images of nonbinary-sexed figures, who (they believed) transgressed or made irrelevant dichotomous roles. Yet, at other times, nonbinary imagery served to tighten and enforce those boundaries.

This interplay between metamorphosis and hybridity, between flux and stasis, was the process by which ideas about nonbinary sex shaped what it meant to be human and, by extension, who could enjoy humanity's safeguards and privileges.[17] As I argue here, a full analysis of such ideas transforms our understanding of sex, gender, and human history. Ideas about nonbinary-sexed figures underpinned how writers imagined all sorts of categories: those of male and female—certainly—but also those of species and nature, and of belief and culture. What is more, when we analyze this history, I suggest we cannot help but reenvision our own categories, too.[18]

MODERN SCHOLARSHIP AND PREMODERN PERSPECTIVES

My perspective in this book is informed by much recent theorizing in queer, feminist, intersex, and transgender studies, in critical animal studies and posthuman studies, and in Black feminist and decolonial thought. Scholars in these fields have been pioneers in dismantling any easy separation of humans from nonhumans, foregrounding the role of sex and gender in defining humankind, and making clear how ontological categories are inflected by race and place. This book adopts certain frameworks and observations by those scholars, who (for the most part) study modern society and culture, but it also revises some of their chronologies and approaches. As we shall see, episodes from the distant past are often strikingly similar to our own current debates about sex, gender, and identity, and they expand our modern chronological view. Yet, in other ways, premodern categories are foreign to us, suggesting that sex and gender have starkly different meanings when viewed across time.

Up until the mid-twentieth century, "hermaphrodite" was a common term in medical and sexological literature used to describe variations in sexed characteristics that, as the scholar Iain Morland dryly observes, "some people find confusing."[19] During the late twentieth century, affected individuals begin to view "hermaphrodite" as an offensive and outdated term. For a new generation of thinkers, the word was misleading: it conjured up an individual who, like Ovid's mythic creature, had two complete sexes—a physiological impossibility. It also connoted sexual fetishes and fantasies that stigmatized individuals and negatively affected their experience of health care. A group of activists and scholars instead proposed "intersex" as the preferred term, and they began to describe intersex variations not as pathologies but as sources of identity and pride. Even more recently, many individuals have embraced the term "DSD" (an acronym for *disorders* or *differences of sex development*), signaling that they view—or at least find it beneficial to describe—their variations as disorders warranting medical attention, although others have rejected this nomenclature.[20]

Both intersex and DSD operate as umbrella terms for dozens of diagnoses, encompassing perceived ambiguities or disagreements among components of sex: internal sex organs, chromosomes, hormones, and external genitalia.[21] Some variations are apparent at birth, while others become obvious only at the time of puberty. Researchers estimate that one or two of every two thousand people possesses an intersex variation, a common-enough incidence that scholars and activists have suggested that multiple gradations of sex between male and female should be considered normal.[22] In general, in today's global north, when an infant with an intersex variation is born, doctors assign a male or female sex to that infant and, in many cases, they also perform surgeries or other medical interventions to make that infant's body look more like what they think a male or female person should look like.[23] Although activists have denounced cosmetic genital surgeries on intersex infants for decades, physicians have been slow to curtail them. In addition, because certain physicians have advised parents to keep their children's diagnoses secret from them, some people with intersex variations describe being unable to access or understand their own medical histories.[24] Some have experienced feelings of "dread and horror" stemming from unwanted or damaging treatments or from confusing exams. Some describe having never felt at home in their assigned sex.[25]

The surge in intersex studies of the 1990s and early 2000s grew out of a desire to address these ethical violations and the secrecy that surrounded them. Pioneering scholars and writers such as Bo Laurent (Cheryl Chase), Morgan Holmes, Iain Morland, Thea Hillman, Suzanne Kessler, Alice Dreger, Elizabeth Reis, David A. Rubin, and Katrina Karkazis, among others, have written important studies of intersex within different social and medical contexts, advocating for the health of affected individuals and their right to bodily autonomy (many of them writing from their own perspectives as people with intersex variations).[26] A number of scholars in this field have, in addition, grounded contemporary thinking about intersex within a larger historical framework, creating an expanded account of intersex and its treatment across time.

Scholars in transgender studies (also known as trans or trans* studies) have also been at work creating a broader history of transgender self-perceptions and practices. Their efforts date back to Leslie Feinberg's *Transgender Warriors*, a groundbreaking study that identified figures from the historical past as "transgender," that is, as individuals whose sense of gender identity or whose gender practices did not match the sex to which they were assigned at birth.[27] While Feinberg's initial effort, now more than twenty years old, has been criticized for anachronism, scholars and readers have also recognized the immense power of identifying historical ancestors. If anti-transgender sentiments now often rely on ideas about "traditional" gender (i.e., the assumption that transgender practices are new and historically unprecedented), transgender histories can offer a way for trans people to "arm themselves" against charges that "nobody like them ever existed before 1990 or so," as the scholar Alex Baldassano explains.[28] In their book *Transgender Studies Reader 2*, editors Susan Stryker and Aren Z. Aizura suggest that transgender history brings together "different methods for excavating pasts that certainly contained gender-variant cultural practices, without necessarily imposing the name 'transgender' on historical moments."[29] Transgender history, then, allows us to foreground different kinds of gender-crossings from the past, making them legible and meaningful to readers now. Such histories can foster a sense of connection between gender-crossing individuals across time, and they can make the existence of such communities in the future more imaginable.[30] They can also educate non-gender-marginalized people, enabling them to understand that diverse categories of sex and gender are significant, and that they cannot be left out of our standard histories.

Intersex people—that is, those born with bodies that are not considered typically male or female—and transgender people—in simple terms, those born with bodies that do not fit their gender identity or whose practices defy gender norms in some way—are distinct groups.[31] Most people with intersex variations do not identify as transgender (although some do). But the two communities have commonalities: above all, both groups argue that they should be allowed to live according to their own gender identities and to control what is done (or not done) to their bodies. They view these demands as a matter of human rights. Both groups face discrimination and, because certain intersex activists and scholars have aligned with the LGBT community, their political and intellectual movements are in certain respects linked.[32]

The interrelation of transgender and intersex is particularly important for my book because some of the gender-crossings attributed to "hermaphrodites" in premodern Europe more closely resemble what we now call "transgender" than what we now call "intersex." As a result, this study grounds its subjects in the history of both groups. Because it is the least pathologizing term and the one most often used in social science scholarship, I use "intersex" when referring to individuals with sex-variant bodies in the past, although "intersex," too, has its critics.³³ Intersex is a modern term, but it is analogous to, and hence descriptive of, a category of intermediate sex that some thinkers identified during the premodern period. I also use "transgender" as an analytical, rather than an identitarian term, to speak of past gender-crossing practices, as I explain in chapter 5. When discussing ideas and myths about sex and gender categories, however, I often retain the specific vocabulary of my primary sources: "hermaphrodite," "androgyne" (Greek for "man-woman"), and "neither" or "both" sexes.³⁴ I also consider a range of other bodies that fit uneasily into premodern male-female binaries, including asexuals, sodomites, eunuchs, castrates, impotent men, women with "enlarged" genitals, and others. I use "nonbinary" to encompass all of these ancient and medieval categories, although I am aware that many intersex and transgender people do not today identify as nonbinary. I am also aware that many people now view "hermaphrodite" as an offensive and retrograde term, rightly relegated to the dustbin of history in favor of less stigmatizing vocabulary. I hope readers will accept my use of it here as I engage critically with my primary sources. In the course of that engagement, I try to avoid reifying derogatory language and concepts while also remaining attentive to historical specificity.³⁵ Because ancient and medieval ideas about hermaphroditism and those about modern intersex or transgender are not precisely equivalent, the terms cannot always be used interchangeably, nor can we place all the subjects of this study into a teleological arc in which premodern categories eventually become what we now recognize as modern ones.³⁶ In some cases, to be sure, ancient and medieval ideas about sex and gender are very similar to, and even seem to anticipate, our own. In other cases, however, premodern ideas are starkly different: sometimes they are far more restrictive and derogatory than our current ones, but at other times they are more accepting and can present themselves in rich and imaginative ways. While similarities between past and present speak to the deep roots of our current assumptions about sex and gender, the many differences between them also unsettle those assumptions. Recent scholarship has already taken up this point, suggesting how earlier models of sex and gender might give voice to transgender, intersex, or queer identities in new and unexpected ways, both supporting and challenging the ways in which we talk about sex and gender today.³⁷

This relatively new dialogue between intersex studies, transgender studies, and premodern history does more than just show us that sex- and gender-variant people have a long presence in the historical record. It also opens up insights into the formation of classificatory systems themselves, the very structures that render certain anatomies and individuals "variant." Through historical analysis, we can document how hierarchical and oppositional modes of sex and gender come into being, rather than accepting them as natural, real, or immutable.³⁸ This mode of historical analysis is often called a "denaturalization" of sex and gender, and it follows the historian Joan W. Scott's famous observation that a fixed male-female binary reflects neither nature nor consensus but rather "overt contests" and "the refusal or repression of alternative possibilities."[39] Exploring such contests across time can persuade us to view with new skepticism the seemingly unambiguous categories of "male" and "female."[40] It can also help us to remember that societies in the distant past thought about sex and gender deeply and creatively, just as we do now.

NONBINARY SEX AT THE BEGINNING AND END OF TIME: A CHRONOLOGY

The chronological arc of this book is simple, even as the ideas are anything but: we find an embrace of the idea of nonbinary sex among authorities in early Christianity, its rejection at the turn of the thirteenth century, and a new enthusiasm for its novel and expanded properties at the dawn of the Renaissance. I begin my first chapter in the third century, but I move quickly to the European medieval period, which is the main focus of this book. Each chapter leads us through a different cluster of related texts, tracing the twists and turns of people who were thinking about—and through—the concept of nonbinary sex and exploring the often-vast ramifications of that thinking.[41]

In chapter 1, we find ancient and medieval Christians who hailed "androgyny" as a transcendent combination of male and female—the original condition of humanity, created by God and chronicled in the first chapters of the biblical book of Genesis. By this argument, Adam was made initially as an "androgyne" (or "man-woman")—a state of pure and primal undifferentiation and at odds with the divisive male and female sexes that followed thereafter. While a number of authorities rejected this opinion—often conflating androgynes with what they described as deviant and double-sexed "hermaphrodites"—a countertradition persisted, claiming nonbinary sex as a divine and human ideal. The distinctive relationship between Adam and Eve, moreover, set the stage for broader social structures of family, kingdom, and church; therefore, belief in a "primal androgyne" had the power to undermine society's foundational order. This chapter also considers the Christian theology of the resurrection, another fundamental doctrine that developed during the period, and one that held that all humans would reclaim their bodies at the end of time as they entered the afterlife. This chapter explores the ways in which theology defined human sex by considering which bodies were perfect enough to experience eternity.

If some early Christians believed androgyny to be a human ideal, shifting political currents eventually led to more ambivalent attitudes toward nonbinary sex. In the twelfth and thirteenth centuries, a heightening of religious tensions between Christians and Jews in northern Europe, as well as a worsening of prospects for crusaders in what Christians called the "holy land," prompted Christians to more adamantly distinguish and demote the "others" around them. Chapters 2 and 3 reveal two manifestations of this broader trend, discussing how authors portrayed hermaphrodites as both monsters and beasts in an effort to substantiate differences between Christians, Muslims, and Jews. In chapter 2, I begin with a "world map"—the English Hereford *mappamundi*—which invoked both nonbinary sex and the legend of the so-called "monstrous races" to comment upon the crusades. The map depicted a turbaned figure as a mythical, bilaterally split "hermaphrodite," drawing upon ancient and medieval myths to brand its subject as monstrous, sexually deviant, and dubiously human. Here and elsewhere, authors were concerned with characterizing geographic, religious, and racial "others" as different from Christians—and inferior to them—on the basis of both bodily and cultural traits. In that capacity, ideas about nonbinary sex actively shaped the reality of the period, suggesting which bodies could not fit within Christian territory and justifying violence that was all too real.

Chapter 3 continues this approach by looking at a virulently polemical image of a nonbinary-sexed hyena in the Aberdeen Bestiary, which served to dehumanize Jews, as well as to paint them as duplicitous agents of spiritual pollution. Such connections contributed to an ongoing campaign in thirteenth-century England to remove Jews from Christian society. The production of this and other similar images presaged or coincided with violent massacres of Jews in England, as well as the expulsion of Jewish communities from the region in 1290. Here again, I show how medieval Christians used images of nonbinary-sexed figures to substantiate divisions and to displace non-Christians elsewhere, outside the territorial and ritual bounds of Christian kingdoms. Once more, ideas about nonbinary sex played an important role in demarcating limits and demonizing religious and racial outsiders, and then removing them from Christian society.

Chapter 4 considers natural philosophers and legal theorists as they struggled to define which sexes were human ones. The thirteenth century saw an influx of naturalist ideas into Latin Europe from the classical Greek and Islamic worlds. Those texts offered new ways of systematizing distinctions between men and women, as well as between different kinds of creatures. Their appearance in Latin Europe shaped a new and foundational belief among some European naturalists that what we now call intersex—generally called "hermaphroditism" by medieval authors—did not exist in the human species. Beginning in the mid-thirteenth century, certain natural philosophers claimed male and female to be the only proper human sexes, a theoretical model that complemented their views that lower creatures such as plants and "imperfect" animals could express multiple sexes but that higher creatures such as humans came in just male and female types. As a result, intersex became for them a "monstrosity" rather than one of several natural possibilities of human sex, as previous medical models had imagined. In this chapter, I also examine the opinions of Roman and canon lawyers, who proposed a different way of dividing humanity into sexed categories but who also enforced male-female binaries in their approaches to inheritance, baptism, ordination, and other matters.

Chapter 5 confronts efforts not only to think about nonbinary sex in the abstract but also to alter the physical bodies of actual individuals. In Italy and France in the late thirteenth and early fourteenth centuries, surgeons devised ways of "correcting" atypical sex anatomies by surgically removing parts of people's bodies. These brutal surgeries, and the textbooks that justified them, reveal contradictory efforts to define sex by means of behavior, sexual desire, and physical shape. Chapters 4 and 5 demonstrate how considerations of nonbinary sex categories prompted authorities to define the human sexes, to place humanity within a larger natural order, and to manipulate their fellow humans to fit within that imagined order. Their conclusions led to new bodily ideals along with new roles for medicine to play in their regulation.

As my first five chapters demonstrate, writers and thinkers from the twelfth to the fourteenth century generally favored the erasure of nonbinary sex from both the human body and the broader community (although their arguments were never unidirectional nor monolithic). But as new theories about the body surfaced at the end of the period, so too did new ideas about sexual difference.[42] Even as actual people with sex-variant anatomies were steeped in a history that overwhelmingly viewed them as defective or atavistic, novel arguments in the fourteenth century began to exalt ideas about nonbinary sex as a path to utopic and forward-looking freedom. As chapter 6 shows, indebted to growing optimism about the possibility of metamorphosis, as well as to developing ideas about sex in medieval art and literature, fourteenth- and fifteenth-century authors proposed a new and ideal figure, the "alchemical hermaphrodite." This figure shared much with its antecedents, yet it also diverged from them sharply. This alchemical hermaphrodite was a transformative concept—as well as a chemical product—that could reportedly change other objects and people. As a figure of metamorphosis, the alchemical hermaphrodite suggested new ways of being in the world—and ones that went far beyond ordinary categories and divisions. Some alchemical authors even claimed that Jesus combined not only human and divine attributes but also masculine and feminine ones. This alchemical "Jesus hermaphrodite" possessed awesome powers of transmutation, purifying both bodies and spirits. Contemporary authors claimed that the emergence of the Jesus hermaphrodite was crucial because the apocalyptic end of time was near. While the early "Adam androgyne" represented early human society, the "Jesus hermaphrodite" assured humanity's ultimate salvation. These two figures, which flourished at the beginning and the end of the period I survey here, identified nonbinary sexes as the anchors of eschatological time: its origin and its final reconciliatory end.

It is not always clear what premodern history—so remote from us in time and intellectual context—has to offer to people now, who might crave both a usable past and a more radically transformative future. Yet because this history is so removed from us, I argue it has exceptional power. Where we do find resonances between past and present, we are reminded that our own current controversies are far from unique. And where the premodern period stands as a world completely apart, it testifies to the simple fact that dramatic change has happened, and that it is indeed still possible. When we perceive an earlier period in all its alterity and, further, when we see the profound shifts that occurred even within that period, we can see how new futures come into being—how, as Susan Stryker says, "The flesh can, at times, come to signify anew."[43] This book follows these new futures as they unfold in the distant past, demonstrating that our ordering of sex, gender, and embodiment in our own era "is not natural, inevitable, or eternal."[44] We might also consider how our own ordering shapes the questions we ask about the past—how we make the past, too, signify anew.

The book's title, *The Shape of Sex*, refers to the shape of the body, the focus of so much inquiry and contestation during the premodern period. Yet it also speaks to the ways in which bodily sex came to "shape" the ancient and medieval worlds, transforming their social, religious, and natural landscapes. It also, further, points to how sex still continues to shape our cultural views. The scholars M. W. Bychowski and Ruth Evans have recently and helpfully suggested that, with respect to nonbinary sex, we might move across temporal registers, acknowledging "the presence of the past in the now and of the now in the past," and noting how such dislocations can "disorien[t] claims over what genders exist when and where."[45] I devote this study to such sentiments. Premodern ideas about nonbinary sex—uniting fusions, mixtures, and negations; in the service of medical decisions, social and religious dilemmas, and cartographies of people and places—are all different from each other, and they are all different in certain respects from what we now call transgender or intersex. And yet, even as we acknowledge these differences between past and present—between categories, vocabularies, and imperatives—it is important to point out that, just as in the premodern era, our modern debates have at their heart who gets to be human.

To declare oneself "human" is to define what is "not human." Such articulations force us to contend with, or at least imagine, those who are not "us"—and to decide whether to assimilate or reject those outsiders. Each time we make these decisions, we define our relations with the world and with ourselves. It is through narrating these acts, we might say, that we write a story of our self. I document here a premodern story of self that entangled male and female, human and animal, and race and religion in ways familiar (inviting modern thinkers to consider an expanded timeline for our own modern exclusions) and unfamiliar (suggesting that those exclusions are not inevitable but the result of specific historical circumstances). *The Shape of Sex* tells a premodern story of self that enabled thinkers to define who they were, who they were not, and who was deserving of a livable life. If we look and read carefully, as I suggest here, this premodern story of self might prompt us to engage more effectively with our own humanity. It might help us to see more clearly how we write our own stories of self and other—of representation, symbol, and image—and it might illuminate how we piece together, both in the past and the future, the direction of historical change.

I
The Perfect Sexes of Paradise

In the late fourteenth century, an English clerk of the Exchequer, James le Palmer, devoted a chapter of his colossal, 1100-page encyclopedia, the *Omne bonum*, to "hermaphrodites," who seemed, as James put it, "neither man nor woman and . . . both man and woman."[1] *Omne bonum* offered summaries of topics of interest to contemporary readers, drawing its wide-ranging wisdom from legal, medical, theological, and mythological sources. In it, James asked whether or not "hermaphrodites" could claim descent from Adam, the first human. He answered in the affirmative, citing Augustine's *City of God*:

> Whoever is anywhere born a man, that is, a rational, mortal animal, no matter how unusual he is to our senses in his shape, color, movement, or sound, or in any natural power, part, or quality, no believer will doubt that he springs from that first-created man [Adam].[2]

A historiated initial illustrates the section: a praying figure, an amalgam of male and female profiles tucked inside a gilded letter "H" (see fig. 1.1). Adam, whose creation was described in the first chapters of the biblical book of Genesis, was also sometimes imagined as a bicephalic figure.[3] Double faces could signify duplicity in the Middle Ages, and the *Omne bonum* image could refer to Adam's disobedience and the fall into sin. But the illumination might hint at something else: at Adam's sexual duality.[4] According to Genesis, Adam's body contained within it the rib that formed Eve; for some readers, that meant that Adam's maleness was inherently joined with femaleness. Some went so far as to claim Adam himself as an "androgyne," or a "man-woman."

FIGURE 1.1 "Hermaphrodite." James le Palmer, *Omne bonum*. London, British Library, Royal MS 6 E VII/1, fol. 205r (c. 1360–1375).

Beginning in late antiquity, certain Christian theologians described Adam as sexually undifferentiated, a lost prototype of human nature that reflected divine innocence and simplicity at the beginning of time. This concept of "primal androgyny" entered Christian theology during the first decades of the third century, and I take that period as the starting point for this book. Although the idea of an androgynous Adam encountered deep skepticism from critics, at the beginning of Christianity and among its first proponents, a strong current embraced nonbinary sex as an ideal—that is, as a perfect union of male and female.[5] The first half of this chapter looks at ideas about "primal androgyny" as they appear in late antique and medieval commentaries on the biblical book of Genesis. As we shall see, tales about the creation of Adam and Eve staged a theological debate: Was sexual unity (androgyny) or sexual division (binary sex) the first and intended state of humanity? What sort of bodies existed at the beginning of time?

While some early theorists imagined sexual undifferentiation to be the original and most pristine state of humanity, authors in later centuries expressed more ambivalent attitudes. During the twelfth and thirteenth centuries, theologians conflated the primal androgyne with a corporeal, double-sexed "hermaphrodite," which they described in deeply negative terms. To this new wave of theologians, sex existed ideally as "diverse, divided, and distinct," that is, as only discrete male and female forms. According to this view, androgynes and hermaphrodites were a defective sex and an unfortunate devolution from natural and biblical perfection. Even further, certain thinkers began to connect androgynes and hermaphrodites to the crimes of sodomy, heresy, and murder.

The ancient and medieval controversy over primal androgyny is fairly well-known to scholars but less familiar are similar discussions that focused not just on the beginning of time but on its end, and not just on extraordinary figures such as Adam and Eve but on ordinary, rank-and-file Christians. The second half of this chapter examines how nonbinary sex fared in the theology of the resurrection. According to medieval Christian doctrine, at the conclusion of time, the dead would rise in a general resurrection, taking up their former bodies to face a final judgment. Theologians speculated that resurrected human bodies would be immortal, perfect, and free from all defects, much like the original, first-created body of Adam in paradise. In conversations about the resurrection, as in those about the creation, questions about "androgyny" or "hermaphroditism" surfaced repeatedly. Sexual difference became central to how theologians theorized human nature, and nonbinary sex, in particular, became a locus for thinking about the fundamental qualities of humankind.

Thus, the stakes were high for determining what God intended when he first created sex. For the Christian faithful, the distinction of the sexes and the sequential order of Adam and Eve's creation, as described in Genesis, legitimated the doctrines of both marriage and patriarchy. Moreover, because Christian thinkers drew correspondences between the subordination of women to men, on the one hand, and subjects to rulers, on the other, political authority depended at least in part on the precedent of Eve's inferiority. In addition, for certain authors, primal androgyny was about much more than an intellectual conceit. It was a way to refuse conventions of gender and kinship that ordered daily life. Debates about sexual difference thus represented efforts to work out critical issues regarding humanity's rightful shape, with profound consequences for how Christians viewed their bodies, their selves, and their places in a transcendent order. Along the way, sex—in both its binary and nonbinary forms—became a crucial component of the creation story, one of the best-known and most important narratives of European history, with far-reaching consequences for life in the Middle Ages and beyond.

BODIES AT THE BEGINNING

The biblical book of Genesis opens with what appear to be two different accounts of creation. The first, succinctly told in Genesis 1:27, says that God created Adam and Eve simultaneously: "And God created man to his own image: to the image of God he created him: male and female he created them." In a second, more detailed story, God created Adam from the slime of the earth before turning his attention to Eve, whom he shaped from Adam's rib (Genesis 2:7, 21–25). From the patristic texts of late antiquity to the hexaemeral traditions of the Middle Ages—and even today—Christians have looked to the opening chapters of Genesis as a record of the first days of human existence.[6] While modern biblical scholars have identified multiple scribal voices within Genesis, ancient and medieval readers believed the text to have only one author.[7] Apparent contradictions stemmed not from plural perspectives but from faulty human understanding, which could be addressed through careful exegesis (scholarly interpretation). The opening passages of Genesis were important in many respects but especially because they provided a theological and historical foundation for gender relations. Had man and woman emerged simultaneously and on equal footing, as God created *them*? Or was woman the inferior sex, ancillary to her mate and under his dominion? Was sexuality a positive, even indispensable, part of human nature, or was it a regrettable consequence of the fall? Genesis was so spare in its description of the events in question that scholars were left to scrutinize the text for clues to the nature of Adam and Eve and their legacy for later humans.[8]

As the historian Daniel Boyarin has shown, a late antique Jewish midrashic tradition imagined Adam as a fused physical body of male and female forms, with two faces and two sets of genitals. According to this tradition, Adam comprised both sexes until Eve was extracted from him, and the creation story in Genesis 2 described the splitting of that conjoined figure into two male and female halves:

> When the Holiness (Be it Blessed) created the first human, He created him androgynous, for it says, "Male and female he created them." R. Samuel the son of Nahman said: When the Holiness (Be it blessed) created the first human, He made it two-faced, then He sawed it and made a back for this one and a back for that one. They objected to him: but it says, "He took one of his ribs (*tsela'*)." He answered [that it means], "one of his sides," similarly to that which is written, "And the side (*tsela'*) of the tabernacle" [Exodus 26:20].[9]

The idea that the first human was two-sexed also had precedent in ancient Greek philosophy. It was attested to as early as Empedocles, and it appeared, famously, in a speech by Aristophanes in Plato's *Symposium*.[10] In that version of the tale, Zeus cleaved the first proto-humans, who were double-bodied and mostly androgynous, into distinct male and female forms. Scholars have suggested that the Platonic androgyne story drew from a widespread mythology of primal gender that also appeared in Zoroastrian, Sidonian, and other ancient traditions, and which imagined masculo-feminine entities that could self-procreate.[11] In some of these myths, the first humans were multiple-sexed, animalian, or doubled—with twinned or Janus-like heads. But ancient Greek versions of the primal androgyne had limited direct influence on Christian notions of creation: Plato's *Symposium* survives only in a few dozen medieval manuscripts, and it does not appear to have been widely read during the period.[12]

Greek myths of androgyny did, however, exercise power over the Greek-speaking Jewish philosopher Philo of Alexandria (20 BCE–40 CE), who proposed a spiritual interpretation of the biblical creation myth.[13] An influential commentator on the Torah, he attempted to reconcile the seeming conflict between the two Genesis stories by viewing them as two stages of a single process. Accordingly, the first human was a spiritual androgyne—pre-gendered and hence simultaneously *both* male and female and *neither* male nor female. Philo imagined this primal state not as inherently egalitarian but as a more masculine form of androgyny; the female component was more or less subsumed into the dominant male one. God later split this spiritual figure into two corporeal sexes, as narrated in the second story of creation.[14] Philo's writings were well respected by Christians, earning him the honorific "Philo the bishop" and placing him on par with the early Christian fathers.[15] His vision of sexual undifferentiation therefore came with a honorable pedigree, as well as a certain plausibility.[16] The division of a spiritual androgyne into two embodied sexes seemed to harmonize the incongruities of scripture, and it appealed to a Hellenized Jewish culture steeped in the precepts of Greek philosophy.[17]

During the same period, Christian Gnostic texts—early Christian teachings that purported to offer "secret" knowledge of God or Jesus—praised God as a union of paternal and maternal elements, one who spoke in both male and female voices.[18] Some of these texts drew on the creation story of Genesis 1:27 to portray God as androgynous, and at least one text claimed that Adam was "discovered to be two: a male-female being that bears the female within it."[19] Irenaeus, a second-century theologian who catalogued and refuted contemporary heresies, rejected the absurd (as he viewed it) Gnostic belief "that one human was formed after the image and likeness of God, masculo-feminine, and that this was the spiritual human; and that another was formed out of the earth."[20] Gnostic texts expressing such ideas were copied throughout the third and fourth centuries, suggesting they continued to generate both interest and debate.

During this same period, two influential Greek Christian fathers, Origen of Alexandria (c. 185–254) and Gregory of Nyssa (c. 335–395), adopted the theory of an androgynous, first-created human. Origen, a radical ascetic who worked in the Neo-Platonic tradition, interpreted the first creation story as describing a human who was both incorporeal and sexually undifferentiated. As he saw it, the second creation story described the infusion of an incorporeal soul into a body and, with it, the initiation of sexual difference.[21] In the following century, the bishop and theologian Gregory of Nyssa placed this theory more squarely within the context of the fall into sin. In his version, before the advent of sin, the first humans experienced a sort of "serene undifferentiation" in which sexual difference existed only in potential.[22] Adam and Eve were angelic androgynes, a lost prototype of human nature that reflected God's purity and simplicity and transcended the need for bodily distinctions. Adam and Eve's sin, however, prompted the activation of their latent anatomical sexes, dividing them into male and female types. As a result, binary sexes reflected the fallen condition of humans, who experienced only a greatly diminished version of their immortality through sexual reproduction.[23] For Gregory of Nyssa, the most elevated state of humanity was the *absence* of binary sex. Sexual difference, as he viewed it, was not an inherent part of human nature: God had placed a capacity for sex within humans because he knew they would fall. But humans had existed before differentiated sex, and they would exist after it. Gregory claimed that humans would regain their lost angelic state following the general resurrection at the end of time.[24]

For both Origen and Gregory, and others who accepted their view, the first humans were incorporeal and undifferentiated, with the ability to reproduce like the angels. Scholars have called this state "primal androgyny," although Origen and Gregory had in mind what we might call an "agender" or "asexual" state, not the physically doubled sex described by the *Symposium* and certain Jewish texts.[25] By Gregory's logic, this condition suspended biological processes: before the fall, humans exhibited the sort of stasis and immutability—that is, freedom from earthly cycles of "generation" and "corruption"—associated with heaven. Because angelic androgynes were not so much *both* sexes but an undifferentiated *neither*, they exhibited not a surplus of sex but a freedom from it that at least some patristic authors regarded with nostalgia.[26] The Christian fathers were perhaps moved by their own experiences of desire that seemed to arise uncontrollably from the flesh (Origen reputedly had himself castrated to escape such urges).[27] Whatever the reason, they claimed that the absence of bodily difference—and its release from sexual temptation—was the original condition for which humans were made. Rather than viewing nonbinary sex as especially linked to improper sexuality and sin, as later authors would do, Gregory of Nyssa suggested instead—in a rather radical claim—that it was expressed sexual difference, and not the simplicity of undifferentiated sex, that was "fallen."

AUGUSTINE OF HIPPO AND THE DUAL SEXES OF CREATION

If some early Christian fathers championed undifferentiated sex as the apex of human existence, exegetes in later centuries envisioned a very different kind of perfection. Key to this shift was Augustine of Hippo (354–430 CE), a foremost architect of Christian orthodoxy and the proponent of a much more optimistic view of sexuality than many of his predecessors. Augustine's theology was intensely focused on Genesis, upon which he commented in no fewer than six works.[28] He took up the question of Adam's sex multiple times, suggesting that it merited serious consideration.

In *The Literal Meaning of Genesis* (*De Genesi ad litteram*, 401–15), Augustine interpreted Genesis 1:27 to argue that Adam and Eve were not disembodied, angelic spirits. He rejected the idea, advanced by Origen and Gregory, that the first human was incorporeal and androgynous. Instead, Adam and Eve were male and female forms made of flesh, ideally suited for the physical joys of intercourse, parturition, and child rearing.[29] While theologians such as Gregory of Nyssa claimed that sexuality was part and parcel of the regrettable decline of humans from their original celestial nature, Augustine located sexuality in the bodies of humans from the first moment of creation. In paradise, he argued, humans could enjoy the whole panoply of physical acts made possible by complementary sexes (although they would have done so without the lust that corrupted sexuality thereafter). Humans, for Augustine, were always corporeal and heterogeneous, and sexuality was in no way at odds with the original innocence of Eden.

Augustine's argument was to some extent a result of the domestication of Christianity at the turn of the fifth century. As Christianity shifted from a subcultural movement at the fringes of society to the official religion of the Roman Empire, church leaders became increasingly sensitive to the needs of laypeople, whose lives were centered on issues of marriage and lineage. Authorities were also eager to moderate the extremity of certain Christian radicals who rejected sexual relations altogether.[30] Toward this end, Augustine emphasized the value of the flesh, which served to counter contemporary heresies, as well as to refute his colleague, Jerome, who delivered scathing attacks on marriage.[31] For Augustine, the creation of Adam and Eve provided a prophecy of Jesus's incarnation and an allegory for the church and the bond of marriage. His argument, in fact, shares much with early rabbinic explanations of marriage as a fulfillment of humanity's desire to return to its primal male-female union. For those authors, as for Augustine, marriage was a laudable institution whose roots were implanted in the very bodies of the first humans. And yet Augustine distanced himself from the rabbinic view that Adam was literally androgynous. He wrote: "Moreover, lest anyone suppose that this creation took place in such a way that both sexes appeared in one single human being (as happens in some births, in the case of what we call androgynes [*androgynos*]), the sacred writer shows that he used the singular number [i.e., *Male and female He made him*] because of the bond of unity between man and woman, and because woman was made from man."[32] Augustine wrote the scripture as "male and female He made *him*," but he made it clear that despite their bond of love, man and woman were never joined in a single physical body.

In another work, *On the Trinity* (*De trinitate*, 404), Augustine clarified the matter further, fearing that "something monstrous, as it were, should be understood [by this interpretation], just as are those whom they call hermaphrodites [*hermaphroditos*]."[33] And yet Augustine allowed that "in this case the singular number could also be correctly understood of both, because of what was said 'two in one flesh.'"[34] In this passage, Augustine alluded to Paul's letter to the Corinthians (11:7), in which the creation story functioned as a parable for marriage. The primeval relationship of Adam and Eve, he claimed, should be understood as an expression of marital concord between man and woman, Christ and church, and heaven and earth—the final unity that beckoned on the eschatological horizon.[35]

Augustine, however, recognized the possibility of a junction of male and female qualities within an individual body in certain respects. In *The Literal Meaning of Genesis*, he proposed a theory of human psychology in which human traits were categorized into male-female binaries:

> There is, of course, the subtle theory that the human mind that, being a form of rational life and precisely the part in which he is made to the image of God, is partly occupied with the contemplation of eternal truth and partly with the administration of temporal things, and thus it is made, in a sense, masculine and feminine, the masculine part as the planner, the feminine as the one that obeys. But it is not in this double function that the image of God is found, but rather in that part which is devoted to the contemplation of immutable truth.[36]

Augustine introduced in this passage a series of oppositions and hierarchies—timelessness and temporality, contemplation and administration, mastery and servitude. For Augustine, the inferior of each pair was feminine, just as Eve was the helpmeet to Adam, and yet all were collapsed into a single divine image. Augustine's classifications are complex: he subdivides the masculine-inflected rational mind into a further male-female binary. But Augustine's characterization of a single human being in terms of binary-sexed qualities also suggested that masculine and feminine principles were inherent in each individual. Later thinkers would adopt this notion to make a very different claim about sex in later centuries, one that idealized the unification of male spirit and female flesh into a bi-sexed figure, which gave rise to the "Jesus hermaphrodite," as I explain later in this book.

Augustine was keen to reject both the incorporeal androgyne of the Greek tradition and the corporeal androgyne of the rabbinic tradition.[37] In using the terms *androgynos* (androgynes) and *hermaphroditos* (hermaphrodites), Augustine may have signaled his opposition to both theories. Yet Augustine also appeared to envision an androgyne in purely physical terms, as a body with both male and female attributes ("as happens in some births"), and with a supposed superfluity of sex rather than its absence. This interpretation is further supported by Augustine's remarks in *City of God*, in which he uses "androgyne" and "hermaphrodite" as synonyms, writing that "androgynes" (*Androgyni*) are also called "hermaphrodites" (*Hermaphroditi*).[38] In any case, subsequent theologians tended to adopt Augustine's terminology, identifying "androgyny" with "hermaphroditism." The two concepts were to remain linked for the rest of the period, although authors used them in different ways.

We might find it curious that Augustine would set down in writing so many clarifications of the sexes of Adam and Eve. But we can also see how much depended on a clear rejection of the primal androgyne. Few narratives were more familiar to medieval Christians than the creation story. For many, the distinctions enacted by Adam and Eve legitimated the doctrine of marriage and, with it, the entire edifice of patriarchal rule (although Origen and others who rejected what was to become the orthodox view of creation were hardly gender egalitarians).[39] Nevertheless, because medieval theorists often imagined correspondences between the microcosm of the family and the macrocosm of the kingdom, the origins of subordination in Genesis underpinned political rule writ large.[40] Augustine's writings on the primal androgyne were concerned with the materiality of the first bodies and the ways in which women participated in the divine image—in response to current debates about marriage, virginity, and the essential goodness of the human body—but his arguments shaped long-lived ideas about both sex and power. According to Augustine's view, God fashioned Adam and Eve as resolutely male and female, and only men and women fit the biblical definition of human perfection. And yet, his writings hinted that some aspects of sexual difference lay outside of rigid binaries.

THE PRIMAL ANDROGYNE EMBRACED

Even as Augustine denounced it, the idea of the primal androgyne continued to exercise a certain influence: in fact, a countertradition of texts and images persisted from earliest Christianity to the thirteenth century that idealized androgyny and envisioned a masculo-feminine Adam. Despite repeated efforts at suppression, androgyny and the creation remained firmly connected in the minds of certain Christian thinkers.

Ideas about sexual egalitarianism and the creation story proved compelling, for instance, among the mixed-sex intellectual circle surrounding Priscillian, a late fourth-century bishop of Avila and a contemporary of Augustine.[41] After some of the group's leaders were executed, the survivors produced a set of writings known as the Priscillianist *tractates* to defend themselves from charges of heresy. The Priscillianists promoted gender-egalitarian ideals and called upon Genesis 1:27 for textual support. The historian Felice Lifshitz argues that the Priscillianists' doctrines were likely interpreted as expressing belief in a masculo-feminine God, a stance that led to further persecution by authorities.[42] Such notions were hard to suppress, however, and the Priscillianist *tractates* eventually found their way to the eighth-century Rhine Valley of Francia and an aristocratic community of monastic women. This same network of women also had access to a copy of the *Apocryphal Acts of the Apostles*, written for female spiritual communities in the late second or early third century and containing egalitarian rhetoric, as well as descriptions of an androgynous God. These topics were still relevant and volatile enough in the eighth century to stir controversy, if the *Admonitio generalis* of 789—which ruled that such texts be burned—is any indication.[43]

Just a few decades later, the ninth-century Irish philosopher and theologian John Scottus Eriugena revived a version of the primal androgyne in his treatise the *Periphyseon* (also known as *On the Division of Nature [De divisione naturae]*, c. 860s). Building on the Greek and Latin fathers, and especially on Origen and Gregory of Nyssa, John described the original state of humanity before the fall as one that transcended the polarizing categories of male and female. In the text, John offered an idiosyncratic retelling of the creation story: he explained that while Adam was still alone in paradise, he experienced a sexual fantasy in his sleep. The transgression constituted the fall from grace and led to the creation of Eve. John described the event from God's point of view:

> Man, whom we made to our image and likeness, does not think it good to be alone (that is, simple and perfect), altogether and permanently without the division of his nature into sexes, being wholly in the likeness of the angelic nature, but prefers to tumble headlong into earthly coitus like the beasts. . . . Let us therefore make for him a companion like unto him, through whom he can perform what he longs to do, that is to say, with a woman who is fragile and unstable like the male, and is eager for earthly lusts.[44]

This transgression, John argued, introduced sexual division into the world, alienating humanity from its singular, undifferentiated nature, and joining it to the irrational world of beasts.[45] If humans had never sinned, John claimed, they would have retained their sexless forms and multiplied like angels, rather than through the sexual congress common among animals. Sexual reproduction was not a human necessity, John argued; it derived from Adam's sin, and division and heterogeneity were a part of the fallen, corrupt nature of this world.

This vision of primal unity was apparently compelling enough that it inspired writers even centuries later. In the first quarter of the twelfth century, the monk Honorius of Autun borrowed from John's *Periphyseon* to advocate for a similarly sexless view of the creation in his *Clavis physicae*.[46] Around the same time, the Benedictine historian Guibert of Nogent's *Moral Commentary on Genesis* described Adam as undivided before the fall into sin. Guibert's choice of vocabulary was strikingly reminiscent of early Christian conceptions of unity and the primal androgyne. Although he was careful to state that sexual diversity was original to humanity, for Guibert, male and female were also intertwined in the first creation.[47] Apparently, seven centuries after Augustine's refutation, the promise of an undivided human still exercised a certain power.

THE PRIMAL ANDROGYNE REJECTED (AGAIN)

In fact, other writers were wrestling with the problem of the primal androgyne soon after thanks to the reinvigorated exegetical tradition of the twelfth-century revival of learning. Interpretive innovation regarding Genesis had fallen out of favor for much of the early Middle Ages, and authors generally quoted from earlier works without too much elaboration. But with the "twelfth-century renaissance" in full swing, rigorous exegesis resurfaced once more, as did new interpretations of the creation story in a variety of contexts.[48] Such texts tended to adopt Augustine's language linking androgyny to "hermaphroditism," which authors now viewed as a physically doubled—and undesirable—sex.

The *Glossa ordinaria*, for instance, the standard commentary on the Bible for much of the Middle Ages, includes a brief rejection of the primal androgyne, arguing, "Lest it be thought that both sexes were in one human, like those they call hermaphrodites, [the scripture] explains several times, '[God] created them,' [and] although woman had not yet been divided from man, she was materially pre-begotten."[49] Drawing from Augustine, the gloss preserved the oneness of human creation that so inspired early Jewish and Christian interpreters. Yet, according to its argument, Eve was already "pre-begotten"—that is, she was conceived with Adam in anticipation of her later material creation in time. The plural "them" of the passage, then, referred to both Adam and Eve rather than to two sexes within a single undifferentiated human. Andrew of St. Victor (d. 1175), a canon at the abbey of St. Victor in Paris and one of the influential "Victorines," adopted this approach, too, rejecting the primal androgyne on the grounds that Eve had participated in the first creation, if only in potential.[50]

Other theologians also denied the existence of an androgynous creation. In about 1170 the Parisian theologian Peter Comestor addressed the problem in his influential *Scholastic History*. Like Andrew of St. Victor, to whom he was indebted, Peter disapproved the primal androgyne theory, arguing, "Truly, God created them man and woman. . . . it says 'them' in the plural, however, lest we think that that they were made as androgynes or hermaphrodites."[51] He specified that God made *them*, male and female, but he avoided any sustained reconciliation of the two accounts of creation in Genesis. As the historian Constance Brittain Bouchard notes, contemporary glossators tended to avoid a logical account for differences between the two Genesis stories (and hence for the sex of Adam), instead rejecting the primal androgyne out of hand without clear explanation.[52] While Christian theologians debated Jewish experts on the Bible in public disputes, and those who read the Talmud and midrashic texts were likely aware of diverse ideas about sex and creation, they did not engage in any serious textual criticism of the original Hebrew on Adam and Eve until the second quarter of the fourteenth century.[53]

The Spanish archbishop Rodrigo Jiménez de Rada (c. 1170–1247), who studied at the University of Paris in the early 1200s, offered a slightly different analysis of the androgyne problem in his work. Rodrigo observed in his *Breviary in Catholic History* that "some say that the pronoun 'him' should not be taken as one but as two, as if collectively, and therefore it is rightly made in relation to the plural; or [it is] placed first in the singular and after in the plural, lest one hermaphroditic human, that is, one divided in love or in sex, were imagined."[54] His wording suggested that it was "hermaphrodites," and not binary sexes, that were "divided." This division extended not only to anatomy but to *love*, that is, emotional or sexual desire, an element that was to take on a more sinister meaning in subsequent commentaries, some of which now imagined the primal androgyne as a sinful sodomite.

ANDROGYNES, SODOMY, AND HERESY

Indeed, at the turn of the thirteenth century, certain authors began to equate androgynes and hermaphrodites with sexual deviants who provoked the judgment of God. Peter the Chanter (d. 1197), a master of theology in Paris and the author of a gloss on Genesis, provided perhaps the most striking rhetoric connecting the primal androgyne and sodomy:

> It says 'God created man,' not only one man, but two, nor just in one sex, but in both, since *male and female he created them*, not as androgynes, that is, not as hermaphrodites who have the instrument of a man and woman at the same time. Therefore, it says [it] in several places, in order to prevent a sodomite man from claiming that he could abuse a man in place of a woman, as if a man had both instruments.[55]

Peter assumed that androgynes, conflated here with dual-sexed "hermaphrodites," had "both instruments," that is, both male and female sexual organs, which led them to commit sodomitic acts. Peter made a similar claim in another text, his *Verbum adbreviatum* (c. 1190s), which also drew upon the Genesis story to reject sodomy and the primal androgyne theory. "Lest any should believe they [Adam and Eve] to have been androgynes," Peter claimed, the scripture says, "'Male and female he created them,' as if to say, 'There was not any intercourse of men with men or women with women, but only of men with women and vice versa.'"[56] For this reason, Peter added, church law in his own time required a living intersex person—here called an "androgyne"—to choose either an active male role (that is, the role of a sexual penetrator in sexual intercourse) or a passive female one (that is, the person who was sexually penetrated), and to marry accordingly. According to this argument, such a person must perform sexually as either male (active) or female (passive) —but never as both—in order to avoid any inversion of sexual roles.[57] Peter continued, saying, "If however, [an androgyne] should fail with one organ, the use of the other can never be permitted, but the person must be perpetually celibate so that the terrible sin [of sodomy] is extirpated."[58] Alternations of sexual roles were strictly forbidden, and Peter included the shocking charge that sodomy was comparable in its gravity to murder. Again, androgyny was elided with "hermaphroditism"—here indicating an intersex person—and both terms were associated with a transgression of "male" (active) and "female" (passive) sexual roles.

As the art historian Robert Mills has suggested, scholastic thinkers in thirteenth-century France—where many of these commentators were based—were engaged in intense debate over sodomy's intellectual and moral dimensions. Churchmen imagined sodomy not so much as a particular genital sex act but as a transgression of prescribed gendered roles.[59] Singled out for special censure was any inversion of position, as, for instance, when a man took on a passive, "feminine" role or when a woman took on an active, "masculine" one.[60] Perhaps even more disturbing was the prospect that one person might switch roles during a single sexual liaison, a behavior that at least one author regarded as "hermaphroditic."[61] As a result, sodomy drew some of its stigma from its supposed reversals of gender, which were comparable to hermaphroditism, even as hermaphroditism was stigmatized by its association with sodomy.[62]

Peter the Chanter's *Verbum adbreviatum* indeed reflected concerns about sodomy and gender inversion that were emerging in the thirteenth century. Despite (or perhaps because of) its hyperbolic tone, Peter's connection between "hermaphroditism" and sodomy proved influential, and further equations of the two soon followed. The argument was repeated by Stephen Langton and Nicholas of Tournai, and the Dominican master Hugh of Saint-Cher (c. 1200–1263) vehemently denied that Adam was a "hermaphrodite," warning that God in the creation story "names the two sexes separately, and [he] distinctly damns the sodomitical vice."[63]

Around this same time, another important development was further shaping views of the primal androgyne. By the late twelfth century, churchmen increasingly worried about a diverse group of heretics who later came to be known as the "Albigensians" or "Cathars."[64] While the Cathar heresy seems in retrospect to have been more a product of church paranoia than any cohesive sect or doctrine, Christian polemicists accused Cathar heretics of dualist doctrines denigrating material embodiment and erasing divisions of sex and gender. According to inquisitorial testimony, some heretics apparently believed that the devil had lured humans, who were originally celestial or angelic spirits, into corporeal "tunics" of skin, a crude existence that could be escaped only through a heretical rite called the *consolamentum*, which released humans from endless cycles of mortal reincarnation and returned them to their noncorporeal, angelic forms.[65] Such an argument, of course, could imply that humans were originally incorporeal—an echo of the primal androgyne theory. Cathars were believed to reject the inherent goodness of the human body: they saw the flesh as inherently demonic, and they envisioned a future freed from bodily sex.[66]

Around the same time, a different heretical group, the Amauricians (named for their leader Amalric of Bena), allegedly made a similar set of claims. Amalric, possibly influenced by John Scottus Eriugena, was reported to believe that "if man had not sinned he would not have been divided into the twofold sexes." In addition, at the end of time, he argued, "There will be a union of the sexes, or there will be no distinction of sex." These positions were strongly condemned at a Paris synod in 1210, and the threat of heresy cast a heavy pall of suspicion over the primal androgyne theory.[67] The bishop and jurist Hostiensis, who wrote about Amalric's case, singled out such belief as a serious doctrinal threat.[68] In both doctrine and practice, church authorities and their supporters increasingly prioritized the body as a fundamental part of human perfection, and they viewed androgyny as unacceptable—now for two reasons. If primal androgyny was corporeal, then it was connected to the supposed physical and sexual excess of "hermaphroditism." And if it was incorporeal, then it smacked of the beliefs of Cathars, Amauricians, and other suspected heretics.

With the arrival of new Aristotelian and Islamic naturalist texts early in the thirteenth century, particularly the translation from Arabic into Latin of Aristotle's *On the Generation of Animals* by mathematician and scholar Michael Scot, theologians had a new body of theory on which to base their refutations. The story of Aristotelian natural philosophy unfolds, for the most part, in chapter 4 of this book, which looks at naturalist theories of sexual difference in detail. Suffice it to say that scholastic theologians could now situate their arguments in the systematic language of medieval biology. The preeminent scholastic philosopher and theologian Albert the Great (Albertus Magnus) (1200–1280), for instance, cited the zoological writings of Aristotle to dismiss the prospect of Adam's androgyny and asexuality at the time of creation. Albert rejected the primal androgyne on the basis of naturalist ideas about reproduction, an approach that was also taken up by Nicholas of Lyra's *Postilla*, which denied that God would have given Adam, his most perfect creation, the form of a "monster."[69]

Albert's most famous student, the theologian Thomas Aquinas, argued from a different standpoint, but he too rejected the primal androgyne theory. As he explained in his *Summa theologiae* (1260–70s), the text of the Bible—"male and female he created them"—was rendered in the plural precisely "so that it not be thought that both sexes were conjoined in a single individual."[70] Aquinas argued that two distinct sexes had always existed, even in the prelapsarian paradise of Eden. God established both male and female sexes as essential parts of human nature before the fall, and "just as variety in the grading of things contributes to the perfection of the universe, so variety of sex makes for the perfection of human nature."[71] Aquinas inverted the logic that had once privileged the singularity of androgyny over the divisiveness of binary sex. Drawing on longstanding arguments that lauded the diversity of the macrocosm as a wondrous expression of God's creativity, Aquinas praised the diversity of sexes—that is, two sexes—within the microcosm of humanity.[72] Sexual heterogeneity, by this argument, was not a deviation from pure and original oneness. It was the root of perfection itself. The *Ordinary Reading on the Sacred Scripture* (*Lectura ordinaria super sacram scripturam*, 1275–76, attributed to the Parisian theologian Henry of Ghent), seemed to approve this view, claiming that Adam and Eve were created not as "one hermaphrodite" but as two "diverse, divided, and distinct" sexes.[73]

At this point, we should pause to observe the dramatic shift in the fates of the primal androgyne. At the beginning of the period, theologians claimed that undifferentiated sex—angelic and incorporeal—was the most desirable configuration of human sex on earth. For them, androgyny epitomized the perfect and original state of humanity that preceded the fall. Even theologians who stopped short of belief in a primal androgyne nevertheless praised oneness over division. As Jerome observed in his *Against Jovinianus*, the oft-repeated phrase "And God saw that it was good" was absent from Genesis's description of the second day of creation. That lapse, for Jerome, signaled that God was not entirely satisfied, "leaving us to understand that two is not a good number because it destroys unity."[74]

And yet in stark contrast, by the end of the Middle Ages, theologians could claim that androgyny, now often equated with "hermaphroditism," was fallen, even damnable—linked to the crimes of sodomy and heresy. Division was, by this argument, superior to primal singularity, and androgyny's sense of angelic transcendence was lost. Nonbinary sex disappeared from the narrative of biblical creation to uphold the dyadic relationship between man and woman, spirit and body, church and adherent. Such a genealogy assured Christians that their society stemmed, not from an accident of history, but from the will of God, as it was implanted in the very flesh of humanity. Much then rested on the fates of the primal androgyne.

NONBINARY SEX AT THE END

Questions about sexual difference emerged in the context of debates not only about the creation of humanity but also about its resurrection, a similarly complex belief that prompted similarly spirited debates. I am not, of course, the first to notice the significance of the sexed body to the theology of the resurrection. As the historian Caroline Walker Bynum has shown in her pioneering work, the resurrection surfaced as a central theme in Christian theology as early as the second century CE, with important ramifications both for the trajectory of the faith and contemporary views of sex and gender.[75] More recently, scholars have focused on how the doctrine of resurrection interacted with notions of sexual desire and sexual difference, as well as what it meant for understanding the medieval disabled body.[76]

As Bynum has shown, late antique and medieval thinkers engaged in vigorous debates about exactly what kind of body would be resurrected at the end of time: Would it be old or young? Tall or short? Male or female? A number of theologians seized on the latter question in particular, wondering whether humans would retain in death the sexes they had possessed in life. Biblical passages such as Romans 8:29 and Ephesians 4:13, as well as certain early Christian texts, could be read to suggest that women would be changed into men to better conform to the image of Christ.[77] In addition, some theologians viewed salvation as a process of reconciling all opposites, including opposite sexes. As St. Paul had famously claimed in Galatians 3:28, in Christ "there is neither Jew nor Greek: there is neither bond nor free: there is neither male nor female. For you are all one in Christ Jesus." Some writers ventured, as a result, that post-resurrection bodies would be without sexual difference: certain theologians imagined humans would rise in the end like androgynous angels, without any sexual attributes at all.[78] Gregory of Nyssa once more provides an example: he argued that humans would regain their lost state of sexual undifferentiation at the end of time.[79] Such conclusions revealed how ideas about prelapsarian and post-resurrection androgyny were entangled in the minds of certain early Christians. They suggested that sexual difference was a temporary aspect of earthly existence and not an essential part of human nature.

Sentiments along these same lines appeared again in John Scottus Eriugena's ninth-century tract, the *Periphyseon*. As we have already seen, John described the state of humanity before sin as one that transcended the polarizing categories of male and female. He also claimed that humans would one day return to this state of undifferentiated sex, which he considered the lost apogee of human existence.⁸⁰ Jesus had sloughed off biological sex at the time of his resurrection, John argued, and humans would undergo a similar transformation:

> When rising, [Christ] had no sex; although to confirm the faith of His disciples, after the resurrection He appeared to them in the masculine form.... But none of the faithful may believe or think in any sense that He was held fast by sex after the resurrection, "For in Jesus Christ there is neither male nor female," but only the true and whole man, I mean body, soul, and intellect, without sex or comprehensible form.... The humanity of Christ, made one with deity, is contained in no place, moved in no time, circumscribed by no form or sex because it is exalted above all these things.... What He fulfilled particularly in Himself, He will fulfill generally in human nature as a whole at the time of resurrection.⁸¹

For John, the state of being after death and resurrection eliminated any base categorizations of sex that constrained earthly bodies. Just as Christ had dispensed with sex upon death, humans would follow his example. After the resurrection, Christ would "unit[e] man by mystically removing and transforming to spirit the distinction into male and female," drawing all humans into the sexless glory of angels, and dissolving the barrier between heaven and earth.⁸²

Although John's ideas continued to find supporters, by the twelfth and thirteenth centuries, the majority of Christian theologians rejected the view that resurrected persons were sexless or androgynous, instead favoring claims by Tertullian, Jerome, and others that the resurrected body would be fundamentally the same as the one that had lived, with all its structures and idiosyncrasies, including its genitals (although not its sexual desires and practices). By this reasoning, individuals who rose with different physical forms could not be the same as those individuals who had lived. Sexual difference *was* an essential part of human identity: the distinct size, shape, and qualities of the body had to be preserved in the afterlife because they were central to what made one uniquely oneself.⁸³ Thereafter, Christian writers predicted the survival of a particular, unique body that was materially one's own—an "identical" body, with a continuity of size and shape and structure. And yet they also asserted the need for a body that was "perfect," that is, free from all defects and impairments. But what of intersex individuals, whose sex was considered by many to be a defect or an imperfection—something "monstrous," as Augustine and Nicholas of Lyra had put it?

The chronicle of the Cistercian monk Otto of Freising, whose historical writings synthesized various theological opinions in the twelfth century, offers some answers. Relying heavily on Augustine, Otto recounted in his *Chronicle, or*

History of the Two Cities (completed in 1157) a number of doctrines surrounding the resurrection of the body, to which he attached his own deliberative (if not always consistent) conclusions. First, he refuted the idea that women would be transformed into men in the resurrection: "Some believe that women will not rise in the female sex, but all of them in the male, since God created man alone out of clay and woman from man. But I find more wisdom in those who do not doubt that both sexes will rise."[84]

For Otto, it was crucial that individuals be reunited with the sexed bodies that they possessed in life; that is, they would "without a doubt return to the original substance that they had when they lived in the world."[85] Not so, however, for "hermaphrodites," Otto specified, "whom a mistake of nature has badly joined or badly divided."[86] While bodies forged in the resurrection would arise "free from every defect and spot," a body with apparent attributes of both sexes, Otto wrote, was a "deformity" resulting from a deviation from the ordinary course of nature. Otto grouped together hermaphroditism with other supposed defects of the body, such as short stature, dark "Ethiopian" skin, and lameness.[87] According to Otto's argument, all such conditions would be corrected in the afterlife:

> Therefore all defects will be taken from bodies, but the natural state of the bodies will be preserved. . . . But where there is no harmony of parts, a body offends either because it is deformed, that is, because there is a defect or because there is an excess. Accordingly, there will be no deformity such as lack of harmony of the parts produced when those parts which are misshapen are corrected; and what is less than is seemly shall be supplied from a source known to the creator, and that which is more than is comely shall be removed, though the integrity of the matter is preserved.[88]

In Otto's view, all bodies would return to the ideal form of human nature, that is, its most elevated state of physical integrity and perfection: dwarves would grow tall, Ethiopians' skin would become pale, and intersex people would transform into properly shaped men and women.[89] This divine correction of such individuals erased their purported cosmetic deficiencies, perfecting their corporeal parts, and making them worthy of eternity. We should also note how Otto's position reveals a strikingly narrow sense of material perfection—one manifested only in bodies that were able, light-skinned, and of a standard enough form to merit Christian European recognition as ideal.

As Caroline Bynum has observed, by the twelfth century, Christian scholastic theologians had come to view the body as both the purveyor and the expression of each person's unique qualities. Given the consensus that all the parts of one's body, including one's sexual organs, were indispensable aspects of self, it is notable that people with nonbinary-sexed bodies were not imagined to retain their sexes in the afterlife but were rendered decisively male or female by God. Irina Metzler points out that medieval theorists of the body viewed far fewer physical characteristics as intrinsic to the self than we do now: while sex and age mattered to identity, physical impairments—what Otto calls "deformities"—did not.[90] Authors stressed the need for morphological continuity between the mortal and resurrected body, including a continuity of sex, and yet Otto dismissed what we now call intersex as a category admissible to the afterlife. By this logic, nonbinary bodies were not legitimate roots of personhood nor identity; they were considered a morphological defect—akin to dwarfism, obesity, physical disability, or dark skin—that supposedly detracted from the body's intended perfection. Nor were Otto's conclusions unique. The influential scholastic Albert the Great similarly assured readers in his *On the Resurrection* that "the general resurrection will correct two things in nature, namely error and defect—error in the monstrosity of the members [*in monstruositate membrorum*], [and] defect in a body's diminished stature."[91]

We see, then, that during the twelfth and thirteenth centuries, a number of writers were making similar arguments about both the creation and the resurrection. In both cases, they imagined only a very restricted set of sexes to be worthy of eternity. For Otto and his interlocutors, nonbinary sex was not an immortal ideal. It was for him, instead, an unfortunate and transitory state. Like other supposed physical defects, it reflected the broken nature of this world. Sex in his view existed ideally as distinct and binary, and people with sex-variant bodies were denied a central Christian promise of an afterlife—an eternity spent in their own unique bodies.

As we see, nonbinary sex was summarily excluded from the perfection of paradise, both in the beginning and in the end of time. And yet such conclusions were perhaps not absolute. The sources I focus on in this chapter originated in the elite atmosphere of late antique and medieval intellectual society. We cannot know for sure how deeply their opinions resonated with those who were not of that class, nor with those who were but who didn't leave behind written records. There are some hints that such ideas weren't shared by all. While most visual images depicted resurrected bodies as distinctly male or female, the scholar Deborah Markow has found several images that conflated disembodied souls—often considered sexless—with resurrected humans.[92] In addition, certain illustrations of the creation emphasized Adam and Eve's physical symmetry and sexual undifferentiation. Ninth-century Carolingian Bibles produced in Tours, for instance, portray Adam and Eve as nearly identical in size and gesture, without apparent distinction in their sexual anatomy. This same composition appears on the eleventh-century bronze doors of the German cathedral of Hildesheim, which foregrounded the symmetry of Adam and Eve, omitting any clear sign of their physical distinction. We find yet another example in an illustrated *Bible moralisée* of the thirteenth century, which called attention to Adam and Eve's apparent sexual undifferentiation.[93] Other examples of visual art, too, showed Adam and Eve as conjoined in a single Y-shaped body, a trope I explore in chapter 6. These images hint at complex understandings of the creation of humanity and the nature of sexual difference, as I argue later in that chapter.[94]

Moreover, the alarmed reactions of church authorities to heretical views on nonbinary sex in the creation and resurrection indicate that, despite near-constant refutation, plural ideas about Adam, Eve, and sexual difference were difficult to stamp out. The fact that we find so many rejections of the primal androgyne in so many texts over so many centuries suggests that authors were addressing real confusion about the issue. Of course, androgynes and hermaphrodites were by no means at the center of medieval theology—discussions of them are generally brief and within the context of broader questions—but the brevity of these discussions should not blind us to their significance. Offhand or indirect comments betray deep assumptions at the heart of a culture, and—as scholars have noted— ideas implicit in premodern texts are often more revealing than explicit ones.[95] Repeated references to nonbinary sex categories in twelfth- and thirteenth-century texts suggest that theologians had reason to worry about such ideas, and that the appeal of nonbinary sex was not so easily dispelled.

I do not intend here to smooth over the different sexual categories and historical contexts that I discuss in this chapter. "Androgny" was, of course, not precisely the same thing as "hermaphroditism," nor were concerns about the creation identical to those about the resurrection. Androgyny could be a category of neuter or undifferentiated sex, as in the texts of Origen, Gregory of Nyssa, and John Scottus Eriugena, or a morphologically doubled one, as we find in certain classical Greek texts or in the Jewish midrashim. Some rhetors seem to have distinguished androgyny from hermaphroditism, viewing the former as a desirable spiritual state (the most perfect reflection of God) and the latter as an undesirable bi-corporeal physical state (often, but not always, meaning what we now call intersex, and then considered a defective and unfortunate devolution from natural and biblical perfection). But androgyny could be an embodied state, too, and some writers used the two terms interchangeably. To the extent that medieval theorists conflated the two categories, they tended to view both negatively. Yet, in all this variability, what stands out are the ways in which sexual difference became key to how theologians theorized human nature. Nonbinary sexes became loci for thinking about the fundamental or ideal qualities of humankind at crucial points in human history.

Indeed, it is notable that ideas about nonbinary sex appear at the most dramatic and critical thresholds of Christian time—at the Beginning (the creation) and at the End (the resurrection). Why did medieval thinkers keep coming back to these nonbinary figures at such pivotal points in sacred time? Certainly, the unification of opposites was a prominent aspect of Christian symbolism (a motif shared by a number of other ancient religions). As scholars have observed, premodern Christianity placed great value on acts of reunification, cohesion, and completion. Certain early Christian texts seemed to suggest that ascension toward God entailed the increasing reconciliation of divisions, including sexual divisions.[96] Such traditions prompted at least some thinkers to imagine the resolution or transcendence of contrary sexes as a necessary step in the reconciliation of humanity with God.

Nor were these explorations of sexual difference mere academic exercises. Theological studies were among the chief means of ordering the premodern world and, as such, they provided answers to all manner of questions, from the esoteric to the practical. Analyses of the original state of humanity, as it was intended by God, could legitimate distinctions that regulated not just marriage and family but also king and subject, church and believer, God and human. These structures depended upon a separate and sequential creation of man and woman by God, not the formation of a single neuter or undifferentiated person that placed the sexes on equal footing—or that undermined them altogether.[97] And yet it is important to point out that the supporters of nonbinary interpretations of Genesis were not necessarily proponents of women's equality. Philo, for instance, was a noted misogynist, and Christian texts were sometimes internally inconsistent in their views on the subordination of women and the order of creation.[98]

But we might interpret at least some of the distaste for nonbinary sex in the twelfth and thirteenth centuries as rooted in its potential to upend the social order. At least some early Christians craved a release from sexual and social conventions, preferring a path toward the agender, asexual emulation of God. As Dale B. Martin has pointed out, there was nothing so radical in these claims: for ancient writers, androgyny was less a matter of gender equality than "unity in masculinity" that subsumed the weaker female into the stronger male. A human who was neither male nor female was really, at the heart of it, just *not female*.[99] This idea resonates with contemporary legal efforts to assimilate people with sex-variant anatomies into what was considered the superior male sex, as we shall see in chapter 4. And yet it is far from certain that all medieval authors viewed androgyny as merely not female because some used the terms *androgynus* and *hermaphroditus* interchangeably, and in doing so, they did not always distinguish between a male-inflected state of androgyny and a body displaying both traditionally understood male and female sex traits. The *Omne bonum* encyclopedia, which opened this chapter, defined a "hermaphrodite" as a person with two sexes, who nevertheless seemed "neither man nor woman and . . . both man and woman." The accompanying image, split down the center, recalls Plato's androgyne or the double-faced *Adam* of the Jewish midrashim, holding male and female in tension within a single form.

Part of my aim in this book is to show how traditional ideas about binary sex came into being, rather than accepting them as natural, timeless, and ahistorical. The idea that God created humans as distinctly binary-sexed was by no means self-evident to all premodern thinkers. On the contrary, theologians felt compelled to repeat this claim over and over again for more than a millennium to secure its acceptance. As Elizabeth Clark writes, repetition of this kind functions "to obscure the notion that ideas and beliefs are particular and local, situated in specific times, places, and groups; to the contrary, it encourages the view that our society's values *have* no history, but are eternal and 'natural.'"[100] As we can see, the creation of Adam and Eve as male and female was not the only, nor even the most obvious, reading of the creation story. Nor did readers find it abundantly clear why humans needed their sexual organs and their gender identities in the afterlife. Precisely because they were not timeless truths, authoritative teachings on the creation, the resurrection, and sexual difference had to be bolstered and enforced for centuries— to the exclusion of all other views. The development of these teachings, which conceptualized the creation and resurrection, and which invested them with meaning, constitute an important history of sexual difference and the ascendancy of the binary model.

We might also witness in ancient and medieval arguments the process by which Christians constructed the category of "the human." Modern scholars of queer, transgender, and critical race studies have produced important studies exploring the ways in which definitions of humanity have been crucially shaped by discourses of sex and gender. As they have shown, sex and gender play central roles in legitimizing personhood, often by granting humanity only to those who fit into accepted, privileged categories, while withholding it from those whose bodies or gendered identities are considered unnatural and unacceptable.[101] We might make a parallel argument about early analyses of Adam and Eve, as well as those of resurrected persons: authors placed limits on which sexes were natural or worthy of humanity, and they established parameters for how the human body might look or act in its most rarified state. In these sources, we witness how medieval Christians accepted only certain sexes as perfect, proper, and free of "defect." After all, humans with nonbinary bodies could not enter the afterlife—a core human experience in the Christian tradition—without having their sexes corrected into male or female ones.

As we move through the chapters of this book, we will see that nonbinary sexes were to become a recurring—if much debated—means for thinking about important aspects of premodern society and spirituality. Not only Adam, but also demons, angels, and even Christ himself, were all depicted in some sources as nonbinary-sexed figures. This convention, at least in certain contexts, could represent a perfect unity of unlike parts—not only masculine and feminine, but also divine and human, eternal and temporal. Such arguments located nonbinary sex outside the strictures of time and sexuality, encompassing the perfect equilibrium of elements. Over the course of more than a millennium, when certain theorists central to the European tradition imagined human perfection—whether at time's paradisiacal beginning or at its apocalyptic end—they imagined it in the form of a nonbinary figure. This impulse demonstrates the continuing attractiveness of nonbinary sex: it was in some texts monstrous, immoral, even damnable, and yet it spoke to an alternative past and an imagined future that was seductive and potent—the untainted perfection of all creation.

2

The Monstrous Races

Mapping the Borders of Sex

The known world spreads across the surface of the English Hereford *mappamundi*, a massive "world map" and the largest surviving one of its kind. Fashioned from a single sheet of vellum around 1300, and measuring over five feet in height, the map populates Europe, Asia, and Africa with intricate scenes drawn from scripture, history, and myth.[1] Among the map's inhabitants is a turbaned figure with a full breast on one side, a flat chest on the other, and both a penis and vulva below. According to the map's inscription, the figure represents "a race of both sexes, unnatural in many of their customs."[2] The turbaned figure appears within a row of strange creatures—the so-called "monstrous races"—that curve along the map's right edge, skirting the border of Africa on the banks of the Nile River (see fig. 2.1B).

The Roman historian Pliny the Elder (23–79 CE) had long before popularized the legend of the "monstrous races"—supposedly exotic, humanoid creatures with extraordinary anatomies and customs—thought to live in regions distant from Europe, often in Africa, Asia, or at the very edges of the earth. Pliny's encyclopedic *Natural History* described a host of these figures: "cynocephali" (with dog's heads), "blemmyes" (with faces on their chests), and "androgyni" or "hermaphrodites" (male on one side and female on the other), among other unusual characters.[3] Myths about the monstrous races were repeated by trusted writers such as Augustine of Hippo and Isidore of Seville, and included in bestiaries, travelogues, and *mappaemundi*. Descriptions of monsters were no doubt entertaining, but they also performed the serious work of defining what Europeans viewed as civilized cultural practices and establishing antipathy toward bodies and desires at odds with a European Christian ideal.[4]

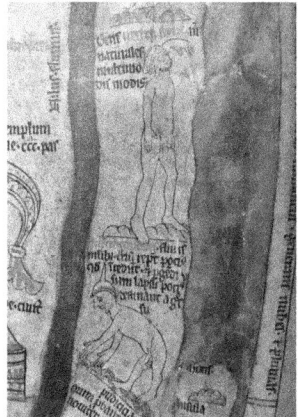

FIGURE 2.1 "Monstrous races." Hereford *Mappa Mundi* (detail). (a) Two "monstrous" figures along the Nile River: (b) nonbinary-sexed figure with turban; (c) himantopodes with *pileum cornutum*. Hereford Cathedral (c. 1300).

Much scholarship in recent years has focused on monsters and the monstrous races, but little attention has been directed toward the myth of the "hermaphroditic" monstrous race in particular. In the first part of this chapter, I look closely at that myth, considering its appearance in a series of encyclopedias written between the second and thirteenth centuries. *Mappaemundi* were encyclopedias of a sort, too. They were highly subjective renderings of space, less concerned with topographical accuracy than with capturing and ordering all of God's creation, intertwining the natural, the theological, and the historical.[5] As I show, encyclopedic sources used the hermaphroditic race's imagined bodily and behavioral differences to draw boundaries between spatial, species, religious, and racial categories. In the second part of this chapter, I use the Hereford Map's image of its turbaned figure as an entry point into a series of similar pictorial images of mythic hermaphrodites. As I explain, these images appeared as binaries that deconstructed themselves before the viewer's eyes, showing (and suppressing) alternative sex and gender possibilities that were imagined to exist in foreign lands.[6]

At the end of this chapter, I return to the specific context of late thirteenth-century England and the Christian holy wars now known as the crusades. As I show, the Hereford Map capitalized on long-standing meanings attached to the legend of the hermaphroditic race to debase its turbaned, two-sexed subject as exotic, dubiously human, and racially distinct.[7] Such impulses reflected contemporary events, especially the fall of the city of Acre (in the Kingdom of Jerusalem) in 1291. The loss, devastating for Christians, preceded the creation of the Hereford Map by just a decade or so. Because the mythic hermaphroditic race connoted boundaries, I argue, it was an especially apt tool to demarcate territorial borders and, at the same time, to express doubt about the inviolability of those borders. I suggest that ideas about monstrous-race hermaphrodites and their complex crossings came into play at a moment when the actual borders of Christian kingdoms were under great pressure.

MONSTERS AND DEFINITIONS OF THE HUMAN

In the twentieth and twenty-first centuries, emerging technologies and modes of thought have prompted a reevaluation of the very meaning of "the human." The definition of humanity as a cohesive category, distinct from animals and other creatures, often rests on the assumption that humans possess some crucial trait—whether language, reason, tools, culture, a soul, or something else—that distinguishes them from nonhuman creatures and entitles them to special ethical consideration. An explosion of scholarship in "critical animal studies," "posthuman studies," and "multispecies theory," however, has developed in recent years to question the existence of any true divide between humans and nonhumans, historicizing the production of those categories, and challenging human exceptionalism.[8] "The human," by this view, becomes comprehensible as a distinct category only in relation to its foil—in many cases, "the animal"—upon which its identity (through its actual or imagined encounters) is based. Moreover, as many scholars have observed, human-nonhuman boundaries are often worked out through ideas about sex and sexuality.[9]

During the Middle Ages, efforts to define the human often centered on "monsters." The word "monster" (*monstrum*) had variable meanings during the period but, in essence, monsters were different in their physical appearance or social practice from the person who was describing them.[10] Monsters came in a variety of forms, including outsized or hybridized animals (such as giant ants or griffins) and humanoid species whose bodies or customs were considered odd or threatening (such as headless blemmyes or cannibal anthropophages). Scholars such as John Block Friedman, Jeffrey Cohen, Dana Oswald, and Asa Mittman, among others, have produced insightful studies explaining how medieval monster-making delineated boundaries crucial to human identity.[11] As Jeffrey Cohen explains, a monster is above all a "cultural body," that is, it always "signifies something other than itself."[12] Monsters appear at times of cultural crisis to gleefully violate binaries and to create new possibilities—especially in the areas of politics, religion, and gender. They thus confound but also instantiate and enforce the binaries in which they take part. Dana Oswald adds that monsters inhabit "geographies of ambiguity" that establish "what it means for a body to appear *different*."[13] The fourteenth-century English *Mandeville's Travels* seems to affirm this sense of monsters' fundamental difference, inasmuch as it calls a monster "a thing deformed against kind, both of man or of beast or of anything else."[14] By occupying a position "against kind"—that is, outside the bounds of what man or beast should be—monsters made visible and meaningful the limits of "kind."[15]

In the European Middle Ages, monsters often appeared in efforts to consider the nature of humankind. When medieval authors struggled to evaluate the humanity of the monstrous races, they often defined the qualities they considered most basic to human identity. Augustine of Hippo, for instance, expressed an especially generous attitude toward human diversity, accepting as human any rational creature, no matter how odd its physical appearance. As he saw it, the monstrous races were a part of God's creation and a source of beauty and pleasure. But Augustine did not commit himself so fully to the monstrous races' human status. Instead, he equivocated, writing, "Let me then tentatively and cautiously state my conclusion. Either the written accounts of certain races are completely unfounded or, if such races do exist, they are not human; or if they are human, they are descended from Adam."[16] Augustine avoided any definitive position on the monstrous races' humanity, even considering the possibility that some monsters did *not* descend from Adam.[17]

The question of monsters' ontological status was important because if they were human, they could be converted to Christianity. In the ninth century, the French monk Ratramnus of Corbie considered missions to the dog-headed cynocephali, writing that the creatures' social organization and use of clothing was evidence enough of their rational souls. In the twelfth century, Peter Abelard affirmed this position, stating that an unusual body presented no obstacle to the possession of a human soul—as he claimed, even the hybrid satyrs of legend were human.[18] But the Flemish Dominican encyclopedist Thomas of Cantimpré, writing in around 1240, rejected these arguments, suggesting that the monstrous races were not human because they did not have the physical organization needed for intellectual reason to be informed by sense perception. Thomas addressed this issue in his encyclopedic *On the Nature of Things (De natura rerum)*, in a section called "On the Monstrous Humans of the East." The section's very title seemed to acknowledge monsters' humanity but, within the preface, Thomas substituted the word *animal* for *homo* (human) before confessing that "truly, we do not believe the monstrous animals to have a soul."[19] For Thomas, an unorthodox bodily shape precluded a human soul and, hence, a human status.

Nor was Thomas the only thinker to suggest that bodily difference could disrupt the self's engagement with the exterior world and, as a result, its humanity.[20] Other authors also believed that the soul required a certain type of body—whether upright or bipedal or in the possession of a head or hands—to correctly perceive the world, an operation that made possible rational thought, the *sine qua non* of humanity.[21] Even the medieval prohibition on abortion was based on the idea that an individual's humanity was deeply connected to the shape of the body. Abortion was often allowed until a fetus developed past a corporeal tipping point, after which it qualified as a human. According to legal and theological views on the subject, the form of the body, with its limbs and members in the correct numbers and places, was key to a fetus's passage from nonhumanity into humanity.[22] In the eyes of some Christian thinkers, then, bodily differences—such as those of the monstrous races—could disqualify one from the human race or render one an inferior form of human. Such exclusions were not, however, absolute.[23]

Thomas of Cantimpré's *On the Nature of Things* was a popular text: it survives in dozens of Latin manuscripts, as well as in Dutch, French, and German translations.[24] It continued the tradition of earlier encyclopedias such as Pliny the Elder's *Natural History* and Isidore of Seville's *Etymologies*, which compiled natural, medical, historical, and mythological information into quasi-comprehensive reference works. *On the Nature of Things* was just one of a cluster of great thirteenth-century encyclopedias, including Bartholomew the Englishman's *On the Properties of Things* (fl. c. 1245), Vincent of Beauvais's *Great Mirror* (c. 1240–60) and Jacob van Maerlant's *Flower of Nature* (c. 1270), among others.[25] These encyclopedias were among the most authoritative collections of naturalist knowledge before the spread of Greek and Arabic texts later in the century, and they remained popular even after.

Encyclopedias tended to impose hierarchical order on the wealth of information they collected.[26] *On the Nature of Things*, for instance, guided the reader in a descending catalogue from highest living thing to lowest: Thomas devoted his first two books to the human body and soul before turning to the monstrous races in book three; he covered beasts, fish, and insects in books four through nine. His organization, meaningfully, placed the monstrous races—with "hermaphrodites" among them—at the border between humans and nonhumans.[27] Bartholomew the Englishman's *On the Properties of Things*, widely read in England, also demonstrated ambivalence about the place of monsters within the order of nature. He discussed "pygmies" twice, once among humans and again among beasts, suggesting they did not fit easily within either category.[28] Indeed, the humanity of pygmies became a source of lively debate among scholastic philosophers during the thirteenth century. The famed philosopher Albert the Great, for instance, claimed that pygmies lacked true human language and reason, while his fellow scholastic, Peter of Auvergne, thought pygmies to be heliotropic, like plants.[29] Like their fellow members of the monstrous races, pygmies seemed to blur a line between humans and nonhumans, and they constituted a special opportunity to work out such distinctions. Shirin Khanmohamadi observes that during the thirteenth century, scholars devoted special attention to establishing definitions of the human through such arguments.[30]

Taken together, lists and images of the monstrous races formed what the scholars Asa Mittman and Susan Kim call a "hideous aggregate," prompting audiences to take stock of their own bodies, as well as their clothing, diets, dwellings, speech, and social practices, identifying themselves as human on the basis of those traits.[31] By contrast, a monster was, as Jeffrey Cohen says, a "morally and physically deformed creature arriving to demarcate the boundary beyond which lies the unintelligible, the inhuman."[32] As a result, traditional depictions of the monstrous races constituted a visual catalogue that made palpably clear monsters' physical distinction from humanity, as well as their collective exclusion from Christendom. Images of mythic hermaphrodites, which appeared side by side with aberrant characters such as cyclopes and blemmyes, were deemed strange; they were formed "against kind," and they were thus, inescapably, implicated in how authors defined "kind."[33]

But wherever boundaries existed, they could be crossed or hybridized and, indeed, not all of the monstrous races were monstrous in every way. The race of mythic hermaphrodites were bipedal; they had a head and hands and a shape too familiar to be summarily dismissed as nonhuman.[34] As Mittman points out, we might better characterize certain monstrous races as "monstrous peoples." They intermingled the traits of humans and nonhumans, bridging any firm divide between categories.[35] Medieval monsters, then, were not merely an "other" that lay incontestably outside of humanity; monsters crossed or confounded binaries and resisted simple classifications.[36] Members of the monstrous races—including mythic hermaphrodites—constituted a special impetus, as Karl Steel writes, for audiences to reflect "on and past the limits of their humanity."[37]

"QUITE OTHERWISE": SPATIAL DIFFERENCES BETWEEN EAST AND WEST

As members of the "monstrous races," mythic hermaphrodites were implicated in an ontological line that divided humans from nonhumans. As it turns out, tales of a foreign race of hermaphrodites participated in other kinds of boundary-marking, too. They separated a reader's homeland from the places outside it, defining geographical regions, and placing the monstrous races at a distance—at the earth's most remote edges. The strangeness of those purportedly marginal places offered a counterpoint for more ordinary communities at home in Europe and England.[38]

A moralizing French version of Thomas of Cantimpré's *On the Nature of Things* (c. 1290), for instance, gave a breathless catalogue of the exotic habits of the "East," which differed in every way from the local mores of ordinary peoples:

> In foreign lands they are not a bit
> like they are here. You know
> truly that the Easterners are quite otherwise than we are.[39]

By being "quite otherwise," that is, by doing the opposite of what Europeans were supposed to do, monsters in the "East" helped to establish rules for proper behavior in the "West."[40] As I explain, images and tales of a monstrous race of hermaphrodites crossed a boundary between male and female, making clear the division of sexes that was expected of audiences at home.

Drawing upon the foundational work of Edward Said and other postcolonial scholars, specialists in medieval studies have suggested in recent years that medieval Europeans, much like their modern counterparts, defined their "self" in opposition to an unfamiliar and distant "other," often in the East.[41] During the medieval period, the "East" was a rather nebulous category: it encompassed the Near or Middle East, as well as parts of Asia and Africa. The "South" could be an "other," too, and encyclopedic texts often favored a tripartite division of the world into Europe, Asia, and Africa, which also overlapped with East-West binaries.[42] Michael Uebel has suggested that imaginative engagements with foreign others were crucial during the Middle Ages, for they performed "the cultural and psychological work of imagining a Western self and Oriental other in dialectical relation."[43] Yet Uebel, Albrecht Classen, and Kim Phillips have added that medieval encounters between "self" and "other" were never just clashes between opposites. They were complex and open-ended negotiations, allowing Europeans to see parallels between themselves and their eastern counterparts, as well as to identify the "other" within themselves.⁴⁴

In the next two sections of this chapter, I explore this interplay between "self" and "other" within European visions of nonbinary-sexed figures. First, I consider pictorial images of foreign and mythic hermaphrodites in medieval visual art. Several genres of sources featured such images, including *mappaemundi*, bestiaries, travel writings, and monster catalogues such as *Marvels of the East*. I offer no exhaustive survey of such images here, instead confining myself to a few representative examples: they date from the twelfth to the fifteenth centuries, and they range in geographic origin and circumstances of production. Despite their diversity, I argue that these images share some important visual and rhetorical elements. The turbaned figure of the Hereford Map—with which I began this chapter—turns out to be but one of a long-lived set of images in which a mythic race of nonbinary-sexed figures was presented as bilaterally split.⁴⁵

Such iconography reflected an equally long-standing belief that monstrous-race hermaphrodites had half-male and half-female bodies. Pliny's *Natural History* (first century CE), a standard book of reference during the Middle Ages and one of the Hereford Map's known sources, cited the existence of a mythic race of hermaphrodites—here called "Androgynes"—who lived in Africa:

> Above the Nassamones, and the Machlyae, who border upon them, are found, as we learn from Calliphanes, the nation of the Androgynes, a people who unite the two sexes in the same individual, and alternately perform the functions of each. Aristotle also states that their right breast is that of a male, the left that of a female.⁴⁶

Isidore of Seville's *Etymologies* (c. 600–20), another source of the Hereford Map and a foundational text for medieval Europe, made a similar claim: "Hermaphrodites are so named because both sexes appear in them.... These, having a male right breast and a female left breast, in sexual intercourse sire and bear children in turn."⁴⁷ As Isidore stated, hermaphrodites, thanks to their dual anatomy, oscillated between sexual roles, playing the "father" in one instance and the "mother" in another. Such individuals also supposedly switched between social roles: each had "a male right breast for performing work, and a left female breast for nourishing children," as the seventh- or eighth-century teratological encyclopedia, the Anglo-Latin *Book of Monsters*, reported.⁴⁸ These details highlighted the reputedly cyclical nature of hermaphrodites' activities: they labored as men at work, and they labored as women at childrearing. Other texts also repeated these myths, sometimes illustrating them with a bilaterally split figure, much like we see on the Hereford Map.

An illustration from a twelfth-century Anglo-Latin copy of *Marvels of the East*, for instance, pictures a bifurcated hermaphrodite with both traditionally understood male and female traits (see fig. 2.2).[49] Parroting Isidore of Seville, the accompanying text states that "hermaphrodites are so called because both sexes appear in them. . . . These, having a male right breast and a female left breast, in sexual intercourse sire and bear children in turn."[50] A colorful

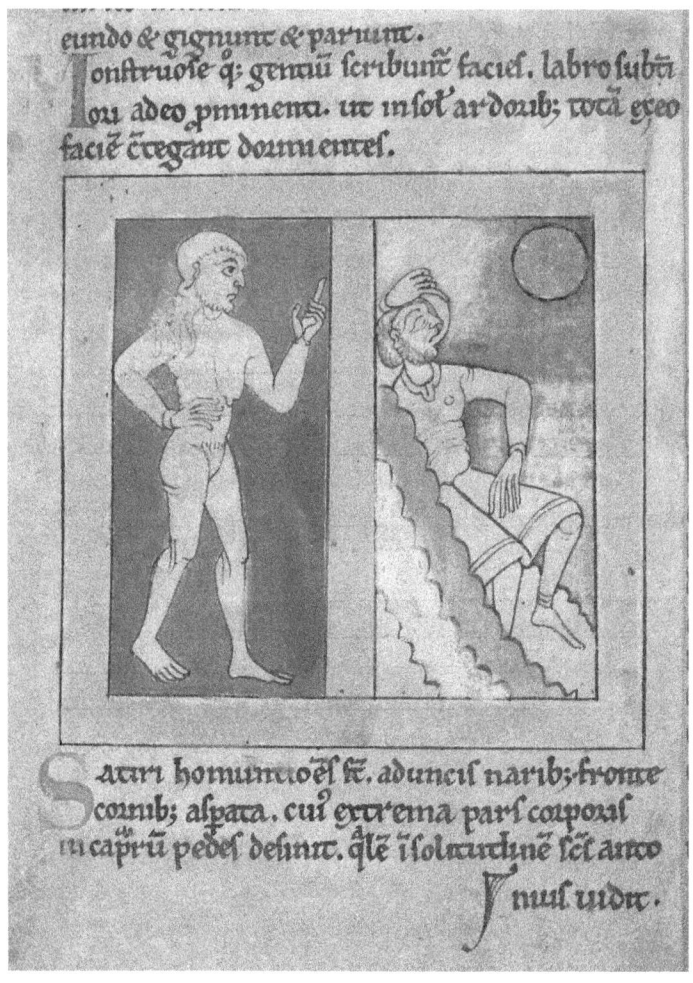

FIGURE 2.2 Nonbinary-sexed figure (left). *Marvels of the East*. Oxford, University of Oxford, Bodleian Library, MS Bodley 614, fol. 050v (mid-twelfth century). Permission of the Bodleian Libraries.

illustration accompanies the passage: a nude nonbinary-sexed figure turned to the right, left arm raised, feet poised in almost the same position as the figure on the Hereford Map. In this image and others like it, such figures basked in shameless nudity, calling attention to their titillating attributes and satisfying viewers' more prurient interests at a time when sexually explicit images were few.[51] The absence of modesty in such images also implied irrationality, for some authors argued that the ability to recognize decency was a hallmark of human status.[52] Moreover, such images drew attention to mythic hermaphrodites' imagined behavioral reversals, which transgressed social boundaries and "traveled" between male and female. We might imagine that medieval readers enjoyed a vicarious journey across both geographical and sexual terrain when they viewed such images.

Other manuscripts shared these pictorial conventions. As we have already seen, the *Omne bonum*, an English encyclopedia attributed to the fourteenth-century clerk James le Palmer, includes an image of a dual-sexed figure with two Janus-like faces (see fig. 1.1). Nor was such imagery unique to English manuscripts. A fifteenth-century *mappamundi* in a French copy of Giovanni Colonna's (c. 1298–1340) *Mare historiarum* features a group of split mythic hermaphrodites (see fig. 2.3), who parade across Africa and Asia, positioned at left and separated by a river from the civilized (and clothed) Europeans at far right.[53] The hermaphrodites occupy the map's center, facing Europe on one side and the continents of Africa and Asia on the other. The medieval theory of climate zones held that foreign regions with very hot or very sunny climates, such as Africa and Asia, produced inhabitants with unusual anatomies and customs. Climate-based theories varied, but they contributed to an overall impression that the monstrous races clustered in extreme, non-European environments.[54] The *Mare historiarum* drew heavily from the thirteenth-century encyclopedic tradition and, in a dramatic expression of Eurocentrism, its *mappamundi* placed naked and unrefined split hermaphrodites in stark contrast to the clothed men and women of Europe.[55] At a spatial remove, and untouched by the sartorial markers of binary gender, the map's double-faced hermaphrodites were imagined outside of civilization.

Another related image, from a famous fifteenth-century manuscript known as the *Livre des merveilles* (*Book of Marvels*), shows a group of dual-sexed figures in a rich and verdant landscape (see fig. 2.4).[56] The manuscript, a gift from John the Fearless to the Duke of Berry, illustrates the adventures of Marco Polo, John Mandeville, Odoric of Pordenone, and others (the nonbinary-sexed figures appear in the Mandeville section). Travel manuscripts of this kind were often intended for wealthy "armchair travelers" and were less concerned with

FIGURE 2.3 "Monstrous races." Giovanni Colonna, *Mare historiarum*. Paris, Bibliothèque nationale de France, MS latin 4915, fol. 26v (1447–1455).

FIGURE 2.4 Nonbinary-sexed figures. *Livre des merveilles (Mandeville's Travels)*. Paris, Bibliothèque nationale de France, MS français 2810, fol. 195v (c. 1410–1412).

the moralizing impulses of bestiaries and encyclopedias and more focused on showcasing strange peoples in fanciful, pleasure-inducing scenes.[57] The *Livre des merveilles* extracts its monstrous races from the rectangular frames that encase them in earlier images (for instance, fig. 2.2), allowing the figures to roam freely across exotic settings. While the author of *Mandeville's Travels* mentions "hermaphrodites" only briefly, the illustrators of the *Livre des merveilles* seemed to delight in depicting the monstrous races. A nearby page reveals a similar scene, this one featuring the headless blemmyes and epiphagi (see fig. 2.5).[58]

Illustrated by the anonymous painter known as the Egerton Master, the nonbinary figures of the *Livre des merveilles* appear with three animals in an unblemished wilderness, itself a symbol of the primordial, pre-societal, and pre-familial.[59] Another contemporary manuscript copy of *Mandeville's Travels* preserves the split-bodied style of the earlier programs (see fig. 2.6), but the *Livre des merveilles*

FIGURE 2.5 Blemmyes and epiphagi. *Livre des merveilles (Mandeville's Travels)*. Paris, Bibliothèque nationale de France, MS français 2810, fol. 194v (c. 1410–1412).

FIGURE 2.6 Wild man and nonbinary-sexed figures. Jean de Mandeville, *Antichrist (Travels of Sir John Mandeville)*. St. Gallen, Stiftsarchiv St. Gallen, (Abtei Pfäfers), Cod. Fab. XVI, fol. 66v (second quarter of fifteenth century). Photo: www.e-codices.ch.

diverges from the longstanding "bifurcated" convention. Its hermaphrodites have undivided bodies and doubled male and female genitals, and they are engaged in identical pursuits, gathering food from the abundant trees. The environment is peaceful, almost Edenic, and, indeed, the scholar Henri Auguste Omont has identified this illustration as a portrait of Adam and Eve in paradise.[60]

The *Livre des merveilles* thus evoked not only the legend of the monstrous races but also perhaps that of prelapsarian Eden. The monstrous races shared with the earthly paradise a geographic location: Eden was sometimes thought to exist in the "East," proximate to the lands of the monstrous races.⁶¹ The *Livre des merveilles* possibly gestured at the nonbinary-sexed undercurrents of the creation story, as discussed in the previous chapter. Nakedness among monsters could connote wildness and bestiality, yet in this image, the nonbinary-sexed figures' nudity and peaceful coexistence with animals suggested an innocence and closeness to nature in its most positive sense, one in defiance of those who would brand them as unnatural.⁶² In the *Livre des merveilles*, nonbinary behaviors were not to be avoided, nor shunned as "otherwise"; they were marvelous—even desirable.⁶³ These mythic hermaphrodites' lack of sexually divided labor may also have hinted at remaking society outside of conventional structures of kinship, an effort that—if earlier writings on the primal androgyne were any indication—at least some Christians longed for as a return to the condition of paradise.

The group of manuscripts I've just discussed differs markedly from a series of well-known ancient bi-corporeal images, some of which depicted the Greek deity Hermaphroditus. As Aileen Ajootian writes, by the fourth century BCE, Hermaphroditus had acquired both a cult and a fairly consistent iconography that emphasized the figure's dual sexes.⁶⁴ Early depictions included the *anasyromenos* style, that is, a standing feminine figure that revealed a hidden penis and testicles. Terracotta sculptures of this type were produced far into the Roman period, and they were disseminated widely in Greece, Italy, and Asia Minor. Literary and archaeological evidence suggests that ancient audiences viewed Hermaphroditus's purported two sexes, not as a monstrosity, but as a transcendent union of male and female, associated with fertility, healing, and protection. In addition, at least as early as the first century BCE, a genre of Roman sculpture known as the "Borghese hermaphrodite" or "sleeping hermaphrodite" portrayed an apparently female figure whose reclining position similarly obscured a penis and testicles. These ancient sculptures generally capitalized on a dramatic moment of revelation when a viewer realized that a seemingly female form was more complex than initially met the eye.⁶⁵

In formal terms, these ancient antecedents were quite distinct from later medieval images of mythic monstrous-race hermaphrodites. But medieval mythic hermaphrodites resembled another traditional figure: Janus, the Roman god of travel, doorways, and thresholds. In ancient mythology, Janus ruled over portals and boundaries, with two faces (or sometimes two heads) pointing in different directions. In the ancient world, Janus's temple stood sentry over the Roman forum: situated on an east-west axis, it opened its doors in wartime and closed them in peace.⁶⁶ A millennium later, during the twelfth and thirteenth centuries, Janiform images proliferated in Gothic art, particularly in calendars and "labors of the months" cycles, in which Janus appeared as "January" (see fig. 2.7). While ancient and late antique Roman calendars tended to illustrate January with a person making a religious offering, Janus-as-January images—either with two faces (*bifrons*) or two heads (*biceps*)—were ubiquitous in Gothic churches in France, Germany, Italy, Spain, and England, as well as in manuscript illuminations.⁶⁷

Information about Janus had long circulated in older writings by Ovid, Macrobius, and Isidore of Seville, and his attributes may have been well entrenched in medieval oral culture. Jacopo de Varagine, for instance, recorded in his thirteenth-century history of Genoa several legends about Janus, about which he said: they "cannot be found in any ancient history-book, [but] they are testified as true by public and consolidated fame."⁶⁸ In the fourteenth century, the English

FIGURE 2.7 Janus and two doors. *Psalterium ad usum ecclesiae Trecensis*. Paris, Bibliothèque nationale de France, MS latin 238, fol. 1r (late twelfth or thirteenth century).

poet Chaucer could assume a certain familiarity with Janus among readers of his *Merchant's Tale*, full of bawdy jokes about the vigilant but easily duped Januarie.[69] Further, Chaucer used Januarie's tale to allude not only to Janus but also to Hermaphroditus. When Januarie's wife, May, had an adulterous affair with Damyan, the result was a Hermaphroditus-like figure (created by the lovers' fused bodies) that makes a clever reference to Ovid's *Metamorphoses*.[70] A connection between the visual attributes of Janus and those of monstrous-race hermaphrodites can be no more than speculative. But at least some medieval split images of mythic hermaphrodites may have gestured to the ancient tradition of Janus (perhaps connected to Hermaphroditus) and signified a threshold between two spatial fields.

Whatever their influences, medieval images of mythic hermaphrodites drew a line that separated not only male from female, but also geographic center from margin. To the extent that authors and artists imagined distant peoples to flout the man-woman binary, while those at home were compelled to adhere to it, we can see how sex and gender were calibrated in relation to (imagined) encounters with regions that were "quite otherwise."

The English Hereford Map, in a similar fashion, placed its turbaned male-female figure at a geographic edge, in an area representing Ethiopia. The surface of Ethiopia was rocky and barren, in contrast to the architecturally developed areas that elsewhere on the map represented civilization.[71] The scholar M. W. Bychowski writes that the Hereford Map's turbaned figure embodied all that was spatially remote, a distant "them" that existed elsewhere and outside of a local "us." By displacing nonbinary sex to the margins, she writes, people at the center could recognize, by contrast, their own binary difference. Nonbinary sex, in Bychowski's view, "becomes shorthand for 'not here' or 'not us' in order that the here and now, the 'us,' can become defined."[72] According to this logic, the monstrous races, including mythic hermaphrodites, contributed to a much larger model of civilizational order: sex was one thing at the center, and something "quite otherwise" outside it.

Bychowski's observation fits well within a long-standing view that a society's identity is constructed in relation to its borders.[73] As the art historian Michael Camille famously argued, a center is perpetually in dialogue with its margins, an interaction that catalyzes definitions of self as distinct from periphery. But the monsters of medieval *mappaemundi* played an ambiguous role in such divisions: while monsters helped to solidify boundaries, they also threatened to tear them down. As Michael Uebel writes, monsters "expose[d] classificatory boundaries as fragile by always threatening to dissolve the border between other and same, nature and culture, exteriority and interiority."[74] The expulsion of nonbinary monsters to the world's farthest edge neutralized the peril that they supposedly presented, facilitating the creation of European—and human—identity. And yet we can detect a counternarrative in such texts too—one that located nonbinary sex not only geographically outside, but also inside—intrinsic to authors' and audiences' own identity.

"MONSTROUS BIRTHS": INTERSEX INFANTS IN THE WEST

Indeed, the monstrous races were not the only supposed monsters who populated medieval teratological texts: so-called "monstrous births" were also standard fare in contemporary writings on marvels and monstrosity. "Monstrous births" referred to local infants who were born with what medieval people viewed as too few, too many, or unusually shaped body parts that strayed beyond what the author Isidore of Seville called "common human nature."[75] Individual "monsters" were born to families who did not look like them, in contrast to the monstrous races, whose members were all imagined to be monsters. So-called monstrous births sometimes, but not always, referred to people whom we might now describe as having disabilities or morphological differences, including conjoined twins, intersex infants (here called "hermaphrodites"), and others with unusual physical features.[76] During the medieval period, tales of monstrous births were a source of perennial fascination for writers, who pondered their causes, as well as their deeper meanings. The Latin word for "monster"—*monstrum*—reputedly derived from either the verb *monstrare*, meaning "to show or to instruct," or *monere*, "to warn," and monstrous births were thought to show God's will by communicating predictive messages or by warning of collective or hidden sin.[77] During the thirteenth century and after, medieval theorists tended to draw clear distinctions between the monstrous races and monstrous births: the former was a manifestation of God's diverse creation, while the latter was a troubling transgression of natural law.[78]

Monstrous births, however, shared with the monstrous races an instrumental role in defining the limits of humankind. As scholars have shown, medieval jurists, theologians, and other authorities struggled to define humanity on the basis of fundamental traits, which determined whether or not a particular infant was to be accepted as human. Essential to their understanding of human status was *reason*, that is, the capacity to separate oneself from one's surroundings, as well as to exercise free choice and abstract thinking.[79] But the shape of the body—believed inseparable from its mental faculties—was crucial to such evaluations. In judging the ontological status of monsters, medieval authorities pondered how far a body could go past "kind" before it no longer qualified as a human in their view. Such evaluations were not mere theoretical exercises: an infant's ontological status affected matters of lineage (could this person eventually inherit, marry, and name heirs?) and of culpability (if someone killed such an infant, was it murder?). Human status was important from the moment of birth, moreover, for it determined whether or not an infant could be baptized and enter the Christian community.[80]

Medieval thinkers tended to deny personhood to people with physical anomalies that departed too much from what they considered "common human nature," such as if a person lacked a head or was deemed to be exceedingly small or misshapen. Intersex individuals—generally included among monstrous births—were subject to this process of evaluation, too. According to Roman law on the subject, if an individual had what were viewed as simple corporeal deficiencies or multiplications—such as four fingers on a hand or two sets of genitals (as per the medieval understanding of intersex)—then they were accepted as indubitably human. Intersex infants could be baptized, although whether they were to be baptized with a male or female name was another matter entirely, as I discuss in chapter 4.[81] Given these rules, those whom medieval writers labeled "hermaphrodites" occupied a "double place" in medieval culture: they existed as mythic races at the earth's farthest edges but also as clearly human members of the local community. While the former's status was an open question, the latter group enjoyed participation in human institutions—although within certain limits.[82] But we should not divide intellectual approaches to the two groups too definitively. Myths about the monstrous races functioned as much more than escapist entertainment: as Caroline Walker Bynum and Brian Stock have noted, monsters and marvels were an instigation for medieval classification and analysis. The aspects of monstrosity that were legendary, on the one hand, and those that were verifiable and real, on the other, constituted a single spectrum of knowledge that revealed the natural and transcendent order. Both types of "monsters," moreover, could have moral significance.[83]

Beyond this, in certain ancient and medieval writings, including some sources of the Hereford Map, the monstrous races and individual intersex people were even more closely related. After highlighting the exotic Nation of Androgyni in his *Natural History*, for instance, Pliny the Elder turned his attention to the question of intersex individuals, saying they were prized in Rome as local entertainments.[84] In his *City of God*, Augustine jumped from a discussion of the mythic monstrous race of hermaphrodites, presumably located abroad, to a description of intersex infants and the problems they raised for baptismal procedure.[85] As Lisa Verner notes, Augustine made little to no distinction between the foreign monstrous races and individual "monsters" within his own region.[86] Isidore of

Seville, too, intermingled the two categories, eliding his discussion of the monstrous races with that of domestic monstrous births, both of which could convey divine messages.[87]

Certain thirteenth-century encyclopedic texts adopted a similar approach, too, interrupting their descriptions of the monstrous races with observations about people with intersex anatomies who lived nearby in Europe.[88] In his *History of the East, or Jerusalem* (c. 1215), the cleric Jacques de Vitry moved abruptly from tales of exotic monstrous races to marvels nearer to home, including "hermaphrodites" with "twin sexes" found in the heart of France.[89] A few decades later, Thomas of Cantimpré repeated trivia about the monstrous races before noting without pausing that in France, "humans of the male and female sex have been seen."[90] In a similar vein, the *Omne bonum* passed seamlessly from a gloss on canon law and intersex infants to a description of the mythic monstrous races, whose bodies were half-male and half-female.[91] In this series of texts, the monstrous races of the East and the sex-variant individuals of the West appear in quick succession. Such narratives shifted the reader rapidly from "there" to "here"—from "them" to "us." Far from relegating nonbinary sex to a safely distant margin, these texts emphasized that "we" could also include such variations.

In other texts too, the categories of here and there were not so clearly defined. As A. J. Ford notes, divisions between East and West were never absolute: some material from *Marvels of the East* transposed local phenomena onto foreign places, and vice versa.[92] Asa Mittman observes that the English viewed themselves as marginal, far from the cultural and spiritual center of Jerusalem, the central point of the Hereford Map.[93] The Hereford *mappamundi* located the British Isles in the extreme lower orbit of the world, in the same geographic band that also contained the monstrous races of Africa, suggesting that England too was a borderland.[94] Scholars have noted that English thinkers sometimes identified with monsters; they viewed their own homeland as proximate to monstrosity; and they drew particular connections between England and Africa.[95] Monsters, including "hermaphrodites," could therefore function as a means to reflect not only on the supposed strangeness of distant lands but also on the strangeness that existed within.

The locality of such monsters did not, however, allay all hostility toward them.[96] As Lorraine Daston and Katharine Park explain, medieval thinkers tended to view proximate monsters with much greater horror than they did foreign marvels: both Jacques de Vitry and Thomas of Cantimpré, for their part, expressed antipathy toward so-called monsters who appeared closer to home in Europe.[97] Attitudes toward monsters were ambivalent and contradictory, and in encyclopedic texts—of which the *mappaemundi* were a part—we find that nonbinary "others" were not merely externals to be banished to the distance. They were both inside and outside: *out there*, in Africa or the East, and *right here*, in Rome or France. They straddled categories, bridging a line between human and monster, between here and there—between "us" and "them." As I discuss next, medieval thinking about nonbinary sex became a way of thinking about sexual boundaries, too. As ideas about nonbinary sex shifted across territories, they broached the line that separated the sexes, challenging the contours of those categories but also upholding their difference.

NONBINARY SEX, GENDER-CROSSING, AND SEXUAL BOUNDARIES

From Pliny onward, textual accounts of the monstrous races tended to describe the mythic hermaphroditic race as having bifurcated, half-male and half-female bodies. This imagined morphology allowed authors and artists to depict hermaphrodites as switching back and forth between genders. What was at stake in these writings, then, was not only that mythic hermaphrodites had remarkable physical shapes but also that they crossed between distinct male and female social spheres. Pictorial images of mythic hermaphrodites, however, depicted them not as serially sexed—not as male to female and back again—but as hybrids or a paradox, a simultaneous embodiment of two contraries in one form.[98]

The English illustrated Westminster Abbey Bestiary, created in a Franciscan friary, possibly in York (c. 1270–80) (see fig. 2.8), includes just such an image. Its mythic hermaphrodite (lower right corner) has a split physique, much like that of the Hereford Map, with a sword on the right side and a pair of scissors on the left.[99] Such symbols signaled the figure's two distinct halves: the masculine side fights with a phallic weapon, while the feminine side is busied with the domestic arts (the scissors' prominent vulvar opening also no doubt refers to the female anatomy). Unlike the other images discussed earlier, this nonbinary member of the monstrous races has no visible genitals at all, only a smooth surface in the region of the groin. The image further communicates the figure's sex through its spectacularly schismatic gendered activities, which are carried out by the body's two sides. The figure seems equally suited to both male and female pursuits, yet the image cleaves the body firmly in two. If monsters were, as Dana Oswald has suggested, "intermediate, interstitial, [and] in transition," this image, in contrast, united contraries and held them apart simultaneously.[100] This mythic hermaphrodite was no integrated mixture, no midpoint between; the figure was a union of opposites in unresolved

FIGURE 2.8 "Monstrous races." *Bestiary*. London, Westminster Abbey Library, MS 22, fol. 3r (c. 1270–1280).

tension. The image reveals the extent to which nonbinary sex threw into relief questions about daily life and its tidy division into male and female spheres. By making its composite parts so visible, the bestiary's image defined what it meant to be a man or woman. But it suggested other possibilities, too: the sword's and scissors' symmetrical blades perhaps hinted that the gendered spheres were not so separate after all. The unromanticized figure—bluntly rendered, almost spectral—conveys notable ambivalence about such a possibility, however: it marvels at a person who was both male and female, but it shudders at the prospect of unfixed roles.

Ideas about sex were undergoing rapid development in the thirteenth century, thanks to the arrival of new Greek and Arabic texts in Latin translation, which offered readers sophisticated theories regarding embryology and human sexual difference. Thirteenth-century encyclopedias subscribed to the newly arrived ideas (Bartholomew the Englishman's *On the Properties of Things*, for example, mentioned the fetal development of intersex anatomies in quasi-scientific terms), but they did not engage in the sustained biological analysis that would characterize Albert the Great's writings on sexual difference just a decade later.[101] (I will have much more to say about naturalist theories of sex in chapters 4 and 5.) The traditional myth of the monstrous races pictured hermaphrodites as two horizontally arrayed sexes, emphasizing their lateral polarity.[102] In such images, mythic hermaphrodites were "both sexes" not only because they confounded sexual dimorphism but also because they confounded binaries of sexual and social labor.

Writings on the monstrous races collapsed what we now view as separate categories of sex, gender, and sexuality into a single form of difference that they called, simply, *sexus* ("sex"). *Sexus* existed in four ways: external and internal reproductive anatomy, secondary sex characteristics such as breasts or beards, active or passive roles in sexual intercourse and generation, and social roles in labor. The former two are components of what we now call morphological or endocrinologic "sex," while the latter two we tend to call "gender"—that is, "a social category imposed on a sexed body" (to use the phrasing of Joan Scott), and a way of signifying social roles based on "biological differences related to the 'labor of procreation and reproduction.'"[103] Yet medieval authorities did not think of sex and gender (nor sexual orientation) as separable fields of difference.[104]

Of course, scholars have written extensively about the complex relationship between sex and gender in modern contexts. Biological "sex" and social "gender" still operate as distinct modes of classification (which may or may not line up within a given individual), but feminist and queer academics have also emphasized the ways in which categories of sex and gender are never wholly separate. Anne Fausto-Sterling, Katrina Karkazis, and Rebecca Jordan-Young, for instance, point out how seemingly objective, biological signs of sex in modern science reflect what amount to cultural gendered biases, making biological sex to some degree a product of social gender. Judith Butler's landmark book, *Gender Trouble*, similarly locates the "iteration," or ritual repetition, of gendered acts at the heart of subject creation.[105] Sex, by her argument, is "not simply what one has, or a static description of what one is" but the effects of what one *does* within a normative structure of heterosexuality.[106] Butler's theory of "performativity" is not a perfect match for the Middle Ages—a period during which "norms" and "heterosexuality" would have been alien concepts—but Butler makes clear the prioritization of gender in the formation of sexual difference.[107] Gayle Salamon adds that sex is created not by the body's physical attributes but by its social relationships with others and its "intentionality toward the other and toward the world."[108] In medieval monstrous-race discourse, too, sex emerges not just through a body's physical attributes but also through its encounter with the outside world, through its acts and affiliations. Sex was not the result of inert biology for these medieval thinkers; it was an open-ended process or activity shored up by sociality rather than any single destiny of the flesh.

I will discuss the details of medieval sex-based distinctions in much greater detail in chapters 4 and 5, but, in short, both medical and religious authorities cited various binaries that separated male from female, with the male sex clearly superior to its female counterpart.[109] Medieval gender also existed, simultaneously, on a spectrum, admitting to a number of intermediate categories of peoples—including those viewed as positive, such as virgins and celibate clergy. Despite the range and complexity of medieval models of sex, individuals who transgressed male-female binaries were for the most part, as Ruth Karras and Tom Linkinen note, "the exception that prove[d] the rule of the gender binary": that is, they were "monsters" because they did not fit.[110] Mythic hermaphrodites were "monsters" for this very reason: they did not conform to a single sex but rather transitioned back and forth between stereotypically male and female positions or occupied them simultaneously. Images of the monstrous races made visibly clear the unsettling nature of such transitions. The ease with which mythic hermaphrodites confounded the gendered order—switching back and forth between sexes—tested the dichotomy that underlay so much of medieval culture and revealed it to be quite fragile indeed. After all, a mythic hermaphrodite was merely one individual capable of both male and female tasks, one who could not help but challenge the necessity of binary divisions.[111]

But if the legend of the monstrous races emphasized hermaphrodites' potential for transgression, visual images of mythic hermaphrodites also sought to rein in that potential. "Bifurcated" hermaphrodites—as I call the convention here— were junctions of distinct, unaltered sexes, and they made a herculean effort to reinforce binaries. Such images kept within sight an intact, male-female division of the body, rejecting any true confusion of categories. Even as authors marveled at the "sex changes" of a foreign monstrous race, images of mythic hermaphrodites attenuated that change. The figure's female side did the female work while the male did the male work, and the two sides of the body remained easily identifiable. Such images emphasized doubling and dissimilitude, and not the more radical prospect of change via metamorphosis.[112] While the sources played with fluidity and boundary crossing, they also maintained the boundaries themselves as recognizable. Mythic hermaphrodites in these contexts were not indiscriminate mixtures of male and female, nor were they intermediates on a sexual spectrum. Instead, they were binaries that deconstructed themselves before their viewer's eyes, joining and making visible their contrary parts.

We might see in such images, therefore, both transgressive and conservative elements. They are a good example of how monsters, as Jeffrey Cohen argues, confound but also instantiate and enforce the binaries in which they take part.[113] Mythic hermaphrodites—who supposedly switched from male activity to female passivity, from male labor to female caretaking—crossed the male-female boundary even as they upheld it. As figures who were "quite otherwise," the monstrous races provided an anti-model for the gendered practices expected of viewers and readers at home. But they created new possibilities too: by breaching the line that separated male from female, images of monstrous-race hermaphrodites could not help but hint at the possibility of escaping such strictures. Not through travel to other lands, as their putative subject suggested, but through imaginative possibility in Europe: through a reconstitution of categories outside the realm of binary difference.

THE HEREFORD MAP, MUSLIMS, AND CRUSADING ENGLAND

Thus far in this chapter, I have offered wide-ranging analyses of medieval ideas about hermaphrodites for the most part as foreign "monsters," drawing on chronologically expansive and translocal texts and images. I return here to the particular setting of turn-of-the-fourteenth-century England and the Hereford Map, taking up the map and its turbaned figure within their specific historical contexts.

The Hereford Map was created in Hereford soon after 1300, placing it in a critical phase of what is now often called the crusades, the large-scale campaign of territorial and religious wars that reached their zenith during the twelfth and thirteenth centuries.[114] Initiated in 1095 by Pope Urban II's call to arms at the Council of Clermont, the crusades purported to reclaim Jerusalem for Christianity and extend the Christian faith throughout the region. The crusades coincided with other projects of European religious and military conquest, including the Iberian "Reconquista" and Norman consolidation of Sicily, both of which brought Christian overlordship to areas with sizable Jewish and Muslim populations. These shifts in power and demography initiated dynamic engagements between peoples of different faiths. They also prompted Christians to distinguish themselves more clearly from non-Christians, whether through legal means or through textual and visual polemics.

The Hereford Map chose Jerusalem as its geographic center, emphasizing the significance of the so-called holy land and the crusades to the map's visual rhetoric.[115] Historians have noted that the English were single-minded in their zeal for the crusades, especially in the fight for Jerusalem. English soldiers were heavily involved in efforts to claim or hold the region, an effort subsidized by a system of local taxes and revenues that historians have taken as evidence of broad-based support.[116] Yet the thirteenth century also saw declining confidence in Christian control over the area. The expansion of the Mongol Empire, as well as reports of Muslim attacks on Christians, led to both disillusionment and outrage in the years just before the Hereford Map's creation.[117] The year 1291, in particular, marked the fall of the city of Acre, a critical center for Christians in the Crusader Kingdom of Jerusalem. The loss of Acre dealt a considerable blow: its fall is often read by scholars as a watershed moment—the beginning of the end of Latin imperialism and significant crusader influence in the region. For Christians in Europe and England, the defeat was bitter, and it elicited hostile feelings toward Muslims.[118] Coming closely on the heels of Acre's fall, the Hereford Map and its vision of the world were strongly informed by this recent history.[119]

Scholars have offered contrasting views of the turbaned headdress worn by the Hereford Map's nonbinary figure. Christof Rolker argues that the turban is a sign of generalized exoticism, while M. W. Bychowski sees it as a symbol of non-Christian faith.[120] But the art historian Debra Strickland argues persuasively that the figure's turban and beard would have been instantly recognizable to viewers as pictorial signs of a "Saracen"—the medieval term for a Muslim that encompassed both Islamic faith and a fundamental physical difference from Christians.[121] The Hereford Map's hermaphrodite stands above a crawling "himantopodes," another member of the monstrous races, and one who wears a *pileum cornutum*, a pointed hat that was a contemporary sign of Judaism (see figs. 2.1A and 2.1C).[122] The himantopodes appears in profile, with one large visible eye and a hooked nose, stereotypical features that link it to other derisory images of Jews on the map (see, for instance, a similar image of a Jew on the Exodus path, who worships a defecating idol labeled "mahun," a likely reference to Muhammad, and an image that appears to conflate Islam and Judaism).[123] The juxtaposition of the two monstrous-race figures—the Muslim hermaphrodite and the Jewish himantopodes—suggests that non-Christian religion was deliberately conflated with monstrosity on the map.[124] The map's turbaned hermaphrodite thus takes on additional meanings: after all, the Hereford Map displaced its turbaned figure to its edge, farthest from the central territory of Jerusalem. In doing so, the map symbolically ejected turbaned foes—that is, Muslims—from Jerusalem's spatial limits.

Viewing the Hereford Map's hermaphrodite through this lens suggests a range of further interpretations. During the crusades, a number of Christian texts condemned the Muslim faith in explicitly monstrous terms. Alan of Lille's twelfth-century *Against Heretics* (*Contra haereticos*), for instance, railed against "Muhammad's monstrous life, more monstrous sect, and most monstrous end."[125] As Naomi Kline observes, Muslims in certain respects were familiar to the English—missionizing activity recognized Muslims' humanity and their capacity for conversion—but in the decades leading up to the Hereford Map's creation, news of "inhuman" atrocities committed by Mongol armies reached virtually every parish in England.[126] From the twelfth century on, English art and literature sometimes portrayed Muslims as bestial, hybridized, or misshapen, and *chansons de geste* (French military epics) could show Muslims with distorted, and even frankly monstrous, bodies.[127] Albrecht Classen argues that in crusading literature, Muslims were depicted as on par with beasts, stereotyped as a "photographic negative of the self-perception of an ideal Christian."[128] As the influential abbot Peter the Venerable (1092–1156) claimed, the Saracen religion was a hybrid constructed "monstrously" from preexisting religious doctrine, distorting the body of Christian belief.[129] Importantly, split bodies could connote religious schism, too: Dante's *Inferno* imagined Muhammad as corporeally divided, "cleft from the chin to the part that breaks wind," much like the bifurcated hermaphrodite on the Hereford Map. As Steven Kruger observes, the fragmented bodies of Muslims in medieval literature visualized Islam "as both a schismatic departure from Christianity and itself a religion rent by schism."[130]

The Hereford Map's inscription characterized its turbaned hermaphrodite as "a race of both sexes, unnatural in many of their customs." The illustration featured exposed genitals, suggesting that "unnatural customs" were to be understood, at least in part, as sexual. Contemporary Christian polemics linked Muslims to erotic excess—a result of both their purported spiritual failings and origin in warmer climes, which were thought to produce lustier and impetuous bodies.[131] As Christians argued, the Muslim faith was a "carnal cult for a carnal people," inextricably bound to sexual vices of polygamy and sodomy.[132] Africans could be rendered in similar terms, too: just after 1300, the Montpellier-based physician Arnold of Villanova wrote that "black men" were both uncivilized and perverse, driven to sexual intercourse with any partner, "regardless of sex, age, or species."[133] "Unnatural," of course, was the standard descriptor in the Middle Ages for sodomy, the quintessential "sin against nature," and one with which nonbinary-sexed figures were repeatedly linked.[134] As we have seen, biblical commentators such as Peter the Chanter and Hugh of St. Cher drew multiple connections between androgyny, hermaphroditism, and sodomy. Twelfth-century moralists such as Bernard of Cluny and Alan of Lille also compared hermaphrodites to sodomites.[135] In his *Summa of Confession* (c. 1216), Peter of Poitiers cited nonbinary sex as a part of his polemic against masturbation, which Peter claimed was more monstrous than sodomy, "since the person practicing it is both active and passive, and thus as if man and woman, and as if a hermaphrodite."[136] As John Boswell noted in his now-classic *Christianity, Social Tolerance, and Homosexuality*, ideas about "hermaphroditism" and sodomy were fluidly associated in the minds of many medieval thinkers.[137] Moreover, sodomy was for some Christians not only a matter of moral choice but also of essential biological difference.[138] The mythic hermaphrodite image on the Hereford Map thus evoked the sensual excess associated with foreign lands, while also suggesting that Africans and Muslims were hypersexual and corporeally distinct from the residents of Christendom.

Scholars have further shown how medieval disparagements of Africans and Muslims in terms of monstrosity are invocations of what we now call "race" and "racism."[139] Historians have long been cautious about using modern racial terms to describe premodern phenomena, but a wave of new scholarship has made a persuasive case that we must identify elements of race and racism in the medieval world. Scholars such as Geraldine Heng, Suzanne Akbari, Cord Whitaker, Thomas Hahn, and Dorothy Kim, among others, have argued that medieval rhetoric cannot be dismissed as innocent of racial animus. A growing number of scholars now view claims of African, Muslim, or Jewish inferiority on the basis of a matrix of embodied and cultural traits as compelling evidence of what we now call racial sorting and derogation.[140] Geraldine Heng, in particular, identifies thirteenth-century England as central to the articulation of racial difference and the construction of an English collective identity. According to Heng, the monstrous Africans on the Hereford Map concretized racial stratifications, indexing "each vector of the world according to its relative distance from Europe in human, as well as spatial, terms."[141] Similarly, for Debra Strickland, the myth of the monstrous races provided "an enduring blueprint for the condemnation and exclusion of real-world, non-Christian cultural outsiders," including Jews, Muslims, and Africans.[142]

Medieval Christian literature could sometimes idealize Africans: Prester John, a legendary king imagined to live in Africa, held out the promise of a Christian ally abroad in the fourteenth century.[143] But the Hereford Map portrayed its African hermaphrodite in terms of cultural difference ("unnatural customs") and physical difference (a monstrous body), placing it within an expanded field of medieval race-making, one in which embodied sexual traits contributed to hierarchies of peoples, and they created racialized distinctions between self and other.[144] The map's dehumanizing portrait of Ethiopia also lends further credence to scholarly claims that medieval marvels were not just fanciful celebrations of pleasure-inducing diversity but also instruments of violence that assigned alien and subhuman status to fellow peoples.[145] The Hereford Map assigned grotesque bodies and uncivilized practices to Ethiopians, who became grist for the cultural mill of the monstrous races, the derogation of foreign lands, and the overarching project of English self-identification.

Such messages were conveyed to a relatively broad and diverse public. The Hereford *mappamundi*'s original position inside the Hereford Cathedral—likely affixed to the wall on the south choir aisle—located the map near the terminus of a pilgrimage.[146] This placement would have made it accessible to clergy, monarchs, nobles, merchants, peasants, and pilgrims from all over Europe. With pictorial content that was comprehensible to illiterate viewers, and Latin and Anglo-Norman inscriptions suited to more sophisticated audiences, the map could accommodate a flexible and "international" society of readers and onlookers. Moreover, as some scholars have suggested, church-commissioned *mappaemundi* were essentially works of public art. Along with songs, plays, monumental sculptures, stained glass, and other artistic productions meant for broad audiences, the Hereford Map contributed to and communicated prevailing ideologies of the day, including exclusionary views of foreign, religious, and racial others, and their supposed expressions of monstrous sexual difference and sexuality.[147]

Drawing from the centuries-old tradition of the monstrous races, the Hereford Map pictured its turbaned subject as corporeally and culturally distinct, removed from the imagined physical standards and bodily ideals of English Christianity. The art historian Michael Camille has called the medieval *mappamundi* a cartographic space for the "banished, outlawed, leprous, scabrous outcasts of society" relegated to the global margins.[148] The Hereford Map conjured up the curious spectacle of an Ethiopian turbaned nonbinary figure, only to thrust the figure to the map's most scabrous and alien edge. And yet multiple links between nonbinary sex and boundary-crossing complicated any straightforward message of alterity and distance. The map held out the possibility that the figure's location "outside" was not absolute. The turbaned figure might come to violate the imagined borders of Christendom once again.

Monsters were central to medieval culture, shaping the limits of human identity and establishing what kind of bodies mattered to society.[149] As this chapter argues, monstrous figures with nonbinary sex traits lay at numerous conceptual borders in the Middle Ages, fashioning and making visible the categories of sex, geography, race, and species. If all human knowledge is corporeal (that is, if the human body is a primary source of knowledge and ordering of the world), then sexual difference—often imagined to be the first and most basic difference among humans—is uniquely suited to making sense of other kinds of difference. Sexual difference was instrumental to medieval monster-making: as scholars have noted, a number of other monsters besides mythic hermaphrodites also expressed nonbinary sex.[150] The myth of the monstrous races, moreover, implied a central question: What is a human? The inclusion of nonbinary-sexed figures within this legend meant that they were bound up with fundamental problems concerning human nature and identity. As a result, ideas about nonbinary sex were a vehicle for exploring the boundaries that touched on all peoples.

Anthropologists have pointed out that the worldviews of many societies can be reduced to binary oppositions of human/nonhuman and us/them, which often overlapped. According to this argument, medieval texts about monsters were engaged in hyperbolic speech that made caricatures of those groups medieval authors deemed inferior, establishing a clear distinction between "us" and "them" and bolstering group identity.[151] More recently, scholars in critical race, critical animal, and post/decolonial studies have offered new perspectives on the process by which certain individuals become human and worthy of ethical consideration, while others do not.[152] Exclusions from the human often depend on the rhetoric of gender and sexuality; that is, individuals considered racially or geographically "other" are often assumed to express gender and sexuality in ways that differ from normative subjects.[153] In the medieval period, too, the racial and sexual derogation of groups outside of Europe could be used to forge and stabilize the bodies and statuses of those within it. By picturing a nonbinary monster in Ethiopia, the Hereford Map aimed to keep apart Christendom and those others whose shapes and customs were imagined to transgress its limits. Such images cast geographical and racial others outside, "hermaphroditizing" them, and rationalizing their purported inferiority. Moreover, by labeling outsiders as "hermaphrodites" and "monsters," Europeans could by contrast define the sexual binary, and those who adhered to it, as ideal.

In light of these parallels between medieval and modern hierarchies of peoples based on purported embodied and cultural differences, it is reasonable—and important—to note that aspects of colonial and racist thinking can be identified in medieval discourse about the monstrous races.[154] It is also important to point out that the establishment of the binary sexual model as ideal in Christian Europe emerged from Europe's real and imagined encounters with its Muslim territorial neighbors. Yet binary frameworks do not encompass fully the heterogeneity of medieval thinking. With respect to nonbinary sex, there was no clear-cut East-West divide that can be mapped onto medieval classifications. We cannot place nonbinary-sexed monstrosity firmly beyond or in opposition to English or European identity. Nonbinary-sexed monsters could exist on both sides of a line between human and nonhuman, here and there, and self and other. Nonbinary figures could be imagined as members of unknowable tribes in the distance but also as intimates at home in the West. As residents of nearby regions, even neighbors, they were people that "we" might know and who might confuse our ability to distinguish *them* from *us*.

3

The Hyena's Unclean Sex

Beasts, Bestiaries, and Jewish Communities

Brimming with evocative tales and illustrations, bestiaries—as medieval guides to animals were known—became tremendously popular during the twelfth and thirteenth centuries, especially in England.[1] Underpinning the genre was belief that the natural world was a "book of nature" parallel to the biblical "book of scripture" and, like it, filled with religious import.[2] Bestiaries offered not only zoological information—drawn from scriptural, mythological, and naturalist sources—but also moral lessons exemplified by the behavior of animals and upheld by divine writ.

Animals with unusual sexes paraded across the pages of bestiaries and related animal lore. Some beasts were praiseworthy—such as beavers who, texts claimed, castrated themselves in an allegory of chastity—but others were much less admirable.[3] Hares were double-sexed: their tendency to multiply quickly earned them a reputation for promiscuity, fluctuating sex, and autonomous reproduction.[4] Other animals, too, were imagined to be asexual or nonbinary sexed. But the nonbinary beast par excellence was the hyena. A macabre illustration in an English manuscript known as the Aberdeen Bestiary (c. 1200) highlights a hyena's monstrous body and savage fangs as it feasts on a nude human corpse (see fig. 3.1). Ancient authorities sometimes described hyenas as "hermaphrodites," and the bestiary's graphic image pictures the animal with both a vagina and a prominent penis.[5] As the accompanying passage argued, the hyena's two sexes represented the "uncleanness" of Jews.[6]

In the first section of this chapter, I look closely at the Aberdeen Bestiary's hyena. As I show, the bestiary drew upon the biblical book of Leviticus to explore binary divisions, the transgression of which led to "uncleanness"—a formula used to denigrate contemporary Jews. Next, I place the binaries so important

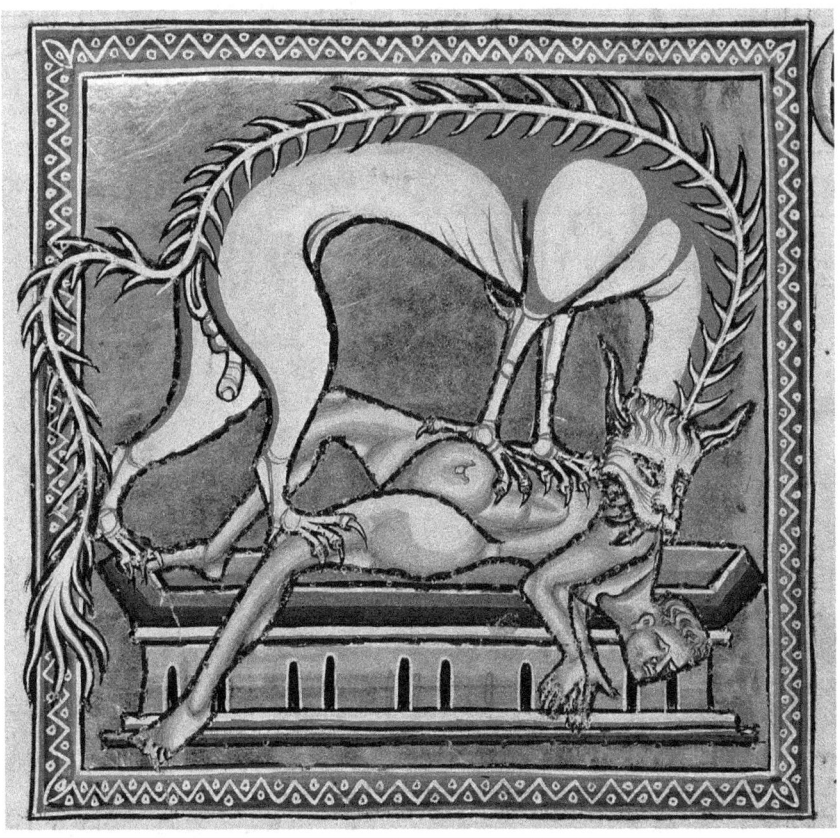

FIGURE 3.1 Hyena. *Aberdeen Bestiary*. Aberdeen, University of Aberdeen Library, MS 24, fol. 11v (c. 1200).

to the Aberdeen Bestiary within a broader "discourse of opposites" that pervaded the twelfth century. In this section, I cast my net rather widely to look at a series of texts and images that used the idea of nonbinary sex as an analogy for boundary-crossing, especially when that boundary separated spirituality from materiality (the latter often in the form of money). In addition, I consider texts that accused sodomites and demons of gender inversion, condemning their sexual unfixity and uncleanness, which were thought to jeopardize the Christian faith.

Finally, I place ideas about nonbinary sex, boundaries, and uncleanness within the context of Jewish-Christian relations in late twelfth- and thirteenth-century England. This period witnessed growing interreligious tensions, which erupted in repeated massacres of Jews and the cruel expulsion of Jewish communities from the kingdom at the end of the century. Although I focus on England in this chapter, a parallel trajectory was taking place in France, which saw similar expulsions in 1306, 1322, and 1394.[7] A number of scholars have documented how images from bestiaries contributed to anti-Jewish sentiment during the period. But as of yet, no one has looked at the specific role that ideas about nonbinary sex played in such polemics. By identifying Jews with nonbinary anatomies and practices, the Aberdeen Bestiary mobilized the supposedly negative qualities of nonbinary sex to depict Jews as unclean and dangerous pollutants. Much as in the texts of the previous chapter, we find a similar logic at work in shaping the Christian community. The Aberdeen Bestiary and its dual-sexed hyena were part of a climate that identified Jews as confounders of categories and threats to the Christian community.

THE ABERDEEN BESTIARY

The Aberdeen Bestiary was just one of a cluster of bestiaries created in England during the twelfth and thirteenth centuries, when the bestiary genre was reaching the height of its artistic production and popularity. A number of English bestiaries included a hyena allegory, along with a pictorial illustration of a hyena with both male and female sex traits (as traditionally understood) attacking a dead human body.[8] The Aberdeen Bestiary, the focus in this section, features a particularly evocative and hyperbolic version of this image, and it may have been a model for other bestiaries. The Aberdeen Bestiary's specific origin remains unknown, but scholars such as Willene Clark and Xenia Muratova point to a possible genesis in the northeast Midlands or in south England.[9] The manuscript may have been intended for a monastic audience or, alternatively, for a higher clerical or aristocratic patron. Accent markings for stressed pronunciation, along with finger imprints suggesting a pattern of use, indicate that the Aberdeen Bestiary was probably read aloud and then turned upside-down to display its illustrations.[10] Its complementary text-and-image format may have helped students—perhaps illiterate lay brothers at a monastery, or the young members of an aristocratic household—to understand the bestiaries' moral lessons.

Its eye-catching hyena image appears alongside a detailed passage that compares Jews to hyenas, who could allegedly alternate their sex:

> There is an animal called the hyena, which inhabits the tombs of the dead and feeds on their bodies. Its nature is that it is sometimes male, sometimes female, and it is therefore an unclean animal.... In its search for buried bodies, the hyena

digs up graves. The sons of Israel resemble the hyena. At the beginning they served the living God. Later, addicted to wealth and luxury, they worshipped idols. For this reason the prophet compared the synagogue to an unclean animal: "My heritage is to me as the den of a hyena." Therefore those among us who are slaves to luxury and greed, are like this brute, since they are neither men nor women, that is, neither faithful nor faithless, but are without doubt those of whom Solomon says: "A double-minded man is unstable in all his ways"; of whom the Lord says: "You cannot serve God and mammon."[11]

The text of the bestiary deems certain behaviors and attributes "unclean," a word evoking the biblical book of Leviticus and the law of the ancient Israelites, who used designations of "clean" and "unclean" to organize ritual and daily life.[12] As anthropologists have suggested, many societies make use of purity taboos to establish the social order, as well as to remove sources of pollution from the community. Analyzing such taboos, scholars say, gives us crucial insight into a culture and its social organization: that is, whenever an "order of things" is violated, we get a glimpse into that society's system of values.[13]

We see just such a violation with the hyena and its transgressive behavior. Much like the prohibitions of Leviticus, the bestiary's hyena reveals a classificatory system at work: the bestiary's text and image establish a series of binary oppositions (male and female, living and dead, material and spiritual), the crossing or confounding of which results in "uncleanness." We also see an overlap between the bestiary and the monstrous-race literature I surveyed in chapter 2. According to that tradition, mythic hermaphrodites had both male and female traits that allowed them to switch between roles, occupying neither sex permanently. Here, too, the Aberdeen Bestiary described hyenas as "sometimes male, sometimes female," and "neither men nor women." In a departure from the monstrous-race tradition, however, the bestiary identified the hyena's praiseworthy qualities with masculinity: the hyena represented not only sexual duality but also the degeneration of a positive male body into a more negative female one.[14]

While the bestiary emphasized the duplicatory aspect of nonbinary sex by comparing a hyena to a "double-minded man," the image depicted its hyena not as bifurcated (as we saw in the split and Janiform mythic hermaphrodites of chapter 2), but as a combination of traditionally male-female and anthropomorphic-theriomorphic traits. The assertion that "mixed" bodies were ritually unclean had precedent in Hebrew law. According to anthropologist Mary Douglas, Leviticus identified as abominations those animals that blurred categorical divisions between species. As Douglas writes, "Those species are unclean which are imperfect members of their class, or whose class itself confounds the general scheme of the world."[15] Creatures that lived in water but moved with legs (such as shellfish) or animals with cloven feet that did not chew cud (such as pigs) were considered abominations, and they were rejected by Leviticus as sources of food and sacrifice.[16] In the Aberdeen Bestiary, a creature with both male and female genitals exhibited a similar confusion of categories and a similar unclean status.

The graveyard setting of the bestiary's image also epitomized uncleanness. A living creature that made its home among tombs and ate decaying flesh was a transgressor of multiple boundaries regarding space and food. The hyena, who in "its search for buried bodies . . . digs up graves," was a desecrator of the cemetery, a space generally reserved for the dead. Although corpses were hardly a rare sight in the Middle Ages, rotting bodies were still a horrifying presence: scholars have pointed to the ways in which nearly all cultures deny or hide the processes of decay that immediately follow death.[17] Also, because the bestiary image depicted necrophagy, it evoked rules that sorted foods into permissible and impermissible types (for instance, the raw and the cooked, or the fresh and the spoiled).[18] In medieval life, dietary distinctions could differentiate humans from both monsters and beasts, which consumed foul and stomach-churning foods forbidden to humans—such as raw, rotting, or human flesh.[19] Eating the flesh of humans, in particular, signaled both monstrosity and inhumanity. A different man-eating monster, a lion-human hybrid known as the manticore, also appears in certain contemporary bestiaries.[20] In MS Bodley 764 (England, c. 1240–60), for instance, a manticore wears a Phrygian hat—often interpreted as a sign of Jewishness—as it devours a severed human leg (see fig. 3.2).[21] The scholar Peter Hulme suggests that cannibalism has often been imagined as a category diametrically opposed to humanity, a barbaric other against which human civilization strives. By featuring an allegedly Jewish hybrid beast consuming human flesh, a bestiary could portray a non-Christian figure as a violator of the fundamental taboos that defined humankind.[22]

If monstrosity was often centered on eating, eating in the Middle Ages was also inextricably tied to sexuality. Sexual and gastronomic sins were not always discrete categories of transgression in the Middle Ages. Writers frequently conflated or juxtaposed the two, which arose from desires that enveloped the whole body, finding expression in a variety of forms.[23] In many texts, the mouth and vagina were homologous symbols of unquenchable appetite, the nature of their indulgence rendered imprecise.[24] Further, the prominence of the hyena's genitals in the Aberdeen Bestiary alluded not only to sexuality but also to the genitals' role in fecal and urinary elimination, foregrounding the animal's bodily excretions and their link to filth and pollution.[25] Contemporary Christian texts often spoke of sinfulness in terms of bodily excrement, and we also find scatological language used to describe Jews.[26] The grotesque aspects of excretory matter derived

FIGURE 3.2 Manticore. *Bestiary*. Oxford, University of Oxford, Bodleian Library, MS Bodley 764, fol. 25r (c. 1240–1260). Permission of the Bodleian Libraries.

from ideas about the body's leaky openings and convexities, which allowed for encounters with the outside world, as well as with other bodies. Such was Mikhail Bakhtin's "bodily lower stratum" that linked digestion and defecation to ribald expressions of fertility—as well as grim reminders of death.[27] Around the turn of the twelfth century, the bishop Odo of Tournai described what was a common sensory-based reaction to excretory functions in the Middle Ages, a "gut-feeling" that "despises our genitalia, viscera, and excrement, and judges them unclean."[28]

"Unclean" in the Aberdeen Bestiary also characterized Jews, who according to the text were "neither men nor women, that is, neither faithful nor faithless." The uncanny, humanlike appearance of the animal's sexual organs also proposed a resemblance between the hyena and a Jewish body. The illumination placed the hyena's vagina dorsally to the extent that it resembled an anus, further suggesting the hyena's suitability for deviant, even sodomitical, sex.[29] As scholars have noted, common anti-Jewish tropes in medieval literature portrayed Jewish men as effeminate, libidinous, or androgynous. Some Christian sources explained such physical characteristics in "scientific" terms that asserted the innate, biological otherness of Jewish bodies. Jewish men, for instance, were reported to suffer from a monthly bloody flux from the anus that differentiated them from Christians and linked them to the oozing, uncontrollable physicality associated at that time with women.[30] Like the abominations of the biblical book of Leviticus, the bestiary's Jewish hyena was believed to confound the binaries that ordered the world.

The Aberdeen Bestiary also accused Jews of greed and indulgence by placing money before God. In the bestiary, Jews strayed from the proper and fixed path of spirituality: they betrayed God in favor of a lust for riches that was both vulgar and unclean. During this same time period, complaints about monetization and taxation were on the rise in England, and Jews—who, beginning in 1180, were forced by Henry II to become de facto tax collectors—were often resented by Christians, who associated them with usury, debt, and the exploitative side of the money economy.[31] Contemporary texts, such as the *Bible moralisée*, made it clear that Jews' occupation as moneylenders was evidence enough for many Christians that they "idolatrously worshipped money."[32] Over the course of the thirteenth century, English Jews were targeted repeatedly for money-related offenses, such as coin-clipping and counterfeiting, so much so that some scholars have argued that Jews came to personify money and the sins of avarice and fraud in the view of Christians.[33] In the Aberdeen Bestiary, Jews were "double-minded" men who could not serve two masters—that is, both God and wealth—and they therefore occupied an unclean space between male-female and spirituality-materiality.

A number of authors have also analyzed how bestiaries adopted their structure from an anonymous text known as the *Physiologus (The Naturalist*, sometimes translated as *The Allegorist)*, a treatise written in Alexandria between the second and fourth centuries CE. The *Physiologus* took active part in Alexandria's climate of anti-Judaism, which also spawned "*Adversus Iudaeos*" literature such as the *Epistle of Barnabus* and Justin Martyr's *Dialogue with Trypho*.[34] As Debra Strickland indicates, bestiaries refashioned these ancient tropes to express contemporary grievances against Jews. When the Aberdeen Bestiary identified Jews as violators of binary categories and vectors of pollution, it borrowed from Leviticus and the *Physiologus* to elevate current political and economic conflicts to biblical proportions. The categories of clean and unclean established by the Hebrew Bible functioned to preserve the communal purity of the Israelites in exile.[35] These were crucial tools of inclusion and exclusion, central to the ways in which objects and practices were sorted and perceived. In the case of the Aberdeen Bestiary, Christian creators transformed the ancient rhetoric of cultic impurity into a weapon against Jews, sorting them into the category of the unclean.[36]

The Aberdeen Bestiary also charged that hyenas were both sexes, unfixed in their serial shifts between male and female.[37] According to the charges of Christian authors, Jews were similarly inconsistent in their religious fidelity. A thirteenth-century manuscript illumination—a "before" and "after" portrait in a copy of the Anglo-Norman *Bestiaire*, written by Guillaume le Clerc in around 1210—placed Jews firmly in the category of serial shifters (see fig. 3.3).[38] The image, which illustrates the "sermon of the hyena," includes two related temporal fields. The upper register shows Jews kneeling in front of the burning bush, in which Christ's face appears, while the lower register shows Jews idolatrously worshipping the Golden Calf.[39] The latter image illustrates the backslide of the Israelites into idolatry before their correction by Moses, a story that appears in Exodus 32:4. By showing this scene, the *Bestiaire* argued that Jews had previously alternated between belief and unbelief, and it held out the hope that they would once again return to the purportedly proper faith. By emphasizing the supposed impermanence of Jews' religious practice, the bestiary compared their behavior to the gendered inconstancy of hyenas and, at the same time, it pointed to the possibility of their future conversion. In this case, sexual mobility might also have intersected with notions of Jews as nomadic or wandering: an older eastern legend of the "wandering Jew" was apparently known in thirteenth-century England.[40]

The Aberdeen Bestiary denounced Jews by likening them to gender-crossing hyenas, a comparison that highlighted their supposed spiritual instability and animal nature. Such accusations also resonated with other polemics that similarly designated Jews as bestial and subhuman. In the eyes of the influential abbot Peter the Venerable, who flourished in the twelfth century, the Jewish rejection of Christianity meant that Jews lacked reason and hence should be regarded as mere "wild animal[s]" or "beast[s]." For other authors, too, the purported blindness of Jews to the truth of Christianity proved that Jews were irrational and, as a result, less than human.[41] The Aberdeen Bestiary, moreover, expressed concern that Christians, the bestiary's primary audience, were in danger of deteriorating

FIGURE 3.3 Jews with burning bush and golden calf (Sermon of the hyena). Guillaume le Clerc, *Bestiaire*. Paris, Bibliothèque nationale de France, MS français 14969, fol. 29v (c. 1265–1270).

into subhumans, too. Using its nonbinary-sexed hyena as a warning, the bestiary cautioned Christians against imitating their Jewish neighbors' inconstant faith and unclean reverence for money, which would lead to diminished spiritual superiority and threaten their human status.

Although scholars have noted that each bestiary manuscript is unique, they have also argued that bestiaries nevertheless shared common purposes.[42] However distinct their details, bestiaries tended to repeat a great deal of material, and the allegory of the hyena was routinely featured in such manuscripts. Very similar

FIGURE 3.4 Hyena. *Northumberland Bestiary*. Pen-and-ink drawing tinted with body color and translucent washes on parchment.

Leaf: 21 × 15.7 cm (8 1/4 × 6 3/16 in.), (England, about 1250 – 1260). Los Angeles, The J. Paul Getty Museum, MS 100, fol. 12v.

wording and imagery appear in members of the "Morgan" or "transitional" group, including the Northumberland Bestiary (England, c. 1250–60) (see fig. 3.4); Worksop Bestiary (England, possibly in Lincoln or York before 1187), St. Petersburg Bestiary (England, c. 1180–90); and Royal 12 C.XIX (England, c. 1200–10). In addition, the British Library Add. MS 11283 (England, c. 1175–1200), Ashmole Bestiary (England, c. 1200), Bodley 764 (England, c. 1240–60) and other exemplars of "second-family" bestiaries also include virtually the same text.[43] Bestiaries delivered their messages to a substantial Christian audience: scholars have identified them as one of the most popular and widespread genres of literature in the Middle Ages.[44] By the thirteenth century, the bestiaries' content had moved beyond elite circles to more diverse audiences. Far from being available to only the highest echelon of religious and secular authorities, the moral lessons of the bestiaries were used by teachers to clarify religious principles, and preachers mined them for *exempla* to illustrate sermons. Sarah Kay notes that, taken together, the audiences of bestiaries included aristocratic courts, "twelfth-century *literati*, thirteenth-century arts students, scholars of natural science, and theologians of all kinds," as well as the young students with which they are often associated. As Joyce Salisbury suggests, bestiaries worked to "change the medieval mental landscape."[45]

CONFOUNDING OPPOSITIONS: WORLDLINESS AND SPIRITUALITY

While ostensibly a compilation of animal curiosities, the Aberdeen Bestiary was also a regulator of human behavior. As we have seen, the bestiary used the language of opposition to draw attention to the nonbinary-sexed results of conflicting loyalties. The book shared its method with other contemporary texts that were also theorizing opposed ideas in terms of sexed qualities. As we shall see, when authors struggled to describe categories that could not be reconciled—or when they pictured dangerous or polluting combinations of things—they repeatedly imagined them in the form of "hermaphrodites."

During the twelfth century, in particular, medieval thinkers conceived of many aspects of life—from religious conversion to romance to legal disputes—in light of paired oppositions. Dyads, paradoxes, and dichotomies were common rhetorical devices in both classical and medieval culture and, despite the centrality of the trinity and other triads, the Christian church was also an enthusiastic purveyor of dualities (Christ was both human and God; human beings were both body and soul). In schools, courts, monasteries, and beyond, medieval thinkers wrestled with the tension between unity and diversity, and they explored with great interest contraries, dichotomies, and binaries, ordering their world through a "discourse of opposites."[46]

But even as such opposed categories necessitated and reflected each other, they also remained distinct. "Mixtures" (*mixtiones, confusiones*), in contrast, carried negative connotations in both ancient and medieval thought, where they were described as sources of chaos and incoherence. Ancient rhetoricians, for instance, warned authors to preserve the "integrity" and "dignity" of different stylistic elements rather than blending them together into an unintelligible mixture. Authors praised the dynamism of *varietas* (variety), a polyfocality that encouraged harmony, but they nevertheless viewed mixtures with suspicion.[47] For the famous twelfth-century abbot Bernard of Clairvaux, *puritas* (purity) was the opposite of *mixtio*, and a term that connoted monsters, category violations, and other combinations of unlike qualities.[48] But, as Bernard himself noted, Christ was a mixture—as was the Virgin birth, and the creation. About the latter, Bernard mused, "God mixes the vile slime of earth with vital force" and to honor humans more, "he united in his person God and slime, majesty and lowliness, such vileness and such sublimity."[49] These mixtures of high and low, spirit and flesh, were so marvelous that they were, as the scholar Mary Carruthers puts it, "a kind of a monstrosity."[50] Extraordinary mixtures aroused wonder, but they discomfited Christians, too.

Scholasticism, the intellectual approach of high medieval schools, also explored ideas in terms of binaries. The reception of Aristotle's "New Logic" during the twelfth century joined with the "Old Logic" that had already been a part of European high intellectual culture for centuries.[51] Boethius's Latin translations of Aristotle's *Prior Analytics*, *Topics*, and *Sophistical Refutations*, along with James of Venice's translation of the *Posterior Analytics*, appeared or reappeared between 1115–59, and they came to play important roles in twelfth- and thirteenth-century scholastic analyses.[52] Such texts emphasized approaches based on proofs and counterproofs, propositions and negations, and other pairs of contraries.[53] Moreover, much like the varied models of nonbinary sex that I discuss throughout this book, scholastic models were polyvalent, with some scholars embracing unresolved opposition (such as Abelard) and others preferring integration (such as Peter Lombard). By the thirteenth century, scholasticism tended to emphasize a unitary truth: at its core was an encounter between thesis and antithesis—statements juxtaposed in such a way that they could be reconciled.[54] By this view, the stronger argument claimed victory over the weaker, and harmony won out over confusion.

JOHN OF SALISBURY

A conflict between harmony and confusion is precisely what troubles the writings of the twelfth-century English philosopher John of Salisbury, a former student of the French scholastic Peter Abelard. Abelard was, of course, the author of *Sic et non* (*Yes and No*), a famous work that placed in glaring contrast the contrary teachings of the Bible, the church fathers, and other authorities, encouraging (but not accomplishing) their resolution.[55] Resolution was far from the result, however, when opposites collided in John's *Policraticus* (1159). In this work, he lamented the fates of men who were both philosophers and courtiers: such irreconcilable commitments, John claimed, produced "hermaphrodites."

As John explained to readers, courtly life was full of "disgusting uncleanness [*illuuio feda*] and cancerous affliction," so much so that "it is hardly possible to retain one's innocence among courtiers."[56] To support his argument, John turned to Ovid's *Metamorphoses* and the ill-fated encounter between Hermaphroditus and Salmacis. According to the tale, after entering Salmacis's fountain, Hermaphroditus fused with Salmacis into a male-female creature that seemed, according to Ovid, "neither [sex], and yet both."[57] For John of Salisbury, court life—like Salmacis' fountain—degenerated the virility of philosophers and enervated them to such a degree of weakness that like effeminate men they are deprived of the nobler sex; and none stepped out from it other than those who were stunned and distressed to be changed into women. For either their sex, vanishing entirely, had degenerated into the inferior gender or they retained enough of the vestiges of their former dignity to assume the identity of a hermaphrodite, who, by a sort of foolish error of nature, exhibits the likeness of both sexes, yet retains the true qualities of neither of them.[58]

In John's account, court life caused a philosopher's sex to "vanish entirely," replaced by the inferior sex of a woman. This transformation entailed the substitution of one thing (female) for another thing (male), a "stunning" and "distressing" change that weakened, or even obliterated, the philosopher's sex. If, however, the philosopher retained some of his manly qualities, he became an attenuated man, that is, one who was neither male nor female but who encompassed both sexes. John continued:

He who engages in the trifles of the courtier and undertakes the obligations of the philosopher or the good man is a hermaphrodite, whose harsh and prickly face disfigures the beauty of women and who pollutes and dishonors virility with effeminacy. For indeed the philosopher-courtier is a monstrous thing; and, while he affects to be both, he is neither one because the court excludes philosophy and the philosopher at no time engages in the trifles of the courtier.[59]

In this passage, we find a number of statements comparable to those of the Aberdeen Bestiary. John's courtier-philosopher, poised between two irreconcilable opposites, is a "hermaphrodite" and a "monstrous thing" who serves neither court nor philosophy faithfully. In John's view, moreover, a hermaphrodite was a mixture: a beard mars feminine beauty, effeminacy "pollutes and dishonors" virility, and superficialities foul philosophical truth. Two opposites combine, one weakening the other, diluting it and subsuming it into *neither*.

Court life in the twelfth century was inherently itinerant and unstable, subject to fluctuating fashions and favorites, and contemporary clerics often complained about the faddish hairstyles and clothes that sunk courtly youth "in effeminacy."[60] To John, court life resembled the imagined inconstancy of hermaphrodites, who were thought to flit between the sexes and confuse the spheres of male and female.[61] John's rhetoric revealed yet another important claim, too: because he thought hermaphrodites were adulterations of pure maleness and femaleness, their presence occasioned what he called "disgusting uncleanness." Proximity to moral filth was enough to infect one with it. As John himself noted,

" 'He who touches pitch is dirtied by it'; and 'contact with one bunch of grapes produces spoilage in another.' "[62] In the *Policraticus*, ideas about hermaphrodites and their alleged unfixed natures were comparable to an aristocratic court and its ever-shifting ground. But ideas about hermaphrodites also symbolized a failure to keep separate that which must not be mixed. Such sentiments invoked the regulatory system of Leviticus and a seeping "uncleanness" that polluted whomever it touched. Elsewhere in his writings, John advocated for a middle ground—an alternative to the oppositions so championed by his scholastic colleagues—but in the passage just cited, the middle ground yielded only uncleanness.[63] Notably, John's conclusions diverged markedly from that of his contemporary, Bernard of Clairvaux, who advised a similarly conflicted figure, Eugene III, to practice an ethical mean between two extremes (quiet contemplation as a monk and worldly administration as a pope). But, for John, intermediacy of this type was contaminating, disfiguring, and even monstrous.[64]

NONBINARY TRANSGRESSIONS

John of Salisbury's text fits well into a long-lived set of associations between nonbinary sex and spiritual transgression among Christian authors. John might have found inspiration, for instance, in Gregory the Great's sixth-century *Pastoral Care*, a veritable "best seller" of the Carolingian era that denounced as "lukewarm" a Christian who was neither a fervent believer ("hot") nor a potential convert ("cold") and who deserved to be "vomited out" from society.[65] According to the historian Lynda Coon, the elemental qualities used by Gregory to describe faith indicated that the tepid believer was neither man nor woman but a nonbinary figure "suspended between orthodoxy and paganism, an aberrant creature on account of its [sic] mixing of the feminine (cold/inconstant) and the masculine (hot/constant) and its [sic] inability to fulfil either gender."[66] In *Pastoral Care*, climatic opposites—sexed as male and female—came to reflect on spiritual categories, staging a contrast between truth and falsity, religion and idolatry— and necessitating the removal, or "vomiting out," of those who fell between.

Another early medieval text, the Benedictine monk Remigius of Auxerre's ninth-century commentary on Martianus Capella's influential school text, *The Marriage of Philology and Mercury*, placed nonbinary sex in a similarly compromising position between truth and falsity. For the author, Hermaphroditus signified a "lasciviousness of speech that [is] obtain[ed] when the reasoned search for truth is neglected and the superfluous adornment of speech above all pursued."⁶⁷ As in the *Policraticus*, in which frivolity compromised philosophical truth, a figure suspended between ephemerality and eternity is once again a hermaphrodite.

A twelfth-century polemic that predated the *Policraticus* by a few decades also used similar imagery to describe split loyalties—this time among Christians who betrayed the faith and supported Jews. The French monk Guibert of Nogent was a relentless critic of Judaism and an early promoter of anti-Jewish tropes that were to gain even greater currency in later centuries.⁶⁸ In his virulently anti-Jewish *Treatise on the Incarnation Against the Jews* (*Tractatus de incarnatione contra Judaeos*, written in 1111), Guibert invented a neologism: *neutericum*—"neither one nor the other"—as a slur for a "Judaizer."⁶⁹ Guibert's Judaizing *neutericum* was probably the Count Jean of Soissons, the brother of the local bishop and a vocal Jewish sympathizer. The count apparently consorted with Jews and questioned the tenets of the Christian faith, leading Guibert to complain that he followed neither Jewish nor Christian law.⁷⁰ The word *neutericum* occurs in Guibert's meditation on the incarnation of Christ, in which he denounced Jews for their faithlessness. According to the treatise, Jewish errors stem from their carnality, which led Jews to focus on the physical aspects of Christ's life rather than on its spiritual meaning.⁷¹ As we have seen, "neitherness" also characterized those who served no single master faithfully, a point that Guibert also makes. Given its context, Guibert's *neutericum* was also likely a reference to "hermaphroditic" loyalties—indeed, some scholars have read the term *neutericum* as meaning "neither male nor female."⁷² Furthermore, according to Guibert, Jean's status as *neutericum* placed him in a no-man's-land shared by suffers of leprosy, an unclean disease in Leviticus.⁷³ In the text, "neitherness" characterized the seepage of the material world into spirituality, contaminating the faith and threatening Christians who, by supporting Jews, became "neither" too.

Other authors also made similar use of "hermaphrodites" to characterize mixtures of the spiritual and material. The Italian jurist Baldus de Ubaldis, a towering legal figure of the fourteenth century, analyzed the right of "advowson" (that is, when a lay patron recommended a candidate for a benefice) by an analogy to hermaphroditism. As Baldus observed, advowson entailed both laical and clerical elements and therefore was a mix of the temporal and spiritual, just like a hermaphrodite.⁷⁴ Baldus's argument is complex, but in it a nonbinary-sexed figure once more stood for obligations that blended the temporal and spiritual.

A final example demonstrates the continuing use of this equation, albeit in a more negative context. A fourteenth-century English pro-Lollard manifesto against clerical hypocrisy, *The Twelve Conclusions of the Lollards*, used the concept of hermaphroditism to describe the improper mixture of worldliness and holiness in priests who held both secular and ecclesiastical office. The manifesto's Sixth Conclusion compared any cleric who retained worldly power to a hermaphrodite: "Temporality and spirituality are two parts of the holy church, and therefore he who has taken himself to the one should not mix [*medlin*] himself with the other, 'because no one can serve two masters.' It seems to us that 'hermaphrodite' or 'ambidexter' would be a good name for such manner of men of double estate."[75] Like the *Policraticus*, the *Twelve Conclusions* denounced the loyalties that resulted from mixed temporal and spiritual obligations as irreconcilable. According to the text, any priest who occupied temporal office "took fees from both sides" (the contemporary meaning of "ambidexter"), seizing secular power and neglecting parishioners' souls.[76] This comparison once more relied on understandings of hermaphrodites as double and "playing both roles," and it suggested that hermaphrodites served neither master faithfully. Like the Jews of the Aberdeen Bestiary, such priests pursued worldliness over spiritual duty, placing God and *mammon* (the evil influence of wealth) in conflict. As in earlier texts, the idea of doubled or alternating sex was invoked when the integrity of Christianity was at stake.

The writings I've discussed in this section range over several centuries and geographic contexts. But for that very reason, I argue, the recurring theme of nonbinary sex and gender inversion is suggestive. The broadly dispersed and long-lived nature of this trope indicates that thinking about the transgression of opposed categories—especially those of materiality and spirituality—as nonbinary or hermaphroditic was likely understood and widely accepted by readers between the sixth and fourteenth centuries.

NONBINARY AND UNCLEAN SEX

In the decades leading up to the Aberdeen Bestiary's composition, authors were also making use of similar imagery to identify yet another source of uncleanness: the sexual pollution of sodomy. Two mid-twelfth-century texts, Alan of Lille's *Plaint of Nature* and Bernard of Cluny's *Scorn for the World*, both invoked the idea of nonbinary sex to denounce sodomitical sin and its perceived association with moral and material filth.

The *Plaint of Nature*, written by the theologian Alan of Lille around the 1160s, is well-known by scholars for its clever comparison of sex to irregular grammar.[77] But also notable is the way in which Alan used scatological language to characterize hermaphrodites as category violators and sources of moral decay.

In the text, Alan extolls Nature as a series of beautiful oppositions, which operate in harmony while maintaining their contradistinction.[78] But Alan lashes out at that category of defects, the sodomite, whose boundary confusion "blackens the honor of his sex and the art of magical Venus turns him into a hermaphrodite."[79] According to Nature's complaint, a sodomite's sexual perversity emits a "stench of the dung heap," an excretive foulness that it induces "many to vomit in the nausea of indignation."[80] In strikingly visceral language, Alan denounces sodomy as an unclean, sickening, gender-inverting transgression of boundaries. Alan also plays upon the both-neither qualities associated with nonbinary sex in the text, writing that the narrator is "neither alive nor dead but being tormented as neither . . . floated in a state in between."[81] Elsewhere, the goddess Nature expresses her outrage at humankind, whose nonbinary tendencies "contriv[e] to split me in two by eliding two attributes into one."[82] Nonbinary sex is here an alteration or "blackening" of God's work that fractures the oppositions so beloved by Alan. According to *Plaint of Nature*, like the *Policraticus*, "hermaphroditism" corrupts a man's sex, spoiling virility and muddying sex's boundaries.

Alan's contemporary, the twelfth-century Benedictine friar Bernard of Cluny, also denounced sodomy in his *Scorn for the World* (*De contemptu mundi*, c. 1140), a satirical poem that raged against society's current decadence. Bernard's verse adopts the language of Leviticus, singling out sodomites, hyenas, and hermaphrodites for special censure:

> O madness! O terror! The male forgetful of manliness is like a *hyena*!
> Look how many men in unnatural filth, buried in it;
> In what category, what name does this abomination have?
> Alas! the impious horror of that sin resounds even to the stars.
> The naked deed occurs, the clamor for it occurs; O chaste soul, be mournful!
> By turns this man becomes that one's accomplice, and that one becomes his.
> O Christ your law, your word, your portion are nearly dead. . . .
> O final madness! There is many a *Hermaphrodite* now. . . .
> The leprosy clings to the lowly and the mighty.
> The law of natural appetite perishes, and acknowledged custom ceases because of this plague. . . . I call them half-male who defile themselves.[83]

According to the text, like hyenas and hermaphrodites, sodomites departed from the category of man and became abominations—sources of exceptional filth. The poem is awash in scenes of deterioration: the laws of Christ and nature become half-dead, and men forget their sex and become half-men. This nonbinary destruction of categories leads to ruination, leprosy, and plague: the gruesome punishments of the Hebrew Bible. Once more in this text, hermaphrodites (and hyenas) and their allegedly mixed-up natures are identified as sources of contagious pollution. Like the Aberdeen Bestiary, which praised Jews' past devotion to the true God, Bernard's *Scorn* and Alain's *Plaint* looked back to an age when the boundaries of sex and the law were clear. In each case, the author denounced nonbinary-sexed figures as impure violators of a natural or ritual order.

DEMONIC UNCLEANNESS

In the illuminated Aberdeen Bestiary, the hyena is pictured as a threatening, gender-transgressing beast that dines on dead human flesh. With its sharp fangs and gaping mouth, the hyena image raised the disturbing possibility of the dead being unearthed, torn apart, and digested by animals. In this respect, the Aberdeen Bestiary's illustration resembled contemporary images of the "hellmouth," a demonic gateway that devoured sinners as they passed through its jaws.[84] (See fig. 3.5) For Christian theologians, damnation constituted a sort of eternal swallowing. Heaven promised immutability, bodily integrity, and freedom from decay, but hell was its opposite—mastication, partition, and consumption.[85] Eating was, of course, another dissolver of boundaries. Theories of digestion were undergoing rapid development around 1200, and some thinkers were at pains to admit any real incorporation of food into the substance of the body. But a consensus was also emerging that whatever one ate was actually absorbed into the body's flesh, changing eaten into eater, and unraveling firm distinctions between self and other.[86] The central characteristics of hell—change, process, and digestion—thus resonated with the characteristics of the Aberdeen Bestiary's hyena. The animal was visibly diabolical, with a barbed spine and hornlike ears. As we have seen, the hyena allegedly practiced reversals that confused the categories of male-female, human-animal, and truth-falsity. These tendencies linked the creature to another group of duplicitous, diabolical, nonbinary figures: demons.

Christian theologians held that demons and angels were essentially the same type of being: demons were fallen angels, banished to the infernal regions for the sins of pride and rebellion.[87] Scholastic treatises of the period noted that neither angels nor demons had material bodies, but they could transform their aerial forms into the appearance of men and women at will to better communicate

FIGURE 3.5 The Harrowing of Hell. *Psalter.* Tempera colors, gold leaf, and ink on parchment.

Leaf: 23.5 × 16.5 cm (9 1/4 × 6 1/2 in.), (Flemish, mid-1200s). Los Angeles, The J. Paul Getty Museum, MS 14, fol. 110.

with humans.[88] A demon could thus choose to assume either a male or female form, and shape-shifting demons appear with regularity in medieval hagiography and preaching *exempla*. In one story, for instance, the devil tries to seduce Saint Anthony in the guise of a woman before transforming into a black-skinned boy.[89]

Angels, too, were thought to transcend sexual boundaries. The historian Dyan Elliott notes that, at least for some authors, sexual difference was the principal quality that separated humans, with their distinct binary sexes, from the "male-inflected androgyny" of the angels.⁹⁰ Henry Mayr-Harting adds that twelfth- and thirteenth-century depictions of angels became more "caelesticized," meaning that they took on a more heavenly appearance. As angels became more divine, they also became more androgynous. Harting points to mid-thirteenth-century sculptures of angels on the portals of Reims Cathedral as emblematic of medieval views of angels as "amiable hermaphrodites."⁹¹ Indeed, medieval iconography rendered angels consistently as "androgynous and sylph-like, rather than with anatomically specific bodies indicative of earthly physicality."⁹² It was therefore a common perception by the thirteenth century that both demons and angels defied dichotomous sex. They fluctuated between the sexes, or they expressed an androgyny that altogether transcended binary sex.

As writers cautioned during the period, demons delighted in luring humans into sexual sin—so much so that historians have observed among medieval thinkers a virtual obsession with the prospect of demon-human sex.⁹³ Scholastics debated the mechanics of such unions, suggesting that demons played both male and female sexual roles, assuming the form of a female "succubus" to have sex with men before changing into a male "incubus" to impregnate women.⁹⁴ In their (at least apparent) shifts between the sexes, demons resembled the alternations of sex attributed to the mythic hermaphroditic race or to hyenas who, as we have already seen, were depicted as having "played both roles." Some scholastics also made an explicit comparison between demons and intersex people: the thirteenth-century Flemish theologian Henry Bate (a pupil of Thomas Aquinas) used the metaphor of a human with both male and female sexual organs to characterize the mechanics of demonic impregnation.⁹⁵ Demon-human sex was also linked to bestiality: the devil was thought to metamorphose into an animal—often a snake, dog, or goat—to have sex with humans.⁹⁶ Like the bestiary's hyena, Satan and his demons troubled the divisions of both sex and species.

Despite their lack of physicality, demons appeared in visual and literary sources as palpably incarnate. Visual illustrations sometimes pictured demons with mixed male and female traits, and with hybridized, theriomorphic bodies. As early as the fifth century, the Council of Toledo catalogued Satan's rather fearsome traits, a chimerical mixture of animal parts (claws, cloven hooves, horns, ass's ears), along with exaggerated sexual features.⁹⁷ This transgression of sexual and species boundaries signaled demons' radical assault on the social and spiritual order. Pictorial attention to their morphological distortions also conveyed sexual perversion.⁹⁸ Although there was no one way of depicting demons during the Middle Ages, a number of illustrations clothed their bodies in ventral, mask-like faces that obscured their genitals, avoiding overt obscenity while highlighting demons' penchant for sexual sin. These faces featured large noses, tongues, and goat's beards: such protrusions were likely recognizable to medieval viewers as phallic signs (see, for instance, fig. 3.6).⁹⁹ Yet demonic masks indicated not only purportedly active, masculine sexual organs but also passive, feminine ones. Comparisons between the mouth and the vagina appeared widely in both learned and popular writings during the Middle Ages, and an image of a demonic head with an open mouth fastened around the lower part of the body, usually at the belly or pubis, signaled the vaginal orifice.¹⁰⁰ This strategy of locating both traditionally imagined male and female sexual symbols at the groin portrayed

FIGURE 3.6 Lucifer with Christ in majesty. *Livre de la Vigne nostre Seigneur*. Oxford, University of Oxford, Bodleian Library, MS Douce 134, fol. 67v (c. 1450–1470). Permission of the Bodleian Libraries.

the demonic body as sexually multiple and polyvalent. (See, for instance, the southern English Huntingfield Psalter, contemporary with the Aberdeen Bestiary (see fig. 3.7), which pictured demons with both "male" and "female" sexual features.)[101] Such images differed markedly from the Janus-faced hermaphrodites of chapter 2, which held binary sexes in eternal suspension. These demonic bodies were violative mixtures of human and animal, active and passive, traits. Their unseemly mixtures made visible their uncleanness—and, indeed, medieval writers often referred to demons as "unclean spirits."[102]

FIGURE 3.7 Temptation of Christ. *Huntingfield Psalter*. New York, The Morgan Library & Museum, MS M.43, fol. 20v (Oxford, c. 1212–20). Purchased by J. Pierpont Morgan in 1902.

92   THE HYENA'S UNCLEAN SEX

By the end of the Middle Ages, however, theologians began to consider the sex-shifting qualities of demonic activity to be so unpalatable that even demons refrained from them. Theologians began to claim that demons had sex with human men or women without oscillating between the sexes (perhaps making them less transgressive than the allegedly gender-inverting sodomites and hermaphrodites of medieval discourse).[103] Nevertheless, some manuscript illuminations continued to portray demons as having both male and female sexual features. An illustration from a fifteenth-century copy of *Histoire ancienne universelle* shows a dual-sex devil besieging Job with a string of tragedies (see fig. 3.8).

FIGURE 3.8   A devil burns Job's house. *Histoire ancienne universelle*. Rouen, Collections de la Bibliothèque municipale de Rouen, MS 1139 (U. 005), fol. 134 (fifteenth century).

Photographer: Thierry Ascencio-Parvy.

THE HYENA'S UNCLEAN SEX 93

A close look at the flying demon reveals a hybridized body of human and animal traits, as well as breasts and a penis.

Christian authors routinely compared Jews to demons, or portrayed Jews as in league with demonic forces. Some images linked Jews explicitly to both demons and nonbinary sex.[104] Guillaume le Clerc's Anglo-Norman *Bestiaire*, roughly contemporary with the Aberdeen Bestiary, rehearses what are by now familiar accusations: Jews were denounced in the text as sexually and spiritually inconstant and duplicitous; they were said to serve two masters but satisfied neither.[105] An illumination from a manuscript copy of the text, MS français 14969—likely produced in London or Oxford around 1265–70—includes an image of Jesus at right, hanging in crucifixion, a solemn crowd of Christians gathered on his right side (see fig. 3.9).[106] At left, however, a vastly different

FIGURE 3.9 Allegory of the Redemption. Guillaume le Clerc, *Bestiaire*. Paris, Bibliothèque nationale de France, MS français 14969, fol. 9 (c. 1265–1270).

FIGURE 3.10 Demons with *rouelle*. *Der Juden Erbarkeit* (1571). Munich, Bayerische Staatsbibliothek, 4 P.o.germ. 45 m, frontispiece.

scene unfolds: a carnivalesque demon shoves jeering Jews into a hellmouth that engulfs their bodies in fanglike flames. The hellmouth inverts the image of the biting Jewish-hyena that appears elsewhere in the manuscript—the two monsters share similar features, with deep-set eyes, pointed ears, and doglike snouts. In the visual rhetoric of the bestiary, Jews get their comeuppance through a descent into a toothy maw that proposes a horrifyingly visible link between Jews and the demonic.[107]

Such connections appeared in later centuries, too: a frontispiece of the sixteenth-century *Der Juden Erbarkeit* pictures a horned and hooved Satanic figure whose open cloak reveals breasts and an erect penis. Fastened on the figure's clothing is coin-shaped *rouelle* that the scholar Henry Abramson interprets as a sign of Judaism (see fig. 3.10).[108] In yet another image, this one from Pierre Boaistuau's sixteenth-century *Histoires prodigieuses*, a heavy-breasted Satan is attended by Jews at his throne, a masklike demonic face covering an otherwise naked body. The face grins malevolently, its chin projecting a sharp, swordlike appendage that gestures at the demon's doubled sex (see fig. 3.11).[109]

FIGURE 3.11 Satan with attendants. Pierre Boaistuau, *Histoires prodigieuses extraictes de plusieurs fameux autheurs, grecz & latins, sacrez & prophanes* (Paris: Robert LeMangnier, 1566), fol. 1.

JEWISH-CHRISTIAN RELATIONS IN ENGLAND

Like these texts, English bestiaries such as the Aberdeen Bestiary contained viciously negative portrayals of Jews, reflecting, no doubt, the volatile nature of interreligious relations in contemporary England. By the late twelfth century, greater Christian enmity toward Jews was on the rise, and a series of Christian massacres of Jews took place in English towns, including in Westminster, London, Lynn, Norwich, Stamford, and York.[110] In addition, in the years surrounding the Aberdeen Bestiary's creation, a notable shift in Christian religiosity was taking place. New devotional practices emphasized the humanity and vulnerability of Christ's body, amplifying Christians' sense that Christ and his followers were susceptible to attack. This shift also accompanied increasingly negative attitudes toward Jews among Christians. Medieval theologians had long held that Jews had willfully, rather than ignorantly, crucified Christ and rejected the truth of Christianity. They argued that not only ancient—but also living—Jews were responsible for his death.[111]

At this same time, repressive laws were emerging throughout the region to distinguish Christians from non-Christians.[112] Despite the relatively small number of Jews living in England (a few thousand before the expulsion of 1290), Jewish communities were visible and prominent. Jews often resided in the prestigious centers of towns, with their homes interspersed among those of Christians.[113] Beginning in 1217, English Jews were compelled to wear badges on their chests, an obligation reaffirmed by statutes from 1222 to 1275, although historians are uncertain to what extent such rules were enforced.[114] Christians increasingly worried about Jews living among them and committing "blasphemies" that threatened the integrity of the Christian faith. Derogatory rhetoric began to pervade sermons, plays, and other literature, often portraying Jews as greedy and traitorous. Moreover, visual traditions—which had begun to show Jews with stereotyped features such as heavy brows, long beards, and hooked noses—also became more negative.[115] At a time when Jews were protected, albeit inconsistently, by the English crown and other powerful patrons (who benefited from Jews' roles as moneylenders and taxable subjects), anti-Jewish images, such as those of the Aberdeen Bestiary, reflected growing Christian fear and antagonism.

In addition, the Aberdeen Bestiary emerged in the wake of rumors that Jews constituted not only a spiritual but also a physical threat to Christians. According to contemporary rumors, Jews in Norwich conspired to murder a twelve-year-old Christian child in 1144. A few decades later, Jews in Bristol supposedly roasted a Christian child on a spit "like a fat chicken."[116] Additional charges emerged in Gloucester in 1168, Bury St. Edmunds in 1181, and (possibly) Winchester in 1192.[117] Between 1235 and 1279, accusations of ritual cannibalism proliferated, including cases in London, Lincoln, and Northampton. Contemporary hagiographers and chroniclers such as Thomas of Monmouth and Matthew of Paris dramatized the murders, stirring up anti-Jewish sentiment years after the supposed incidents took place.[118] These tales rendered Jews in terms not so far removed from the bestiaries' manticores and hyenas: they were killers and cannibals, their behavior outside the bounds of both civility and humanity.

The Aberdeen Bestiary also provided visual confirmation of what seemed to be an existential threat: the hyena's sharp teeth tear into a naked, defenseless, and (presumably) Christian body. It was common in the Middle Ages to imagine the "body of society" as an actual human body, with all of its physical limbs and organs.[119] According to this schema, what viewers witnessed in the Aberdeen Bestiary was a nonbinary-sexed Jewish aggressor devouring a vulnerable Christian body politic. Despite the massacres and expulsions of Jewish communities that had recently occurred or were soon to take place in the region, the Aberdeen Bestiary argued forcefully that it was Christians—and not Jews—who were under attack in thirteenth-century England.

ANTI-JEWISH POLEMIC IN HISTORICAL PERSPECTIVE

It is important to note that Christian views of Jews were far from univocal in the period, and bestiaries made up just one strain of invective that flourished mainly in England and northern Europe. A generation ago, R. I. Moore published his now-classic *The Formation of a Persecuting Society*, which analyzed medieval violence against minority groups.[120] In it, Moore argued that deliberate and habitual violence began to be directed against Jews, heretics, and lepers during the high Middle Ages, not as a result of popular demand, but as a way of consolidating power into the hands of an emerging clerical class. As a result, minority groups were defined and stereotyped as sources of social contamination by an act of "collective imagination." Moore claimed that this shift, which he linked to the rise of centralized governments and the growth of a monetary economy, led to a persecuting mentality that has survived to this day.

Much recent scholarship has downplayed this narrative of unrelenting hostility, instead pointing to the multiplicity of Christian attitudes toward religious others.[121] In southern Europe, particularly in Spain, Christians interacted with Jews and Muslims on a daily basis, sharing territories, meals, and sexual liaisons. Paola Tartakoff writes that modern scholarship on Christian-Jewish relations in Europe—which often contrast an intolerant north with a tolerant south—have overstated regional variations, and that intermittent enmity, accommodation, and mutual influence characterized both the north and south.[122] Shirin Khanmohamadi has shown how Christians who traveled abroad expressed an openness to non-Christian communities and cultures, with which they formed fluid and complex relationships.[123] Moreover, Christians were prone to expressing confused and contradictory notions about non-Christians within a single work. We should thus be cautious about viewing English discourse about Jews, or non-Christians more generally, as reductive or Manichean.[124]

Yet one would not want to paint too rosy a picture. The most powerful Christian monarchs and churchmen exploited Jewish communities and fostered anti-Jewish views. Limited zones of contact and intercultural exchange existed, but Christians and non-Christians lived for the most part separate lives, and many Christians viewed non-Christians negatively.[125] While some Christian kings were eager to convert Jews, and indeed theologians considered the conversion of Jews a necessary step in the march toward an apocalyptic end, Christians also expressed antipathy toward Jewish converts, who possessed a lingering "Jewishness" that many Christians thought survived any change of faith.[126] Despite any diversity of attitudes, by the thirteenth century, Christians were proposing quasi-biological, racist theories that Jews possessed essential physical traits, whether a foul smell, a humoral complexion, or some other mark of difference, that could not be eliminated, even by baptism.[127]

The nonbinary-sexed hyena of the Aberdeen Bestiary was thus an important rhetorical tool in portraying Jews as bestial and outside of the Christian community. The text charged that Jews combined traits in a foul fashion, and they represented sources of pollution that—like John of Salisbury's grapes—contaminated whomever they touched. Contemporary sources also described Muslims in strikingly similar terms. Christians justified the crusades with accusations that Muslims desecrated the so-called Christian holy land: the twelfth-century monk Fulcher of Chartres, for instance, likened Muslims to sources of spoilage: "rotten apples" that "disfigured" the sacred sites of Jerusalem with idolatry.[128] Both the expulsion of Jews from England and the conquest of Jerusalem, including violence against non-Christians, were widely viewed by Christians as divinely sanctioned acts that wiped away abominations.[129]

In these arguments, non-believers were sources of uncleanness that, like spoiled fruit, made rotten their surroundings. But external threats to the Christian faith were not the sole danger. As we have seen, Guibert of Nogent warned of Judaizing Christians who supported Jews and as a result descended, like them, into "neitherness." The Aberdeen Bestiary condemned not only Jewish but also Christian errors, warning against Christians who betrayed their faith, rejoiced in luxury, and worshipped money to the extent that they, like Jews, became "hermaphrodites" and animals too.

We are now quite far afield from the "bifurcated" mythic hermaphrodites of the previous chapter. While the mythic monstrous races and the bestiary's hyena belong to the same umbrella category of nonbinary sex, they represented different modes of sexual difference, as well as different rhetorical strategies. Bifurcated hermaphrodites—as we have already seen—were junctions of distinct, unaltered sexes: they kept within sight the male-female division of the body, rejecting any true mixture of categories. Even as authors marveled at these figures' "sex changes," they illustrated them in ways that suppressed that change. The figure's female side did the female work while the male did the male work; body parts joined, but their sexes remained identifiable. In addition, such texts represented an entertaining, if moralizing, escape into distant and alternative realities, even as their rhetoric did real-life damage to human communities of Muslims.

The images of nonbinary sex within this chapter, in contrast, emphasized deterioration and corruption. Lines of demarcation fell away, contraries lost cohesion, and other subsumed self.[130] These figures stressed not polarity but confusion, and through them, boundaries revealed themselves to be distressingly permeable. This schema was invoked, moreover, not in fanciful inquiries into foreign lands but in urgent questions about the here and now. How could Christians choose between spirituality and materiality in a society that demanded both? How could they reconcile commerce with poverty and work with withdrawal? Images of nonbinary sex illuminated the uncomfortable compromises of medieval life—especially those that had to do with money. In his classic work, *Religious Poverty and the Profit Economy in Medieval Europe*, historian Lester K. Little identified new anxieties about wealth that accompanied the growth of monetary activity in the twelfth century, prompting the proliferation of new religious orders that embraced poverty in response.[131] Caroline Bynum has pointed to the emergence of "hybridized" religious roles, which led to profound ambivalence about conflicting ideals. As she observes, a number of churchmen during the period described their dual commitments to the sacred and profane in terms of monstrosity.[132]

In the Aberdeen Bestiary, nonbinary sex categories were described as similarly monstrous. Because of the ways in which Christians identified spirituality and temporality with the masculine and feminine, ideas about nonbinary sex provided an especially powerful analogy for thinking about the irreconcilable demands of power and piety—and one that tapped into ancient rules of Leviticus decrying the mixing of parts. Mixtures, of course, could be admirable. For Bernard of Clairvaux, they represented the highest figures of Christianity: the martyrs, the Virgin, the Savior. But in the texts that I analyze here, they also represented the lowest: the sodomites, the idolaters, the demons. Nonbinary sex categories were not just imagined as hybrids but as abominations. For the theologians, they confounded the world's order, bringing into violative contact that which should remain separate. In varied texts—from the Aberdeen Bestiary to moralizing guides to polemical poetry—authors used the concept of nonbinary sex to describe what they saw as ritually unclean: the intrusion of the profane into the sacred. While the art historian Michael Camille warned us against seeing medieval culture in terms of spiritual or worldly binaries because medieval people enjoyed ambiguity, in these cases, ambiguity represented both contamination and soteriological danger.[133]

Nonbinary-sexed figures were, of course, not the only, nor even the primary, source of purported pollution in medieval culture. Women's bodies were still viewed as the ultimate threat to communal purity, so much so that male contact with menstrual blood was thought to cause leprosy and decimate crops. Dyan Elliott has shown how priests shielded the Eucharist from female contamination through clerical celibacy. Sara Alison Miller has argued that medieval thinkers envisioned the female body as a putrid, contaminating "sewer," even as they acknowledged its positive role in birth and salvation.[134] Denunciations of sodomy by writers such as Alan of Lille, Bernard of Cluny, and others repeatedly associated effeminacy with what they called hermaphroditism, suggesting that intersex people were sexually inverted and womanish, and hence they shared in the venomous, contagious aspects of femaleness. With this in mind, we can see how denunciations of nonbinary sex relied on a fundamentally misogynistic logic. Male repugnance for women and all things feminine formed a basis for authors' horror at the prospect of effeminates, half-men, and other figures that departed from approved standards of medieval masculinity.

Throughout this book thus far, I have suggested that ideas about nonbinary sex were tools for thinking about categories and their boundaries. Images of nonbinary-sexed figures often appeared between or beyond categories, providing a means to explore fundamental ideas and their classification. For that reason, despite the divergence of their organizing principles and purposes, mythic monstrous-race hermaphrodites (as we saw in the last chapter) and the bestiary's hyena (as we see in this chapter) shared a certain common mission. In works such as the *Marvels of the East* and the Hereford Map, nonbinary figures were pictured as subhuman or dubiously human members of the monstrous races, ejected (for the most part) from a Christian ecumene. In the case of the Aberdeen Bestiary, we see similar efforts to displace nonbinary Jews elsewhere, outside the communal and territorial bounds of English Christendom. Once more, nonbinary sex played an important role in demarcating limits, and in demonizing or "hermaphroditizing" those who were cast outside.

Finally, images of nonbinary sex in this chapter also participated in a broader medieval conversation about "the human." Scholars have long been interested in human-animal relations, studying how medieval thinkers elevated aristocrats, enforced religious difference, and justified the abuse of peasants based on their subjects' proximity to beasts.[135] Such scholarship has looked carefully at the role that bestiaries, in particular, played in constructing human-animal boundaries. The Aberdeen Bestiary's hyena was one of a number of allegories that shored up "the human" by pointing out the differences between human and bestial behavior.[136] In this way, bestiaries helped readers to form human identities by overcoming their animality—that is, by subjecting themselves to (impossible) moral demands, which prompted them to voice ever more definitively their unique, oppositional identity vis-à-vis beasts.[137] At the same time, scholars have also noted how bestiaries blurred the lines between species. Joyce Salisbury has argued that the ontological separation of species was breaking down after the twelfth century, and that Christian thinkers began to imagine humans and beasts as closer than they had formerly liked to admit.[138] Sarah Kay and Susan Crane have shown that despite their investment in human exceptionalism, the bestiaries asserted common ground between humans and animals, which shared natural capacities.[139] The Aberdeen Bestiary contributed to this process of defining the human, encouraging readers to embrace their humanity, in part by avoiding polluting behaviors (and those who indulged in them). But it also suggested that such boundaries were far from firm.

A number of scholars have observed how English Christians depicted Jews as agents of contamination—a form of rhetoric that was used to justify the cruel expulsion of Jewish communities in 1290. By identifying Jews with the alleged impurity of nonbinary anatomies and practices, bestiaries and other texts charged that Jews were ritually unclean. Their bodies were maligned as sources of pollution that impinged on Christian space and necessitated their collective removal.[140] The images at the heart of the chapters 2 and 3—the Hereford Map's turbaned figure and the Aberdeen Bestiary's hyena—show how the concept of nonbinary sex could be mobilized as a vicious tool to denigrate non-Christian and racially-"othered" subjects. Such images provided a means by which their creators could present Africans, Muslims, or Jews as bestial or subhuman figures and advocate for their removal from Christianity's borders. In the case of the Hereford Map, its turbaned hermaphrodite spoke to the marginalization of Africans and Muslims, who were banished to the cartographic edge. In the Aberdeen Bestiary and other sources, nonbinary sex—here, a symbol of transgression and contamination—signaled that Jews and their purported polluting qualities belonged "outside."

4
Sex and Order in Natural Philosophy and Law

A richly decorated manuscript copy of Albert the Great's *On Animals*—MS Latin 16169, now housed at the Bibliothèque nationale de France—pictures a group of illuminated birds and animals, some of which copulate with wild abandon in the manuscript's bas-de-page (see fig. 4.1).[1] On a nearby folio, a delicate drawing of a nonbinary-sexed human hovers at the manuscript's edge, keeping company with four other figures: two human-animal hybrids, a hairy beast, and a set of conjoined twins (see fig. 4.2 and fig. 4.3).[2] The manuscript itself is an exceptional object, purchased in the fourteenth century by the masters at the College of Sorbonne in Paris, possibly as a reference work for the college's great library.[3] The manuscript's illuminations are perfectly suited to the text, a great compendium of living creatures and their properties based on Aristotle's *On Animals*. In the mid-thirteenth century, new translations of Greek and Arabic medical and natural philosophical works had just recently reached audiences in Latin-speaking Europe. They were soon to exercise great power in scholastic circles, with considerable consequences for ideas about sex and sexuality thereafter.

MS Latin 16169's rich decorations illuminate not only the surface of its pages but also some of the themes of this chapter. Some of the authors I discuss here wrote in starkly negative terms about intersex people—individuals perceived at that time to have nonbinary-sexed morphologies, described as "hermaphrodites" in the texts.[4] According to those authorities, the sexual acts of such individuals were "unclean" or "confused," a state from which nature and human judgment "recoiled." In their opinion, moreover, nonbinary sex was "monstrous," outside the ordinary course of nature. Yet ideas about nonbinary sex appeared in neutral and quotidian contexts, too, linked to common birth anomalies such

FIGURE 4.1 Copulating animals. Albert the Great, *De animalibus*. Paris, Bibliothèque nationale de France, MS latin 16169, fol. 209v (fourteenth century).

as twins and—in the eyes of certain medieval thinkers—women. In the view of such authors, nonbinary sex continued to cross boundaries: it was masculine and feminine, natural and unnatural, pedestrian and alien. MS Latin 16169's copulating animals offer further context, too, for the purportedly paradoxical qualities of nonbinary sex were often worked out in the realms of sexual behavior and reproduction.

This chapter once more takes up a recurring question: What is a human? As philosophers and historians have long argued, to participate in human society is

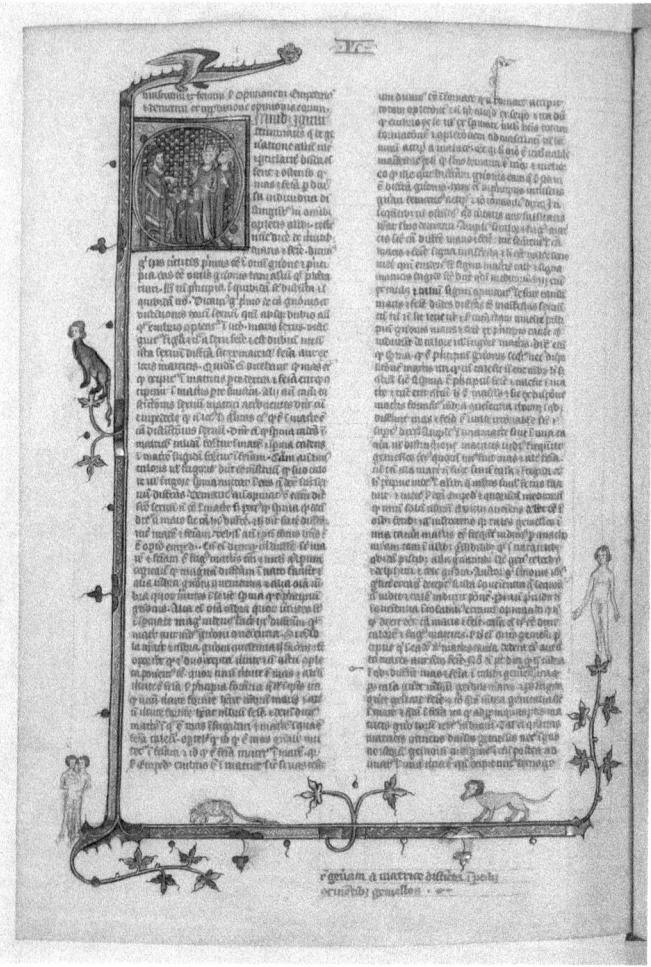

FIGURE 4.2 Marginal figures (full page). Albert the Great, *De animalibus*. Paris, Bibliothèque nationale de France, MS latin 16169, fol. 233v (fourteenth century).

to be both physically sexed and culturally gendered: physical sex is thus among the most central and definitive of human experiences.[5] Beginning in the 1250s, as this chapter explains, a series of naturalist writers in Latin Europe began to deny participation in that human experience to intersex individuals. In the view of these authors, nonbinary sex was a natural feature of lower organisms, including plants and "imperfect" animals, but among higher animals—including humans—it was an impossibility. For them, nonbinary genitals were a cosmetic

FIGURE 4.3 Marginal figure (detail). Albert the Great, *De animalibus*. Paris, Bibliothèque nationale de France, MS latin 16169, fol. 233v (fourteenth century).

defect that obscured an underlying sex that was "really" male or female. Whereas earlier medical models had identified "hermaphroditism" as a less common but no less natural sex—one possibility among many on a multi-sex spectrum—a new group of scholars began to claim that all humans came in only two types: male or female.[6]

The experts who subscribed to such theories, as a result, assigned all individuals to a binary sex. Their decisions relied on authoritative traditions drawn from the distant past, especially from Greek antiquity and the Islamic ʿAbbāsid dynasty. Among the most respected representatives of those traditions were the writers Aristotle and Abū Alī al-Husayn ibn Sīnā (or Ibn Sīnā, known in Latin Europe as Avicenna), whose ideas deeply influenced medieval European naturalist teachings—that is, the premodern traditions of medicine and natural philosophy (the theoretical study of the natural world) and their views on sex and the human body.[7] In the first part of this chapter, I consider Aristotle and Ibn Sīnā's writings about sexual difference and their impact on scholastic naturalist theories. Next, I turn to the judgments of Roman and canon law: although jurists followed their own traditions and trajectories, legal approaches to nonbinary sex intersected with naturalist ones in many ways. Both naturalist and legal authorities assimilated intersex individuals to a male or female sex and, for the most part, they made nonbinary sex disappear as a social problem and a biological category.

The texts at the heart of this chapter were diverse in their genres and aims. They offer no single model of sex development nor just one theory of how humans fit into sexual categories. Authors expressed contrasting views on whether sex should be judged according to genital anatomy, overall "complexion," sexual function, disposition, or an individual's own choice. Nevertheless, discussions of nonbinary sex allowed medieval thinkers to sort out fundamental questions regarding human nature: How many sexes were there really? How did men and women differ from each other? How did humans fit into a larger natural and social order? An influential group of scholars of the thirteenth and fourteenth centuries limited the range of legitimate, natural configurations of sex to just male and female—and, in a related fashion, they constrained human behavior to just two mutually exclusive types: active and passive (male and female). By selecting which sexes and sexualities were legitimate and natural, I argue, authorities constructed a very particularized vision of "the human." This vision determined how authorities reconciled intersex individuals to the demands of families, lineages, and institutions, forcing diverse bodies into restrictive binary categories.

ARISTOTELIAN THEORIES

The thirteenth century was an exciting period for intellectuals, with scholars at the newly founded universities of Western Europe poring over recently rediscovered naturalist texts, including those of the Greek philosopher Aristotle (384–22 BCE). In the last chapter, I described how Aristotle's "New Logic" (which arrived in Latin translation over the course of the twelfth century) contributed to a "discourse of opposites" in diverse parts of medieval culture.

Aristotle's zoological texts, translations of which reached Europe in the thirteenth century, were similarly transformative. They activated lively debates about sexual difference and human biology, giving scholars new tools for thinking systematically about sex and sexuality, as well as for judging how nonbinary sexes fit into a larger order of being.

Important to these discussions was Aristotle's *On Animals* (made up of three related writings, *The History of Animals*, *On the Parts of Animals*, and *On the Generation of Animals*). *On the Generation of Animals* dealt with subjects of direct relevance to medieval medicine and biology, including how different organisms expressed bodily sex and generated offspring.[8] Aristotle did not assume a radical distinction between humans and animals, which were part of the same continuum of existence (although humans occupied a higher plane), and so his writings dealt with human generation in the context of the larger animal world. Because one of Aristotle's aims in *On the Generation of Animals* was to create systematic typologies, he provided criteria for dividing organisms into discrete and hierarchical categories.[9] Means of generation was an important tool of organization for him, and sexual difference was tightly bound to this issue. Aristotle took up the topic of sexual difference numerous times in his work, revealing its significance to his overall project.[10]

Unlike other stalwarts of the medieval biological tradition—Hippocrates (that is, the corpus of texts compiled between the fifth and fourth centuries BCE and attributed to Hippocrates of Cos) and Galen (c. 130–210 CE), both ostensibly physicians with pragmatic concerns about disease—Aristotle focused less on medical therapeutics and more on naturalist explanations within a broader system of philosophy. Part of his inquiry entailed "final causes," or *teleologies*, which explained the overarching purpose of a body part or a process.[11] What, then, was the *telos* of the sexes? Aristotle explained that by definition mortal organisms cannot live forever, and yet all things strive for continued existence. Their only chance at immortality is through the survival of their offspring, which necessitates reproduction of the self and, in higher animals, sexual difference. Aristotle made it clear that sexual differentiation per se was superior to a lack of differentiation. The male—who was active and spiritually elevated—was in all ways better than the female—who was passive and yoked to the lower realms of matter. As a result, Aristotle thought it best for the active to be fully divided from the passive: "So far as possible, the male is separate from the female," he wrote, because the active male is superior to the passive female, who constitutes mere matter.[12] Aristotle described the process of sexual generation in a way that privileged the separation of male (active) and female (passive) principles from each other, while also emphasizing female inferiority.[13]

According to Aristotle, every act of sexual generation involved form (semen provided by the male) and matter (menstrual material provided by the female). At the time of conception, he wrote, nature always strove to produce a superior male offspring. In some cases, however, insufficient heat prevented the formative male principle from dominating, and a female offspring, characterized by her lesser heat, would be conceived instead.[14] A female, then, was the result of a less successful generative process—a mistake—and a departure from nature's intended course. By this argument, females were contrary to nature, although Aristotle elsewhere assured readers that females were in other ways a "necessity required by nature."[15] Nevertheless, females were, in Aristotle's view, "deformed" or failed males, and therefore an inferior version of men, rather than merely men's opposite.[16]

On the Generation of Animals also addressed other imagined deviations from nature's intended course, which resulted in the birth of what Aristotle called "monsters." Monsters included two-headed snakes and other unusual creatures, although for Aristotle any organism that failed to resemble its parents was to some extent a monster.[17] He also described the creation of "monstrosities" or "deformities" that resulted when maternal matter was too excessive to produce just one fetus but was not enough for two. This matter could be overabundant enough to produce conjoined twins, but in lesser cases, it could also create extra organs or digits on an individual's body. As Aristotle explained, when excessive maternal matter was located in the groin, and when it was further shaped by equal male and female generative contributions, it could produce an offspring with both male and female sexual organs. Aristotle wrote: "Sometimes an offspring is born having too many fingers, and sometimes having one only; and it is the same with the other parts, since some are superfluous, and some are too few. Sometimes an offspring is born with [both] a penis and a female organ. This happens in human women and also in goats."[18] Nevertheless, only one set of sexual organs was functional in such a case, and the other was a redundant growth, much like a tumor, with no bearing on the affected individual's actual sex. While Aristotle argued that such individuals were both monstrous and contrary to nature, he was not particularly troubled by them because their underlying sex was always either male or female. Sex was determined by the heat of the heart, which established the "complexion" of the whole of the body.[19]

Aristotle's decision to assimilate all individual humans to either a male or female category, and to deny that they belonged to a truly nonbinary sex, made sense in light of his broader attempt to categorize creatures. Aristotle argued that the sexes were especially distinct among the most noble creatures—or "perfect" animals, as he called them—who occupied the top tier of creatures on earth.

According to this model, the qualitative superiority of organisms rose as they ascended a graduated scale from the lowest to the highest, with humans at the pinnacle. The highest creatures had hot, fluid, and mobile natures, and they produced viviparous young in the most perfect manner—through sexual intercourse between male and female partners.[20] In contrast, the lower creatures came in a variety of differentiated and undifferentiated sexes, and they reproduced in a variety of ways. Eels and certain fish and insects, for instance, lacked dichotomous sex. Plants and what Aristotle called *Testacea*—an intermediary between plants and animals that included shelled invertebrates—also created offspring without dimorphic mates and without sexual generation. These examples were fodder for Aristotle's argument that in lower beings, the active and passive principles might be united in a single form, which could reproduce asexually, while in the higher animals, male and female always came in separate and distinct pairs. Humans, who enjoyed a position at the highest level of existence, displayed the most extreme form of sexual dimorphism.[21]

As a result, in Aristotle's view, humans could not be born as sometimes male, sometimes female, and sometimes a combination of both sexes as part of nature's routine course. A human who appeared to have features of both sexes only superficially belonged to a nonbinary sex and could be classified as male or female upon further investigation. Aristotle's willingness to acknowledge the diversity of sex in lower creatures only underscored his insistence on binary clarity in the higher ones. In accordance with Aristotle's view, sex among higher animals—including humans—came only in two types.

IBN SĪNĀ AND MUSLIM TRADITIONS OF SEX

The opinions of "The Philosopher," as Aristotle was called in the Middle Ages, stimulated much discussion after his biological texts became available to European audiences in the thirteenth century. But Aristotle's naturalist works did not arrive in a vacuum. Instead, they were accompanied by a rich tradition of naturalist commentary and analysis, originating for the most part in the Muslim ʿAbbāsid caliphate. That polity, which thrived from 750–1258 CE, and which stretched, for a time, from the coast of the eastern Mediterranean to Central Asia in the north, and from North Africa to the Arabian Peninsula in the south, produced a wealth of scholarship on the properties of the human body, weaving together diverse strains of naturalist thought into a new and intellectually vigorous tradition.

Regional politics were key to the development of the 'Abbāsid caliphate. In 750 CE, the 'Abbāsids overthrew the Umayyad dynasty and moved the caliphal capital from Damascus to the Mesopotamian city of Baghdad. This transition thrust the 'Abbāsids into a multicultural and multilingual region, promoting a ready exchange of ideas, technologies, and practices, and facilitating ready access to learned communities further south and east. That period ushered in an efflorescence of art, science, and literature that united intellectual currents from pre-Islamic Persia, the Indian subcontinent, and the Mediterranean, drawing from, among other sources, natural philosophical, mathematical, and other intellectual disciplines, including those of Greek antiquity.[22] A massive translation project began under the 'Abbāsids, especially from the eighth to tenth centuries, to appropriate the wealth of Greek learning, including the major works of Aristotle and Galen. While much of this activity happened in the heart of the kingdom, in the modern Middle East, other regions, including Central Asia and Andalusian Spain, were centers of learning, too, and they too enlarged the sphere of naturalist thought.[23]

Islamic naturalism expanded upon and integrated Greek antecedents with indigenous scholarly works, creating a body of knowledge extensive in its scope and theoretical sophistication. Drawing on Hippocratic texts on embryology, gynecology, and obstetrics; Aristotelian texts on natural philosophy; and Galenic texts on medicine and anatomy, Muslim authors synthesized and innovated in each of those fields.[24] Luminaries such as Abū Bakr Muhammad ibn Zakarīyā al-Rāzī, Alī ibn al-'Abbās al-Majūsī, and Ibn Sīnā (known in the West, respectively, as Rhazes, Haly Abbas, and Avicenna), among others, composed dynamic and richly detailed medical and philosophical works. Along with translators, compilers, and other theorists, they developed a vibrant and learned discourse that was all their own.[25]

Such discourse explored, among other topics, the nature of the human body, including its modes of generation and its sexual development. Islamic approaches to sexual difference were variable, but a prevailing view (also shared by a number of classical works) held that the "complexion"—that is, the balance of qualities (hot, wet, cold, and dry), in the form of the four humors (blood, phlegm, black bile, and yellow bile)—determined the shape and operations of the human body. Males tended to be hot and dry in complexion, while females were cold and wet—distinctions, in turn, that led to sex-based physiological and social differences. As Katharine Park has noted, writings in the Islamic tradition were deeply concerned with sexuality, and they explored the distinctive aspects of male and female anatomy—including the genitals—in detail, rather than dismissing them as largely unimportant (as had some early Christian texts, which were focused on virginity and abstinence). Muslim theorists proposed other sex-based distinctions, too, such that males were natural penetrators and females were naturally penetrated with respect to their roles in sexual intercourse.[26]

Among the most important of Muslim naturalist authors was the physician and philosopher Ibn Sīnā (980–1037) whose *al-Qānūn fī at-tibb* (*The Canon of Medicine*, or *Liber canonis* in Latin), was completed around 1025. Among its topics, the *Canon* considered questions of sexual difference, drawing from Galenic medical and Aristotelian natural philosophical theories. Ibn Sīnā identified clear differences between male and female bodies, which constituted two distinct sexes separated by discrete physiologies, anatomical structures, and potential pathologies.[27] And yet Ibn Sīnā also proposed the existence of several nonbinary sex categories. As he wrote, some individuals have

> [neither] a male organ nor a female organ. Others have both, but one is more hidden and weaker as opposed to the other, and [a person] urinates from one and not the other. In others, the two [organs] are the same [in size and appearance]. I was told that some of them can penetrate and be penetrated, but I can hardly credit this account. In many cases, they are treated by cutting the hidden organ and treating the wound.[28]

Ibn Sīnā described here several intersex categories, each displaying a different genital morphology. One variety was characterized by two sets of functioning genitals; another had neither set functioning; and a third type had one dominant set and another less dominant set. As scholars have suggested, Islamic anatomical and physiological treatises tended to accept a diverse range of human sexes that included not only *khuntha* (intersex), but also feminine males and masculine females, none of which were assimilable to binary categories.[29] Evidence from the Ottoman period further suggests that Islamic authorities considered nonbinary sexes to be neither a deformity nor a monstrosity. As the historian Sara Scalenghe notes, attitudes toward intersex individuals were, instead, consistently pragmatic and neutral.[30]

Ibn Sīnā and his contemporaries offered analyses of sexual difference that were far ranging, richly detailed, and carefully nuanced. And yet—as scholars have pointed out—such analyses were also multivalent and internally contested. Because Muslim scholars borrowed from diverse textual disciplines, and because their ancient sources often disagreed with each other, experts never settled on a single authoritative view of sex and sexuality.[31] Traditions of Islamic knowledge—both deeply learned and deeply plural—were conveyed to Western Europe through another massive translation project, this time from Arabic to Latin. The resulting texts, which reached Western Europe in a piecemeal fashion from the late eleventh to the late thirteenth century, transformed the intellectual atmosphere of Western Europe. Latin scholars delved into the new naturalism, absorbing its lessons on sex and sexuality and, along the way, drawing their own conclusions.

SEX DIFFERENTIATION IN LATIN EUROPE

As we have seen, medieval Muslim scholars operated within a multilingual, multi-faith urban milieu that allowed for easy engagement with contemporary and ancient sources. Medieval scholars in the Latin-speaking West, in contrast, had little direct knowledge of the core writings of Aristotle and Galen on the human body up until the late eleventh century. Decentralized political authority and social organization in the West, along with a lack of direct contact with the Greek-speaking East, had contributed to an overall decline in familiarity with the Greek language and with Greek naturalist ideas. Scholars in Western Europe were forced to contend with a relatively small number of Greek writings that had been translated into Latin during late antiquity and the early Middle Ages, along with some eclectic synopses and compilations. In comparison to their Muslim counterparts, Western European scholars developed only a rudimentary knowledge of Greek anatomy and physiology. All of this changed, however, with the arrival of the new translations.[32]

In the last decades of the eleventh century, while living at the Italian monastery of Monte Cassino, the North African monk (and likely native Arabic speaker) Constantine the African translated al-Majūsī's *Complete Book of the Medical Art* (*Pantegni*) and Johannitius's *Isagoge*, along with other soon-to-be influential works. Constantine's compositions and translations, together with those of Gerard of Cremona, Burgundio of Pisa, and other translators, provided a ready stimulant to naturalist thinking across Latin Europe.[33] As the historian Joan Cadden notes, Latin analyses of sex thereafter became more explicit, more complex, and more complete than ever before.[34] Christian views of sex, formerly dependent on the likes of Soranus and Isidore of Seville, were transformed by the new translations, which taught the fundamentals of Hippocratic- and Galenic-influenced theories on sexual difference, including the belief that men and women had different complexions, different physiologies and psychologies, and that both men and women emitted procreative "sperm" during conception.[35]

In the twelfth and early thirteenth centuries, Latin scholars drew heavily on the new, chiefly Galenic-Arabic theories (Aristotle's natural philosophical texts were not yet available, although Galenic-Arabic texts were infused with Aristotelian precepts), as well as older versions of Hippocrates and Galen that were already available in Latin Europe. Scholars copied manuscripts and authored new works on the structure and functions of the human body, including its sexual generation and its fetal development. As the texts explained, the sex of a fetus, in general, derived from the relative dominance and heat of both male and female "sperm" at the moment of conception, along with the location in which an embryo implanted in the uterus.[36] Such texts tended to theorize sex, not as a binary, but as a spectrum, anchored by masculine men and feminine women at the poles, but with several additional categories—including feminine males, masculine females, and individuals "of both sexes"—in the middle.

The pseudonymous tract *On Sperm* (*De spermate*, attributed falsely to Galen but perhaps a real translation of Constantine the African) provides a good example. The text circulated in England and southern France in the mid-twelfth century before becoming widely disseminated across Europe in later decades.[37] *On Sperm* emphasized the continuity of the sexes rather than their vast difference, which resulted from natural variables at the time of conception:

> Note that if the seed falls into the right-hand part of the uterus, the child will be male. . . . However, if the man's weak sperm falls in the right part [of the uterus] and there is combined with a woman's sperm stronger than itself, then [the infant], although male, will be feminine. And the man's seed can come to be so weak that the infant will be of both sexes. If, however, the sperm falls into the left part [of the uterus], it will transform into a female nature . . . and if the man's sperm prevails over the woman's seed in the left part, [the infant] will turn into the female sex but retain certain masculine traits, such as hairiness, a beard, a deep voice, etc. And the female sperm can be so weak that a child of both sexes is created.[38]

Another text, the *Prose Salernitan Questions* (c. 1200), a series of natural-philosophical questions that may have originated in Salerno, offers a similar view of fetal sexual development, along with an etiology of nonbinary sex:

> If more of the womanly sperm is set in the right part [of the womb], a manly woman [*femina virago*] will be generated. If more in the left than the right, and there is more of the manly seed than the womanly, an effeminate man [*vir effeminatus*] will be born. If [the sperm is] in the middle chamber, so that it is subject to the impression of both parts, there will be a hermaphrodite, since it will have and produce the equipment of the body of both one [sex] and the other.[39]

According to these texts, sex existed across a spectrum that encompassed masculine men, feminine women, and "hermaphrodites," the latter of which balanced male and female sexual traits in equilibrium.[40] A central contributor to sex development was the shape of the uterus, which was thought to have multiple chambers—medieval thinkers differed in whether these chambers numbered three, five, or seven—the middle of which produced an offspring with features of both sexes (see fig. 4.4). Both *On Sperm* and the *Prose Salernitan Questions*

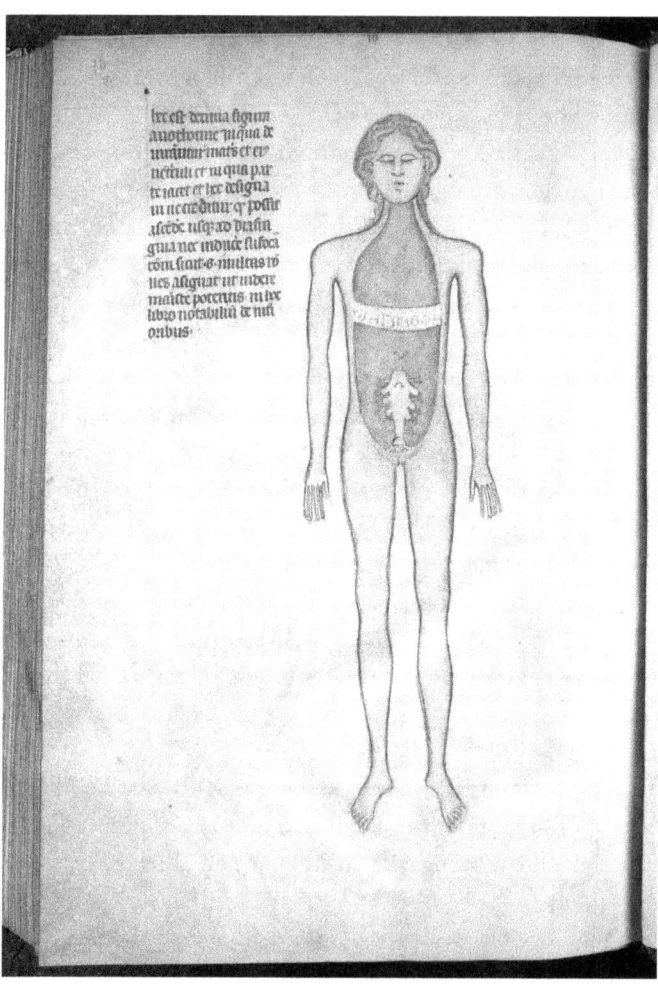

FIGURE 4.4 Seven-celled uterus. Guido da Vigevano, *Liber notabilium Philippi (VI) regis Francorum*. Chantilly, Bibliothèque du musée Condé, MS 003 (0569), fol. 267v (c. 1345). © Cliché CNRS-IRHT.

also described sexual difference in terms of right-left and hot-cold polarities: that is, the left side of the body was colder, favoring the creation of females, while the right side was warmer, favoring the creation of males.[41] Classical Greek and Islamic teachings on "sperm" were complex, but the two previous passages focused on the relative quality and quantity of male and female sperm, which battled for dominance at the moment of conception.[42] For instance, if a man provided a greater quantity of sperm than a woman, the offspring would be male; if the opposite, then the offspring would be female. If the two sperms were present in equal proportions, then an infant with "both sexes" would be born. In these and other writings, we also find musings about the "disposition" of the testicles, the age of the father, and the position of the stars, which interacted with these conditions to further influence an infant's sex.[43]

For these authors, the important difference between male and female was a matter of continuity and degree, rather than of bipolar distinction, and a number of intermediate sexual categories could result from natural variables during conception and gestation.[44] Analyses of this type were for the most part neutral; they did not express any moral outrage about nonbinary sexes, and they did not use the language of monstrosity.

As additional Arabic and Greek texts became available in the thirteenth century, however, new ideas began to extend and challenge these Galenic-influenced anatomical and physiological theories. Ibn Sīnā's *Canon*—itself a synthesis of Galenic medicine, Aristotelian natural philosophy, and other texts—was translated into Latin by Gerard of Cremona during the second half of the twelfth century (although it took several decades before it was fully absorbed by medical scholars). Aristotle's biological theories also became available in Latin, indirectly, through Muslim summaries and, directly, through Michael Scot's translation of Aristotle's *On Animals*, completed around 1220. All of this activity complicated ideas about sexual difference—including analyses of nonbinary sex—from about the mid-thirteenth century on.[45]

A rapid shift in social organization in Western Europe, along with the arrival of new institutions of learning, facilitated this activity. During the twelfth century, a revival of scholarly activity was in full swing in Western Europe. Towns and courts—both secular and ecclesiastic—were fast becoming increasingly vibrant. In Italy, secular urban schools were grappling with the new translations, while in the north, cathedral schools (formed under the auspices of bishops) were multiplying, and new scholastic methods were quickly gaining influence.[46] From these beginnings, the foundation of universities around 1200 soon followed, and scholastic masters and students became intensely engaged with Greco-Arabic naturalist works, developing from them new theories and new modes of textual analysis.[47] After the foundation of the mendicant orders in the thirteenth century, members of the Dominican Order, initially advocates of itinerancy and preaching, became leading schoolmasters. This cascade of changes allowed for greater personal mobility for scholars, who—now no longer cloistered in monasteries—were able to disseminate their ideas more widely. One would not want to overstate the distinction between rural monastic and urban scholastic circles, however; the Italian city of Salerno saw both monks and medical practitioners (not mutually exclusive groups) using the new texts in innovative ways.[48] Even before the advent of the mendicant orders, certain monks traveled or lived at court and participated in a relatively wide exchange of ideas.

Yet the specific transformations of the thirteenth century focused the bulk of intellectual activity on the universities, where scholars interpreted classical texts, including the biological works of Aristotle, with great care and precision. By the 1250s, university masters at Paris were required to cover Aristotle's *On Animals* in lecture (although Aristotle's natural philosophical works were also technically banned by church authorities anxious to suppress their pagan content).[49] As we have seen, Aristotle's *On the Generation of Animals* stressed the asymmetry of male and female generative contributions (only males contributed formative sperm), as well as the inferiority of females (who were defective or failed males).[50] Aristotle also regarded a truly intermediate sex among humans as an impossibility. In higher creatures, any individual with the apparent characteristics of both sexes was merely a case of doubled or superfluous genitals, a redundancy with no bearing on the individual's actual sex.[51] Aristotle tended to view human sex in binaries and not continuities—a conceit that would prove formative for new Latin writings on sexual difference. But Arabic naturalist texts—so central to scholastic innovation—also combined theories from diverse and even contradictory sources, conveying to audiences multifaceted views about sex and gender.[52]

Latin Christians were thus recipients of a tradition that allowed for both complexity and dissent. As Lorraine Daston and Katharine Park point out, Hippocratic- or Galenic-influenced "medical" theories recognizing a continuum of sexes and Aristotelian-influenced "philosophical" ones asserting only two sexes, continued to coexist in tension, complicating any definitive ruling on human sexual difference for centuries. But the binary model—favored by the Aristotelian camp—became increasingly influential after the 1250s.[53] According to the group of Latin European writers I turn to next, sex was no longer believed to encompass a range of diverse points on a continuous spectrum. Nonbinary sex was, instead, deemed a "monstrosity" that lay outside of nature's order.

ALBERT THE GREAT

By the mid-thirteenth century, scholastic thinkers, including the theologian and philosopher Albert the Great, drew on the new naturalism to propose novel explanations of fetal development and human sexual difference. A Dominican scholar based in Paris and Cologne, Albert wrote voluminously and achieved great renown during his life.[54] Along with his student Thomas Aquinas, Albert was perhaps the greatest Christian synthesizer of Aristotle, but his work drew on Hippocratic and Galenic writings, too, as well as on Ibn Sīnā's *Canon* and *On the Nature of Animals*, which strongly informed his views.[55]

Albert was especially interested in Aristotelian zoology, to which he devoted a series of lectures, *Questions Concerning Aristotle's On Animals* (delivered in 1258 and compiled in 1260), as well as his own lengthy commentary, *On Animals* (completed c. 1263), the latter of which became a textbook for medieval and early modern medical students.[56] Albert mentioned what he called "hermaphroditism" several times in these works and also in his *Physics*, *Summa of Theology*, *On Vegetables and Plants*, and *On Minerals*. In them, Albert characterized individuals with atypical sex anatomies as a "monstrosity"—a flaw in nature's creation.

In fact, Albert devoted special attention to such individuals within the context of "monstrous births," which he explained in naturalistic terms. With the greater systematization of nature that followed the scholastic revival and the new naturalism, the conceptual gap between the so-called monstrous races and monstrous births was only increasing.[57] Albert, for his part, dismissed as ridiculous the birth of a fetus who was male on the right side and female on the left, effectively refuting the legend of the bilaterally split hermaphroditic monstrous race in terms of biology.[58] Using Aristotle and Ibn Sīnā as guides, Albert placed questions of sexual difference instead within the new naturalist theories of human reproduction and embryology. As Luke Demaitre and Anthony Travill observe, Albert was "fascinated" by human sexual generation and fetal development.[59]

In *Questions Concerning Aristotle's On Animals*, Albert touched on sexual difference as a part of his inquiry into reproduction. In a discussion that borrowed from Aristotle's *On the Generation of Animals*, as well as *On Plants* (a pseudonymous text that medieval thinkers believed to be a genuine work of Aristotle), Albert explained that sex was "confused [*confusus*] among plants, but . . . distinct in animals" because of their greater physiological complexity.[60] Albert claimed that plants and some lower creatures generated offspring naturally without two consistently divided sexes, but more complex animals required more complex generative processes.[61] Humans exhibited the most complicated form of generation; that is, they always had two distinct sexes and always reproduced sexually. Such conclusions were in keeping with Aristotle's assertion that only the lower creatures of earth were asexual and could self-reproduce, while reproduction in higher animals required male (active) and female (passive) sexual partners. "Perfect" animals, Albert argued—quadrupeds and humans—could not alternate between the sexes nor could they exhibit nonbinary sex across the species. For that reason, Albert denied that hyenas, hares, and other perfect animals were either dual-sexed or capable of self-fertilization, which were common assertions in bestiaries and related animal lore. Those traditions were mistaken because the active and passive principles of generation in higher animals had to be separated into two distinct forms, as Aristotle had explained.[62]

While higher animals could not be nonbinary-sexed throughout the species, individuals with both male and female sex traits, Albert argued, were nevertheless sometimes born. He wrote, "For various reasons, male and female can occur in the same individual owing to a flaw in nature, as is evident in a hermaphrodite, who has each [sexual] member. But this is a monster in nature."[63] Albert claimed that such individuals were the exception that proved the rule: they were "monsters" who strayed beyond the bounds of ordinary nature, although he also wrote that "hermaphrodites" were in other ways natural because they resulted from a natural cause.[64] For him, such individuals in some respects resembled women, who (in the medieval view) resulted from both natural and unnatural processes. But, unlike women, intersex individuals were thought to serve no natural purpose in the mechanics of reproduction.[65]

In *On Animals*, Albert also argued that the morphology of these individuals, whose etiology was closely related to that of twins, resulted from excess matter in the region of the groin which, along with equal hot and cold generative contributions from the parents, caused the genital flesh to divide into distinct male and female members.[66] Albert's explanation, drawn from both Aristotle and Ibn Sīnā, diverged from the opinions of *On Sperm* and the *Prose Salernitan Questions*, which said nonbinary sexes resulted from an encounter between male and female sperm or from the placement of the embryo within a multicellular womb.[67]

But Albert rejected those explanations in another, even more fundamental way. A truly nonbinary sex in humans, Albert argued, was impossible. By his argument, individuals who appeared to have the features of both sexes actually had only one functional organ; the "other has little more than shape" and is similar to a growth.[68] Concerning such an individual's sex, Albert wrote:

> Sometimes the shape of each [genital] member is so complete to the sight and touch that one cannot discern which sex is dominant. And there is nothing

preventing such a young also from having two bladders and emitting urine through each of them, or during intercourse playing both the active and the passive role, lying both on top and below. I do not think that [such a person] can both impregnate and become impregnated. Certainly, however, the sex will be the more principal which is aided by the complexion of the heart. Nevertheless, sometimes the complexion of the heart is so much in the middle that one can scarcely discern which sex is dominant.[69]

To determine the predominant sex of such a person, Albert relied first on a visual inspection, which he claimed generally revealed one organ or the other to be dominant. But, as Albert added, such an examination was not always effective. Sometimes both organs are "so complete to the sight and touch that one cannot discern" which sex is primary. In that case, Albert turned to the complexion of the heart, which always indicated a dominant sex (even if it was sometimes difficult to determine). Albert did not specify which parts of the body revealed the heart's complexion, but elsewhere he listed a number of physical traits, including secondary sex characteristics, that distinguished men from women in complexionary terms.[70]

Complexion, of course, existed on a continuum, with hot and cold at the extremes and, between them, a range of intermediates. And yet Albert could not admit to any true midpoint with respect to human sex. He argued that even if an individual's sex was difficult to discern, every human had to be *really* male or female.[71] What is important here is that Albert, like Aristotle before him, denied to humans a truly nonbinary sex: male and female differed from each other not in degree, but in *kind*. In his view, humans who appeared to have both male and female sex traits were merely defective men or women rather than members of their own distinct and natural category of sex that lay beyond the binary division.

Albert also went beyond Aristotle's analysis to consider intersex individuals' potential sexual role.[72] People with combined sex traits, Albert claimed, could perform either actively or passively in sexual intercourse ("on top or below"), but Albert waxed uncertain about whether such a person could both impregnate and be impregnated. In his *Questions on Animals*, however, Albert firmly stated that such an individual could not conceive as a woman. The individual's female member was always infertile, he argued, because the wombs of all mannish women (*viragines*) were unsuitable for conception. Albert speculated that such a person could be fertile as a man, but a human could never self-impregnate.[73] This distinction was important because otherwise humans with both male and female sex traits might seem to resemble plants, which Albert believed capable of self-fertilization. But the "confused" sex of plants, Albert explained, was different from the distinct sexes that characterized higher creatures. The active and passive generative principles could never be united in a single human being, and unlike a plant, a human could never procreate as both male and female.[74]

In his analysis, Albert recognized the humanity of intersex people without the equivocation of, say, Thomas of Cantimpré, who questioned their ontological status in his *On the Nature of Things*.[75] Yet Albert denied the existence of any real sex category between male and female. For him, a human could not be one of a variety of intermediate sexes, as previous texts such as *On Sperm* or the *Prose Salernitan Questions* had proposed. In contrast, Albert defined hermaphroditism as a perfect equilibrium of male and female traits in a single body that could reproduce asexually. In his view, lower forms of life, such as plants, could display nonbinary sex, but humans could not. From a modern standpoint, Albert was correct: a human cannot have both complete male and female sexual anatomies, nor self-fertilize, as certain plants do. Yet this was hardly the only definition of nonbinary sex available to Albert in the thirteenth century. As we have seen, texts that were already in circulation, such as Ibn Sīnā's *Canon of Medicine* or the pseudonymous *On Sperm*, viewed nonbinary sexes as recognizable categories of human sex that combined traits traditionally considered male and female. In contrast, Albert effectively erased nonbinary sex from human nature. To accept intermediate sexes as natural and routine among humans would be to unsettle the binary that distinguished the highest level of creatures, as well as the natural order that depended on it.[76]

To his discussion in *On Animals*, Albert appended a striking anecdote about a contemporary individual with unusual sex anatomy:

> In a certain person born in our time, the testicles were contained higher up within the skin in such a way that their outward bulge gave the suggestion of the two lips of a woman's vulva. There also seemed to be a split in the middle which was closed over by skin. Since the parents thought [this person] was a girl, and that the split should be opened to facilitate sexual intercourse, an incision was made, from which burst forth testicles and a penis. And afterward [this person] took a wife and bore many children from her.[77]

Albert counted a number of physicians in Cologne among his friends, with whom he apparently discussed medical cases—perhaps they were the origin of this tale.[78] The outline of the case foreshadowed later recommendations by surgeons such as Lanfranc of Milan and Guy de Chauliac, who were to describe surgical interventions on nonbinary bodies in similar terms. (Albert's narrative seems more formulaic and less nuanced than those of the surgeons, as we shall see in the next chapter.)[79] But Albert's writings reveal an early manifestation of what was to develop even further in later decades: the certainty that all humans belonged to one of just two sexes, which often could be revealed or corrected through surgery. In previous chapters, we have already seen how authors imagined mythic hermaphrodites and hyenas who shifted between the categories of male and female sex, undermining, in some respects, a clear and dichotomous line between them. But in Albert's view, humans who appeared to have both male and female traits only served to make that boundary more palpable and definitive.

Albert's treatises were studied in medical schools and cited with reverence by medieval medical writers, who accepted the authority of few post-classical authors.[80] Universities trained a relatively small population of students, but they were responsible for concepts and techniques that traveled far beyond scholastic circles.[81] As Maaike van der Lugt observes, after Aristotle's theories spread in Latin Europe, most physicians and scholastic philosophers came to deny the existence of a sex category that lay between male and female.[82] This denial became part of a broader intellectual landscape regarding sexual difference, and it contributed to a host of ideas that developed outside of the university. For instance, the thirteenth-century Franciscan treatise *On the Human Body*, which I turn to next, married the new Aristotelian zoology to an analysis of biblical creation, resulting in a deeply pessimistic view of the place of nonbinary sex within not only the natural but also the moral order.

ON THE HUMAN BODY

Alexander of Hales, an influential Franciscan philosopher and founder of the Franciscan school in Paris, was the main authority behind the *Summa of Theology*, a massive compendium of theology compiled by his students and disseminated under his name. Sometime after Alexander's death, a lengthy treatise on biblical creation, written sometime in the 1250s by an anonymous Franciscan, became appended to his work.[83] This treatise, known as *On the Human Body (De corpore humano)*, explored, among other topics, the relationship between biblical creation and human sexual difference. Composed outside the scholastic milieu of the universities, the treatise nevertheless engaged readily with new natural philosophical theories on sex and the body. Using Augustine's *On the Literal Meaning of Genesis* as a guide, *On the Human Body* integrated Aristotelian zoology with a decidedly Christian view of creation.

The biblical creation story and Aristotelian natural philosophy were in many ways compatible: both placed living creatures within a broad and meaningful hierarchy.[84] Yet Aristotle had been almost completely unconcerned with the boundaries of the human—for him, humans and quadrupeds were indistinguishable from each other from the standpoint of generation. *On the Human Body*, in contrast, was sharply focused on the unique origins and features of humanity. Moreover, when *On the Human Body* considered generation within the context of Genesis, it emphasized how humans were set apart by the circumstances of their reproduction.

On the Human Body began with a fundamental question: Why did God create male and female bodies? The author immediately dispensed with the notion that the first man required a woman to help him work or to keep him company. A male companion for Adam would have been, on both accounts, infinitely preferable. Woman had to fulfill some other purpose, then—perhaps, the author hypothesized, it was procreation. But was a woman really necessary for procreation? Why should man, who was the most powerful and virtuous of all creatures, require anything beyond himself to reproduce? As was common in scholastic treatises, the author began with the position that he would argue against:

> Nature works however it can most quickly, and in a way appropriate to its nobility and dignity; therefore, if human generation had been made from one sole principle, that is, from one person and one sex, human nature would have been made worthier and more perfect; therefore, it seems that God should not have created human nature in a plurality of sexes.[85]

In other words, the simplicity and efficiency of a single individual who comprised both sexes—that is, a primal androgyne—was preferable to two distinct individuals (one male, one female), which entailed needless complications of sexual differentiation. Here the author pictures an androgynous first-created man as an asexual and self-reproducing creature—much like a plant—and potentially the most perfect form of humanity.

Indeed, Aristotle had argued that nature generally prefers the simplest and most efficient path. But, as the author of *On the Human Body* added, Aristotle also asserted that natural perfection required the separation of active and passive principles. Plants, for example, which were of a lower class of being, had no apparent division of the sexes. Animals were of a higher class, *On the Human Body* claimed, and so they beget themselves in a two-fold manner: that is, some animals had clearly divided binary sexes while others lacked them. But, as *On the Human Body* made clear, the human is the most perfect of all animals; hence, it is fitting that humans exist with a distinction of the sexes [. . ..] man is better suited to that mode of generation which is the more noble than others; the more noble mode is that in which the active is distinguished from the passive rather than that in which the [sexes] are confused.[86]

For the author of *On the Human Body*, as for Aristotle, the sexes were distinct among the "perfect" animals. Human perfection demanded distinct male and female, active and passive, pairs—thanks to what the author called their "nobility," which elevated humans above lesser creatures, and raised them to the top tier of existence on earth.[87] According to the author, "nature desires perfection and avoids confusion" and, as a result, "woman was formed distinct from man so that no plurality of the sexes might be found together in one and the same person, which would cause confusion [*confusionem*]—from which nature and the judgment of right thinking recoil—just as we see in a hermaphrodite."[88] The author grumbled that "such an operation, that is, of the propagation of the human [without distinct sexes], is not fitting of human dignity, to put up with the confusion of the active and passive."[89] According to the author, a self-propagating Adam was comparable to a "hermaphrodite," a confusion of active-passive roles that resembled plants and other inferior organisms, and which constituted an "abomination" [*abusio*] from which nature and human judgement "recoil[ed]."[90] As the author argued, nonbinary sex was at odds with both human dignity and the right intention of nature, which preferred binary clarity over sexual "confusion."

Finally, *On the Human Body* emphasized the social and spiritual consequences of binary sex. God could have had humans procreate in any manner, but God implanted in humans binary sexual difference to foster a mutual relationship between men and women.[91] Binary sexes had an allegorical and anagogical meaning, too: God created humans "so that in the distinction of the sexes and in sexual intercourse, during the union of the flesh, [this act] signified the joining of Christ and the Church."[92] Moreover, the conjunction of man and woman signified the soul's union with God and its potential for salvation.[93] The division of the sexes was rooted in man's position vis-à-vis woman, vis-à-vis the church, and vis-à-vis God. The author of *On the Human Body* reconciled Aristotelian philosophy to the moral and spiritual order dictated by Christian doctrine, showing binary sex to have vast societal implications.[94]

The author of *On the Human Body*, much as Augustine of Hippo had centuries before, rejected the theory of an androgynous Adam, which the author associated with "hermaphroditism." Moreover, for the author, intersex people, who supposedly transgressed the separation of active and passive principles, become violators of the natural and divine order.⁹⁵ The author's tone differed dramatically from the neutral characterizations of nonbinary sex that appeared in texts such as *On Sperm* and the *Prose Salernitan Questions*. No longer one of several sexes to which humans might naturally belong, hermaphroditism, the author noted with distaste, was unnatural and inferior, a condition fit for plants and imperfect animals but revolting in humans.

We can see how this argument played out just a few decades later, for instance, in the early fourteenth-century *Commentary on the Sentences* of French theologian Peter of Palude. In it, Peter posed the hypothetical problem of an intersex priest (described as a "hermaphrodite"), arguing that such a person should not be ordained because they were both monstrous in nature and "deformed in body." Humans may appear to possess both sexes, Peter added, but "nevertheless they must be either one or the other [sex], because the masculine and the feminine force can be joined perfectly in plants, but never in perfect animals, and most of all [not] in humans."⁹⁶ Following the same logic that animated *On the Human Body*, Peter identified binary sex as a necessary attribute of all perfect animals, and especially humans, thanks to their rarefied place in the order of being.

ROMAN AND CANON LAW

Peter's questions about ordination gestured at another set of problems that intersex people purportedly raised: If such a person had to "be either one [sex] or the other," as Peter insisted, how were authorities to decide which one? This was especially important in a world that assigned vastly different legal privileges to men and women. Civil and canon lawyers pondered the question after the twelfth century, when jurists expressed new interest in legal synthesis and proposed new ways of classifying the sexes. Determinations and assignments of sex were important because they affected not only the individual in question but also the individual's extended family and community. Whether one could marry a particular person, name heirs, offer witness testimony, or enter the priesthood depended on one's legal status as male or female. Efforts to provide clarity for individuals born with atypical sex anatomies, as well as their families, relied on a system of disambiguation that differed from but also intersected with naturalist approaches in their division of humans into binary categories.

Previously, in Republican Rome, officials had interpreted intersex infants as "prodigies," or signs of rupture in the natural order. Elaborate expiatory rites were required to purify the Republic, and the infants in question were put out to sea (presumably to drown), if the ancient historian Livy is to be believed.[97] Attitudes soon shifted, however, and post-Republican authorities began to consider such individuals as a legal rather than a religious problem.[98] Centuries later, following the precedents of ancient law, medieval jurists adopted and expanded these approaches. Although some scholars have suggested that intersex individuals were persecuted, or even executed, in the Middle Ages, no documentary evidence appears to support these assertions and, instead, medieval jurists approached the prospect of sex variance rather pragmatically, with no particular moral outrage, and sometimes with a measure of empathy.[99] This pragmatism coincided with parallel impulses in other faiths: medieval Muslim lawyers considered the fraught gender status of *khuntha mushkil* for the purposes of ritual, marriage, and inheritance, while rabbinic law deliberated on nonbinary sex categories such as *tumtum* and *androginos* with great seriousness.[100]

In Latin Christendom, among the most influential of legal texts was the *Corpus Iuris Civilis*, a codification of Roman law that dated to the sixth century and formed the backbone of much later legal reasoning. In the *Digest* (a part of the *Corpus Iuris Civilis*), the jurist Ulpian argued that an intersex person—designated here as a "hermaphrodite"—could name posthumous heirs if the male sex predominated in that individual.[101] In the same work, the jurist Paulus added that whether such a person could institute heirs or witness wills "depends on the development of the sexual qualities [*qualitas sexus incalescentis*]."[102] The historian Mathew Kuefler explains that *qualitas sexus incalescentis*—which literally means the "quality of the heating of the sex"—was a reference to the heat of the body, since the blood of males was believed to be hotter than that of females. But Monica Green translates the phrase somewhat differently, that is, as that sex which is "able to be heated" or, in modern speech, "sexually aroused."[103] In either case, the sexual organs of the individual in question were central to determining whether or not that individual could access male privileges, an opinion that was reiterated in a number of later texts.

By the twelfth century, the rediscovery of Roman law invigorated medieval jurisprudence, and legal texts relied heavily on ancient sources in their approach to classifications of persons. The Italian jurist Azo, for instance, writing in Bologna around 1200, invoked the *Digest* to suggest that all humans came in one of three types—man, woman, or hermaphrodite—as a basic division of humankind. But Azo also argued forcefully that for legal purposes, members of the third group had to be classified as a "man only, or as a woman only, according to the prevalence of the sexual development [*sexus incalescentis*]."[104] Azo's analysis prompted him to turn explicitly to the varying legal statuses of men and women: "Women are different from men in many things," he wrote, "because the legal status of women is lower than that of men"—a pronouncement that initiated his list of women's legal impediments.[105]

In the following century, other civil jurists reinforced earlier approaches to such dilemmas, with the English law codes of Bracton (c. 1220–30, with additions through the 1250s) and Fleta (c. 1290) arguing that individuals with both male and female attributes had to be "classed with male or female according to the predominance of the sexual qualities [*sexus incalescentis*]."[106] A thirteenth-century Italian notarial guide, Rolandus Passagerii's (d. c. 1300) *Summa on the Notarial Art* (*Summa artis notariae*), placed first the distinction between man, woman, and hermaphrodite, indicating that sexual difference played a central role in classificatory systems.[107] Yet Rolandus also stressed that members of the third group had to be assimilated to a male or female sex, so that "the threefold division can be reduced to a binary division."[108] Given that Rolandus's textbook was intended for notaries, we can imagine that such categorizations were not only theoretical but also practical in nature. Rolandus's guide was widely read, influencing readers beyond Italy, including in Poland, Austria, and Hungary.[109] His approach to sex variance, along with that of other contemporary texts, suggests that by the end of the thirteenth century, both in England and on the continent, a consensus was emerging to sort humans into three types, but only two binary sexes, for legal and notarial purposes.[110]

Canon law was closely related to Roman law, and Gratian's famous twelfth-century collection of canon law, the *Decretum*, drew from the *Digest* to conclude that a person with both male and female anatomical traits "can witness a testament depend[ing] on the development of the sexual qualities [*qualitas incalescentis sexus*]."[111] Canonists applied Gratian's maxim to other questions, including those of marriage and priestly ordination, and they evaluated affected individuals on the basis of dominant masculine or feminine physical traits.[112] *Incalescentis sexus* would seem to require an inspection of the genitals, but jurists left behind little indication of how it was to be judged. In other words, authorities took the liberty of assigning intersex individuals to a male or female sex without recording explicit instructions considering the individual's own preference, that of their family, or the sex of their rearing. This silence belies the potential cruelty of the legal process and how a court's assignment of sex—perhaps one unwanted by the subject—could upend that person's world.

Toward the end of the twelfth century, however, the Italian decretist Huguccio's *Summa on the Decretum* (c. 1188) addressed the topic in a manner that offered at least some agency to the individuals whose lives hinged on his decision:

> As to a hermaphrodite, if he has a beard and always wants to engage in manly activities and not in those of women, and if he always seeks the company of men

and not of women, it is a sign that the masculine sex predominates in him and then he can be a witness where a woman is not allowed, namely with regard to a last will and testament, and that he also can be ordained a priest. If he however lacks a beard and always wants to be with women and be involved in feminine works, the judgment is that the feminine sex predominates in him and he should not be admitted to giving any witness wherever women are not admitted, namely at a last will and testament, neither can he be ordained. In addition, in this distinction, the inspection of the genitals is frequently effective.[113]

Huguccio's discussion of "manly" company and activities indicates the power of social roles and networks in establishing masculinity and femininity. Huguccio focused on self-selected practices and proclivities, prioritizing an individual's internally felt sense of self—akin to what would we now call "gender identity." In doing so, Huguccio also relied on culturally mediated gender stereotypes to assign manhood or womanhood—for instance, a person who liked "female" things was female, while one who liked "male" things was male, although a number of contemporary texts documented the existence of effeminate males and masculine females who were nonetheless male or female.[114] Huguccio also relied on hair—specifically, the ability to grow a beard—as a means to assign sex. Secondary sex characteristics and homosocial bonds thus seem to have possessed much explanatory power in Huguccio's text. And yet Huguccio ultimately fell back upon the genitals as a final arbiter of difference, closing his discussion with the observation that an inspection of the sexual organs is "frequently effective."[115]

Elsewhere, Huguccio discussed once more whether a person with attributes of both sexes was eligible for the priesthood. If this person was more female than male, Huguccio argued, they could not be ordained because a woman could not receive ordination, nor could a person who was equal in the sexes. If such a person was predominately male, Huguccio wrote, they could receive ordination, but *should* not, because of "deformity" and "monstrosity," which rendered such a person unsuitable for the priesthood.[116] Huguccio's decision was in keeping with certain twelfth-century decretals that barred men with bodily impairments—what we would now call disabilities—from receiving higher holy orders.[117] Irina Metzler argues that intersex individuals were viewed as impaired during the period, in the sense that their anatomy "was an incurable, permanent, physical aberration from the anatomical norm which excluded the affected individual from certain aspects of *normal* social life."[118] Not all impairments were equally serious, however: missing fingers and even eunuchism did not necessarily disqualify one from the priesthood.[119] But for Huguccio, a person with both masculine and feminine anatomical traits was an unsuitable candidate for ordination.

Was the body, then, the ultimate determinant of an individual's assigned sex? A few decades later, in the mid-thirteenth century, the Italian canonist Hostiensis (c. 1200–71) seemed to demur. He argued that an oral commitment was preferable to a physical inspection, at least in the case of a so-called "perfect hermaphrodite" (that is, one who was equally male and female). Such a person, Hostiensis wrote, should swear an oath to the bishop promising to use only one set of genitals—either male or female—instead of alternating between roles.[120] Hostiensis recognized the ability of such a person to choose their own sex, but he prohibited any change after that initial sex assignment; there was to be no further crossing over between male and female thereafter.

An interesting case comes from the last decade of the fourteenth century, when the Italian lawyer Baldus de Ubaldis produced a *consilium* (case study) on the contested inheritance of Giovanni Malaspina, an individual with atypical genital anatomy who identified as male, and who petitioned to succeed in his late father's fief. The lawyer Baldus, whose own father had been a physician, brought diverse perspectives drawn from medicine, anatomy, and natural philosophy to bear upon the case. In his analysis, Baldus quoted Hostiensis's ruling that a person with both male and female sexual traits should choose their own path as a man or a woman, especially after the person had reached the age of puberty and had a firm sense of their own masculinity or femininity.[121] Baldus noted that such a choice was permanent, and that an individual could not transition between the sexes after an initial assignment.

Although Baldus emphasized the role of individual choice, the body also played an important role in his opinion. Giovanni, who had a beard and a "manly spirit," also lacked a penis—a detail made clear in a description of Giovanni's anatomy that accompanied the case—apparently the result of an earlier medical exam that did not reach a definitive conclusion regarding Giovanni's status.[122] Guided by the Aristotelian concept that generative capacity was central to sex, Baldus struggled to identify Giovanni as either male or female, instead settling on the observation that Giovanni's sex was "mixed" or "confused." But Baldus found Giovanni eligible for his inheritance on the common-sense grounds that Giovanni was not a woman, and that his disposition favored riding horses, handling weapons, and giving wise counsel—all manly duties associated with his feudal inheritance. If Giovanni had been fragile and feminine, Baldus added, he would have been considered female.[123] Baldus, like Huguccio and Hostiensis before him, tried to account for Giovanni's self-directed habits and preferences (again, what we might call gender identity) as distinct from his exterior physical traits. But Baldus also upheld rules preventing individuals from switching back and forth between active and passive sexual roles, a practice long associated with nonbinary-sexed figures in other texts. Baldus, like other jurists of the period, thought an assignment of binary sex to be required in such cases, but his *consilium* also recognized the role of an individual in determining their own sex.

This set of legal opinions from the twelfth through fourteenth centuries allows us to draw some general conclusions. First, jurists proposed a nonbinary sex category in which both sexes were equal, as well as what Baldus described a "confused" sex, although this latter opinion may have been unique in legal contexts. Second, Huguccio, Hostiensis, and Baldus exercised a degree of latitude in evaluating such cases, although they ultimately enforced sexual binarism in their decision-making. Jurists assigned to sex-variant individuals a male or female sex to address issues of inheritance, witness testimony, ordination, and marriage, ascribing to men and women different legal obligations and privileges. The subject's own preference was given significant weight by at least some jurists, who evaluated a person's activities and relationships, as well as their personal identity, to arrive at a decision about their sex.[124] Jurists also relied on stereotypical gender markers to assign sex, such as judging a person who liked "female" things to be female, while one with a "virile spirit" and a penchant for horseback-riding was male. As the historian Christof Rolker points out, jurists did not consider people with sex-variant anatomies to be legal "monsters"—their humanity was never in question, but some sources did use the language of monstrosity, perhaps to denote a body that did not conform to nature's ordinary course in their view.[125]

We might also observe that at least some jurists were apt to assign a male sex in such cases, likely reflecting a strong preference for males in a society that assigned to them greater social and economic value. Baldus, for his part, judged Giovanni eligible for his inheritance despite his lack of a penis and, in other cases too, authorities allowed such individuals to marry as men even if they possessed physical characteristics that were interpreted as feminine.[126] Augustine of Hippo offered some early evidence of this tendency, writing that the "prevalent usage" assigned infants with both male and female physical traits "to the superior sex; for no one has ever used the feminine names androgynesses [*Androgynaecas*] or hermaphroditesses [*Hermaphroditas*]."[127] The same sentiment appears in a thirteenth-century medical text known as the *Secrets of Women*, attributed to Albert the Great but likely written by his disciples. That text argued that even if a person had "both natures" they should receive "the worthier male species"—that is, an assignment of male status.[128] Whether jurists preferred the male sex, legal imperatives required binary clarity; that is, each person was to live as a "man only, or as a woman only," rather than alternating between male and female roles.

SUMMA "OMNES HOMINES"

A final text—the *Problemata Aristotelis ac philosophorum medicorumque complurium*, also known by its incipit (opening words), as *Summa "Omnes homines"*—brings together many of the various ideas of this chapter. The text belongs to the encyclopedic "natural questions" genre, loosely connected to Aristotle's *Problems* and written in a question-and-answer format.[129] Natural-questions collections enjoyed great popularity and circulation between the fourteenth and the seventeenth centuries, and they appeared in both Latin and vernacular versions.[130] One copy of the *Summa "Omnes homines"* (probably early fourteenth century, recorded in a fifteenth-century Bolognese manuscript) posed hundreds of questions about human anatomy and physiology, answering them with snippets of wisdom from Aristotle, Galen, and Ibn Sīnā, among other authorities.[131] The text was aimed at well-educated readers, perhaps even physicians.[132]

In its exploration of human nature, including sexual reproduction, the text integrated teachings from medical, legal, and theological traditions. With regard to individuals who, in its view, possessed anatomical traits of both sexes, the author repeated Aristotelian doctrine, noting that it was possible for an "indisposition" of matter and a "disobedience" of sperm to prevent the male parent from perfecting a fetus to its superior male form, resulting in a child with features of both sexes. How, the author asked, should such a person be classified? The author answered that "the size of one [genital] member over the size of the other member" should be evaluated, along with the member's sexual capacity, to determine "to what extent one member is more potent in the sexual act, and if in the male, then he is a man, and if in the other, then she is a woman."[133]

The author also considered access to the sacraments, asking whether such an infant should be baptized as male or female. It is unclear why baptism required any immediate ruling because all human infants were baptized, regardless of sex. Nevertheless, the author claimed that such a child should be baptized as male because the male is the "more worthy of the sexes, and the active [is] better than its passive."[134] With respect to ordination, the text deferred to what was "just said," presumably that such a person could receive holy orders if the male sexual organs dominated.[135] Like other writings of the period, it sorted sex-variant individuals into binary categories (preferring the male) while seizing an opportunity to denigrate women. The author repeated the chestnut that a woman was a failed male, an error that he connected to the phenomenon of monstrous births. Among so-called monstrous births, he mentioned both conjoined twins and a cow that gave birth to a calf-human hybrid, an anecdote that also appears in *Secrets of Women*, attributed falsely to Albert the Great.[136]

Finally, the text explained, "according to the rule of law," a person with both male and female sex traits must

> swear before being admitted to judgment which [genital] member is able to be used and, according to this, he must be admitted following the use and potency of such a member, and if both members are used then, according to the universal faith, he is unclean. [According to holy mother church he ought not to be tolerated.]¹³⁷

Here again, legal exigencies required individuals to use only one sexual organ, either a male one or a female one, and never to switch between roles. But disobedience was no mere legal transgression: according to the passage, it was a source of ritual pollution. The passage's invocation of "unclean" recalls the textual sources of the previous chapter, in which authors reacted with horror to spiritually contaminating active and passive boundary violations. According to the *Summa "Omnes homines,"* too, the alternations of sexual roles associated with nonbinary sex anatomies were "unclean," the threatening nature of which foregrounds how much was at stake in policing binary sexual difference. Its identification and rigorous enforcement were seen as crucial to the maintenance of both the natural and the moral order.

The linkage of nonbinary sex, conjoined twins, and a cow-human hybrid in *Summa "Omnes Homines"* also brings us back to Latin 16169, the manuscript of Albert the Great's *On Animals*, with which I began this chapter. Its marginal drawings placed a nonbinary-sexed human in the company of a hairy beast (perhaps a hyena), a pair of conjoined twins, and two human-animal hybrids. This juxtaposition speaks to the various ways in which intersex individuals were characterized during the period. They were judged as similar to women and twins because of their presumed failed generation. Yet in Latin 16169, the nonbinary figure's bestial companions hint at the more alien qualities associated with nonbinary sex—ones from which, authors claimed, nature and human judgment "recoiled." Here, a nonbinary body butts up against representatives of the hybrid, the monstrous, and the bestial. In the texts surveyed in this chapter, nonbinary sex was singled out as a source of confusion, one that might trouble the central categories that ordered the world.

Much like modern scientists, medieval naturalists assumed their beliefs about sexual difference to be objective facts. But sex is not an unchanging reality. As historian Ahmed Ragab explains, sex is a "historically contingent category" rooted in a "specific discourse about nature, a discourse that was produced and dominated by particular groups whose claimed expertise was the human body."[138] In analyzing medieval discourse, some historians have explicitly distinguished between *sexing* the body (identifying its physical category) and *gendering* the body (identifying its social role). But, as feminist and queer studies scholars have argued, our bodies are never really sexed outside of considerations of gender. The biologist Anne Fausto-Sterling writes:

> Our bodies are too complex to provide clear-cut answers about sexual difference. The more we look for a simple physical basis for "sex," the more it becomes clear that "sex" is not a pure physical category. What bodily signals and functions we define as male or female come already entangled in our ideas about gender.[139]

That is not to say that there is no material basis for sexual difference; rather, how we view that material difference is wrapped up in what we think about gender. The physical features that medieval experts identified as meaningful to sex assignment were not based on timeless or natural biological truths. They depended on historically contingent ideas about what made a person male or female and what made one "monstrous" or "defective." When thirteenth- and fourteenth-century authorities spoke of "discerning" a sex that already existed in the body, they were not describing any corporeal reality but rather the effects of their own ideology, which caused them to interpret bodies in ways that suited cultural, as well as biological, imperatives. The apparently straightforward question of "Is this person male or female?" occludes the process by which historically contingent societies must decide what males and females are.[140]

As this chapter has argued, authors imagined certain bodies to pose a challenge to binary categories of sex, as well as the natural, social, and divine order that hinged on them. Some of those authors, in response, suppressed nonbinary possibilities: intersex (generally described as "hermaphroditism") was an anomaly rather than a basic category of human sex. All humans had to be either male or female, or at least regarded "as a man only, or as a woman only" so that sexual diversity was reduced "to a binary division." The multifaceted inheritance of classical Greek and Muslim naturalism, as well as that of Roman and canon law, meant that expert views on sex in the thirteenth and fourteenth centuries were never monolithic. Naturalist and legal authors differed in their understandings of sex, which could arise from complexion, genital anatomy, sexual capacity, disposition, or an individual's own choice. Despite the plurality of traditions and opinions that we find, however, we can see such discourse moving in a discernible direction. To be a human was (in nearly all cases) to be male or female—or at least to be recognized "as a man or a woman only."

How a society treats unusual bodies is an important historical question that goes to the heart of what it means to be human.[141] We have already seen how debates about the creation and resurrection of humans in medieval theology limited which sexes were worthy of perfection and the eternity of paradise. In the twelfth century, as we learned in chapter 1, the bishop Otto of Freising assured readers that intersex people would rise with their bodies perfected and all "deformities" erased in the afterlife by the hand of God. Otto proposed a limited view of humanity, one in which only binary men and women could be admitted to an everlasting human experience. The naturalist and legal writers of this chapter, too, offered a similarly narrow view of human nature. They too naturalized or legitimized only certain sexes, granting admission to the human community on the basis of division into only male or female categories; for the most part, they erased other possibilities from the human species. As I have argued here, Aristotelian-influenced naturalist theories (and, to a certain extent, legal opinions) effectively made nonbinary sex among humans "disappear." We saw in chapter 2 that the Hereford Map ejected its turbaned mythic hermaphrodite to the spatial margins of the earth. In chapter 3, the Aberdeen Bestiary contributed to a climate in which allegedly nonbinary Jews were expelled from the boundaries of the kingdom. By deciding that humans had to be either male or female, the naturalist authors of this chapter similarly erased nonbinary sex from the human species.

5

The Correction of Nature

Sex and the Science of Surgery

This chapter returns us to Berengaria Castelló of Castelló d'Empúries, whose contested marriage, as we have already seen, came before a court in fourteenth-century Perelada (see fig. 0.1). As I explained in the first pages of this book, the surgeon Vesianus Pelegrini examined Berengaria's anatomy and found in it a "preponderance" of the masculine. Pelegrini's approach mirrored decisions by contemporary jurists, who classified individuals like Berengaria into binary categories for legal matters. But, as I argue in this chapter, some thinkers went beyond mere classification. Between about 1250 and 1350, a group of elite European surgeons began to propose that nonbinary bodies could be corrected by means of surgery. These surgeons followed the precedents of legal and naturalist traditions, placing sex-variant anatomies into yet another categorical system: one that prized polarity in assigning sex and justified its invasive procedures as natural and benevolent "cures." Keeping the story of Berengaria Castelló in my focus, I will piece together a history of sexual difference within the medieval world of surgery.

I begin with Latin surgical manuals of the thirteenth and fourteenth centuries—an important period for the development of surgery and, as I suggest, for ideas about the nature of sex itself. Efforts to "cure" unusual sex anatomies, as proposed in a new genre of surgical manuals, drew on translations of Arabic and Greek texts, which complemented ideas about the gendered body already present in Latin European circles. I argue that close inspection of surgical writings complicates orthodox narratives in the history of sex and sexuality: medieval thinkers approached sex and gender in a sophisticated manner that belies any simple opposition of premodern and modern paradigms. In addition, because surgical treatments of nonbinary sex anatomies in the medieval world prefigure those of the modern world, this history has the power to offer new perspectives on our current practices, revealing the ways we manipulate bodies to suit shifting ideas about sex and gender.

I trace surgery through several different traditions and contexts in this chapter, each of which shaped surgical views of bodies. I first follow the development of the profession of surgery, showing how an ambitious group of surgeons began to argue that surgery was a rational, literate, and professional discipline. To bolster the stature of their field, members of this elite group of surgeons created a new type of surgical manual that drew its wisdom, in part, from authoritative traditions of Greek and Arabic medicine. The new manuals adopted the language and conceptual frameworks of those traditions, as well as their presumptions about how sexed bodies should look and behave.

Next, I consider how surgeons discussed a group of bodies that challenged conventions of binary sex, including those described as hermaphrodites, impotent men, eunuchs, and women with enlarged sex organs. These bodies prompted inspections by medieval medical experts, who judged their size, shape, and capacity for sexual activity. Medical approaches toward this group of bodies that did not appear to fit the sexual binary offer insight into how surgeons came to view themselves as arbiters of sex. I then place the treatments they recommended within the context of traditional ideas about sex, gender, and power that pervaded Latin Europe during the period, which demanded certain congruities between body and demeanor for the sake of the Christian community. This context reminds us of a central point: how much was at stake in the surgical evaluation of nonbinary sex.

HOW SURGEONS BECAME EXPERTS

Until the thirteenth century, aspiring surgeons trained by apprenticeship, learning from more experienced surgeons through oral and practical instruction rather than in formal schools or with standardized texts.[1] The field of surgery lacked the prestige of internal "medicine," a separate discipline focused on the balance of the four fluids of the body (known as the humors), which was taught in European universities.[2] University-trained physicians occupied the top tier of medical practitioners in Europe, and with the arrival of the new Arabic-language texts in the eleventh and twelfth centuries, physicians were expected to be well versed in contemporary medical theory.[3] Surgeons, who ranked somewhat lower than academic physicians in the medical hierarchy, competed in a rough-and-tumble marketplace alongside barber surgeons, empirics, and other practitioners, many of whom were informally trained.[4] Yet by the mid-thirteenth century, a group of ambitious surgeons in Italy and France began to call for greater respect for their vocation. They created a new genre of "rational" surgery manuals, portraying themselves as members of a rigorously trained group with a learned textual tradition that rivaled that of university physicians.[5] Members of this elite group, including Bruno Longobucco, William of Saliceto, Lanfranc of Milan, and Guy de Chauliac, among others, became among the most authoritative and widely read surgeons in European history. Under their aegis, surgery developed from a craft restricted to treating growths, wounds, and other injuries into a lofty profession expansive in its applications, as well as in its social and academic pretensions.[6] These new surgical manuals provided the first systematic approach to surgery in Western Europe, distinguishing the surgeons who wrote and read them from their less educated competitors, whom they denounced as ignorant and even dangerous.[7]

During this same period, medieval health care was undergoing a process of broader professionalization. As the historian Monica Green has shown, medical knowledge was becoming both increasingly literate and increasingly regulated: laws in Spain, France, Italy, England, and parts of Germany restricted medical practice to those who were licensed and authorized, and different groups of practitioners struggled to limit the professional aspirations of their competitors.[8] The Italian-born, Paris-based surgeon Lanfranc of Milan—the focus of much of this chapter—wrote his surgical manual in the wake of efforts by university-trained physicians to limit surgical practice and place surgery under the supervision of Paris physicians.[9] To convince readers that surgery was a legitimate science, Lanfranc (like other surgeons) borrowed from Greek and Arabic medical writings, bringing surgery into better conformity with accepted medical teachings by authorities such as Galen and Ibn Sīnā. Lanfranc and his colleagues claimed that their discipline relied on reason, expert training, and an established textual tradition, just as medicine did.[10]

The growing ambitions of surgeons went hand in hand with a widening of their professional interests. Surgeons expanded into new areas, including cosmetic medicine—a discipline meant to preserve, or in some cases to embellish, the appearance of the human body.[11] Medical cosmetics were becoming a highly profitable business, and surgeons were able to take advantage of that growth, thanks to their acknowledged expertise over the body's surface.[12] The French surgeon Henri de Mondeville, for instance, cited cosmetic concerns when explaining the removal of a cyst: he advised readers to trim the skin before suturing in order to avoid puckers in the scar, which would disfigure the patient. Other aesthetic remedies also appear in the surgical manuals, including recipes for curing baldness, changing the color of a patient's hair, and removing skin discolorations.[13] In these and other examples, attention to health and functionality was joined with concern about the appearance of the human body.[14]

Surgeons also expanded into women's and reproductive medicine. While surgeons had previously avoided the intimate details of women's bodies because of concerns about propriety, the new surgical manuals began to describe the anatomy of each body part. By the late thirteenth century, surgeons such as Lanfranc were describing maladies of the genitals with new confidence.[15] It was in this context that they broached the topic of patients with morphological sexual traits that appeared to those surgeons to be neither clearly male nor female. In Lanfranc and his colleagues' view, surgeons should evaluate such patients on the basis of a number of factors, including urinary function, the size and character of the genitals, and sexual responsiveness. This process of evaluation culminated in a pronouncement on whether or not the patient was masculine enough to achieve male status or too feminine to qualify. If the patient was deemed male, surgeon sometimes recommended interventions to restore the masculine surface of the body. For patients deemed female, surgeons recommended amputations of masculine-looking genitals to return the body to a "natural form."

The surgical science of sex went hand in hand with surgeons' rivalry with physicians, leading them to seek out new naturalist and medical teachings and prompting new analyses of sexual difference. Yet surgeons were never wholly isolated from physicians: surgeons relied on humoral theories from the discipline of medicine, while physicians adopted practical methods developed by surgeons. Guy de Chauliac, an influential surgical writer, for instance, worked as both a surgeon and a physician.[16] By the second half of the thirteenth century, expert medical authorities, in general, were asserting their authority over the evaluation and alteration of bodies that seemed to stray beyond the confines of male and female.

"CORRECTING" SEX IN THE MEDIEVAL SURGICAL TRADITION

Arabic naturalist texts were once more instrumental to the development of a naturalist discourse of sex in Latin Europe. We have already seen how medieval natural philosophers such as Albert the Great built on Muslim medical texts to develop new theories of fetal development and the appropriate traits of sexed bodies.[17] The discipline of surgery followed a similar trajectory, with surgeons in the West eagerly reading and citing the opinions of Muslim forebears such as

Al-Zahrāwī, Al-Majūsī, and Ibn Sīnā. These thinkers in particular recommended a rather radical intervention for sex-variant individuals—the surgical removal of body parts that did not fit clearly into a male-female binary.[18]

The Andalusian physician Al-Zahrāwī's (d. c. 1013, known in the West as Albucasis) *On Surgery and Instruments* included a short chapter devoted to "hermaphroditism." The text, which circulated independently as a surgical manual, was an excerpt from Al-Zahrāwī's thirty-book medical opus, written in c. 1000, probably while the author was living near Cordoba.[19] In it, Al-Zahrāwī suggested identifying the primary sex of affected individuals on the basis of manner of urination, dividing them into distinct binary categories.[20] In the case of "male hermaphrodites," Al-Zahrāwī explained,

> there appears in the skin of the testicles or in the space between the two testicles a figure that has the appearance of a woman's vulva with hair. Sometimes also urine flows through that which is the skin of the testicles. There is also one kind among women, in which there is above the female vulva, on the pubes, what resembles small male organs projecting outwards. One of these is just like a penis and the two others are like two testicles. This is the treatment of all three kinds, two male and one female: you cut away the superfluous pieces of flesh until the mark of them is eliminated; then cure the wounds left over with the usual treatment.[21]

Al-Zahrāwī explained that "male hermaphrodites" have vulva-like flesh in the region of the groin, while some women have what "resembles" or is "like" a penis and testicles. This flesh—"superfluous" in his view—mimicked the form of an incongruous sex. Al-Zahrāwī's solution was to excise such parts until the "mark of them [was] eliminated."

Al-Zahrāwī's near contemporary, Al-Majūsī, who lived in Shirāz and Baghdad (d. between 982 and 995, and was known in the West as Haly Abbas), offered a similar analysis in his *al-Kāmil fī al-sinā'ah al-tibbiyyah* (*Complete Book in the Medical Art*). He described four classifications—three male and one female type—of hermaphrodite. He concluded that one type of male hermaphrodite could not be cured because surgery would obstruct the patient's ability to urinate, but the others should be treated surgically by removing the extraneous genital flesh. Al-Majūsī's language also betrayed a certain disdain for these patients, for he added that this condition was the "most vile affliction in men."[22]

In a similar manner, Ibn Sīnā's *Canon of Medicine* recommended surgical interventions on certain types of nonbinary bodies. As we saw in the previous chapter, Ibn Sīnā sorted such morphologies into three different groups: one with equally dominant sets of genitals; a second with neither set dominating; and a third group with one dominant set and one less dominant set. Ibn Sīnā concluded that "in many cases, [such conditions] are cured by a removal of the more hidden [i.e., less dominant] member and by treating the wound."[23] Like Al-Zahrāwī and Al-Majūsī before him, Ibn Sīnā interpreted parts of patients' genitals as superfluous tissue in need of surgical removal.

It is important to note that circumcision was a common practice in the medieval Muslim world, and descriptions of circumcision in Arabic-language manuals appeared alongside those of surgeries on sex-variant bodies. Al-Zahrāwī, for instance, instructed readers to remove the foreskin using a knife, scissors, or a thread ligature.[24] Other Islamic texts described the excision of female genitals, a practice now known as female circumcision or female genital cutting.[25] Genital cutting was thought to confer ritual purity on an individual; however, as scholars have pointed out, genital excision also promoted systems of marriage and reproduction by further distinguishing men's and women's anatomies and by constraining female sexuality.[26] According to some accounts, female genital cutting dampened female desire: the reduction of a woman's sexual organ supposedly curbed her lust, limiting her sexual activities to socially approved liaisons.[27] Some authors suggested that smaller genitals also made a woman more sexually appealing to men.[28] We cannot draw an unambiguous line between ritual circumcision and proposed surgeries on sex-variant bodies, yet both types of surgery were based on similar assumptions about the proper appearance and function of the genitals, as well as how surgery might regulate sexual behavior.

By the thirteenth century, Al-Zahrāwī, Al-Majūsī, and Ibn Sīnā were cited with enthusiasm by the new elite surgeons of Latin Europe. Al-Zahrāwī's *On Surgery and Instruments* appeared in Latin translation in the twelfth century, shaping surgical teachings in both Italy and France between 1250 and 1325–50.[29] Al-Majūsī's text was translated into Latin by Stephan of Antioch in 1127, after which it also became an authoritative source for Latin surgeons.[30] A portion of Ibn Sīnā's *Canon of Medicine* began to circulate independently under the name of *Avicenna's Surgery*, and it too deeply influenced European surgery after the mid-thirteenth century. In the fourteenth century, the French surgeon Guy de Chauliac cited Al-Zahrāwī 175 times and Ibn Sīnā more than 600 times, revealing their centrality to his system of thought. He placed Al-Zahrāwī within a pantheon of celebrated authorities that also included Hippocrates and Galen.[31]

The authors of Latin surgical manuals adopted, for the most part, the conclusions of their Muslim predecessors with regard to sex-variant anatomies. The Paduan surgeon Bruno Longobucco, for instance, wrote his *Great Surgery* (1252) in an effort to synthesize Al-Zahrāwī, Al-Majūsī, and Ibn Sīnā, along with other authorities.³² Bruno, who learned his craft in Bologna under the famed surgeon Ugo Borgognoni of Lucca (f. 1205–40), claimed that his surgical recipes derived from personal experience, but he followed Al-Majūsī's writings on the topic so closely that it is difficult to imagine he ever treated such a person:

> The first [type] of men is that which appears in the skin of the testicles, in which there is between the testicles a form like that of the vulva of a woman, and there are hairs in there. The second type is following the same mode except that urine flows through it. The third is similar, but urine does not come out from it. Indeed, that which is in women is when above the vulva of a woman in the pubic hair, it is just as if small male organs hang down: and there are three bodies altogether projecting outside, of which one is just like a penis and two are just like testicles.³³

Influenced by his Arabic sources, Bruno apparently settled on manner of urination as a way to assign a primary sex.³⁴ He concluded that surgeons should afterwards cut off the "leftover, superfluous parts" and, repeating Al-Majūsī, he denigrated nonbinary morphologies as both "unnatural" and a "most vile disease, especially in men."³⁵

A few decades later, the surgeon Lanfranc of Milan offered a much more detailed analysis of sex-variant anatomies in his *Great Surgery* (1296). Lanfranc's innovative vocabulary—the "saddlebags" of men and the "muscular" erectile tissue of women—does not appear in any of the above surgical works, and his language may have stemmed from treating actual patients in the field.³⁶

Lanfranc's discussion appears in a part of his *Great Surgery* entitled "On the Closure of a Hermaphrodite and on the Added Pannicle of a Woman." Lanfranc began his section by describing growths that prevented a woman from engaging in sexual intercourse and conceiving a child. As he explained, extraneous skin could cover the vaginal opening, blocking it and allowing only urine to exit:

> The cure of which is quick: separate the cleft skin of the vulva with a razor, moving lengthwise and [separating] the disordered form from the tissues of fat with the razor, lest the skin is fastened together further.³⁷

Lanfranc also noted that the vulva could sometimes be hindered by "muscular and hard flesh," which should "be removed until it may arrive at the natural form."³⁸ In addition, the uterus could close too tightly, preventing semen from entering. A surgeon should cut away the extraneous matter blocking the entrance, taking care not to remove too much tissue. The goal, as Lanfranc made clear, was sexual intercourse with a man and successful impregnation.

Lanfranc's next paragraph takes up the question of sex organs that appeared to him neither wholly male nor female. He claimed that some individuals possessed both male and female genital characteristics in such a way that

> [the person] is able to be active and passive. Some of these have one [sex] that is fully formed, the other not fully formed, and some have neither fully formed. Indeed, these have in the orifice of the vulva some added flesh, which is sometimes soft, fleshy, of a small and weak character, other times of a strong and sinewy character. The fleshy piece is removed swiftly with cutting instruments, and those parts left behind with light cauterization; the natural flesh must always be taken care of by means of iron, or through a ligature with thread until all superfluity is taken off.[39]

As Lanfranc argued, some individuals had both male and female genital tissue, leading them to be able to perform both actively and passively in sexual intercourse. Some individuals had only one functional sex (one "fully formed, the other not fully formed"), while others had neither sex functioning. Lanfranc seems to have dispensed with the Muslim focus on manner of urination as a way to assign a primary sex, and he has added new material that does not come verbatim from Ibn Sīnā, Al-Zahrāwī, or Al-Majūsī.[40]

Like his predecessors, however, Lanfranc described a serious and potentially life-altering process of evaluation. He argued that in such cases, "added flesh" in the genital area required a careful inspection to assess its size and consistency, that is, whether it was "truly hard and strong and sinewy" or "soft, fleshy, [and] of a small and weak character." If it was soft and fleshy, Lanfranc wrote, the piece was to be excised by cutting or ligature and then cauterized with a hot iron. But, he continued, if "the [seemingly excess] flesh is truly hard and strong and sinewy so that it resembles the male penis and, most of all, if it becomes erect by touching a woman, in no way touch that with the iron nor think to treat it with anything."[41]

Lanfranc's discussion reflected similar opinions by contemporary jurists who, as we saw in the last chapter, assigned a male or female sex to sex-variant individuals on the basis of anatomy or, perhaps, on a subject's experience of sexual arousal [*incalescentis sexus*]. A focus on arousal appears in another medical text, too, a late-twelfth-century anatomical work from Monte Cassino, which concluded that sexual desire revealed such a person's *de facto* sex: "Although [this person] has both sexes," it states, "according to the decrees of the princes [the person] has the privilege of whichever sex [the person] uses more and in which [the person] takes [sexual] delight."[42] In Lanfranc's manual, too, a fleshy piece aroused by a woman apparently met the minimum criterion for masculinity: a surgeon should not touch the member with an iron, "nor think to treat it with anything." The warning suggested that a phallus that was hard, strong, sinewy, and capable of erection when aroused by a woman was sufficient to establish masculinity in such a way that surgical intervention was not only unnecessary, but also unthinkable.

In the same chapter, Lanfranc offered a very different treatment for "men" with partially formed vulvas and vaginal orifices. He wrote:

> There are also certain men who have beyond their testicles two additional "saddlebags" and, in the middle, a pit resembling the vulva of women. In certain of them there is in this pit an opening through which they pass urine. If it was [there] like that, abandon the cure. But if it was not a deep pit, touch that place with a hot iron little by little, and then apply butter and expect the occurrence of the cautery scab. If you followed your plan, you grow back the skin. But if not, repeat with the cauterizer until that place has become well filled in and returns to the natural form.[43]

Lanfranc cautioned against any intervention that might obstruct a patient's ability to urinate but, barring that complication, the surgeon should close the vulva-like pit through repeated cauterizations and, as a result, return the body to a "natural form." As Lanfranc suggested, a man with a vagina-like orifice was at odds with what he considered the natural shape of the male body—closed, integral, and impenetrable. This was in contrast to a woman's body, which had long been imagined in ancient and medieval thought to be lacking in physical stability and subject to uncontrollable leaking and sexual penetration.[44] Here, the bodies of men with "saddlebags" failed to form the boundaries that divided the interior body from its exterior. Yet surgery offered a cure, eliminating the individual's perceived femininity (and potential for sexual passivity) and rendering the body decisively—and "naturally"—male.[45]

Lanfranc's language throughout the *Great Surgery* indeed reveals a striking conception of the "natural." With respect to men with vaginal pits, Lanfranc advised cauterizing the flesh until it returned "to the natural form." Earlier in the chapter, Lanfranco wrote that "nature erred seriously" in creating bodies with both male and female sexual traits. Repeatedly, he encouraged surgeons to restore the body to a "natural form" through surgery.[46] For Lanfranc, nonbinary genitals were unnatural, but surgery *was* natural, restoring the body to the form that nature had intended.

By the time Lanfranc wrote *Great Surgery*, Aristotle's zoological texts had been available in Western Europe for decades, and surgeons were very familiar with them.⁴⁷ Aristotle's *On the Generation of Animals*, as we have seen, argued that people with sex-variant bodies were not members of a natural category of nonbinary sex; they were instead, for him, an unnatural and defective type of man or woman. He proposed that an individual's actual sex could be discovered through careful examination, which would reveal an underlying male or female complexion.⁴⁸ The scholastic natural philosopher Albert the Great drew upon these ideas to argue that cases of apparently nonbinary genitals were really incidences of redundant, tumor-like growths on the sexual organs. Such individuals, by his argument, were *really* male or female: their unusual genitals were an unfortunate mistake of nature. Lanfranc of Milan was likely aware of such theories: he cited Aristotle on embryology in his surgical manual, and Albert's *On Animals* was taught in the same medical faculty in which Lanfranc taught a popular class on rational surgery to medical students in the 1290s.⁴⁹ The idea that nonbinary genitals were "unnatural" appears to have been persuasive for Lanfranc and his colleagues. If an apparently nonbinary body was a mistake, they argued, then surgeons could correct it; their expertise allowed them to restore natural forms through surgery.

Surgeons, in fact, spoke of themselves explicitly as the helpers of nature, who were able to correct nature's mistakes. When discussing wounds, for instance, Lanfranc explained that "nothing is impossible for powerful nature, most of all when a good physician assists her with helpful things, and she is aided to increase her effort."⁵⁰ Elsewhere, he claimed that surgery could enhance nature's potency, even to the point of making the seemingly impossible possible.⁵¹ A decade later, the surgeon Henri de Mondeville added that a surgeon was neither nature's servant nor assistant but her master: "Nature works neither alone nor with the aid of the professional," he wrote. "It is the professional alone who works."⁵² Henri's bold assertion underscored the extent to which surgeons believed themselves capable of assisting or even approving upon nature's handiwork.

The final member of this learned group of surgeons and perhaps the most widely read, Guy de Chauliac, seemed to approve of the sentiments of his surgical predecessors. In his *Inventarium, or Great Surgery* (1363), he explained that

> hermaphroditism [*hermafrodisia*] is the nature of doubled sex, and, according to Albucasis, it appears in men in two ways; since sometimes there is a vulva with hair between the two testicles, and sometimes [it is] in the place that is visible below. In women, however, there is one type, in which above the vulva there appears a penis and testicles. And many times they are cured through incision, as says Avicenna, but not, however, that kind which emits urine, as says Albucasis.⁵³

Guy's offhand mention of pubic hair, also noted in Bruno Longobucco's *Great Surgery*, suggests that surgeons imagined their patients to be post-pubescent, rather than infants, when they encountered the surgeon.[54] It is difficult to determine at what point in the life cycle individuals with sex-variant anatomies would have received medical attention, if indeed they ever did. Infants during this period were usually delivered by "traditional birth attendants," that is, informal female healers who assisted women during childbirth.[55] Outside of elite circles, childbirth was for the most part an all-female affair, and only a small number of female practitioners owned books. It thus seems unlikely that most birth attendants would have been familiar with the learned treatises of surgeons.[56] The historian Irina Metzler speculates that when encountering an infant who was interpreted as neither conclusively male nor female, birth attendants may well have chosen to do nothing; such a birth could have "just been considered part and parcel of life and not something to get particularly excited about."[57] After all, the classification of an infant's sex was not immediately needed for baptism, so if there was any question, the infant could be simply be baptized as male, as many authors suggested.[58] It is possible that a definitive sex assignment from a medical practitioner could generally wait until later, for instance, if a dispute prompted further examination, as when Vesianus Pelegrini was summoned to render a decision about Berengaria— who had presumably been raised as female.

JUDGING BODIES: IMPOTENT AND "CASTRATED" BODIES

As we learned in Lanfranc's *Great Surgery*, a person who was not typically male or female could avoid a painful and potentially dangerous operation if that individual was sexually aroused by a woman. But how did a surgeon know whether his patient experienced sexual desire in this way? It is possible that the surgeon merely asked the patient, yet this odd test of arousal resembled contemporary impotence tests, in which medical practitioners evaluated an accused spouse's physical capacity for erection. Lanfranc may have had such tests in mind when he described his own inspection of a patient's sexual response.

During the thirteenth century, an ecclesiastical court could dissolve a marriage if a spouse was deemed "impotent"—that is, incapable of sexual intercourse. Legal interpretations of consummation were complex and regionally variable, but a group of twelfth-century treatises concluded that legitimate marriage could only take place between two individuals who were capable of contracting it.[59] Because consent to marry generally involved consent to sexual intercourse, impotence caused by illness, "defective" genitalia, or "frigidity" (more on that last term in a moment) was considered incompatible with marriage. If an impotent partner married anyway, then the marriage could be dissolved because impotence had made the original marriage contract invalid.[60] Women could suffer from "impotence," too, that is, from a physical impairment that prevented them from engaging in sexual intercourse or conceiving. A twelfth-century marriage tract attributed to Walter of Mortagne (d. 1174) discussed female "impotence," and Pope Alexander III recognized *arctatio*, or vaginal narrowness, as a basis for marital annulment.[61] Despite heated debates among medieval intellectuals about whether impotence truly invalidated a marriage contract, dissatisfied spouses did in fact petition courts to dissolve their marriages for that very reason.[62] Judges were apparently reluctant to take the two unhappy partners at their word, however, because at least some men seemed to miraculously regain their potency after remarrying. To secure independent verification, the courts asked midwives, laypeople and, eventually, medical practitioners to determine whether or not the accused person was in fact incapable of intercourse.[63]

Church courts officiated over marriage disputes, and the diocesan courts of England, particularly in York, left behind court depositions describing their procedures in great detail.[64] When a wife accused her husband of impotence, the courts of York and Canterbury sometimes gathered together a "congress," that is, a motley group of examiners (including prostitutes), who tried to sexually arouse the man before reporting on their observations.[65] Much as Lanfranc, in *Great Surgery*, evaluated his patient's ability to achieve an erection, congresses judged the sexual potency of an accused husband, testing whether or not he could become erect enough to engage in sexual intercourse.[66] The York records make up an important body of documents in which examiners—including medical practitioners—judged the anatomy and sexual responsiveness of the human body.

Impotence examinations were not dispassionate observations. Examiners were expected to touch, stroke, prod, and otherwise help along arousal, a response that in some cases constituted manhood. In one 1432 case, examiners fondled the subject's penis and testicles, making him touch their bare bodies. A sex worker named Margaret Bell called on one husband to "for shame show... his manhood if he were a man," suggesting that an individual without a capacity for erection and penetrative sex was not a real man at all.[67] In the fourteenth-century case of a man named John Sanderson, a female examiner "felt and took between her hands the penis of the said John," but it stayed flaccid "just like the end of an empty intestine [i.e., sausage skin]."[68] The size of a man's genitals was important, too. One physician reported on a penis that was no larger than that of a "two-year-old boy," while another penis was "far too weak and too short and small" to be potent.[69]

According to contemporary medical theory, a man's virility depended not so much on the size of his penis, but on his internal complexion, of which his penis was merely a sign.[70] Most illness was caused by an imbalance of complexion (that is, heat, cold, wetness, and dryness within the body).[71] Male *frigiditas*, or "coldness"—a common accusation in impotence cases—was not a matter of emotional coldness (as in its modern sense) so much as a failure of the male complexion, which was ideally hot and dry. A man with a cold complexion was not only sexually inadequate but also closer to the sex of a woman; hence, he was imagined to suffer from effeminacy, underdeveloped genitals, and sexual impotence.[72] Examiners, as a result, tried to heat up the bodies of their examinees, nudging their complexions into a hotter masculine range. In the case of Barlay v. Barton, for instance, William Barton "warmed himself and his members" by a fire before submitting to an examination by a mixed group of men and women.[73] The historian Jacqueline Murray explains that an examinee's sex was to some extent indeterminate until examiners prompted an erection and established his male status or, instead, they judged him incapable. Such a judgment was not merely symbolic. If the court established a legal impediment, a man could face the dissolution of his marriage—as well as the "shame" alluded to by Margaret Bell. A man who failed an impotence test was to some extent "unsexed"—dismissed in the record as "less than a 'real man.'"[74]

Medical practitioners were also active participants in these impotence evaluations. Guy de Chauliac described in *Inventarium* a scene much like those recorded in York:

> The *medicus*, having license from the court, must first of all examine the complexion and structure of the generative organs. Then he must go to a matron used to such [procedures] and he must tell [the husband and wife] to lie together on several successive days in the presence of the said matron. She must administer spices and aromatics to them, she must warm them and anoint them with warm oils, she must massage them near the fire, she must order them to talk to each other and to embrace. Then she must report what she has seen to the *medicus*, and when he will have been well informed, he is able to bear testimony about the truth before justice.[75]

Here, a *medicus* ("healer")—either a physician or a surgeon—examined the man in question and judged his complexion and genital anatomy.[76] The *medicus* was responsible for treating sexual dysfunction through a variety of therapeutics and for offering sworn testimony before the court. The historian Katharine Park notes that by the early fourteenth century, male medical practitioners were frequently called upon to testify in civil and ecclesiastical courts about such matters, further legitimizing their role as experts on sexual anatomy and function.[77]

Another marriage dispute, this one between Katherine Paynell and her husband Nicholas, further demonstrates how accusations of impotence could prompt evaluations of the body's masculine status. After four years of marriage, in around 1368, Katherine petitioned the court of York to dissolve her marriage because she had never had sex with her husband. According to testimony, the "aforesaid Nicholas was from the time of his birth, and still is, *castratus* [castrated], such that the natural organs required as tools of procreation were and are lacking. And that if the said Nicholas ever had at any time, or has, any such organs, the same organs were and are unfit, completely defective, and useless for any procreation whatsoever."[78] The archdiocesan court directed Nicholas to submit to a medical examiner to settle the matter, but Nicholas apparently ignored the summons. Even without an examination, the court ruled in Katherine's favor, granting an annulment and judging Nicholas physically inadequate to contract and consummate his marriage.

Yet Nicholas's allegedly unusual anatomy did not appear to have affected his masculine status in other matters. The court consistently used male pronouns for Nicholas, and his anatomy did not interfere with his inheritance of a substantial estate from his father. Even after the annulment, Nicholas did not lose his properties nor his ability to administer as a man. But the scholar Derek Neal speculates that the court's judgment likely stung, preventing Nicholas from marrying again—and perhaps provoking the "shame" that hung over the congresses of York. The historian Ruth Karras suggests that marriage was a defining feature of manhood during this period, separating adult men from mere adolescents.[79] Nicholas died just a few years after, possibly in the process of appealing his case before the papal court in Avignon. In the end, Derek Neal writes, Nicholas was found to be not masculine enough to be a full man nor to exercise all the privileges generally extended to males. A man judged as "impotent" might be denied certain masculine rights while still retaining others, and this mixed legal status likely reflected an equally confused social status.

Notably, in Nicholas's court case, Katherine Paynell used the word *castratus* to describe Nicholas's body, showing how classifications of "impotence" might intersect with those of "eunuchism." Centuries earlier, in ancient Roman law, the category of eunuchs could include "made eunuchs" (that is, individuals who suffered an injury or underwent a medical procedure to remove or alter their genitals), as well as eunuchs "by nature" (that is, those born with what were considered inadequate sexual organs or those whose organs did not develop with maturity). In both cases, eunuchs lacked the sexual organs and reproductive capacities associated with adult masculinity in ancient Roman society.[80] Moreover, eunuchs were generally not assimilable to a male or female binary sex and, hence, their existence in the later Roman Empire, as the historian Mathew Kuefler writes, "greatly upset" notions of masculine identity.[81] The Roman emperor Severus Alexander (r. 222–35) placed eunuchs in a "third sex" or a "third type of human being," while the poet Claudius Mamertinus dismissed eunuchs as "exiles from the society of the human race."[82] Such individuals revealed the precarious nature of binary sexual difference, Kuefler argues, as well as the fragility of the male privileges that derived from it.

In the Western Middle Ages, those described as eunuchs and castrates continued to make routine appearances in textual sources, including in satirical literature, where they were often depicted as ridiculous or even monstrous.[83] Given the severe fines and penalties levied against those who attacked or wounded male genitals, male sexual organs were apparently highly valued in Western medieval society. A male body that lacked genitals, in contrast, received social censure, and Jacqueline Murray observes that intense fear among medieval men led castration to occupy a "central place in theological, legal, and popular discourses."[84] Although eunuchs "for the sake of the kingdom of Heaven"—that is, celibate men—were widely praised in early Christian texts, other categories of eunuchs were generally detested in Western medieval discourse, where they continued to occupy an intermediary position between male and female.[85] Castrated individuals, Murray adds, were virtually "unsexed," and those who lacked a penis were to some extent robbed of their very humanity.[86]

In addition, a number of medieval texts described "castration" and "hermaphroditism" as closely linked; multiple sources drew upon Ovid's story of Hermaphroditus to describe emasculation, and the influential *Catholicon* encyclopedia claimed that "a hermaphrodite is said to be castrated, since [this person] seems to be neither man nor woman."[87] Hence, an impotent man who failed to "show . . . his manhood" during a congress was in some sense reduced to the ambiguous status of those regarded as eunuchs, castrates, and hermaphrodites, all of whom were thought to deviate from socially acceptable standards of masculinity.

In cases of impotence, men could find themselves deemed insufficiently masculine, as was Katharine's husband Nicholas. In the parallel case of Berengaria, a woman could also fall short of feminine ideals for sexual and procreative performance. By the end of the fourteenth century, courts increasingly valued medical practitioners to make sense of such cases.[88] Given this context, we can surmise that surgeons such as Lanfranc reasonably thought of themselves as experts who could judge the sexual capacities of all kinds of bodies, including those that did not fit standard expectations of binary sex. Marriage disputes over impotence, and the role of medical practitioners in adjudicating them, provided an ideological and institutional underpinning for surgeons' decisions about a range of bodies that challenged conventions of manhood and womanhood.

WOMEN WITH "ENLARGED" SEXUAL ORGANS

Lanfranc and his colleagues expressed concern about a range of nonbinary bodies and their sexual capacities, including those of "women" whose genitals were perceived to be excessively large and who, surgeons worried, might use their genitals to have sex with other women. Surgeons viewed "enlarged" female genitals as distinct from "hermaphroditism," yet both kinds of bodies raised questions about the boundaries between men and women, as well as their mutually exclusive roles in sexual intercourse. Surgeons here recommended a treatment much like that for individuals designated as "hermaphrodites": the amputation of body parts that were considered harmful, unnatural, and aesthetically offensive.

Concerns about overly large clitorises appear in some of the same early Arabic texts we have already surveyed, and they once more served as an inspiration for later Latin surgeons. Immediately after discussing those individuals designated as hermaphrodites, for instance, the physician Al-Zahrāwī considered *tentigo* ("tension"), that is, when a clitoris was large enough that it achieved a penis-like erection. In such cases, Al-Zahrāwī claimed, the female organ might grow in size until it is "above the order of nature, and its appearance is shamefully ugly; and in certain women it is so large that it becomes erect just like [the organs of] men and it attains to coitus. You must grasp the growth with your hand or a hook and cut it off."[89] Al-Zahrāwī's discussion assumed that large female organs were outside the natural order to the extent that they were shameful and excessively masculine. This opinion was later taken up by Al-Zahrāwī's Latin successor Guy de Chauliac, who discussed *tentigo* in his *Inventarium* (1363). He explained that the "cure of this (following Albucasis) is that it is cut with a ligature or razor, but not all the way to the bottom, for fear of bleeding."[90] Guy, like Al-Zahrāwī (Albucasis), recommended the amputation of a larger-than-usual clitoris, a source of "discontent" and even "harm" to patients.

Similarly, the physician Ibn Sīnā discussed a set of fleshy growths called "*ragadias*" or "*baccara*," which he thought could produce among women a desire for illicit sexual contact with other women:

Sometimes there arises additional flesh in the mouth of the womb, and sometimes there appears on a woman a thing that is just like the penis aroused in coitus. And sometimes it occurs to her to have coitus with [other] women similar to what is done to them by men. And sometimes it is one large *baccarum*.[91]

Latin translations used a host of terms to indicate the clitoris—*baccarum*, *nymphe*, *tentigo*, *landica*, and *virga*, among other words.[92] As early as Galen, medical authorities seem to have been aware of the clitoris, although there was no agreement on its name, function, or precise location. Galen, for his part, pointed to the vulva as the seat of female sensuality, while the fourteenth-century medical writer Peter of Abano thought women experienced sexual pleasure due to stimulation of the upper pubis, which he compared to the tip of the penis.[93] (Early modern writers, who supposedly "discovered" or "rediscovered" the clitoris, it must be said, also disagreed on such matters.)[94] Here, Ibn Sīnā used the term *baccarum*, a word for the clitoris, but he seems to be describing something that is not quite a clitoris but perhaps a prolapsed uterus or some other type of swelling.[95] Whatever the growth in question, Ibn Sīnā feared that it might prompt a woman to adopt a masculine role in sexual intercourse with other women.

In his *Summa of Preserving and Curing* (c. 1270), the Italian surgeon William of Saliceto (Guglielmo da Saliceto) (1210–76/80), a student of Ugo Borgognoni and the teacher of Lanfranc, highlighted similar concerns with respect to purportedly large female genitals.[96] Like Ibn Sīnā, William worried that female fleshy protrusions might become erect like a male penis. He explained, "Sometimes a thing appears on a woman that is just like a penis aroused during coitus; and sometimes it occurs to her to do what men do with women, that is, have coitus with women."[97] Here, a woman's genitals were considered disturbing not only because they resembled a man's genitals—confusing sexual anatomy—but also because they facilitated sex with other women, confusing sexual roles. For William, a masculine piece of flesh carried with it a masculine sexual appetite for women: its possessor was labeled as a woman and yet the libido it engendered was both active and inappropriately masculine.

A final example comes from Lanfranc, who used the word "pannicle"—a term for the clitoris in certain contexts—to express analogous concerns in his *Great Surgery*.[98] Sometimes, Lanfranc wrote, "muscular" flesh on a woman's pubis became enlarged to the extent that it hung down from the body. A woman with such imposing genitals might be loved less by men, he warned, and he advised the surgeon to amputate the "superfluity of that skin, [and] afterwards, cauterize it with gold until you reduce it to the natural form."[99] Lanfranc seemed to view a large "pannicle" as an obstacle to passive sexual intercourse and childbearing, much like the growths over the vagina and cervix that he described earlier in the chapter. Moreover, this large female organ strayed, in his view, beyond the very bounds of nature. But surgery, Lanfranco made clear, could reduce the organ's size and restore it to a "natural form."

Women were often thought in the Middle Ages to be the more sexually voracious of the sexes, and yet these texts suggest that it is the acquisition of a phallus that activated a woman's lust and (mis)directed it toward other women.[100] Sexual responsiveness to a woman could be a crucial sign of male sex—for Lanfranc it meant an escape from the surgeon's knife. But, here, sexual response did not establish male status. Perhaps it was the experience of passive sexual intercourse that disqualified such patients from maleness? Or the possession of a penetrable vagina? The surgical manuals give us too little information to be sure. Yet the diversity of criteria for maleness expressed here suggests that there was no stable or definitive anatomical trait or somatic experience that defined the male sex. Surgeons recommended excision of those masculine anatomical parts that were on the body but, remarkably, not of it.[101]

Educated men such as Guy, William, and Lanfranc were likely privy to the theory that each part of the body had a "final cause," or *telos*—a single purpose for which it was designed.[102] Reports varied on the purpose of the external female sexual organ (Galen thought it to shield the interior parts in some way), but the idea that it should sexually penetrate another body was out of the question: sex between two women—that is, sodomy—was against "nature's order in the manner of generation, which [was] the starting point for the whole of nature."[103] The physical shapes of men and women, as well as their corresponding roles in sexual activity, underpinned the binary sexes and their places in the order of nature. Upholding that order, as the surgeons purported to do, was a correction of nature, too.

HARD AND SOFT BODIES, ACTIVE AND PASSIVE BODIES

Surgeons' approaches to nonbinary bodies depended on factors that went well beyond matters of size and shape. Surgeons also considered gendered polarities that were widely accepted in thirteenth- and fourteenth-century Europe. Lanfranc, for instance, drew from medieval stereotypes about the body's gendered qualities: while men's sexual organs were supposed to be strong and vigorous, women's were soft and weak, a characterization that appeared commonly in a range of medieval texts.[104] According to Isidore of Seville's *Etymologies* (c. 600–25), man (*vir*) received his name from the Latin word for vigor or power (*vis*), from which also derived the word strength, *virtus*, an attribute that extended to man's anatomy and actions.[105] The word for woman, *mulier*, according to Isidore, was from *mollior*, or "softer," and such softness—both physical and behavioral—was a distinctive feature of femininity and of effeminacy.[106] According to Isidore, a man could not be soft and yielding in the manner of a woman without sacrificing his manhood: for him, a man became soft (*mollis*) when he "disgraces the vigor of his sex with his enervated body, and is softened (*emolliatur*) like a woman (*mulier*)."[107] This linkage of *mollis* and effeminacy appeared at least as early as Roman antiquity, when the word *mollis* conveyed impotence, castration, and a general lack of manly vigor. The famous spring in Halicarnassus—where the mythical nymph Salmacis joined with Hermaphroditus—was reputed to make men who entered the waters *mollis*, *impudicus* (shameless), or *obscenus* (lewd), all terms that connoted male sexual passivity.[108]

The equation of softness with effeminacy continued to have currency during the later period, too. In the mid-thirteenth century, Thomas of Aquinas identified a "softness of complexion" as a cause of lust in women and "phlegmatic" men (i.e., those with an overabundance of the humor phlegm and hence an unbalanced and feminized body). Thomas followed the ancients in their linkage of physical softness, sexual impropriety, and moral weakness.[109] In the early fourteenth century, surgeon Henri de Mondeville singled out eunuchs, phlegmatic men, and effeminate men as the "soft" parts of the public that constituted the body of society.[110] Effeminacy had not only undesirable sexual consequences but also broader ones that could jeopardize a community's very survival. A lifestyle of feminine vanity, torpor, and decadence "unmans" potential warriors, as the poet Peter of Eboli wrote: "For this soil gives birth to effeminate men;/ Restful shade unmans those born to the mirror/ And reared on a soft couch amidst tender roses."[111] Medieval cultural imperatives demanded that men expressed firmness, strength, and stability in both their bodies and demeanors, qualities that determined not just individual destiny but also the collective fate of the community.

Another gendered criterion for judging sex—aesthetics—seems to have been applied differently to the bodies of individuals deemed either male or female. Lanfranc's discussion of men with vaginal pits did not explicitly mention the attractiveness of the male body nor its potential to repulse female partners. But those individuals classified as women with large genitals were judged by vastly different criteria. An allegedly large female sexual organ was spared or removed based on its supposed ugliness, not on its sexual function.[112] In fact, when the sexual function of such organs was considered, it was to prohibit women from using such organs for penetrative sex with other women—a forbidden appropriation of male sexual privilege. This contrast suggests that with respect to patients judged female, surgeons strived to produce cosmetically pleasing genitals while eliminating barriers to reproduction. In the case of individuals with variant anatomies who were judged men, the surgeon removed the semblance of femininity while preserving the male capacity for arousal. In each case, the surgeon altered a nonbinary body to restore what was assumed to be the proper operation and appearance of the genitals, either by removing purportedly superfluous flesh or by closing superfluous orifices, and further promoting gendered views of the body's aesthetic and functional qualities.

What we do not see in these surgical manuals is any attentiveness to a patient's personal sense of self or stated preference to live as a man or a woman (or otherwise). As my last chapter suggested, thirteenth- and fourteenth-century jurists such as Hostiensis and Baldus ruled that gender identity should play a central role in determining a sex-variant person's legal status as male or female. But the opinions of Hostiensis and Baldus likely had little bearing on the elite surgeons' decisions. Baldus's *consilium* postdates the surgical texts I discuss here, and Hostiensis's text was absent from many reference works of canon law, which were compiled early in the thirteenth century, before the apex of Hostiensis's career. The canonist Huguccio, however, enjoyed wide influence during the period. As we have seen, he privileged an inspection of the genitals in such cases—although he still allowed intersex individuals some agency in choosing their sex.[113]

We do find an emphasis on agency in another contemporary text that drew from both legal and surgical thinking, and which upheld the widely acknowledged gendered binaries of activity and passivity. A French encyclopedic text entitled *Placides and Timeus, or the Secrets of the Philosophers*, written in the late thirteenth century, linked the legal closure of sexual options to the surgical closure of the nonbinary-sexed human body. The author wrote:

> The ancient judges established that no one should allow such people to use both natures, but that one should put to them rather what nature they would want, to do it or to suffer [it to be done to them]. And when they have taken the one or the other, that is to say the nature of the man or the woman, if someone finds them practicing that which they had denied, then they must be punished bodily, because it is against nature to use both. And such people, who wish to use both natures, must not be tolerated among the populace, and so the ancients judged that if they chose to be passive, then one had to cut off their testicles and then close up the skin of the penis in the front, and if they chose to be active, that is to say to use the nature of a man, then one closed the orifice, and if by malice they unclose it, than they are punished bodily for doing so.[114]

According to *Placides and Timeus*, a nonbinary-sexed individual's male or female organ was to be rendered unusable by surgery so that they could not "use both natures." But nature was more than just anatomy here. In the passage, an individual's nature was also a complicated intersection of one's expressed object of desire and one's role within a binary schema of sexual activity and passivity. According to Ruth Karras, sex in the Middle Ages was something someone did to another person, and the dichotomous categories of activity and passivity distinguished the vastly different experiences of sexual intercourse that the two partners were thought to have, as well as the asymmetry of their social positions.[115] Therefore, according to the text, people with "two natures" had to specify "what nature they would want, to do it or to suffer [it to be done to them]." Such people could not opt to have both active and passive sex alternately. "Nature" was also in *Placides and Timeus* a set of laws: "It is against nature to use both." Nature dictates the proper use of each body part, which had a natural (and, as we saw in *Summa "Omnes Homines,"* a divine) purpose for which it was made.

"Nature" was therefore crucial to the regulation of both gendered and sexual behavior. Surgeons restored natural forms and corrected nature's failings, an approach that revealed how much was at stake in preserving the hardness or softness of the flesh. The task of surgeons was not only to decide whether a male or female sex prevailed in an individual, but also to "cure" or, as the texts put it, to "close" nonbinary bodies. Such closures were not only physical but also metaphorical. Surgeries on nonbinary bodies closed off sexual functions, preventing individuals from using their bodies for both active and passive roles. In order to avoid engaging in illicit acts, an individual could perform as "male" or "female" but never as both. Surgeons were thus responsible for hewing humans to a natural and moral order.

As I have explained, the surgeon Vesianus Pelegrini inspected Berengaria Castelló's genitals in 1331 and found in them a preponderance of the masculine. The surgeon's observations focused on the contours of Berengaria's body and her role in sexual intercourse. "No man can lie with her," he testified, revealing the extent to which Berengaria's passive, gendered sexual performance was key to her legal and medical sex. It is worth noting that the surgeon found Berengaria to be primarily male on the basis of her failure as a female (her inability to fulfill her marital debt to a man), not on the affirmative criteria advanced by Lanfranc. The surviving record of Berengaria's case gives us no further insight into her own sense of femininity or masculinity, nor what, if any, "cure" she received from the surgeon. It is possible that Vesianus Pelegrini had already studied the rational surgery manuals, some of which were already circulating in translation around the time of Berengaria's examination. Al-Zahrāwī's *Surgery* was available in Catalan as early as 1313, and a Jewish surgeon in Perelada—the same town in which Berengaria was examined—apparently had a copy of it in 1346. Bruno Longobucco's *Surgery* could be found in a Barcelona surgeon's library in 1338, and Lanfranc's *Great Surgery* appeared in Catalan at least as early as the mid-century.[116] But we cannot know whether Pelegrini ever read such manuals.

It is also impossible to know how many people with sex-variant anatomies encountered a learned surgeon. Miri Rubin has found a single case of a surgery on an apparently intersex person in fourteenth-century Bologna, recorded in the *Annals of the Friars Minor of Colmar*.[117] We do not know how many affected individuals received medical attention nor whether the procedures described in the surgical manuals were even intended to be performed.[118] But Berengaria's meeting with Vesianus Pelegrini during this critical period suggests that the processes of sex assignment described in the surgical manuals were no mere theoretical exercises. Surgeons surely, if infrequently, evaluated such cases, although we might imagine that other nonbinary-sexed individuals never saw a surgeon nor endured surgery.

During the thirteenth and fourteenth centuries, an influential group of rational surgeons believed that nonbinary sex was a problem that could be solved, at least in part, by surgery. To determine the proper treatment, surgeons assigned their patients to a male or female sex, subjecting them to physical examinations and recommending operations to restore the "natural form" of the body. In making such decisions, surgeons drew on ancient, as well as contemporary, traditions to conceptualize and enforce sexual difference in new and consequential ways. The conviction that surgery could prevail where nature had failed supported beliefs that binary sex was natural and that nonbinary sex was both unnatural and defective.

It is important to point out that much more was at play in medieval surgical texts than the "one-sex model" popularized by Thomas Laqueur's well-known book *Making Sex: Body and Gender from the Greeks to Freud*. According to Laqueur, until the eighteenth century, medical thinkers believed male and female sexual organs to be the same anatomical structure: the vagina was an inverted penis that appeared internally or externally, depending on the heat of an individual's complexion.[119] Laqueur argued that, with respect to "hermaphrodites," enlarged clitorises were unambiguously female anatomies that did not count in establishing male status; the internal phallic/vaginal structure had to descend to mark maleness.[120] As number of other scholars have countered, however, far from adhering to a one-sex model, medieval writers subscribed to plural theories of sexual difference.[121] While it is true that certain medieval surgeons mentioned the homologies between male and female identified by Laqueur, they also subscribed to a much more nuanced view of sex that went beyond the presence or absence of a descended vagina.[122] Lanfranc of Milan, for instance, shows how surgeons evaluated the size and function of a phallic-clitoral structure to determine a patient's optimal sex and potential therapy. In these cases, the clitoris and penis were separated by a fuzzy line that counted crucially in establishing sex. Laqueur writes that there was no essential sex in the premodern world but "neither were there two sexes juxtaposed in various proportions."[123] But this is just what we find in Lanfranc's "men" with penises, vulvar "saddlebags," and vaginal pits alongside a seeming testicular structure. It seems that, in the case of medieval surgeons, understandings of sexual difference cannot be reduced to a simple one-sex model; we must give voice to the full range of complicated, and even contradictory, ideas that medieval theorists of the body found significant.

In addition, the rational surgeons' approach to nonbinary bodies suggests far less freedom to choose one's sex in the Middle Ages than has been suggested by the influential French theorist Michel Foucault. Foucault claimed in his introduction to the memoirs of the nineteenth-century figure Herculine Barbin that, during the premodern period, people with intersex (hermaphroditic) genitals enjoyed a sort of "free choice" to determine which sex they preferred, rather than being forced to accept a sex that was chosen for them by authorities.[124] Foucault viewed the premodern period as rather fluid in its approach to sexual difference, prior to the biopolitical regulatory practices that demanded from the body a single "true sex" starting in the eighteenth century. While a number of scholars have already challenged Foucault on multiple grounds, the writings of Lanfranc and his colleagues offer yet further counterevidence.[125] Surgeons actively intervened to fit nonbinary bodies into restrictive categories. While self-reported desires and proclivities figured into certain evaluations of people with atypical genitals in the Middle Ages, a narrative focused on self-determination takes too little account of the expert surgeon, whose interrogations and operations eradicated from the body sexual and anatomic possibilities.

MEDIEVAL SURGERY IN MODERN PERSPECTIVE

As I have already suggested, the medieval science of sex resembles our own modern one in some startling ways. The psychologist Suzanne Kessler, who has written extensively on intersex in contemporary medicine, notes that in the modern world, intersex genitals are deemed unacceptable "not because [they are] threatening to the infant's life but because [they are] threatening to the infant's culture."[126] Medical approaches to intersex in recent decades have been, much like medieval surgeries on nonbinary-sexed bodies, dominated by stereotypical notions about how men and women's bodies should look and behave, as well as by restrictive notions of what constitutes sexually functional or aesthetically appealing bodies. As scholars have suggested, the existence of intersex people challenges the myth of humanity as a "perfectly dimorphic species."[127] In addition, modern ideas about sex and surgical intervention often rely on what Vernon A. Rosario calls "neo-Aristotelian" thinking in their dedication to mutually exclusive gendered categories of male activity and female passivity.[128]

Efforts to enforce sex and gender congruence and to eliminate bodily "ambiguity" seem to be well entrenched in medical practice in the twentieth and twenty-first centuries, even as new policies advocated by clinicians (and a strongly worded statement by three former U.S. Surgeons General in 2017) have called for an end to irreversible cosmetic surgeries on infants with intersex variations, which can lead to partial or total destruction of sexual sensation among patients, as well as other serious health complications.[129] Scholars, activists, and allies have welcomed new medical guidelines and patient-centered practices, but several scholars have noted that the "extent to which these guidelines have been put into practice remains disappointingly unclear."[130] A recent report by Human Rights Watch notes that despite decades of advocacy, children with intersex variations continue to be traumatized by "normalizing procedures" and repetitive genital exams, the latter of which patients describe as akin to sexual abuse.[131]

Even with the medical advances and technologies of our recent decades, our contemporary conventions of masculinity and femininity have notable similarities to medieval ones. Parallels between past and present, while not absolute, speak to a shared set of ideas about the interplay between gender, sexuality, and embodiment. The bioethicist Alice Dreger has identified our current "age of surgery" as a new phase in approaches toward intersex, but the surgical documents I explore here suggest that modern impulses to surgically reshape bodies have antecedents in the distant past, even if they are expressed in (sometimes) divergent terms.[132]

For when we compare the medieval and modern, we also see a range of historically contingent ideas about masculine and feminine bodies. Today, a larger-than-average clitoris is generally considered an intersex variation, but medieval medical experts categorized women with large clitorises as distinct from "hermaphrodites." In the Middle Ages, a man born without a penis might be considered a "hermaphrodite," an "impotent" man, or a "castrate." Some "eunuchs" had genital variations that medical practitioners would now consider intersex. As a result, what we now call "intersex" constituted several different (and not entirely consistent) medieval categories, and hence there is no one single category of premodern nonbinary sex that is precisely equivalent to the modern category of "intersex."

Moreover, what medieval people worried about with respect to nonbinary bodies is not precisely what modern doctors focus on with respect to intersex. No one talks today much about male superfluous labial folds, an issue that so preoccupied Lanfranc. A penis with a variably positioned urethra, on the other hand, is much more concerning to doctors now than it was once to medieval practitioners. Intersex variations now vex pediatrics in much the same way that their medieval analogues once troubled adult medicine in the Middle Ages. Such distinctions suggest the divergent ways in which medieval and modern authorities interpreted the human body, as well as the different ways in which bodily attributes come to matter during different moments in our life cycles. Nevertheless, the manuals of Lanfranc and his colleagues constitute an important prehistory of genital surgery, and they hint at an expanded chronology of efforts to manipulate sexed bodies, efforts that continue even now.

Beyond this, medieval authorities expressed concern that a person with a nonbinary body might abandon their assigned sex and adopt a new sex, or, worse, that they might switch back and forth between male and female roles. Legal and medical experts, in response, recommended policies to prevent such crossings because they thought that gender inversion, and not just nonbinary anatomy per se, was the salient threat to the natural, social, and spiritual order. It is for this reason that I suggest here that we read medieval discourse about nonbinary-sexed categories not only through the history of "intersex," but also through that of "transgender."

A number of scholars have already embraced the term "transgender" to talk about figures who transgressed boundaries of sex and gender in the distant past. Kadin Henningsen, Ruth Karras, and Tom Linkinen, for example, argue that the sex worker John/Eleanor Rykener, who faced accusations of crossdressing and sodomy in fourteenth-century London, might productively be labeled as "transgender." New edited volumes on medieval "trans feminisms" and Ovidian gender "transversions" have further directed our attention to a range of transgender practices in premodern history and literature.[133] The art historian Robert Mills suggests that transgender can function "as a prism for understanding medieval encounters with sex change and other modes of gender variance, as well as interrogating the category's associations (or not) with homoerotic behavior."

In Mills's view, "transgender" is a strategic anachronism that illuminates the lives of medieval actors, including gender-switching sodomites and saintly crossdressing monks, even as Mills acknowledges that modern language is necessarily experimental and provisional when it is applied to the distant past.[134] In a similar fashion, I argue that viewing the examples of medieval nonbinary sex that I discuss throughout this book through the modern analytic of transgender offers an opportunity to foreground their alleged sex/gender/sexual crossings, even as we recognize that parallels between medieval and modern categories are always only partial.

"Transgender" is, of course, a category of recent import, tied to twentieth- and twenty-first-century understandings of sex and rooted in subjective experiences of self-identification.[135] Transgender is a tricky word to define, not only because it is a flexible category, but also because it is currently (perhaps always?) in flux and under challenge.[136] Transgender (also written as trans or trans*) encompasses a wide variety of non-normative gender identities and practices in the modern world, drawing its sense of crossing from the Latin prefix of "trans"—meaning "across, through, over, to or on the other side of, beyond, outside of, from one place, person, thing, or state to another."[137] While there is no single definition of transgender, scholars often use the term to refer to a person whose internal sense of gender differs from the gender (or sex) assigned to them at birth. As a result, some individuals choose to "transition" from one gender to another, with or without changing their bodies. (Many transgender people, of course, reject gender binarism altogether and prefer nonbinary or genderqueer identities and practices.) Transgender can describe not only permanent, unidirectional transitions, but also temporary and multidirectional ones.[138] For some thinkers, transgender relies on a clear distinction between "gender identity" and "sexual orientation"— that is, an individual can be transgender no matter what kind of sexual partner they desire, if they desire any—while others draw together gendered and sexual categories in complex ways.[139]

Medieval thinkers, of course, did not make any distinction between sex, gender, and sexuality, all of which were all wrapped up in the single and composite category of "*sexus*."[140] They did not use the language of transgender nor would they have recognized the concept. But we often use contemporary terms to describe past individuals and societies that lack our modern language. (After all, no one used the word "medieval" in the Middle Ages.)[141] As an analytic tool, transgender can describe any movement away from an assigned sex or gender regardless of whether or not an individual in question has explicitly identified as transgender.[142] Using transgender in this way, as an analytical method rather than as a category of identity, as Susan Stryker and Aren Z. Aizura have suggested in their *Transgender Studies Reader 2*, allows us to explore "different methods for excavating pasts that certainly contained gender-variant cultural practices" without labeling those past figures as "transgender" in an ahistorical fashion.[143] An expanded chronology of transgender can enlarge our available archive of gender and its histories, and it can further our awareness that gender, sex, and sexuality have always generated complicated and variable ideas.

By placing medieval ideas about nonbinary bodies within the purview of both intersex and transgender history, I mean to direct our attention toward the centrality of *transition* to medieval thinking about nonbinary sex. In other words, we should take special note of the repeated rhetorical focus on the supposed penchant for gender-crossing and sexual inversion among nonbinary bodies.[144] As we have seen, texts repeatedly argued that individuals should be forced to choose a single and fixed sex, in accordance with the rules of binary, active-passive sexual performance. Of course, there is a fair amount of variability in how medieval experts described atypical genitals, and not all of them were centered on gendered "confusion" nor coercive measures to contain it. Nevertheless, "transgender" brings into sharper focus the preoccupation with gender-crossing that pervades medieval writings on gender-challenging bodies and that animated medieval attempts to stabilize sexual and social practices. Writings on the monstrous races and hyenas, as we saw in chapters 2 and 3, emphasized not only those nonbinary figures' allegedly unusual bodies but also their tendency to cross back and forth between gendered positions. In addition, as the last chapter showed, jurists suppressed the supposed propensity for gender-crossing among people with sex-variant anatomies by subjecting them to fixed sex assignments and sexual roles. Finally, medieval surgeons enforced congruence between such individuals' interior and exterior selves through surgery, validating or erasing certain desires, and assigning a medical status that conferred admission to a human community.

Humans are more than their bodies, but they are their bodies, too. How bodies are treated by their society—that is, whether they are accepted, rejected, contested, or altered—in part defines those bodies, as well as what it means to occupy them as a human.[145] Modern scholars of queer, intersex, and transgender studies have produced important scholarship documenting the ways in which "the human" has been deeply inflected by our beliefs about gender and sexuality. As these scholars have shown, gender plays a central role in legitimizing personhood, granting only the full range of human privileges (including those of bodily integrity and self-determination) to individuals who fit into accepted, natural categories, while withholding it from those whose bodies or gendered practices are considered unnatural or unacceptable.[146] I have already suggested that medieval authorities sorted individuals into binary sexes in order to assimilate them into a natural, social, and divine order. This sorting may have resulted in sex assignments that contradicted an individual's lived experience, and—horrifyingly—resulted in amputations of body parts that were deemed unattractive, shameful, or unnatural. Furthermore, naturalists and theologians of the period constructed a definition of the human that excluded nonbinary sex from the species, and even from the afterlife (as we learned in chapter 1, and in a striking parallel to surgeons' corrections of nonbinary bodies)—in effect, making nonbinary sex disappear.

In the modern world, too, transgender activists such as Laverne Cox have described experiencing a level of "stigma so intense and pervasive that trans folks are often told we don't exist."[147] The legal scholar Dean Spade has documented how trans people are often considered "impossible people," dismissed as unreal and unable to fit in anywhere.[148] A host of scholars and activists have documented the brutal force directed at "non-existing" people, and intersex activists and allies, in particular, have decried the disambiguation of infants with intersex variations through surgeries that, in effect, render intersex "invisible."[149] In a comparable manner, medieval people with sex-variant anatomies faced the prospect of medical treatments that similarly forced their erasure—eradicating from their bodies the traces of a purportedly incongruous sex and remaking them over into "natural" men and women. By collecting these cases across a broad temporal span, we can see an equally broad pattern. Using the institutional forces of law and medicine, authorities accepted or rejected bodies according to their intelligibility to binary systems of sex and gender. The consequences were devastating for nonbinary, atypically-sexed, and otherwise gender-nonconforming people.

Finally, we must acknowledge the ways in which the medieval story I tell here is constrained by the premodern historical archive. Our knowledge of individuals such as Berengaria is circumscribed by the observations of medical and legal authorities, whose goals and assumptions shaped the records they left behind. Their methods rarely allowed subjects to speak for themselves (and even if they did, we could hardly accept them as transparent records of anyone's innermost thoughts and desires). Yet even if this history is limited, it is nevertheless important. Medieval history does not operate as an uncomplicated origin of modern ideas about sex or gender variance, nor should we view medieval nonbinary categories as straightforward teleological precursors to what only finds its full expression in modern ideas. And, over and over again we see that in the Middle Ages, ideas about nonbinary sex operated not only as descriptions of anatomic reality but as capacious symbols with diverse meanings. Yet we should not imagine that the ideas and bodies articulated in the past have nothing to do with the present. The scholar Gayle Salamon explains, "[W]hat we are able to imagine about what our bodies are or may become—even to decide what 'counts' as a body and what does not—is structured by the history of how bodies have been socially understood, by what bodies have been."[150]

I suggest here that, with respect to nonbinary sex categories, we should allow the past and present to resonate productively. In that resonance we might find that our contemporary debates about the body are less new and exceptional than they at first appear. Such resonances may help us pose more critical questions about our own world. What categories are upheld, challenged, or created by our institutions? What cultural demands for activity/passivity, hardness/softness, or beauty/ugliness still, or yet again, animate our bodily choices? What unacknowledged allegiances might we have to a perceived natural or moral order, a transcendent sense of the way that things are or should be, that influences our care for others and ourselves? The surgical texts I discuss here demonstrate the complicated ways in which bodies in the Middle Ages came to belong to the masculine, the feminine, and the human, revealing their history and the consequences of accepting and enforcing their demands.

In my last chapter, I return to some of the ideas with which I began this book, but now I present those ideas through a different lens. As we shall see, ideas about nonbinary sex, which figured so prominently in stories about the world's creation, also played a role in its imagined end. In my final section, I explore how understandings of nonbinary sex as primal and generative combined with other traditions to claim one of the most exalted humans in Christian history—Jesus Christ—as a nonbinary-sexed figure, one with wondrous powers. At the end of the Middle Ages, the ideal of transcendent androgyny was embraced by alchemists, who proposed new ways to shape both time and flesh. In late medieval alchemy, writers conflated Christ with the "philosopher's stone," a chemical substance that elevated contraries and transmuted human bodies. This union of opposites led not to charges of deviance or monstrosity but to the realization of new and idealized forms. In alchemy, the primal androgyne reached its logical conclusion: in fevered, visionary imagery, impossible combinations crystallized into a novel figure, a sun-moon-mother-son-God-man who was also Christ, the singular agent of human salvation.

6

The Jesus Hermaphrodite

*Alchemy in the Late Middle Ages
and Early Renaissance*

In Book IV of Ovid's *Metamorphoses*, a lovestruck water nymph named Salmacis attempts to seduce Hermaphroditus, the son of Hermes and Aphrodite, at the edge of her fountain. Despite the youth's apparent lack of interest, Salmacis follows him into the water, forcibly kissing and fondling him. When he rejects her advances, she boldly asks the gods to join them forever. The result is a single creature of fused male and female body parts:

> As when one grafts a twig on some tree,
> he sees the branches grow one,
> and with common life come to maturity,
> so were these two bodies knit in close embrace:
> they were no longer two, nor such as to be called, one, woman,
> and one, man. They seemed neither, and yet both.[1]

Ovid's *Metamorphoses* was widely distributed during the Middle Ages, as documented by a large number of extant manuscript copies, as well as the many glosses and notes that circulated after the late eleventh century. By the thirteenth century, as scholars have noted, the poem was central to the curricula of the medieval schools, inspiring new attitudes toward change, and especially toward the possibility of metamorphosis.[2] Medieval vernacular poets, including Dante, Chaucer, Chrétien de Troyes, Guillaume de Lorris, Jean de Meun, John Gower, Christine de Pizan, and Boccaccio, among others, all made extensive use of Ovidian material in their writings, and the myth of the hermaphrodite, in particular, found many admirers and interpreters.[3]

Among the readers most fascinated with this myth were alchemists, that is, naturalists who explored the properties and composition of matter, as well as the possibility of making precious metals through human technology. Visual illustrations of nonbinary-sexed figures constitute some of the most intriguing and widely reproduced images from medieval alchemical texts, but they have not so far received much attention from historians.[4] In the mid-twentieth century, scholars such as C. G. Jung and Mircea Eliade made undeniably important contributions to the study of alchemical imagery, but they tended to view the images I analyze here as either evidence of an unchanging psychological "collective unconscious" or as part of a cross-cultural mythological system, rather than as a result of specific historical circumstances.[5]

But the emergence of a nonbinary, compound-sexed "alchemical hermaphrodite" within the specific history of the European Middle Ages is crucial for our understanding of its purpose and power. This final chapter traces how alchemical literature used an image of a "hermaphrodite" to describe a chemical agent believed to transmute base metals into gold or silver. I end this book with alchemy because we can see in it how preexisting ideas about human/nonhuman, male/female, and earthly/heavenly binaries joined to construct a singularly important and influential figure: the "Jesus hermaphrodite." In fact, alchemy's investment in what they called hermaphroditism, particularly in the fourteenth and fifteenth centuries, represented a re-embrace of nonbinary sex parallel to that of early Christianity—but with a twist. Bringing together numerous preexisting ideas about sexual difference, the "Jesus hermaphrodite," as I explain in this chapter, represented a new stage in nonbinary imagery. In chapters 2 and 3, nonbinary sexes for the most part represented troubling or unclean hybrids, but in this new context, nonbinary sex's supposed capacity for joining opposites became a productive symbol of physical and spiritual transformation.

We thus see at the end of the medieval period a return to the optimism that graced the primal androgyne in the early Church. Yet the Jesus hermaphrodite did more than merely replace negative images with positive ones. The concept provided new possibilities for generation, performance, and action, and it offered new ways of being in the world. Here, the idea of nonbinary sex was nothing less than an escape from the corrupt nature of postlapsarian earth.[6] The development of the alchemical hermaphrodite also dovetailed with the historical trajectories of other genres of thought and literature, which by the later Middle Ages were embracing a similarly more dynamic sense of change, while also viewing matter as increasingly plastic and open to transformation.[7]

Late medieval alchemy tended to view hermaphrodites as a combination of masculine and feminine traits, as well as of human and divine ones. Indeed, whether the boundaries in question divided the sexes or the categories of matter and spirit, the nonbinary figures of alchemical literature showed such boundaries to be crossable through human action. Furthermore, such crossings led not to disorder or confusion, as we have seen in other areas of art and literature; instead, they created something precious. The idea of nonbinary sex was a necessary agent in the transmutation of gold and silver; it was a means to understand the God-man that was Jesus, the agent of human salvation.

ALCHEMICAL KNOWLEDGE IN MEDIEVAL EUROPE

Alchemy is usually defined today as an attempt to transmute base metals into gold and silver by means of a chemical agent, often called the "philosophers' stone." But medieval alchemy comprised a wide variety of goals, techniques, and theories. Its research focused not only on transmuting precious metals but also on treating human bodies through medical remedies. Moreover, alchemy was the branch of science devoted to the analysis and manipulation of matter and, hence, many scholars now view alchemy as the forerunner to the modern science of chemistry.[8]

Alchemy became a topic of increased interest in Europe beginning in the mid-twelfth century, when a number of influential Greek and Arabic natural philosophical and alchemical texts became available in Latin translation.[9] Aristotelian texts such as *On Generation and Corruption*, which treated different kinds of natural change; *Meteorology*, which discussed the generation of minerals by dual "exhalations" of the earth; and the pseudonymous *Sciant artifices (Let the Artificers Know)*, which discussed (and rejected) certain alchemical theories, led to controversy in the thirteenth century about whether or not alchemists could effect real changes in matter.[10] If matter could be manipulated through alchemy, then one could transform one substance into another with the correct approach. A number of scholars, including Albert the Great, Roger Bacon (c. 1214–92), and Petrus Bonus of Ferrara (fl. 1330s), among others, engaged in heated debates about alchemists' ability to accomplish such transformations.

Alchemy drew many of its underlying principles from the university-taught disciplines of medicine and natural philosophy, with which it shared basic assumptions about the natural world, as well as about human bodies and their functions. Alchemists borrowed language from those better-known disciplines to describe the novel and complicated concepts that were becoming central to alchemical debates, as well as to legitimize alchemy as an academic discipline.

Because alchemy was relatively new among Latin-speaking audiences in the high Middle Ages, its apparent connection to more familiar bodies of scholastic knowledge helped to bolster its credibility.

Since metals had no obvious means to reproduce themselves, alchemists drew from medicine and natural philosophy the metaphor of sexual reproduction to explain metal formation, as well as to theorize the "philosophers' stone," as they called alchemy's transformative chemical agent. The stone (also sometimes called the "elixir" or the "quintessence") automatically converted base metals into pure silver and gold by balancing their constituent elements. This was possible because precious metals were thought to exemplify a perfect (or nearly perfect) balance of the four elements. Perfect elemental balance—sometimes called "equality"—was also associated with immortality, immutability, and even the perfected nature of Adam's prelapsarian body.

The natural philosopher and aspiring alchemist Roger Bacon claimed, for instance, that the equal complexion created by alchemy was the same as the principle of immortality that existed in prelapsarian and post-resurrection bodies and which suppressed those bodies' potential for change and decay. He wrote:

> For this condition will exist in our bodies after the resurrection. For an equality of elements in those bodies excludes corruption forever. For this equality is the ultimate end of the natural matter in mixed bodies, because it is the noblest state, and therefore in it the appetite of matter would cease, and would desire nothing beyond.[11]

Bacon speculated that Adam's body in the Garden of Eden approached equality, and he elsewhere explained that at the moment of resurrection human bodies also achieved incorruptibility through equality, a perfect balance of complexionary elements that ceased all cycles of generation and corruption.[12] The historian Joel Kaye has shown that during this same period a new theory of equilibrium was developing across Western Europe, replacing older static models with a theory identifying balance as a dynamic, self-regulating guarantor of order.[13] Alchemists likewise seized on the idea of balance—a harmonious mixture of male and female complexionary qualities—as a source of eternal incorruptibility. This was the activating principle of the philosophers' stone, which could also bring about quasi-immortality in humans.[14] Alchemists believed they could produce the philosophers' stone through the arduous process of refining their working materials until they reached the highest level of purity, but precisely how to do this was the most sought-after secret in the field. Numerous theorists and practitioners claimed to have discovered the secret, but following their instructions was no easy matter.

Alchemical writers used symbolic or analogical language not only to clarify the methods by which they worked, but also to obscure them. Would-be alchemists spent much of their time trying to decipher the often-lyrical code names used for alchemical materials, many of which relied on complex metaphorical systems. For instance, the *Emerald Tablet* (*Tabula smaragdina*), one of the foundational texts of alchemy, stated that the father of the philosophers' stone "is the Sun; its mother the Moon."[15] Commentators on the *Emerald Tablet* equated this "father" and "mother" with sulfur and mercury (the two materials generally thought to be the building blocks of metals in the Islamic alchemical tradition), which they identified as components of an alchemical reproductive process. For instance, in his *Letter of a Good Man (Epistola boni viri)*, John Dastin quoted from the *Emerald Tablet*, as well as from the Muslim alchemists Jābir ibn Hayyān and Abū Bakr Muhammad ibn Zakariyyā al-Razi, before concluding that "the stone is nothing other than the male and female, sun and moon, heat and cold, sulfur and mercury."[16] That is, the philosophers' stone was produced in a manner parallel to sexual generation among humans, with hot sulfur taking on the sexual role of the male and cold mercury, the female.

The *Emerald Tablet* was not the only alchemical text that required decoding. During the thirteenth century, European alchemists encountered Latin translations of Arabic writings, some of which included an unidentified alchemical base material, the "rebis." Latin-speaking alchemists such as Constantine of Pisa and Richard Anglicus attempted to decipher the word, apparently a transliteration of a still-unknown Arabic term.[17] Richard interpreted "rebis" as an abbreviation for "res bina," or "two thing," which he identified with the philosophers' stone.[18] The struggle to solve such linguistic puzzles was part of how aspiring alchemists proved their worthiness among the company of adepts.[19] But while alchemists could have interpreted a "two thing" in any number of ways, they generally solved the riddle by imagining a "hermaphrodite," in this context, a combination of male and female qualities. Even authors who did not explicitly use the word rebis eventually began to think of the alchemical agent as a hermaphroditic substance.

The idea of nonbinary sex had almost wholly positive connotations in these conversations, which posited a parallel between metal transmutation and sexual reproduction. Alchemical writers also used other analogies, too—such as plant-grafting and spontaneous generation—to explain metal transmutation, but those other explanations were limited in their power to explain change in terms of the sexed elemental qualities with which alchemists believed they worked.[20] As a result, alchemists preferred the image of a hermaphrodite to describe the philosophers' stone: according to their theories, the philosophers' stone combined male and female elemental qualities into a compound substance that was capable of transmutation. Because the alchemical process forced elemental contrarieties into a perfect stasis, this new body (since chemicals and metals were often called "bodies" in alchemy)[21] was both male and female, a new substance that was outside the bounds of binary division.

SCHOLASTIC CONTRIBUTIONS

Scholastic thinkers Albert the Great and Petrus Bonus of Ferrara (fl. c. 1330) used sexual and reproductive analogies in their work, and they made crucial contributions to the development of the hermaphrodite metaphor as it appeared in mineralogy and alchemy. Although Albert the Great's *On Minerals* was not strictly an alchemical work, Albert drew from alchemical sources in order to supplement the Aristotelian natural philosophical corpus, which lacked an extensive analysis of minerals. He explained how stones and metals developed by using a prolonged comparison to sexual generation, which was rendered in language drawn from Aristotle's *On the Generation of Animals*. Albert's explanations agreed with contemporary medical theories, and he described the development of metals as parallel to the growth of a human fetus in the womb.[22] Moreover, he described sulfur (which he believed was simultaneously hot, cold, wet, and dry) as a "hermaphroditic," plantlike substance.[23] For him, a substance that contained all four qualities was in some sense both male and female and thus capable of asexual self-reproduction. Although Albert did not develop further this theme, his understanding of metal formation as similar to embryology, and of sulfur as similar to a composite male-female sex, was formative. His identification of nonbinary sex with asexual reproduction elsewhere in his biological works led him to discount the possibility of a truly nonbinary sex in humans, as well as to dismiss the primal androgyne theory. But his proposal of the plantlike, self-generative qualities of sulfur would prove fruitful for later medieval imaginings of an "alchemical hermaphrodite" and its potential for human salvation.

Petrus Bonus of Ferrara seems to have been among the first to connect the idea of hermaphroditism explicitly to the alchemical agent of transmutation, the substance that reputedly transformed metals into gold and silver upon contact. Unlike Albert's *On Minerals*, Petrus's text, *The New Pearl of Great Price* (c. 1330), was wholly concerned with alchemy and particularly with the philosophers' stone,[24] which Petrus described as a combination of sulfur and mercury and explained in terms of sexual reproduction:

[They] call the milk that is coagulated the female, and the male that which coagulates, since activity is attributed to the male, and passivity to the female. For when this stone arises, since it is itself liquid and flowing and passive, it is called female. Its coagulum, that which coagulates it, when it is solid, firm, permanent, and active in it, is called male. The combination of these is called the compound stone, perfect and composite, and in the mixing they become altogether one.... Therefore the male and female are joined, and become one.[25]

The aftermath of this conjunction did not follow the same trajectory as human reproduction, however. According to both Hippocratic/Galenic and Aristotelian models of conception, nearly all human pregnancies would result in a male or female child; a child of nonbinary sex was born only in a rare case. At the end of a successful alchemical gestation, in contrast, a "hermaphrodite" was always the result. Petrus noted that when the process was complete, the philosophers' stone embodied both male and female complexionary qualities:

And it must be known that the male and the female are the same and in the same substance, and they have diverse powers in such unity of subject.... [s]uch a union is able to be called *Hermaphrodita*: since plants and seeds impregnate wherever, and are also impregnated, and this denotes that activity and passivity in the same subject are mixed together into a certain unity. When, therefore, the stone arises, it has in it a mixture of male and female.[26]

Since the stone was capable of both active and passive sexual functions, it was able to generate new forms, much like a vegetable seed or an egg, and to transmute metals. For Petrus, the alchemical hermaphrodite was a unity of contrary qualities. Petrus's alchemical stone was a new chemical compound (neither the female nor male that had existed before), yet he preferred to discuss it in terms that preserved the distinct identities of its components (both male and female). The alchemical hermaphrodite was not merely a midpoint between opposites but a body that held contraries in stasis and conversation. While Petrus's comments suggested that he imagined the stone in terms of a nonbinary-sexed plant or egg, he also referred to the substance as a "woman," "king," or "wife," adding an anthropomorphic dimension to his analogy.[27]

Nor was the metaphor of biological reproduction the only image that Petrus used to characterize the philosophers' stone. He noted that the stone had a comprehensive nature that allowed it to be likened to multiple pairs of opposites, including "the corporeal and incorporeal ... corruptible and incorruptible, visible and invisible, to spirit, soul, and body, and their union and separation," among other concepts.²⁸ For Petrus, the stone was both nature and divinity, corruptibility and incorruptibility, and by extension, it was parallel to Christ. According to the historian Chiara Crisciani, Petrus believed that the stone bore the chief aspects of Christ and his life: it was a union of divine and natural elements, the product of a miraculous birth, and subject to death and resurrection.²⁹ Other alchemical treatises of the thirteenth and fourteenth centuries also drew parallels between Christ and the alchemical stone. In the fourteenth-century *On the Philosophers' Stone*, for instance, the author compared the alchemical operation to the life of Christ, ending the work with a symbolic death and resurrection.³⁰ During the same period, the alchemist John of Rupescissa explained that after its death, the stone was entombed in the alchemist's equipment "just like Christ inside the sepulcher."³¹ Analogies between the philosophers' stone and Christ played upon the supposed similarities between alchemy and Christianity. Like Christ, the philosophers' stone was a combination of nature and divinity, of corporeality and incorporeality, of opposites united in one subject. Moreover, such alchemical "mixtures" resulted not in impurity nor corruption but in the kind of marvelous unities of high and low, spirit and flesh, heaven and earth that Bernard of Clairvaux had praised in the twelfth century.³²

Manuscript illuminations by the late Middle Ages also began to depict the alchemical stone visually in terms of Christian imagery. A fourteenth-century manuscript of Gratheus's *Introduction to Alchemy* illustrated alchemical sublimation with a picture of Christ's resurrection.³³ Another alchemical text, *The Book of the Secrets of My Lady Alchemy* (second half of the fourteenth century), brought the pictorial tradition of biblical creation to bear on alchemy. A circular diagram, which depicted transmutation, mimicked the Genesis-cycle illustrations found in much medieval hexaemeral literature (see fig. 6.1).³⁴ This particular illustration, which Barbara Obrist calls the "creation diagram," drew an unmistakable parallel between biblical and alchemical creation. The hand of God appears at upper left, and metals and planets join with the creation of birds, fish, and animals—the origin of creatures described in the first chapters of Genesis.³⁵ This drawing, along with other similar images, made visible the Christian language that was already permeating alchemical sources, and it anticipated connections that later theorists would draw between God—the divine creator—and the alchemist, the creator of new chemical forms.

This group of textual and visual sources reveals some early stages in the development of the alchemical hermaphrodite. Both Albert and Petrus appear to have drawn from notions of nonbinary sex as a fusion of male and female attributes. The alchemical hermaphrodite was not a midpoint between opposites; instead, it was a mixture and a union of contrary parts that remained distinct. Such texts and illustrations also demonstrated the multiplicity of analogies used to characterize the philosophers' stone: the stone was Christ, the stone was a king, and the

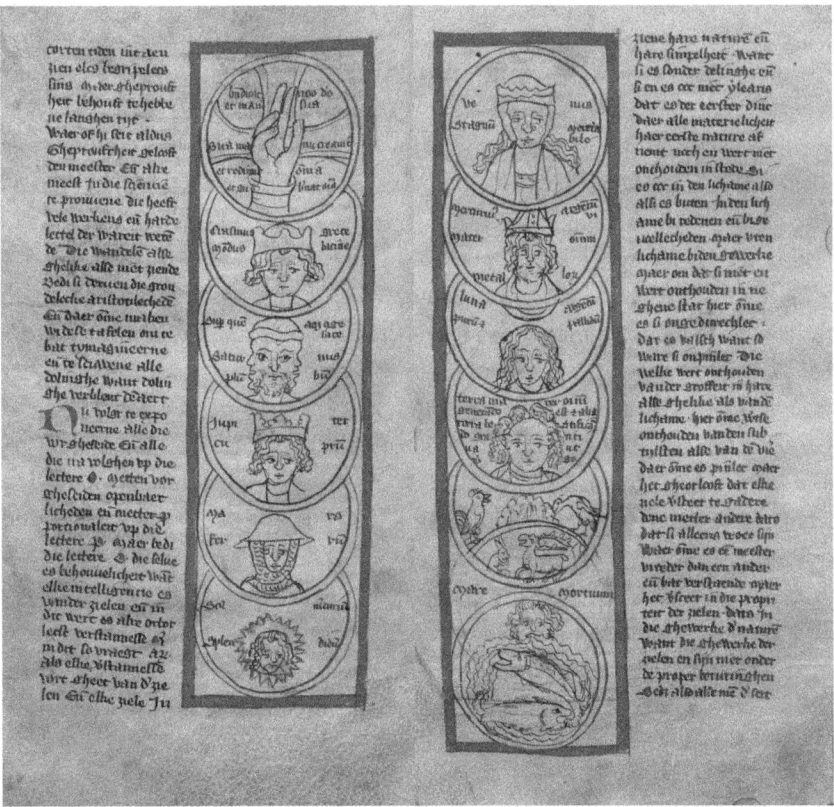

FIGURE 6.1 Creation diagram. *The Secrets of My Lady of Alchemy (Adaptation of Constantine of Pisa, The Book of the Secrets of Alchemy)*. Vienna, Österreichische Nationalbibliothek, Codex Vindobonensis Palatinus 2372, fols. 46vb-47ra (second half of fourteenth century).

stone was a hermaphrodite. These analogies were carried further in the works of other alchemical authors, who combined preexisting images in new ways, exploring the imagined interplay of balance and doubling in a nonbinary body and borrowing from a longstanding tradition of viewing Jesus as both male and female.

AURORA CONSURGENS

During the fourteenth century, an influx of religious language and imagery was transforming Latin alchemy. No longer a self-consciously scholastic discipline, wedded to the language of Aristotelian natural philosophy, certain alchemical texts were becoming increasingly religious both in their sentiment and their vocabulary.[36] The concept of the hermaphrodite became crucial to these new writings, as can be seen from the text and manuscript illuminations of a fourteenth-century alchemical text known as *Aurora consurgens* (*Rising Dawn*) and another anonymous, early fifteenth-century treatise called *The Book of the Holy Trinity*.[37] While Albert the Great and Petrus Bonus tended to view the philosophers' stone as a hermaphroditic plant or egg, these texts clearly represented the philosophers' stone as a nonbinary-sexed human.

While the precise composition date of *Aurora consurgens* remains uncertain, the earliest exemplar of the text is a lushly illustrated manuscript produced in the 1420s and now housed at the Zentralbibliothek of Zürich (Codex Rhenoviensis 172).[38] The text of the anonymous work exemplifies the trend of religious language in alchemy, as well as the symbolic use of the alchemical hermaphrodite. The writing drew from an array of Arabic and Latin alchemical authors, as well as from the sapiential theology of the biblical books of wisdom, to create a tapestry of biblical quotations and poetic imagery more akin to a mystical tract than a practical book of alchemy. It opens with a paean to the female figure of Sapientia, or Wisdom, who is a "gift and sacrament of God and a divine thing, which most of all and in many ways has been hidden in figurative speech by the wise."[39] In the second section, Sapientia herself speaks in seven "parables" that ostensibly reveal the secrets of alchemy but are delivered in highly metaphorical prose. The personified wisdom of biblical scripture, which patristic and medieval authors identified variously with the female Virgin Mary or the male Christ, is equated here with personified alchemy—the *lapis*, or stone.[40] The voice of alchemy in *Aurora consurgens* is thus chiefly female but also sometimes male. In one passage, the feminine Sapientia describes herself in distinctly masculine terms:

> [To the one for] whose love I languish, in whose ardor I melt, in whose fragrance I live, by whose taste I regain my health, by whose milk I am nourished, in whose embrace I grow young, in whose kiss I receive the breath of life, in sleeping with whom my whole body is emptied of life, I will yet be as a father to him and he will be to me as a son.[41]

Sapientia here shows herself to be youthful and aged, revivified and drained, united with a male who is both sexual partner and son (and who may be either the aspiring alchemist or the chemical sulfur, the "male" component of the alchemical stone). Alchemy is described in a series of opposing images, much like those cited by Petrus Bonus in *The New Pearl*. More important, the usually feminine protagonist in *Aurora consurgens* is transformed into a father, suggesting that Sapientia and the alchemical stone have both masculine and feminine properties.

A series of unusual illustrations accompany the text, and they explore the theme of the alchemical hermaphrodite in new ways. While illuminations appear in a number of its manuscripts, the earliest extant copy—the Zentralbibliothek manuscript—is perhaps the most interesting.[42] One particularly evocative painting from this Zürich cycle depicts Sapientia, the personified alchemy, as a Black Madonna who gestures toward a window into her womb to reveal a caduceus, the symbol for Mercury—both the chemical and the deity, also known as Hermes (see fig. 6.2). This image brings to mind a passage in Senior's *Tabula chemica*, a source for *Aurora consurgens*, in which the moon, evoking the language of the *Tabula smaragdina*, claims to carry the soul of the sun in her womb.[43] In this illustration from *Aurora consurgens*, the Virgin Mary, conflated with the goddess Aphrodite, carries Christ, who is also Hermes, within her body. The union of Aphrodite and Hermes in classical mythology gave birth to Hermaphroditus, and here they are representative of both the philosophers' stone and the alchemical hermaphrodite. Hermaphroditism is here imagined as the conjunction of male and female bodies through pregnancy. The illustrator also plays with the traditional sex identification of alchemical materials, designating mercury, rather

FIGURE 6.2 Alchemical "hermaphrodite." *Aurora consurgens*. Zürich, Zentralbibliothek Zürich, MS Rh. 172, fol. 29v (1420s). Photo: www.e-codices.ch.

FIGURE 6.3 Alchemical "hermaphrodite." *Aurora consurgens*. Zürich, Zentralbibliothek Zürich, MS Rh. 172, front paste-down (1420s). Photo: www.e-codices.ch.

than sulfur, as the male component by identifying it with Christ. The depiction of the impregnated Virgin suggests that the alchemical stone could be understood as a physical union of male and female bodies, with Christ and Mary standing in for these two sexes.

Another illustration from the same manuscript envisions the alchemical stone as a conjoined figure in the clutches of a blue eagle (see fig. 6.3). In this illumination, the alchemical hermaphrodite is a physical fusion of male and female bodies, a biform person with two heads, two pairs of arms, two chests, and two sets of genitals. The image draws upon the understanding of the stone as a combination of sulfur (represented by its male half) and mercury (represented by its female half). As in the works of Albert the Great and Petrus Bonus, this alchemical hermaphrodite is imagined as a balance of male (hot and dry) and female (cold and moist) qualities, but the figure's doubled heads and sexual organs also invoke the Aristotelian notion of nonbinary sex as the result of a superfluity of matter.

In the imagery of *Aurora consurgens*, the hands of the alchemical hermaphrodite clasp two animals, adding yet another level of meaning. The bat, symbolizing alchemical "volatility," invoked the double-sexed or split nature of bats in the medieval bestiary tradition.[44] The hare, symbolizing alchemical "fixity," hinted at the well-known legend of hypersexuality and auto-generation among hares. But because hares were thought to be capable of reproducing without a mate, they were also associated with chastity and the supernatural birth of Christ.[45] These iconographical gestures hinted at the contradictory aspects of the alchemical hermaphrodite. This version of the hermaphrodite concept was connected to hypersexuality but, at the same time, to chaste, even miraculous, generation.

THE VISUAL TRADITION OF THE *AURORA CONSURGENS* HERMAPHRODITE

This *Aurora consurgens* illustration joins multiple rhetorical and imagistic strains in such a complex manner that it is worth pausing to consider its elements in detail. First, the image closely resembles a fifteenth-century manuscript illumination of *Ovide moralisé* (*Moralized Ovid's Metamorphoses*) (see fig. 6.4), which depicted the crucial moment in the Ovidian hermaphrodite story as two bodies conjoined at the waist, each embracing the other. The similarity between the two images indicates the debt of the alchemical imagination to Ovid's tale. Change was at the heart of Ovid's metamorphoses, and its hermaphrodite myth in particular provided an apt model for alchemists. It described a fusion of male and female sexed parts into a biform body that was, as Ovid claimed, both and neither. In both images, male and female bodies were fused into a new shape that retained the distinct characteristics of its parts.

Second, the doubled figure in *Aurora consurgens* recalls similar images of conjoined twins, who, as we have seen, were thought to derive from similar conditions at the time of conception. Conjoined twins were linked to nonbinary sex categories in Aristotelian natural philosophy, including in texts by Albert the Great and by the pseudonymous *Secrets of Women*.[46] MS Latin 16169, the richly

FIGURE 6.4 Hermaphroditus and Salmacis. *Ovide moralisé*. Paris, Bibliothèque nationale de France, MS français 137, fol. 49r (c. 1470–1480).

decorated university copy of Albert the Great's *On Animals* that I discussed in chapter 4, includes an image of conjoined twins that shares some of the features of *Aurora consurgens*'s alchemical hermaphrodite.[47] In contemporary manuscript illustrations, moreover, the twins of the zodiac, known as Gemini, were also sometimes depicted as "Y"-shaped figures conjoined at the waist (see fig. 6.5) and sometimes as Janus-faced figures that closely resemble the bifurcated hermaphrodites of *Omne bonum* and the *Mare historiarum* map (see fig. 6.6, and fig. 1.1

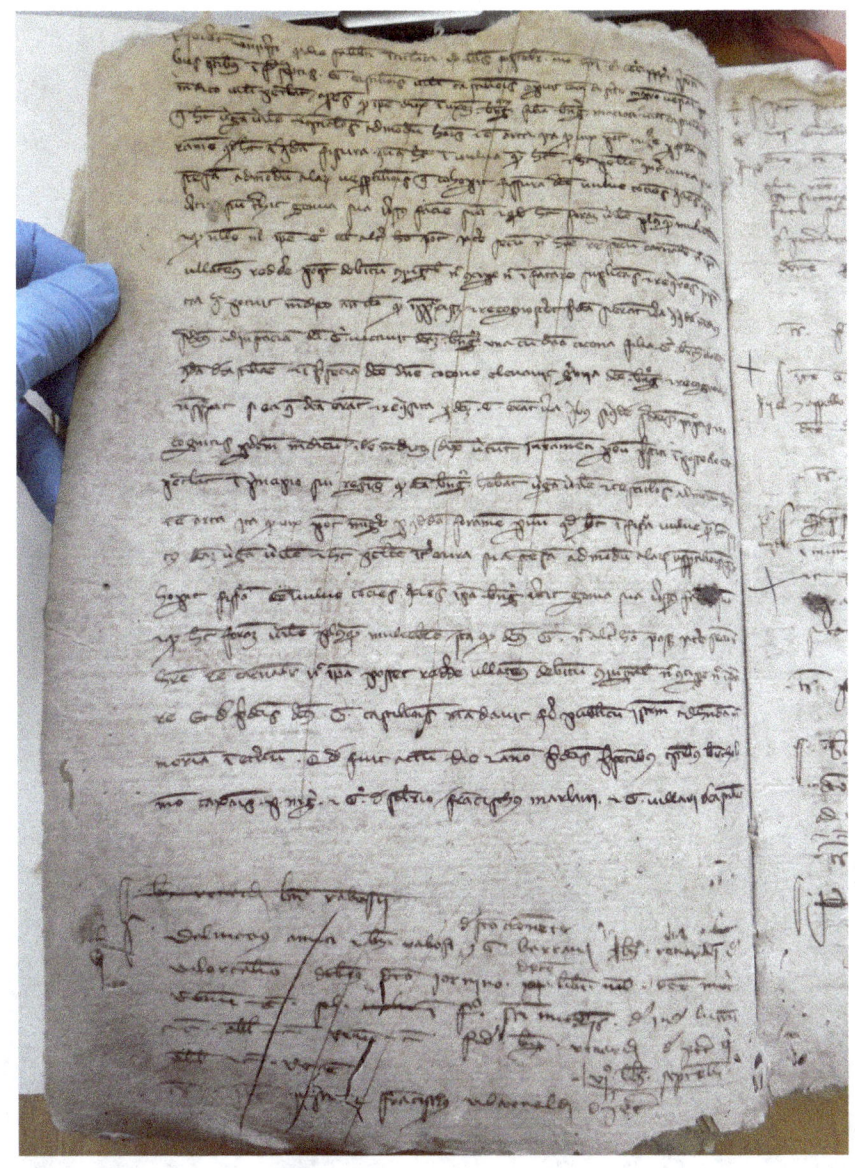

Plate 0.1 Berengaria's story. Arxiu Històric de Girona.

PLATE 1.1 "Hermaphrodite." *Omne bonum.*

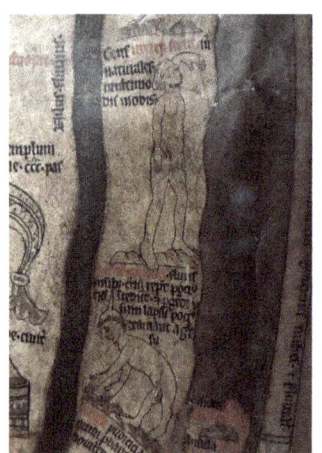

PLATE 2.1 "Monstrous races." *Hereford Mappa Mundi* (detail), Hereford Cathedral.

PLATE 2.2 Nonbinary-sexed figure (left). *Marvels of the East*, University of Oxford, The Bodleian Libraries, MS Bodl. 614, fol. 50v.

PLATE 2.3 "Monstrous races." *Mare historiarum*, BNF.

PLATE 2.4 Nonbinary-sexed Figures. *Livre des merveilles (Mandeville's Travels)*, BNF.

PLATE 2.5 Blemmyes and epiphagi. *Livre des merveilles (Mandeville's Travels)*, BNF.

PLATE 2.6 Wild man and nonbinary-sexed figures. Jean de Mandeville, *Antichrist (Travels of Sir John Mandeville)*, St. Gallen, Stiftsarchiv, Cod. Fab. XVI, f. 66v. Photo: www.e-codices.ch.

PLATE 2.7 Janus and two doors. *Psalterium ad usum ecclesiae Trecensis*, BNF.

PLATE 2.8 "Monstrous races." *Bestiary*, Westminster Abbey Library.

PLATE 3.1 Hyena. *Aberdeen Bestiary*, University of Aberdeen.

Sz cu iudex histrick' pertratis malis iram suā
ad feriendum p̄mouet. tunc omnis ille de
cor laudis uelut fumus euanescat.

In india nascit bestia que manticora dicit.
Triplici dentium ordine coeūte uicib3; alternis. Facie hominis. glaucis oculis. sang-
uineo colore. corpore leonino. cauda uelut scor-
pionis aculeo spiculata. uoce tanq̄ in sibila-

PLATE 3.2   Manticore, *Bestiary*, University of Oxford, The Bodleian Libraries, MS Bodl. 764, fol. 25r.

PLATE 3.3 Jews with burning bush and golden calf (Sermon of the Hyena), Guillaume le Clerc, *Bestiaire*, BNF.

PLATE 3.4 Hyena. *Northumberland Bestiary*. Pen-and-ink drawing tinted with body color and translucent washes on parchment.

Leaf: 21 × 15.7 cm (8 1/4 × 6 3/16 in.), Ms. 100, fol. 12v (England, about 1250 – 1260). Permission of the J. Paul Getty Museum, Los Angeles.

PLATE 3.5 The Harrowing of Hell. *Psalter*. Tempera colors, gold leaf, and ink on parchment. Leaf: 23.5 × 16.5 cm (9 1/4 × 6 1/2 in.), Ms. 14, fol. 110 (Flemish, mid-1200s). Permission of the J. Paul Getty Museum, Los Angeles.

PLATE 3.6 Lucifer with Christ in Majesty. *Livre de la Vigne nostre Seigneur*, University of Oxford, The Bodleian Libraries, MS Douce 134, f. 67v.

PLATE 3.7 Temptation of Christ. *Huntingfield Psalter*, The Morgan Library & Museum, MS M.43, fol. 20v. Photo: The Morgan Library & Museum.

PLATE 3.8 A devil burns Job's house. *Histoire ancienne universelle*. Permission of Collections de la Bibliothèque municipale de Rouen.

Photo: Thierry Ascencio-Parvy.

PLATE 3.9 Allegory of the Redemption. Guillaume le Clerc, *Bestiarie*, BNF.

PLATE 3.10 Demons with *rouelle*. *Der Juden Erbarkeit* (1571), Bayerische Staatsbibliothek München, 4 P.o.germ. 45 m, frontispiece.

PLATE 3.11 Satan with attendants. Pierre Boaistuau, *Histoires prodigieuses*, BNF.

PLATE 4.1 Copulating animals. Albert the Great, *De animalibus*, BNF.

PLATE 4.2 Marginal figures (full page). Albert the Great, *De animalibus*, BNF.

PLATE 4.3 Marginal figure (detail). Albert the Great, *De animalibus*, BNF.

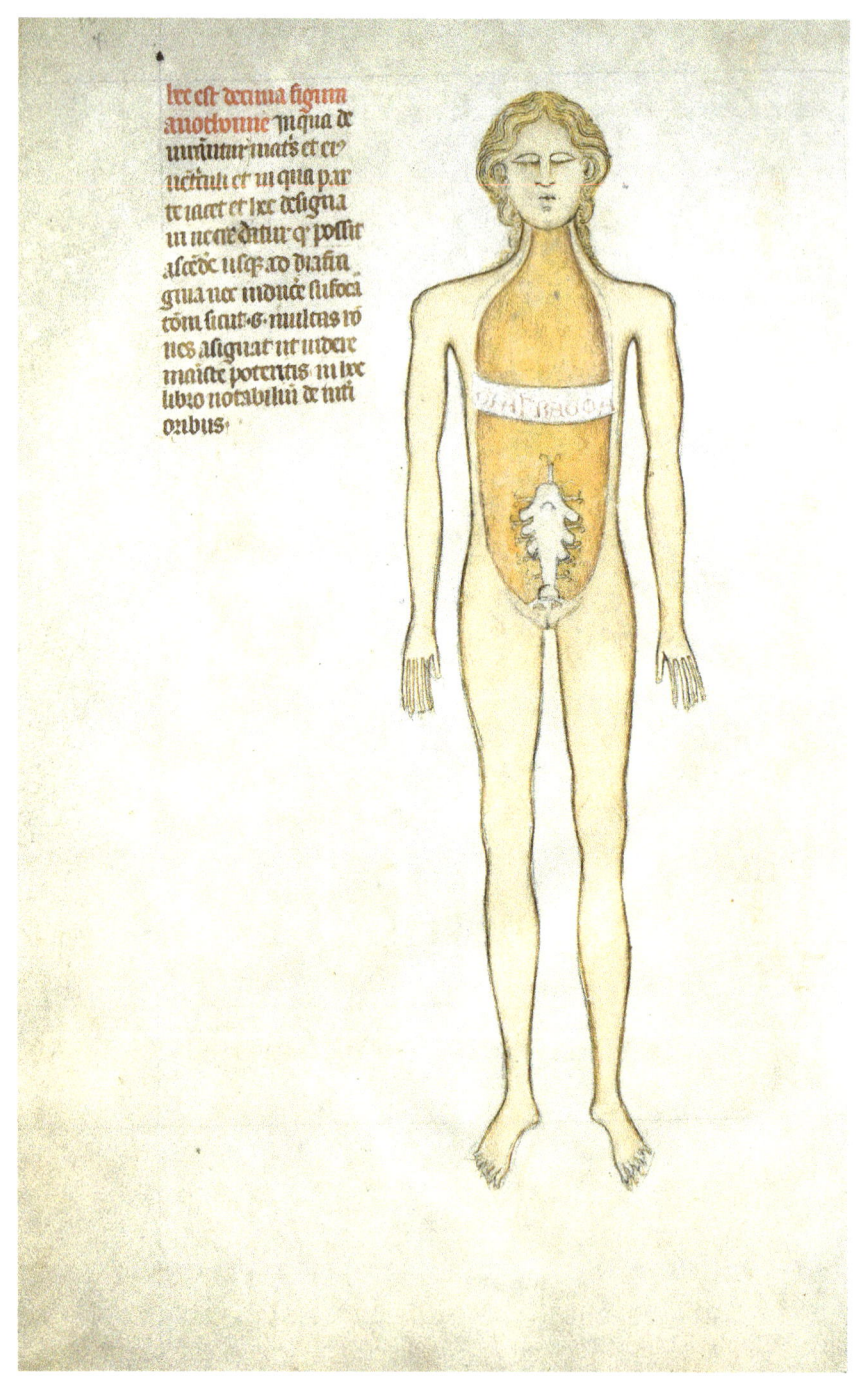

PLATE 4.4 Seven-celled uterus. Guido da Vigevano, *Liber notabilium Philippi (VI) regis Francorum*. Chantilly, Bibliothèque du musée Condé.

MS 003 (0569, f. 267 v) © Cliché CNRS-IRHT

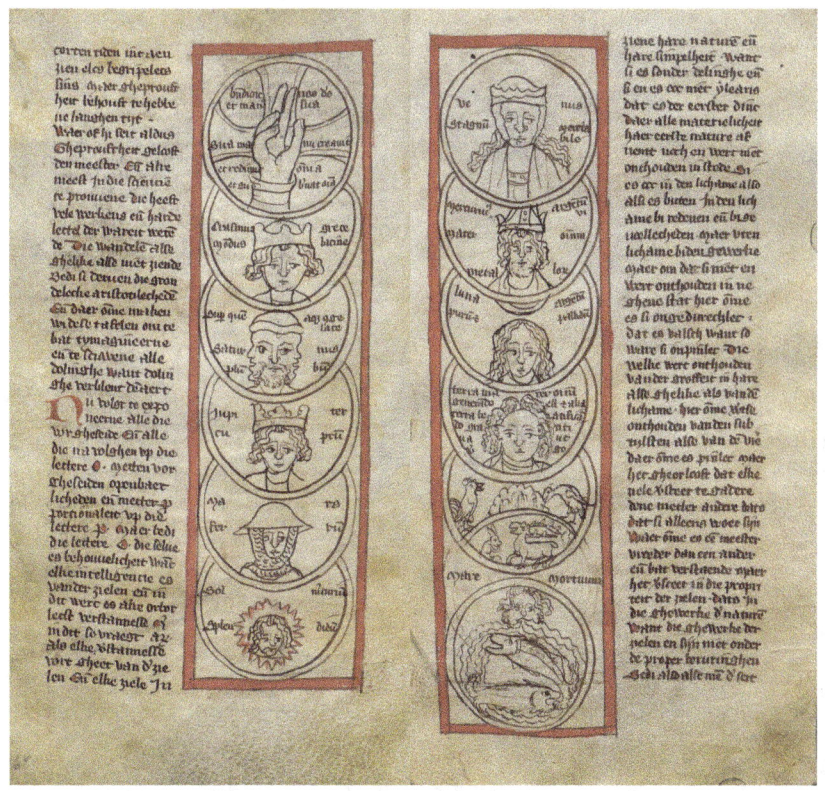

PLATE 6.1 Creation diagram. *The Secrets of My Lady of Alchemy.*

PLATE 6.2 Alchemical "hermaphrodite." *Aurora consurgens*, Zentralbibliothek Zürich, MS Rh 172, fol. 29v.

PLATE 6.3 Alchemical "hermaphrodite." *Aurora consurgens*, Zentralbibliothek Zürich, MS Rh 172, front paste-down.

PLATE 6.4 Hermaphroditus and Salmacis. *Ovide moralisé*, BNF.

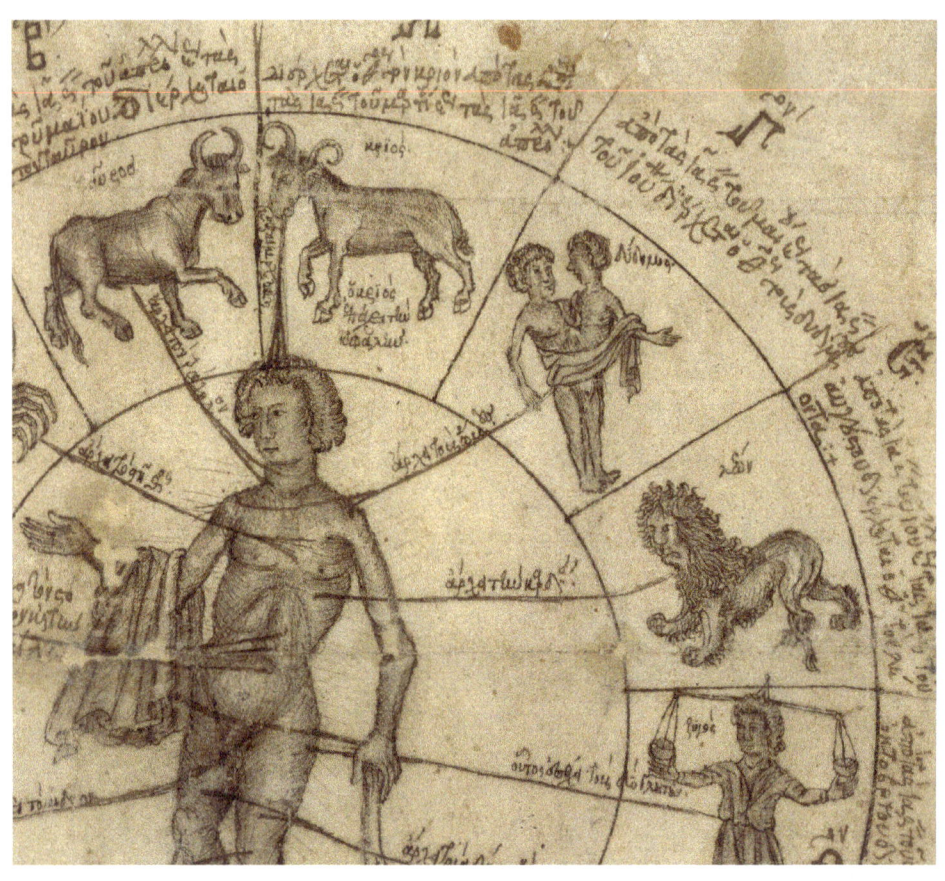

PLATE 6.5 Gemini. *Opuscula astrologica*, BNF.

PLATE 6.6 Gemini. *Liber astrologiae*, BNF.

PLATE 6.7 Adam and Eve as Gemini. *Book of Hours*.

PLATE 6.8 Creation of the world. *Stammheim Missal*. Tempera colors, gold leaf, silver leaf, and ink on parchment bound between wood boards covered with alum tawed pigskin.

Leaf: 28.2 × 18.9 cm (11 1/8 × 7 7/16 in.), Ms. 64 (97.MG.21), fol. 10v (probably 1170s). Permission of the J. Paul Getty Museum, Los Angeles.

PLATE 6.9 Creation of Eve. *Bible historiale*, Master of Jean de Mandeville (French, active 1350–1370). Tempera colors, gold, and ink on parchment.

Leaf: 34.9 × 26 cm (13 3/4 × 10 1/4 in.), Ms. 1, vi, fol. 8v (about 1360–1370). Permission of the J. Paul Getty Museum, Los Angeles.

PLATE 6.10 Scenes from the creation. *Histoire ancienne jusqu'à César*, First Master of the Bible historiale of Jean de Berry (French, active about 1390–about 1400).

Tempera colors, colored washes, gold leaf, and ink on parchment Leaf: 37.7 × 29.8 cm (14 13/16 × 11 3/4 in.), Ms. Ludwig XIII 3, leaf 1 (83.MP.146.1.recto) (about 1390–1400). Permission of the J. Paul Getty Museum, Los Angeles.

PLATE 6.11 Creation of Eve. Saint Ambrose, *Hexaemeron*.

PLATE 6.12 Hermaphroditus and Salmacis. Christine de Pizan, *Epistre Othea*, BNF.

PLATE 6.13 Alchemical "hermaphrodite." *Buch der heiligen Dreifaltigkeit*, Hs 80061, fol. 100r. © Germanisches Nationalmuseum.

PLATE 6.14 Crucifixion of Christ and creation of Eve. *Bible moralisée*, University of Oxford, The Bodleian Libraries, MS Bodl. 270b, fol. 6r.

PLATE 6.15 Androgynous wisdom. Henry of Suso, *Vie du bienheureux Henri Suso*.

FIGURE 6.5 Gemini. *Opuscula astrologica*. Paris, Bibliothèque nationale de France, MS grec 2419, fol. 1 (fifteenth century).

and fig. 2.3).[48] In many astrological images, however, Gemini twins were separate figures, often embracing each other or clasping a shield. Yet it is possible that the illustrator of *Aurora consurgens* was influenced by medical literature or pictorial traditions that associated nonbinary sex with twins. At least some medieval illustrations also portrayed the Gemini twins as Adam and Eve (see fig. 6.7).[49]

The biblical creation story was the focus of a rich visual tradition that used similar Y-shaped iconography to depict the creation of Eve. As I explained in chapter 1, the story of Genesis inspired certain commentaries and illustrations that imagined Adam as an "androgyne" or a "hermaphrodite." And, in a common iconographical strategy, visual images throughout the period imagined the first humans at the moment of creation to be morphologically conjoined. Some visual images went so far as to visualize Adam and Eve in a single bi-sexed form.

As early as the ninth century, certain illustrations of creation rendered Adam and Eve in ways that seemed to emphasize the sexual unity of the first humans.

FIGURE 6.6 Gemini. *Liber astrologiae*. Paris, Bibliothèque nationale de France, MS latin 7330, fol. 11r (thirteenth century).

As I already suggested in chapter 1, a group of ninth-century Carolingian Bibles produced in Tours showed Adam and Eve without apparent differentiation in their sexual anatomy. Similarly, the eleventh-century bronze doors in the German cathedral of Hildesheim also emphasized the symmetry of Adam and Eve and their lack of physical distinction. Other images also assumed this artistic convention, and we find another example in a *Bible moralisée* of the thirteenth century.[50] Also, beginning around the tenth or eleventh century, a common artistic trope within Europe began to picture Eve at the moment of creation, just as she

FIGURE 6.7 Adam and Eve as Gemini. *Book of Hours*. Aix-en-Provence, Bibliothèque Paul-Arbaud, MS 13, fol. 5v (c. 1480–1490).

emerged from an incision in Adam's side. The art historian Johannes Zahlten has surveyed roughly 275 extant images of this type of "Creation of Eve" image, and the exemplars are quite uniform in content.[51] Such images capture Adam and Eve at the crucial moment in which they are not yet completely separated: they are joined in a "Y" formation, split at the waist into two torsos, two heads, and four arms, with Eve's lower limbs still contained within Adam's body.[52] Jack Greenstein suggests that this iconography was inspired not only by the wording of Genesis 1:27 but also by Jesus's remarks in Matthew 19:4–6: "Have ye not read, that he who made man from the beginning made them male and female? And he said: For this cause shall a man leave father and mother, and shall cleave to his wife, and they two shall be in one flesh. Therefore now they are not two, but one flesh."[53] Such iconography made reference to the sacrament of marriage while visualizing Adam's body as a container of female flesh: in these images, God removes from Adam not just a rib but a woman (figs. 6.8, 6.9, 6.10).[54] We can find many different examples of iconography that illustrate this principle over several centuries.

But some versions of the "Creation of Eve" drew the bodies of Adam and Eve even more closely together. A twelfth-century German copy of Ambrose's *Hexaemeron* depicts Adam and Eve as two halves of a single form with both male

180   THE JESUS HERMAPHRODITE

FIGURE 6.8 Creation of the world. *Stammheim Missal*. Tempera colors, gold leaf, silver leaf, and ink on parchment bound between wood boards covered with alum tawed pigskin.

Leaf: 28.2 × 18.9 cm (11 1/8 × 7 7/16 in.), (probably 1170s). Los Angeles, The J. Paul Getty Museum, MS 64 (97.MG.21), fol. 10v.

and female features (see fig. 6.11): Adam and Eve are oriented in the same "Y" formation, but rather than showing Eve emerging from an aperture in Adam's body, Eve and Adam are joined together in a seamless male-female body.[55] Like other exemplars of the "Creation of Eve," Adam and Eve are separated from the waist up, with two heads and two pairs of arms. Eve has prominent breasts while Adam sports a flat chest, but they share only one abdomen and one pair of legs. Their

FIGURE 6.9 Creation of Eve. *Bible historiale*, Master of Jean de Mandeville (French, active 1350–70). Tempera colors, gold, and ink on parchment.

Leaf: 34.9 × 26 cm (13 3/4 × 10 1/4 in.), (about 1360–70). Los Angeles, The J. Paul Getty Museum, MS 1, vi, fol. 8v.

groin is smooth and devoid of sexual markers, their belly swollen and round, as if pregnant—perhaps an allusion to the pair's procreative qualities. Theological writings could speak lyrically of Adam's fecundity: in his *Confessions*, Augustine attributed to "Adam" a womb, which poured forth that "salt sea-water the human race." Scholars have suggested that Augustine intended with that phrase to describe the unity of Adam and Eve, as this image conveys.[56] The illustration bears a strong resemblance to contemporary monstrous-race images in which mythic hermaphrodites appeared with bicephalic or conjoined anatomies.[57] Notably, the composition of the figures is also nearly identical to the fused figure in the manuscript illustration of the *Ovide moralisé*. The interrelation of the two figures of Adam and Eve—separate yet coherent—makes vivid the unity of female and male into one flesh at the moment of creation, and it confounds any

FIGURE 6.10 Scenes from the creation. *Histoire ancienne jusqu'à César*. First Master of the *Bible historiale* of Jean de Berry (French, active about 1390–about 1400). Tempera colors, colored washes, gold leaf, and ink on parchment.

Leaf: 37.7 × 29.8 cm (14 13/16 × 11 3/4 in.), (about 1390–1400). Los Angeles, The J. Paul Getty Museum MS Ludwig XIII 3, leaf 1 (83.MP.146.1.recto).

FIGURE 6.11 Creation of Eve. Saint Ambrose, *Hexaemeron*. Amiens, Bibl. mun., MS Lescalopier 030, fol. 10v (twelfth century).

easy binary division of sex. The similarities between visual depictions of Ovidian, monstrous-race mythic hermaphrodites and Adam and Eve may indicate that viewers read the nonbinary undercurrents of the creation story into such images.

Another important set of images of the alchemical hermaphrodite also appeared during this same period, and they also help us to better understand *Aurora consurgens*. Christine de Pizan's *Epistre Othéa*, or the *Letter of Othea to Hector*, written around 1400 and dedicated to Louis of Orléans, includes a lengthy gloss on Ovid's hermaphrodite story, a scene that was illustrated in several manuscript copies.[58] Certain illustrations picture Hermaphroditus and Salmacis as submerged in the nymph's fountain. Hermaphroditus extends his left arm to touch Salmacis's shoulder with affection, and Salmacis mirrors his gesture with her right arm. Marilynn Desmond and Pamela Sheingorn interpret one version of this illustration as symbolizing equality and mutuality, inasmuch as the bodies are symmetrical, with neither figure dominating the embrace (see fig. 6.12).[59] In their view, the image in this context is a code for a "union of souls," and it exemplifies romantic love between a man and woman.

In the accompanying text, Christine de Pizan emphasizes the compassion hidden within the Ovidian story: "Do not be hard in granting that which you can use well. See yourself in Hermaphroditus, who was harmed for refusing.... The good spirit must not be hard in giving consent where it sees the necessity but rather to comfort the needy to its ability."[60] In Christine's hands, Ovid's tale of Hermaphroditus and Salmacis reveals not feminine aggression but an inspiration for empathy. Christine also alludes to the idea of the hermaphrodite in alchemical literature, writing that "subtle learned philosophers have hidden their great secrets under the cover of fable, and so it can be understood [as] a statement pertaining to the science of astronomy and also of alchemy."[61] With this, Christine remakes the hermaphrodite myth into a paragon of virtue and romantic surrender, and she explicitly connects the Ovidian story to alchemy. It is possible that Christine was hearkening back to early conceptions of nonbinary sex as a symbol of the complete union of two lovers. Certain Christian theorists had interpreted the Christian creation story, with its undercurrent of sexual undifferentiation, as a tale of marital unity. In pagan myth, moreover, Hermaphroditus was born from Hermes and Aphrodite, who were viewed as marriage deities in certain contexts.[62] Christine's positive reading of Ovid's myth leads, perhaps surprisingly, to a vision of male-female union with a high degree of mutuality and non-dominance, a theme that we also see expressed in the Edenic nonbinary-sexed figures of the *Livre des merveilles* manuscript (see fig. 2.4). But, despite Christine's emphasis on unity, the illustrations that accompany her *Letter of Othea* show Hermaphroditus and Salmacis as physically separate individuals, not the bicorporeal bodies

FIGURE 6.12 Hermaphroditus and Salmacis. Christine de Pizan, *Epistre Othea*. Paris, Bibliothèque nationale de France, MS français 606, fol. 38v (1406–1408).

that appear in *Livre des merveilles*, in the fifteenth-century *Ovide moralisé*, or in *Aurora consurgens*.

In that last image—the alchemical hermaphrodite of *Aurora consurgens*—we see an amalgam of male-female bodies that transcends any simple sexual binary. The image is original—and yet it has much in common with other medieval visual interpretations of zodiacal twins, biblical creation, and Ovidian metamorphosis. It seems likely that the alchemical hermaphrodite distilled ideas from natural philosophical, poetic, and hexaemeral traditions to conceive of a new creation.

Taken together, these sources deliver an important message, one that diverges markedly from earlier texts that emphasized the dangers of nonbinary sex and its potential to unsettle gender roles. Here, such unsettling offers profound rewards.

THE JESUS HERMAPHRODITE

The images of the alchemical hermaphrodite in the Zurich manuscript of *Aurora consurgens* also link the text to a similar program of miniatures attached to an anonymous alchemical text known as *The Book of the Holy Trinity* (*Das Buch der heiligen Dreifaltigkeit*), also from the early fifteenth century and from the same southern German area of production.[63] Although we cannot identify the author, we know that he visited the Council of Constance in order to promote his work before the Emperor Sigismund, and that he attracted the interest of other nobles, including the emperor's brother, Wenceslas of Prague, and the margrave Friedrich of Brandenberg, who subsequently became his patron. Perhaps due to the enthusiasm of aristocrats for the alchemical manufacture of gold, the book enjoyed enough success to survive in at least twenty manuscripts, many of which are vividly illustrated. Its illuminations resemble those of *Aurora consurgens* inasmuch as they also depict the alchemical stone as a biform, nonbinary-sexed human. They also further explore medieval understandings of Christ as male and female to develop a new pair of images: the Jesus-Mary hermaphrodite and the Antichrist hermaphrodite.

Central to *The Book of the Holy Trinity* is the author's claim that Christ contains within him his mother, the Virgin Mary, who comprises his feminine principle, as well as the principle of his humanity.[64] The author states that "one can never see the mother of God without also seeing that God eternally hides and intermingles [his mother] within him. God was and is eternally his own mother and his own father, human and divine, his divinity and his humanity intermingled within. And he depends on that which he wishes to be hidden most of all within himself, the divine and the human, the feminine and the masculine."[65] Next, the author emphasizes the inseparable nature of Christ and Mary:

> The humanity of bright Mary was the interior and exterior humanity of God Jesus Christ all made together; he had not and has no other humanity. The two are thus eternal without end.... And they have been eternally one, the Divinity Jesus Christ, which cannot and could not be separated eternally from his exterior humanity, thus Jesus-Mary is and was one being in the same substance.[66]

According to this view, Christ is the ultimate nonbinary figure, a unity of contrary parts—the human and the divine, the male and the female—much as Petrus Bonus described the philosophers' stone as multiple pairs of incongruous qualities. The book's author also explicitly equates the male-female Christ with the male-female stone, writing, "[There] rose Christ, Jesus-Mary, the red stone, the carbuncle, throughout all the same thing. They could not be separated, and they will never be separated. And in the same way, Jesus and Mary are one blood, one moon, one sun."[67]

The author relies here upon the traditional understanding of the philosophers' stone as male and female, sulfur and mercury, and, invoking the astronomical imagery of the *Tabula smaragdina*, sun and moon. The red stone that transmutes metals into gold is also synonymous with the fusion of Jesus and Mary, whose union epitomizes the yoking of contraries that characterized an alchemical hermaphrodite in other texts. The author of *The Book of the Holy Trinity* borrowed and conflated earlier images of the philosophers' stone as Christ with understandings of the stone as "hermaphroditic," arriving at a vision of a nonbinary-sexed Christ-stone. As in Petrus Bonus's text, the narrative of the stone's life and Christ's life become one. They are both nature and supernature, male and female, human and divine—the poles of the spectrum tethered together. The alchemical hermaphrodite is thus an eminently desirable union of opposites that transcends the normal operations of nature, a disruption akin to metal transmutation, the ultimate goal of the alchemist's work.

The idea of nonbinary sex is also for the author such a significant trope that it characterizes not only Christ but also Antichrist. The anonymous writer was very likely a descendent of the "Spiritual Franciscans," a radical sect of Franciscan friars who advocated absolute poverty and expected the imminent appearance of Antichrist and the apocalyptic climax of history.[68] As a result, the author's interests extended not only to Christ but also to Antichrist. Because Antichrist was in all senses a perversion of Christ, he had to share in and subvert all of Christ's attributes, including his male-female nature. As Jesus contained the Virgin Mary and the female sex within him, so Antichrist also would contain his own mother.[69] A dramatic pair of illuminations represents these paired entities—the good Jesus-Mary hermaphrodite and the evil Antichrist hermaphrodite—a melding of male and female bodies in the costumes of kings and queens. In the image of the Antichrist hermaphrodite, a serpentine monster extends two snakelike appendages to wrap around the legs of the figure (see fig. 6.13). One appendage ends in a male head, the other in a female head; they press their faces together near Antichrist's groin, suggesting the figure's nonbinary genitalia.

FIGURE 6.13 Alchemical "hermaphrodite." *Buch der heiligen Dreifaltigkeit (The Book of the Holy Trinity)*. Nuremberg, Germanisches National Museum, MS 80061, fol. 100r (early fifteenth century). © Germanisches Nationalmuseum.

SCHOLASTIC THEOLOGICAL APPROACHES

The "Jesus hermaphrodite" must also be read in the light of wider conversations about Jesus as feminine or dual-sexed in contemporary religious literature. Considerations of nonbinary sex surfaced not only in commentaries on the creation of Adam and Eve, as we have already seen, but also in those on the incarnation of Christ—the central miracle upon which the Christian religion rested. As I argue here, these ideas also combined with traditions that viewed Nature as masculine and feminine, active and passive, to suggest a novel character: an alchemical creator who was both male and female.

In about 1150, the theologian Peter Lombard mused in his *Four Books of Sentences*—arguably the most influential theology textbook of the Middle Ages—whether it would have been possible for Christ to have been born a woman instead of a man. While Lombard gives a fairly brief answer (a female incarnation would have been possible, but it would have been less appropriate than a male incarnation), his work inspired a host of other commentators who were anxious to build on his opinion in new ways. Following the dissemination of Lombard's text, more than a dozen theologians over a century considered whether Christ could have or should have assumed female form.[70] These medieval commentaries ultimately rejected the idea of a female savior, but their considerations raised thorny questions about how male/female and human/divine natures could coexist in one being. They even raised the possibility that Christ was nonbinary sexed.

It is important to note that the creation of Adam and the incarnation of Christ were thought to mirror each other. Just as one woman, Eve, was thought to instigate the fall of humanity, another woman, Mary, was thought to facilitate its redemption. This parallelism was so well known that Jesus was often depicted in literature and iconography as a "second Adam." A French Genesis cycle from c. 1240, for instance, juxtaposes two similar images: a "Creation of Eve" illustration and a "Crucifixion of Christ." The two illuminations portray Christ as a new Adam who gives birth to a female-incarnated Church through an aperture in his side, just as Adam gave birth to Eve (see fig. 6.14).[71] The recognizable "Y" formation—Christ and Church joined at the waist, with the female Church contained within Christ's male body—made absolutely clear the parallels between the two episodes. In light of this symmetry between creation and incarnation, it is perhaps unsurprising that we find a robust tradition of asking questions about the sex not only of Adam but also of Christ. Such inquiries also emerged logically from debates about the relative strengths of men and women within the Christian religion. The existence of a female savior, in fact, might have suggested certain advantages: a woman's purported weakness was all the better to shame the powerful; a female-sexed Christ was also arguably a more sensible counterweight for Eve and her transgression. Moreover, a feminine God capitalized on the nurturing and generative functions associated with maternity.[72]

Albert the Great, always one to weigh in on novel ideas, devoted some effort to exploring whether Christ should have assumed female rather than male form.[73]

FIGURE 6.14 Crucifixion of Christ and creation of Eve. *Bible moralisée*. Oxford, University of Oxford, Bodleian Library, MS Bodley 270b, fol. 6r (c. 1240). Permission of the Bodleian Libraries.

Albert's contributions to the debate lay for the most part outside of our interests, but he offers one point worth noting. Writing in about 1249, Albert argued that if Christ had been female, he would have been both a daughter (temporally) and a son (eternally).[74] Christ's nature, Albert noted, was not divided in such a way that his sex could belong solely to his human or divine aspect. As a result, if Christ had been born a woman, his humanity would have been both male and female at the same time. Following this logic, a female Christ would have been simultaneously both sexes—a possibility that Albert was quick to dismiss.

In a similar vein, a contemporary of Albert's, the philosopher and theologian Roland of Cremona, asked in his commentary on Peter Lombard's *Sentences* whether a female Christ would have been the same person as Jesus. Could a woman who was also the Son of God be both a woman and a man? Roland argues that in circumstances beyond ordinary nature, it is possible for a woman to be a man:

> Certainly I concede that a woman in so far as she is woman is not a man in so far as he is man; that is, femininity is not masculinity. But it does not follow.... therefore that a woman is not a man. This is a fallacy *secundum quid* and *simpliciter*. I say confidently that, given this situation, this man is this woman, and this woman is this man.... Nor is this a valid argument: "femaleness is not maleness, therefore a woman is not a man" just as it is not valid to say "whiteness is not musical, therefore a white thing is not a musician." In creatures it follows validly; "it is a woman therefore not a man" and vice versa. This however is not the case here, which is beyond nature. Therefore, he speaks falsely when he says "It is impossible that a woman is a man."[75]

If we venture through the thicket of this nearly incoherent argument, we find that in certain circumstances beyond the quotidian rules of nature—for instance, in the event of a divine incarnation—it is possible for the human-God that is Christ to be both female and male. That is not to say that Roland believed Christ to be morphologically intersex; in fact, like Albert, subsequent theologians were cautious to reject this conclusion. Bonaventure of Bagnoregio (c.1217–74), for instance, wrote that although it would seem logical for Christ to exhibit both sexes because he came to redeem both men and women, a Christ whose body was both male and female would have been an abomination.[76] Thomas Aquinas, writing in the 1250s, also added that when Christ took on human flesh, he could not adopt a "neuter" sex (which would have left him indistinct and improperly formed) nor "both sexes" (which would have been "monstrous and unnatural"). For Thomas, the only appropriate choice was a single, distinct male or female sex, in keeping with the natural and divinely ordained condition of humanity.[77]

In a later attempt to sort out the ramifications of Christ's sex, Gabriel Biel (d. 1495) adopted in his commentary a position that associated human flesh with femininity. Christ's incarnation in male form, he argued, dignified both men and women because Christ "assumed human nature in the male sex and took it [human nature] from the virgin mother."[78] If Christ had been female, he would have elevated women above men by dignifying them twice—first, through his female form and, second, through the femininity of human nature. According to Biel's argument, even in his male form Christ embodied both sexes because his human nature was inherently feminine. This position identified the fleshy, material aspects of existence—and hence humanity—with the female sex.[79] We have already seen a similar logic at work in Augustine's identification of woman with certain temporal and earthly aspects of humanity. (Medieval writers and modern scholars alike have made much of an equation of flesh with femininity.)[80] Here, Biel imagined Jesus as a fusion of the male divine principle joined to the female human nature, which was furnished by Jesus's mother. We might conclude that because Christ was believed to be both human and divine he was also, in some sense, seen as both male and female. Medieval theologians were careful to note that Christ was not what we would call intersex in any literal, anatomical sense, but such discussions indicate that nonbinary sex was an important means for thinking through extraordinary examples of generation such as the creation and incarnation.

THE FEMINIZED CHRIST IN AFFECTIVE DEVOTION AND HAGIOGRAPHY

The growing significance of affective piety in the late Middle Ages, which embraced the trope of the feminized Christ, also provides an important context for the so-called Jesus hermaphrodite. Early Christian depictions of Jesus from the fourth through the sixth century sometimes envisioned Jesus as a feminine male or an androgynous figure, with a smooth, beardless face, long hair, and even breasts. Several late antique images of Jesus are so androgynous that until recently art historians assumed them to portray women. Thomas Mathews suggests that the rich tradition of these images in later centuries, too, indicates that Christians were not uncomfortable with a feminized savior.[81] Descriptions of God or Jesus as feminine found new popularity in the twelfth through fourteenth centuries, particularly in the writings of Cistercian monks such as Bernard of Clairvaux, William of St. Thierry, and Aelred of Rievaulx, who spoke of Christ in feminine, sometimes maternal, language—even attributing to him breasts or a womb.[82] An image of an androgynous Christ-*Sapientia* (the female personification of Wisdom) appears in an illuminated manuscript of the mystic Henry Suso's *Exemplar* (c. 1371), making visible the ways in which Suso embraced the feminine aspects of divinity in several of his written works (see fig. 6.15).[83] Christ appeared in female guise in other medieval spiritual texts, too, including as a seamstress, washerwoman, and maid. Christ's body was often depicted as bleeding, nourishing, and giving birth, behaviors that medieval people associated with femininity. Hugh of St. Cher (c. 1200–63) noted that churchmen emulated this Christlike, male-female quality, explaining that just as the hare is at once male and female, so the good prelate is both father and mother to those in his care.[84]

FIGURE 6.15 Androgynous wisdom. Henry of Suso, *Vie du bienheureux Henri Suso*. Strasbourg, Bibliothèque nationale et universitaire, MS 2.929, fol. IV (c. 1371).

Such imagery, while particularly attractive to male authors, also appeared in the writings of certain female visionaries. The thirteenth-century Dutch visionary Hadewijch of Brabant described an apocalyptic Christ who was simultaneously a female deity. A century later, the English anchorite Julian of Norwich wrote her *Showings* in language that also emphasized the feminine characteristics of God.[85] Some of these writers identified the material, and hence human, component of Christ as feminine: the visionary Elizabeth of Schönau, for instance, referred to Christ's humanity as a female virgin in her *Visiones*.[86] She, like other female mystics, posited herself as an androgynous embodiment of Christ—a "woman-Christ," as Barbara Newman has memorably called these saintly women.[87] By imagining their own female flesh as symbolizing the humanity of Christ, some medieval religious women, as scholars have rightly observed, "carried the concept *human* beyond any male/female dichotomy."[88]

These examples point to a long tradition of assigning female gender traits to Christ. Such texts, however, do not portray God as physically nonbinary sexed, nor do they cite Jesus-Mary as an inseparable being in the way that *The Book of the Holy Trinity* does. But the *Ovidius moralizatus* of Pierre Bersuire (first half of the fourteenth century) makes clear the connection between the tale of the Ovidian hermaphrodite and Christ, writing that "for that son of Mercury [Hermaphroditus] is the son of God, bridegroom above all ... he descended to the fountain of mercy, that is the blessed Virgin, where at once that nymph, that is, human nature, joined itself to him, and thus he adhered to himself through the blessed incarnation, since from two natures one being resulted."[89] In this text, a nonbinary union of male and female principles draws explicitly from the narratives of both Christian mysticism and Ovidian poetry. The human and divine natures within Christ create a male-female conjunction facilitated by the impregnated body of the Virgin Mary. Although this understanding of Christ is not identical to that of the *Book of the Holy Trinity*, it is clear that by the fourteenth century a number of circulating texts identified Jesus as a feminine or nonbinary figure while noting the role of the Virgin in furnishing his humanity.

But Jesus was not the only dual-sexed creator upon whom alchemists could call for inspiration. Nature, another quintessential creator according to the medieval Christian worldview, was also depicted pictorially as male, female, or both sexes at once. From Macrobius's fifth-century commentary on the *Dream of Scipio* to Alan of Lille's twelfth-century *Plaint of Nature*, Natura could be imagined as a feminine goddess who also wielded stereotypically masculine tools.[90] In *Plaint of Nature*, Alan of Lille describes Nature as a scholar who adopts the language and the authority of a clerical male. Nature is both mother and virgin, yet Alan shows the goddess creating humans by means of a hammer and stylus, tools he uses principally to designate male sexual activity. Nature is thus for Alan in possession of both a womb and a phallus.[91] An illustration of Nature from a manuscript copy of *Plaint of Nature* shows Nature at a podium dressed in clerical garb, perhaps lecturing or preaching; a related image from Alan's *Anticlaudianus* shows Nature fashioning a man with an axe, a decidedly masculine tool of creation.[92] Because alchemy was often described as an imitation of nature, it is possible that alchemical authors and illustrators also drew from textual and visual portraits of

Nature as simultaneously male and female, prompting them to imagine alchemy as a similarly compound-sexed agent of creation.

For alchemists pondering the philosophers' stone, the metaphor of nonbinary sex was an attractive solution. Ovid's stories of metamorphoses mirrored the alchemists' goal in metal transmutation: the change of one thing into another. The hybrid nature associated with nonbinary sex also provided a useful model for the hybrid philosophers' stone. It satisfied the need to solve the linguistic puzzle of the "rebis," or "two thing," and it fit readily within the conventional vocabulary of sexual reproduction in scholastic natural philosophy and medicine. Moreover, traditional stories of creation, whether by God or by Nature, played upon the supposedly masculine and feminine aspects of the creator. Alchemical authors and illustrators were possibly aware of the tradition of the primal androgyne, and with it, the conceit that Adam was made in the image of a masculo-feminine deity. The widely held notion that Christ was a second Adam might have implied that he, too, transcended binary sex. If the original, untainted perfection of creation went beyond divisions of earthly sex, then a masculo-feminine Christ might have been an attractive—and even necessary—solution.

The goal of alchemical writing was to explain and defend the processes of metal generation, particularly the generation of gold and silver. How better to explain generation than by means of a generator that was both male and female, active and passive? The rationale behind the philosophers' stone was even more persuasive when one imagined the substance as simultaneously both mother and father. When alchemists portrayed their art as creative, they did so by using the models of creation at their disposal: the medical language of sexual generation, the biblical language of genesis, and the literary language of metamorphosis.

NONBINARY SEX AND METAMORPHOSIS

The history of the alchemical hermaphrodite provides us with an opportunity to think about the fluidity of boundaries between metals, as well as between other sorts of bodies. Alchemy was perhaps in a unique position to capitalize upon the hybridity of nonbinary sex that we have seen proposed in so many other genres of art and literature. The mixture of sulfur and mercury in alchemy reportedly produced a hybrid of male and female components; this product was also a new and paradoxical third substance. Alchemy held that real and unexpected change was possible, both in the creation of the philosophers' stone from its contrary parts, and in its transmutation of metals. The analogy of nonbinary sex thus tapped into the fertility of Ovid's story of metamorphosis, invoking the playfulness and instability of its reality. Yet Ovid's hermaphrodite, like the philosophers' stone, was not a complete transformation; the result was a third thing that held aspects of the previous two in tension. Beyond that, the result was a mixture, an intermingling of unlike parts that heralded, in this case—not pollution—but possibility. An alchemical hermaphrodite was thus a dramatic, and sometimes unsettling, union of opposites—male and female, natural and artificial, heavenly and earthly. Alchemy's advocates followed this argument to its logical conclusion: Christ—the ultimate union of contraries—must also be in some sense both male and female.

Authors and illustrators appeared to have solved the problem of the "two thing" by relying on earlier models of nonbinary sex in medical, theological, and mythological sources. But how closely did the alchemical hermaphrodite really correspond to the models that inspired it? The philosophers' stone was not really an intermediate point on a continuum of sexual difference, as the Galenic medical model held, nor could it be the result of excessive generative matter, as the Aristotelian philosophical model argued (and no matter what illustrations from *Aurora consurgens* and *The Book of the Holy Trinity* might have suggested). Similarly, the alchemical hermaphrodite did not follow the narrative of Ovid's tale precisely. The substance was not "enfeebled" by its change, as Hermaphroditus lamented in the *Metamorphoses*, and alchemical authors tended to emphasize the *bothness* of male-female rather than the perhaps to them more disturbing idea of *neitherness*.[93] The alchemical hermaphrodite, much like mythic monstrous-race hermaphrodites, forced opposites together, highlighting their differences. This process is evident in the imagery of *The Book of the Holy Trinity*, which knits together male-female bodies into the Jesus-Mary hermaphrodite. Although Jesus-Mary comprises one substance that cannot be separated, the two constituent characters retain their discrete identities and qualities. This achievement of paradox was outside the ordinary course of nature. It was believed to be the agent of wondrous transformative possibilities, such as the salvation of humankind and, on a lesser scale, metal transmutation.

The alchemical hermaphrodite stands in stark contrast to the ambiguous position of the nonbinary-sexed figures that appear in much other medieval literature. Unlike the mythic monstrous races, or the hyena of the Aberdeen Bestiary, the Jesus-Mary hermaphrodite of *The Book of the Holy Trinity* is presented as an ideal. The nonbinary philosophers' stone and the nonbinary Jesus purportedly transmuted metals and redeemed humans by means of their special and paradoxical natures. So why was nonbinary sex celebrated in alchemy but not in society?

The idea of nonbinary sex in alchemy was of course a purely intellectual conceit. There was no fear that alchemical hermaphrodites might commit sodomitic acts or create confusion about their gendered statuses in medical or juridical contexts. Nevertheless, there was something transgressive about them. The fluidity of sexes in the alchemical hermaphrodite hinted at the fluidity of boundaries between metals, which alchemy argued could be changed through the art of the alchemist. Whether the boundaries in question divided the sexes or the categories of humanity and divinity, the idea of nonbinary sex in alchemical literature indicated that such boundaries were crossable. Furthermore, the crossing of boundaries in alchemy was linked not to confusion but to the creation of something miraculous. The alchemical hermaphrodite was a means to understand the God-man that was Jesus, the agent of human salvation and a singularly important figure in European and Christian history.

The alchemical hermaphrodite may at first appear an obscure figure, part of a literary genre known, if nothing else, for its esotericism, and an odd way to close our study. Yet the alchemical hermaphrodite interrogated the stability of some of the most inviolable categories of the premodern world, and it offered a discourse of fluidity and transcendence often overlooked by scholars. By considering the specific images, tropes, and metaphors that appear in these late medieval and early Renaissance alchemical texts, we can learn a great deal about authors' (and readers') assumptions about the human body and its place in the narrative of history. Although alchemy was never a university discipline, its proponents and audiences were among the elites most likely to discuss and construct the boundaries of the natural world. Manuals of alchemy and "books of secrets" that included alchemical recipes were popular among literate audiences, and these texts became even more available with the advent of the printing press.[94] Despite prohibitions against the art, alchemical research was long supported by royal and papal courts, and many of its known practitioners were physicians, university masters, and prelates.[95] Alchemical texts therefore provide valuable insights into late medieval and early Renaissance presuppositions about social, natural philosophical, and theological standards, and the ways in which contemporaries imagined their world's ability to confound categorization. Because alchemy existed alongside sanctioned academic disciplines, borrowing from them and informing them, it also offered a view of the natural and social world that had enormous—yet generally unacknowledged—influence. In later centuries, alchemical hermaphrodites would provide an opportunity to explicitly question contemporary gender roles and sexuality, as scholars such as Kathleen P. Long and Ruth Gilbert have argued, a challenge that we also see expressed implicitly in some of the images and texts I have analyzed here.[96]

When scholastic theologians spoke of heaven, they often did so in the language of incorruptibility, immutability, and stasis. Hell, on the other hand, was where change took place: early medieval theologians detailed in horror the corporeal processes and metamorphoses that broke down the stable boundaries of the self in hell.[97] Ideas about nonbinary sex, as I have argued throughout this book, were linked to transition, whether through their associations with gender inversion, or their imagined ability to create new and potentially volatile forms. As medieval authors often claimed, nonbinary figures were appetitive, fluid, and unstable—the opposite of how scholastics imagined heaven, a crystalline state of solids and certainty that arrested both appetite and fluidity.[98] Bodies in heaven would never die, feel pain, or transform in any way. They were satiated, static, and complete. In many respects, they were the antithesis of the mobility and mutability that characterized ideas about nonbinary sex. Even the pure and ethereal androgyny of angels—shared by prelapsarian and post-resurrection bodies according to some theologians—enjoyed an undifferentiated state of agender and asexuality that was at first glance incompatible with the excessive corporeality attributed to other nonbinary figures. Yet, as this book suggests, such ideas were reconcilable. Medieval audiences possessed powerful tools for imagining sex as open to contradiction and difference. The primal androgyne and the Jesus hermaphrodite fused husband and wife, mother and son, creator and created, dismantling and reconstituting kinship outside its ordinary boundaries and proposing heterogeneous systems that confounded simple oppositions.

Alchemical writers depended on contemporary understandings of nonbinary sex and its supposed links to inhumanity, transformation, and fertile potentiality. Nonbinary sex could be a symbol of both hypersexual deviance and asexual chastity. Nonbinary figures could represent both societal decay and a desirable means to transcend this world. Understandings of nonbinary sex as primordial, incorruptible, and outside of time suggested to medieval thinkers that it contained within it a seed of paradise that could be harnessed to perfect both metallic and human bodies. This perfection was the key to not only individual health but also—as *The Book of the Holy Trinity* made clear—the collective fate of the Christian community on the brink of an apocalyptic age.

I have already noted that ideas about nonbinary sex appear in theological writings at the most dramatic and critical thresholds of Christian time—the

Beginning, the Incarnation, and the End. It is worth repeating that the unification of opposites was a prominent aspect of Christian symbolism (a motif shared by a number of ancient religions). From Paul's remark in Galatians 3:28 to the experiences of late medieval visionaries, Christianity placed great value on acts of unification, junction, and completion. As we have seen, a number of Christian texts emphasized that ascension toward God prompted a greater and greater reconciliation of divisions, including sexual divisions.[99] In addition, a prevalent mode of thought in scholastic circles, as well as in other aspects of medieval culture, focused on opposed categories and their resolution.[100] Such spiritual and intellectual approaches may have prompted at least some thinkers to imagine the resolution of what they viewed as contrary sexes as a necessary step in the reconciliation of humanity with God. Finally, Christianity offered a narrative that was inextricably connected to the processes of death, decay, and fertility. Fertility, in particular, was seen as a generative melding of male and female principles, a union of unlike qualities that created something new—but that retained the trace of its contrary and constituent parts.[101]

The alchemical hermaphrodites of *Aurora consurgens* and *The Book of the Holy Trinity* also demonstrate how ideas about nonbinary sex crossed not only sexual but also temporal and eschatological boundaries, uniting biblical, alchemical, and apocalyptic transformations. Authors argued that nonbinary-sexed figures traversed, or even dissolved, the boundary between human and nonhuman, earth and heaven, time and timelessness. For them, nonbinary figures represented a coincidence of opposites and, with it, a manipulation of the continuities of time and space. Nonbinary sex, as a result, was not simply a category of gender or sex but also one of creation and transformation—processes that were both strenuously objected to and enthusiastically embraced by premodern Christians. Transformation was, after all, at the heart of Christian theology, and its most transformative figure, Christ, was believed to be the most perfect of all bodies and the chief reconciler of unlike parts. Nonbinary-sexed figures' alleged capacity for shifting between contraries, and for uniting and transcending them, was thus at the root of both their greatest offense and their greatest appeal. As I have suggested throughout this book, premodern Christians used ideas about nonbinary sex to define themselves and to distinguish their community from outsiders. Strong cultural forces no doubt coerced individuals into very restricted expressions of masculinity and femininity in practice. But this final chapter serves as a reminder that breaking free of those confines was not always undesirable.

The premodern ideas about nonbinary sex that I have described here were soon to undergo their own transformation. Medieval theories of sex, monstrosity, and geography continued to reverberate through the expansionary, colonial projects of the early modern period, ensconced in pseudo-Aristotelian texts, and spread by European colonizers to the Americas, with immeasurably destructive results.[102] Yet, in many ways, developments during the early modern period were to change fundamentally the conversation about nonbinary sex. Plato's *Symposium* became widely available to Western European readers again at the end of the fifteenth century, offering new ways of thinking about androgyny, femininity, and embodiment. The sixteenth century saw increasing interest in "hermaphroditism," leading to an explosion of inquiries into its causes and classificatory meanings. During that period, a Hippocratic revival introduced once more the possibility of a truly intermediate sex, with all its incumbent challenges to the social and sexual order. At that same time, considerations of intersex people in medical and legal sources became intensely hostile, linking them to the supposed deviance of sodomy and pornography in new and now urgent ways. In many respects, the narrative arc that we have followed in this book came to a close at the end of the fifteenth century, giving way to a host of new ideas about gender and nature in the sixteenth and seventeenth centuries, and in manners that both intensified and departed from medieval interpretations.[103]

But in the Middle Ages, ideas about nonbinary sex still upended chronology: they suspended, ruptured, and compressed time. They hearkened back to creation and accelerated forward toward its end. Through this temporal juncture of idyllic past and revelatory future I suggest that we might find our way back to the opening image of my first chapter, the Janus-faced figure of *Omne bonum*, poised on the cusp of before and after—and a symbol of the generative, liminal space in which past and future meet. That Janus-faced image, so similar to the alchemical images we have seen in this last chapter, provides us with a particularly rich emblem of nonbinary sex as it was understood throughout the period. Much as Janus's face united opposite directions, ideas about nonbinary sex embodied opposite meanings. Medieval thinkers shunned nonbinary figures as foreign, unstable, and in some ways less than human, but they also praised those same traits as miraculously and uniquely productive. Ideas about nonbinary sex offered a triumph over the boundaries of life and death. They presented a generative core, one that yielded yet further paradoxes. As medieval thinkers imagined, nonbinary sex was a return to the old, a hastening of the new, an affirmation of the mortal, and a path to the divine. The concept of nonbinary sex had the potential to break apart the linear march of time and unleash something expansive, something at the very source of life: an existence that was both earthly and everlasting.

Conclusion

Tension and Tenses

Our story begins and ends with opposition. At the start, in the third century, we have the "primal androgyne." At the end, more than one thousand years later, we have the "Jesus hermaphrodite." These Janus faces (see figures 1.1 and 6.13) are rich emblems of medieval sexual difference: each image fuses and separates its constituent parts, it arrests and extends time, and it forces contraries into a single and visible form. These images are useful examples of how premodern thinkers viewed encounters between purportedly opposed sexes, ideas, and situations. Yet they are also emblematic of how we might approach history from our own vantage point in the twenty-first century. This book, too, is about junctures of time, space, and history—about the hybrid nature of our own position in a never-finished now. This history, like all histories, is about the present: the point of tension in which past and future meet.

What lessons should we take from this story of nonbinary sex? I hope I have made clear that sexual binarism was neither a natural nor a timeless phenomenon. As I have shown, monsters on maps, hyenas and demons in psalters and bestiaries, and even Christ and the Virgin Mary were all part of a changing narrative of sexual difference, one shaped by a range of specific historical circumstances. Over the course of a thousand years, nonbinary sex was understood in varying ways by varying authors and audiences, with profound consequences for actual living individuals whose bodies or practices were perceived as nonbinary. In the art and literature that I've surveyed here, ideas about nonbinary sex joined multiple vectors of power and identity during the Middle Ages, signifying different things to different people at different times. Moreover, there is no essential truth that underlies all of the nonbinary figures that populate this book. Instead, we find a messy assemblage of living people and abstract ideas that premodern rhetors laid upon life to facilitate their theories of sex, gender, and embodiment.

Intersex people, to be sure, had a relatively small presence in the historical record. But ideas about nonbinary sex played an outsized role in premodern history. For the better part of a millennium, nonbinary sex operated as a delivery system for thoughts extending far beyond those of sex and gender, to questions of geography, nature, race, religion, and the very meaning of life on earth. In their writings, premodern authors used the concept of nonbinary sex to warn against impurity, fluctuation, and adulteration, all of which threatened the contours of the community and the integrity of the self. Authors also used images of mythic and monstrous "hermaphrodites" to exaggerate and eliminate enemies, and to unite ancient traditions and contemporary concerns in authoring a whole new reality. Ideas about nonbinary sex in these contexts worked to secure certain subjects within an interior while relegating others to the exterior, outside the spatial bounds of society, the ritual bounds of faith, and the social bounds of humanity. In this capacity, nonbinary sex participated in a staggering range of historical narratives in different intellectual, political, and social contexts. Even as a marginal subject, nonbinary sex played a pivotal role in the formation of categories and definitions fundamental to the European Christian tradition.

As I have suggested, nonbinary language and imagery in the Middle Ages elevated daily conflicts to cosmic proportions. Thinking with nonbinary sex allowed theorists to liken political and spiritual struggles to the horrors of demons and hell. But inasmuch as they mirrored the divine and angelic, nonbinary sexes also brought to mind the purity of heaven. Drawing inspiration from biblical exegesis, natural philosophy, and mythic poetry, among other traditions, thinkers imagined nonbinary characters as perfected figures from the edges of time, linked to idyllic pasts and futures. Those figures' reputed potential to undergo transformation and to bring about transformation in others was at the heart of their appeal. Even as medieval actors and institutions tried to force actual intersex individuals into restrictive categories, and even as they used nonbinary rhetoric to justify the expulsion of Jews and Muslims from their territories, European Christian thinkers and institutions also created imaginative spaces for nonbinary ideas and practices to thrive.

Of course, when medieval Europeans theorized sex, gender, and embodiment, they didn't do so in the terms we use now, not in the language of critical race, transgender, or intersex studies. They talked, instead, about Adam and Eve, about beasts and monsters, about the (to them) faraway lands of Africa and Asia. European Christians debated why God created the sexes, how the sexes were to be managed during life, and what happened to them after death. When they talked about these topics, however, authors were engaged in serious theorizations of sex, gender, and humanity. Their conclusions were sometimes far more vicious and vilifying than present-day rhetoric, especially when they focused on religious and racial exclusions. Yet at other times, people living a thousand years before us seem to have been far more comfortable with genitals that did not ostensibly match gender identity, and they were in some cases more accepting of nonbinary sex categories than our own modern medical and legal institutions are.

Indeed, this book has emphasized how ideas about sexual difference during the premodern period differ in many ways from our own. To be sure, medieval authors did describe a range of intermediate sex categories parallel to our modern notion of intersex (although not necessarily as part of a ternary model, since some authors imagined the sexes to number five or six).[1] Yet others saw nonbinary sex in terms of fused or bi-corporeal sex, or of negation or transcendence—models that have little purchase in the modern world. Medieval medical practitioners evaluated atypical sex anatomies and argued for their correction at different points in the human life cycle than do modern physicians now. Further, the gender-crossings attributed to nonbinary figures in some ways more closely resemble "transgender" practices than intersex morphologies. "Androgynes" and "hermaphrodites" were also repeatedly identified as a human ideal, with conjoined, split, or Y-shaped bodies that defy modern anatomies of any type. Perhaps above all, medieval texts often identified nonbinary sexes as abstract ideas rather than as the properties of actual living people. The concept of nonbinary sex that exercised so much power in the premodern world has no modern analogue.

Even if we can't identify premodern nonbinary sex as precisely equivalent to our categories of intersex or transgender, neither can we isolate it from our own modern moment. Placing the premodern and modern in conversation allows us to recognize a pattern in thinking about human bodily diversity that continues, or perhaps recurs, in science and medicine across a long chronological framework. Whether medical practitioners relied on the new science of surgery, as they did in the Middle Ages, or on novel technologies of imaging, chromosomal, and hormonal testing, as they do now, physicians nevertheless have applied subjective, historically contingent assumptions about masculinity and femininity to their treatment of people with uncommon anatomies. This pattern makes it possible for us to acknowledge the many harms visited upon sex- and gender-variant people over the centuries, especially by the scientific and medical authorities considered most expert during those times. Parallels between past and present, while not absolute, speak to an expanded timeline of efforts to manipulate bodies to fit the binary sexual and social categories of male and female. A deep history helps us to shine a light on harmful and even violent practices in the past, as well as to make further challenges to ones that exist even today. We can see that even as the science of sex has changed dramatically since the end of the Middle Ages, it has also remained in some respects remarkably consistent.

Activists have in recent years urged us to notice that "life chances"—that is, the ability to survive and thrive in our current environment—often elude those who disrupt sex and gender's binary logic.[2] If prevailing wisdom recognizes only male and female sexes as legitimately human, then people who are not typically male or female can be dismissed as inferior or defective types of human. Even now, centuries after the texts and events that occupy this volume, people whose bodies seem to depart from common sex morphologies or whose gender differs from their assigned "biological" sex face enormous pressure to conform to a binary male or female category. People with intersex variations still face widespread discrimination, hostile scrutiny, and unwelcome medical intervention. We can see a salient example in the recent pressure on elite athletes who have intersex variations (especially those athletes from the global south) to undergo forced surgeries and unwanted hormonal treatments in order to compete in sporting events at the international level.[3] Unnecessary treatments aimed at maintaining a gender binary, along with their devastating effects on people's lives, demonstrate over and over again how individuals with intersex variations are marked as "non-human, sub-human or pre-human," as one scholar observes, and denied the right to bodily integrity.[4]

In a similar manner, even as transgender communities have become increasingly visible in media and popular culture, and even as new nonbinary gender-markers have become available in certain legal and social contexts, we are also witnessing a backlash of negative rhetoric, repressive legislation, and physical violence against transgender communities—and especially against transgender women of color. Beyond this, institutional and systemic forms of transphobia continue to subject trans people to poverty, incarceration, and early death at alarmingly disproportionate rates.[5] These and other examples speak to the violence enabled by rendering individuals and communities "outside" and undeserving of full ethical consideration.

As I write this conclusion, new laws and policies are being proposed or enacted in the United States, including "bathroom bills," religious liberty laws, and restrictions on offering medical care to transgender children.[6] For the most part, these developments are aimed at reducing sex to "biology," at challenging the validity of transgender and other gender-marginalized identities, and at codifying a definition of sex that, as one former government official observes, "quite simply negates the humanity of people."[7] Efforts to define sex as merely "biological" also figure prominently into position papers by U.S. evangelical Christian advocacy groups, some of which draw from the biblical book of Genesis to condemn gender nonconformity on the grounds that God created humans "distinct as male and female."[8] Certainty about what God intended when God first created humans, however, shrouds the historical events and diverse conversations that I study in this book, the latter of which persisted for over a thousand years to secure that certainty.

These new developments in the twenty-first century further reveal the persistence of ancient and medieval Christian thought in establishing which configurations of sex and gender are acceptable, and which lives are redeemable, even now. In other words, premodern histories of sex and gender are far from an obscure, outdated episode: they have ramifications in contemporary culture and politics, as well as in the survival of very real intersex and trans people. Given this reality, it is more vital than ever that we examine the historical contexts through which ideas about sex and gender emerged and developed, rather than imagining that they are merely natural and unchanging categories. Such histories have the power to disrupt our certainties now about which sexes and genders are legitimate, natural, and human, as well as how we shape our schools, governments, hospitals, and other social spaces to accommodate those certainties. Histories can also prompt us to note that traditional Christian ideas about sex and gender were not historically consistent, nor were they always restrictive. An expansive chronology of sexual difference can be a powerful corrective to assertions that sex and gender binaries have simply always been with us. The complex notions of sex and gender that preceded our era by many centuries, and the heated debates that surrounded them, whether or not we know about those debates, continue to affect our world.

Activists and allies have been rightly critical of scholarship that uses people with intersex variations or transgender people *instrumentally*—that is, as mere bodies to "think with"—and that, in the process, displays little consideration for people's actual perspectives and lived experiences, nor the very real peril that they face. Certainly, my efforts here represent scholarly "thinking with" sex- and gender-marginalized people in the premodern world. Yet I hope that such thinking can be done in the service of trans, intersex, and nonbinary readers of all genders now. I wrote this book, in part, to understand the social and intellectual landscape navigated by people like Berengaria, in the interest of recovering their stories and perspectives. Through my research, however, I found that the voices of these past figures are all but lost to us. We can just barely glimpse them in the archives, and we can't piece together much, if any, of their own subjectivities, experiences, and agencies. What we know offers us little in the way of inspiring examples of resistance and survival, or of a past era of fluidity and choice—before the biopolitical practices that surveil and manage populations today. When we page through the fragmented manuscripts that contain the lives of individuals like Berengaria, we find no clearly drawn personalities to touch across time, nor any radically transformative politics to emulate. Perhaps such research can advance what Andrea Long Chu and Emmett Harsin Drager have recently called a history of "messiness, contradictions, disappointments, and unexpected outcomes."[9] Perhaps this history can kindle not only disappointment in what we cannot know about the past but also a better sense of how that past might lead to unexpected outcomes in the future.

In contrast to premodern Europe, today is a moment when—despite and because of the urgency of our political situation—the voices of sex- and gender-marginalized people are louder and more widely heard than ever before. In light of the volume and power of that speech, we might now ask: how can historians amplify those speakers, speakers who now can call out to express their own subjectivities, experiences, and agencies in their own voices? As we have seen, thinkers in the Middle Ages used Janus-faced images to invent a whole new world: they looked back to a vanishing past in one direction, toward an unfolding future in the other, and they created boundaries that included or excluded others in their present. Could we not direct that bi-form Janus image toward a different end? Could we not face the past head-on, support the future already being envisioned by intersex, trans, and nonbinary communities, and allow history to support a new world as it emerges into reality?

I have written this book as a collection of narratives that, I argue, adds up to a premodern story of self. Narrative conventions require a story to adopt a recognizable shape—one dependent on orderly passage from beginning to middle to end. Yet the bifurcated premodern illustrations of nonbinary sex confound any sense of narrative order. They reorient our attention toward a bilateral line, a point of *tension*, where bodies and genders meet. "Tension," from the word *tendere*, means "to stretch thin," and it is also at the root of the word "tense," which refers to a moment in time (past, present, future) in which an action takes place. "Tension" is therefore closely connected to how we perceive our position within time.[10] In premodern ideas about nonbinary sex, too, we witness an encounter of tension and tenses. The bi-form images that open and close this book upend chronology: they suspend, compress, and rupture time. They evoke a sense of time doubling over on itself, of retreating to origin. Yet they also offer a forward-looking opportunity for reform and renewal. These visionary emblems of nonbinary sex, the subjects of this study, constitute not merely time's beginning nor its final conclusion, but a rethinking of time altogether. The linkage of before and after, of times held in tension, points to how historians might work in different tenses, too, and how we might draw past, present, and future into new relation.

For there is no doubt that premodern ideas about nonbinary sex are temporally remote from us and yet also strikingly proximate. Ideas about sex and gender in the distant past, as we have seen, share much terrain with how we conceptualize some of our most closely held categories today. The assumptions encapsulated in past ideas—including those about female "passivity" and male "activity," the hierarchy of nature, and entrenched ideas about race, geography, and species—still, or perhaps yet again, animate our beliefs about who now deserves a livable life. Given these complex resonances between past and present, we might ask: is it our task now to overcome the vestiges of a history that still contaminates our worldview? Should we aim, in other words, to eliminate past ideas that prevent us from reaching a just and more transformative future? Or should we conclude that our current conceptions of sex, religion, race, and species are so time-bound that we have little to learn from those of a distant past?

I would like to suggest a reading that is neither teleological nor dismissive of the ways in which we carry our inheritances. From our vantage point in the present—our own moment of tension—we might benefit from a considered form of temporal play. No direct link binds us to our premodern forerunners. The political and social structures that surround us, our daily lives and expectations, share little with those that existed a thousand years ago. Yet our sense of what qualifies as an acceptable human subject, a natural human body, or a proper human desire has much to do with the ways in which prior theorists solved problems of sex and gender over the centuries. Perhaps our task at this moment, then, is to let the past intrude, to be attentive to its iterations, and to keep the future open. What is at stake is a world that rests not on the politics of exclusion—on the ejection of disfavored sexes, genders, and races—but on a rethinking and remaking of the human itself.

Notes

INTRODUCTION

1. Arxiu Històric de Girona, Notaria de Peralada, 26 bis. *Llibre de Bernat Sunyer*, years 1331–32, fol. 52v:

    habebat virgam virilem et testiculos ad modum hominis et est arta ita quod vix potest mingere per quoddam foramen parvum quod habet in fissura vulve quam habet suptus dictam virgam virilem et habet pellem inter crura sua stensam ad modum alarum vespertilionis que cohoperit fissuram dicte vulve tociens quociens ipsa Berengaria vertit genua sua versus faciem suam et quod habet formam virilem plus quam muliebrem, ita quod dictus Guillelmus nec alter homo posse iacere secum nec habere rem carnaliter nec ipsa posset reddere ullatenus debitum coniugalis nec concipere nec infantare.

    Michael R. McVaugh discovered the case and discusses it and Vesianus Pelegrini briefly in his *Medicine Before the Plague: Practitioners and the Patients in the Crown of Aragon, 1285–1345* (Cambridge: Cambridge University Press, 1993), 206. As I have noted, I use female pronouns for Berengaria, following the vocabulary of the primary source, and in an effort to avoid imposing further pronouns on Berengaria.

2. Husbands were obligated to render the conjugal debt, too. I discuss impotence cases in chapter 5.
3. On Vesianus Pelegrini, see McVaugh, *Medicine*, 206n56.
4. Michelle Armstrong-Partida, "Priestly Wives: The Role and Acceptance of Clerics' Concubines in the Parishes of Late Medieval Catalunya," *Speculum* 88:1 (2013): 166–214.
5. Armstrong-Partida, 182, 182n47.
6. On publicizing a marriage, see Marie A. Kelleher, "'The Fragility of the Female Sex': Women and the Law in the Fourteenth-Century Crown of Aragon," PhD diss., University of Kansas, 2003, 88–90; for the many different opinions and rules on what constituted legitimate marriage, see James Brundage, *Law, Sex, and Christian Society in Medieval Europe* (Chicago: University of Chicago Press, 1987).

    If Berengaria and Guillem's marriage was annulled (as the historian Christof Rolker suspects), then the two families were obliged to return the marital gifts they exchanged. Such payments could be substantial, as well as the source of considerable dispute. Christof Rolker, "The Two Laws and the Three Sexes: Ambiguous Bodies in Canon Law and Roman Law (12th to 16th Centuries)," *Zeitschrift der Savigny-Stiftung für Rechtsgeschichte kanonistische Abteilung* 100 (2014): 207; for marital payments and disputes, see Kelleher, 119–28, 149, and passim. For Pope Alexander III's ruling on annulments for *arctatio* ("anatomical impediments to intromission"), see Thomas G. Benedek and Janet Kubinec, "The Evaluation of Impotence by Sexual Congress and Alternatives Thereto in Divorce Proceedings," *Transactions and Studies of the College of Physicians of Philadelphia* 4:2 (1982): 129–30, and chapter 5 in this volume.

7. Christof Rolker, however, has identified medieval marriage cases in which a rather relaxed attitude toward intersex pervades. See "Der Hermaphrodit und seine Frau: Körper, Sexualität und Geschlecht im Spätmittelalter," *Hist. Z.* 297 (2013): 593–620. It is also possible that Berengaria's unusual body caused a stir at the time of her birth, as, for instance, in a case of 1437–1438. See my discussion of birth and birth attendants in chapter 5.

8. Armstrong-Partida, 197, 208.

9. See chapter 4 for a discussion of Roman and canon law on intersex.

10. Marisa J. Fuentes, *Dispossessed Lives: Enslaved Women, Violence, and the Archive* (Philadelphia: University of Pennsylvania Press, 2016), 6.

11. See discussion of legal categories in chapter 4 in the section devoted to Roman and canon law.

12. For "life chances," see Dean Spade, *Normal Life: Administrative Violence, Critical Trans Politics, and the Limits of the Law* (Brooklyn, NY: South Bend, 2011), 11–13, 19–47.

13. For theories of opposition, see G. E. R. Lloyd, *Polarity and Analogy: Two Types of Argumentation in Early Greek Thought* (Cambridge: Cambridge University Press, 1966); Rodney Needham, ed., *Right and Left: Essays on Dual Symbolic Classification* (Chicago: University of Chicago Press, 1973). For borderlands and nonbinaries in classification, see Geoffrey C. Bowker and Susan Leigh Star, *Sorting Things Out: Classification and Its Consequences* (Cambridge, MA: MIT Press, 1999), 300–305; Jenny L. Davis, Lal Zimman, and Joshua Raclaw, "Opposites Attract: Retheorizing Binaries in Language, Gender, and Sexuality," in *Queer Excursions: Retheorizing Binaries in Language, Gender, and Sexuality* (New York: Oxford University Press, 2014), 1–12.

14. *Oxford English Dictionary (OED) Online* (Oxford: University of Oxford Press, 2017).

15. M. W. Bychowski, "The Isle of Hermaphrodites: Disorienting the Place of Intersex in the Middle Ages," *postmedieval: a journal of medieval cultural studies* 9:2 (2018): 163.

16. Ovid, *Metamorphoses*, trans. Frank Justus Miller, 2 vols. (Cambridge, MA: Loeb Classical Library, Harvard University Press, 1971), 4.375–9 (I: 204): "velut, si quis conducat cortice ramos/ crescendo iungi pariterque adolescere cernit/ sic ubi conplexu coierunt membra tenaci/ nec duo sunt et forma duplex, nec femina dici/ nec puer ut possit, neutrumque et utrumque videntur." As scholars have pointed out, Hermaphroditus was already to some extent gender-nonconforming before his transformation in *Metamorphoses*. Other legends held that Hermaphroditus was born with male and female attributes. M. Robinson, "Salmacis and Hermaphroditus: When Two Become One: (Ovid, Met. 4.285–388)," *Classical Quarterly* 49:1 (1999): 212–23; Georgia Nugent, "This Sex Which Is Not One: De-constructing Ovid's Hermaphrodite," *differences* 2:1 (1990): 160–85. See also Ruth Evans, "Gender Is not Genitals," along with other works collected in Evans, ed., *Medieval Intersex: Language and Hermaphroditism*, special issue of *postmedieval: a journal of medieval cultural studies* 9:2 (2018); Vanda Zajko " 'Listening With' Ovid: Intersexuality, Queer Theory, and the Myth of Hermaphroditus and Salmacis," *Helios* 36:2 (2009): 175–202; Cary J. Nederman and Jacqui True, "The Third Sex: The Idea of the Hermaphrodite in Twelfth-Century Europe," *Journal of the History of Sexuality* 6:4 (1996): 497–517.

17. My argument is indebted to Caroline Walker Bynum, *Metamorphosis and Identity* (New York: Zone, 2001).

18. See, as a parallel, Joy Ladin's moving statement that modern transgender experience is above all a "human experience," and that the questions transgender people face are shared by all: "Everyone, transgender or not, must decide what aspects of ourselves we will and won't express, when we can't and when we must subordinate our individuality in order to fulfill our roles in relationships, families,

and communities. . . . the crisis [this experience] dramatizes is . . . the crisis of realizing that either we live what makes us different or we cannot live at all." Ladin, "In the Image of God, God Created Them: Toward Trans Theology," *Journal of Feminist Studies in Religion* 34:1 (2018): 56.

19. Iain Morland, "Intersex," *TSQ: Transgender Studies Quarterly* 1–2 (2014): 111.

20. The nomenclature is controversial, and DSD is also the subject of much criticism. See Ellen K. Feder, "Imperatives of Normality: From 'Intersex' to 'Disorders of Sex Development,'" *GLQ: A Journal of Lesbian and Gay Studies* 15:2 (2009): 225–47; see also the statement of ISNA on their shift to the term DSD, accessed March 4, 2019, http://www.isna.org/node/1066. C. G. Costello, "Intersex and Trans* Communities: Commonalities and Tensions," in *Transgender and Intersex: Theoretical, Practical, and Artistic Perspectives*, ed. Stefan Horlacher (New York: Palgrave MacMillan, 2016), 83–108.

21. Alice D. Dreger and April M. Herndon, "Progress and Politics in the Intersex Rights Movement: Feminist Theory in Action," *GLQ: A Journal of Lesbian and Gay Studies* 15:2 (2009): 199–224; Morland, "Intersex," 111.

22. Melanie Blackless et al. put the figure at two percent of live births in "How Sexually Dimorphic Are We? Review and Synthesis," *American Journal of Human Biology* 12 (2000), 151–66. This figure is disputed in Katrina Karkazis, *Fixing Sex: Intersex, Medical Authority, and Lived Experience* (Durham, NC: Duke, 2008), 23–24.

23. David A. Rubin, *Intersex Matters: Biomedical Embodiment, Gender Regulation, and Transnational Activism* (Albany, NY: SUNY Press, 2017); Lisa Downing, Iain Morland, and Nikki Sullivan, *Fuckology: Critical Essays on John Money's Diagnostic Concepts* (Chicago: University of Chicago Press, 2015); Georgiann Davis, *Contesting Intersex: The Dubious Diagnosis* (New York: NYU Press, 2015); Julie A. Greenberg, *Intersexuality and the Law: Why Sex Matters* (New York: NYU Press, 2012); Elizabeth Reis, *Bodies in Doubt: An American History of Intersex* (Baltimore, MD: Johns Hopkins University Press, 2009); Morgan Holmes, ed., *Critical Intersex* (Aldershot, UK: Ashgate, 2009); Iain Morland, *Intersex and After*, special issue, *GLQ: A Journal of Lesbian and Gay Studies* 15:2(2009); Karkazis, *Fixing Sex*; Sharon E. Sytsma, ed., *Ethics and Intersex* (Dordrecht, The Netherlands: Springer, 2006); Anne Fausto-Sterling, *Sexing the Body: Gender Politics and the Construction of Sexuality* (New York: Basic, 2000); Suzanne Kessler, *Lessons from the Intersexed* (New Brunswick, NJ: Rutgers University Press, 1998); Alice Domurat Dreger, *Hermaphrodites and the Medical Invention of Sex* (Cambridge, MA: Harvard University Press, 1999); Alice Domurat Dreger, ed., *Intersex in the Age of Ethics* (Hagerstown, MD: University Publishing Group, 1999); Cheryl Chase (now Bo Laurent), "Hermaphrodites with Attitude: Mapping the Emergence of Intersex Political Activism," *GLQ: A Journal of Lesbian and Gay Studies* 4:2 (1998): 189–211; as well as the information collected by the Intersex Society of North America (http://www.isna.org/) and Accord Alliance (http://www.accordalliance.org).

24. Morland, "Intersex," 111; Karkazis, *Fixing Sex*.

25. Sherri G. Morris, "Twisted Lies: My Journey in an Imperfect Body," in *Surgically Shaping Children: Technology, Ethics, and the Pursuit of Normality*, ed. Erik Parens (Baltimore: The Johns Hopkins University Press, 2006), 3–12; Human Rights Watch/interACT, "'I Want to Be Like Nature Made Me': Medically Unnecessary Surgeries on Intersex Children in the US" (July 2017), accessed March 4, 2019, available at https://www.hrw.org/node/306688/.

26. Dreger and Herndon, 203–8.

27. Leslie Feinberg, *Transgender Warriors: Making History from Joan of Arc to Dennis Rodman* (Boston: Beacon , 1996).

28. A. Baldassano, "Bodies of Resistance: On (Not) Naming Gender in the Medieval West," PhD diss., The City University of New York, 2017, 1.

29. Susan Stryker and Aren Z. Aizura, eds., *The Transgender Studies Reader 2* (New York: Routledge, 2013), 11.

30. For community across time, see Carolyn Dinshaw, *Getting Medieval: Sexualities and Communities, Pre- and Postmodern* (Durham, NC: Duke University Press 1999); Carolyn Dinshaw et al., "Theorizing Queer Temporalities: A Roundtable Discussion," *GLQ: A Journal of Lesbian and Gay Studies* 13:2–3 (2007): 177–95; Elizabeth Freeman, *Time Binds: Queer Temporalities, Queer Histories* (Durham, NC: Duke University Press, 2010).

31. For definitions of transgender, see Susan Stryker, *Transgender History* (Berkeley, CA: Seal, 2008), 19; Jack Halberstam, *Trans*: A Quick and Quirky Account of Gender Variability* (Oakland: University of California Press, 2017), 1–21; David Valentine, *Imagining Transgender: An Ethnography of a Category* (Durham, NC: Duke University Press, 2007). I am aware that the definitions I offer in this introduction are, by necessity, simplifications. Both intersex and transgender are umbrella terms for a spectrum of complex bodies, identities, and practices. Please see my discussion in chapter 5 in the section entitled Medieval Surgery in Modern Perspective.

32. See Thea Hillman's memoir, which describes complicated engagements between queer, trans, and intersex communities: *Intersex (For Lack of a Better Word)* (San Francisco: Manic D, 2008), 76, 129–37. Trans and intersex studies constitute distinct fields, but trans studies often seeks to engage intersex studies, historical studies of intersex have recently engaged trans studies, and some prominent works of theory discuss both trans and intersex. On the two fields' interaction, see David Rubin, 74–76; Stefan Horlacher, "Transgender and Intersex: Theoretical, Practical, and Artistic Perspectives," in *Transgender and Intersex: Theoretical, Practical, and Artistic Perspectives*, ed. Stefan Horlacher, 1–27. Among other recent examples are Kathleen P. Long, "Intersex/Transgender," in *The Bloomsbury Handbook of 21st-Century Feminist Theory*, ed. Robin Truth Goodman (London: Bloomsbury, 2019), 121–41, and Paul B. Preciado, *Countersexual Manifesto*, trans. Kevin Gerry Dunn (New York: Columbia University Press, 2018), 106–19.

33. For criticism, see Karkazis, *Fixing Sex*, 18–21. In using "intersex" for medieval individuals, I follow recent scholarship in premodern disability studies, including Sara Scalenghe, *Disability in the Ottoman Arab World, 1500–1800* (Cambridge: Cambridge University Press, 2014), and Richard H. Godden and Asa S. Mittman, eds., *Monstrosity, Disability, and the Posthuman in the Medieval and Early Modern World* (Cham, Switzerland: Palgrave, 2019).

34. That is *hermaphroditus*, *androgynus* (from the Greek for "man-woman"), *nec* and *utriusque sexus* ("neither" and, in this context, "both sexes").

35. See Intersex Society of North America, "What's the History Behind the Intersex Rights Movement?" accessed March 4, 2019, http://www.isna.org/faq/history; April Herndon, "Getting Rid of 'Hermaphroditism' Once and For All" (2005), accessed March 4, 2019, http://www.isna.org/node/979; Hillman, 25–29. A number of affected individuals in Europe now identify themselves as "hermaphrodites" or "herms," but this terminology remains pejorative in the United States. Costello, 85.

36. For a characterization of transgender historical studies, among many examples, see Joanne Meyerowitz, *How Sex Changed: A History of Transsexuality in the United States* (Cambridge, MA: Harvard University Press, 2002); Bernice L. Hausman, *Changing Sex: Transsexualism, Technology, and the Idea of Gender* (Chapel Hill, NC: Duke University Press, 1995); Stryker, *Transgender History*, 19; Stryker and Aizura, *Transgender Studies Reader 2*, 317–70; Leah DeVun and Zeb Tortorici, "Trans, Time, and History," in DeVun and Tortorici, eds., "Trans*historicities," special issue of *TSQ: Transgender Studies Quarterly* 5:4 (2018): 518–39, and the forthcoming *Trans Historical: Gender Plurality Before the Modern*, ed. Greta LaFleur, Anna Kłosowska, and Masha Raskolnikov. Others have proposed "trans temporality" as a method for thinking about transgender's relation to time and history. See Kadji Amin, "Temporality," *TSQ: Transgender Studies Quarterly* 1:1–2 (2014): 219–22; Jacob Lau, "Between the Times: Trans-Temporality, and Historical Representation," PhD diss., University of California, 2016; Simon D. Elin Fisher, Rasheedah Phillips, and Ido H. Katri, eds., "Trans Temporalities," special issue of *Somatechnics* 7:1 (2017).

37. M. W. Bychowski, Howard Chiang, et al., "Trans*historicities: A Roundtable Discussion," *TSQ: Transgender Studies Quarterly* 5:4 (2018): 658–85; Baldassano, 1–32, 270–73. Strassfeld notes some have claimed premodern categories such as *tumtum* and *androginos* as a part of trans/intersex Jewish history: "Classically Queer: Eunuchs and Androgynes in Rabbinic Literature." PhD diss., Stanford University, 2013, 97n164.

38. For trans as a methodological approach, see Susan Stryker, "Transgender Studies: Queer Theory's Evil Twin," *GLQ: A Journal of Lesbian and Gay Studies* 10:2 (2004): 212–15; Susan Stryker, Paisley Currah, and Lisa Jean Moore, "Introduction: Trans-, Trans, or Transgender?" *WSQ* 36:3–4 (2008): 11–22; for questions about what constitutes "cultural studies from an intersex perspective," see Iain Morland, "Afterword: Genitals Are History," *postmedieval: a journal of medieval cultural studies* 9:2 (2018): 209–15.

39. Joan W. Scott, "Gender as a Useful Category of Historical Analysis," *American Historical Review* 91:5 (1986): 1068, 1074.

40. Sharon Block, "Making Meaningful Bodies: Physical Appearance in Colonial Writings," *Early American Studies: An Interdisciplinary Journal* 12:3 (2014): 524–47.

41. My work builds on some excellent and path-breaking histories of ancient and early modern intersex, usually discussed as "hermaphroditism," as well as a range of older and new studies in medieval studies that bring nonbinary sex categories and "transgender" figures to the fore in new ways. See Marie Delcourt, *Hermaphrodite: Myths and Rites of the Bisexual Figure in Classical Antiquity*, trans. Jennifer Nicholson (London: Studio, 1956); Ruth Gilbert, *Early Modern Hermaphrodites: Sex and Other Stories* (New York: Palgrave, 2002); Kathleen P. Long, *Hermaphrodites in Renaissance Europe* (Aldershot, UK: Ashgate, 2006); Joan Cadden, *The Meanings of Sex Difference in the Middle Ages: Medicine, Science, and Culture* (New York: Cambridge University Press, 1993); Lorraine Daston and Katharine Park, "The Hermaphrodite and the Orders of Nature: Sexual Ambiguity in Early Modern France," *GLQ: A Journal of Lesbian and Gay Studies* 1:1 (1995): 419–38. Evans, *Medieval Intersex: Language and Hermaphroditism*; M.W. Bychowski and Dorothy Kim, eds., "Visions of Medieval Trans Feminism," special issue of *Medieval Feminist Forum* 55:1 (2019); David Rollo, *Kiss My Relics: Hermaphroditic Fictions of the Middle Ages* (Chicago: University of Chicago Press, 2011); Irina Metzler, "Hermaphroditism in the Western Middle Ages: Physicians, Lawyers and the Intersexed Person," *Studies in Early Medicine I—Bodies of Knowledge: Cultural Interpretations of Illness and Medicine in Medieval Europe*, BAR International Series 2170, ed. Sally Crawford and Christina Lee (2010): 27–39; Max Strassfeld, "Translating the Human: The *Androginos* in *Tosefta Bikurim*," *TSQ: Transgender Studies Quarterly* 3:3–4 (2016): 587–604; Daniel Burton-Rose, "Gendered Androgyny: Transcendent Ideals and Profane Realities in Buddhism, Classicism, and Daoism," in *Transgender China*, ed. Howard Chiang (New York: Palgrave Macmillan, 2012), 67–96; Karl Whittington, "Medieval," *TSQ: Transgender Studies Quarterly* 1:1–2 (2014): 125–9; Nederman and True, 497–517; Maaike Van der Lugt, "Sex Difference in Medieval Theology and Canon Law: A Tribute to Joan Cadden," *Medieval Feminist Forum* 46:1 (2010): 101–21; Van der Lugt, "Pourquoi Dieu a-t-il créé la femme? Différence sexuelle et théologie médiévale," in *Ève et Pandora: la création de la femme*, ed. Jean-Claude Schmitt (Paris: Gallimard, 2001), 89–113 (notes on 262–67); Van der Lugt, "L'humanité des monstres et leur accès aux sacrements dans la pensée médiévale." Accessed on March 20, 2019, https://halshs.archives-ouvertes.fr/halshs-00175497/document. Published in *Monstres, humanité et sacrements dans la pensée médiévale*, ed. A. Caiozzo et A.-E. Demartini, 135–161. Paris: Créaphis, 2008.

42. As theorists of sexuality have pointed out, even as discourse produces expressions of power, it also simultaneously exposes and undercuts that power: that is, the language of domination might be used to oppose that dominance, and identical terms might come to support opposite goals. In this way, dominant discourse can become "reversed": it can become a stumbling block, or even a starting point for opposition and resistance. Foucault, *The History of Sexuality, Vol. 1: An Introduction* (New

York: Vintage, 1990), 92–102; Heather Love, *Feeling Backward: Loss and the Politics of Queer History* (Cambridge, MA: Harvard University Press, 2007), 18–28.
43. Susan Stryker, "General Editor's Introduction," in DeVun and Tortorici, 516.
44. Stryker, "General Editor's Introduction," 516.
45. Evans, "Gender," 122; Bychowski, "The Isle of Hermaphrodites," 175.

1. THE PERFECT SEXES OF PARADISE

1. James le Palmer (attributed), *Omne bonum*, BL Royal MS 6 E VII/1 (Ebrietas-Humanus), fol. 205r: "Et quia talis homo nec uir nec mulier esse uidetur et utrumque uidetur." On this manuscript, see Lucy Freeman Sandler, *Omne Bonum: A Fourteenth-Century Encyclopedia of Universal Knowledge*, 2 vols. (London: Harvey Miller, 1996).
2. *Omne bonum*, fol. 205r-v: "quisquis uspiam nascitur homo id est animal rationale mortale quamlibet nostris inuisitatam sensibus gerat formam corporis seu colorem seu motum sensuum seu sonum seu qualibet ui qualibet parte qualibet qualitate naturam ex illo uno protoplausto originem ducere nullus fidelium dubitauerit." He cites from Augustine of Hippo, *De civitate Dei*, Libri XXII, ed. B. Dombart, 2nd ed., 2 vols. (Leipzig: Teubner, 1877), 16:8 (II: 135–36). English trans. in *Concerning the City of God Against the Pagans*, trans. Henry Bettenson (Harmondsworth, UK: Penguin, 1972), 663.
3. See Robert Graves and Raphael Patai, *Hebrew Myths: The Book of Genesis* (New York: McGraw Hill, 1963), 66–67; Wayne A. Meeks, "The Image of the Androgyne: Some Uses of a Symbol in Earliest Christianity," *History of Religions* 13:3 (1974): 186n90; Elliot R. Wolfson, "Bifurcating the Androgyne and Engendering Sin: A Zoharic Reading of Gen. 1–3," in *Hidden Truths from Eden: Esoteric Readings of Genesis 1–3*, ed. Caroline Vander Stichele and Susanne Scholz (Atlanta: SBL, 2014), 97; the Midrash Rabbah describes Adam as two-sexed and "double-faced." See Ruth Gilbert, *Early Modern Hermaphrodites*, 15. The Roman god Janus was also frequently pictured as double-faced in medieval iconography. Janus symbolized cosmic generation and the propagation of the human race; he was also identified with Adam. For Janus's connection to cosmic generation and the four elements, see Jane Chance, *Medieval Mythography: From Roman North Africa to the School of Chartres, A.D. 433–1177* (Gainesville: University Press of Florida, 1994), 76–77, 142–44, and 570–71n46. Maria Grazia Cittadini Fulvi and Vania Gasperoi Panella, *Dal mondo antico al cristianesimo sulle tracce di Giano: il simbolismo della porta e del passaggio in relazione al dio bifronte* (Perugia: Morlacchi Editore, 2008).
4. David Williams, *Deformed Discourse: The Function of the Monster in Medieval Thought and Literature* (Montreal: McGill-Queen's University Press, 1996), 128–31, 171; for duplicity as two-faced, see Debra Higgs Strickland, *Saracens, Demons, and Jews: Making Monsters in Medieval Art* (Princeton, NJ: Princeton University Press, 2003), 74.
5. On primal androgyny, see Meeks, 165–208; Maryanne Cline Horowitz, "The Image of God in Man—Is Woman Included?" *Harvard Theological Review* 72:3–4 (1979): 175–205; Van der Lugt, "Pourquoi," 95–103; Daniel Boyarin, *Carnal Israel: Reading Sex in Talmudic Culture* (Berkeley: University of California Press, 1993), 35–61; Taylor G. Petrey, *Resurrecting Parts: Early Christians on Desire, Reproduction, and Sexual Difference* (London: Routledge, 2016); Dale B. Martin, *Sex and the Single Savior: Gender and Sexuality in Biblical Interpretation* (Louisville, KY: Westminster John Knox Press, 2006), 77–90; Benjamin H. Dunning, *Specters of Paul: Sexual Difference in Early Christian Thought* (Philadelphia: University of Pennsylvania Press, 2011). Martin wonders if the term should continue to be used, given its connotations of male-female equality, which I address in this chapter. I use the term here because it is so well known.
6. "Hexaemeron" refers to the "six-day work" of creation by God.

7. For distinctions between the Priestly and Yahwist accounts of creation, see Edward Noort, "The Creation of Man and Woman in Biblical and Ancient Near Eastern Traditions," in *The Creation of Man and Woman: Interpretations of the Biblical Narratives in Jewish and Christian Traditions*, ed. Gerard P. Luttikhuizen (Leiden: Brill, 2000), 1–18.
8. My analysis follows closely that of Van der Lugt's "Pourquoi," 95–103.
9. Quoted in Boyarin, *Carnal Israel*, 42–43; "On the History of the Early Phallus," in *Gender and Difference in the Middle Ages*, ed. Sharon Farmer and Carol Braun Pasternack (Minneapolis: University of Minnesota Press, 2003), 27. See also Horowitz, 185–86.
10. Plato's *Timaeus* also suggested that the original state of human perfection lacked sexual division. Giulia Sissa, "The Sexual Philosophies of Plato and Aristotle," in *A History of Women in the West*, vol. 1, *From Ancient Goddesses to Christian Saints*, ed. Pauline Schmitt Pantel (Cambridge, MA: Belknap Press, 1992), 60. On Jewish interpretations of androgyny, which were diverse, see Boyarin, *Carnal Israel*, 42–46; Max K. Strassfeld, "Classically Queer: Eunuchs and Androgynes in Rabbinic Literature." PhD diss., Stanford University, 2013; Marianne Schleicher, "Constructions of Sex and Gender: Attending to Androgynes and Tumtumim Through Jewish Scriptural Use," *Literature and Theology* 25:4 (2011): 422–35.
11. Shai Secunda, "The Construction, Composition, and Idealization of the Female Body in Rabbinic Literature and Parallel Iranian Texts: Three Excursuses," *Nashim: A Journal of Jewish Women's Studies & Gender Issues* 23 (Spring-Fall 2012): 62–67; M. L. West, *Early Greek Philosophy and the Orient* (Oxford: Clarendon Press, 1971), 28–36; Aileen Ajootian, "The Only Happy Couple: Hermaphrodites and Gender," in *Naked Truths*, ed. A. O. Koloski-Ostrow and C. L. Lyons (New York: Routledge, 1997), 226; Robert Garland, *The Eye of the Beholder: Deformity and Disability in the Graeco-Roman World* (Ithaca, NY: Cornell University Press, 1995), 174–75. Scholars have observed the ubiquity of binary categories and a focus on their reconciliation in numerous mythological systems; see, for example, Mircea Eliade, *The Two and the One* (New York: Harper, 1965), 78–124.
12. John Flood, *Representations of Eve in Antiquity and the English Middle Ages* (New York: Routledge, 2011), 135n86.
13. For divine androgyny in Greek and Roman paganism, Anthony Corbeill, *Sexing the World: Grammatical Gender and Biological Sex in Ancient Rome* (Ithaca, NY: Cornell University Press, 2015), 104–35; 145–51. Boyarin deals with the relationship between Greek and Gnostic texts and Philo in *Carnal Israel*, 35–46.
14. Dunning, 21; Martin, 77–90. For Philo and his successors, see Boyarin, *Carnal Israel*, 37–60; "Early Phallus," 3–44.
15. David T. Runia, *Philo in Early Christian Literature: A Survey* (Assen, The Netherlands: Van Gorcum, 1993), 3; Flood, 17.
16. Flood, 42.
17. Stephen Greenblatt, *The Rise and Fall of Adam and Eve* (New York: W. W. Norton, 2017), 77.
18. Elaine Pagels, *The Gnostic Gospels* (New York: Vintage, 1989 [first pub. 1979]), 48–57.
19. Pagels, *Gnostic Gospels*, 56; "The Gnostic Vision: Varieties of Androgyny Illustrated by Texts from the Nag Hammadi Library," in *Parabola* 3/4 (1978), 6–9; Karen L. King, "Sophia and Christ in the *Apocryphon of John*," in *Images of the Feminine in Gnosticism*, ed. Karen L. King (Philadelphia: Fortress Press, 1988), 158–76; Meeks, 188–97; Horowitz, 185.
20. Irenaeus, *Adversus haereses seu Detectio et eversio falso cognominatae Gnoseos* (Turnhout, Belgium: Brepols, 2010), 1.18.2: "Quidam autem et alterum esse uolunt qui secundum imaginem et similitudinem Dei factus est homo masculofeminus, et hunc esse spiritalem, alterum autem qui ex terra plasmatus sit." Dennis Ronald MacDonald, "Corinthian Veils and Gnostic Androgynes," in *Images of the Feminine in Gnosticism*, 283.
21. Van der Lugt, "Pourquoi," 101; "Sex Difference," 106–7; Marian Rothstein, *The Androgyne in Early Modern France: Contextualizing the Power of Gender* (New York: Palgrave, 2015), 9–11.

22. Van der Lugt, "Sex Difference," 107; Peter Brown, *The Body and Society: Men, Women, and Sexual Renunciation in Early Christianity* (New York: Columbia University Press, 1988), 293–96.
23. Gregory did, however, believe that procreation took place in Eden. Jeremy Cohen argues that Gregory was never quite able to reconcile reproduction with primal innocence; see *"Be Fertile and Increase, Fill the Earth and Master It": The Ancient and Medieval Career of a Biblical Text* (Ithaca, NY:: Cornell University Press, 1989), 258.
24. Brown, 293–94; Van der Lugt, "Pourquoi," 101–2.
25. Boyarin notes the primal androgyne myth was widespread in late antiquity; see "Paul and the Genealogy of Gender," *Representations* 41 (1993): 10.
26. Van der Lugt, "Pourquoi," 102; Martin, *Sex and the Single Savior*, 77–90; Lone Fatum, "Image of God and Glory of Man: Women in the Pauline Congregations," in *The Image of God and Gender Models in Judaeo-Christian Tradition*, ed. Kari Elisabeth Børresen (Oslo: Solum Forlag, 1991), 67–69; Boyarin, "Paul and the Genealogy of Gender," 4.
27. Brown, 168. Some have disputed the story as apocryphal; see Bruce Chilton, "Resurrection in the Gospels," in Jacob Neusner and Alan J. Avery-Peck, eds., *Judaism in Late Antiquity, Part 4: Death, Life-After-Death, Resurrection and the World-to-Come in the Judaisms of Antiquity* (Leiden: Brill, 2000), 231.
28. Flood, 24.
29. Such an approach differed from his earlier spiritual interpretation of creation in *De Genesi contra Manichaeos*. See Elizabeth A. Clark, "Adam's Only Companion: Augustine and the Early Christian Debate on Marriage," *Recherches Augustiniennes* 21 (1986): 143. Augustine drew precise distinctions between the "seminal" creation, in which man and woman are coeval, and their sequential formation in time, in which man precedes woman. See Kari Elisabeth Børresen, *Subordination and Equivalence: The Nature and Role of Women in Augustine and Thomas Aquinas*, trans. Charles H. Talbot (Washington, DC: University Press of America, 1981), 20–21; Jack M. Greenstein, *The Creation of Eve and Renaissance Naturalism: Visual Theology and Artistic Invention* (Cambridge: Cambridge University Press, 2016), 17–22.
30. Clark, "Adam's Only Companion," 139–62.
31. Elizabeth A. Clark, "Heresy, Asceticism, Adam and Eve: Interpretations of Genesis 1–3 in the Later Church Fathers," in *Ascetic Piety and Women's Faith: Essays on Late Ancient Christianity* (Lewiston, NY: Edwin Mellen, 1986), 353–86.
32. Augustine, *De Genesi ad litteram*, ed. J. Zycha, Corpus Scriptorum Ecclesiasticorum Latinorum 28 (Vienna: F. Tempsky; Leipzig: G. Freytag, 1894), 89–90: "rursus ne quisquam arbitraretur ita factum, ut in homine singulari uterque sexus exprimeretur, sicut interdum nascuntur, quos androgynos uocant, ostendit se singularem numerum propter coiunctionis unitatem posuisse et quod de uiro mulier facta est." English trans. in Augustine's *The Literal Meaning of Genesis*, trans. John Hammond Taylor, SJ., 2 vols. (Mahwah, NJ: Paulist, 1982), I: 99. See also Augustine, *De Genesi contra Manichaeos*, ed. D. Weber, Corpus Christianorum Ecclesiastorum Latinorum 91 (Vienna: Verlag der Österreichischen Akademie der Wissenschaften, 1998), book 3, chap. 34 (p. 22).
33. Augustine, *De trinitate*, ed. W. J. Mountain and F. Glorie, Corpus Christianorum: Series Latina [hereafter CCCL], vols. 50 and 50A (Turnhout, Belgium: Brepols, 1968), 12.6.8 (50: 363): "quidam enim timuerunt dicere: *Fecit eum masculum et feminam* ne quasi monstrosum aliquid intellegeretur sicuti sunt quos hermaphroditos uocant." See English trans. in *On the Trinity: Books 8–15*, ed. Gareth B. Matthews and trans. Stephen McKenna (Cambridge: Cambridge University Press, 2002), 88.
34. Augustine, *De trinitate*: "cum etiam sic non mendaciter possit intellegi utrumque in numero singulari propter id quod dictum est: *Duo in carne una*[.]"
35. Brown, 401–3.

1. THE PERFECT SEXES OF PARADISE   217

36. Augustine, *De Genesi ad litteram*, 89:

> Licet enim subtilissime disseratur ipsam mentem hominis, in qua factus est ad imaginem dei, quandam scilicet rationalem uitam, distribui in aeternae contemplationis ueritatem et in rerum temporalium administrationem, atque ita fieri quasi masculum et feminam illa parte consulente, hac obtemperante: in hac tamen distributione non recte dicitur imago dei, nisi illud, quod inhaeret contemplandae incommutabili ueritati.

> Eng. trans. in *Literal Meaning of Genesis*, I:98. Greenstein, 156–8; Flood, 25.

37. Van der Lugt, "Pourquoi," 96, 102; Greenstein, 118–19.
38. Augustine, *De civitate Dei*, 16.8 (II:136): "Androgyni, quos etiam Hermaphroditos nuncupant, quamvis ad modum rari sint, difficile est tamen ut temporibus desint, in quibus sic uterque sexus apparet." English trans. p. 663.
39. Gemma Wain, "*Nec ancilla nec domina*: Representations of Eve in the Twelfth Century," PhD diss., Durham University, 2013; Van der Lugt, "Sex Difference," 105–6; Meeks, 176–77. Kari Vogt, "'Becoming Male': A Gnostic and Early Christian Metaphor," in *The Image of God and Gender Models in Judaeo-Christian Tradition*, 172–86; Martin, 83–85.
40. On the political implications of the creation story in Genesis, see Elaine Pagels, *Adam, Eve, and the Serpent: Sex and Politics in Early Christianity* (New York: Random House, 1988); Cadden, *Meanings*, 193.
41. Felice Lifshitz, "The Persistence of Late Antiquity: Christ as Man and Woman in an Eighth-Century Miniature," *Medieval Feminist Forum* 38:1 (2004): 18–27.
42. Lifshitz, "Persistence," 20.
43. Lifshitz, "Persistence," 19–21; *Religious Women in Early Carolingian Francia: A Study of Manuscript Transmission and Monastic Culture* (New York: Fordham University Press, 2014), 30.
44. John Scottus Eriugena, *Periphyseon (De divisione naturae): Liber quartus*, ed. Édouard A. Jeauneau, Corpus Christianorum Continuatio Mediaevalis [hereafter CCCM] 164 (Turnhout, Belgium: Brepols, 2000), 148–49:

> Non uidetur homini, quem ad imaginem et similitudinem nostram fecimus, bonum esse solum (hoc est simplicem atque perfectum) uniuersaliterque diuisione naturae in sexus, ad similitudinem angelicae naturae, absolutum permanere, sed pronum procliuumque ad terrenos coitus pariter cum bestiis ruere.... Faciamus ergo ei adiutorium simile, quo id quod appetit peragere possit, feminam uidelicet, quae similiter ut masculus fragilis ac lubrica terrenas appetat concupiscentias.

> Donald F. Duclow, "The Sleep of Adam, the Making of Eve: Sin and Creation in Eriugena," in *Johannes Scottus Eriugena: Eriugena and Creation*, ed. W. Otten and M. I. Allen (Turnhout, Belgium: Brepols, 2014), 240.

45. Duclow, 235–61.
46. Honorius Augustodunensis, *Clavis physicae, critical edition of the first part (§§ 1–315)*, ed. Paolo Lucentini (Rome: Edizioni di Storia e Letteratura, 1974), 49–53; Dyan Elliott, "Rubber Soul: Theology, Hagiography, and the Spirit World of the High Middle Ages," in *From Beasts to Souls: Gender and Embodiment in Medieval Europe*, ed. E. Jane Burns and Peggy McCracken (Notre Dame, IN: University of Notre Dame Press, 2013), 97–98; Caroline Walker Bynum, *The Resurrection of the Body in Western Christianity, 200–1336* (New York: Columbia University Press, 1995), 147.
47. Constance Brittain Bouchard, *"Every Valley Shall Be Exalted": The Discourse of Opposites in Twelfth-Century Thought* (Ithaca, NY: Cornell University Press, 2003), 126; Guibert of Nogent, *Moralium in Genesim* I, in Migne, *Patrologia Latina* (hereafter PL) 156: 57: "Primo in homine quaedam fuit identitas, sed ex peccati poena accidit demum diversitas, ut in duo divideretur humanitas."

48. See Ryan P. Freeburn, *Hugh of Amiens and the Twelfth-Century Renaissance* (Farnham, UK: Ashgate, 2011), 116–17. On hexaemeral literature, Frank E. Robbins, *The Hexaemeral Literature: A Study of the Greek and Latin Commentaries on Genesis* (Chicago: Chicago University Press, 1912); Willemien Otten, "Reading Creation: Early Medieval Views of Genesis and Plato's *Timaeus*," in *The Creation of Heaven and Earth: Re-Interpretation of Genesis I in the Context of Judaism, Ancient Philosophy, Christianity, and Modern Physics*, ed. George H. van Kooten, Themes in Biblical Narrative 8 (Leiden: Brill, 2005): 225–43.

49. *Biblia Latina cum Glossa Ordinaria: Facsimile Reprint of the Editio Princeps Adolph Rusch of Strassburg 1480/81*, ed. Karlfield Froehlich and Margaret T. Gibson (Turnhout, Belgium: Brepols, 1992), 15: "Rursus ne in uno homine uterque sexus deputaretur sicut quos androgenos vocant pluraliter subiecit fecit eos: quamvis mulier nondum esset a viro divisa sed materialiter praeseminata." The *glossa*'s dates of composition are c. 1080–1130 but it has a complicated history and continued to take shape over subsequent decades. Margaret T. Gibson, "The Place of the *Glossa ordinaria* in Medieval Exegesis," in *Ad litteram: Authoritative Texts and their Medieval Readers*, ed. Mark D. Jordan and Kent Emery, Jr. (Notre Dame, IN: University of Notre Dame Press, 1992), 5–27.

50. Andrew of St. Victor, *Expositionem super Heptateuchum*, ed. Charles Lohr and Rainer Berndt, CCCM 53 (Turnhout, Belgium: Brepols, 1986), I: 21:

> Rursus ne in uno homine uterque sexus putaretur, sicut quos 'androgynos' uocant, pluraliter subiecit: *creauit eos*, quamuis mulier nondum esset a uiro diuisa, sed materialiter praeseminata. Mulier enim per prolepsim hic simul cum uiro dicitur facta, cum non simul in tempore—etsi in praescientia—facta sit, quippe qui de eius costa postea facta fuisse legitur.

51. Peter Comestor, *Scolastica historia: Liber Genesis*, ed. Agneta Sylwan, CCCM 191 (Turnhout, Belgium: Brepols, 2005), 21: "Masculum et feminam creauit eos. Hoc quantum ad corpus tamen dicitur creasse propter animam. Eos autem dicitur pluraliter, ne androgeos, id est hermafroditos, factos putaremus." David Luscombe, "Peter Comestor," in *The Bible in the Medieval World: Essays in Memory of Beryl Smalley*, ed. Katherine Walsh and Diana Wood (Oxford: Blackwell, 1985), 111–2.

52. Bouchard, 124.

53. Flood, 41–2; Van der Lugt, "Pourquoi," 93–97; Steven F. Kruger, *The Spectral Jew: Conversion and Embodiment in Medieval Europe* (Minneapolis: University of Minnesota Press, 2006), 31; Horowitz, 184. Mystical readings of Genesis that dealt with the androgyny of creation also circulated in Jewish kabbalistic texts, particularly in Iberia. See Wolfson, 87–119.

54. Roderici Ximenii de Rada (Rodrigo Jiménez de Rada), *Breviarium historie catholice (I-V)*, ed. Juan Fernández Valverde, CCCM 72A-B (Turnhout, Belgium: Brepols, 1992), A: 23: "quidam dicunt hoc pronomen 'illum' non pro uno set duobus poni quasi collectiue, et ideo bene fit relatio in plurali; uel prius posuit in singulari et postea in plurali ne unus homo hermafroditus, id est, diuisus in uenere siue sexu, putaretur."

55. Petrus Cantor, *Glossae super Genesim: Prologus et Capitula 1–3*, ed. Agneta Sylwan (Gothenburg: Acta Universitatis, 1992), 40–41:

> *Masculum et feminam creavit eos.* Sic construe ut locum habeat ratio, quasi dicat: 'Deus creavit hominem,' non solum unum hominem, sed duos, nec in uno tantum sexu, sed in utroque, quia *masculum et feminam creavit eos*, non androgynos, id est non hermafroditos qui viri et mulieris simul habent instrumentum. Ergo pluraliter dicit, ne putaret homo sodomita posse abuti homine loco mulieris, quasi homo utrumque haberet instrumentum.

Van der Lugt, "Pourquoi," 98–100; "Sex Difference," 106, 116n19. Rolker notes that canon law was not decided on this issue; see "Two Laws," 195–97.

56. *Petri Cantoris Parisiensis Verbum Adbreviatum: Textus Conflatus*, ed. Monique Boutry CCCM 196 (Turnhout, Belgium: Brepols, 2004), 775: "ne crederet eos quis androgeos, preocupans formationem mulieris ait: *Masculum et feminam creauit eos*, quasi non erat consortium uiri ad uirum uel mulieris ad mulierem, sed tantum uiri ad mulierem, et econuerso." See John Boswell's translation in *Christianity, Homosexuality, and Social Tolerance: Gay People in Western Europe from the Beginning of the Christian Era to the Fourteenth Century* (Chicago: University of Chicago, 1980), 375–76n50. Boswell views the passage as a confusion or conflation of intersex ("hermaphroditism") and homosexuality, which was born of ignorance.
57. Boswell, 375–78.
58. *Petri Cantoris Parisiensis Verbum Adbreviatum*, 775: "Si autem in illo instrumento defecerit, nunquam conceditur ei usus reliqui, sed perpetuo continebit, ut sic uicium istud extirpetur et nullatenus agentis et pacientis officium sequens uestigia alternitatis uicii sodomitici adeo detestabilis posse conuenire uni et eidem persone credatur." (Both Boswell and Rolker read *adeo* as possibly meant to be *a Deo*.)
59. Robert Mills, *Seeing Sodomy in the Middle Ages* (Chicago: University of Chicago Press, 2015), 75; Karma Lochrie, *Covert Operations: The Medieval Uses of Secrecy* (Philadelphia: University of Pennsylvania Press, 1999), 191–99; "Presumptive Sodomy and Its Exclusions," *Textual Practice* 13:2 (1999): 295–310. See also Cadden, *Nothing Natural Is Shameful: Sodomy and Science in Late Medieval Europe* (Philadelphia: Pennsylvania University Press, 2013); Bernadette J. Brooten, *Love Between Women: Early Christian Responses to Female Homoeroticism* (Chicago: University of Chicago Press, 1996), 235.
60. Mills, *Seeing Sodomy*, 81–82 and passim.
61. See, for instance, Peter of Poitiers (Petrus Pictaviensis), *Summa de Confessione: Compilatio praesens*, ed. Jean Longère, CCCM 51 (Turnhout, Belgium: Brepols, 1980), 18.
62. Mills points out that sodomites were a distinct category from—and distinctly less acceptable than—intersex people. *Seeing Sodomy*, 107.
63. Van der Lugt, "Pourquoi," 98. Hugo de Sancto Caro, *Hugonis Cardinalis Opera Omnia in Universum Vetus, et Novum Testamentum: Tomi Octo. 1 in Libros Genesis . . .* (Venice: Pezzana, 1703), 3v: "Deus creavit hominem, non solum unum, sed duos, et in duplici sexu, quia masculum, et foeminam creavit, id est, plasmavit, id est, non hermaphroditos, qui viri, et mulieris simul habent instrumentum. Et quod dicitur hic de muliere, praeoccupatio est, quia infra agetur de formatione muleris. Et quod nominat duos sexus divisim, et distincte, vitium sodomiticum damnat."
64. Mark Pegg, *A Most Holy War: The Albigensian Crusade and the Battle for Christendom* (Oxford: Oxford University Press, 2008); R. I. Moore, *The War on Heresy* (Cambridge, MA: Belknap Press, 2012).
65. Dyan Elliott, *Fallen Bodies: Pollution, Sexuality, and Demonology in the Middle Ages* (Philadelphia: University of Pennsylvania Press, 1999), 144–46; see the resonance of the "tunic" language with Origen's remarks on the creation in "Rubber Soul," 93.
66. Bynum, *Resurrection*, 216.
67. Duclow, 257; Bynum, *Resurrection*, 153–54; Elliott, "Rubber Soul," 98–100.
68. Duclow, 257–58.
69. Irven Resnick, "Albert the Great on Nature and the Production of Hermaphrodites: Theoretical and Practical Considerations," *Traditio* 74 (2019): 330; Van der Lugt, "Pourquoi," 100.
70. Thomas Aquinas, *Summa theologiae: Latin text and English translation, Introductions, Notes, Appendices, and Glossaries* (New York, Blackfriars, 1964–81), 13: 60 (pt. 1a, q. 93, art. 4): "Unde *Gen.*, cum dixisset *ad imaginem Dei creavit illum*, scilicet hominem, subdidit, *masculum et feminam creavit eos*; et dixit pluraliter *eos*, ut Augustinus dicit, ne intelligatur in uno individuo uterque sexus fuisse conjunctus."

71. Aquinas, *Summa theologiae*, 13: 164 (pt. 1a, q. 99, art. 2): "Sicut autem ad perfectionem universi pertinent diversi gradus rerum, ita etiam diversitas sexus est ad perfectionem humanae naturae."
72. See, for instance, Augustine, *City of God*, 16.8. On *varietas* and *diversitas* as sources of beauty, see Mary Carruthers, *The Experience of Beauty in the Middle Ages* (Oxford: Oxford University Press, 2013), 135–164.
73. Henricus de Gandavo, *La "Lectura ordinaria super sacram scripturam" attribuée à Henri de Gand*, ed. Raymond Macken (Louvain, Belgium: Éditions universitaires de Louvain, 1972), 167: "Rursus ne credatur Deus sexus in homine creasse permixtos in uno homine hermaphrodito, sed in diversis, divisis, et distinctis, addit illud quod dicit: *eos*." See also his comments on Genesis 2:18 (207).
74. Jerome, *Against Jovinianus*, in *Nicene and Post-Nicene Fathers, Vol. 6: Jerome: Letters and Selected Works*, ed. Philip Schaff and Henry Wace (New York: Charles Scribner's Sons, 1912), 1.16 (360); John M. Fyler, *Language and the Declining World in Chaucer, Dante, and Jean de Meun* (Cambridge: Cambridge University Press, 2007), 8.
75. Bynum, *Resurrection*, passim.
76. Petrey, passim; Irina Metzler, *Disability in Medieval Europe: Thinking about Physical Impairment During the High Middle Ages, c. 1100–1400* (London: Routledge, 2006), 55–64.
77. Vogt, 172–87; Joyce E. Salisbury, "The Latin Doctors of the Church on Sexuality," *Journal of Medieval History* 12 (1986): 280; Bynum, *Jesus as Mother: Studies in the Spirituality of the High Middle Ages* (Berkeley: University of California Press, 1982), 138–39.
78. Paul, of course, tempered this statement with pronouncements on women's inferiority in 1 Cor. 11:7–8. Elliott, "Rubber Soul," 91–93; Petrey, 20; for Origen, see Bynum, *Resurrection*, 67; for Gregory of Nyssa, 82–91.
79. Cohen, *Be Fertile*, 238; Brown, 293–94.
80. Bynum, *Resurrection*, 142–46.
81. John Scottus Eriugena, *Periphyseon: Liber Quintus*, ed. Jeauneu, CCCM 165 (Turnhout, Belgium: Brepols, 2003), 49–51:

    Resurgens quippe nullum sexum habuit. Quamuis enim in ipso sexu (masculi uidelicet), in quo ex uirgine natus et inter homines usque ad passionem conuersatus, post resurrectionem discipulis suis ad confirmandam illorum fidem apparuit . . . nulli fidelium licet credere aut ullo modo cogitare ipsum post resurrectionem ullo sexu detineri. In Christo enim Iesu "neque masculus est neque femina," sed solum uerum et totum hominem (corpus dico et animam et intellectum) absque ullo sexu uel aliqua comprehensibili forma. . . . Humanitas siquidem Christi unum cum deitate facta nullo loco continetur, nullo tempore mouetur, nulla forma seu sexu circumscribitur, quia super haec omnia exaltata est. . . . Et quod in se ipso particulariter perfecit, generaliter resurrectionis tempore in tota humana natura perfecturus est.

    English trans. in *Periphyseon: On the Division of Nature*, trans. Myra L. Uhlfelder (Indianapolis, IN: Bobbs-Merrill Company, Inc., 1976), 296–97.
82. Eriugena, *Liber Quintus*, 52: "Adunauit enim hominem, ipsam secundum masculum et feminam differentiam mystice in spiritum auferens, et proprietatibus quae per passiones sunt in ambobus liberam naturae rationem constituens." English trans., 298.
83. Bynum, *Resurrection*, 37; Petrey, passim.
84. Otto of Freising, *Chronica sive historia de duabus civitatibus*, ed. Adolf Hofmeister, Scriptores rerum Germanicarum in usum scholarum ex Monumentis Germaniae Historicis separatim editi (Hanover: Hahn, 1912), 408: "nec in sexu femineo resurrecturas feminas credunt, sed in virili omnes, quoniam Deus solum hominem fecit ex limo, feminam ex viro. Sed mihi melius sapere videntur, qui utrumque sexum resurrecturum esse non dubitant." English trans. in Otto of Freising, *The Two Cities: A Chronicle of Universal History to the Year 1146 A.D.* Ed. and trans. Charles Christopher Mierow (New York: Columbia University Press, 2002), 469.

1. THE PERFECT SEXES OF PARADISE 221

85. Hofmeister, 407: "ad pristinam vitae substantiam indubitanter redire."
86. Hofmeister, 409: "Ceterum de ermafroditis, bicipitibus, quos naturae error vel male coniunxit vel male divisit."
87. Hofmeister, 408.
88. Hofmeister, 408 (paraphrasing Augustine, *City of God*, 1060-61):

    Corporibus ergo illis vitia detrahentur, natura servabitur. . . . Ubi autem non est partium congruentia, aut ideo offendit, quia pravum est, aut ideo, quia parum, aut ideo, quia nimium. Proinde nulla erit deformitas, quam facit incongruentia partium, ubi et quae prava sunt corrigentur, et quod minus est quam decet, unde creator novit, inde subplebitur, et quod plus est quam decet, materiae servata integritate detrahetur.

    English trans., 469-71. For Augustine, see John Block Friedman, *The Monstrous Races in Medieval Art and Thought* (Cambridge, MA: Harvard University Press, 1981), 121.
89. Hofmeister, 408; Metzler, *Disability*, 57-58.
90. Bynum, 255-56n108; Metzler, *Disability*, 59-64.
91. Albert the Great (Albertus Magnus), *De resurrectione*, in vol. 26 of *Opera omnia*, ed. Wilhelm Kübel et al. (Münster: Aschendorff, 1956), tr. 3, q. 1, sol. (305): "Dicimus, quod resurrectio communi duo corrigit in natura, scilicet errorem et defectum, in monstruositate membrorum, defectum in statura corporis diminuta." Resnick, "Hermaphrodites," 323. See also his "Conjoined Twins, Medieval Biology, and Evolving Reflection on Individual Identity," *Viator* 44:2 (2013): 343-68.
92. Deborah Markow, "The Iconography of the Soul in Medieval Art," PhD diss., New York University, 1983, 114-20.
93. Adam S. Cohen and Anne Derbes, "Bernward and Eve at Hildesheim," *Gesta* 40:1 (2001): 21-22. On the *Bible moralisée* from Paris c. 1220-25, Vienna Österreichische Nationalbibliothek, cod. 2554, fol. 2r, see Mills, *Seeing Sodomy*, 32.
94. See chapter 6 on the visual tradition of the *Aurora consurgens*.
95. As the scholar Martha Vicinus has advised, when dealing with subaltern subjects, we sometimes must prioritize what is unseen and unsaid. Vicinus, "Lesbian History: All Theory and No Facts or All Facts and No Theory?" *Radical History Review* 60 (1994): 58; Bynum makes a similar argument in *Resurrection*, 7-8.
96. Fyler, 8, 12, and passim.
97. Boyarin, "Paul and the Genealogy of Gender," 11-12; MacDonald, "Corinthian Veils," 276-92.
98. Meeks, 176 and passim; Martin, 84-86. Moreover, for medieval thinkers, diversity did not necessarily mean egalitarianism. Differences were often ranked, for instance, as in the well-known model of the "three orders." Michael Uebel, *Ecstatic Transformation: On the Uses of Alterity in the Middle Ages* (New York: Palgrave, 2005), 16-17; George Duby, *The Three Orders: Feudal Society Imagined* (Chicago: University of Chicago Press, 1982).
99. Martin, 84-86; Petrey, 11-12.
100. Elizabeth A. Clark, "Ideology, History, and the Construction of 'Woman' in Late Ancient Christianity," *Journal of Early Christian Studies* 2:2 (1994): 160. See also Mathew Kuefler's remarks in *The Manly Eunuch: Masculinity, Gender Ambiguity, and Christian Ideology in Late Antiquity* (Chicago: University of Chicago Press, 2001), 11-12.
101. Among many examples, Judith Butler, "Performative Acts and Gender Constitution: An Essay in Phenomenology and Feminist Theory," *Theatre Journal* 40:4 (1988): 528; Mel Y. Chen, *Animacies: Biopolitics, Racial Mattering, and Queer Affect* (Durham, NC: Duke University Press, 2012); C. Riley Snorton and Jin Haritaworn, "Trans Necropolitics: A Transnational Reflection on Violence, Death, and the Trans of Color Afterlife," in *The Transgender Studies Reader 2*, ed. Susan Stryker and Aren Z. Aizura (New York: Routledge, 2013), 66-76; C. Riley Snorton, *Black on Both Sides: A Racial History of Trans Identity* (Minneapolis: University of Minnesota Press, 2017).

2. THE MONSTROUS RACES: MAPPING THE BORDERS OF SEX

1. For the map, Scott Westrem, *The Hereford Map: A Transcription and Translation of the Legends with Commentary* (Turnhout, Belgium: Brepols, 2001); Marcia Kupfer, *Art and Optics in the Hereford Map: An English Mappa Mundi c. 1300* (New Haven, CT: Yale University Press, 2016); Naomi Reed Kline, *Maps of Medieval Thought: The Hereford Paradigm* (Woodbridge, UK: Boydell & Brewer, 2001); P. D.A. Harvey, *Mappa Mundi: The Hereford World Map* (Toronto: University of Toronto Press, 1996); P. D. A. Harvey, ed., *The Hereford World Map: Medieval World Maps and Their Context* (London: British Library, 2006). For medieval maps in general, Evelyn Edson, *The World Map, 1300–1492: The Persistence of Tradition and Transformation* (Baltimore, MD: Johns Hopkins University Press, 2007); David Woodward, "Medieval *Mappaemundi*," in *The History of Cartography, I: Cartography in Prehistoric, Ancient, and Medieval Europe and the Mediterranean*, ed. J. B. Harley and David Woodward (Chicago: University of Chicago Press, 1982), 286–370. Dan Terkla has recently suggested a slightly later date for the map (after 1303), given its inclusion of the *triregnum* tiara. I thank Asa Mittman for bringing this to my attention via personal correspondence.
2. "Gens uterque sexus innaturales multimodis modis." South Side of the Nile River, Hereford Map. See Kline, 143, 151. I modify her translation slightly. Westrem translates *uterque* as "either" sex, 379.
3. For Pliny, see Friedman, *The Monstrous Races*, 5–25; Lisa Verner, *The Epistemology of the Monstrous in the Middle Ages* (New York: Routledge, 2005), 12–21; for monsters and the Hereford map, Kline, 146–64; for other medieval teratological sources, see Karl Steel, "Centaurs, Satyrs, and Cynocephali: Medieval Scholarly Teratology and the Question of the Human," in Asa S. Mittman and Peter Dendle, eds., *The Ashgate Research Companion to Monsters and the Monstrous* (Aldershot, UK: Ashgate, 2013), 259–61.
4. For wonders as entertainment, see Lorraine Daston and Katharine Park. *Wonders and the Order of Nature, 1150–1750* (New York: Zone, 2001), 33–34 and passim.
5. Asa S. Mittman, *Maps and Monsters in Medieval England* (New York: Routledge, 2006), 27–31; Edson, 11, 30–31.
6. This characterization emerged from a conversation with María Bullón-Fernández. I thank her for her assistance with this image.
7. I am indebted to intersectionality, assemblage theory, and queer of color critique in my analysis of intersecting vectors of marginalization. I do not engage with these theories explicitly in the body of this chapter, however, because I cannot attend to all their nuances and to the complexity of the debates surrounding them. On these theories, among many sources, see Jennifer C. Nash, *Black Feminism Reimagined: After Intersectionality* (Durham, NC: Duke University Press, 2019); Jasbir K. Puar, *Terrorist Assemblages: Homonationalism in Queer Times* (Durham, NC: Duke University Press, 2007); Kimberlé Crenshaw, "Demarginalizing the Intersection of Race and Sex: A Black Feminist Critique of Antidiscrimination Doctrine, Feminist Theory and Antiracist Politics," *The University of Chicago Legal Forum* 140 (1989): 139–67; Sumi Cho, Kimberlé Williams Crenshaw, and Leslie McCall, "Toward a Field of Intersectionality Studies: Theory, Applications, and Praxis," *Signs* 38:4, *Intersectionality: Theorizing Power, Empowering Theory* (2013): 785–810.
8. The literature in critical animal studies, multispecies theory, and other related fields is vast. See, for instance, Jacques Derrida, *The Animal that Therefore I Am* (New York: Fordham University Press, 2008 [orig. pub. 1999]); Donna J. Haraway, *When Species Meet* (Minneapolis: University of Minnesota Press, 2008); *The Companion Species Manifesto: Dogs, People, and Significant Otherness* (Chicago: Prickly Paradigm, 2003); Cary Wolfe, ed., *Zoontologies: The Question of the Animal* (Minneapolis: University of Minnesota Press, 2003), and *Animal Rites: American Culture, the Discourse of Species, and Posthumanist Theory* (Chicago: University of Chicago Press, 2003); H. Peter Steeves, ed., *Animal Others: On Ethics, Ontology and Animal Life* (Albany: State University of New York

Press, 1999); and the essays collected in Julie Livingston and Jasbir Puar, eds., *Interspecies*, special issue of *Social Text* 29:1 (2011); and Lori Gruen and Kari Weil, eds., *Animal Others*, special issue of *Hypatia* 27:3 (2012). Some scholars point out that the perceived division between humans and other organisms is for the most part a western phenomenon; for instance, Graham Harvey, "Animals, Animists, and Academics," *Zygon* 41:1 (2006): 9–19.

9. Myra J. Hird, "Animal Trans," in *Queering the Non/Human*, ed. Noreen Giffney and Myra J. Hird (Aldershot, UK: Ashgate, 2008), 227–47; Mel Y. Chen, *Animacies: Biopolitics, Racial Mattering, and Queer Affect* (Durham, NC: Duke University Press, 2012). See also the works in the section entitled "Transsexing Humanimality," in *TSR 2*, 145–88; Eva Hayward and Jami Weinstein, eds., *Tranimalities*; Dana Luciano and Mel Y. Chen, *Queer Inhumanisms*, special issue of *GLQ: A Journal of Gay and Lesbian Studies* 21:2–3 (2015); Nikki Sullivan and Samantha Murray, eds., *Somatechnics: Queering the Technologisation of Bodies* (Aldershot, UK: Ashgate, 2009); J. Halberstam and I. Livingston, *Posthuman Bodies* (Bloomington: Indiana University Press, 1995), among others.

10. Friedman, *Monstrous Races*, 1. On the difficulty of defining monstrosity, see Verner, 1–10; Asa S. Mittman, "Introduction: The Impact of Monsters and Monster Studies," in Asa S. Mittman and Peter Dendle, eds., *The Ashgate Research Companion to Monsters and the Monstrous* (Aldershot, UK: Ashgate, 2013), 7–8. In modern contexts, Susan Stryker, Anson Koch-Rein, and other transgender studies scholars have recast the word "monster" in an effort to plumb its history and to dispel its "ability to harm." Susan Stryker, "My Words to Victor Frankenstein above the Village of Chamounix: Performing Transgender Rage," *GLQ: A Journal of Lesbian and Gay Studies* 1:3 (1994): 237–54, quotation at 240; Anson Koch-Rein, "Monster," in *TSQ: Transgender Studies Quarterly* 1–2 (2014): 134–35; Max Strassfeld, "Transing Religious Studies," *Journal of Feminist Studies in Religion* 34:1 (2018): 44–49. Yet Jinthana Haritaworn asks "How do inhuman 'orientations' intersect with different proclivities toward life and death? For whom might identifying with the nonhuman be too risky a move?" See "Decolonizing the Non/Human," *GLQ: A Journal of Lesbian and Gay Studies* 21:2–3 (2015): 212.

11. Friedman, *Monstrous Races*; Williams, *Deformed Discourse*; Jeffrey Jerome Cohen, ed., *Monster Theory: Reading Culture* (Minneapolis: University of Minnesota, 1996); *Of Giants: Sex, Monsters, and the Middle Ages* (Minneapolis and London: University of Minnesota Press, 1999); *Hybridity, Identity and Monstrosity in Medieval Britain: On Difficult Middles* (New York: Palgrave, 2006); Bettina Bildhauer and Robert Mills, eds., *The Monstrous Middle Ages* (Toronto: University of Toronto Press, 2003); Andy Orchard, *Pride and Prodigies: Studies in the Monsters of the Beowulf-Manuscript* (Cambridge: Boydell & Brewer, 1995); as well as Mittman's numerous works on monstrosity, including, most recently, Mittman and Sherry C. M. Lindquist, *Medieval Monsters: Terrors, Aliens, Wonders* (New York: Morgan Library and Museum, 2018).

12. Jeffery Jerome Cohen, "Monster Culture (Seven Theses)" in *Monster Theory*, 4.

13. Dana M. Oswald, *Monsters, Gender and Sexuality in Medieval English Literature* (Cambridge: Boydell & Brewer, 2010), 3; "Monstrous Gender: Geographies of Ambiguity," in in Asa S. Mittman and Peter Dendle, eds., *The Ashgate Research Companion to Monsters and the Monstrous* (Aldershot, UK: Ashgate, 2013), 343.

14. *Mandeville's Travels*, ed. P. Hamelius, Early English Text Society 153 (Milwood, NY: Kraus Reprint, 1987), 30: "a monstre is a þing difformed aȝen kynde bothe of man or of best or of ony þing elles & þat is cleped a Monstre." Oswald, *Monsters, Gender, and Sexuality*, 2.

15. Verner, 5–6.

16. Augustine, *De civitate Dei*, 16.8 (II:137): "Quapropter ut istam quaestionem pedetemtim cauteque concludam: aut illa, quae talia de quibusdam gentibus scripta sunt, omnino nulla sunt; aut si sunt, homines non sunt; aut ex Adam sunt, si homines sunt." Van der Lugt, "L'humanité," 2–4.

17. Friedman, *Monstrous Races*, 92.

18. Van der Lugt, "L'humanité," 5–6; Friedman, *Monstrous Races*, 188–89.

19. Thomas of Cantimpré, ed. Helmut Boese, *Liber de natura rerum* (Berlin: Walter de Gruyter, 1973), 97: *Animalibus vero monstruosis animam inesse non credimus*. Karl Steel, *How to Make a Human: Animals and Violence in the Middle Ages* (Columbus: Ohio State University Press, 2011), 52–60. See also Brigitte Resl, ed., *A Cultural History of Animals in the Medieval Age*, vol. 2 of *A Cultural History of Animals*, ed. Linda Kalof and Brigitte Resl (Oxford: Berg, 2007).
20. Steel, "Centaurs," 266.
21. In his *Image of the World*, Honorius of Autun noted that some monsters should be accepted as humans, while others were more rightly called beasts. Steel, "Centaurs," 266; *How to Make a Human*, 44–60; Williams, 126–27; Dorothy Yamamoto, *The Boundaries of the Human in Medieval English Literature*. Oxford: Oxford University Press, 2000), 8.
22. Katharine Park, "Birth and Death," in Linda Kalof, ed., *A Cultural History of the Human Body in the Medieval Age*, vol. 2 of *A Cultural History of the Human Body*, ed. Linda Kalof and William Bynum (Oxford: Berg, 2010), 18–19; Luke E. Demaitre and Anthony A. Travill, "Human Embryology and Development in the Works of Albertus Magnus," in *Albertus Magnus and the Sciences: Commemorative Essays 1980*, ed. James A. Weisheipl (Toronto: Pontifical Institute of Mediaeval Studies, 1980), 424.
23. Friedman, *Monstrous Races*, 178–196.
24. Thomas of Cantimpré, "Thomas of Cantimpré, *De naturis rerum*: Prologue, Book III, Book XIX," ed. John Block Friedman, in *Cahiers d'Etudes Medievales* 2: *La Science de la Nature* (Montreal: Vrin, 1974), 108–9; Monica H. Green, *Making Women's Medicine Masculine: The Rise of Male Authority in Pre-Modern Gynaecology* (Oxford: Oxford University Press, 2008), 79, 149.
25. On the genre, see Michel de Boüard, "Encyclopédies médiévales: Sur la 'connaissance de la nature et du monde' au moyen âge," *Revue des questions historiques* 112 (1930): 258–304; Peter Murray Jones, "The Medieval Encyclopedia: Science and Practice," in *The Cambridge Illuminations: Ten Centuries of Book Production in the Medieval West*, ed. Paul Binski and Stella Panayotova (London: Harvey Miller, 2005), 297–303.
26. Verner, 14–15.
27. Steel, *How to Make a Human*, 53.
28. Lynn T. Ramey, *Black Legacies: Race and the European Middle Ages* (Gainesville: University Press of Florida, 2014), 97. On pygmies, see Friedman, *Monstrous Races*, 190–96; Shirin A. Khanmohamadi, *In Light of Another's Word: European Ethnography in the Middle Ages* (Philadelphia: University of Pennsylvania Press, 2014), 22–25; Van der Lugt, "L'humanité," 8–10.
29. Steel, "Centaurs," 267.
30. Khanmohamadi, 20.
31. Asa S. Mittman and Susan M. Kim, "Monsters and the Exotic in Early Medieval England," *Literature Compass* 6:2 (2009): 332–48, at 344; for monstrous attributes, see Khanmohamadi, 21–22.
32. Cohen, *Of Giants*, xiv.
33. Verner, 5.
34. Jeffrey Jerome Cohen makes this point about medieval giants. "Introduction: Midcolonial," to *The Postcolonial Middle Ages*, ed. Cohen (New York: St. Martin's, 2000), 5; *Of Giants*, xi-xx.
35. Mittman, *Maps and Monsters*, 105–6.
36. Michael Camille, "Prophets, Canons, and Promising Monsters," *Art Bulletin* 78:2 (1996): 198–201; Michael Uebel, "Unthinking the Monster: Twelfth-Century Responses to Saracen Alterity," in *Monster Theory*, 266.
37. Steel, "Centaurs," 263.
38. Kathy Lavezzo, *Angels on the Edge of the World: Geography, Literature, and English Community, 1000–1534* (Ithaca, NY: Cornell, 2006), 14.
39. Alfons Hilka, ed., "Eine alt-französische moralisierende Bearbeitung des *Liber de Monstruosis Hominibus Orientis* aus Thomas von Cantimpré. *De Naturis Rerum*," in *Abhandlungen der*

Gesellschaft der Wissenschaften zu Gottingen: Philologisch-Historische Klasse 7 (Berlin: Weidmannsche Buchhandlung, 1933), 23: "Me covient pener et retraire/Chose qui tourt a examplaire,/Selonc la nature des gens/Qui ore sont, dont biaus et gens/I a (d)aucuns en ces parties;/Mais es estranges ne sont mies/Itel com il sont ci aval./Sachiés de voir: Oriental/Sont tout autre que nos ne soumes[.]" I slightly alter the translation in Friedman, *Monstrous Races*, 130, and Debra Higgs Strickland, *Saracens, Demons, and Jews: Making Monsters in Medieval Art*. (Princeton: Princeton University Press, 2003), 7.

40. As Dana Oswald observes, the "gendered bodies of the monstrous both disrupt and reaffirm the social hierarchy—that is, monsters reveal and enforce the standards for appropriate human appearance and behavior. They demonstrate the boundaries beyond which humans should not proceed." *Monsters, Gender, and Sexuality*, 30.

41. See Mary Baine Campbell, *The Witness and the Other World: Exotic European Travel Writing, 400–1600* (Ithaca, NY: Cornell University Press, 1988); Uebel, *Ecstatic Transformation*; Suzanne Conklin Akbari, *Idols in the East: European Representations of Islam and the Orient, 1100–1450* (Ithaca, NY: Cornell University Press, 2009), 280; Strickland, *Saracens*, 20. This work is quite nuanced, admitting to middle areas and ambiguous contacts between regions.

42. For what constituted the East, see Mittman and Kim, "Monsters and the Exotic," 335–37; for the interrelation of binary, ternary, and quaternary divisions, see Suzanne Conklin Akbari, "From Due East to True North: Orientalism and Orientation," in *The Postcolonial Middle Ages*, 19–34, and *Idols*, 20–66.

43. Uebel, *Ecstatic Transformation*, 5.

44. Uebel, "Unthinking the Monster," 264–91; Albrecht Classen, "Introduction: The Self, the Other, and Everything in Between: Xenological Phenomenology of the Middle Ages," in *Meeting the Foreign in the Middle Ages*, ed. Albrecht Classen (New York: Routledge, 2002), xi–lxxiii (quotation at xv); Sharon Kinoshita, *Medieval Boundaries: Rethinking Difference in Old French Literature* (Philadelphia: University of Pennsylvania Press, 2006); Kim M. Phillips, *Before Orientalism: Asian Peoples and Cultures in European Travel Writing, 1245–1510* (Philadelphia: University of Pennsylvania Press, 2014); see also Paul Freedman, "The Medieval Other: The Middle Ages as Other," in *Marvels, Monsters, and Miracles: Studies in the Medieval and Early Modern Imaginations*, ed. Timothy S. Jones and David A. Sprunger (Kalamazoo, MI: Medieval Institute Publications, 2002), 1–24.

45. There were exceptions to this iconographic strategy; see, for instance, The Hague, KB, KA 16, fol. 43r (fourteenth century); The Hague, KB 76 E 4, fol. 6r (late fifteenth century).

46. Pliny the Elder, *Natural History*, Vol. II, Books 3–7, ed. H Rackham (Cambridge, MA: Harvard University Press, 1942), VII, 2, 15–17 (p. 516): "Supra Nasamonas confinesque illis Machlyas Androgynos esse utriusque naturae inter se vicibus coeuntes Calliphanes tradit. Aristoteles adicit dextram mammam is virilem, laevam muliebrem esse." For Pliny and his legacy, see Verner, 11–21. For the sources of the Hereford Map, see Evelyn Edson, 24–29; Westrem, xxvii–xxxvii.

47. Isidore of Seville, *Etymologiarum*, vol. II, bk. XI, iii, 11 (translated in Barney et al., 244).

48. *Liber monstrorum*, in Orchard, 271: "Et in his incredibilibus quoddam genus utriusque sexus describitur, qui dexteram mammam uirilem pro exercendis operibus et ad fetus nutriendo sinistram habent muliebrem. Quos inter se uicibus coeundo ferunt alternis generare."

49. The text survives in three famous English illustrated manuscripts; on them, Asa S. Mittman and Susan M. Kim, eds., *Inconceivable Beasts: The Wonders of the East in the Beowulf Manuscript* (Tempe, AZ: ACMRS, 2013); A. J. Ford, *Marvel and Artefact: The "Wonders of the East" in Its Manuscript Contexts* (Leiden: Brill, 2016); Orchard; Oswald, *Monsters, Gender, and Sexuality*, 27–65; Mittman, *Maps and Monsters*, 67–81.

50. University of Oxford, Bodleian Library, MS Bodley 614, fol. 50: "Sunt homines ermafrodite nuncupati eo, quod eis uterque sexus appareat.... Hii dexteram mammam virilem sinistram muliebrem habentes. Vicissim coeundo et gignunt et pariunt." See also Orchard, 22.

51. Mittman, "Are the 'Monstrous Races' Races?" *postmedieval: a journal of medieval cultural studies* 6:1 (2015): 41.
52. Robert Bartlett, *The Natural and the Supernatural in the Middle Ages* (Cambridge: Cambridge University Press, 2008), 99–100; Friedman, *Monstrous Races*, 189.
53. The map was painted in 1447–55. Chet Van Duzer, "A Neglected Type of Medieval *Mappamundi* and its Re-Imaging in the *Mare Historiarum* (BNF MS Lat. 4915, Fol. 26v)," *Viator* 43: 2 (2012): 277–301.
54. Akbari, *Idols*, 48, 140–54 and passim; Strickland, *Saracens*, 30. The twelfth-century *Summa parisiensis*, for instance, noted that hotter regions produced "many" hermaphrodites. *The Summa Parisiensis on the Decretum Gratiani*, ed. Terence P. McLaughlin (Toronto: Pontifical Institute of Mediaeval Studies, 1952), 126. Climate-related traits were described as mutable or heritable; see Francisco Bethencourt, *Racisms from the Crusades to the Twentieth Century* (Princeton, NJ: Princeton University Press, 2015), 13–14; Ziegler, "Physiognomy, Science, and Proto-Racism, 1200–1500," in *The Origins of Racism in the West*, ed. Miriam Eliav-Feldon, Benjamin Isaac, and Joseph Ziegler (Cambridge: Cambridge University Press, 2008), 195–98.
55. Van Duzer, 285.
56. On this manuscript, see Rosemary Tzanaki, *Mandeville's Medieval Audiences: Studies in the Reception of the Book of Sir John Mandeville (1371–1550)* (London: Ashgate, 2003), 27, 125, 252 and passim; Henri Omont, ed., *Livre des merveilles: Reproduction des 265 miniatures du manuscrit français 2810 de la Bibliothèque Nationale*, 2 vols. (Paris: Berthaud Frères, 1907).
57. Friedman, *Monstrous Races*, 131–2.
58. On nonbinary sex in Mandeville, see Bychowski, "Isle," 169–76; for the manuscript, see Friedman, *Monstrous Races*, 154; Bibliothèque nationale de France, Département des Manuscrits, accessed May 30, 2019, at https://archivesetmanuscrits.bnf.fr/ark:/12148/cc77943x.
59. Robert Pogue Harrison, *Forests: The Shadow of Civilization* (Chicago: University of Chicago Press, 1992); see also Friedman, *Monstrous Races*, 163–77.
60. Metzler, "Hermaphrodites," 32; Omont, II:6, 164. The figures in this image are indistinguishable from portraits of Adam and Eve, pictured as submerged in a lake of tears on a neighboring folio page (193r). Adam and Eve share with the nonbinary figures the same facial features and hairstyles, and they are attended by the same three animals, whose heads emerge from a similar landscape.
61. Sharae Deckard, *Paradise Discourse, Imperialism, and Globalization: Exploiting Eden* (New York: Routledge, 2010), 6; Alessandro Scafi, *Maps of Paradise* (Chicago: University of Chicago Press, 2013), 41–76. The Hereford Map also placed Eden near the marginal monsters of the East. Kline, 150.
62. Friedman, *Monstrous Races*, 31. On nakedness and monstrosity, see Mittman and Kim, *Inconceivable Beasts*, 103–36.
63. Bildhauer and Mills, "Introduction," in *Monstrous Middle Ages*, 4. For a parallel reading of a cynocephalus image in the *Livre des merveilles*, see Daston and Park, *Wonders*, 35–38.
64. Ajootian, 220–31. See also Ruth Evans, "The Intersex Look," *postmedieval: a journal of medieval cultural studies* 9:2 (2018): 117–119.
65. Ajootian, 231–35; see also variations on this genre that depicted an encounter between a nonbinary-sexed figure and a sexually predatory satyr. Katharine T. Von Stackelberg, "Garden Hybrids: Hermaphrodite Images in the Roman House," *Classical Antiquity* 33:2 (2014): 395–426.
66. On Janus, see Louise Adams Holland, *Janus and the Bridge* (Rome: Publications of the American Academy in Rome, 1961); Bessie Rebecca Burchett, "Janus in Roman Life and Cult: A Study in Roman Religions," PhD thesis, University of Pennsylvania. Menasha, WI: George Banta Publishing Company, 1918; Simona Cohen, *Transformations of Time and Temporality in Medieval and Renaissance Art* (Leiden: Brill, 2014), 35–37. Rabun Taylor, "Watching the Skies: Janus, Auspication, and the Shrine in the Roman Forum," *Memoirs of the American Academy in Rome* 45 (2000): 1–40. Taylor points out that Janus in the ancient world signaled not a binary nature but a "single divine faculty."

67. For Janus in the Middle Ages, see Jane Chance, *Medieval Mythography*, 142–44, and 570–71n46; Jill Meredith, "The *Bifrons* Relief of Janus: The Implications of the Antique in the Court Art of Emperor Frederick II," in *The Brummer Collection of Medieval Art*, ed. Carol Bruzelius with Jill Meredith (Durham, NC: Duke University Press, 1991), 102; Manuel Antonio Castiñeiras, "Gennaio e Giano bifronte: dalle 'anni januae' all'interno domestico (secoli XII–XIII)," *Prospettiva* 66 (1992): 53–63; Charles Boutell, "Symbols of the Seasons and Months Represented in Early Art," *Art Journal*, new series 3 (1877): 233–36; James Carson Webster, *The Labors of the Months in Antique and Mediaeval Art: To the End of the Twelfth Century* (Evanston, IL: Northwestern University, 1938).
68. Quoted in Stefania Gerevini, "Written in Stone: Civic Memory and Monumental Writing in the Cathedral of San Lorenzo in Genoa," in *Viewing Inscriptions in the Late Antique and Medieval World*, ed. Antony Eastmond (Cambridge: Cambridge University Press, 2015), 216.
69. Jane Chance, *The Mythographic Chaucer: The Fabulation of Sexual Politics* (Minneapolis: University of Minnesota Press, 1995), 240–3; V. A. Kolve, *Telling Images: Chaucer and the Imagery of Narrative II* (Stanford, CA: Stanford University Press, 2009), 97–104.
70. Chance, *Mythographic Chaucer*, 232–43, 344n31.
71. Kline, 150–51.
72. Bychowski, "Isle," 168–69; see also Uebel, "Unthinking the Monster," 267.
73. Among many examples, Peter Stallybrass and Allon White, *The Politics and Poetics of Transgression* (Ithaca, NY: Cornell University Press, 1986), 20, 200; Yamamoto, 4. Such scholars often draw on the work of Michel Foucault.
74. Uebel, "Unthinking the Monster," 266.
75. *Etymologiarum*, vol. II, bk. XI, iii, 7–9 (translated in Barney et al., 244). For various categories of monsters, see Verner, 3; Bildhauer and Mills, "Introduction," 14–15; Williams, 107–215.
76. Some modern intersex communities embrace a disability model, while others reject it. For medieval disability and definitions of monstrosity, see Eliza Buhrer, " 'If in Other Respects He Appears to Be Effectively Human': Defining Monstrosity in Medieval English Law," in *Monstrosity, Disability, and the Posthuman in the Medieval and Early Modern World*, ed. Richard H. Godden and Asa Simon Mittman (Palgrave, 2019), 63–83.
77. Resnick, "Conjoined Twins," 343–68. *Etymologiarum*, vol. II, bk. XI, iii, 3–4 (translated in Barney et al., 244). Authors described the functions of monsters variously: see Van der Lugt, "L'humanité," 2; Verner, 3, 36–39; Metzler, *Disability*, 89.
78. Daston and Park, *Wonders*, 48–66.
79. Van der Lugt, "L'humanité," 2–23; Buhrer, 63–83; Friedman, *Monstrous Races*, 178–83; Steel, "Centaurs," 267; "How to Make a Human," *Exemplaria* 20:1 (2008): 3–27, at 11. For parallel arguments in Jewish contexts, see David I. Shyovitz, " 'Unearthing the Children of Cain': Between Humans, Animals, and Demons in Medieval Jewish Culture," in *Monsters and Monstrosity in Jewish History: From the Middle Ages to Modernity*, ed. Iris Idelson-Shein and Christian Wiese (London: Bloomsbury, 2019), 157–86, esp. 163.
80. Van der Lugt, "L'humanité"; Daston and Park, *Wonders*, 57.
81. Opinions varied on the significance of size; see Van der Lugt, "L'humanité," 9–23; on legal arguments, Rolker, "Two Laws," 183, 188; Buhrer, 63–83.
82. I borrow the "double place" phrase from Akbari, who uses it to characterize the ambivalent position of Jews. See *Idols*, 139. For limits, see chapters 4 and 5.
83. Brian Stock, *Myth and Science in the Twelfth Century: A Study of Bernard Silvester* (Princeton, NJ: Princeton University Press, 1972), 3; Bynum, *Metamorphosis*, 37–75. See also Susan Crane, *Animal Encounters: Contacts and Concepts in Medieval Britain* (Philadelphia: University of Pennsylvania Press, 2012), 89; Susan Kim, "Man-Eating Monsters and Ants as Big as Dogs: The Alienated Language of the Cotton Vitellius A. XV 'Wonders of the East,' " in *Animals and the Symbolic in Mediaeval Art and Literature*, ed. L.A.J.R. Houwen (Groningen, The Netherlands: Egbert Forsten, 1997), 43.

84. Pliny, VII, 3, 34 (528): "Gignuntur et utriusque sexus quos Hermaphroditos vocamus, olim androgynos vocatos et in prodigiis habitos, nunc vero in deliciis." Verner, 20.
85. Augustine, *De civitate Dei*, 16.8 (II:135–36). Kline notes that although Augustine was not specifically cited as a source of the Hereford Map, an Augustinian message pervades the map (and Augustine's image appears on it). Kline, 147.
86. Verner, 2–3; see also Bildhauer and Mills, 9.
87. Verner, 37–39. See also the seventh- or eighth-century *Book of Monsters*, whose author claimed firsthand knowledge of a presumably local gender nonconforming person "of both sexes" (*utriusque sexus*). The author described this individual in precisely the same terms as a distant tribe of nonbinary-sexed peoples (*utriusque sexus*). People of "both sexes" were, for the author, both remote exoticisms and recognizable members of the human community. *Liber monstrorum*, in Orchard, 258: "Me enim quendam hominem in primordio operis utriusque sexus cognouisse testor, qui tamen ipsa facie plus et pectore uirilis quam muliebris apparuit; et uir a nescientibus putabatur, sed muliebria opera dilexit, et ignaros uirorum more meretricis, decipiebat; sed hoc frequenter apud humanum genus contigisse fertur."
88. For high medieval encyclopedias as Augustinian in their approach, see Daston and Park, *Wonders*, 41–49, 175.
89. Jessalynn Bird, "The *Historia Orientalis* of Jacques de Vitry: Visual and Written Commentaries as Evidence of a Text's Audience, Reception, and Utilization," *Essays in Medieval Studies* 20 (2003): 56–74. Jacques de Vitry, *Histoire orientale: Historia orientalis*, ed. Jean Donnadieu (Turnhout, Belgium: Brepols, 2008), 406–410, at 410: "Quidam etiam hermaphroditi seu gemini sexus in partibus Francie a multis visi fuerunt." Elsewhere, in his *Historia occidentalis*, Jacques described individual monsters in the West chiefly in negative terms. See Daston and Park, *Wonders*, 51.
90. Thomas of Cantimpré, 100: "Homines quidam silvestres in partibus orientis capti sunt in silvis, qui postquam inter homines veniebant, manducare renuentes moriebantur vel evadebant. Homines etiam hermofrodite in Francia visi sunt, masculini sexus et feminini." While Thomas placed the wild men in the East, Jacques of Vitry located the same figures in the West ("partibus occidentis") in his *Historia orientalis*, 410. Vincent of Beauvais repeated the anecdote about hermaphrodites in his *Speculum Naturale* in *Speculum quadruplex, sive, Speculum maius: naturale, doctrinale, morale, historiale* (Graz, Austria, 1964–1965), 1: 2394: "Homines etiam Hermaphroditi visi sunt in Francia masculini sexus, et foeminini." Jacob van Maerlant also noted it in his *The Flower of Nature*, or *Der naturen bloeme*, ed. Maurits Gysseling (The Hague: Martinus Nijhoff, 1981), 29: "jnt vran/ kerike eist worden/ mare/ datmen lieden/ heuet ghesien./ die hadden tusschen hare dien/ vorme van wiue ende van manne."
91. James le Palmer, *Omne bonum*, BL Royal MS 6 E VII/1 (Ebrietas-Humanus), fol. 205r-v.
92. Ford, 138–40.
93. For Jerusalem as center, see Edson, 20–21; Suzanne Conklin Akbari, "From Due East to True North," 21.
94. Mittman, *Maps and Monsters*, 32–43.
95. Mittman, *Maps and Monsters*, 43–44, 46; Kim "Man-Eating Monsters," 48–50.
96. Mittman and Kim, "Monsters and the Exotic," 332–48; Mittman, *Maps and Monsters*, 99; Kline, 162–64; Kruger, *Spectral Jew*, 25; Bilhauer and Mills, 8–9.
97. For negative glosses of western monsters, see Daston and Park, *Wonders*, 51; Steel notes that Thomas of Cantimpré appeared eager to exclude all monsters from the category of the human, 54.
98. On paradox, see Caroline Walker Bynum, "Why Paradox? The Contradictions of My Life as a Scholar," *Catholic Historical Review* 98:3 (2012): 435.
99. On the manuscript, Ron Baxter, *Bestiaries and Their Users in the Middle Ages* (Stroud, UK: Sutton Publishing, 1998), 132–141; Ilya Dines, "The Earliest Use of John of Salisbury's *Policraticus*: Third Family Bestiaries," *Viator* 44:1 (2013): 107–118. The makers of the Hereford Map likely relied on

100. Oswald, "Monstrous Gender," 343.
101. Bartholomaeus Anglicus, *De rerum proprietatibus: Frankfurt 1601* (Frankfurt: Minerva, 1964), bk. 18, cap. XLIX (p. 1070). Päivi Pahta, *Medieval Embryology in the Vernacular: The Case of* De spermate (Helsinki: Société Néophilologique, 1998), 75. For Albert on embryology, see chapter 4 below.
102. They generally reflect ancient theories that identified the right side of the body with the male sex and the left side with the female sex; the Hereford Map, with its female side on the right, is an exception. Fridolf Kudlien, "The Seven Cells of the Uterus: The Doctrine and Its Roots," *Bulletin of the History of Medicine* 39 (1965): 417; Cadden, *Meanings*, 33, 198–99.
103. Scott, 1053–75. Scholars have documented how John Money, Joan G. Hampson, and John L. Hampson developed a particularized definition of "gender" as distinct from biological "sex" during the course of their research on intersex during the mid-twentieth century. For Money's work, see Downing et al., *Fuckology*, 215 and passim; Karkazis, *Fixing Sex*, 47–86 and passim.
104. Katherine Park, "Medicine and Natural Philosophy: Naturalistic Traditions," in *The Oxford Handbook of Women and Gender in Medieval Europe*, ed. Judith Bennett and Ruth Karras (Oxford: Oxford University Press, 2013), 84; Ruth Mazo Karras and Tom Linkinen "John/Eleanor Rykener Revisited," in *Founding Feminisms: Essays in Honor of E. Jane Burns*, ed. Laine E. Doggett and Daniel E. O'Sullivan (Cambridge: Boydell & Brewer, 2016), 113.
105. Fausto-Sterling, *Sexing the Body*; Rebecca M. Jordan-Young and Katrina Karkazis, *Testosterone: An Unauthorized Biography* (Cambridge, MA: Harvard University Press, 2019); Judith Butler, *Gender Trouble: Feminism and the Subversion of Identity* (New York: Routledge, 1990). See also Londa Schiebinger, *Nature's Body: Gender in the Making of Modern Science* (New York: Beacon, 1993) and Suzanne Kessler and Wendy McKenna, *Gender: An Ethnomethodological Approach* (New York: John Wiley and Sons, 1978).
106. Butler, *Bodies That Matter: On the Discursive Limits of Sex* (New York: Routledge, 1993), 2–3.
107. On norms and heterosexuality in the Middle Ages, see Lochrie, *Heterosyncrasies*, 1–25; James A. Schultz, "Heterosexuality as a Threat to Medieval Studies," *Journal of the History of Sexuality* 15:1 (2006): 14–29.
108. Gayle Salamon, paraphrasing Maurice Merleau-Ponty, in *Assuming a Body: Transgender and Rhetorics of Materiality* (New York: Columbia University Press, 2010), 50.
109. Jacqueline Murray, "One Flesh, Two Sexes, Three Genders?" in *Gender and Christianity in Medieval Europe: New Perspectives*, ed. Lisa M. Bitel and Felice Lifshitz (Philadelphia: University of Pennsylvania Press, 2008), 34–51.
110. Karras and Linkinen, 113, 121. Murray, "One Flesh," 36, 48–51; Jo Ann McNamara, "Canossa and the Ungendering of the Public Man," in *Render Unto Caesar: The Religious Sphere in World Politics*, ed. Sabrina Petra Ramet and Donald W. Treadgold (Washington, DC: American University Press, 1995), 131–49; "An Unresolved Syllogism," in *Conflicted Identities and Multiple Masculinities: Men in the Medieval West*, ed. Jacqueline Murray (New York: Garland, 1999), 1–24; "Chastity as a Third Gender in the History and Hagiography of Gregory of Tours," in *The World of Gregory of Tours*, ed. Kathleen Mitchell and Ian Wood (Leiden: Brill, 2002), 199–209; Anke Bernau, Ruth Evans, and Sarah Salih, "Introduction: Virginities and Virginity Studies," in *Medieval Virginities*, ed. Anke Bernau, Ruth Evans, and Sarah Salih (Toronto: University of Toronto Press, 2003), 1–13. Mythic hermaphrodites were in some respects comparable to "crossdressers," who transitioned between male and female roles for various reasons. Although crossdressing saints were sometimes praised, crossdressing was also condemned, for instance, by Hildegard of Bingen. Robert Mills, "Visibly Trans? Picturing Saint Eugenia in Medieval Art," *TSQ: Transgender Studies Quarterly* 5:4 (2018): 540–64 at 541. See also Vern L. Bullough, "Transvestism in the Middle Ages," in *Sexual Practices and the*

Medieval Church, ed. Vern L. Bullough and James A. Brundage (Buffalo, NY: Prometheus, 1982), 43–54; Valerie R. Hotchkiss, *Clothes Make the Man: Female Cross Dressing in Medieval Europe* (New York: Garland, 1996).

111. Oswald, "Monstrous Gender," 362. Mathew Kuefler makes a similar argument about eunuchs, who he argues "constantly tested the division between men and women, between the manly and unmanly, and continually revealed that division as an arbitrary and constructed one." *Manly Eunuch*, 36.

112. In monstrous-race discourse, hermaphrodites did not really "change" sex: they exhibited neither "evolution-change," that is, the unfolding or development of an essential self, nor "replacement-change," that is, the substitution of one thing for another. On types of change in the Middle Ages, see Bynum, *Metamorphosis*, esp. 15–36.

113. Cohen, "Monster Culture (Seven Theses)," 3–25.

114. For provenance, see Debra Higgs Strickland, "Edward I, Exodus, and England on the Hereford World Map," *Speculum* (2018): 423. The identity of Richard of Haldingham, the map's attributed creator, remains uncertain. See P. D. A Harvey, *The Hereford Map: Introduction* (London: The Folio Society, 2010), 33; Kupfer, 31–32; Westrem, xxiv.

115. For the relationship between the map and the Crusades, see Kline, 194–218; Strickland, "Edward," 452; Woodward, 340–42; Akbari, "Due East," 21.

116. Kline, 196.

117. A bishop of Lincoln, for instance, responded to unfortunate news from abroad with near hysteria, offering to preach the Gospel "in the farthest regions of the Saracens, even to death." Kline, 203.

118. See, for instance, the lament of the Dominican Riccoldo of Monte Croce in 1291. John Tolan argues that after the defeats of the Crusades, Christian discourse about Muslims became more hostile and less interested in finding common ground. *Saracens: Islam in the Medieval European Imagination* (New York: Columbia University Press, 2002), viii–xiv, 172–73; see also Jaroslav Folda, *Crusader Art in the Holy Land, From the Third Crusade to the Fall of Acre, 1187–1291* (Cambridge: Cambridge University Press, 2005). Kline argues that attention to the Crusades in England intensified in response to the fall of Acre; Kline, 196.

119. Strickland, "Edward," 431.

120. Bychowski, "Isle," 168; Christof Rolker, "Off the Map? Hermaphrodites on the Hereford Map," in Männlich-weiblich-zwischen, 03/06/2016, https://intersex.hypotheses.org/?p=3305.

121. Strickland, *Saracens*, 187–88; Geraldine Heng, *The Invention of Race in the European Middle Ages* (Cambridge: Cambridge University Press, 2018), 110–80. The terms "Muslim" and "Islam" do not enter the Western lexicon until the sixteenth century. For the meaning of "Saracen," which encompassed both Islamic faith and racial difference from Christians, see Suzanne Conklin Akbari, *Idols*, 155; Tolan, *Saracens*, xv.

122. See, for instance, an English manuscript illumination (c. 1265–70) of Jews wearing similar hats in Guillaume le Clerc, *Bestiarie*, Paris, Bibiothèque nationale de France, MS français 14969, fol. 29v (fig. 19).

123. On the pointed hat, or *pileum cornutum*, as a sign of Jewishness, see Sara Lipton, *Images of Intolerance: The Representation of Jews and Judaism in the Bible moralisée* (Berkeley: University of California Press, 1999), 15–21; *Dark Mirror: The Medieval Origins of Anti-Jewish Iconography* (New York: Metropolitan, 2014), 16–39; Ruth Mellinkoff, *Outcasts: Signs of Otherness in Northern European Art of the Late Middle Ages*, 2 vols. (Berkeley: University of California Press, 1993), I: 59–94. For a conflation of Jews and Saracens on the Hereford Map, see Strickland, "Edward," 430–31 and figure 2; Heng, "Jews, Saracens, 'Black Men,' Tartars: England in a World of Racial Difference," in *A Companion to Medieval English Literature, c. 1350–1500*, ed. Peter Brown (London: Blackwell Publishing, 2007), 256.

124. Strickland, *Saracens*, 186–88.

125. Uebel, "Unthinking the Monster," 274.

126. Kline, 203. Kline's volume would seem to offer evidence against interpreting the turbaned hermaphrodite as Muslim, inasmuch as she points out that Jews and Muslims on the map were generally depicted as clothed.
127. Strickland, "Monstrosity and Race," 376–79; Heng, *Invention*, 118, 187–88; "Jews, Saracens, 'Black Men,' Tartars," 259–60; Akbari, *Idols*, 156.
128. Classen, xlix.
129. Uebel, "Unthinking the Monster," 275–76.
130. Kruger, *Spectral Jew*, 41, and passim.
131. For the production of different bodies in hotter climates; and for Muhammad or Islam as reputedly sexually decadent, see Akbari, *Idols*, 161–64; 257–58. See also Brian A. Catlos, *Muslims of Medieval Latin Christendom, c. 1050–1614* (Cambridge: Cambridge University Press, 2014), 326–28. On Christian views of Muslim sexual perversity in general, see Norman Daniel, *Islam and the West: The Making of an Image* (Edinburgh: University Press, 1960), 135–61.
132. Tolan, *Saracens*, 166.
133. "Sunt etiam in cibo parcissimi, modicum valde comedentes, licet frequenter luxuriam vero bestialiter exercent, nec sexum nec etatem nec speciem attendentes." Quoted from the *Speculum medicine* in Peter Biller, "Proto-Racial Thought in Medieval Science," in *Origins of Racism*, 175 and 175n74 (translation is mine); on the *Speculum*'s composition, Michael R. McVaugh, "The Writing of the *Speculum Medicine* and Its Place in Arnau de Vilanova's Last Years," *Arxiu de textos catalans antics* 30 (2011–3): 293–304.
134. On sodomy as *contra natura*, see Mark D. Jordan, *The Invention of Sodomy in Christian Theology* (Chicago: University of Chicago Press, 1997), 136–58 and passim.
135. See "Nonbinary and Unclean Sex" in chapter 3 below.
136. Peter of Poitiers, *Summa de Confessione*, 19: "In hoc quidem distans ab illo quod in hoc corrumpitur una sola persona, et in illo duae, sed in eo monstruosius est quam illud, quia hic eadem persona fit agens et patiens, et ita quasi uir et mulier, et quasi hermaphroditus." See John W. Baldwin, *The Language of Sex: Five Voices From Northern France Around 1200* (Chicago: University of Chicago Press, 1994), 316n66.
137. Boswell, 375–76n50. Glenn W. Olsen notes a relationship between the terms "sodomite," "effeminate," "hermaphrodite," and "androgyne," which might function as descriptors of male sexual passivity; *Of Sodomites, Effeminates, Hermaphrodites, and Androgynes: Sodomy in the Age of Peter Damian* (Toronto: Pontifical Institute of Mediaeval Studies, 2011), 65.
138. Kruger, *Spectral Jew*, 74; Cadden, *Meanings*, 214–15, and *Nothing Natural Is Shameful*.
139. Debra Higgs Strickland, "Monstrosity and Race in the Late Middle Ages," in *The Ashgate Research Companion to Monsters and the Monstrous*, ed. Asa S. Mittman and Peter Dendle (Aldershot, UK: Ashgate, 2013), 375.
140. See, for instance, Geraldine Heng, *Invention*; Heng, *England and the Jews: How Religion and Violence Created the First Racial State in the West* (Cambridge: Cambridge University Press, 2019); Akbari, *Idols*; Cord J. Whitaker, ed., "Making Race Matter in the Middle Ages," special issue of *postmedieval: a journal of medieval cultural studies* 6:1 (2015); *Black Metaphors: How Modern Racism Emerged from Medieval Race-Thinking* (Philadelphia: University of Pennsylvania Press, 2019); Sierra Lomuto, "The Mongol Princess of Tars: Global Relations and Racial Formation in The King of Tars (c. 1330)," *Exemplaria* 313:3 (2019): 171–92; Dorothy Kim, "Introduction to *Literature Compass* Special Cluster: Critical Race and the Middle Ages," *Literature Compass* 16:9–10 (2019); Thomas Hahn, ed., "Race and Ethnicity in the Middle Ages," special issue of the *Journal of Medieval and Early Modern Studies* 31:1 (2001); Eliav-Feldon et al., *Origins of Racism*; Bethencourt; Jeffrey Jerome Cohen, "On Saracen Enjoyment: Some Fantasies of Race in Late Medieval France and England," *Journal of Medieval and Early Modern Studies* 31:1 (2001): 113–46; "Race," in *A Handbook of Middle English Studies*, ed. Marion Turner (Chichester: Wiley-Blackwell, 2013), 109–22. Among those medievalists

skeptical of the appropriateness of "race" for the Middle Ages, see Robert Bartlett, *The Making of Europe: Conquest, Colonization, and Cultural Change, 950–1350* (Princeton, NJ: Princeton University Press, 1993), 197–242; William Chester Jordan, "Why 'Race'?," *Journal of Medieval and Early Modern Studies* 31:1 (2001): 165–74, at 169. Other works by non-medievalists have also identified race as a uniquely modern phenomenon; see, for instance, Nell Painter, *The History of White People* (New York: W.W. Norton, 2010).

141. Heng, *Invention*, 35. As we have seen, the Hereford Map denigrated Jews by showing them worshipping a simian and defecating demon (see Kupfer, 46). Strickland views anti-Judaism on the map as instrumental in the formation of English nationhood, "Edward I," 420–69.

142. Strickland, *Saracens*, 42; see also "Monstrosity and Race," 366.

143. Heng, *Invention*, 133–37, 218 and passim. Prester John was first thought to live in India, before being relocated to Africa in the European imagination in the fourteenth century.

144. Heng, "The Invention of Race in the European Middle Ages I: Race Studies, Modernity, and the Middle Ages," *Literature Compass* 8:5 (2011): 315–31; Kruger, *Spectral Jew*, 85–109.

145. For the map as inspiring wonder, see Kupfer, 47–48; for a different view, see Mittman and Kim, "Monsters and the Exotic"; Heng, *Invention*, 35; Heng, "Jews, Saracens, 'Black Men,' Tartars," 263.

146. Thomas de Wesselow, "Locating the Hereford Mappa Mundi," *Imago Mundi* 65 (2013): 180–206 at 198; Strickland, "Edward," 424.

147. Strickland, "Edward," 452–69; Strickland, *Saracens*, 13.

148. Camille, *Image on the Edge: The Margins of Medieval Art* (Cambridge, MA: Harvard University Press, 1992), 16.

149. Miller, *Medieval Monstrosity*, 1; Bildhauer and Mills, 6.

150. Asa S. Mittman and Susan M. Kim, "The Exposed Body and the Gendered *Blemmye*: Reading the *Wonders of the East*," in *Sexuality in the Middle Ages and Early Modern Times: New Approaches to a Fundamental Cultural-Historical and Literary-Anthropological Theme*, ed. Albrecht Classen (Berlin: Walter de Gruyter, 2008), 171–201; Amanda Lehr, "Sexing the Cannibal in the *Wonders of the East* and Beowulf," *postmedieval: a journal of medieval cultural studies* 9:2 (2018): 179–95.

151. Elaine Pagels, *The Origin of Satan* (New York: Random House, 1995), xviii–xix.

152. Among many examples, C. Riley Snorton *Black on Both Sides*; Eva Hayward and Jami Weinstein, "Tranimalities,"; Alexander G. Weheliye, *Habeas Viscus: Racializing Assemblages, Biopolitics, and Black Feminist Theories of the Human* (Durham, NC: Duke University Press, 2014); Chen, *Animacies*; Neel Ahuja, "Postcolonial Critique in a Multispecies World," *PMLA* 124:2 (2009): 556–63; Ann Laura Stoler, *Race and the Education of Desire: Foucault's History of Sexuality and the Colonial Order of Things* (Durham, NC: Duke University Press, 1995).

153. For instance, Hortense J. Spillers, "Mama's Baby, Papa's Maybe: An American Grammar Book," *Diacritics* 17:2 (1987): 64–81, esp. 68; Weheliye, 41–42; Cathy Cohen, "Punks, Bulldaggers, and Welfare Queens: The Radical Potential of Queer Politics?," *GLQ: A Journal of Gay and Lesbian Studies* 3:4 (1997): 437–65; María Lugones, "Heterosexualism and the Colonial/Modern Gender System," *Hypatia* 22:1 (2007): 195; Hilary Malatino, "Gone, Missing: Queering and Racializing Absence in Trans and Intersex Archives," in *Queer Feminist Science Studies Reader*, ed. Cyd Cipolla, Kristina Gupta, David A. Rubin, and Angela Willey (Seattle: University of Washington Press, 2017), 157–71; Rubin, *Intersex Matters*, 121–39.

154. As have argued Jeffrey Cohen, *Postcolonial Middle Ages*; Lisa Lampert-Weissig, *Medieval Literature and Postcolonial Studies* (Edinburgh: Edinburgh University Press, 2010); and Akbari, *Idols*. Others are skeptical, for instance, Michael W. Twomey, "Inventing the Encyclopedia," in *Schooling and Society: The Ordering and Reordering of Knowledge in the Western Middle Ages*, ed. Alasdair A. MacDonald and Michael W. Twomey (Leuven: Peeters, 2004), 73–92; Simon Gaunt, "Can the Middle Ages be Postcolonial?" *Comparative Literature* 61: 2 (2009): 160–76.

3. THE HYENA'S UNCLEAN SEX: BEASTS, BESTIARIES, AND JEWISH COMMUNITIES

1. On bestiaries, see M. R. James, *The Bestiary: Being a Reproduction in Full of the Manuscript Ii. 4. 26 in the University Library, Cambridge, with Supplementary Plates from other Manuscripts of English Origin, and a Preliminary Study of the Latin* Bestiary *as Current in England* (Oxford: Oxford University Press, 1928); Florence McCulloch, *Mediaeval Latin and French Bestiaries* (Chapel Hill: University of North Carolina Press, 1962); Debra Hassig (now Strickland), *Medieval Bestiaries: Text, Image, Ideology* (Cambridge: Cambridge University Press, 1995); Willene B. Clark, *A Medieval Book of Beasts: The Second-Family Bestiary: Commentary, Art, Text and Translation* (Woodbridge, UK: Boydell, 2006); Sarah Kay, *Animal Skins and the Reading Self in Medieval Latin and French Bestiaries* (Chicago: University of Chicago Press, 2017); Elizabeth Morrison, ed., *Book of Beasts: The Bestiary in the Medieval World* (Los Angeles: J. Paul Getty Museum, 2019). Ron Baxter is cautious about identifying a genre of literature that can be called a "bestiary," instead focusing on specific manuscripts and their users. But Willene B. Clark and Meradith T. McMunn use the term "bestiary" to refer to any work that derives from the *Physiologus* (more on this text in note 34 of this chapter) but departs from the Y, C, and B versions of the text through additions and interpolations. See Baxter, *Bestiaries and Their Users*; Willene B. Clark and Meradith T. McMunn, eds., *Beasts and Birds of the Middle Ages: The Bestiary and Its Legacy* (Philadelphia: University of Pennsylvania Press, 1989), 3.
2. For the Book of Nature in medieval literature, see Constant J. Mews, "The World as Text: The Bible and the Book of Nature in Twelfth-Century Theology," in *Scripture and Pluralism: Reading the Bible in the Religiously Plural Worlds of the Middle Ages and Renaissance*, ed. Thomas J. Heffernan and Thomas E. Burman (Leiden: Brill, 2005), 95–122. Susan Crane argues that scholars often ignore bestiaries' non-religious content, which was substantial, in "Expanding the Bestiary's Meaning: The Case of Bodley MS. 764," in *Book of Beasts*, 77–85.
3. The bestiaries assigned to animals a variety of sexual categories, including male, female, neuter, or multiple-sexed. See Debra Higgs Strickland, "Sex in the Bestiaries," in *The Mark of the Beast: The Medieval Bestiary in Art, Life, and Literature*, ed. Debra Higgs Strickland (New York: Garland, 1999), 71–97.
4. Ilya Dines, "The Hare and its Alter Ego in the Middle Ages," *Reinardus* 17 (2004): 73–84; Beryl Rowland, *Animals with Human Faces: A Guide to Animal Symbolism* (Knoxville: University of Tennessee Press, 1973), 88–93.
5. Boswell, 138–39, and 138-39n5 and 139n6; Luc Brisson, *Sexual Ambivalence: Androgyny and Hermaphroditism in Graeco-Roman Antiquity*, trans. Janet Lloyd (Berkeley: University of California Press, 2002), 137–40.
6. Salisbury, *The Beast Within*, 89–107. Scholars disagree about whether bestiaries were generally more interested in naturalism than in moralism; see, for instance, Crane, *Animal Encounters*, 69–100.
7. Portugal and Spain exiled their Jewish populations in the following century.
8. See, for instance, comparable images in four manuscripts that share textual and imagistic features: the "transitional" Worksop Bestiary, New York, Morgan Library, MS M.81, fol. 14v (England, possibly in Lincoln or York before 1187); the St. Petersburg Bestiary, Saint Petersburg, Saint Petersburg Public Library, Latin Q.v.V.1, fol. 15v (England, c. 1180–90); Bestiary, London, British Library, Royal 12 C.XIX, fol. 11v (England, c. 1200–10), and the Northumberland Bestiary (see fig. 3.2). See also the "second-family" Ashmole Bestiary, University of Oxford, Bodleian Library, MS Ashmole 1511, fol. 17v (England, early thirteenth century). In the interest of space, I cannot trace here the genesis and history of each of these manuscripts nor their specific users. Some scholars have divided these bestiaries into "families" of recensions, but others have criticized such classifications. See Clark, *Medieval Book of Beasts*, 23–27, 34–50; and Baxter's discussion of the so-called "transitional" (or "Morgan") and "second-family" bestiaries, including the luxury bestiary manuscripts, 100–24, 124–32, and

9. Willene B. Clark, *The Medieval Book of Birds: Hugh of Fouilloy's* Aviarium (Binghamton, NY: State University of New York, 1992), 76–85; Clark, *Medieval Book of Beasts*, 68–71; Xenia Muratova, "The Bestiaries, An Aspect of Medieval Patronage," in ed. S. Macready and F. H. Thompson, *Art and Patronage in the English Romanesque* (London: Society of Antiquaries of London, 1986), 118–44; Muratova, "Workshop Methods in English Late Twelfth-Century Illumination and the Production of Luxury Bestiaries," in Willene B. Clark and Meradith T. McMunn, 53–63; M. R. James, "The Bestiary in the University Library," *Aberdeen University Library Bulletin* 36:6 (1928): 529–31.

177–78; Dines, "The Problem of the Transitional Family of Bestiaries," *Reinardus* 24 (2011–12): 29–52. Images of hyenas from this group are discussed by Strickland in *Medieval Bestiaries*, 145–55.

10. Clark, *Medieval Book of Beasts*, 68, 97, 112; Beryl Rowland, "The Art of Memory and the Bestiary," 12–25. James classified the Aberdeen and Ashmole bestiaries as "second-family" bestiaries, and they are considered by Clark to be of the highest rank of illumination. Scholars believe the Aberdeen and Ashmole bestiaries are closely related, perhaps produced in the same workshop, and perhaps using a common source. For Clark, the Ashmole Bestiary perhaps postdates the Aberdeen by five or more years, but Muratova finds it impossible to determine the order of their composition and considers them contemporary. A portion of their content is drawn from the mid-twelfth-century canon Hugh of Fouilloy's book about birds, the *Aviarium*. See Clark, *The Medieval Book of Birds*, 22–23, 76–85; Muratova, "Workshop Methods," 53–63; Strickland, *Medieval Bestiaries*, 4–5; Aberdeen Bestiary Project, accessed on May 20, 2019, at https://www.abdn.ac.uk/bestiary/history.php.

11. Aberdeen Bestiary, University of Aberdeen, MS 24, 11v-12r:

> Est animal qui\ dicitur yena, in se\pulchris mortu\orum habitans, eorum\que corpora vescens.\ Cuius natura est ut ali\quando masculus\ sit, aliquando fem\ina, et ideo est immun\dum animal. . . . Huic as\similantur filii Israel, qui ab initio deo vivo servierunt. Postea divitiis\ et luxurie dediti ydola coluerunt. Ideo propheta comparavit sy\nagogam in mundo animali dicens: Facta est michi hereditas\ mea quasi spelunca yene. Quicumque igitur inter nos luxurie et\ avaricie inserviunt, huic belue comparantur cum nec viri nec\ femine sint id est nec fideles, nec perfidi sunt, sed sunt sine dubio, de\ quibus ait Salomon: Vir duplex animo, inconstans est in omnibus\ viis suis. De quibus ait dominus: Non potestis deo servire et mamone.

> A transcription and translation of the manuscript with commentary appears at the Aberdeen Bestiary Project: www.abdn.ac.uk/bestiary/.

12. Debra Higgs Strickland, "The Jews, Leviticus, and the Unclean in Medieval English Bestiaries," in *Beyond the Yellow Badge: Anti-Judaism and Antisemitism in Medieval and Early Modern Culture*, ed. Mitchell B. Merback (Leiden and Boston: Brill, 2008), 203–32; Baxter, 84.

13. Mary Douglas, "Pollution," in *Implicit Meanings: Essays in Anthropology*, ed. Mary Douglas (London: Routledge, 1975), 50–51.

14. Kay, 70.

15. Mary Douglas, *Purity and Danger: An Analysis of the Concepts of Pollution and Taboo* (London: Routledge, 2003), 56.

16. Douglas, *Purity and Danger*, 42–58; William J. Bouwsma, "Anxiety and the Formation of Early Modern Culture," in *After the Reformation: Essays in Honor of J. H. Hexter*, ed. Barbara C. Malament (Philadelphia: University of Philadelphia Press, 1980), 215–46.

17. Louis-Vincent Thomas, *Le cadavre: de la biologie à l'anthropologie* (Brussels: Éditions Complexe, 1980); Caroline Walker Bynum, *Fragmentation and Redemption: Essays on Gender and the Human Body in Medieval Religion* (New York: Zone, 1992), 295. This impulse was also partly responsible for medieval attitudes toward leprosy; see, for instance, Timothy S. Miller and John W. Nesbitt, eds., *Walking Corpses: Leprosy in Byzantium and the Medieval West* (Ithaca, NY: Cornell University Press, 2014).

3. THE HYENA'S UNCLEAN SEX   235

18. Claude Lévi-Strauss, *The Raw and the Cooked*, trans. John and Doreen Weightman (New York: Harper and Row, 1964).
19. Liz Herbert McAvoy and Teresa Walters, ed., *Consuming Narratives: Gender and Monstrous Appetite in the Middle Ages and the Renaissance* (Cardiff: University of Wales Press, 2002).
20. Strickland, *Saracens*, 136; Pamela Gravestock, "Did Imaginary Animals Exist?" in *Mark of the Beast: The Medieval Bestiary in Art, Life, and Literature*, ed. Debra Higgs Strickland (New York: Garland, 1999), 121. On the lamia, another unclean Jewish hybrid beast (also associated with intersex in antiquity), Irven M. Resnick and Kenneth F. Kitchell Jr., "The Sweepings of Lamia: Transformations of the Myths of Lilith and Lamia," in *Religion, Gender, and Culture in the Pre-modern World*, ed. Alexandra Cuffel and Brian Britt (New York: Palgrave Macmillan, 2007), 77–104.
21. Manticore, University of Oxford, Bodleian Library, MS Bodley 764, fol. 25r. For the Phrygian cap as a symbol of the infidel, see Jeanne Fox-Friedman, "Vision of the World: Romanesque Art of Northern Italy and the Hereford Mappamundi," in *The Hereford World Map: Medieval World Maps and Their Contexts*, ed. P. D. A. Harvey (London: The British Library, 2006), 140–41. For Jews depicted as cannibals, see Scott Westrem, "Against Gog and Magog," in *Text and Territory: Geographical Imagination in the European Middle Ages*, ed. Sylvia Tomasch and Sealy Gilles (Philadelphia: University of Pennsylvania Press, 1998), 65–66. Muslims were also subject to such accusations. Vincent of Beauvais wrote in his *Speculum Historiale* that Mongols "devour human meat as lions." See Sophia Menache, "Tartars, Jews, Saracens, and the Jewish-Mongol 'Plot' of 1241." *History* 81:263 (1996): 325.
22. Peter Hulme, "Introduction: The Cannibal Scene," in *Cannibalism and the Colonial World*, ed. Francis Barker, Peter Hulme, and Margaret Iversen (Cambridge: Cambridge University Press, 1998), 1–38.
23. Robert Mills, "Seeing Sodomy in the *Bibles moralisées*," *Speculum* 87:2 (2012): 424; Geraldine Heng, *Empire of Magic: Medieval Romance and the Politics of Cultural Fantasy* (New York: Columbia University Press, 2003), 98.
24. Lynda L. Coon, "Gender and the Body," in *The Cambridge History of Christianity*, vol. 3: *Early Medieval Christianities, c. 600–c. 1100*, ed. Thomas F. X. Noble and Julia M. H. Smith (Cambridge: Cambridge University Press, 2006), 440–47; for a later example, see Kirstie Gulick Rosenfield, "Monstrous Generation: Witchcraft and Generation in *Othello*," in *Consuming Narratives*, 231–32.
25. Kay, 68–73. Scholars have noted that while excrement was viewed negatively in the medieval period, it was also linked to the fertility of manure. Humorous depictions of feces were also a common theme in manuscript marginalia. See Camille, *Image on the Edge*, 111–15; Susan Signe Morrison, *Excrement in the Late Middle Ages: Sacred Filth and Chaucer's Fecopoetics* (New York: Palgrave Macmillan, 2008).
26. Morrison, *Excrement*, 25–41; Bynum, *Resurrection*, 148.
27. Bakhtin, *Rabelais and His World*, trans. Hélène Iswolsky (Bloomington: Indiana University Press, 1984; first pub. 1968), 25–29, 316–18; Maggie Kilgour, *From Communion to Cannibalism: An Anatomy of Metaphors of Incorporation* (Princeton: Princeton University Press, 1990).
28. Odo of Tournai, *On Original Sin and A Disputation with the Jew, Leo, Concerning the Advent of Christ, the Son of God: Two Theological Treatises*, trans. and ed. Irven M. Resnick (Philadelphia: University of Pennsylvania Press, 1994), 96. Odo argues against the value of such visceral reactions, however.
29. Jeffrey Jerome Cohen, "Inventing with Animals in the Middle Ages," in *Engaging with Nature: Essays on the Natural World in Medieval and Early Modern Europe*, ed. Barbara A. Hanawalt and Lisa J. Kiser (Notre Dame, IN: University of Notre Dame Press, 2008), 46–48. Circumcision was seen by some Christians as a feminization of Jewish men. See Irven M. Resnick, *Marks of Distinction: Christian Perceptions of Jews in the High Middle Ages* (Washington, D.C.: Catholic University of America Press, 2012), 53–92. For bestiaries and sexual misconduct, see Kay, 66–67.

30. Irven M. Resnick, "Medieval Roots of the Myth of Jewish Male Menses," *Harvard Theological Review* 93:3 (2000): 241–63; *Marks of Distinction*, 46–51, 182–94: Peter Biller, "A 'Scientific' View of Jews from Paris around 1300," *Micrologus* 9 (2001): 137–68. As Sara Lipton has pointed out, scholastics such as Albert the Great attributed Jewish traits to internal complexion, which could be manipulated. See Lipton, *Dark Mirror*, 176. Suzanne Akbari reads these sources differently, noting that at least one Paris *quodlibet* views Jewish traits as innate and natural. See Akbari, *Idols*, 148–50. For scholarship on innate bodily differences as indications of racialization in the Middle Ages, see, for instance, Heng, *Invention*, 75–81 and passim; Strickland, "Monstrosity and Race in the Late Middle Ages"; Jonathan M. Elukin, "From Jew to Christian? Conversion and Immutability in Medieval Europe," in *Varieties of Religious Conversion in the Middle Ages*, ed. James Muldoon (Gainesville: University Press of Florida, 1997), 171–89; Mary Stroll, *The Jewish Pope: Ideology and Politics in the Papal Schism of 1130* (Leiden: Brill, 1987), 156–68; Steven F. Kruger, "Conversion and Medieval Sexual, Religious, and Racial Categories," in *Constructing Medieval Sexuality*, ed. Karma Lochrie, Peggy McCracken, and James A. Schultz (Minneapolis: University of Minnesota Press, 1997), 158–79; *Spectral Jew*, 67–109, and above in chapter 2 in the section entitled "The Hereford Map, Muslims, and Crusading England." Jews were also sometimes conflated with sodomites, and sodomites with foreigners and heretics; see Mills, "*Bibles moralisées*," 435–50.
31. Robert C. Stacey, "Jewish Lending and the Medieval English Economy," in *A Commercialising Economy: England 1086 to c. 1300*, ed. Richard H. Britnell and Bruce M.S. Campbell (Manchester: Manchester University Press, 1995), 78–101; Lester K. Little, *Religious Poverty and the Profit Economy in Medieval Europe* (Ithaca, NY: Cornell University Press, 1978), 45–46; Heng, *Invention*, 55–75.
32. Strickland, "Leviticus," 210–11.
33. Heng, *Invention*, 60–61.
34. Strickland, "Leviticus," 206; Clark and McMunn, 2–4. On the *Physiologus*, see Michael J. Curley, ed. and trans., *Physiologus: A Medieval Book of Nature Lore* (Chicago: University of Chicago Press, 2009); Salisbury, *Beast Within*, 86–89. Clark and McMunn, 3; for the history of the bestiary and its relationship to the *Physiologus*, see Kay, 7–15. The creators of bestiaries also combined the *Physiologus* with later materials, such as lore drawn from Isidore of Seville's *Etymologies* and other sources.
35. A scholarly consensus asserts that communal integrity is the goal of purity systems in general, but there is some disagreement about whether Israelite taboos preserved the people, the sanctuary, or something else. Douglas's views on this point changed over the course of her career. See T. M. Lemos, "The Universal and the Particular: Mary Douglas and the Politics of Impurity," *The Journal of Religion* 89:2 (2009): 236–51.
36. I draw in this chapter from Kruger, *Spectral Jew*, 12–13 and passim.
37. Curley, 52–53. Baxter places the hyena within a group of chapters devoted to vice and the snares of the devil: 45–47.
38. Paris, Bibliothèque Nationale de France, MS français 14969, fol. 29v; c. 1265–70, likely produced in a Franciscan circle. On Guillaume le Clerc's bestiary, see Kay, 12, 26–27 and passim.
39. Strickland, "Leviticus," 209–10 and 496, fig. 3; Suzanne Lewis, "*Tractatus adversus Judaeos* in the Gulbenkian Apocalypse," *Art Bulletin* 68 (1986): 543–66, at 349.
40. See G. K. Anderson, "Popular Survivals of the Wandering Jew in England," *The Journal of English and Germanic Philology* 46:4 (1947): 367–82.
41. Yamamoto, 13; Resnick, *Marks of Distinction*, 37–45. Anna Sapir Abulafia, "Bodies in the Jewish-Christian Debate," in *Framing Medieval Bodies*, ed. Sarah Kay and Miri Rubin (Manchester: Manchester University Press, 1994), 124.
42. Crane, *Animal Encounters*, 76.
43. See the similar wording of the hyena allegory, for instance, in the Northumberland Bestiary, J. Paul Getty Museum, MS 100, fol. 12v; Worksop Bestiary, Morgan Library, MS M.81, fol. 14v-15r; Saint Petersburg, Saint Petersburg Public Library, Latin Q.v.V.1, fol. 15v; Bestiary, London, British Library,

3. THE HYENA'S UNCLEAN SEX   237

Royal MS 12 C.XIX, fol. 11v-12r; Ashmole Bestiary, University of Oxford, Bodleian Library, MS Ashmole 1511, fol. 17v-18r; Bestiary, British Library Add. 11283, fol. 5r-v (see Clark, *Medieval Book of Beasts*, 131–32); University of Oxford, Bodleian Library, MS Bodley 764, fol. 15r-v; see also BNF, MS français 14969, fol. 29v-31.

44. Strickland, *Medieval Bestiaries*, 145–55; Strickland, "Leviticus," 204; Salisbury, *Beast Within*, 89–107.
45. Kay, quotation at 15; Salisbury, *Beast Within*, 89–107, quotation at 89; Clark, *Medieval Book of Birds*, 23–24; Strickland, *Mark of the Beast*, xi–xvi; Clark and McMunn, 2–7; Baxter, 192–209; Crane, *Animal Encounters*, 69–70; Kay 14. Images of hyenas appear in ecclesiastical architecture, but Baxter is skeptical that we can draw any conclusions about how they would have been understood by viewers without further study, 1–28, 211–13.
46. Bouchard, 1–27 and passim.
47. Carruthers, *Experience of Beauty*, 151–55.
48. Bynum, *Metamorphosis*, 117.
49. Bernard of Clairvaux, *Sermones*, in vol. 4 of *Opera*, ed. J. LeClercq and H. Rochais (Rome: Editiones Cistercienses, 1966), 217: "Huic enim limo terreno vim vitalem miscuit. . . . et in persona una sibi invicem unirentur Deus et limus, maiestas et infirmitas, tanta vilitas et sublimitas tanta." Bynum, *Metamorphosis*, 122.
50. Mary J. Carruthers, "Varietas: A Word of Many Colours," *Poetica* 41:1–2 (2009): 29.
51. Charles Homer Haskins, *The Renaissance of the Twelfth Century* (Cambridge, MA: Harvard University Press, 1993), 98.
52. Robert Pasnau, "The Latin Aristotle," in C. Shields, ed., *The Oxford Handbook of Aristotle* (Oxford: Oxford University Press, 2012), 665–89, at 666.
53. Edward Grant, *God and Reason in the Middle Ages* (Cambridge: Cambridge University Press, 2001), 116–22. Latin translations of Aristotle arrived in waves, with many of the natural philosophical works appearing later; see chapter 4 on "Aristotelian Theories" and "Sex Differentiation in Latin Europe."
54. Bouchard, 28–56.
55. Bouchard, 36–40. Although they shared an interest in oppositions, Abelard and Bernard of Clairvaux, it must be said, were opponents in nearly every way.
56. John of Salisbury, *Ioannis Saresberiensis Episcopi Carnotensis Policratici sive de Nugis Curialium et Vestigiis Philosophorum Libri viii: recognovit et prolegomenis, apparatu critico, commentario, indicibus instruxit*, ed. Clemens C. I. Webb, 2 vols. (Oxford: Clarendon, 1909), bk. 3, chap. 6; bk. 5, chap. 10 (I: 184, 329). See also John of Salisbury, *Policraticus: Of the Frivolities of Courtiers and the Footprints of Philosophers*, ed. and trans. Cary J. Nederman (Cambridge: Cambridge University Press, 1990), 19, 90.
57. Ovid, *Metamorphoses*, 4.375–9 (I: 204); Nederman and True, 506–7.
58. *Policraticus*, bk. 5, chap. 10 (I: 329): "sed tanta mollitie ingredientes eneruat ut uiris effeminatis nobiliorem adimat sexum; nec ante quisquam egreditur quam stupeat et doleat se mutatum esse in feminam. Aut enim cedens omnino sexus in deteriorem degenerat aut ueteris dignitatis aliquo manente uestigio hermafroditum induit, qui quodam delinquentis naturae ludibrio sic utriusque sexus ostentat imaginem ut neutrius retineat ueritatem." English trans. in Nederman, 90–91.
59. *Policraticus*, bk. 5, chap. 10 (I: 329–30): "Qui curialium ineptias induit et philosophi uel boni uiri officium pollicetur, hermafroditus est, qui duro uultu et hispido muliebrem deturpat uenustatem et uirum muliebribus polluit et incestat. Res siquidem monstruosa est philosophus curialis; et, dum utrumque esse affectat, neutrum est, eo quod curia philosophiam excludit et ineptias curiales philosophus usquequaque non recipit." Nederman, 91.
60. Orderic Vitalis, *The Ecclesiastical History of Orderic Vitalis*, ed. and trans. Marjorie Chibnall, 6 vols. (Oxford: Clarendon, 1973), IV: 188: "Femineam mollitiem petulans iuuentus amplectitur."
61. On the instability of court, see Camille, *Image on the Edge*, 99.

62. *Policraticus*, bk. 5, chap. 10 (I:323): "Qui tangit picem inquinatur ab ea; uuaque contacta liuorem ducit ab uua." The passage cites Ecclesiasticus 13:1 and Juvenal's *Saturae* to argue that moral character is affected by social contacts. See Nederman, 85.

63. See, for instance, his advice that a prince should "mix" justice and mercy; or his *Metalogicon* (1159), which dispensed with a discourse of opposites, according to Bouchard, 48–50. Other texts also identified superficiality and excess with effeminacy. See, for instance, Camille, *Image on the Edge*, 69.

64. John was present at the curia for some of Eugene's pontificate and knew his situation well. "Editor's Introduction," in *Policraticus*, xvi; Bynum, *Metamorphosis*, 141.

65. Gregory the Great, *Pastoral Care: Regulae pastoralis*, ed R. R. Bramley (Oxford: James and Parker, 1874): III.34 (p. 374–76): "Aut calidus ergo quisque esse, aut frigidus quaeritur, ne tepidus evomatur." John praised Gregory the Great in his *Policraticus* as the "most holy doctor." See Ann Kuzdale, "The Reception of Gregory in the Renaissance and Reformation," in *A Companion to Gregory the Great*, ed. Bronwen Neil and Matthew Dal Santo (Leiden: Brill, 2013) 359–86, at 368.

66. Lynda L. Coon, "Somatic Styles of the Early Middle Ages (c. 600–900)," in *Gender and Change: Agency, Chronology, and Periodisation*, ed. Alexandra Shepard and Garthine Walker (Chichester, UK: Wiley-Blackwell, 2009), 22.

67. Remigius of Auxerre, *Commentum in Martianum Capellam*, ed. Cora E. Lutz, 2 vols. (Leiden: Brill, 1962), I: 108: "Ermafroditus autem significat quandam sermonis lasciviatatem, qua plerumque neglecta veritatis ratione superfluus sermonis ornatus requiritur." Rollo, *Kiss My Relics*, 45.

68. Elizabeth Lapina, "Anti-Jewish Rhetoric in Guibert of Nogent's *Dei gesta per Francos*," *Journal of Medieval History* 35 (2009): 239–53, esp. 243.

69. Jan M. Ziolkowski, "Put in No-Man's Land: Guibert of Nogent's Accusations Against a Judaizing and Jew-Supporting Christian," in *Jews and Christians in Twelfth-Century Europe*, ed. Michael A. Signer and John Van Engen (Notre Dame: University of Notre Dame Press, 2001), 119.

70. Guibert of Nogent, *Tractatus de incarnatione contra Judaeos* PL 156 (Turnhout, Belgium: Brepols, 1990), 490–91: "Plane hunc non incongrue Neutericum novo vocabulo dicam, qui neutrum sectatur, dum ea quae laudat jura non prosequitur, et quae videtur prosequi Christiani studii jura non laudat." Jay Rubenstein, *Guibert of Nogent: Portrait of a Medieval Mind* (New York: Routledge, 2002), 115–16, 254n27.

71. Lapina, 242; Anna Sapir Abulafia, "Christian Imagery of Jews in the Twelfth Century: A Look at Odo of Cambrai and Guibert of Nogent," in *Christians and Jews in Dispute: Disputational Literature and the Rise of Anti-Judaism in the West (c. 1000–1150)* (Aldershot, UK: Variorum, 1998), essay X, 387.

72. Ziolkowski, "Put in No-Man's Land," 119; Kruger, *Spectral Jew*, 43–47.

73. Ziolkowski, "Put in No-Man's Land," 119.

74. Ernst H. Kantorowicz, *The King's Two Bodies: A Study in Medieval Political Philosophy* (Princeton, NJ: Princeton University Press, 1997), 10n8; Baldi Ubaldi Perusini, *In decretalium volumen commentaria*, ed. Franciscus de Parona (Torino: Botttega d'Erasmo, 1971), 152v. Baldus also wrote an opinion on a medical case of an intersex individual in Italy; see Julius Kirshner and Osvaldo Cavallar, "Da pudenda a prudentia: il consilium di Baldo degli Ubaldi sul caso di Giovanni Malaspina," *Diritto e processo* 6 (2010): 97–112 and below, in chapter four, in "Roman and Canon Law."

75. *Annales Ricardi Secundi*, in *Johannis de Trokelow et Henrici de Blaneford Chronica et Annales*, ed. Henry Thomas Riley (Cambridge: Cambridge University Press, 2012), 177: "Temporale et spirituale sunt duae partes activae, et ideo ille qui posuit se ad unum, non intromitteret se de alio; quia— 'Nemo potest duobus dominis servire, etc.' Videtur nobis quod hermaphrodita vel ambidexter essent bona nomina pro talibus hominibus duplicis status." Dinshaw, *Getting Medieval*, 79. See also Chaucer's contemporary association of the Pardoner with a hare and, hence, nonbinary sex. Edward C. Schweitzer, Jr. notes that hares were also associated with Jews—and unbelief in general. See his "Chaucer's Pardoner and the Hare," *English Language Notes* 4 (1966–67): 247–50. Some scholars

have described the Pardoner as intersex; see, for instance, C. David Benson, "Chaucer's Pardoner: His Sexuality and Modern Critics," *Mediaevalia* 8 (1982): 338.

76. Dinshaw, *Getting Medieval*, 80.
77. See, for instance, Ziolkowski, *Alain de Lille's Grammar of Sex: The Meaning of Grammar to a Twelfth-Century Intellectual* (Cambridge, MA: Medieval Academy of America, 1985).
78. Bouchard, 41–42.
79. Alan of Lille, "De Planctu naturae," ed. Nikolaus M. Häring, *Studi medievali serie terza* XIX 2 (1978): ln. 1.17–8 (806): "Femina uir factus sexus denigrat honorem/Ars magice Veneris hermafroditat eum." I use the translation of David Rollo.
80. "De Planctu naturae," ln. 8.188–90 (839): "ne si tanti sterquilinii fetor in nimie promulgationis auras euaderet plerosque ad indignationis nauseantis uomitum inuitaret." On Alan of Lille's text, see Rollo, *Kiss My Relics*, 77–142; Mark D. Jordan, 67–91. For sodomy and nonbinary sex in theological and moral treatises, see chapter 1 on "Androgynes, Sodomy, and Heresy."
81. "De Planctu naturae," ln. 6.4–10 (824–25): "In faciem decidens mentem stupore uulneratus exiui totusque in extasis alienatione sepultus sensuumque incarceratis uirtutibus nec uiuens nec mortuus inter utrumque neuter laboram." For "hermaphroditic speech," and "hermaphroditic contagion" in *Plaint of Nature*, see Alexandre Leupin, *Barbarolexis: Medieval Writing and Sexuality*, trans. Kate M. Cooper (Cambridge, MA: Harvard University Press, 1989), 75–76.
82. "De Planctu naturae," ln. 8.62–3 (834): "Dumque in tali constructione me destruit, in sua syneresi mei themesim machinatur."
83. Bernard of Cluny, *De contemptu mundi* (East Lansing, MI: Colleagues, 1991): 146–48:

    Mas maris immemor, O furor, O temor! Et ut hyaena./Aspice sordibus ingenialibus, aspice multos,/ Quo scelus ordine, quo noto nomine? nempe sepultos./Criminis istius, heu! sonat impius horror ad astra./Nuda fit actio, vociferatio; mens geme casta!/Mutuo conscius, ille fit istius, illius iste./Est prope mortua lex tua, vox tua, sors tua Christe./. . . . O furor ultimus! est modo plurimus Hermaphroditus,/. . . . Lepra minoribus et potioribus ista cohaeret./Lex genii perit, usus et interit hac lue notus./. . . . Semimares voco, semiviros probo, se maculantes,/Debita sexibus inferioribus heu!

    Emphasis is mine.
84. Robert Hughes, *Heaven and Hell in Western Art* (New York: Stein and Day, 1968), 175–201.
85. Honorius of Autun's *Elucidarium* was written in England about 1100 and was popular among readers from the twelfth to the fourteenth century. It expressed horror at being eaten, especially by animals, as well as a general fear of the revolting processes of digestion and putrefaction. Bynum, *Resurrection*, 119, 148–51.
86. On eating, absorption, and "otherness," see Kyla Wazana Tompkins, *Racial Indigestion: Eating Bodies in the Nineteenth Century* (New York: New York University Press, 2012). On medieval theories of biological growth, see Joan Cadden, "The Medieval Philosophy and Biology of Growth: Albertus Magnus, Thomas Aquinas, Albert of Saxony and Marsilius of Inghen on Book I, Chapter V of Aristotle's 'De generatione et corruptione,' with Translated Texts of Albertus Magnus and Thomas Aquinas," PhD diss., Indiana University, 1971; and Bynum, *Metamorphosis*, 145.
87. Some suggested that the lapse was, instead, sexual in nature. See Pagels, *Origin of Satan*, 48–49; David Keck, *Angels and Angelology in the Middle Ages* (New York: Oxford University Press, 1998), 24.
88. There was much debate about the nature of angelic and demonic bodies but, by time of Thomas Aquinas, their forms had been for the most part de-corporealized. See Elliott, *Fallen Bodies*, 127–56. See also Jeffrey Burton Russell, *Lucifer: The Devil in the Middle Ages* (Ithaca, NY: Cornell University Press, 1984), 41–42n28; Alain Boureau, *Satan the Heretic: The Birth of Demonology in the Medieval West*, trans. Teresa Lavender Fagan (Chicago: University of Chicago Press, 2006), 99–111; Gareth

Roberts, "The Bodies of Demons," in *The Body in Late Medieval and Early Modern Culture*, ed. Darryll Grantley and Nina Taunton (Aldershot, UK: Ashgate, 2000), 131–142.

89. David Brakke, "Ethiopian Demons: Male Sexuality, the Black-Skinned Other, and the Monastic Self," *Journal of the History of Sexuality* 10: 3–4 (2001): 501.

90. Dyan Elliott, "Tertullian, the Angelic Life, and the Bride of Christ," in *Gender and Christianity in Medieval Europe: New Perspectives*, ed. Lisa M. Bitel and Felice Lifshitz (Philadelphia: University of Pennsylvania Press, 2008), 30.

91. Henry Mayr-Harting, *Perceptions of Angels in History: An Inaugural Lecture Delivered in the University of Oxford on 14 November 1997* (Oxford: Clarendon, 1998), 17–18. Angelic beauty was for some medieval and Renaissance thinkers a harmonious, androgynous blend of female and male traits. Maya Corry, "The Alluring Beauty of a Leonardesque Ideal: Masculinity and Spirituality in Renaissance Milan," in *Sex, Gender and the Sacred: Reconfiguring Religion in Gender History*, ed. Joanna de Groot and Sue Morgan (Sussex, UK: Wiley Blackwell, 2014), 170–94.

92. Strickland, *Saracens*, 73. Barbara Palmer observes that the iconography of angels was fairly consistent throughout the Middle Ages. Barbara D. Palmer, "The Inhabitants of Hell: Devils," in Clifford Davidson and Thomas H. Seller, eds., *The Iconography of Hell* (Kalamazoo, Mich.: Medieval Institute Publications, 1992), 20.

93. Bynum, "Metamorphosis, or Gerald and the Werewolf," *Speculum* 73:4 (1998): 1000; angels, too, could be celestial "predators" who seduced humans; see Elliott, "Tertullian," 18.

94. Bartlett, *Natural and Supernatural*, 75–77; Elliott, *Fallen Bodies*, 33–34.

95. Maaike van der Lugt, *Le ver, le démon et la vierge: les théories médiévales de la génération extraordinaire: une étude sur les rapports entre théologie, philosophie naturelle et médecine* (Paris: Les Belles Lettres, 2004), 307–8.

96. Salisbury, *Beast Within*, 78.

97. Russell, *Lucifer*, 69n131.

98. Palmer, "The Inhabitants of Hell," 24–35.

99. Coon, "Gender and the Body," 435, 447; Strickland, *Saracens*, 71–73. Sarah Alison Miller, "Monstrous Sexuality: Variations on the Vagina Dentata," in *Ashgate Research Companion to Monsters and the Monstrous*, 311–28.

100. Barbara Obrist, "Les deux visages du diable," in *Diables et diableries: La représentation du diable dans la gravure des XVe et XVIe siècles*, ed. Jean Wirth (Geneva: Cabinet des Estampes, 1976), 19–30 at 25–28; Coon, "Gender and the Body," 440–47; Marie-Christine Pouchelle, *The Body and Surgery in the Middle Ages*, trans. Rosemary Morris (Cambridge: Polity Press, 1990), 182–83.

101. Nell Gifford Martin, "Reading the Huntingfield Psalter (Pierpont Morgan Library Manuscript M.43): Devotional Literacy and an English Psalter Preface," PhD diss., University of North Carolina, Chapel Hill, 1995, 322–23, and plate 40.

102. Russell, *Lucifer*, 153n161; Nancy M. Caciola, *Discerning Spirits: Divine and Demonic Possession in the Middle Ages* (Ithaca, NY: Cornell University Press, 2003).

103. Elliott, *Fallen Bodies*, 152–54. Elliott observes that during this same period, demons became policers of sexuality, expressing disgust at transgressive or unnatural sex acts.

104. See, for instance, a famous drawing on an exchequer's roll, produced in Norwich in 1233, that shows Jews and demons counting bags of money, in Pamela A. Patton, *Art of Estrangement: Redefining Jews in Reconquest Spain* (University Park: Pennsylvania State University Press, 2012), 55, fig. 29. See also Strickland, "Meanings of Muhammad in Later Medieval Art," in *The Image of the Prophet Between Ideal and Ideology: A Scholarly Investigation*, ed. Christiane J. Gruber and Avinoam Shalem (Berlin: De Gruyter, 2014), 147–63, and *Saracens*, 77–78, 122–30; Ziolkowski, "Put in No-Man's Land," 117. Jews were also sometimes said to have horns, or even tails. See Joshua Trachtenberg, *The Devil and the Jews: The Medieval Conception of the Jew and Its Relation to Modern Anti-Semitism* (New York: Harper, 1966), 44–53; Heng, *Invention*, 72.

105. Guillaume le Clerc, *Bestiarie*, Paris, Bibiothèque nationale de France, MS français 14969, fol. 29v-31. See also *The Bestiary of Guillaume le Clerc*, trans. George Claridge Druce (Ashford, UK: Invicta, 1936), 48–50.
106. Guillaume le Clerc, *Bestiarie*, Paris, Bibiothèque nationale de France, MS français 14969, fol. 9; for an analysis of this image, see Strickland, "Leviticus," 208–9.
107. Joan Gregg, *Devils, Women, and Jews: Reflections of the Other in Medieval Sermon Stories* (Albany: State University of New York Press, 1997), 252–53n46.
108. Henry Abramson, "A Ready Hatred: Depictions of the Jewish Woman in Medieval Antisemitic Art and Caricature," *Proceedings of the American Academy for Jewish Research* 62 (1996): 4–5.
109. Trachtenberg, *The Devil and the Jews*, 30; Abramson, "A Ready Hatred," 4n12.
110. Heng, *Invention*, 15.
111. Jeremy Cohen, "The Jews as the Killers of Christ in the Latin Tradition from Augustine to the Friars," *Traditio* 39 (1983): 1–27.
112. The canons of the Fourth Lateran Council of 1215 also required Muslims and Jews to wear identifying clothing, preventing Christians from mixing inadvertently with non-Christians. *Disciplinary Decrees of the General Councils: Texts, Translation and Commentary*, ed. Henry Joseph Schroeder (St. Louis, MO: B. Herder, 1937), 290–91.
113. Kathy Lavezzo, *The Accommodated Jew: English Antisemitism from Bede to Milton* (Ithaca, NY: Cornell University Press, 2016), 64–99. See also Paola Tartakoff, "Segregatory Legislation and Jewish Religious Influence on Christians in the Thirteenth Century," in *Religious Minorities in Christian, Jewish, and Muslim Law (5th-15th Centuries)*, ed. Nora Berend et al. (Turnhout, Belgium: Brepols, 2017), 264–76.
114. Strickland notes that such statutes were weakly enforced because Jews could buy exemptions from the king; see *Medieval Bestiaries*, 254n30.
115. For shifting perceptions of Jews in the twelfth and thirteenth centuries, see David Berger, "From Crusades to Blood Libels to Expulsions: Some New Approaches to Medieval Anti-Semitism," in *Persecution, Polemic, and Dialogue: Essays in Jewish-Christian Relations* (Boston: Academic Studies Press, 2010), 15–39; Robert C. Stacey, "The Conversion of Jews to Christianity in Thirteenth-Century England," *Speculum* 67:2 (1992), 265; David Nirenberg, *Anti-Judaism: The Western Tradition* (New York: W.W. Norton, 2013), 183–216. On Jews in medieval (especially Iberian) art, see Patton, *Art of Estrangement*; Lipton, *Dark Mirror*; Heinz Schreckenberg, *The Jews in Christian Art: An Illustrated History* (New York: Continuum Publishing Co., 1996), 303–40; Cecil Roth, "Portraits and Caricatures of Medieval English Jews," in *Essays and Portraits in Anglo-Jewish History* (Philadelphia: Jewish Publication Society, 1962), 22–25; Mellinkoff, I: 127–30.
116. Robert C. Stacey, "From Ritual Crucifixion to Host Desecration: Jews and the Body of Christ," *Jewish History* 12:1 (1998): 17; Denise L. Despres, "Adolescence and Sanctity: *The Life and Passion of Saint William of Norwich*," *The Journal of Religion* 90:1 (2010): 33–62. Muslims too were accused of ritually attacking Christian children; Boswell, 279–80; 367–69.
117. Little, 51; Lavezzo, *Accommodated Jew*, 71. See also Tartakoff, "Conversion to Ritual Murder," 361–89.
118. Gavin I. Langmuir, "Thomas of Monmouth: Detector of Ritual Murder," *Speculum* 59:4 (1984): 820–46; "The Knight's Tale of Young Hugh of Lincoln," *Speculum* 47:3 (1972): 459–82.
119. The human body was an oft-cited medieval metaphor for a community or kingdom; David Berger points to a growing sense in the central and late Middle Ages that "all of society [was] an organic Christian body" in his *Persecution, Polemic, and Dialogue*, 26. See also Jacques Le Goff, "Head or Heart? The Political Use of Body Metaphors in the Middle Ages," in *Fragments for a History of the Human Body*, ed. Michel Feher, with Ramona Naddaff and Nadia Tazi, 3 vols. (New York: Zone, 1989), 3: 13–27; Kantorowicz, *The King's Two Bodies*. Images of the Jewish-hyena appeared at a time when sexual intercourse between Jews and Christians was prohibited by church decree, and

Strickland interprets one version of the image as a product, in part, of Christian fears about interreligious intimacies. Strickland, *Saracens*, 153–54.

120. R. I. Moore, *The Formation of a Persecuting Society: Power And Deviance In Western Europe, 950–1250* (Oxford: Basil Blackwell, 1987).

121. Maya Soifer, "Beyond *Convivencia*: Critical Reflections on the Historiography of Interfaith Relations in Christian Spain," *Journal of Medieval Iberian Studies* 1 (2009): 27–8. For instance, John Christian Laursen and Cary J. Nederman, eds., *Beyond the Persecuting Society: Religious Toleration Before the Enlightenment* (Philadelphia: University of Pennsylvania Press, 1997); Cary J. Nederman, *Worlds of Difference: European Discourses of Toleration, c. 1100-c. 1550* (University Park: The Pennsylvania State University Press, 2000); and, more recently, David Nirenberg, *Neighboring Faiths: Christianity, Islam, and Judaism in the Middle Ages and Today* (Chicago: University of Chicago Press, 2014); Khanmohamadi, *In Light of Another's Word;* Phillips, *Before Orientalism*.

122. Paola Tartakoff, "Testing Boundaries: Jewish Conversion and Cultural Fluidity in Medieval Europe, c. 1200–1391," *Speculum* 90:3 (2015): 728–62. See also Jerrilynn D. Dodds, María Rosa Menocal, and Abigail Krasner Balbale, eds., *The Arts of Intimacy: Christians, Jews and Muslims in the Making of Castilian Culture* (New Haven, CT: Yale University Press, 2008); David Nirenberg, "Love Between Muslim and Jew in Medieval Spain: A Triangular Affair," in Elena Laurie and Harvey J. Hames, eds., *Jews, Muslims and Christians in and Around the Crown of Aragon: Essays in Honour of Professor Elena Lourie* (Leiden: Brill, 2004), 137–65; *Communities of Violence: Persecution of Minorities in the Middle Ages* (Princeton, NJ: Princeton University Press, 1996), 1–17 and passim.

123. Khanmohamadi, *In Light of Another's World*, 2–6 and passim.

124. In Germany, as David F. Tinsley has documented, Christians described Muslims in diverse, and sometimes positive, ways; similarly, Sharon Kinoshita has shown that Christian attitudes toward Muslims in medieval France were neither homogenous nor absolute. David F. Tinsley, "Mapping the Muslims: Images of Islam in Middle High German Literature of the Thirteenth Century," in Jerold C. Frakes, ed.; *Contextualizing the Muslim Other in Medieval Christian Discourse* (New York: Palgrave, 2011), 65–101; Kinoshita, *Medieval Boundaries*.

125. See, among many examples, Andrew Holt, "Crusading Against the Barbarians: Muslims as Barbarians in Crusades Era Sources," in *East Meets West in the Middle Ages and Modern Times: Transcultural Experiences in the Premodern World*, ed. Albrecht Classen (Berlin: De Gruyter, 2013), 443–56; Tolan, *Saracens*, 105–134 and passim.

126. Heng, *Invention*, 76–77; Tartakoff, "Testing Boundaries," 745–46. Resnick, *Marks of Distinction*, 240–60; Mark M. Smith, "Transcending, Othering, Detecting: Smell, Premodernity, Modernity," *postmedieval: a journal of medieval cultural studies* 3:4 (2012): 380–90.

127. Heng, *Invention*, 30 and passim.

128. Penny J. Cole, " 'O God, The Heathen Have Come Into Thy Inheritance' (Ps 78.1): The Theme of Religious Pollution in Crusade Documents,1095-1188," in *Crusaders and Muslims in Twelfth-Century Syria*, ed. Maya Shatzmiller (Leiden: Brill, 1993), 89–90; Uri Shachar, "Pollution and Purity in Near Eastern Jewish, Christian, and Muslim Crusading Rhetoric," *Entangled Histories: Knowledge, Authority, and Jewish Culture in the Thirteenth Century*, ed. Elisheva Baumgarten, Ruth Mazo Karras, and Katelyn Mesler (Philadelphia: University of Pennsylvania Press, 2017), 229–47.

129. Cole, 94–95.

130. Just this question was at issue in scholastic texts of the period, such as Marius's *De elementis*, which newly posited a *mixtio* of contraries as a third or new thing, unlike Bernard of Clairvaux, who tended to see hybrids as continuous with their constituent parts and not something altogether new. See Bynum, *Metamorphosis*, 146–47.

131. Bynum, *Metamorphosis*, 146–47n31.

4. SEX AND ORDER IN NATURAL PHILOSOPHY AND LAW 243

132. Bynum deals with these concerns in a number of publications, including "Did the Twelfth Century Discover the Individual?" and "Jesus as Mother," both in *Jesus as Mother*, 82–109 and 110–169; *Metamorphosis*, 147–50.
133. Camille, *Image on the Edge*, 29.
134. Elliott, *Fallen Bodies*; Sarah Alison Miller, *Medieval Monstrosity and the Female Body* (New York: Routledge, 2010), 84–89, and passim.
135. Among medieval animal studies, see Crane, *Animal Encounters*; Steel, *How to Make a Human*; Karl Steel and Peggy McCracken, eds., *The Animal Turn*, special issue of *postmedieval: a journal of medieval cultural studies* 2:1 (2011); Bruce Holsinger, "Of Pigs and Parchment: Medieval Studies and the Coming of the Animal," *PMLA* 124:2 (2009): 616–23; Resl, *Cultural History of Animals*; Lorraine Daston and Gregg Mitman, eds., *Thinking with Animals: New Perspectives on Anthropomorphism* (New York: Columbia University Press, 2005); Paul Freedman, "The Representation of Medieval Peasants as Bestial and as Human," in *The Animal/Human Boundary: Historical Perspectives*, ed. Angela N. H. Creager and William Chester Jordan (Rochester, NY: University of Rochester Press, 2002), 29–49. See also the still useful Esther Cohen, "Animals in Medieval Perceptions: The Image of the Ubiquitous Other," in *Animals and Human Society: Changing Perspectives*, ed. Aubrey Manning and James Serpell (London: Routledge, 1994), 59–80.
136. Yamamoto, 12–33; Crane, *Animal Encounters*, 94–95.
137. Steel discusses this process with respect to violence against animals, 5–15, quotation at 15.
138. Salisbury, *Beast Within*, 1, 80.
139. Crane, *Animal Encounters*, 69–100.
140. Heng, *Invention*, 81.

4. SEX AND ORDER IN NATURAL PHILOSOPHY AND LAW

1. Albert the Great, *De animalibus*, Paris, Bibiothèque nationale de France, MS Latin 16169, fol. 209v. My observation reflects Michael Camille's characterization of a similar image in *Image on the Edge*, 47–48. I also rely on Robert Mills, "The Birds and the Bees: Sexual Diversity and Animality in Medieval Art," Unpublished Lecture, Rutgers University, April 2016. I thank him for sharing the text of his lecture with me.
2. Albert the Great, *De animalibus*, Paris, Bibiothèque nationale de France, MS Latin 16169, fol. 233v.
3. Amandine Postec, "Un exemplaire singulier du *De animalibus* d'Albert le Grand et son illustration (Paris, Bibiothèque nationale de France, Manuscrits, Latin 16169)," *Reinardus: Yearbook of the International Reynard Society* 26 (2014): 137–40.
4. I use "intersex" in this chapter to describe individuals with sex-variant anatomies, although as I explain in my next chapter, medieval and modern sex categories are not precisely equivalent.
5. My discussion in this chapter is influenced by writings on modern intersex, especially Reis, *Bodies in Doubt*, ix–xv and passim; Dreger, *Hermaphrodites*, 1–14, 167–201 and passim; Karkazis, *Fixing Sex*; Rubin, *Intersex Matters*. Monica H. Green identifies sex as the most significant of bodily differences in medieval society in "Bodily Essences: Bodies as Categories of Difference," in *A Cultural History of the Human Body*, volume 2 of *A Cultural History of the Human Body*, ed. Linda Kalof and William Bynum (Oxford: Berg Publishers, 2010), 150.
6. My argument follows that of Daston and Park, "The Hermaphrodite and the Orders of Nature," 419–38.
7. During the premodern period, "natural philosophy" was the body of knowledge that focused on the operations of the physical world, comparable (but not precisely equivalent) to what we now call

"science." Following other scholars, I call this body of quasi-scientific thought "naturalism" and its practitioners "naturalists." Natural philosophy was closely tied to medicine, and I touch on medical ideas here, but I discuss medical and surgical procedures in a more detailed fashion in the next chapter.

8. Daston and Park, "The Hermaphrodite," 421.
9. Giulia Sissa, "Philosophies of Sex," 55. See also Lloyd, "The Development of Aristotle's Theory of the Classification of Animals," *Phronesis* 6:1 (1961), 59–81.
10. A. L. Peck, "Preface" to Aristotle, *On the Generation of Animals* (London: Harvard University Press, 1963) [hereafter, GA], xxxviii–lxx, at lxx.
11. Cadden, *Meanings*, 22–25, 189; Peck, "Preface." xxxix–xl; Sherry Sayed Gadelrab, "Discourses on Sex Differences in Medieval Scholarly Islamic Thought," *Journal of the History of Medicine and Allied Sciences* 66:1 (2010): 49. Aristotle distinguished between natural philosophy and medicine, but the two fields overlapped: ancient medicine was influenced by philosophical concepts, and Aristotle's work included medical topics. Galen, moreover, engaged in philosophical and teleological thinking. Siraisi, *Medieval and Renaissance Medicine: An Introduction to Knowledge and Practice* (Chicago: University of Chicago Press, 1990), 2–5; Brooke Holmes, *Gender: Antiquity and Its Legacy* (London: I. B. Tauris, 2012), 36.
12. GA II, 1, 732a2-6; Aristotle, *De Animalibus: Michael Scot's Arabic-Latin Translation, Part Three, Books XV-XIX: Generation of Animals*, ed. Aafke M. I. Van Oppenraaij (Leiden: Brill, 1992 [hereafter, VO]), 58: "Et quia causa prima movens est melior, et debet esse illa causa forma, quoniam est melior materia, et quod est melius semper debet separari a peiori in omnibus rebus possibilibus, fuit mas separatus a femina, quoniam mas est melior et propinquior ut sit sicut forma, femina autem est sicut materia." Long, *Hermaphrodites*, 13.
13. Sissa, "Philosophies of Sex," 65–71.
14. GA IV, 1, 766a14-30; GA IV, 3, 767b10-13; VO, 170–71; 175–76. Sissa, "Philosophies of Sex," 75; Karen M. Nielson, "The Private Parts of Animals: Aristotle on the Teleology of Sexual Difference," *Phronesis* 53:4/5 (2008): 373–405.
15. GA IV, 3, 767b1-14; VO, 175. For woman as a "failed" male, see Nielson, 376–77, 384; Cadden, *Meanings*, 23–4.
16. GA II, 3, 737a25-34; IV, 1, 766a14-30; VO, 76; 170–71. Nielson, 386, 400–5.
17. GA 769b10-770a30; VO, 182–5; Sissa, "Philosophies of Sex," 75; Long, *Hermaphrodites*, 13–14.
18. GA IV, 4, 770b28-37; VO, 186–87: "Quoniam forte aliquando paritur filius habens multos digitos et forte habens unum digitum tantum, et similiter in aliis membris, quoniam forte erunt superflui et forte erunt diminuti. Et forte parietur filius habens virgam et membrum mulieris, et hoc accidit etiam mulieribus et capris quae dicuntur graece traganez, quoniam ista habent membrum maris et feminae."
19. GA IV, 4, 772b26-33-773a3; VO, 193–94; Daston and Park, "Hermaphrodite," 421.
20. Lloyd, 76–77; Sissa, *Sex and Sensuality in the Ancient World*, trans. George Staunton (New Haven, CT: Yale University Press, 2008), 4.
21. GA I, 1, 715b1-30; GA II, 4–5, 741a4-b5; GA III, 5, 755b21-25; VO, 2–4; 88–90; 136. Peck, "Preface," lxiii, lxix.
22. F. Jamil Ragep, "Islamic Culture and the Natural Sciences," and Emilie Savage-Smith, "Medicine in Medieval Islam," in D. Lindberg and M. H. Shank, ed., *The Cambridge History of Science*, ed. D. Lindberg and M. H. Shank (Cambridge: Cambridge University Press, 2013), 27–61, 139–67; Peter E. Pormann and Emilie Savage-Smith, *Medieval Islamic Medicine* (Washington, DC: Georgetown University Press, 2007).
23. Ragep, 29–32 and passim; Savage-Smith, "Medicine," 139–45; Gadelrab, 45–46, 53–59; Dimitri L. Gutas, *Greek Thought, Arabic Culture: The Graeco-Arabic Translation Movement in Baghdad and Early 'Abbasid Society, 2nd–4th/8th–10th Centuries* (London: Routledge, 1998); John A. C. Greppin,

4. SEX AND ORDER IN NATURAL PHILOSOPHY AND LAW 245

24. Savage-Smith, and John L. Gueriguian *The Diffusion of Greco-Roman Medicine in the Middle East and the Caucasus* (Delmar, NY: Caravan, 1999).
24. Gadelrab, 45–81.
25. Gadelrab, 53–79; Savage-Smith, "Medicine," 145–54.
26. Pormann and Savage-Smith, 43–45; Park, "Medicine and Natural Philosophy," 86–90. Per-Gunnar Ottosson, *Scholastic Medicine and Philosophy: A Study of Commentaries on Galen's Tegni* (c. 1300–1450) (Naples: Bibliopolis, 1984), 129–94.
27. Ahmed Ragab, "One, Two, or Many Sexes: Sex Differentiation in Islamicate Medical Thought," *Journal of the History of Sexuality* 24:3 (2015): 444–45.
28. Quoted in Ragab, 450, from the Arabic. The Latin translation renders the text slightly differently. Avicenna, *Liber canonis Avicenne* (Venice, 1507; facsimile reprint, Hildesheim, Germany: Georg Olms, 1964), bk. 3, fen. 20, tr. 2, chap. 43 (fol. 358):

> Illi qui est hermaphroditus non est membrum viri neque membrum mulieris. Et de illis est qui habet utrumque: sed vnum eorum est occultius et debilius et aliud est econtrario et descendit sperma ex vno eorum absque alio. Et de illis est in quo ambo sunt equalia. Et peruenit ad me quod de illis est qui agit et patiatur sed parum verificatur hoc. Et multotiens curantur per incisionem membrum occultioris et regimen vulneris eius.

29. Abū Bakr al-Rāzī (d. c. 930) observed that some individuals have both male and female tissue in their genital area, and they might suffer from sterility or other ailments that arose from their specific constitution. See Ragab, 430, 447–50; Gadelrab, 80–81; Sara Scalenghe, *Disability in the Ottoman Arab World*, 124–62; "Being Different: Intersexuality, Blindness, Deafness, and Madness in Ottoman Syria," PhD diss., Georgetown University, 2006, 44–106.
30. Scalenghe, "Being Different," 82.
31. Gadelrab, 43–44; see also Ragab, 428–54; Cadden, *Meanings*, 37.
32. Siraisi, *Medieval and Renaissance Medicine*, 6–7; Park, "Medicine and Natural Philosophy," 85–86; Cadden, *Meanings*, 46–53. Influential works were by the likes of Soranus, Dioscorides, and Isidore of Seville. See, for instance, Ann Ellis Hanson and Monica H. Green, "Soranus of Ephesus: Methodicorum Princeps," *Aufstieg und Niedergang der Römischen Welt* 37 (1994): 968–1075; Caelius Aurelianus, *Gynaecia*, ed. Miriam F. Drabkin and Israel E. Drabkin (Baltimore, MD: Bulletin of the History of Medicine, Suppl. 13, 1951); Pedanius Dioscorides of Anazarbus, *De materia medica*, Lily Y. Beck (Hildesheim: Olms-Weidmann, 2017); Isidore of Seville: *The Medical Writings. An English Translation with an Introduction and Commentary*, ed. and trans. William D. Sharpe, *Transactions of the American Philosophical Society* 54:2 (1964): 1–75.
33. Siraisi, *Medieval and Early Renaissance Medicine*, 13–16, 48–50 and passim; Luis García-Ballester, "Introduction: Practical Medicine from Salerno to the Black Death," in *Practical Medicine from Salerno to the Black Death*, ed. Luis García-Ballester, Roger French, Jon Arrizabalaga, and Andrew Cunningham (Cambridge: Cambridge University Press, 1994), 10. Charles Burnett and Danielle Jacquart, eds., *Constantine the African and Ali ibn al-Abbas al-Majusi: The Pantegni and Related Texts*, Studies in Ancient Medicine, vol. 10 (Leiden: Brill, 1994).
34. Cadden, *Meanings*, 167.
35. Park, "Medicine and Natural Philosophy," 93–94; for ancient sources and their role in medieval debates about sexual difference, see Cadden, *Meanings*, 13–21 (for Aristotle), 30–39 (Galen), 117–34 (scholastic views on seed and sex differentiation) and passim. For specific physiological and anatomical differences in anatomical texts, see Green, "Bodily Essences," 153–54; Siraisi, *Medieval and Early Renaissance Medicine*, 102–14.
36. Daston and Park, "Hermaphrodite," 421.
37. Outi Merisalo, "The Early Tradition of the Pseudo-Galenic *De spermate* (Twelfth-Thirteenth Centuries)," *SCRIPTA: An International Journal of Codicology and Palaeography* 5 (2012): 99–109; Päivi

Pahta, *Medieval Embryology in the Vernacular*, 94–120; Green, *Making Women's Medicine Masculine*, 22n65; Nederman and True, 503–5.

38. London, British Library, Cotton MS Galba E IV, fol. 234:

> Notandum quia si sperma ceciderit in dextram partem matricis; masculus erit. . . . Si autem sperma uiri existens debile cadit in dextram partem et associatur spermati mulieris fortiori se licet masculus fiat, tamen muliebris est . . . et tantam debilitatem potest uenire sperma, quod infans utriusque sexus erit. Si autem ceciderit sperma in sinistram partem, in femineam naturam uertitur. . . . Quod si sperma uirile preualuerit spermati mulieris in sinistra parte, licet uertatur in femineum sexum, tamen retinet quedam uirilia ut gernones et barbam et grossos sermones et cetera. Et ad tantam debilitatem potest uenire femineum sperma quod utriusque sexus efficitur.

> See *An Electronic Edition of the Pseudo-Galenic Treatise Variously Entitled De spermate, Microtegni, and De XII portis*, ed. Outi Merisalo, available online at https://staff.jyu.fi/Members/merisalo/galbanorm.pdf. See also Danielle Jacquart and Claude Thomasset, *Sexuality and Medicine in the Middle Ages*, trans. Matthew Adamsom (Oxford: Polity, 1988), 141; for a Middle English version, see Pahta, 173–75.

39. Brian Lawn, ed., *The Prose Salernitan Questions: Edited from a Bodleian Manuscript (Auct. F. 3. 10)* (London: British Academy, 1979), 103:

> Si vero plus de muliebri spermate in dextra parte collocetur, femina virago generatur. Si plus in sinistram quam in dextram, et si plus sit de virili semine quam muliebri, vir effeminatus nascitur. Si in media cellula ita ut utriusque partis suscipiat impressionem, hermofroditus erit, quoniam et unius et alterius corporis habebit et geret supplementa.

> Trans. in Cadden, *Meanings*, 201. See also Lawn, *The Salernitan Questions: An Introduction to the History of Medieval and Renaissance Problem Literature* (Oxford: Clarendon, 1963).

40. Nederman and True, 503; Cadden, *Meanings*, 198–202; Daston and Park, "Hermaphrodite," 420–22.
41. Kudlien, 415–23; Cadden, *Meanings*, 198–99; Pahta, 102.
42. For seed theories, see Ragab, 431–41; Pahta, 34–43; Gadelrab, "Discourses on Sex Differences in Medieval Scholarly Islamic Thought," 48–49.
43. Cadden, *Meanings*, 131, 197–203; Sissa, "Philosophies of Sex," 68–75; Helen Rodnite Lemay, "The Stars and Human Sexuality: Some Medieval Scientific Views," *Isis* 71:1 (1980): 132; Anna Kłosowska, "Premodern Trans and Queer in French Manuscripts and Early Printed Texts," *postmedieval: a journal of medieval cultural studies* 9:3 (2018): 354–59.
44. Nederman and True, 504–5.
45. Aafke M. I. Van Oppenraaij, "Michael Scot's Arabic-Latin Translation of Aristotle's Books *On Animals*," in *Aristotle's Animals in the Middle Ages and Renaissance*, ed. Carlos Steel, Guy Guldentops, and Pieter Beullens (Leuven, Belgium: Leuven University Press, 1992), 31–43; Siraisi, *Medieval and Early Renaissance Medicine*, 80–81; Cadden, *Meanings*, 106–9. Another Greco-Latin translation of *On Animals* appeared after 1260, and the texts are still extant in 115 manuscript copies. Peter Biller, "Proto-Racial Thought in Medieval Science," 167.
46. Cadden, *Meanings*, 110–11.
47. Siraisi, *Medieval and Early Renaissance Medicine*, 57–66; John W. Baldwin, *The Scholastic Culture of the Middle Ages, 1000–1300* (Lexington, MA: Heath, 1971).
48. Cadden, *Meanings*, 56, 66–69.
49. Kenneth F. Kitchell Jr. and Irven Michael Resnick, "Introduction: The Life and Works of Albert the Great," in Albertus Magnus, *De animalibus*, translated as *On Animals: A Medieval Summa Zoologica*, trans. and ed. Kenneth F. Kitchell Jr. and Irven Michael Resnick, 2 vols. (Baltimore, MD: Johns Hopkins University Press, 1999), I: 20–21 [hereafter SZ]; Pasnau, "The Latin Aristotle," 666–67.

50. Park, "Medicine and Natural Philosophy," 95–96.
51. Daston and Park, "Hermaphrodite," 420–22.
52. Ragep, 41; Pahta, 30, 35; Park, "Medicine and Natural Philosophy," 90–91; Siraisi, *Medieval and Early Renaissance Medicine*, 100; Danielle Jacquart, "Anatomy, Physiology, and Medical Theory," in *The Cambridge History of Science*, ed. David Lindberg and M. Shank (Cambridge: Cambridge University Press, 2013), 591.
53. Daston and Park, "Hermaphrodite," 420–22.
54. Kitchell and Resnick, "Introduction," I: 2. A Latin edition of *De animalibus* appears in Hermann Stadler, ed., *Albertus Magnus de animalibus libri XXVI: Beiträge zur Geschichte der Philosophie des Mittelalters: Texte und Untersuchungen*, 15–16, 2 vols. (Münster: Aschendorff, 1916–21) [hereafter Stadler]. My observations in this section are indebted to Irven M. Resnick, and I thank him for sharing his work with me.
55. Cadden, *Meanings*, 113; Kitchell and Resnick, "Introduction," 34; Demaitre and Travill, 411. On Albert's sources, see Miguel J. C. de Asúa, "The Organization of Discourse on Animals in the Thirteenth Century: Peter of Spain, Albert the Great, and the commentaries on *De animalibus*," PhD diss., University of Notre Dame, 1991, and the essays collected in Weisheipl, ed., *Albertus Magnus and the Sciences*.
56. *Questions Concerning on Animals* was based on a series of lectures on Aristotle's *On Animals* given at the university in Cologne in 1258 and preserved in the notes of Albert's student Conrad of Austria in around 1260. "Introduction," in Albertus Magnus, *Questions Concerning Aristotle's On Animals*, trans. Irven M. Resnick and Kenneth F. Kitchell, Jr. (Washington, DC: Catholic University of America Press, 2008), 5–6. Nancy Siraisi, "The Medical Learning of Albertus Magnus," in *Albertus Magnus and the Sciences: Commemorative Essays, 1980*, ed. James A. Weisheipl (Toronto: Pontifical Institute of Mediaeval Studies, 1980), 380.
57. Demaitre and Travill, 437; Van der Lugt, "L'humanité," 2.
58. Albertus Magnus, *Quaestiones super de animalibus*, ed. Ephrem Filthaut, vol. 12 of *Opera omnia* (Münster: Aschendorff, 1955), bk. 18, q. 1 (296). English trans. in *Questions Concerning Aristotle's On Animals*, 531.
59. Demaitre and Travill, 405, 410–11.
60. Filthaut, bk. 15, q. 4–5 (262): "Oppositum dicit Philosophus. Dicit enim, quod in plantis sexus est confusus, sed in animalibus distinctus." English trans. in *Questions Concerning Aristotle's On Animals*, 445.
61. *De animalibus*, 4.2.4–5.1.1.1–4 (SZ I: 484–8; Stadler 1: 403–9). For Albert on plants, see Karen Meier Reeds, *Botany in Medieval and Renaissance Universities* (New York: Garland, 1991), 7–9.
62. Resnick, "Hermaphrodites," 329–34; *De animalibus* 17.1.5.38–39 (SZ 2: 1255–56; Stadler 2: 1164–65).
63. Filthaut, bk. 15, q. 4–5 (262): "Verumtamen per occasionem naturae mas et femina concurrere possunt in eodem ratine diversorum, sicut patet in hermaphrodita, qui habet utrumque membrum; sed hoc est monstrum in natura." English trans. in *Questions Concerning Aristotle's On Animals*, 445–46.
64. Filthaut, bk. 18, q. 2 (297); English trans. in *Questions Concerning Aristotle's On Animals*, 553.
65. Cadden, *Meanings*, 133; Resnick, "Hermaphrodites."
66. Resnick, "Hermaphrodites"; Demaitre and Travill, 437–38; *De animalibus* 18.2.3.65–66 (SZ II: 1312–13; Stadler 2: 1224–25); J. M. Thijssen, "Twins as Monsters: Albertus Magnus's Theory of the Generation of Twins and its Philosophical Context," *Bulletin of the History of Medicine* 61:2 (1987): 237–46.
67. On Albert's theory of division, see Thijssen, "Twins as Monsters," 241, 245–46.
68. *De animalibus* 18.2.3.66 (SZ II: 1312; Stadler 2: 1224): "propter quod etiam unum membrorum est principale et aliud parum habet plus quam figuram."

69. *De animalibus*, 18.2.3.66 (SZ II: 1313; Stadler 2: 1225):

    Et aliquando est ita figura utriusque membri completa quod ad visum et tactum discerni non potest quis sexus praevaleat: et non est inconveniens quin talis partus etiam habeat duas vesicas et urinam emittat per utrumque et quod in coitu et agat et patiatur, et incumbat et succumbat: sed non puto quod et impraegnet et impraegnetur. Sed pro certo sexus erit principalior qui a cordis iuvatur complexione: tamen aliquando etiam complexio cordis ita media est quod vix discerni potest quis sexuum praevaleat.

70. Resnick, "Hermaphrodites"; *De animalibus* 3.2.2.90–1 (SZ I: 389; Stadler 1: 316–17); 9.1.1.1–15 (SZ I: 774–79; Stadler 1: 674–79); 15.1.2.8–12 (SZ II: 1088–90; Stadler 2: 993–95) and passim; Cadden, *Meanings*, 185.
71. Resnick, "Hermaphrodites," 327–34.
72. Cadden, *Meanings*, 212.
73. Resnick, "Hermaphrodites," 332. Filthaut, bk. 18, q. 2 (297); *Questions Concerning Aristotle's* On Animals, 532–34. Other texts, including Gérard de Breuil's commentary on *De animalibus* (1260–4) and a quodlibet from the faculty of the arts of Paris (c. 1300) attributed to Henry of Germany and Henry of Brussels also debated whether hermaphrodites could both sire and bear offspring, or whether auto-fertilization was possible. Van der Lugt, *Le ver*, 119–23, 307–8.
74. Albertus Magnus, *Mineralium libri quinque*, in *Opera omnia*, vol. 5, ed. A. Borgnet (Paris: Apud Ludovicum Vivès, 1890), bk. IV, chap. 1 (82); see chapter 6 on "Scholastic Contributions." See also Filthaut, bk. 15, q. 4–5 (261–62); *Questions Concerning Aristotle's* On Animals, 444–46. For Albert on plants, see Karen Reeds, "Albert on the Natural Philosophy of Plant Life," in *Albertus Magnus and the Sciences: Commemorative Essays, 1980*, ed. James A. Weisheipl (Toronto: Pontifical Institute of Mediaeval Studies, 1980), 341–54.
75. Steel notes that Thomas sought to exclude all monsters from humanity, *How to Make a Human*, 54; and see chapter 2 above on "Monsters and Definitions of the Human." For Albert on the humanity of monsters, Demaitre and Travill, 434, 436.
76. Nederman and True, 497–517; Cadden, *Meanings*, 212.
77. *De animalibus*, 18.2.3.69 (SZ II: 1314; Stadler 2: 1226): "In quodam etiam nostri temporis nato testiculi infra pellem contenti erant superius, ita quod prominentia eorum repraesentabat duo labra vulvae muliebris: et fissure videbatur esse in medio clausa per pellem: et cum putaretur esse puella a parentibus et deberet aperiri fissura ut habilitaretur ad coitum, incisione facta prosilierunt testiculi et virga: et postea duxit uxorem et genuit ex ea plures filios." Note the resemblance to a similar case in Bern in 1300 from the *Annales Colmarienses Minores*, cited by Miri Rubin, "The Person in the Form: Medieval Challenges to Bodily 'Order,' " in *Framing Medieval Bodies*, ed. Sarah Kay and Miri Rubin (Manchester: Manchester University Press, 1994), 101–2.
78. Demaitre and Travill, 409; Siraisi, "Medical Learning," 384.
79. Albert's account resembles mythic sex-change stories recounted by Pliny the Elder (first century CE) and Diodorus of Sicily (first century BCE), and later by Ambroise Paré (sixteenth century), all of which seem to support Thomas Laqueur's "one-sex" theory. These stories differ from the more nuanced observations of Lanfranc of Milan, whom I discuss in chapter 5. See Pliny the Elder, *Natural History, Volume II: Books 3–7*, (7.4), 2:530; *Diodoros of Sicily*, ed. and trans. Francis R. Walton, 12 vols. (Cambridge, MA: Harvard University Press, 1957), XI: 446–55. Bernadette J. Brooten discusses Diodorus's text in *Love Between Women*, 277–80. For the famous case of Marie-Germain, see Ambroise Paré, *On Monsters and Marvels*, trans. Janis L. Pallister (Chicago: University of Chicago Press, 1995), 31–33.
80. Siraisi, "Medical Learning," 379–80.
81. Pahta, 7; García-Ballester, "Introduction," 4–9.
82. Van der Lugt, "Pourquoi," 99.

83. I rely on Van der Lugt's extensive treatment of the text in her "Sex Difference," 103–13, and "Pourquoi," 103–13. *On the Human Body* (*De corpore humano*) is published as 'De corpore muliebri' in Alexander of Hales (attrib.), *Doctoris irrefragabilis Alexandri de Hales Ordinis Minorum Summa theologica*, 4 vols. (Quaracchi, Italy: Collegium S. Bonaventurae, 1928), II, inq. iv, tract. ii, sect. ii, q. ii, 463–8 (II: 610–30).
84. Cadden, *Meanings*, 190.
85. *De corpore humano*, II: 611: "Quia natura operatur in quantum brevius potest, et hoc spectat ad eius nobilitatem et dignitatem; ergo, si generatio humana fieret ab uno solo principio, videlicet ab una persona, et uno sexu, natura humana dignius et perfectius esset instituta; ergo videtur quod Deus non debuerit eam condere in sexuum pluralitate."
86. *De corpore humano*, II: 612:

> homo perfectissimum est omnium animalium, videtur quod conveniens fuerit hominem fieri in distinctio sexuum [. . ..]; ergo debet communicare in modo generandi cum animalibus brutis; sed, cum sit duplex modus—est enim quidam modus generandi in distinctione sexus, quidam sine—magis convenit homini illa communicatio quae est per modum nobiliorem quam alia; modus autem nobilior est quo distinguitur agens a patiente quam ille quo confunduntur in eodem.

87. Van der Lugt, "Pourquoi," 105–6.
88. *De corpore humano*, II: 612–13:

> Litteralis quidem, quia natura desiderat perfectionem et refugit confusionem, et ideo debuit homo fieri taliter ut esset in eo perfectio ad actum propagandi, et ita in primaria hominis conditione debuit fieri agens et patiens, et haec inconfusa. Et hinc est quod mulier formata fuit a viro distincta, ne, si pluralitas sexuum in unam personam concurreret confusionem faceret, quam refugit natura et rectum rationis iudicium, sicut videmus circa hermaphroditum.

89. *De corpore humano*, II: 613: "Praeterea, non decuit humanam dignitatem in tali opere, scilicet propagationis humanae, confusionem agentis et patientis sustinere."
90. Van der Lugt, "Sex Difference," 107.
91. Van der Lugt, "Sex Difference," 106–10.
92. *De corpore humano*, II: 613: "Ratio allegorica fuit ut in illorum sexuum distinctione et coniunctione in carnis unitatem significaretur coniunctio Christi et Ecclesiae."
93. *De corpore humano*, II: 613.
94. Elsewhere in the *Summa*, the author argued that monsters' bodily differences derived from sin. The purported deformity of intersex people supposedly rendered them an inferior form of humanity, both aesthetically and morally. Van der Lugt, "L'humanité," 7; Friedman, *Monstrous Races*, 187.
95. Van der Lugt, "Pourquoi," 106.
96. Petrus de Palude, *Exactissimi et q[ua]m maxime probati ac clarissimi doctoris Petri de Palude Predicatorij Ordinis Hierosolimitani quonda[m] Patriarche dignissimi Quartus Sententiaru[m] liber* (Paris: Petit, Regnault, & Chevallon, 1514), 133rb: "Oportet tamen quod sit alterum tantum: quia in plantis possunt coniungi vis masculina et femina perfecte: sed nunquam in animalibus perfectis et maxime hominibus."
97. Corbeill, 151–59; Luc Brisson, *Sexual Ambivalence*, 7–40.
98. Corbeill, 166; Jane F. Gardner, "Sexing a Roman: Imperfect Men in Roman Law" in *When Men Were Men: Masculinity, Power, and Identity in Classical Antiquity*, ed. Lin Foxhall and John Salmon (New York: Routledge, 1998), 136–52.
99. Rolker "Two Laws," 181–211.
100. Paula Sanders, "Gendering the Ungendered Body: Hermaphrodites in Medieval Islamic Law," in *Women in Middle Eastern History: Shifting Boundaries in Sex and Gender*, ed. Nikki R. Keddie and

Beth Baron (New Haven, CT: Yale University Press, 1991), 74–95; Max Strassfeld, "Translating the Human," 587–604.

101. *The Digest of Justinian*, ed. Theodor Mommsen, Paul Kreuger, and Alan Watson (Philadelphia: University of Pennsylvania Press, 1985), 28.2.6. 2 (II: 820). Rolker, "Two Laws," 187–89.

102. *The Digest of Justinian*, 22.5.15 (II: 652): "Hermaphroditus an ad testamentum adhiberi possit, qualitas sexus incalescentis ostendit."

103. Kuefler, *Manly Eunuch*, 23; Green, "Caring for Gendered Bodies," in *Oxford Handbook of Medieval Women and Gender*, ed. Judith Bennett and Ruth Mazo Karras (Oxford: Oxford University Press, 2013), 356.

104. Azo of Bologna, *In ius civile Summa* (N.p.: Lyon, 1564), 281ra: "Hermaphroditus comparatur masculo tantum, vel foeminae tantum, secundum praeualentiam sexus incalescentis."

105. Kirshner and Cavallar, 107.

106. "Hermaphroditus comparatur masculo tantum vel foeminae tantum secundum praevalescentiam sexus incalescentis." Metzler, "Hermaphroditism," 28.

107. Rolker, "Two Laws," 205.

108. Rolandino de' Passageri, *Summa artis notariae* (Lyon: Apud haeredes Iacobi Iuntae, 1559), 806: "Et sic ista diuisio trimembris potest reduci ad bimembrem: quia si magis incalescunt in masculino sexu, sunt in primo membro: si magis incalescunt in foeminino sunt in secundo." Christof Rolker, "Roman Law on Hermaphrodites," accessed on April 11, 2019, https://www.academia.edu/8962918/Roman_law_on_hermaphrodites.

109. Rolker, "Two Laws," 205.

110. This is the view of Kirshner and Cavallar, 107; Rolker and Nederman and True use different language, describing the law as denoting two sexes and three "genders," Nederman and True, 511–17; Rolker, "Two Laws," 178–222.

111. Gratian, *Decretum Magistri Gratiani (Concordia discordantium canonum)*, ed. Emil Friedberg, in *Corpus Iuris Canonici* (Leipzig: Tauchnitz,1879), pars 2, c. 4, q. 2, canon 3: § 22: "Hermaphroditus an ad testamentum adhiberi possit, qualitas sexus incalescentis ostendit."

112. Rolker, "Two Laws," 190–98.

113. Huguccio, *Summa decretorum*, Vatican City, BAV, MS Vat. Lat. 2280, fol. 140v:

> Si quidem habet barbam et semper vult exercere virilia et non feminea et semper vult conversare cum viris et non cum feminis signum est quod virilis sexus in eo prevalet et tunc potest esse testis ubi mulier non admittitur scilicet in testamento et in ultimis voluntatibus tunc etiam ordinari potest. Si vero caret barba et semper vult esse cum feminis et exercere feminea opera iudicium est quod feminini [sic] sexus in eo prevalet et tunc non admittitur ad testimonium ubi femina non admittitur, scilicet in testamento sed nec tunc ordinari potest quia femina ordinem non recipit. Praeterea ad talem discretionem multum valet inspectio genitalium. Quid si illi duo sexus equales per omnia inveniuntur in eo credo quod debeat iudicari de eo tamquam femineus sexus in eo praevalet quia verum est virilem sexum in eo non praevalere.

> On Huguccio, see Kenneth Pennington and Wolfgang P. Müller, "The Decretists: The Italian school," in *The History of Medieval Canon Law in the Classical Period, 1140–1234: From Gratian to the Decretals of Pope Gregory IX*, ed. Wilfried Hartmann and Kenneth Pennington (Washington, DC: Catholic University of America Press, 2008), 142–60.

114. See Barbara Newman, *From Virile Woman to WomanChrist* (Philadelphia: University of Pennsylvania Press, 1995); Bynum, "Jesus as Mother," 110–69.

115. On hair, Cadden, *Meanings*, 181–83; see also Van der Lugt, "Sex Difference," 111. Rolker notes the ambiguity of Huguccio's "company," "Two Laws," 193–94.

4. SEX AND ORDER IN NATURAL PHILOSOPHY AND LAW   251

116. Rolker, "Two Laws," 195; A. J. Minnis, "*De impedimento sexus*: Women's Bodies and Medieval Impediments to Female Ordination," in *Medieval Theology and the Natural Body*, ed. Peter Biller and A.J. Minnis (York: University of York, York Medieval Press, 1997), 109–39.
117. Metzler, *Disability in Medieval Europe*, 40–41. Metzler explains distinctions between impairments and their social construction as disabilities.
118. Metzler, "Hermaphroditism," 36.
119. Metzler, *Disability*, 274n77.
120. Rolker, "Two Laws," 198–200; Kirshner and Cavallar, 109.
121. Kirshner and Cavallar, 108–9.
122. Kirshner and Cavallar, 108–9.
123. Kirshner and Cavallar, 110–12.
124. Charlotte Fonrobert makes a similar observation with respect to rabbinic law; see her "Regulating the Human Body: Rabbinic Legal Discourse and the Making of Jewish Gender," in *The Cambridge Companion to the Talmud and Rabbinic Literature*, ed. Charlotte Elisheva Fonrobert and Martin S. Jaffee (Cambridge: Cambridge University Press, 2007), 270–94. For modern analogues, Anne Fausto-Sterling, "The Five Sexes: Why Male and Female Are Not Enough," *The Sciences* 33 (March/April 1993): 20–25.
125. Rolker, "Two Laws," 183–84, 202.
126. Rolker, "Der Hermaphrodit und seine Frau," 593–620; "Two Laws," 208–10.
127. *De civitate Dei*, 16.8 (136): "ut, ex quo potius debeant accipere nomen, incertum sit ; a meliore tamen, hoc est a masculino, ut appellarentur, loquendi consuetudo praevaluit. Nam nemo umquam Androgynaecas aut Hermaphroditas nuncupavit." English trans., 663.
128. Albertus Magnus, *De secretis mulierum: Item De virtutibus herbarum lapidum et animalium* (Amsterdam: Apud Iodocum Ianssonium 1655), 98: "Et a viro tanquam digniori recipit speciem secundum naturam, licet hae naturae fiant in ipso." English trans. in Ps.-Albertus Magnus, *Women's Secrets: A Translation of Pseudo-Albertus Magnus's De Secretis Mulierum with Commentaries*, ed. and trans. Helen Rodnite Lemay (Albany, NY: State University of New York Press, 1992), 117.
129. Ann Blair, "Authorship in the Popular 'Problemata Aristotelis,' " *Early Science and Medicine* 4:3 (1999): 189–227. The *Prose Salernitan Questions* (which I discuss earlier in this chapter, in the section entitled "Sex Differentiation in Latin Europe") is another example of a natural questions text.
130. Iolanda Ventura, "*Quaestiones* and Encyclopedias: Some Aspects of the Late Medieval Reception of Pseudo-Aristotelian *Problemata* in Encyclopedic and Scientific Culture," in *Schooling and Society*, 24, 30–32.
131. This version has been published as *Problemata Varia Anatomica: The University of Bologna MS 1165*, ed. L. R. Lind (Lawrence: University of Kansas Press, 1968); for dating and sources see his introduction, 1–6.
132. Ventura, 32.
133. *Problemata Varia Anatomica*, 67: "Respondetur quod in eo consideranda est quantitas unius membri super quantitatem alterius membri et debet considerari in quo membro sit potens in actu uenereo et si in uirili, tunc est uir et si in alio tunc est mulier."
134. *Problemata Varia Anatomica*, 67: "Respondetur quod nomine uiri quia nomina imponuntur ad placitum et a digniori debet fieri denominatio quia uir est dignior muliere ex quo agens praestantius est suo passo." Van der Lugt, "Sex Difference," 112.
135. Resnick, "Hermaphrodites"; *Problemata Varia Anatomica*, 67: "ergo dicunt naturales quod hermofrodita semper sit impotens in membro uirili."
136. *Problemata Varia Anatomica*, 67–68; Ps.-Albertus Magnus, *Women's Secrets*, 115–16. Van der Lugt points out that this story is not found in Albert's oeuvre, although he discusses hybrids in his *Physica*. See "L'humanité," 11 and 11n45.

137. *Problemata Varia Anatomica*, 67: "Respondetur secundum regulam iuris quia debet iurare antequam admittatur ad iudicium quo membro potest uti et secundum hoc est admittendus secundum usum et potentiam talis membri, et si utentur ambobus membris tunc secundum catholicam in.c. mundus [secundum sanctam matrem ecclesiam non est tolerandus *text of 1500*]."
138. Ragab, 430.
139. Fausto-Sterling, *Sexing the Body*, 4; Monica H. Green extends this reasoning to the medieval period, writing that historical actors were always "both sexed and gendered simultaneously." *Making Women's Medicine Masculine*, 30. See also Rubin, *Intersex Matters*, 12–14.
140. Thomas Laqueur makes this important point about the constructed nature of sex in his *Making Sex: Body and Gender from the Greeks to Freud*. Cambridge: Harvard University Press, 1990). See also Kirshner and Cavallar, 105; Karkazis, *Fixing Sex*, 94, 287–90 and passim.
141. Reis, ix–xv.

5. THE CORRECTION OF NATURE: SEX AND THE SCIENCE OF SURGERY

1. Michael R. McVaugh, *The Rational Surgery of the Middle Ages* (Florence: SISMEL, 2006), 13–87.
2. Siraisi, *Medieval and Early Renaissance Medicine*, 153–86.
3. Pahta, 11; Green, *Making Women's Medicine Masculine*, 38–39 and passim.
4. For medical practitioners, their licensing and training, and their approach to medicine, see McVaugh, *Medicine Before the Plague*, 38–42; Monica H. Green, "Bodies, Gender, Health, Disease: Recent Work on Medieval Women's Medicine," *Studies in Medieval and Renaissance History*, 3rd ser. vol. 2 (2005): 1–46; Danielle Jacquart, "Medical Practice in Paris in the First Half of the Fourteenth Century," in *Practical Medicine*, 186–210; Siraisi, *Medieval and Early Renaissance Medicine*, 17–36; Pouchelle, 13–22.
5. McVaugh, *Rational Surgery*, 35, 89–134, and passim.
6. The surgeons were not completely successful in their goals to institutionalize surgical instruction in the universities, however. See *Rational Surgery*, 229–66.
7. Green, *Making Women's Medicine Masculine*, 14; McVaugh, *Rational Surgery*, 40–41, 53–54 and passim.
8. Green, *Making Women's Medicine Masculine*, viii–9, 107, 120–62. Universities did not, however, exercise a monopoly over the training and licensing of physicians; regulation was variable with respect to time, place, and discipline; see Siraisi, *Medieval and Early Renaissance Medicine*, 17–20, 179–81. For apprenticeships, see Cornelius O'Boyle, "Surgical Texts and Social Contexts: Physicians and Surgeons in Paris, c. 1270 to 1340," in *Practical Medicine*, 159–60.
9. McVaugh, *Rational Surgery*, 38–39.
10. McVaugh, *Rational Surgery*, 35–41, 54–59. Not all surgeons argued for integration of medicine and surgery, however.
11. Luke Demaitre, "Skin and the City: Cosmetic Medicine as an Urban Concern," in *Between Text and Patient: The Medical Enterprise in Medieval and Modern Europe*, ed. Florence Eliza Glaze and Brian K. Nance (Florence: SISMEL, 2011), 97–120. See also Sander L. Gilman, *Making the Body Beautiful: A Cultural History of Aesthetic Surgery* (Princeton, NJ: Princeton University Press, 1999), 8–10, 338n11–13.
12. Demaitre, "Skin and the City," 97–98, 110; cosmetics were a regular feature of surgical manuals beginning with Teodorico's *Venerabili* (1260s). McVaugh, *Rational Surgery*, 30–32; 215–28.
13. Demaitre, "Skin and the City," 101–2. See, for instance, Lanfranc of Milan, *Chirurgia magna* (Venice: Per Bonetus Locatellus, 1498), 181-82rb, as well as some of the recipes concerned with the head

and face within Guy de Chauliac, *Inventarium sive chirurgia magna*, ed. Michael R. McVaugh, with commentary by McVaugh and Margaret S. Ogden, 2 vols. (Leiden: Brill, 1997), I: 309–23.

14. McVaugh, *Rational Surgery*, 122–26, 216. Jacques Rovinski, "La cosmétologie de Guy de Chauliac," in *Les soins de beauté, Moyen Age; début des temps modernes. Actes du IIIe Colloque international, Grasse (26–28 avril 1985)* (Nice: Centre d'Études Médiévales, 1987), 171–82. Medieval medicine also worked toward the aesthetic enhancement of the body. Demaitre, "Skin and the City," 100–9.

15. Lanfranc explicitly identified the treatment of nonbinary sex anatomies (described as hermaphroditism) as one of a surgeon's duties. Green, *Making Women's Medicine Masculine*, 97–111, esp. 105n89; "Bodily Essences," 155–56. McVaugh, *Rational Surgery*, 67–68.

16. Siraisi, *Medieval and Early Renaissance Medicine*, 154–55, 174–80; McVaugh, *Rational Surgery*, 203, 230–41; *Inventarium*, xi–xii.

17. See chapter 4.

18. For Islamicate surgery and its Greek antecedents, see Savage-Smith, "The Exchange of Medical and Surgical Ideas Between Europe and Islam," in *Diffusion of Greco-Roman Medicine*, 37–55.

19. Monica H. Green, "From Philology to Social History: The Circulation and Uses of Albucasis's Latin *Surgery* in the Middle Ages," *Micrologus* 39 (2011): 331–72. For bibliography on Al-Zahrāwī, see Emilie Savage-Smith, "Zahrāwī, Abū 'l-Qāsim," in *Encyclopedia of Islam*, 2nd ed., ed. P. Bearman et al., vol. 11 (Leiden: Brill, 1960–2004): 398–99; "Medicine in Medieval Islam," 158–60.

20. Green, "Caring for Gendered Bodies,"355; Scalenghe, "Being Different," 61.

21. Albucasis, *Cyrurgia Albucasis cum cauterijs et alijs instrumentis*, in *Cyrurgia parua Guidonis* (Venice: Per Bonetum Locatellus, 1500), chap. 70 (23v):

    Apparet in eo quod sequitur spacium aut in cute testiculorum in eo quod est inter duos testiculos figura quasi vulua mulieris in qua sunt pili: et quandoque currit vrina ex eo quod est in cute testiculorum. In mulieribus autem est species vna et est vulua mulieris super pectinem sicut testiculi viri parui omino eminentes ad exteriora. Quorum vnus est sicut priapus viri: et duo sicut duo testiculi. Et curatio trium specierum, duarum ex viris: et speciei vnius ex mulieribus est: quia oportet vt incidas carnes additas donec effugiat impressio earum, deinde cura eas curatione reliquorum vulnerum.

    For his reliance on the Byzantine physician Paul of Aegina, see Albucasis, *On Surgery and Instruments*, ed. M. S. Spink and G. L. Lewis (Berkeley: University of California Press, 1973), 454.

22. Haly Abbas, *Liber totius medicine* (Lyon: Typis Jacobi Myt, 1523), 282v (*Practica* IX, liiii): "et est in viris turpissima passio."

23. Avicenna, *Liber canonis*, bk. 3, fen. 20, tr. 2, chap. 43 (fol. 358): "Et multotiens curantur per incisionem membrum occultioris et regimen vulneris eius." On the text, see Ragab, 428–54; on its influence on surgeons, see McVaugh, "Surgical Education in the Middle Ages," 287; *Rational Surgery*, 23.

24. Albucasis, chap. 57, fol. 21r.

25. Surgical methods and goals in circumcision and excision varied considerably according to geography and culture. See Mary Knight, "Curing Cut or Ritual Mutilation? Some Remarks on the Practice of Female and Male Circumcision in Graeco-Roman Egypt," *Isis* 92:2 (2001): 317–38; Jonathan P. Berkey, "Circumcision Circumscribed: Female Excision and Cultural Accommodation in the Medieval Near East," *International Journal of Middle East Studies* 28:1 (1996): 19–38; Janice Boddy, *Wombs and Alien Spirits: Women, Men, and the Zār Cult in Northern Sudan* (Madison: University of Wisconsin Press, 1989); Boddy, "Violence Embodied? Circumcision, Gender Politics, and Cultural Aesthetics," in *Rethinking Violence Against Women*, ed. R. Emerson Dobash and Russell P. Dobash (Thousand Oaks, CA: Sage Publications, 1996), 77–110. On circumcision in Jewish contexts, see Paola Tartakoff, "From Conversion to Ritual Murder: Re-contextualizing the Circumcision Charge," *Medieval Encounters* 24 (2018): 368–76. Kathleen Biddick, *The Typological Imaginary: Circumcision, Technology, History* (Philadelphia: University of Pennsylvania Press, 2003), 66–68; Leonard B. Glick,

254   5. THE CORRECTION OF NATURE

Marked in Your Flesh: Circumcision from Ancient Judea to Modern America (Oxford: Oxford University Press, 2005), 55–90.

26. Boddy, *Wombs and Alien Spirits*, 49–61; Otto Meinardus, "Mythological, Historical and Sociological Aspects of the Practice of Female Circumcision Among the Egyptians," *Acta Ethnographica Academiae Scientiarum Hungaricae* 16 (1967): 387–97. The meaning of circumcision in medieval Jewish contexts was distinct. See, for instance, Eva Frovmovic, "Reframing Gender in Medieval Jewish Images of Circumcision," in *Framing the Family: Narrative and Representation in the Medieval and Early Modern Periods* ed. Rosalynn Voaden and Diane Wolfthal (Tempe: Arizona Center for Medieval and Renaissance Studies, 2005), 221–43; Resnick, *Marks of Distinction*, 53–79; Tartakoff, "From Conversion to Ritual Murder," 361–89.
27. Berkey, 31–33.
28. Berkey, 32.
29. Green, "From Philology to Social History," 331–72; the characterization of the text is McVaugh's, *Rational Surgery*, 23.
30. Ragab, 437.
31. Albucasis, *On Surgery and Instruments*, x; McVaugh, *Rational Surgery*, 23; *Inventarium*, xiii; Green, "Philology," 338.
32. McVaugh, *Rational Surgery*, 17, 25–27.
33. Bruno Longobucco, *The Cyrurgia magna of Brunus Longoburgensis: A Critical Edition*, ed. S. P. Hall, D Phil thesis, Oxford University, 1957 (book II, chap. 13), 290:

    Et prima uirorum est que apparet in cute testiculorum, in eo quod est inter duos testiculos figura quasi sit uulua mulieris et sunt in ea pili. Et secunda species est secundum eundem modum tamen per eam fluit urina, et tertia quidem similis tamen ex ea urina non effunditur. Illa uero que in mulieribus fit est quoniam super uuluam mulieris in pectine tanquam masculi parui dependent uirilia, et tunc sunt tria corpora omnino foras eminentia, quorum unum est sicut uirga et duo sunt sicut testiculi.

    I repeat Monica Green's assessment of the originality of his text. On Bruno's claims to originality in general, see McVaugh, *Rational Surgery*, 26.
34. Green, "Caring for Gendered Bodies," 355.
35. Bruno Longobucco, 290–91: "Et modus curationis est ut seces illas carnes superfluas sectione qua non remaneat ex eis aliquid. Deinde cura locum cum reliqua curatione uulnerum donec sanetur. " See also Hall, ed., 290: "Hermofrodita, ut dicit Haly, est passio innaturalis et turpissima ualde uiris."
36. Green, "Caring for Gendered Bodies," 355; *Making Women's Medicine Masculine*, 99–100. Surgeons sometimes included empirical observations alongside theoretical material from authoritative sources; see McVaugh, *Rational Surgery*, 37–38.
37. Lanfranc of Milan, *Chirurgia*, cap. IX, 198v: "Cuius cura leuis est: pellicula secundum longituginem vulue scissa cum rasorio et forma de stupis cum rasura lardi permixta ne dimittat vlterius pelliculam solidari."
38. Lanfranc of Milan, *Chirurgia*, 198v: "Si vero ex alia re fortiori claudatur, vt aliqua lacertosa duraque carne totam illam duriciem remoueri opportet: donec in forma veniat naturali."
39. Lanfranc of Milan, *Chirurgia*, 198v:

    Hermaphroditus est ille qui habet utrumque sexum perfectum: ita quod agere potest et pati: quorum aliqui habent vnum perfectum alium imperfectum: aliqui nec vtrumque perfectum: immo habent in orificio vulue aliquid carnis addite: que aliquando est mollis carnea parue et debilis tenacitatis: aliquando fortis et neruosa. Carnea vero remouetur de leui cum instrumentis incidentibus: et cum leui cauterizatione residui, carnem semper cauendo naturalem a ferro: vel cum ligatione cum filo: quod quotidie plus stringatur donec tota superfluitas auferatur.

5. THE CORRECTION OF NATURE   255

40. Green, "Caring for Gendered Bodies," 355.
41. Lanfranc of Milan, *Chirurgia*, 198v: "Si vero dura sit et fortis: et neruosa: ita quod virge virili assimiletur: et maxime si tangendo mulierem erigitur: illam nullo modo ferro tangas: nec cum aliquo curare cogites."
42. Quoted in Green, "Caring for Gendered Bodies," 356 (I have slightly adjusted the translation); "Bodily Essences," 165.
43. Lanfranc of Milan, *Chirurgia*, 198v: "Sunt etiam quidam viri qui post testiculos habent additamenta duo lateralia: et in medio foueam quasi vuluam mulierum: in quam in quibusdam est foramen: per quod emittunt vrinam: quod si sic fuerit, curam dimittas. Si vero profunda non fuerit illa loca ferro tangas calido paulatine: deinde butirum appone: et escare casum expecta. Quod si tuum fueris consecutus propositum cutem regenera. Sin autem cauterium itera donec locus optime fuerit repletus et ad formam redierit naturalem."
44. Anne Carson, "Putting Her in Her Place: Woman, Dirt, and Desire," in *Before Sexuality: The Construction of Erotic Experience in the Ancient Greek World*, ed. David Halperin et al. (Princeton, NJ: Princeton University Press, 1990), 135–69.
45. In contrast, contemporary commentators on the *Problemata*, an Aristotelian compilation of questions about naturalist subjects, generally considered genital surgery on defective men who favored passive sex to be poor medical practice; see Cadden, *Nothing Natural Is Shameful*, 64–65.
46. Lanfranc of Milan, *Chirurgia*, 198v: "Nam illud peccatum est in forma vbi natura fortiter errauit."
47. McVaugh, *Rational Surgery*, 69; Siraisi, *Medieval and Early Renaissance Medicine*, 174.
48. Daston and Park, "Hermaphrodite," 421.
49. Green, *Making Women's Medicine Masculine*, 99–100; Siraisi, "Medical Learning," 380. McVaugh, *Rational Surgery*, 38–39; O'Boyle, "Surgical Texts and Social Contexts," 161; Pahta, 76.
50. Lanfranc of Milan, *Chirurgia*, 178ra: "Forti namque nature nihil est impossibile: maxime cum per bonum medicum ex rebus eam iuuantibus: et ad intentionem valentibus adiuuatur."
51. Lanfranc of Milan, *Chirurgia*, 178ra. William, in contrast, emphasized the potency of nature in his *Surgery*; McVaugh, *Rational Surgery*, 90.
52. Quoted in Pouchelle, 39.
53. Guy de Chauliac, *Inventarium*, 1:387: "Hermafrodisia est natura sexus duplicata, et est secundum Albucasim in viris secundum duos modos; quia quandoque est vulva pilosa inter duos testiculos, quandoque in spacio que est apparens subtus. In muliere autem est una species, in qua supra vulvam apparet virga et teesticuli. Et multociens curantur per incisionem, ut dicit Avicenna, non autem illa que facit urinam, ut dicit Albucasis."
54. This timing of this treatment in the medieval period is in sharp contrast to modern surgeries, which have been performed chiefly on infants; see Kessler, *Lessons from the Intersexed*, 12–32.
55. Green, "Caring for Gendered Bodies," 347–49; World Health Organization, "Traditional Birth Attendants: A Joint WHO/UNFPA/UNICEF Statement" (Geneva: WHO,1992), 4. Retrieved May 3, 2019, at http://apps.who.int/iris/bitstream/10665/38994/1/9241561505.pdf.
56. Green, "Caring for Gendered Bodies," 347–49.
57. Metzler, "Hermaphroditism," 37.
58. Van der Lugt, "Sex Difference ," 112. One Catalan case from 1437–38, however, indicates that the birth of an infant with atypical genitals could also draw immediate attention; in this case, a converted Jew was suspected of circumcising his child. Josep Hernando i Delgado, "El procès contra el convers Nicolau Sanxo, ciutadà de Barcelona, acusat d'haver circumcidat el seu fill (1437-1438)," *Acta Hist. Archaeol. Med.* 13 (1992): 75–100. My thanks to Paola Tartakoff for bringing this case to my attention.
59. James A. Brundage, "Impotence, Frigidity, and Marital Nullity in the Decretists and the Early Decretalists," in *Sex, Law, and Marriage in the Middle Ages*, ed. James A. Brundage (London: Variorum, 1993), X: 407–23; Philip L. Reynolds, *How Marriage Became One of the Sacraments: The Sacramental*

Theology of Marriage from its Medieval Origins to the Council of Trent (Cambridge: Cambridge University Press, 2016), 317–20.

60. Reynolds, 319–20.
61. Benedek and Kubinec, 129–30; McVaugh, *Medicine Before the Plague*, 202.
62. Jacquart and Thomasset, *Sexuality and Medicine*, 171–72; Bronach Kane, *Impotence and Virginity in the Late Medieval Ecclesiastical Court of York* (York: Borthwick Institute, University of York, 2008), 5–37.
63. Brundage, "Impotence," 420–21; Benedek and Kubinec, 127–29; McVaugh, *Medicine Before the Plague*, 202–7.
64. On these cases, see Kane, 6; Brundage, *Law, Sex, and Christian Society*, 415, 457; Jeremy Goldberg, "John Skathelok's Dick: Voyeurism and 'Pornography' in Late Medieval England," in *Medieval Obscenities*, ed. Nicola McDonald (Woodbridge: York Medieval Press, 2006), 105–6; Benedek and Kubinec, 131–46.
65. This process reflected a ruling in the *Decretals* of Gregory IX that a congress should be convened to evaluate allegations of impotence and to determine whether a couple should be separated. Benedek and Kubinec, 132. Kane, 9.
66. Goldberg, 117–18; as Kane has noted, the women did not always expose their naked bodies but touching, massaging, and other attempts at sexual arousal seem to have been de rigueur.
67. Goldberg, 119.
68. Derek Neal, *The Masculine Self in Late Medieval England* (Chicago: University of Chicago Press, 2008), 141–42.
69. Jacquart and Thomasset, 171; Neal, 144. Enlarging a small penis by medical means is a serious concern in surgical texts such as William of Saliceto's *Summa conservationis et curationis*. See Helen Rodnite Lemay, "William of Saliceto on Human Sexuality," *Viator* 12 (1981): 168.
70. Joseph Ziegler, "Sexuality and the Sexual Organs in Latin Physiognomy 1200–1500," *Studies in Medieval and Renaissance History*, 3rd ser., 2 (2005), 90–91.
71. Ottosson, *Scholastic Medicine*, 131.
72. See Elspeth Whitney, "What's Wrong with the Pardoner? Complexion Theory, the Phlegmatic Man, and Effeminacy," *Chaucer Review* 45:4 (2011): 360; Neal, 143; Kane, 8–9; Reynolds, 319.
73. Kane, 8–14.
74. Jacqueline Murray, "Hiding Behind the Universal Man: Male Sexuality in the Middle Ages," in Vern L. Bullough and James A. Brundage, eds., *Handbook of Medieval Sexuality* (New York: Garland, 1996), 139.
75. Jacquart and Thomasset, 172; Guy de Chauliac, *Inventarium*, I: 386:

> Et est quod medicus, habita licencia a iusticia, examinet primo complexionem et composicionem membrorum generativorum. Deinde habeat matronam in talibus consuetam, et precipiatur quod iaceant simul per aliquos dies, ipsa matrona presente cum eis, et det eis species et pigmenta et eos calefaciat et inungat cum oleis calidis et fricet iuxta ignem sermentorum et iubeat eos confabulari et amplecti. Deinde quod viderit referat medico; et quando medicus fuerit bene informatus, coram iusticia de veritate deponere potest.

76. *Medicus*, or "healer," could include both groups. McVaugh documents examinations by a physician and a surgeon; *Medicine Before the Plague*, 40, 205–6. For terminology, Green, *Making Women's Medicine Masculine*, 5, 38.
77. Katharine Park, *Secrets of Women: Gender: Generation, and the Origins of Human Dissection* (New York: Zone, 2006), 97.
78. Neal, 143.
79. Ruth Mazo Karras, *From Boys to Men: Formations of Masculinity in Late Medieval Europe* (Philadelphia: University of Pennsylvania Press, 2003), 16–17, 161.

80. Kuefler, *Manly Eunuch*, 32–33.
81. Kuefler, *Manly Eunuch*, 31.
82. Kuefler, *Manly Eunuch*, 36; Shaun Tougher, ed., *Eunuchs in Antiquity and Beyond* (Swansea, UK: Classical Press of Wales and Duckworth, 2002); Keith Hopkins, "Eunuchs in Politics in the Later Roman Empire," *The Cambridge Classical Journal* 9 (1963): 62–80.
83. Kuefler, *Manly Eunuch*, 259, 264–82; Mathew Kuefler, "Castration and Eunuchism in the Middle Ages," in *Handbook of Medieval Sexuality*, 289–91; Robert L. A. Clark, "Culture Loves a Void: Eunuchry in *De Vetula* and Jean le Fèvre's *La Vielle*," *Castration and Culture in the Middle Ages*, ed. Larissa Tracy (Cambridge: Boydell & Brewer, 2013), 280–94.
84. Larissa Tracy, "A History of Calamities: The Culture of Castration," in *Castration and Culture*, 1–28, at 2. Jacqueline Murray, "Sexual Mutilation and Castration Anxiety: A Medieval Perspective," in *The Boswell Thesis: Essays on Christianity, Social Tolerance, and Homosexuality*, ed. Mathew Kuefler (Chicago: University of Chicago Press, 2006), quotation at 255.
85. Kuefler, "Castration," 298.
86. Murray, "Sexual Mutilation," 265–66.
87. Giovanni Balbi, *Catholicon*, under *hermafroditus* (n.p.): "hermafroditus dicitur castratus, quia nec uir nec mulier uidetur." On similar sentiments, see Ellen Lorraine Friedrich, "Insinuating Indeterminate Gender: A Castration Motif in Guillaume de Lorris's *Romans de la rose*," in *Castration and Culture in the Middle Ages*, ed. Larissa Tracy (Cambridge: Boydell & Brewer, 255–79; Clark, "Culture Loves a Void," 280–94. On "congenital eunuchs," see also Strassfeld, "Classically Queer," 38–39, 136–38 and passim.
88. McVaugh, *Medicine Before the Plague*, 206–7 and 207n60.
89. Albucasis, *Cyrurgia Albucasis*, 23vb: "Tentigo fortasse additur super rem naturalem donec sedatur et turpis sit aspectus eius: et quandoque magnificatur in quibusdam mulieribus adeo donec expanditur sicut in viris et peruenit usque ad coitum. Oportet ergo vt teneas superfluitatem tentiginis manu aut cum vncino et incidas: et non vltimes in incisione precipue in profundo radicis vt non accidat fluxus sanguinis." See Karma Lochrie, *Heterosyncrasies: Female Sexuality When Normal Wasn't* (Minneapolis: University of Minnesota Press, 2005), 79.
90. Guy de Chauliac, I: 388: "Quandoque illa addicio carnosa que vocatur tentigo in vulva crescit ad tantum quod facit displicenciam et nocumentum. Et cura eius est (secundum Albucasim) quod incidatur cum ligamento aut rasorio, et non usque ad profundum, timore sanguinis; deinde aliorum vulnerum curacione curetur."
91. Avicenna, lib. III, fen. 21, tr. I, chap. 22 (377v): "Quandoque oritur in ore matricis caro addita et quandoque apparet super mulierem res que est sicut virga commouens sub coitu. Et quandoque aduenit ei vt faciat cum mulieribus simile quod fit eis cum quibus coitus. Et quandoque est illud baccarum magnum."
92. Lochrie, *Heterosyncrasies*, 82.
93. Lochrie, *Heterosyncrasies*, 76–89.
94. Katharine Park, "The Rediscovery of the Clitoris: French Medicine and the Tribade, 1570–1620," in *The Body in Parts: Fantasies of Corporeality in Early Modern Europe*, ed. David Hillman and Carla Mazzio (New York: Routledge, 1997), 170–93. See also Valerie Traub, *The Renaissance of Lesbianism in Early Modern England* (Cambridge: Cambridge University Press, 2002), 87–93.
95. Lochrie, *Heterosyncrasies*, 79–80.
96. Green, *Making Women's Medicine Masculine*, 98–99; Lochrie, *Heterosyncrasies*, 83–84.
97. William of Saliceto (Guglielmo da Saliceto), *Summa conservationis et curationis* (Venice: Marinus Saracenus, 1490), chap 168, 63rb: "Ragadie sunt scisure cum quibusdam eminentii carnosis a quibus per fricationem cum virga et etiam per se emanat sanguis. . . . quandoque preter ragadias oritur in ore matricis caro addita: et quandoque apparet res super muliere que est sicut virga commouens sub coitu: et quandoque aduenit ei vt faciat cum mulieribus similiter quod fit eis cum quibus

coitus: et quandoque est bothor magnum vel eminentia." Helen Rodnite Lemay, "Human Sexuality in Twelfth- through Fifteenth-Century Scientific Writings," in *Sexual Practices and the Medieval Church*, ed. Vern L. Bullough and James A. Brundage (New York: Prometheus, 1982), 196; "William of Saliceto," 179. Lochrie, *Heterosyncrasies*, 83–84.

98. Lochrie, *Heterosyncrasies*, 77.
99. Lanfranc of Milan, *Chirurgia*, 198v: "Quibusdam etiam accidit mulieribus quod panniculus quidam lacertosus: qui est in orificio vulue: adeo augmentatur: quod multum dependeat: ita quod mulierem afficit tedio: et a viro multo minus amatur: quam sic cures superfluum illius incide pellicule: postea cum auro calido cauteriza donec ab formam naturalem reducas."
100. Cadden, *Meanings*, 178; Neal, 138. Men were also thought of as active sexual initiators, however.
101. On the contingency of masculinity, see Erika Lorraine Milam and Robert A. Nye, "An Introduction to Scientific Masculinities," in "Scientific Masculinities," special issue of *Osiris* 30:1 (2015), 6–7. Lemay, "William of Saliceto," 179.
102. If the *telos* of a phallus was to ejaculate semen into the womb of a female, then no other use of it could be judged natural. Jordan, *Invention of Sodomy*, 132. See also Daston and Park, "Hermaphrodite," 427.
103. Jordan, *Invention of Sodomy*, 127.
104. The word *nervus* (tendon or sinew) was a common Roman term for penis, and the description of the penis as "sinewy" was repeated by many medieval interpreters of the body. Some writers, including Galen, viewed the penis as a tendon or collection of tendons. James Noel Adams, *The Latin Sexual Vocabulary* (Baltimore, MD: Johns Hopkins University Press, 1990), 38. On ancient Roman ideas about masculine hardness and feminine softness, see Kuefler, *Manly Eunuch*, 21.
105. *Etymologiarum*, vol. II, bk. XI, ii, 17 (Translated in Barney et al., 242).
106. *Etymologiarum*, vol. II, bk. XI, ii, 18–9 (Translated in Barney et al., 242).
107. *Etymologiarum*, vol. I, bk. X, M, 179–80 (Translated in Barney et al., 224).
108. Robinson, "Salmacis and Hermaphroditus," 212–13. A *mollis* who took on the passive role in sexual acts with other men was classified as an "adulteress" in the early medieval English *Penitentials of Theodore*, suggesting that he violated not only sexual conventions but also the category of maleness. Allen J. Frantzen, *Before the Closet: Same-Sex Love from Beowulf to Angels in America* (Chicago: University of Chicago Press, 1998), 151–52.
109. Thomas Aquinas, *Summa theologiae*, 44:20–23 (pt. 2a2ae, q. 156, art. 2): "sicut e contrario contingit quod aliquis non persistat in eo quod consiliatum est, ex eo quod debiliter inhaeret propter mollitiem complexionis, ut de mulieribus dictum est, quod etiam videtur in phlegmaticis."
110. Pouchelle, 112–13.
111. Quoted in Demaitre, "Skin and the City," 113.
112. Medical and surgical treatises devoted attention to enhancing the attractiveness of the female body, and female cosmetics were a thriving business in urban centers—although medical practitioners also catered to male vanity. Demaitre, "Skin and the City," 111–14. On women's cosmetics, see Monica H. Green, ed., *The Trotula: An English Translation of the Medieval Compendium of Women's Medicine* (Philadelphia: University of Pennsylvania Press, 2002).
113. Hostiensis's opinion ultimately exercised great influence in the fourteenth through seventeenth centuries. Rolker, "Two Laws," 199–200.
114. Claude Thomasset, ed., *Placides et Timéo, ou, Li secrés as philosophes* (Geneva and Paris: Droz, 1980), 153–4:

> Les anchiens justichiers establirent que nuls ne laissast tels hommes user de .II. natures, mais c'on les meist enchois a quois de prendre quelle nature qu'il vorroient, de faire ou de souffrir. Et quant il aroient prins l'un ou l'autre, c'est assavoir le nature de l'omme ou de le femme, qui les trouveroit ouvrans de celle qu'il avoient renoÿe qu'ilz fussent punis du corps, car c'est contre nature d'user de deux. Et tels hommes, qui de deux natures veulent user, ne devroient

5. THE CORRECTION OF NATURE 259

estre souffers entres gens, et si jugerent les anchiens que, s'i eslisoient a souffrir, que on leur copast les testicules et si closist on le pel de le vergue par devant, et, s'i eslisoient a faire, c'est assavoir d'user de nature d'omme, que on closist l'orefice, et se ilz par malice le destoupoient, que il en fussent pugnis du corps.

115. Ruth Mazo Karras, *Sexuality in Medieval Europe: Doing unto Others*, 3rd ed. (New York: Routledge, 2017), 3–5.
116. Green, "From Philology to Social History," 338; Carmel Ferragud, "Wounds, Amputations, and Expert Procedures in the City of Valencia in the Early Fifteenth Century," in *Wounds and Wound Repair in Medieval Culture*, ed. Larissa Tracy and Kelly DeVries (Leiden: Brill, 2015), 250; Lluís Cifuentes, "Las traducciones catalanas y castellanas de la *Chirurgia magna* de Lanfranco de Milán: Un ejemplo de intercomunicación cultural y científica a finales de la edad media," *Essays on Medieval Translation in the Iberian Peninsula*, ed. Tomàs Martínez Romero and Roxana Recio (Castelló: Publicacions de la Universitat Jaume I; Omaha: Creighton University, 2001), 99. Lanfranc's chapter on "hermaphrodites" also appears in a fifteenth-century Castilian-language manuscript; see Guadalupe Albi Romero, *Lanfranco de Milán en España: Estudio y edición de la Magna Chirurgia en traducción castellana medieval* (Valladolid: Secretariado de Publicaciones, 1988), 62, 320–21. McVaugh, *Rational Surgery*, 241–42.
117. Rubin, "Person in the Form," 101–2.
118. Rolker, "Der Hermaphrodit und seine Frau," 593–620, and "Two Laws," 207–11; Siraisi, *Medieval and Early Renaissance Medicine*, 162.
119. Laqueur, *Making Sex*, 25–62.
120. Laqueur, *Making Sex*, 137–38.
121. Among the many works that challenge Laqueur's thesis, see Cadden, *Meanings*, 3; Park, "Medicine and Natural Philosophy," 96–98; "Cadden, Laqueur, and the 'One-Sex Body,'" *Medieval Feminist Forum* 46:1 (2010): 96–100; Park and Robert A. Nye, "Destiny Is Anatomy," *New Republic* 204 (Feb. 18, 1991): 53–57; Helen King, *The One-Sex Body on Trial: The Classical and Early Modern Evidence* (Farnham, UK: Ashgate, 2013); Gadelrab, 52–53.
122. Galen's homologues between male and female appeared in *De usu partium*, but that text had little influence in the Middle Ages. Park, "Cadden, Laqueur, and the 'One-Sex Body,'" 98–99.
123. Laqueur, *Making Sex*, 124.
124. Foucault, *Herculine Barbin: Being the Recently Discovered Memoirs of a Nineteenth-Century French Hermaphrodite*, trans. Richard McDougall (New York: Pantheon, 1980), vii–viii.
125. Foucault, *Herculine Barbin*, vii–xvii. See, for instance, Gilbert, *Early Modern Hermaphrodites*, 2–3; Rolker, "Two Laws," 181.
126. Kessler, *Lessons from the Intersexed*, 32. See also Katrina Roen, "Clinical Intervention and Embodied Subjectivity: Atypically Sexed Children and Their Parents," in *Critical Intersex*, ed. Morgan Holmes (Aldershot, UK: Ashgate, 2009), 15–40; Rubin, *Intersex Matters*; Karkazis, *Fixing Sex*; Dreger, *Hermaphrodites*, and *Intersex in the Age of Ethics*, and the other works on intersex cited in my introduction in "Modern Scholarship and Premodern Perspectives."
127. Quoted in Rubin, *Intersex Matters*, 3.
128. Kiira Triea, "Power, Orgasm, and the Psychohormonal Research Unit," in *Intersex in the Age of Ethics*, ed. Alice Domurat Dreger (Hagerstown, MD: University Publishing Group, 1999), 142–43; Vernon A. Rosario, "Quantum Sex: Intersex and the Molecular Deconstruction of Sex," *GLQ: A Journal of Lesbian and Gay Studies* 15:2 (2009): 273; Kessler, *Lessons from the Intersexed*; Karkazis, *Fixing Sex*.
129. M. Joycelyn Elders, David Satcher and Richard Carmona, "Re-Thinking Genital Surgeries on Intersex Infants" (2017), accessed March 10, 2019, http://www.palmcenter.org/wp-content/uploads/2017/06/Re-Thinking-Genital-Surgeries-1.pdf; Rubin, *Intersex Matters*, 2–14.

130. Morland, "Intersex," 111; Human Rights Watch/interACT, "'I Want to Be Like Nature Made Me.'"
131. Human Rights Watch/interACT, "'I Want to Be Like Nature Made Me.'"
132. Alice Domurat Dreger, "A History of Intersex: From the Age of Gonads to the Age of Consent," in *Intersex in the Age of Ethics* (Hagerstown, MD: University Publishing Group, 1999), 5–22.
133. Ruth Mazo Karras and Tom Linkinen, "John/Eleanor Rykener Revisited," 111–21; Kadin Henningsen, "'Calling [herself] Eleanor': Gender Labor and Becoming a Woman in the Rykener Case," 249–66; M. W. Bychowski and Dorothy Kim, eds., "Visions of Medieval Trans Feminism," special issue of *Medieval Feminist Forum* 55:1 (2019). These works embrace "transgender" and "trans feminism" as ways of talking about medieval phenomena. See also Valerie Traub, "Introduction," in *Ovidian Transversions: 'Iphis and Ianthe,' 1300–1650*, ed. Patricia Badir, Peggy McCracken, and Valerie Traub (Edinburgh: Edinburgh University Press, 2019), 1–41, and Kathleen P. Long, "Illegible Bodies: Reading Intersex and Transgender in Early Modern France (The Case of Isaac de Benserade's *Iphis et Iante*)," also in *Ovidian Transversions*, 213–40.
134. Mills, *Seeing Sodomy*, 81–132, quotation at 132; Mills, "Visibly Trans?" 540–64.
135. Also at issue is Foucault's understanding of homosexuality as a purely modern phenomenon, inseparable from the formation of modern concepts of sex and selfhood. If we extend Foucault's logic to issues of gender, one cannot write about "transgender" or "transsexual" before the advent of the very vocabulary that generated such subjects; to do so would risk divesting past gender practice of what made it meaningful in its own time and place. See, for instance, the cautions of Peter Boag, "Go West Young Man, Go East Young Woman: Searching for the Trans in Western Gender History," *Western Historical Quarterly* 36:4 (2005): 479–80; Genny Beemyn, "A Presence in the Past: A Transgender Historiography," *Journal of Women's History* 25:4 (2013): 113. I discuss this issue extensively in DeVun and Tortorici, "Trans, Time, and History," 518–39. See also recent engagements with trans history, such as Jen Manion, *Female Husbands* (Cambridge: Cambridge University Press, 2020); Emily Skidmore, *True Sex: The Lives of Trans Men at the Turn of the Century* (New York: New York University Press, 2017); Domitilla Campanile, Filippo Carlà-Uhink, and Margherita Facella, eds., *TransAntiquity: Cross-Dressing and Transgender Dynamics in the Ancient World* (New York: Routledge, 2017); Snorton, *Black on Both Sides;* Clare Sears, *Arresting Dress: Cross-Dressing, Law and Fascination in Nineteenth-Century San Francisco* (Chapel Hill, NC: Duke University Press, 2015); Rachel Hope Cleves, "Beyond the Binaries in Early America: Special Issue Introduction," *Early American Studies: An Interdisciplinary Journal* 12:3 (2014): 459–68, among many examples.
136. Scholars continue to criticize how "trans" both collects and omits diverse subjects in accordance with raced, classed, and regional hegemonies. See Yv E. Nay, "The Atmosphere of Trans* Politics in the Global North and West," *TSQ: Transgender Studies Quarterly* 6:1 (2019): 64–79; Reina Gossett (now Tourmaline), Eric A. Stanley and Johanna Burton, eds., *Trap Door: Trans Cultural Production and the Politics of Visibility* (Cambridge, MA: MIT Press, 2017); Marlon M. Bailey, *Butch Queens Up in Pumps: Gender, Performance, and Ballroom Culture in Detroit* (Ann Arbor: University of Michigan Press, 2013).
137. *Oxford English Dictionary*, s.v. "trans," 1.
138. For definitions of transgender and a guide to transgender studies, see Susan Stryker, "(De)subjugated Knowledges: An Introduction to Transgender Studies," in *The Transgender Studies Reader* 1, ed. Susan Stryker and Stephen Whittle (New York: Routledge, 2006), 1–17; Stryker and Aizura, "Introduction: Transgender Studies 2.0," in *Transgender Studies Reader 2*, 1–12; A. Finn Enke, ed., *Transfeminist Perspectives in and Beyond Transgender and Gender Studies* (Philadelphia: Temple, 2012); Paisley Currah and Susan Stryker, eds., *Postposttranssexual: Key Concepts for a Twenty-First-Century Transgender Studies*, special issue of *TSQ: Transgender Studies Quarterly* 1:1–2 (2014). On multidirectional transitions, see Jesse Bayker, "Before Transsexuality: Transgender Lives and Practices in Nineteenth-Century America," PhD diss., Rutgers University, 2019.

139. Susan Stryker and Paisley Currah, "General Editors' Introduction," *TSQ: Transgender Studies Quarterly* 1:3 (2014): 303–4; Rubin, *Intersex Matters*, 99; Valentine, 157.
140. See chapter 2 above, in "Nonbinary Sex, Gender-Crossing, and Sexual Boundaries."
141. Among many statements of this truism, see Karras and Linkinen, 114; Bychowski and Kim, "Visions of Medieval Trans Feminism," 6–41, at 19–20.
142. Stryker, *Transgender History*, 1.
143. Stryker and Aizura, "Introduction," 11.
144. Robert Mills makes this point with respect to medieval prohibitions of sodomy, which he argues stemmed from fears about gender inversion (a confusion of active and passive roles) rather than any particular genital sexual act. *Seeing Sodomy*, 90.
145. I adapt the wording of Neal's apt observation, 124.
146. Among many examples, Butler, "Performative Acts," 528; *Bodies That Matter*, 7–9; on trans bodies as marked for death, see Snorton, *Black on Both Sides*, vii–xiv; Snorton and Jin Haritaworn, "Trans Necropolitics," 66–76.
147. Laverne Cox, "The Bullies Don't Draw a Distinction," *New York Times*, October 15, 2013, accessed March 10, 2019, www.nytimes.com/roomfordebate/2013/10/15/are-trans-rights-and-gay-rights-still-allies/the-bullies-dont-draw-a-distinction. See also Vivianne Namaste, *Invisible Lives: The Erasure of Transsexual and Transgendered People* (Chicago: University of Chicago Press, 2000).
148. Spade, 209.
149. Emi Koyama, "Being Accountable to the Invisible Community," accessed March 7, 2019, http://www.intersexinitiative.org/articles/invisible-community.html.
150. Salamon, 76–77.

6. THE JESUS HERMAPHRODITE: ALCHEMY IN THE LATE MIDDLE AGES AND EARLY RENAISSANCE

1. Ovid, *Metamorphoses*, 4.375–9 (I: 204): "velut, si quis conducat cortice ramos/ crescendo iungi pariterque adolescere cernit/ sic ubi conplexu coierunt membra tenaci/ nec duo sunt et forma duplex, nec femina dici/ nec puer ut possit, neutrumque et utrumque videntur."
2. Traub, "Introduction," in *Ovidian Transversions*, 2–3. For Ovid and theories of change, see Bynum, *Metamorphosis and Identity*, 86–101.
3. On Ovid's influence in the Middle Ages, Traub, ed., *Ovidian Transversions*; James G. Clark, Frank T. Coulson and Kathryn L. McKinley, ed., *Ovid in the Middle Ages* (Cambridge: Cambridge University Press, 2011); Marilynn R. Desmond, ed., *Mediaevalia: A Journal of Medieval Studies.* Special issue, *Ovid in Medieval Culture* 13 (1987); Lauren Silberman, "Mythographic Transformations of Ovid's Hermaphrodite," *Sixteenth Century Journal* 19:4 (1988): 643–52.
4. Some exceptions are Kathleen P. Long's *Hermaphrodites in Renaissance Europe* (Aldershot, UK: Ashgate, 2006), 109–62; Long, ed., *Gender and Scientific Discourse in Early Modern Culture* (Aldershot, UK: Ashgate, 2010), 1–12, 63–85; Lawrence M. Principe, "Revealing Analogies: The Descriptive and Deceptive Roles of Sexuality and Gender in Latin Alchemy," in *Hidden Intercourse: Eros and Sexuality in the History of Western Esotericism*, ed. Wouter J. Hanegraaff and Jeffrey J. Kripal (New York: Fordham University Press, 2011), 209–30.
5. C. G. Jung, *Jung on Alchemy*, ed. Nathan Schwartz-Salant (Princeton, NJ: Princeton University Press, 1995), 126, 211–13; Mircea Eliade, *The Forge and the Crucible*, trans. Stephen Corrin (New York: Harper & Row, 1962), 58–62, 138, 161; *The Two and the One*, trans. J. M. Cohen (Chicago: University of Chicago Press, 1979), 102-3.

6. See also Leonard Barkan, who suggests that for "all its emphasis upon the blurring of clear categories, metamorphosis is as much concerned with reduction and fixity as with variability or complexity." *The Gods Made Flesh: Metamorphosis and the Pursuit of Paganism* (New Haven, CT: Yale University Press, 1986), 66.
7. This narrative dovetails with Christine Ferlampin-Acher's observation that monsters in narrative literature followed a parallel trajectory: the twelfth-century focus on hybridity waned, only to be replaced in the late Middle Ages by a newfound interest in shape-shifting and the power of metamorphosis. See "Le Monstre dans le romans des XIIIe et XIVe siècles," in *Ecriture et modes de pensée au Moyen Age (VIIIe-Xve siècles)*, ed. Dominique Boutet and Laurence Harf-Lancner (Paris: Ecole Normale Supérieure, 1993), 69–87; see also Bynum, *Metamorphosis and Identity*, 152; *Christian Materiality: An Essay on Religion in Late Medieval Europe* (New York: Zone, 2011), 217–65.
8. Useful surveys of alchemy include W. Ganzenmüller's *Die Alchemie im Mittelalter* (Paderborn: Verlag der Bonifacius-Druckerei, 1938), trans. G. Petit-Dutaillis as *L'Alchimie au moyen âge* (Paris: Aubier, 1940); Frank Sherwood Taylor, *The Alchemists: Founders of Modern Chemistry* (New York: Henry Schuman, 1949); Robert Halleux, *Les textes alchimiques, Typologie des sources du moyen âge occidental* 32 (Turnhout, Belgium: Brepols, 1979); Lawrence M. Principe, ed., *Chymists and Chymistry: Studies in the History of Alchemy and Early Modern Chemistry* (Sagamore Beach, MA: Science History Publications, 2007); Lawrence M. Principe, *The Secrets of Alchemy* (Chicago: University of Chicago Press, 2013); Antoine Calvet, *L'alchimie au moyen âge: XIIe-XVe siècles* (Paris: Vrin, 2018).
9. Leah DeVun, *Prophecy, Alchemy, and the End of Time: John of Rupescissa in the Late Middle Ages* (New York: Columbia University Press, 2009), 54–57.
10. For this debate, see Constantine of Pisa, *The Book of the Secrets of Alchemy. Introduction, Critical Edition, Translation, and Commentary*, ed. Barbara Obrist (Leiden: Brill, 1990), 23–29. For the text, see Pseudo-Geber, *The Summa Perfectionis of Pseudo-Geber: A Critical Edition, Translation, and Study*, ed. William R. Newman (Leiden: Brill, 1991), 2–30, 48–51; Chiara Crisciani and Michela Pereira, "L'ingresso dell'alchimia in Occidente," in *L'arte del sole e della luna: alchimia e filosofia nel medioevo* (Spoleto: Centro italiano di studi sull'alto medioevo, 1996), 3–21.
11. Roger Bacon, *The "Opus Majus" of Roger Bacon*, ed. John Henry Bridges, 2 vols. (Oxford: Clarendon, 1897), II: 212:

> Nam sic erit in corporibus post resurrectionem. Aequalitas enim elementorum in corporibus illis excludit corruptionem in aeternum. Nam haec aequalitas est ultimus finis materiae naturalis in corporibus mixtis, quia nobilissimum est, et ideo in eo quiesceret appetitus materiae, et non desideraret aliquid ultra. Corpus autem Adae non habuit elementa in plena aequalitate, et ideo fuerunt in eo actio et passio elementorum contrariorum, et per consequens deperditio, et ideo indiguit nutrimento. Et propter hoc fuit ei praeceptum, ut non comederet de fructu vitae. Sed quia elementa in eo fuerunt prope aequalitatem, ideo modica fuit in eo deperditio; et propter hoc fuit aptus ad immortalitatem quam posset consequi, si fructum ligni vitae semper comedisset. Hic enim fructus aestimatur habere elementa prope aequalitatem; et ideo potuit continuare incorruptionem in Adam, quod factum fuisset, si non peccasset. Sapientes ergo laboraverunt, ut in aliquo comestibili vel potabili reducerent elementa ad aequalitatem vel prope, et docuerunt vias ad hoc.

12. See also the unattributed passage of Bacon quoted in Agostino Paravicini Bagliani, "Storia della scienza e storia della mentalità: Ruggero Bacone, Bonifacio VIII e la teoria della 'prolongatio vitae,'" in *Aspetti della letteratura latina nel secolo XIII*, ed. Claudio Leonardi and Giovanni Orlandi (Florence: La Nuova Italia, 1986), 259; Zachary Matus, "Roger Bacon's Apocalypticism in Light of His Alchemical and Scientific Thought," *Harvard Theological Review* 105:2 (2012): 218–19.
13. Joel Kaye, *A History of Balance, 1250–1375: The Emergence of a New Model of Equilibrium and Its Impact on Thought* (Cambridge: Cambridge University Press, 2014).

14. Agostino Paravicini Bagliani, *The Pope's Body*, trans. David S. Peterson (Chicago: University of Chicago Press, 2000); DeVun, *Prophecy*, 52–79 and passim.
15. Julius Ruska, ed., *Tabula Smaragdina: ein Beitrag zur Geschichte der hermetischen Literatur* (Heidelberg: Winter, 1926), 2: "Pater ejus est Sol, mater ejus Luna." Identifications of man/woman with binaries such as heaven/earth and sun/moon occur in patristic texts; Aristotle traces them back to the Pythagoreans in his *Metaphysics*. See Flood, 18, 129n72.
16. John Dastin, *Epistola boni viri*, ed. and trans. Wilfred R. Theissen in "John Dastin's Letter on the Philosophers' Stone," *Ambix* 33 (1986): 81: "Non ergo perturbent te haec verba vel alia consilia, quia lapis nihil aliud est quam masculus et femina, sol et luna, calor et frigus, sulphur et mercurium." On Dastin, Michela Pereira, "Projecting Perfection: Remarks on the Origin of the 'Alchemy of the Elixir,' " *Micrologus* 24 (2016): 73–93.
17. Andrée Colinet, "Le livre d'Hermès intitulé 'Liber dabessi' ou 'Liber rebis,' " *Studi medievali* 36 (1995): 1011–52 at 1034.
18. See, for example, Constantine of Pisa, 111, 212n372; Richardus Anglicus, *Correctorium alchemiae*, in Guglielmo Grataroli, ed., *Alchemiae quam vocant artisque metallicae doctrina*, 2 vols. (Basel: Petrum Pernam, 1572), I: 553–55.
19. Halleux, *Les textes alchimiques*, 114–19.
20. William R. Newman, *Promethean Ambitions: Alchemy and the Quest to Perfect Nature* (Chicago: University of Chicago Press, 2004), 64–65.
21. Pereira, 85.
22. *Mineralium libri quinque*, bk. IV (83–93). See Barbara Obrist, "Les rapports d'analogie entre philosophie et alchimie médiévales," in *Alchimie et philosophie à la renaissance*, ed. Jean-Claude Margolin and Sylvain Matton (Paris: Vrin, 1993), 50–51; Obrist, "Art et nature dans l'alchimie médiévale," *Revue d'histoire des sciences* 49:2–3 (1996): 266–67.
23. Albertus Magnus, *Mineralium*, bk. IV, chap. 1 (82): "Sed observandum est quoddam calidum siccum esse conjunctum humido frigido in eadem complexione, et haec complexio est hermaphrodita, sicut in plantis apparet, quae ubique impraegnantur et impraegnant."
24. On Petrus Bonus, see Chiara Crisciani, "The Conception of Alchemy as Expressed in the *Pretiosa Margarita Novella* of Petrus Bonus of Ferrara," *Ambix* 20 (1973): 165–81.
25. Petrus Bonus of Ferrara, *Margarita preciosa novella*, in *Bibliotheca chemica curiosa*, ed. J. J. Manget, 2 vols. (Geneva, 1702 [repr. Bologna: A. Forni, 1976]), II: 51:

    [N]ominantes foeminam ipsum lac quod coagulatur, masculum autem quod coagulat: quia actio attribuitur masculo, passio vero foeminae. Nam in hoc lapide, quando oritur, cum ipse sit liquidus, et fluens et patiens dicitur foemina: suum autem coagulum, a quo cogulatur cum sit solidum, firmum, permanens et agens in illud, dicitur masculus: compositum autem ex iis, dicitur lapis commixtus, perfectus et compositus, et fiunt in commixtione unum omnino.... Masculus ergo et foemina conjunguntur, et unum fiunt, et cetera.

26. Petrus Bonus, II: 51:

    Et est sciendum, quod masculus et foemina sunt idem, et in eodem substantivo, et sunt habentes virtutes diversas in tali subjecti unitate.... talis copulatio potest dici Hermophrodita: quia plantae et semina ubicunque impraegnant, impraegnantur etiam, et hoc denotat agens et patiens in eodem subjecto simul esse commixta in unitate quadam. Quando ergo oritur lapis iste, habet in se mixtionem masculi et foeminae.

27. Petrus Bonus, II: 51.
28. Petrus Bonus, II: 34. "Tam corporeis quam incorporeis... et de corruptibilibus et incorruptibilibus, et visibilibus et invisibilibus, et de spiritu, et anima, et corpore, et ipsorum unione."
29. Crisciani, 171–73.

30. Antoine Calvet, "Alchimie et joachimisme dans les alchimica pseudo-arnaldiens," in *Alchimie et philosophie à la Renaissance*, ed. Jean-Claude Margolin and Sylvain Matton (Paris: Vrin, 1993), 99–100.
31. John of Rupescissa (Giovanni da Rupescissa), *Liber lucis*, in *Il libro della luce*, ed. Andrea Aromatico (Venice: Marsilio, 1997), 24v (142–43): "Sic extrahe ipsum de vase predicto quod vocatur ovum Philosophorum, et Magister Arnaldus dicit quod Lapis est clausus in eo sicut Christus in sepulcro."
32. See chapter 3 in "Confounding Oppositions."
33. Vienna, Österreichische Nationalbibliothek, Cod. Vind. 2372, fol. 57va. See Obrist, "Visualization in Medieval Alchemy," *Hyle* 9:2 (2003): 155.
34. Obrist "Visualization," 131–70; on alchemical imagery in general, see her *Les débuts de l'imagerie alchimique (XIVe–XVe siècles)* (Paris: Sycomore, 1982).
35. Obrist "Visualization," 141–42.
36. Andrew Campbell, Lorenza Gianfrancesco, and Neil Tarrant, "Alchemy and the Mendicant Orders of Late Medieval and Early Modern Europe," *Ambix* 65:3 (2018): 201–9; Tara Nummedal, "Alchemy and Religion in Christian Europe," *Ambix* 60:4 (2013): 311–22; Zachary A. Matus, "Alchemy and Christianity in the Middle Ages," *History Compass* 10:12 (2012): 934–45.
37. I use the Latin title here for the *Aurora consurgens* because it is so well-known by this name.
38. On this text, see Obrist, *Les débuts*, 183–245; Barbara Newman, *God and the Goddesses: Vision, Poetry, and Belief in the Middle Ages* (Philadelphia: University of Pennsylvania Press, 2005), 235–40.
39. *Aurora consurgens*, ed. Marie-Louise Von Franz, trans. R. F. C. Hull and A. S. B. Glover (New York: Bollingen Foundation, 1966), 42: "Est namque donum et sacramentum Dei atque res divina, quae maxime et diversimode a sapientum sermonibus typicis est occultata."
40. On personified Wisdom, see Barbara Newman, *Sister of Wisdom: St. Hildegard's Theology of the Feminine* (Berkeley: University of California Press, 1987), 42–88. For patristic and medieval understandings of Wisdom as feminine, see Jennifer P. Heimmel, *"God Is Our Mother": Julian of Norwich and the Medieval Image of Christian Feminine Divinity* (Salzburg: Institut für Anglistik und Amerikanistik, Universität Salzburg, 1982), 21–24.
41. *Aurora consurgens*, 58: "cuius amore langueo, ardore liquesco, odore vivo, sapore convalesco, cuius lacte nutrimentum suscipio, amplexu iuvenesco, osculo spiraculum vitae recipio, cuius condormitione totum corpus meum exinanitur, illi vero ero in patrem et ipse mihi in filium" (emphasis is mine).
42. Obrist, *Les débuts*, 188–89.
43. Obrist, *Les débuts*, 238–40; Newman, *God and the Goddesses*, 238–40.
44. Alan of Lille describes the bat as a "hermaphroditic bird" ("auis hermafroditica") in *De Planctu naturae,*, 2.192–93 (816).
45. Tom Greeves, Sue Andrew and Chris Chapman, *The Three Hares: A Curiosity Worth Regarding* (Devon: Skerryvore Productions Ltd., 2016).
46. Pseudo-Albertus's *Secrets of Women*, for example, warned against sexual positions that could scatter the male seed within the womb and cause monsters; a nearby passage claimed that semen in the center of the womb could produce an infant who was both male and female. *De secretis mulierum*, 94–98; a different version appears in English translation in Ps.-Albertus Magnus, *Secrets of Women*, 113–18; see also Miller, 87.
47. See chapter 4 passim and fig 4.2.
48. See also similar images in BNF, Ms Arabe 2583, fol. 9v (15th century) and Châteauroux Bibliothèque municipale, Ms 2, fol. 3 (1414).
49. By the late Middle Ages, zodiacal twins are often pictured as a male-female pair, but many illustrations continue to portray them as the same sex. For zodiac twins and Adam and Eve, see Colum Hourihane, ed., *Time in the Medieval World: Occupations of the Months and Signs of the Zodiac in the Index of Christian Art* (Princeton, NJ: Princeton University, 2007), lxi; Strickland, *Saracens*, 33.

50. Cohen and Derbes, 21–22. On the *Bible moralisée* from Paris c. 1220–25, Vienna Österreichische Nationalbibliothek, cod. 2554, fol. 2r, see Mills, *Seeing Sodomy*, 32.
51. Jack M. Greenstein, "The Body of Eve in Andrea Pisano's *Creation* Relief," *Art Bulletin* 90:4 (2008): 577–78; Greenstein, *The Creation of Eve and Renaissance Naturalism: Visual Theology and Artistic Invention* (Cambridge: Cambridge University Press, 2016), 33–40.
52. Such images seem to resonate with cross-cultural depictions of miraculous birth, for instance, the Buddha from his mother's flank. See Patricia Eichenbaum Karentzky, *The Life of the Buddha: Ancient Scriptural and Pictorial Traditions* (Lanham, MD: University Press of America, 1992), 15–16.
53. Greenstein, "The Body of Eve," 578–79.
54. These illustrations also invert contemporary representations of Caesarean birth, comparing God to a physician who surgically removes femaleness from the male body. The surgeon Henri de Mondeville, in fact, made the comparison between God and the surgeon explicitly. Pouchelle, 43. See also Renate Blumenfeld-Kosinski, *Not of Woman Born: Representations of Caesarean Birth in Medieval and Renaissance Culture* (Ithaca, NY: Cornell University Press, 1990).
55. On this convention in later images, see Greenstein, *Creation of Eve*, 120–21.
56. Gillian Clark, "Adam's Womb (Augustine, Confessions 13:28) and the Salty Sea," and "Adam's Engendering: Augustine on Gender and Creation," in *Body and Gender, Soul and Reason in Late Antiquity* (Burlington, VT: Ashgate, 2011), VII: 89–90; X: 18.
57. See chapter 2.
58. Sandra L. Hindman, *Christine de Pizan's "Epistre Othéa": Painting and Politics at the Court of Charles VI* (Toronto: Pontifical Institute of Mediaeval Studies, 1986).
59. Marilynn Desmond and Pamela Sheingorn, *Myth, Montage, and Visuality in Late Medieval Manuscript Culture: Christine de Pizan's Epistre Othea* (Ann Arbor: University of Michigan Press, 2003), 148–51. See also a similar image of two lovers united in a bicephalous body in *Li ars d'amour de vertu et de bonheurté*, a late thirteenth-century French moral treatise. Michael Camille, "The Image and the Self: Unwriting Late Medieval Bodies," in *Framing Medieval Bodies*, ed. Sarah Kay and Miri Rubin (Manchester: Manchester University Press, 1994), 72–73 (fig. 13).
60. Christine de Pizan, *Epistre Othea: Edition critique*, ed. Gabriella Parussa (Geneva: Droz, 1999), 82.1–5; 42–52 (pp. 315–17):

    Ne soyes dur a ottroyer/ Ce que tu peus bien emploier;/ A Hermofrodicus te mire/ A qui mal prist pour escondire. . . . Dur ne doit estre a ottroier le bon esperit la ou il voit la neccessité, mais reconforter le besongneux a son pouoir. Comme dit saint Gregoire es Morales que quant nous voulons reconforter aucun afflict en sa tristece, nous devons premierement douloir avecques lui, car cellui ne peut proprement reconforter le dolent qui ne s'acorde a sa douleur, car ainsi comme l'en ne pourroit joindre l'un fer a l'autre se tous les .ij. ne sont eschauffez et amoliez au feu, ainsi ne pouons nous autrui redrecier se nostre cuer n'est amoli par compassion.

61. Christine de Pizan, 82.26–29 (p. 316): "clercs soubtilz philosophes ayent muciez leur grans secrés soubz couverture de fable, y peut ester entendue sentence appartenant a la science d'astronomie et autressi d'arquemie."
62. Robinson, 215.
63. On this work, see Obrist, *Les débuts*, 117–82; Denis Duveen, "Le Livre de la très sainte trinité," *Ambix* 3 (1948): 26–32; Herwig Buntz, "*Das Buch der heiligen Dreifaltigkeit*: Sein Autor und seine Überlieferung," *Zeitschrift für deutsches Altertum und deutsche Litteratur* 101 (1972), 150–60; W. Ganzenmüller, "Das *Buch der heiligen Dreigfaltigkeit*: Eine deutsche Alchemie aus dem Anfang des 15. Jahrhunderts," *Archiv für Kulturgeschichte* 29 (1939): 93–146.
64. On sculptural figures of opening virgins, see Elina Gertsman, *Worlds Within: Opening the Medieval Shrine Madonna* (University Park: Pennsylvania State University Press, 2015).

65. Anonymous, *Livre de la très sainte trinité*, Beinecke Library, Yale University, Mellon MS 74, fol. 25r-v: "On ne peut iamais voir la mere de Dieu sans voir aussÿ éternellement Dieu ainsÿ caché et meslé ensemble, Dieu étoit et est éternellement sa propre mere et son propre pere humain divin sous sa divinité et sous son humanité ensemble et il depend de luÿ lequel il veut étre le plus caché en soy le divin ou l'humain, le feminin ou masculin."

66. Mellon MS 74, fol. 25r: "La transparente humanité de Marie claire étoit l'humanité interieur et exterieur de Dieu Jesus Christus tout a fait ensemble il n'a eu et n'a point d'autre humanité toutes les deux sont icÿ eternelles sans fin. . . . Et ont esté eternellement un, la Divinité Jesus Christus ne peut et ne peuvent pas éternellement estre separée de son humanité exterieure ainsÿ Jesus Maria est et étoit un en méme substance Jesus Maria."

67. Mellon MS 74, fol. 16v: "Surrexit Christus, Jesus, Maria, lapis, rubeus, carbunculus, par tout une méme chose, ils ne pouvoient pas se separer et il[s] ne se separeront iamais. Ainsi de méme Jesus et Marie sont un sang, une lune, un soleil, ce qui est demontré par tout dans ce livre."

68. Obrist, *Les débuts*, 133. David Burr, *The Spiritual Franciscans* (University Park: Pennsylvania State University Press, 2001).

69. Obrist, *Les débuts*, 160.

70. This section is indebted to Joan Gibson's argument in "Could Christ Have Been Born a Woman? A Medieval Debate," *Journal of Feminist Studies in Religion* 8:1 (1992): 65–82. Gibson argues that interest in the question of God's female sex reached its apogee in the thirteenth century, although discussions continued into the fifteenth century. See also Van der Lugt, "Pourquoi," 89–113.

71. Bynum, *Fragmentation and Redemption*, 97–99, fig. 3.6; Flood, 14.

72. Gibson, "Could Christ Have Been Born a Woman?" 71.

73. Albert the Great, *Commentarii in Tertium Librum Sententiarium*, in *Opera omnia*, ed. A. Borgnet (Paris: Vivès, 1894), 28: 234; Gibson, 72.

74. Gibson, 69–72.

75. *Summae Magistri Rolandi Cremonensis*, ed. A. Cortesi (Bergamo: Edizioni Monumenta Bergomensia, 1962-), 7:47:

> Ad illud quod dicit contra—femina non est vir—dicimus quod falsum est. Immo ista femina est vir, quia sunt eadem persona et idem homo Iehsus et hec femina. Bene concedo quod femina in quantum femina non est vir in quantum vir, idest feminitas non est virilitas. Sed non sequitur . . . ergo femina non est vir. Et est fallacia secundum quid et simpliciter. Confidenter dico quod, facta illa positione, iste vir est ista femina, et hec femina est iste vir . . . Nec valet istud argumentum: 'feminitas non est virilitas, ergo femina non est vir', sicut non valet: albedo non est musica, ergo album non est musicum. In creaturis bene sequitur: est femina, ergo non est vir, et e converso. Hic autem non est ita, quia supra naturam est hoc. Falsum ergo dixit quando dixit: 'Impossibile est quod femina sit vir.'

Gibson, 70.

76. Gibson, 73.

77. Thomas Aquinas, *Scriptum super sententiis Magistri Petri Lombardi*, ed. R. P. Maria Fabianus Moos (Paris: Lethielleux, 1956), 3: 233–35; 385–87; at 3:387: "Unde in eo non potuit esse uterque sexus, quia hoc esset monstruosum et innaturale."

78. *Collectorium circa quattuor libros Sententiarum*, ed. Wilfrid Werbeck and Udo Hofman (Tübingen: J. C. B. Mohr, 1973), 214: "Nunc autem utrumque dignificavit, quia ipse naturam in sexu virili assumpsit et eam de Virgine matre accepit." Gibson, 77. See also Denis the Carthusian's comments on the primal hermaphrodite and Genesis 1:27, citing Peter Comestor's *Historia scholastica* in *Enarratio in Genesim*, in *Doctoris ecstatici D. Dionysii Cartusiani Opera omnia*, 42 vols. (Monstrolii: Typis Cartusiae S. M. de Pratis, 1896), I: 55.

79. It is worth pointing out that while Adam was made from mud, Eve was made from flesh. But identifications of woman with flesh or matter were hardly monolithic, and other traditions identified woman with soul. See, for instance, Flood, 18; Bynum, "Jesus as Mother," 110–69; Bynum, *Fragmentation and Redemption*, 151–79.
80. Bynum, "Why All the Fuss about the Body? A Medievalist's Perspective," *Critical Inquiry* 22:1 (1995): 6–33.
81. See the Würzburg crucifixion; the apse mosaic at Stonecutters' Monastery of Blessed David, Thessalonica; and the so-called "seated poetess" now located in Rome. Lifshitz, "Persistence," 18–27; Thomas F. Mathews, *The Clash of Gods: A Reinterpretation of Early Christian Art* (Princeton, NJ: Princeton University Press, 1999), 115–41; Ilse E. Friesen, *The Female Crucifix: Images of St. Wilgefortis Since the Middle Ages* (Waterloo, ON: Wilfrid Laurier University Press, 2001), 27–30.
82. Bynum, "Jesus as Mother," 110–69.
83. Carolyn Diskant Muir, "Bride or Bridegroom? Masculine Identity in Mystic Marriages," in *Holiness and Masculinity in the Middle Ages*, ed. P. H. Cullum and Katherine J. Lewis (Cardiff: University of Wales, 2005), 60–69; on Suso, see Jeffrey F. Hamburger, *The Visual and the Visionary: Art and Female Spirituality in Late Medieval Germany* (New York: Zone, 1998), 197–232.
84. Schweitzer, 249; Bynum, *Fragmentation and Redemption*, 93–101.
85. Newman, *From Virile Woman*, 156–57.
86. Bynum, "Jesus as Mother," 140n105; Heimmel, 46–102.
87. Newman, *From Virile Woman*, 11–12, 111, and passim.
88. Bynum, *Holy Feast and Holy Fast: The Religious Significance of Food to Medieval Women* (Berkeley: University of California Press, 1988), 292.
89. Pierre Bersuire, *L' 'Ovidius Moralizatus' di Pierre Bersuire*, ed. F. Ghisaberti (Rome: Presso La Societá, 1933), 116: "Iste enim puer filius Mercurii est Dei filius super omnia sponsus. . . . iste in fontem misericordie i. beatam Virginem descendit, ubi statim nimpha ista i. natura humana cum eo se coniunxit, et sic sibi per beatam incarnationem adhesit quod ex duabus naturis una persona resultavit." The *Ovidius moralizatus* was book 15 of his *Reductorium morale*, but it frequently circulated independently. See Kathryn L. McKinley, *Reading the Ovidian Heroine: "Metamorphoses" Commentaries 1100–1618* (Leiden: Brill, 2001), 106.
90. George D. Economou, *The Goddess Natura in Medieval Literature* (Cambridge, MA: Harvard University Press, 1972), 19–20, 72–97; Larry Scanlon, "Unspeakable Pleasures: Alain de Lille, Sexual Regulation and the Priesthood of Genius," *Romanic Review* 86:2 (1995): 213–42, esp. 231–33; Jordan, *Invention of Sodomy*, 70–71; Katharine Park, "Nature in Person: Medieval and Renaissance Allegories and Emblems," in *The Moral Authority of Nature*, ed. Lorraine Daston and Fernando Vidal (Chicago: University of Chicago Press, 2004), 54–55.
91. Jordan, 70–71.
92. Mechtild Modersohn, *Natura als Göttin im Mittelalter: Ikonographische Studien zu Darstellungen der personifizierten Natur* (Berlin: Akademie Verlag, 1997), 35–44 and figs. 10 and 15a.
93. Ovid, *Metamorphoses*, 4.380–81 (I: 204).
94. William Eamon, *Science and the Secrets of Nature: Books of Secrets in Medieval and Early Modern Culture* (Princeton, NJ: Princeton University Press, 1994).
95. See, for instance, Paravicini Bagliani, *Pope's Body*, 204–11; Pamela H. Smith, *The Business of Alchemy: Science and Culture in the Holy Roman Empire* (Princeton, NJ: Princeton University Press, 1994).
96. Long, *Hermaphrodites*; Gilbert, *Early Modern Hermaphrodites*.
97. Bynum, "Fuss," 25.
98. Bynum, "Fuss," 25. As Bynum has noted, other depictions of heaven differed from this scholastic vision.
99. Meeks, 185.

100. Bouchard, 14–23, 28–56. Platonic themes emphasizing the reconciliation of contraries imbued early Christianity, too, as a number of scholars have argued.
101. As Bynum argues, a metamorphosis can never be complete or the sense of the original is lost; as a result, medieval sources tended to emphasize some lingering element of duality. *Metamorphosis*, 163–89.
102. Akbari, *Idols*, 146; Reis, 5–8; Lugones, 195.
103. Daston and Park, "Hermaphrodite," 419–38; Long, *Hermaphrodites*; Sergius Kodera, *Disreputable Bodies: Magic, Medicine, and Gender in Renaissance Natural Philosophy* (Toronto: Centre for Renaissance and Reformation Studies, 2010).

CONCLUSION: TENSION AND TENSES

1. See Long, "Intersex/Transgender," 122.
2. For criticism of scholars who use intersex instrumentally, see Strassfeld, "Classically Queer," 95–97; Karkazis, *Fixing Sex*. For life chances, Spade, 11–13 and passim.
3. David A. Rubin, 125–39; Katrina Karkazis and Rebecca Jordan-Young, "The Powers of Testosterone: Obscuring Race and Regional Bias in the Regulation of Women Athletes," *Feminist Formations* 30:2 (2018): 1–39; Neville Hoad, "'Run, Caster Semenya, Run!' Nativism and the Translation of Gender Variance," *Safundi: The Journal of South African and American Studies* 11:4 (2010): 397–405.
4. Alice Dreger, quoted in Nikki Sullivan, "The Somatechnics of Intersexuality," *GLQ: A Journal of Gay and Lesbian Studies* 15:2 (2009): 323.
5. As certain trans people become more visible, scholars argue, others are increasingly erased, especially those who are economically precarious, who are of color, or whose means of self-representation are limited by systemic racism and sexism. See Reina Gossett (now Tourmaline), Eric A. Stanley, and Johanna Burton, ed. *Trap Door: Trans Cultural Production and the Politics of Visibility* (Cambridge, MA: MIT Press, 2017); Joey L. Mogul, Andrea J. Ritchie, and Kay Whitlock, *Queer (In)Justice: The Criminalization of LGBT People in the United States* (Boston: Beacon Press, 2011); Eric A. Stanley and Nat Smith, ed., *Captive Genders: Trans Embodiment and the Prison Industrial Complex* (Edinburgh: AK, 2011).
6. For a list of current anti-LGBT bills, see American Civil Liberties Union (ACLU), "Legislation Affecting LGBT Rights Across the Country," accessed December, 2019, https://www.aclu.org/legislation-affecting-lgbt-rights-across-country?redirect=other/legislation-affecting-lgbt-rights-across-country. Samantha Allen, "SCOTUS Lets Mississippi HB 1523, America's Most Anti-LGBT Law, Stay in Place," Daily Beast (January 11, 2018), accessed March 3, 2019, https://www.thedailybeast.com/scotus-lets-mississippis-hb-1523-americas-most-anti-lgbt-law-stay-in-place. Dan Levin, "A Clash Across America Over Transgender Rights," *The New York Times*, March 12, 2020.
7. Quoted in Green et al., "Transgender."
8. Council on Biblical Manhood and Womanhood, Nashville Statement, 2017, accessed December, 2019, https://cbmw.org/nashville-statement/. On religious language in so-called bathroom bills, see Strassfeld, "Transing Religious Studies," 37–53.
9. Andrea Long Chu and Emmett Harsin Drager, "After Trans Studies," *TSQ: Transgender Studies Quarterly* 6:1 (2019): 107.
10. My use of "tense" and temporality here is inspired by Alexander Nagel, "The Tenses of Drawing," Public Lecture, Morgan Library and Museum, New York, May 9, 2017; Dinshaw, *Getting Medieval*; Dinshaw et al., "Theorizing Queer Temporalities," 177–95.

Bibliography

PRINTED PRIMARY SOURCES

Alan of Lille. "De Planctu naturae." Ed. Nikolaus M. Häring. *Studi medievali*, serie terza 19:2 (1978): 797–879.
Albert the Great (Albertus Magnus). *De animalibus*. In *Albertus Magnus de animalibus libri XXVI: Beiträge zur Geschichte der Philosophie des Mittelalters: Texte und Untersuchungen*, ed. Hermann Stadler, 15–16, 2 vols. Münster: Aschendorff, 1916–21.
———. *On Animals: A Medieval Summa Zoologica*. Trans. and ed. Kenneth F. Kitchell Jr. and Irven Michael Resnick, 2 vols. Baltimore and London: Johns Hopkins University Press, 1999.
———. *Commentarii in Tertium Librum Sententiarium*, in *B. Alberti Magni Ratisbonensis episcopi, ordinis Prædicatorum*, vol. 28 of *Opera omnia, ex editione lugdunensi religiose castigata*, ed. A. Borgnet. Paris: Vivès, 1894.
———. *De mineralibus*. Ed. and trans. Dorothy Wyckoff. Oxford: Clarendon, 1967.
———. *De resurrectione*. In *Opera omnia*, vol. 26, ed. Wilhelm Kübel et al. Münster: Aschendorff, 1956.
———. *De secretis mulierum: Item De virtutibus herbarum lapidum et animalium*. Amsterdam: Apud Iodocum Ianssonium 1655.
———. *Mineralium libri quinque*. In *Opera omnia*, vol. 5, ed. A. Borgnet. Paris: Apud Ludovicum Vivès, 1890.
———. *Questions Concerning Aristotle's* On Animals. Trans. Irven M. Resnick and Kenneth F. Kitchell Jr. Washington, DC: Catholic University of America Press, 2008.
———. *Quaestiones super de animalibus*. Ed. Ephrem Filthaut. Vol. 12 of *Opera omnia*, 77–351. Münster: Aschendorff, 1955.
———. *Summa theologiae*. In *Opera omnia*, vol. 32, ed. A. Borgnet. Paris: Apud Ludovicum Vivès, 1895.
Albucasis. *Cyrurgia Albucasis cum cauterijs et alijs instrumentis*. In *Cyrurgia parua Guidonis*. Venice: Per Bonetum Locatellus, 1500.
———. *On Surgery and Instruments*. Ed. M. S. Spink and G. L. Lewis. Berkeley: University of California Press, 1973.
Alexander of Hales (attrib.). *Doctoris irrefragabilis Alexandri de Hales Ordinis Minorum Summa theologica*. 4 vols. Quaracchi, Italy: Collegium S. Bonaventurae, 1928.
Andrew of St. Victor. *Expositionem super Heptateuchum*. Ed. Charles Lohr and Rainer Berndt. CCCM 53. Turnhout, Belgium: Brepols, 1986.

Aristotle, *De Animalibus: Michael Scot's Arabic-Latin Translation, Part Three, Books XV-XIX: Generation of Animals*, ed. Aafke M. I. Van Oppenraaij. Leiden: Brill, 1992.
———. *On the Generation of Animals*. Ed. and trans. A. L. Peck. London: Harvard University Press, 1963.
Augustine of Hippo. *Concerning the City of God Against the Pagans (De civitate Dei)*. Trans. Henry Bettenson. Harmondsworth, UK: Penguin, 1972.
———. *De civitate Dei*. Ed. Bernhard Dombart and Alfons Kalb, CCSL 48. Turnhout, Belgium: Brepols, 1955.
———. *De Genesi ad litteram*. Ed. J. Zycha. CSEL 28. Vienna: F. Tempsky; Leipzig: G. Freytag, 1894.
———. *De Genesi contra Manichaeos*. Ed. Dorothea Weber, CSEL 91 (Vienna: Verlag der österreichischen Akademie der Wissenschaften, 1998.
———. *De trinitate*. Ed. W. J. Mountain and F. Glorie. CCSL 50-50A. Turnhout, Belgium: Brepols, 1968.
———. *The Literal Meaning of Genesis*. Trans. John Hammond Taylor, SJ. 2 vols. Mahwah, NJ: Paulist, 1982.
———. *On the Trinity: Books 8–15*. Ed. Gareth B. Matthews and trans. Stephen McKenna. Cambridge: Cambridge University Press, 2002.
Aurora consurgens. Ed. Marie-Louise Von Franz, trans. R. F. C. Hull and A. S. B. Glover. New York: Bollingen Foundation, 1966.
Avicenna, *Liber canonis Avicenne*. Venice, 1507; facsimile reprint, Hildesheim, Germany: Georg Olms, 1964.
Azo of Bologna. *In ius civile Summa*. N.p.: Lyon, 1564.
Baldus de Ubaldis. *In decretalium volumen commentaria*. Ed. Franciscus de Parona. Torino: Botttega d'Erasmo, 1971.
Bartholomaeus Anglicus, *De rerum proprietatibus: Frankfurt 1601*. Frankfurt: Minerva, 1964.
Bernard of Clairvaux. *Sermones*. Vol. 4 of *Opera omnia*, ed. J. LeClercq and H. Rochais. Rome: Editiones Cistercienses, 1966.
Bernard of Cluny. *Scorn for the World (De contemptu mundi)*. Ed. and trans. Ronald E. Pepin. East Lansing, MI: Colleagues, 1991.
Biblia Latina cum Glossa Ordinaria: Facsimile Reprint of the Editio Princeps Adolph Rusch of Strassburg 1480/81. Ed. Karlfield Froehlich and Margaret T. Gibson. Turnhout, Belgium: Brepols, 1992.
Bruno Longobucco. "The *Cyrurgia magna* of Brunus Longoburgensis: A Critical Edition." Ed. S. P. Hall. DPhil thesis, Oxford University, 1957.
Caelius Aurelianus. *Gynaecia*. Ed. Miriam F. Drabkin and Israel E. Drabkin. Baltimore, MD: Bulletin of the History of Medicine, Suppl. 13, 1951.
Constantine of Pisa. *The Book of the Secrets of Alchemy. Introduction, Critical Edition, Translation, and Commentary*. Ed. Barbara Obrist. Leiden: Brill, 1990.
Constantine the African and 'Alī ibn al-'Abbās al-Magūsī. *Constantine the African and 'Alī ibn al-'Abbās al-Magūsī: The* Pantegni *and Related Texts*. Ed. Charles Burnett and Danielle Jacquart. Leiden: Brill, 1994.
Christine de Pizan. *Epistre Othea: Edition critique*. Ed. Gabriella Parussa. Geneva: Droz, 1999.
Curley, Michael J., ed. and trans. *Physiologus: A Medieval Book of Nature Lore*. Chicago: University of Chicago Press, 2009.
Denis the Carthusian. *Doctoris ecstatici D. Dionysii Cartusiani Opera omnia*, 42 vols. Monstrolii: Typis Cartusiae S. M. de Pratis, 1896.
The Digest of Justinian. Ed. Theodor Mommsen, Paul Kreuger, and Alan Watson. Philadelphia: University of Pennsylvania Press, 1985.
Diodoros of Sicily. *Diodoros of Sicily*. Ed. and trans. Francis R. Walton. Cambridge, MA: Loeb Classical Library, Harvard University Press,1957.
Disciplinary Decrees of the General Councils: Texts, Translation and Commentary. Ed. Henry Joseph Schroeder. St. Louis, MO: B. Herder, 1937.
Gabriel Biel. *Collectorium circa quattuor libros Sententiarum*. Ed. Wilfrid Werbeck and Udo Hofman. Tübingen: J. C. B. Mohr, 1973.
Giovanni Balbi. *Catholicon*. Westmead, UK: Gregg, 1971.

BIBLIOGRAPHY

Giovanni da Rupescissa. *Il libro della luce*. Ed. Andrea Aromatico. Venice : Marsilio, 1997.
Gratian. *Decretum Magistri Gratiani*. In *Corpus Iuris Canonici*, vol. 1, ed. Emil Friedberg. Graz, Austria: Akademische Druck-u. Verlagsanstalt, 1959.
Gregory the Great. *Pastoral Care: Regula pastoralis*. Trans. Henry Davis. Westminster, MD : Newman , 1950.
Guglielmo da Saliceto. *Summa conservationis et curationis*. Venice: Marinus Saracenus, 1490
Guibert of Nogent. *Moralium in Genesim*. PL 156: 19–338.
———. *Tractatus de incarnatione contra Judaeos*. PL 156: 489–527.
Guillaume le Clerc. *The Bestiary of Guillaume le Clerc*. Trans. George Claridge Druce. Ashford, UK: Invicta, 1936.
Guy de Chauliac. *Inventarium sive chirurgia magna*. Ed. Michael McVaugh, with commentary by McVaugh and Margaret S. Ogden, 2 vols. Leiden: Brill, 1997.
Haly Abbas. *Liber totius medicine*. Lyon: Typis Jacobi Myt, 1523.
Henricus de Gandavo. *La "Lectura ordinaria super sacram scripturam" attribuée à Henri de Gand*. Ed. Raymond Macken. Leuven, Belgium: Éditions universitaires de Louvain, 1972.
Hilka, Alfons, ed. "Eine alt-französische moralisierende Bearbeitung des *Liber de Monstruosis Hominibus Orientis* aus Thomas von Cantimpré. *De Naturis Rerum*." In *Abhandlungen der Gesellschaft der Wissenschaften zu Gottingen: Philologisch-Historische Klasse* 7, 1–73. Berlin: Weidmannsche Buchhandlung, 1933.
Hillman, Thea. *Intersex (For Lack of a Better Word)*. San Francisco: Manic D, 2008.
Honorius Augustodunensis. *Clavis physicae, critical edition of the first part (§§ 1–315)*. Ed. Paolo Lucentini. Rome: Edizioni di Storia e Letteratura, 1974.
Hugo de Sancto Caro. *Hugonis Cardinalis Opera Omnia in Universum Vetus, et Novum Testamentum: Tomi Octo. 1 In Libros Genesis...* (Venice: Pezzana, 1703).
Irenaeus, *Adversus haereses seu Detectio et eversio falso cognominatae Gnoseos*. Turnhout, Belgium: Brepols, 2010.
Isidore of Seville. *Isidori Hispalensis Episcopi Etymologiarum sive originum*. Ed. W. M. Lindsay. 2 vols. Oxford: Clarendon, 1911.
———. *The Etymologies of Isidore of Seville*. Ed. and trans. Stephen A. Barney et al. Cambridge: Cambridge University Press, 2006.
———. *The Medical Writings. An English Translation with an Introduction and Commentary*. Ed. and trans. William D. Sharpe. *Transactions of the American Philosophical Society* 54:2 (1964): 1–75.
Jacob van Maerlant. *Der naturen bloeme*. Ed. Maurits Gysseling. 'S-Gravenhage: Martinus Nijhoff, 1981.
Jacques de Vitry. *Histoire orientale: Historia orientalis*. Ed. Jean Donnadieu. Turnhout, Belgium: Brepols, 2008.
Jerome. *Against Jovinianus*. In *Nicene and Post-Nicene Fathers, Vol. 6: Jerome: Letters and Selected Works*, ed. Philip Schaff and Henry Wace, 346–416. New York: Charles Scribner's Sons, 1912.
John of Salisbury. *Ioannis Saresberiensis Episcopi Carnotensis Policratici sive de Nugis Curialium et Vestigiis Philosophorum Libri viii: recognovit et prolegomenis, apparatu critico, commentario, indicibus instruxit*. Ed. Clemens C. I. Webb, 2 vols. Oxford: Clarendon, 1909.
———. *Policraticus: Of the Frivolities of Courtiers and the Footprints of Philosophers*. Ed. and trans. Cary J. Nederman. Cambridge: Cambridge University Press, 1990.
John Scottus Eriugena. *Periphyseon: Liber quartus*. Ed. Édouard A. Jeauneau. CCCM 164. Turnhout, Belgium: Brepols, 1996–2003.
———. *Periphyseon: Liber Quintus*. Édouard A. Jeauneau. CCCM 165. Turnhout, Belgium: Brepols, 2003.
———. *Periphyseon: On the Division of Nature*. Trans. Myra L. Uhlfelder. Indianapolis: Bobbs-Merrill, 1976.
Lanfranc of Milan. *Chirurgia magna*. Venice: Per Bonetus Locatellus, 1498.
Lawn, Brian, ed. *The Prose Salernitan Questions: Edited from a Bodleian Manuscript (Auct. F. 3. 10)*. London: British Academy, 1979.
Mandeville, John. *Mandeville's Travels*. Ed. P. Hamelius, Early English Text Society, o.s. 153. Milwood, NY: Kraus Reprint, 1987.

Odo of Tournai. *On Original Sin and A Disputation with the Jew, Leo, Concerning the Advent of Christ, the Son of God: Two Theological Treatises*. Trans. and ed. Irven M. Resnick. Philadelphia: University of Pennsylvania Press, 1994.

Orderic Vitalis. *The Ecclesiastical History*. Ed. and trans. Marjorie Chibnall. 6 vols. Oxford: Clarendon, 1973.

Otto of Freising. *Chronica sive historia de duabus civitatibus*. Ed. Adolf Hofmeister. Scriptores rerum Germanicarum in usum scholarum ex Monumentis Germaniae Historicis separatim editi. Hanover: Hahn, 1912.

———. *The Two Cities: A Chronicle of Universal History to the Year 1146 A.D.* Ed. and trans. Charles Christopher Mierow. New York: Columbia University Press, 2002.

Ovid, *Metamorphoses*. Trans. Frank Justus Miller. 2 vols. Cambridge, MA: Loeb Classical Library, Harvard University Press, 1971.

Paré, Ambroise. *On Monsters and Marvels*. Ed. and trans. Janis L. Pallister. Chicago: University of Chicago Press, 1995.

Pedanius Dioscorides. *De materia medica by Pedanius Dioscorides*. Trans. Lily Y. Beck. Hildesheim, Germany: Olms-Weidmann, 2005.

Peter of Poitiers. *Summa de Confessione: Compilatio praesens*. Ed. Jean Longère. CCCM 51. Turnhout, Belgium: Brepols, 1980.

Petrus Bonus. *Margarita preciosa novella*. In *Bibliotheca chemica curiosa*, ed. J. J. Manget, 2 vols., II: 1–80. Geneva, 1702 (repr. Bologna: A. Forni, 1976).

Petrus Cantor. *Glossae super Genesim: Prologus et Capitula 1–3*. Ed. Agneta Sylwan. Gothenburg: Acta Universitatis, 1992.

———. *Petri Cantoris Parisiensis Verbum Adbreviatum: Textus Conflatus*. Ed. Monique Boutry CCCM 196. Turnhout, Belgium: Brepols, 2004.

Peter Comestor. *Scolastica historia: Liber Genesis*. Ed. Agneta Sylwan, CCCM 191. Turnhout, Belgium: Brepols, 2005.

Petrus de Palude. *Exactissimi . . . doctoris Petri de Palude . . . Quartus Sententiarum*. Paris: Petit, Regnault, & Chevallon, 1514.

Pierre Bersuire. *L'Ovidius Moralizatus di Pierre Bersuire*. Ed. F. Ghisaberti. Rome: Presso La Societá, 1933.

Pliny the Elder. *Natural History*, Vol. II, Books 3–7. Ed. H. Rackham. Cambridge, MA: Harvard University Press, 1942.

Problemata varia anatomica: The University of Bologna MS 1165. Ed. L. R. Lind. Lawrence: University of Kansas Press, 1968.

The Prose Salernitan Questions: Edited from a Bodleian Manuscript (Auct. F. 3. 10). Ed. Brian Lawn. London: British Academy, 1979.

Ps.-Albertus Magnus. *Women's Secrets: A Translation of Pseudo-Albertus Magnus's De Secretis Mulierum with Commentaries*. Ed. and trans. Helen Rodnite Lemay. Albany: State University of New York Press, 1992.

Pseudo-Geber. *The Summa Perfectionis of Pseudo-Geber: A Critical Edition, Translation and Study*. Ed. William R. Newman. Leiden: Brill, 1991.

Remigius of Auxerre. *Commentum in Martianum Capellam*. Ed. Cora E. Lutz. 2 vols. Leiden: Brill, 1962.

Richardus Anglicus. *Correctorium alchemiae*. In *Alchemiae quam vocant artisque metallicae doctrina*, 2 vols., I, ed. Guglielmo Grataroli, 534–76. Basel: Petrum Pernam, 1572.

Riley, Henry Thomas, ed. *Johannis de Trokelow et Henrici de Blaneford Chronica et Annales*. Cambridge: Cambridge University Press, 2012.

Roderici Ximenii de Rada (Rodrigo Jiménez de Rada). *Breviarium historie catholice (I-V)*. Ed. Juan Fernández Valverde. CCCM 72A-B. Turnhout, Belgium: Brepols, 1992.

Roger Bacon. *The "Opus Majus" of Roger Bacon*. Ed. John Henry Bridges, 2 vols. Oxford: Clarendon, 1897.

Rolandino de' Passageri. *Summa artis notariae*. Lyon: Apud haeredes Iacobi Iuntae, 1559.

Julius Ruska, ed. *Tabula Smaragdina: ein Beitrag zur Geschichte der hermetischen Literatur*. Heidelberg: Winter, 1926.

The Summa Parisiensis on the Decretum Gratiani. Ed. Terence P. McLaughlin. Toronto: Pontifical Institute of Mediaeval Studies, 1952.

Thomas Aquinas. *Scriptum super sententiis Magistri Petri Lombardi*. Ed. R. P. Maria Fabianus Moos. Paris: Lethielleux, 1956.

——. *Summa theologiae: Latin text and English translation, Introductions, Notes, Appendices, and Glossaries*. New York: Blackfriars, 1964–81.

Thomas of Cantimpré. "Thomas of Cantimpré, *De naturis rerum*: Prologue, Book III, Book XIX." Ed. John Block Friedman. In *Cahiers d'Etudes Medievales* 2: *La Science de la Nature*, 107–54. Montreal: Vrin, 1974.

——. *Liber de natura rerum*. Ed. Helmut Boese. Berlin: Walter de Gruyter, 1973.

Thomasset, Claude, ed. *Placides et Timéo, ou, Li secrés as philosophes*. Geneva: Droz, 1980.

Vincent of Beauvais. *Speculum quadruplex, sive, Speculum maius: naturale, doctrinale, morale, historiale*. Graz, Austria, 1964–1965.

SECONDARY SOURCES

Aberdeen Bestiary Project. https://www.abdn.ac.uk/bestiary/history.php.

Abramson, Henry. "A Ready Hatred: Depictions of the Jewish Woman in Medieval Antisemitic Art and Caricature." *Proceedings of the American Academy for Jewish Research* 62 (1996): 1–18.

Abulafia, Anna S. "Bodies in the Jewish-Christian Debate." In *Framing Medieval Bodies*, ed. Sarah Kay and Miri Rubin, 123–37. Manchester: Manchester University Press, 1994.

——. "Christian Imagery of Jews in the Twelfth Century: A Look at Odo of Cambrai and Guibert of Nogent." In *Christians and Jews in Dispute: Disputational Literature and the Rise of Anti-Judaism in the West (c. 1000–1150)*, X: 383–91. Aldershot, UK: Variorum, 1998.

Adams, James Noel. *The Latin Sexual Vocabulary*. Baltimore, MD: Johns Hopkins University Press, 1990.

Ahuja, Neel. "Postcolonial Critique in a Multispecies World." *PMLA* 124:2 (2009): 556–63.

Ajootian, Aileen. "The Only Happy Couple: Hermaphrodites and Gender." In *Naked Truths*, ed. A. O. Koloski-Ostrow and C. L. Lyons, 220–42. New York: Routledge, 1997.

Akbari, Suzanne Conklin. "From Due East to True North: Orientalism and Orientation." In *The Postcolonial Middle Ages*, ed. Jeffrey Jerome Cohen, 19–34. New York: Palgrave, 2000.

——. *Idols in the East: European Representations of Islam and the Orient, 1100–1450*. Ithaca, NY: Cornell University Press, 2009.

Allen, Samantha. "SCOTUS Lets Mississippi HB 1523, America's Most Anti-LGBT Law, Stay in Place." *The Daily Beast*, January 11, 2018. https://www.thedailybeast.com/scotus-lets-mississippis-hb-1523-americas-most-anti-lgbt-law-stay-in-place.

American Civil Liberties Union (ACLU). "Legislation Affecting LGBT Rights Across the Country." Accessed December 2019. https://www.aclu.org/legislation-affecting-lgbt-rights-across-country?redirect=other/legislation-affecting-lgbt-rights-across-country.

Amin, Kadji. "Temporality." *TSQ: Transgender Studies Quarterly* 1:1–2 (2014): 219–22.

Anderson, G. K. "Popular Survivals of the Wandering Jew in England." *The Journal of English and Germanic Philology* 46:4 (1947): 367–82.

Armstrong-Partida, Michelle. "Priestly Wives: The Role and Acceptance of Clerics' Concubines in the Parishes of Late Medieval Catalunya." *Speculum* 88:1 (2013): 166–214.

Badir, Patricia, Peggy McCracken, and Valerie Traub, ed. *Ovidian Transversions: 'Iphis and Ianthe,' 1300–1650*. Edinburgh: Edinburgh University Press, 2019.

Bailey, Marlon M. *Butch Queens Up in Pumps: Gender, Performance, and Ballroom Culture in Detroit*. Ann Arbor: University of Michigan Press, 2013.

Bakhtin, Mikhail. *Rabelais and His World*. Trans. Hélène Iswolsky. Bloomington: Indiana University Press, 1984; first pub. 1968.

Baldassano, A. "Bodies of Resistance: On (Not) Naming Gender in the Medieval West." PhD diss, The City University of New York, 2017.

Baldwin, John W. *The Language of Sex: Five Voices from Northern France Around 1200*. Chicago: University of Chicago Press, 1994.

——. *The Scholastic Culture of the Middle Ages, 1000–1300*. Lexington, MA: Heath, 1971.

Barkan, Leonard. *The Gods Made Flesh: Metamorphosis and the Pursuit of Paganism*. New Haven, CT: Yale University Press, 1986.

Bartlett, Robert. *The Making of Europe: Conquest, Colonization, and Cultural Change, 950–1350*. Princeton, NJ: Princeton University Press, 1993.

——. *The Natural and the Supernatural in the Middle Ages*. Cambridge: Cambridge University Press, 2008.

Baxter, Ron. *Bestiaries and Their Users in the Middle Ages*. Stroud, UK: Sutton Publishing, 1998.

Bayker, Jesse. "Before Transsexuality: Transgender Lives and Practices in Nineteenth-Century America." PhD diss., Rutgers University, 2019.

Beemyn, Genny. "A Presence in the Past: A Transgender Historiography," *Journal of Women's History* 25:4 (2013): 113–21.

Benedek, Thomas G. and Janet Kubinec. "The Evaluation of Impotence by Sexual Congress and Alternatives Thereto in Divorce Proceedings." *Transactions and Studies of the College of Physicians of Philadelphia* 4:2 (1982): 122–53.

Benson, David. C. "Chaucer's Pardoner: His Sexuality and Modern Critics." *Mediaevalia* 8 (1982): 337–49.

Berger, David. *Persecution, Polemic, and Dialogue: Essays in Jewish-Christian Relations*. Boston, MA: Academic Studies Press, 2010.

Berkey, Jonathan P. "Circumcision Circumscribed: Female Excision and Cultural Accommodation in the Medieval Near East." *International Journal of Middle East Studies* 28 (1996): 19–38.

Bernau, Anke, Ruth Evans, and Sarah Salih. "Introduction: Virginities and Virginity Studies." In *Medieval Virginities*, ed. Anke Bernau, Ruth Evans, and Sarah Salih, 1–13. Toronto: University of Toronto Press, 2003.

Bethencourt, Francisco. *Racisms from the Crusades to the Twentieth Century*. Princeton, NJ: Princeton University Press, 2015.

Biddick, Kathleen. *The Typological Imaginary: Circumcision, Technology, History*. Philadelphia: University of Pennsylvania Press, 2003.

Bildhauer, Bettina and Robert Mills, ed. *The Monstrous Middle Ages*. Toronto: University of Toronto Press, 2003.

Biller, Peter. "A 'Scientific' View of Jews from Paris around 1300." *Micrologus* 9 (2001): 137–68.

——. "Proto-Racial Thought in Medieval Science." In *Origins of Racism in the West*, ed. Miriam Eliav-Feldon, Benjamin Isaac, and Joseph Ziegler, 157–180. Cambridge: Cambridge University Press, 2009.

Bird, Jessalynn. "The *Historia Orientalis* of Jacques de Vitry: Visual and Written Commentaries as Evidence of a Text's Audience, Reception, and Utilization." *Essays in Medieval Studies* 20 (2003): 56–74.

Blackless, Melanie, Anthony Charuvastra, Amanda Derryck, Anne Fausto-Sterling, Karl Lauzanne, and Ellen Lee. "How Sexually Dimorphic Are We? Review and Synthesis." *American Journal of Human Biology* 12 (2000): 151–66.

Blair, Ann. "Authorship in the Popular 'Problemata Aristotelis.' " *Early Science and Medicine* 4:3 (1999): 189–227.

Block, Sharon. "Making Meaningful Bodies: Physical Appearance in Colonial Writings." *Early American Studies: An Interdisciplinary Journal* 12:3 (2014): 524–47.

Blumenfeld-Kosinski, Renate. *Not of Woman Born: Representations of Caesarean Birth in Medieval and Renaissance Culture*. Ithaca, NY: Cornell University Press, 1990.

Boag, Peter. "Go West Young Man, Go East Young Woman: Searching for the *Trans* in Western Gender History." *Western Historical Quarterly* 36:4 (2005): 477–97.
Boddy, Janice. *Wombs and Alien Spirits: Women, Men, and the Zār Cult in Northern Sudan*. Madison: University of Wisconsin Press, 1989.
——. "Violence Embodied? Circumcision, Gender Politics, and Cultural Aesthetics." In *Rethinking Violence Against Women*, ed. R. Emerson Dobash and Russell P. Dobash, 77–110. Thousand Oaks, CA: Sage Publications, 1996.
Boswell, John. *Christianity, Homosexuality, and Social Tolerance: Gay People in Western Europe from the Beginning of the Christian Era to the Fourteenth Century*. Chicago: University of Chicago, 1980.
Børresen, Kari Elisabeth. *Subordination and Equivalence: The Nature and Role of Women in Augustine and Thomas Aquinas*. Trans. Charles H. Talbot. Washington, DC: University Press of America, 1981.
Bouchard, Constance Brittain. *"Every Valley Shall Be Exalted": The Discourse of Opposites in Twelfth-Century Thought*. Ithaca, NY: Cornell University Press, 2003.
Boureau, Alain. *Satan the Heretic: The Birth of Demonology in the Medieval West*. Trans. Teresa Lavender Fagan. Chicago: University of Chicago Press, 2006.
Boutell, Charles. "Symbols of the Seasons and Months Represented in Early Art." *Art Journal*, new series 3 (1877): 233–36.
Bouwsma, William. "Anxiety and the Formation of Early Modern Culture." In *After the Reformation: Essays in Honor of J. H. Hexter*, ed. Barbara C. Malament, 215–46. Philadelphia: University of Philadelphia Press, 1980.
Bowker, Geoffrey C. and Susan Leigh Star. *Sorting Things Out: Classification and Its Consequences*. Cambridge, MA: MIT Press, 1999.
Boyarin, Daniel. *Carnal Israel: Reading Sex in Talmudic Culture*. Berkeley: University of California Press, 1993.
——. "Paul and the Genealogy of Gender." *Representations* 41 (1993): 1–43.
——. "On the History of the Early Phallus." In *Gender and Difference in the Middle Ages*, ed. Sharon Farmer and Carol Braun Pasternack, 3–44. Minneapolis: University of Minnesota Press, 2003.
Brakke, David. "Ethiopian Demons: Male Sexuality, the Black-Skinned Other, and the Monastic Self." *Journal of the History of Sexuality* 10:3–4 (2001): 501–35.
Brisson, Luc. *Sexual Ambivalence: Androgyny and Hermaphroditism in Graeco-Roman Antiquity*. Trans. Janet Lloyd. Berkeley: University of California Press, 2002.
Brooten, Bernadette J. *Love Between Women: Early Christian Responses to Female Homoeroticism*. Chicago: University of Chicago Press, 1996.
Brown, Peter. *The Body and Society: Men, Women, and Sexual Renunciation in Early Christianity*. New York: Columbia University Press, 1988.
Brundage, James A. *Law, Sex, and Christian Society in Medieval Europe*. Chicago: University of Chicago Press, 1987.
——. "Impotence, Frigidity, and Marital Nullity in the Decretists and the Early Decretalists." In *Sex, Law, and Marriage in the Middle Ages*, ed. James A. Brundage, X: 407–23. London: Variorum, 1993.
Buhrer, Eliza. " 'If in Other Respects He Appears to Be Effectively Human': Defining Monstrosity in Medieval English Law." In *Monstrosity, Disability, and the Posthuman in the Medieval and Early Modern World*, ed. Richard H. Godden and Asa Simon Mittman, 63–83. New York: Palgrave, 2019.
Bullough, Vern L. "Transvestism in the Middle Ages." In *Sexual Practices and the Medieval Church*, ed. Vern L. Bullough and James A. Brundage, 43–54. Buffalo, NY: Prometheus, 1982.
Buntz, Herwig. "*Das Buch der heiligen Dreifaltigkeit*: Sein Autor und seine Überlieferung." *Zeitschrift für deutsches Altertum und deutsche Literatur* 101 (1972): 150–60.
Burchett, Bessie Rebecca. "Janus in Roman Life and Cult: A Study in Roman Religions." PhD thesis, University of Pennsylvania. Menasha, WI: George Banta Publishing Company, 1918.
Burr, David. *The Spiritual Franciscans*. University Park: Pennsylvania State University Press, 2001.

Burton-Rose, Daniel. "Gendered Androgyny: Transcendent Ideals and Profane Realities in Buddhism, Classicism, and Daoism." In *Transgender China*, ed. Howard Chiang, 67–96. Palgrave Macmillan, 2012.

Butler, Judith. "Performative Acts and Gender Constitution: An Essay in Phenomenology and Feminist Theory." *Theatre Journal* 40:4 (1988): 519–31.

———. *Gender Trouble: Feminism and the Subversion of Identity*. New York: Routledge, 1990.

———. *Bodies That Matter: On the Discursive Limits of Sex*. New York: Routledge, 1993.

Bychowski, M. W. "The Isle of Hermaphrodites: Disorienting the Place of Intersex in the Middle Ages." *postmedieval: a journal of medieval cultural studies* 9:2 (2018): 161–78.

Bychowski, M. W., Howard Chiang, et al. "Trans*historicities: A Roundtable Discussion." *TSQ: Transgender Studies Quarterly* 5:4 (2018): 658–85.

Bychowski, M. W. and Dorothy Kim, ed. "Visions of Medieval Trans Feminism." Special issue of *Medieval Feminist Forum* 55:1 (Summer 2019).

Bynum, Caroline Walker. *Jesus as Mother: Studies in the Spirituality of the High Middle Ages*. Berkeley: University of California Press, 1982.

———. *Holy Feast and Holy Fast: The Religious Significance of Food to Medieval Women*. Berkeley: University of California Press, 1988.

———. *Fragmentation and Redemption: Essays on Gender and the Human Body in Medieval Religion*. New York: Zone, 1992.

———. *The Resurrection of the Body in Western Christianity, 200–1336*. New York: Columbia University Press, 1995.

———. "Why All the Fuss about the Body? A Medievalist's Perspective." *Critical Inquiry* 22:1 (1995): 1–33.

———. "Metamorphosis, or Gerald and the Werewolf." *Speculum* 73:4 (1998): 987–1013.

———. *Metamorphosis and Identity*. New York: Zone, 2001.

———. *Christian Materiality: An Essay on Religion in Late Medieval Europe*. New York: Zone, 2011.

Caciola, Nancy M. *Discerning Spirits: Divine and Demonic Possession in the Middle Ages*. Ithaca, NY: Cornell University Press, 2003.

Cadden, Joan. "The Medieval Philosophy and Biology of Growth: Albertus Magnus, Thomas Aquinas, Albert of Saxony and Marsilius of Inghen on Book I, Chapter V of Aristotle's 'De generatione et corruptione,' with Translated Texts of Albertus Magnus and Thomas Aquinas." PhD diss., Indiana University, 1971.

———. *The Meanings of Sex Difference in the Middle Ages: Medicine, Science, and Culture*. New York: Cambridge University Press, 1993.

———. *Nothing Natural Is Shameful: Sodomy and Science in Late Medieval Europe*. Philadelphia: Pennsylvania University Press, 2013.

Calvet, Antoine. "Alchimie et joachimisme dans les alchimica pseudo-arnaldiens." In *Alchimie et philosophie à la Renaissance*, ed. Jean-Claude Margolin and Sylvain Matton, 93–107. Paris: Vrin, 1993.

———. *L'alchimie au moyen âge: XIIe-XVe siècles*. Paris: Vrin, 2018.

Camille, Michael. *Image on the Edge: The Margins of Medieval Art*. Cambridge, MA: Harvard University Press, 1992.

———. "The Image and the Self: Unwriting Late Medieval Bodies." In *Framing Medieval Bodies*, ed. Sarah Kay and Miri Rubin, 62–99. Manchester: Manchester University Press, 1994.

———. "Prophets, Canons, and Promising Monsters." *Art Bulletin* 78:2 (1996): 198–201.

Campbell, Andrew, Lorenza Gianfrancesco, and Neil Tarrant. "Alchemy and the Mendicant Orders of Late Medieval and Early Modern Europe." *Ambix* 65:3 (August 2018): 201–9.

Campbell, Mary Baine. *The Witness and the Other World: Exotic European Travel Writing, 400–1600* (Ithaca, NY: Cornell University Press, 1988.

Campanile, Domitilla, Filippo Carlà-Uhink, and Margherita Facella, ed. *TransAntiquity: Cross-Dressing and Transgender Dynamics in the Ancient World*. New York: Routledge, 2017.

Carruthers, Mary J. "Varietas: A Word of Many Colours." *Poetica* 41:1–2 (2009): 11–32.

———. *The Experience of Beauty in the Middle Ages*. Oxford: Oxford University Press, 2013.

Carson, Anne. "Putting Her in Her Place: Woman, Dirt, and Desire." In *Before Sexuality: The Construction of Erotic Experience in the Ancient Greek World*, ed. David Halperin et al., 135–69. Princeton, NJ: Princeton University Press, 1990.

Castiñeiras, Manuel Antonio. "Gennaio e Giano bifronte: dalle 'anni januae' all'interno domestico (secoli XII–XIII)." *Prospettiva* 66 (1992): 53–63.

Catlos, Brian A. *Muslims of Medieval Latin Christendom, c. 1050–1614*. Cambridge: Cambridge University Press, 2014.

Chance, Jane. *Medieval Mythography: From Roman North Africa to the School of Chartres, A.D. 433–1177*. Gainesville: University Press of Florida, 1994.

———. *The Mythographic Chaucer: The Fabulation of Sexual Politics*. Minneapolis: University of Minnesota Press, 1995.

Chase, Cheryl (now Bo Laurent). "Hermaphrodites with Attitude: Mapping the Emergence of Intersex Political Activism." *GLQ: A Journal of Lesbian and Gay Studies* 4:2 (1998): 189–211.

Chen, Mel Y. *Animacies: Biopolitics, Racial Mattering, and Queer Affect*. Durham, NC: Duke University Press, 2012.

Chilton, Bruce. "Resurrection in the Gospels." In *Judaism in Late Antiquity, Part 4: Death, Life-After-Death, Resurrection and the World-to-Come in the Judaisms of Antiquity*, ed. Jacob Neusner and Alan J. Avery-Peck, 215–42. Leiden: Brill, 2000.

Cho, Sumi, Kimberlé Williams Crenshaw, and Leslie McCall, "Toward a Field of Intersectionality Studies: Theory, Applications, and Praxis." *Signs* 38:4 (2013): 785–810.

Chu, Andrea Long and Emmett Harsin Drager. "After Trans Studies." *TSQ: Transgender Studies Quarterly* 6:1 (2019): 103–16.

Cifuentes, Lluís. "Las traducciones catalanas y castellanas de la *Chirurgia magna* de Lanfranco de Milán: Un ejemplo de intercomunicación cultural y científica a finales de la edad media." In *Essays on Medieval Translation in the Iberian Peninsula*, ed. Tomàs Martínez Romero and Roxana Recio, 95–127. Castelló: Publicacions de la Universitat Jaume I; Omaha: Creighton University, 2001.

Clark, Elizabeth A. "Adam's Only Companion: Augustine and the Early Christian Debate on Marriage." *Recherches Augustiniennes* 21 (1986): 139–62.

———. "Heresy, Asceticism, Adam and Eve: Interpretations of Genesis 1–3 in the Later Church Fathers." In *Ascetic Piety and Women's Faith: Essays on Late Ancient Christianity*, 353–86. Lewiston, NY: Edwin Mellen, 1986.

———. "Ideology, History, and the Construction of 'Woman' in Late Ancient Christianity." *Journal of Early Christian Studies* 2:2 (1994): 155–84.

Clark, Gillian. *Body and Gender, Soul and Reason in Late Antiquity*. Burlington, VT: Ashgate, 2011.

Clark, James G., Frank T. Coulson and Kathryn L. McKinley, ed. *Ovid in the Middle Ages*. Cambridge: Cambridge University Press, 2011.

Clark, Robert L. A. "Culture Loves a Void: Eunuchry in *De Vetula* and Jean le Fèvre's *La Vielle*." In *Castration and Culture in the Middle Ages*, ed. Larissa Tracy, 280–94. Cambridge: Boydell & Brewer, 2013.

Clark, Willene B. *The Medieval Book of Birds: Hugh of Fouilloy's Aviarium*. Binghamton, NY: State University of New York Press, 1992.

———. *A Medieval Book of Beasts: The Second-Family Bestiary: Commentary, Art, Text and Translation*. Woodbridge, UK: Boydell Press, 2006.

Clark, Willene B. and Meradith T. McMunn, ed. *Beasts and Birds of the Middle Ages: The Bestiary and Its Legacy*. Philadelphia: University of Pennsylvania Press, 1989.

Classen, Albrecht. "Introduction: The Self, the Other, and Everything in Between: Xenological Phenomenology of the Middle Ages." In *Meeting the Foreign in the Middle Ages*, ed. Albrecht Classen, xi–lxxiii. New York: Routledge, 2002.

Cleves, Rachel Hope. "Beyond the Binaries in Early America: Special Issue Introduction." *Early American Studies: An Interdisciplinary Journal* 12:3 (Fall 2014): 459–68.
Cohen, Adam S. and Anne Derbes, "Bernward and Eve at Hildesheim." *Gesta* 40:1 (2001): 19–38.
Cohen, Cathy. "Punks, Bulldaggers, and Welfare Queens: The Radical Potential of Queer Politics?" *GLQ: A Journal of Gay and Lesbian Studies* 3:4 (1997): 437–65.
Cohen, Esther. "Animals in Medieval Perceptions: The Image of the Ubiquitous Other." In *Animals and Human Society: Changing Perspectives*, ed. Aubrey Manning and James Serpell, 59–80. London: Routledge, 1994.
Cohen, Jeffrey Jerome. *Monster Theory: Reading Culture*. Minneapolis: University of Minnesota, 1996.
——. *Of Giants: Sex, Monsters, and the Middle Ages*. Minneapolis: University of Minnesota Press, 1999.
——. "On Saracen Enjoyment: Some Fantasies of Race in Late Medieval France and England." *Journal of Medieval and Early Modern Studies* 31:1 (2001): 113–46.
——. *Hybridity, Identity and Monstrosity in Medieval Britain: On Difficult Middles*. New York: Palgrave, 2006.
——. "Inventing with Animals in the Middle Ages." In *Engaging with Nature: Essays on the Natural World in Medieval and Early Modern Europe*, ed. Barbara A. Hanawalt and Lisa J. Kiser, 39–62. Notre Dame, IN: University of Notre Dame Press, 2008),
——. "Race." In *A Handbook of Middle English Studies*, ed. Marion Turner, 109–22. Oxford: Wiley-Blackwell, 2013.
——, ed. *The Postcolonial Middle Ages*. New York: St. Martin's, 2000.
Cohen, Jeremy. *"Be Fertile and Increase, Fill the Earth and Master It": The Ancient and Medieval Career of a Biblical Text*. Ithaca, NY: Cornell University Press, 1989.
——. "The Jews as the Killers of Christ in the Latin Tradition from Augustine to the Friars." *Traditio* 39 (1983): 1–27.
Cohen, Simona. *Transformations of Time and Temporality in Medieval and Renaissance Art*. Leiden: Brill, 2014.
Cole, Penny J. " 'O God, The Heathen Have Come Into Thy Inheritance' (Ps 78.1): The Theme of Religious Pollution in Crusade Documents, 1095–1188." In *Crusaders and Muslims in Twelfth-Century Syria*, ed. Maya Shatzmiller, 84–111. Leiden: Brill, 1993.
Colinet, Andrée. "Le livre d'Hermès intitulé 'Liber dabessi' ou 'Liber rebis,' " *Studi medievali* 36 (1995): 1011–52.
Coon, Lynda L. "Gender and the Body." In *The Cambridge History of Christianity*, vol. 3: *Early Medieval Christianities, c. 600-c. 1100*, ed. Thomas F. X. Noble and Julia M. H. Smith, 433–52. Cambridge: Cambridge University Press, 2006.
——. "Somatic Styles of the Early Middle Ages (c. 600–900)." In *Gender and Change: Agency, Chronology, and Periodisation*, ed. Alexandra Shepard and Garthine Walker, 13–42. Chichester, UK: Wiley-Blackwell, 2009.
Corbeill, Anthony. *Sexing the World: Grammatical Gender and Biological Sex in Ancient Rome*. Ithaca, NY: Cornell University Press, 2015.
Corry, Maya. "The Alluring Beauty of a Leonardesque Ideal: Masculinity and Spirituality in Renaissance Milan." In *Sex, Gender and the Sacred: Reconfiguring Religion in Gender History*, ed. Joanna de Groot and Sue Morgan, 170–94. Sussex, UK: Wiley Blackwell, 2014.
Costello, C. G. "Intersex and Trans* Communities: Commonalities and Tensions," in *Transgender and Intersex: Theoretical, Practical, and Artistic Perspectives*, ed. Stefan Horlacher, 83–108. New York: Palgrave MacMillan, 2016.
Council on Biblical Manhood and Womanhood. "Nashville Statement." Accessed December 2019. https://cbmw.org/nashville-statement/.
Cox, Laverne. "The Bullies Don't Draw a Distinction." *New York Times*, October 15, 2013. www.nytimes.com/roomfordebate/2013/10/15/are-trans-rights-and-gay-rights-still-allies/the-bullies-dont-draw-a-distinction.

Crane, Susan. *Animal Encounters: Contacts and Concepts in Medieval Britain*. Philadelphia: University of Pennsylvania Press, 2012.

———. "Expanding the Bestiary's Meaning: The Case of Bodley MS. 764." In *Book of Beasts: The Bestiary in the Medieval World*, ed. Elizabeth Morrison, 77–85. Los Angeles: J. Paul Getty Museum, 2019.

Crenshaw, Kimberlé. "Demarginalizing the Intersection of Race and Sex: A Black Feminist Critique of Antidiscrimination Doctrine, Feminist Theory and Antiracist Politics." *The University of Chicago Legal Forum* 140 (1989): 139–67.

Crisciani, Chiara. "The Conception of Alchemy as Expressed in the *Pretiosa Margarita Novella* of Petrus Bonus of Ferrara." *Ambix* 20 (1973): 165–81.

Crisciani, Chiara and Michela Pereira. *L'arte del sole e della luna: alchimia e filosofia nel medioevo*. Spoleto: Centro italiano di studi sull'alto medioevo, 1996.

Currah, Paisley and Susan Stryker, ed. "Postposttranssexual: Key Concepts for a Twenty-First-Century Transgender Studies." Special issue of *TSQ: Transgender Studies Quarterly* 1:1–2 (May 2014).

Daniel, Norman. *Islam and the West: The Making of an Image*. Edinburgh: University Press, 1960.

Daston, Lorraine and Gregg Mitman, ed.. *Thinking with Animals: New Perspectives on Anthropomorphism*. New York: Columbia University Press, 2005.

Daston, Lorraine and Katharine Park. "The Hermaphrodite and the Orders of Nature: Sexual Ambiguity in Early Modern France." *GLQ* 1 (1995): 419–38.

———. *Wonders and the Order of Nature, 1150–1750*. New York: Zone, 2001.

Davis, Georgiann. *Contesting Intersex: The Dubious Diagnosis*. New York: New York University Press, 2015.

Davis, Jenny L., Lal Zimman, and Joshua Raclaw. "Opposites Attract: Retheorizing Binaries in Language, Gender, and Sexuality." In *Queer Excursions: Retheorizing Binaries in Language, Gender, and Sexuality*, 1–12. New York: Oxford University Press, 2014.

De Asúa, Miguel J. C. "The Organization of Discourse on Animals in the Thirteenth Century: Peter of Spain, Albert the Great, and the commentaries on *De animalibus*." PhD diss., University of Notre Dame, 1991.

De Boüard, Michel. "Encyclopédies médiévales: Sur la 'connaissance de la nature et du monde' au moyen âge." *Revue des questions historiques* 112 (1930): 258–304.

De Wesselow, Thomas. "Locating the Hereford Mappa Mundi." *Imago Mundi* 65:2 (2013): 180–206.

Deckard, Sharae. *Paradise Discourse, Imperialism, and Globalization: Exploiting Eden*. New York: Routledge, 2010.

Delcourt, Marie. *Hermaphrodite: Myths and Rites of the Bisexual Figure in Classical Antiquity*, trans. Jennifer Nicholson. London: Studio, 1956.

Demaitre, Luke. "Skin and the City: Cosmetic Medicine as an Urban Concern." In *Between Text and Patient: The Medical Enterprise in Medieval and Modern Europe*, ed. Florence Eliza Glaze and Brian K. Nance, 97–120. Florence: Edizione de Galluzzo, 2011.

Demaitre, Luke and Anthony A. Travill, "Human Embryology and Development in the Works of Albertus Magnus." In *Albertus Magnus and the Sciences: Commemorative Essays, 1980*, ed. James A. Weisheipl, 405–40. Toronto: Pontifical Institute of Mediaeval Studies, 1980.

Derrida, Jacques. *The Animal that Therefore I Am*. New York: Fordham University Press, 2008.

Desmond, Marilynn R. ed. *Mediaevalia: A Journal of Medieval Studies*. Special issue, *Ovid in Medieval Culture* 13 (1987).

Desmond, Marilynn R. and Pamela Sheingorn. *Myth, Montage, and Visuality in Late Medieval Manuscript Culture: Christine de Pizan's Epistre Othea*. Ann Arbor: University of Michigan Press, 2003.

Despres, Denise L. "Adolescence and Sanctity: The Life and Passion of Saint William of Norwich." *The Journal of Religion* 90:1 (2010): 33–62.

DeVun, Leah. *Prophecy, Alchemy, and the End of Time: John of Rupescissa in the Late Middle Ages*. New York: Columbia, 2009.

DeVun, Leah and Zeb Tortorici, "Trans, Time, and History." *TSQ: Transgender Studies Quarterly* 5:4 (2018): 518–39.
———, ed. "Trans*historicities." Special issue of *TSQ: Transgender Studies Quarterly* 5:4 (2018).
Dines, Ilya. "The Earliest Use of John of Salisbury's *Policraticus*: Third Family Bestiaries." *Viator* 44:1 (2013): 107–118.
———. "The Hare and Its Alter Ego in the Middle Ages." *Reinardus* 17 (2004): 73–84.
———. "The Problem of the Transitional Family of Bestiaries." *Reinardus* 24 (2011–12): 29–52.
Dinshaw, Carolyn. *Getting Medieval: Sexualities and Communities, Pre- and Postmodern*. Durham, NC: Duke University Press, 1999.
Dinshaw, Carolyn et al. "Theorizing Queer Temporalities: A Roundtable Discussion." *GLQ: A Journal of Lesbian and Gay Studies* 13:2–3 (2007): 177–95.
Dodds, Jerrilynn D., María Rosa Menocal, and Abigail Krasner Balbale, ed. *The Arts of Intimacy: Christians, Jews and Muslims in the Making of Castilian Culture*. New Haven, CT: Yale University Press, 2008.
Douglas, Mary. "Pollution." In *Implicit Meanings: Essays in Anthropology*, ed. Mary Douglas, 106–15. London: Routledge, 1975.
———. *Purity and Danger: An Analysis of the Concepts of Pollution and Taboo*. London and New York: Routledge, 2003.
Downing, Lisa, Iain Morland, and Nikki Sullivan. *Fuckology: Critical Essays on John Money's Diagnostic Concepts*. Chicago: University of Chicago Press, 2015.
Dreger, Alice Domurat. *Hermaphrodites and the Medical Invention of Sex*. Cambridge, MA: Harvard University Press, 1998.
———. "A History of Intersex: From the Age of Gonads to the Age of Consent." In *Intersex in the Age of Ethics*, ed. Alice Domurat Dreger, 5–22. Hagerstown, MD: University Publishing Group, 1999.
———, ed. *Intersex in the Age of Ethics*. Hagerstown, MD: University Publishing Group, 1999.
Dreger, Alice D. and April M. Herndon. "Progress and Politics in the Intersex Rights Movement: Feminist Theory in Action." *GLQ: A Journal of Lesbian and Gay Studies* 15:2 (2009): 199–224.
Duby, Georges. *The Three Orders: Feudal Society Imagined*. Chicago: University of Chicago Press, 1982.
Duclow, Donald F. "The Sleep of Adam, the Making of Eve: Sin and Creation in Eriugena." In *Johannes Scottus Eriugena: Eriugena and Creation*, ed. W. Otten and M. I. Allen, 235–61. Turnhout, Belgium: Brepols, 2014.
Dunning, Benjamin H. *Specters of Paul: Sexual Difference in Early Christian Thought*. Philadelphia: University of Pennsylvania Press, 2011.
Duveen, Denis. "Le Livre de la très sainte trinité." *Ambix* 3 (1948): 26–32.
Eamon, William. *Science and the Secrets of Nature: Books of Secrets in Medieval and Early Modern Culture*. Princeton, NJ: Princeton University Press, 1994.
Economou, George D. *The Goddess Natura in Medieval Literature*. Cambridge, MA: Harvard University Press, 1972.
Edson, Evelyn. *The World Map, 1300–1492: The Persistence of Tradition and Transformation*. Baltimore, MD: Johns Hopkins University Press, 2007.
Elders, M. Joycelyn, David Satcher, and Richard Carmona. "Re-Thinking Genital Surgeries on Intersex Infants" (2017). Available at http://www.palmcenter.org/wp-content/uploads/2017/06/Re-Thinking-Genital-Surgeries-1.pdf.
Eliade, Mircea. *The Two and the One*. Trans. J. M. Cohen. Chicago: University of Chicago Press, 1979.
———. *The Forge and the Crucible*. Trans. Stephen Corrin. New York: Harper & Row, 1962.
Eliav-Feldon, Miriam, Benjamin Isaac, and Joseph Ziegler, ed. *The Origins of Racism in the West*. Cambridge: Cambridge University Press, 2008.
Elliott, Dyan. *Fallen Bodies: Pollution, Sexuality, and Demonology in the Middle Ages*. Philadelphia: University of Pennsylvania Press, 1999.

———. "Tertullian, the Angelic Life, and the Bride of Christ." In *Gender and Christianity in Medieval Europe: New Perspectives*, ed. Lisa M. Bitel and Felice Lifshitz, 16–33. Philadelphia: University of Pennsylvania Press, 2008.

———. "Rubber Soul: Theology, Hagiography, and the Spirit World of the High Middle Ages." In *From Beasts to Souls: Gender and Embodiment in Medieval Europe*, ed. E. Jane Burns and Peggy McCracken, 89–120. Notre Dame, IN: University of Notre Dame Press, 2013.

Elukin, Jonathan M. "From Jew to Christian? Conversion and Immutability in Medieval Europe." In *Varieties of Religious Conversion in the Middle Ages*, ed. James Muldoon, 171–89. Gainesville: University Press of Florida, 1997.

Enke, A. Finn, ed. *Transfeminist Perspectives in and beyond Transgender and Gender Studies*. Philadelphia: Temple University Press, 2012.

Evans, Ruth. "Gender Is not Genitals." In "Medieval Intersex: Language and Hermaphroditism." Special issue of *postmedieval: a journal of medieval cultural studies* 9:2 (2018): 120–31.

———. "The Intersex Look." *postmedieval: a journal of medieval cultural studies* 9:2 (2018): 117–19.

———, ed. *Medieval Intersex: Language and Hermaphroditism*. Special issue of *postmedieval: a journal of medieval cultural studies* 9:2 (2018).

Fatum, Lone. "Image of God and Glory of Man: Women in the Pauline Congregations." In *The Image of God and Gender Models in Judaeo-Christian Tradition*, ed. Kari Elisabeth Børresen, 56–137. Oslo: Solum Forlag, 1991.

Fausto-Sterling, Anne. "The Five Sexes: Why Male and Female Are Not Enough." *The Sciences* 33 (March/April 1993): 20–25.

———. *Sexing the Body: Gender Politics and the Construction of Sexuality*. New York: Basic, 2000.

Feder, Ellen K. "Imperatives of Normality: From 'Intersex' to 'Disorders of Sex Development.'" *GLQ: A Journal of Lesbian and Gay Studies* 15:2 (2009): 225–47.

Feinberg, Leslie. *Transgender Warriors: Making History from Joan of Arc to Dennis Rodman*. Boston: Beacon, 1996.

Ferlampin-Acher, Christine. "Le Monstre dans le romans des XIIIe et XIVe siècles." In *Ecriture et modes de pensée au Moyen Age (VIIIe-Xve siècles)*, ed. Dominique Boutet and Laurence Harf-Lancner, 69–87. Paris: Ecole Normale Supérieure, 1993.

Ferragud, Carmel. "Wounds, Amputations, and Expert Procedures in the City of Valencia in the Early Fifteenth Century." In *Wounds and Wound Repair in Medieval Culture*, ed. Larissa Tracy and Kelly DeVries, 233–251. Leiden: Brill, 2015.

Fisher, Simon D. Elin, Rasheedah Phillips, and Ido H. Katri, ed. "Trans Temporalities." Special issue, *Somatechnics* 7:1 (March 2017).

Flood, John. *Representations of Eve in Antiquity and the English Middle Ages*. New York: Routledge, 2011.

Folda, Jaroslav. *Crusader Art in the Holy Land, From the Third Crusade to the Fall of Acre, 1187–1291*. Cambridge: Cambridge University Press, 2005.

Fonrobert, Charlotte. "Regulating the Human Body: Rabbinic Legal Discourse and the Making of Jewish Gender." In *The Cambridge Companion to the Talmud and Rabbinic Literature*, ed. Charlotte Fonrobert and Martin Jaffee, 270–94. Cambridge: Cambridge University Press, 2007.

Ford, A. J. *Marvel and Artefact: the "Wonders of the East" in Its Manuscript Contexts*. Leiden: Brill, 2016.

Foucault, Michel. *The History of Sexuality*, 3 vols. New York: Pantheon, 1978–1986.

———. *Herculine Barbin: Being the Recently Discovered Memoirs of a Nineteenth-Century French Hermaphrodite*. Trans. Richard McDougall. New York: Pantheon, 1980.

Fox-Friedman, Jeanne. "Vision of the World: Romanesque Art of Northern Italy and the Hereford Mappamundi." In *The Hereford World Map: Medieval World Maps and Their Contexts*, ed. P. D. A. Harvey, 137–51. London: The British Library, 2006.

Frantzen, Allen J. *Before the Closet: Same-Sex Love from Beowulf to Angels in America*. Chicago: University of Chicago Press, 1998.

Freeburn, Ryan P. *Hugh of Amiens and the Twelfth-Century Renaissance*. Farnham, UK: Ashgate, 2011.

Freedman, Paul. "The Medieval Other: The Middle Ages as Other." In *Marvels, Monsters, and Miracles: Studies in the Medieval and Early Modern Imaginations*, ed. Timothy S. Jones and David A. Sprunger, 1–24. Kalamazoo, MI: Medieval Institute Publications, 2002.

———. "The Representation of Medieval Peasants as Bestial and as Human." In *The Animal/Human Boundary: Historical Perspectives*, ed. Angela N. H. Creager and William Chester Jordan, 29–49. Rochester, NY: University of Rochester Press, 2002.

Freeman, Elizabeth. *Time Binds: Queer Temporalities, Queer Histories.* Durham, NC: Duke University Press, 2010.

Friedman, John Block. *The Monstrous Races in Medieval Art and Thought.* Cambridge, MA: Harvard University Press, 1981.

Friedrich, Ellen Lorraine. "Insinuating Indeterminate Gender: A Castration Motif in Guillaume de Lorris's *Romans de la rose.*" In *Castration and Culture in the Middle Ages*, ed. Larissa Tracy, 255–79. Cambridge: Boydell & Brewer, 2013.

Friesen, Ilse E. *The Female Crucifix: Images of St. Wilgefortis Since the Middle Ages.* Waterloo, ON: Wilfrid Laurier University Press, 2001.

Frovmovic, Eva. "Reframing Gender in Medieval Jewish Images of Circumcision." In *Framing the Family: Representation and Narrative in the Medieval and Early Modern Period*, MRTS 280, ed. Rosalynn Voaden and Diane Wolfthal, 221–43. Tempe: Arizona Center for Medieval and Renaissance Studies, 2005.

Fuentes, Marisa J. *Dispossessed Lives: Enslaved Women, Violence, and the Archive.* Philadelphia: University of Pennsylvania Press, 2016.

Fulvi, Maria Grazia Cittadini and Vania Gasperoi Panella. *Dal mondo antico al cristianesimo sulle tracce di Giano: il simbolismo della porta e del passaggio in relazione al dio bifronte.* Perugia: Morlacchi Editore, 2008.

Fyler, John M. *Language and the Declining World in Chaucer, Dante, and Jean de Meun.* Cambridge: Cambridge University Press, 2007.

Gadelrab, Sherry Sayed. "Discourses on Sex Differences in Medieval Scholarly Islamic Thought." *Journal of the History of Medicine and Allied Sciences* 66:1 (2011): 40–81.

Ganzenmüller, W. *Die Alchemie im Mittelalter.* Paderborn: Bonifacius-Druckerei, 1938.

———. "Das *Buch der heiligen Dreifaltigkeit*: Eine deutsche Alchemie aus dem Anfang des 15. Jahrhunderts." *Archiv für Kulturgeschichte* 29 (1939): 93–146.

———. *L'Alchimie au moyen âge.* Trans. G. Petit-Dutaillis. Paris: Aubier, 1940.

García-Ballester, Luis. "Introduction: Practical Medicine from Salerno to the Black Death." In *Practical Medicine from Salerno to the Black Death*, ed. Luis García-Ballester, Roger French, Jon Arrizabalaga, and Andrew Cunningham, 1–29. Cambridge: Cambridge University Press, 1994.

Gardner, Jane F. "Sexing a Roman: Imperfect Men in Roman Law" in *When Men Were Men: Masculinity, Power, and Identity in Classical Antiquity*, ed. Lin Foxhall and John Salmon, 136–52. New York: Routledge, 1998.

Garland, Robert. *The Eye of the Beholder: Deformity and Disability in the Graeco-Roman World.* Ithaca, NY: Cornell University Press, 1995.

Gaunt, Simon. "Can the Middle Ages Be Postcolonial?" *Comparative Literature* 61:2 (Spring 2009): 160–76.

Gerevini, Stefania. "Written in Stone: Civic Memory and Monumental Writing in the Cathedral of San Lorenzo in Genoa." In *Viewing Inscriptions in the Late Antique and Medieval World*, ed. Antony Eastmond, 205–29. Cambridge: Cambridge University Press, 2015.

Gertsman, Elina. *Worlds Within: Opening the Medieval Shrine Madonna.* University Park: Pennsylvania State University Press, 2015.

Gibson, Joan. "Could Christ Have Been Born a Woman? A Medieval Debate." *Journal of Feminist Studies in Religion* 8:1 (1992): 65–82.

Gibson, Margaret T. "The Place of the *Glossa ordinaria* in Medieval Exegesis." In *Ad litteram: Authoritative Texts and their Medieval Readers*, ed. Mark D. Jordan and Kent Emery, Jr., 5–27. Notre Dame, IN: University of Notre Dame Press, 1992.

Gilbert, Ruth. *Early Modern Hermaphrodites: Sex and Other Stories*. New York: Palgrave, 2002.
Gilman, Sander L. *Making the Body Beautiful: A Cultural History of Aesthetic Surgery*. Princeton, NJ: Princeton University Press, 1999.
Glick, Leonard B. *Marked in Your Flesh: Circumcision from Ancient Judea to Modern America*. Oxford: Oxford University Press, 2005.
Godden, Richard H. and Asa S. Mittman, ed. *Monstrosity, Disability, and the Posthuman in the Medieval and Early Modern World*. Cham, Switzerland: Palgrave, 2019.
Goldberg, Jeremy. "John Skathelok's Dick: Voyeurism and 'Pornography' in Late Medieval England." In *Medieval Obscenities*, ed. Nicola McDonald, 105–23. Woodbridge, UK: York Medieval Press, 2006.
Gossett, Reina (now Tourmaline), Eric A. Stanley, and Johanna Burton, ed. *Trap Door: Trans Cultural Production and the Politics of Visibility*. Cambridge, MA: MIT Press, 2017.
Grant, Edward. *God and Reason in the Middle Ages*. Cambridge: Cambridge University Press, 2001.
Graves, Robert and Raphael Patai. *Hebrew Myths: The Book of Genesis*. New York: McGraw Hill, 1963.
Gravestock, Pamela. "Did Imaginary Animals Exist?" In *The Mark of the Beast: The Medieval Bestiary in Art, Life, and Literature*, ed. Debra Higgs Strickland, 119–40. New York: Garland, 1999.
Green, Monica H. "Bodies, Gender, Health, Disease: Recent Work on Medieval Women's Medicine." *Studies in Medieval and Renaissance History*, 3rd ser. vol. 2 (2005): 1–46.
———. *Making Women's Medicine Masculine: The Rise of Male Authority in Pre-Modern Gynaecology*. Oxford: Oxford University Press, 2008.
———. "Bodily Essences: Bodies as Categories of Difference." In *A Cultural History of the Human Body in the Medieval Age*. Vol. 2 of *A Cultural History of the Human Body*, ed. Linda Kalof and William Bynum, 149–71. Oxford: Berg Publishers, 2010.
———. "From Philology to Social History: The Circulation and Uses of Albucasis's Latin *Surgery* in the Middle Ages." *Micrologus* 39 (2011): 331–72.
———. "Caring for Gendered Bodies." In *Oxford Handbook of Medieval Women and Gender*, ed. Judith Bennett and Ruth Mazo Karras, 345–61. Oxford: Oxford University Press, 2013.
———, ed. *The Trotula: An English Translation of the Medieval Compendium of Women's Medicine*. Philadelphia: University of Pennsylvania Press, 2002.
Greenberg, Julie A. *Intersexuality and the Law: Why Sex Matters*. New York: New York University Press, 2012.
Greenblatt, Stephen. *The Rise and Fall of Adam and Eve*. New York: W.W. Norton, 2017.
Greenstein, Jack M. "The Body of Eve in Andrea Pisano's *Creation* Relief." *Art Bulletin* 90:4 (2008): 575–96.
———. *The Creation of Eve and Renaissance Naturalism: Visual Theology and Artistic Invention*. Cambridge: Cambridge University Press, 2016.
Greeves, Tom, Sue Andrew and Chris Chapman. *The Three Hares: A Curiosity Worth Regarding*. Devon: Skerryvore Productions Ltd, 2016.
Gregg, Joan. *Devils, Women, and Jews: Reflections of the Other in Medieval Sermon Stories*. Albany: State University of New York Press, 1997.
Greppin, John A. C., Emilie Savage-Smith, and John L. Gueriguian. *The Diffusion of Greco-Roman Medicine in the Middle East and the Caucasus*. Delmar, NY: Caravan, 1999.
Gruen, Lori and Kari Weil, ed. *Animal Others*. Special issue of *Hypatia* 27:3 (2012).
Gutas, Dimitri L. *Greek Thought, Arabic Culture: The Graeco-Arabic Translation Movement in Baghdad and Early 'Abbāsid Society (2nd–4th/8th–10th Centuries)*. London: Routledge, 1998.
Hahn, Thomas, ed. "Race and Ethnicity in the Middle Ages." Special issue of the *Journal of Medieval and Early Modern Studies* 31:1 (2001).
Halberstam, Jack. *Trans*: A Quick and Quirky Account of Gender Variability*. Oakland: University of California Press, 2017.
Halberstam, Jack and I. Livingston, *Posthuman Bodies*. Bloomington: Indiana University Press, 1995.

Halleux, Robert. *Les textes alchimiques, Typologie des sources du moyen âge occidental* 32 (Turnhout, Belgium: Brepols, 1979).
Hamburger, Jeffrey F. *The Visual and the Visionary: Art and Female Spirituality in Late Medieval Germany*. New York: Zone, 1998.
Hanson, Ann Ellis and Monica H. Green. "Soranus of Ephesus: Methodicorum Princeps." In *Aufstieg und Niedergang der Römischen Welt*, Teilband II, Band 37.2, ed. Wolfgang Haase and Hildegard Temporini. Berlin: Walter de Gruyter, 1994, 968–1075.
Haraway, Donna J. *The Companion Species Manifesto: Dogs, People, and Significant Otherness*. Chicago: Prickly Paradigm, 2003.
——. *When Species Meet*. Minneapolis: University of Minnesota Press, 2008.
Haritaworn, Jinthana. "Decolonizing the Non/Human." *GLQ: A Journal of Lesbian and Gay Studies* 21:2–3 (2015): 212.
Harrison, Robert Pogue. *Forests: The Shadow of Civilization*. Chicago: University of Chicago Press, 1992.
Harvey, Graham. "Animals, Animists, and Academics." *Zygon* 41:1 (2006): 9–19.
Harvey, P. D. A., ed. *Mappa Mundi: The Hereford World Map*. Toronto: University of Toronto Press, 1996.
——. *The Hereford World Map: Medieval World Maps and Their Context*. London: British Library, 2006.
——. *The Hereford World Map: Introduction*. London: The Folio Society, 2010.
Haskins, Charles Homer. *The Renaissance of the Twelfth Century*. Cambridge, MA: Harvard University Press, 1993.
Hassig, Debra (now Debra Higgs Strickland). *Medieval Bestiaries: Text, Image, Ideology*. Cambridge: Cambridge University Press, 1995.
Hausman, Bernice L. *Changing Sex: Transsexualism, Technology, and the Idea of Gender*. Chapel Hill, NC: Duke University Press, 1995.
Hayward, Eva and Jami Weinstein, ed. "Tranimalities." Special issue of *TSQ: Transgender Studies Quarterly* 2:2 (2015).
Heimmel, Jennifer. *"God Is Our Mother": Julian of Norwich and the Medieval Image of Christian Feminine Divinity*. Salzburg: Institut für Anglistik und Amerikanistik, Universität Salzburg, 1982.
Heng, Geraldine. *Empire of Magic: Medieval Romance and the Politics of Cultural Fantasy*. New York: Columbia University Press, 2003.
——. "Jews, Saracens, 'Black Men,' Tartars: England in a World of Racial Difference." In *A Companion to Medieval English Literature, c. 1350–1500*, ed. Peter Brown, 247–69. London: Blackwell Publishing, 2007.
——. "The Invention of Race in the European Middle Ages I: Race Studies, Modernity, and the Middle Ages." *Literature Compass* 8:5 (2011): 315–31.
——. *The Invention of Race in the European Middle Ages*. Cambridge: Cambridge University Press, 2018.
——. *England and the Jews: How Religion and Violence Created the First Racial State in the West*. Cambridge: Cambridge University Press, 2019.
Henningsen, Kadin. " 'Calling [herself] Eleanor': Gender Labor and Becoming a Woman in the Rykener Case." *Medieval Feminist Forum* 55:1 (Summer 2019): 249–66.
Herndon, April. "Getting Rid of 'Hermaphroditism' Once and For All." http://www.isna.org/node/979 (2005).
Hernando i Delgado, Josep. "El procès contra el convers Nicolau Sanxo, ciutadà de Barcelona, acusat d'haver circumcidat el seu fill (1437–1438)." *Acta Historica et Archaeologica Mediaevalia* 13 (1992): 75–100.
Hilka, Alfons, ed. "Eine alt-französische moralisierende Bearbeitung des *Liber de Monstruosis Hominibus Orientis* aus Thomas von Cantimpré. *De Naturis Rerum*." In *Abhandlungen der Gesellschaft der Wissenschaften zu Gottingen: Philologisch-Historische Klasse* 7 1–73. Berlin: Weidmannsche Buchhandlung, 1933.
Hindman, Sandra L. *Christine de Pizan's "Epistre Othéa": Painting and Politics at the Court of Charles VI*. Toronto: Pontifical Institute of Mediaeval Studies, 1986.

Hird, Myra J. "Animal Trans." In *Queering the Non/Human*, ed. Noreen Giffney and Myra J. Hird, 227–47. Aldershot, UK: Ashgate, 2008.

Hoad, Neville. "'Run, Caster Semenya, Run!' Nativism and the Translation of Gender Variance." *Safundi: The Journal of South African and American Studies* 11:4 (2010): 397–405.

Holland, Louise Adams. *Janus and the Bridge*. Rome: Publications of the American Academy in Rome, 1961.

Holmes, Brooke. *Gender: Antiquity and Its Legacy* London: I. B. Tauris, 2012.

Holmes, Morgan, ed. *Critical Intersex*. Aldershot, UK: Ashgate, 2009.

Holsinger, Bruce. "Of Pigs and Parchment: Medieval Studies and the Coming of the Animal." *PMLA* 124:2 (2009): 616–23.

Holt, Andrew. "Crusading Against the Barbarians: Muslims as Barbarians in Crusades Era Sources." In *East Meets West in the Middle Ages and Modern Times: Transcultural Experiences in the Premodern World*, ed. Albrecht Classen, 443–56. Berlin: De Gruyter, 2013.

Hopkins, Keith. "Eunuchs in Politics in the Later Roman Empire." *The Cambridge Classical Journal* 9 (1963): 62–80.

Horlacher, Stefan, ed. *Transgender and Intersex: Theoretical, Practical, and Artistic Perspectives*. New York: Palgrave MacMillan, 2016.

Horowitz, Maryanne Cline. "The Image of God in Man—Is Woman Included?" *Harvard Theological Review* 72:3–4 (1979): 175–205.

Hotchkiss, Valerie R. *Clothes Make the Man: Female Cross Dressing in Medieval Europe*. New York: Garland, 1996.

Hourihane, Colum, ed. *Time in the Medieval World: Occupations of the Months and Signs of the Zodiac in the Index of Christian Art*. Princeton, NJ: Princeton University and Penn State University Press, 2007.

Hughes, Robert. *Heaven and Hell in Western Art*. New York: Stein and Day, 1968.

Hulme, Peter. "Introduction: The Cannibal Scene." In *Cannibalism and the Colonial World*, ed. Francis Barker, Peter Hulme, and Margaret Iversen, 1–38. Cambridge: Cambridge University Press, 1998.

Human Rights Watch/interACT. "'I Want to Be Like Nature Made Me': Medically Unnecessary Surgeries on Intersex Children in the US." July 2017. https://www.hrw.org/report/2017/07/25/i-want-be-nature-made-me/medically-unnecessary-surgeries-intersex-children-us#.

Intersex Society of North America. "What's the History Behind the Intersex Rights Movement?" http://www.isna.org/faq/history. 2008.

Jacquart, Danielle. "Medical Practice in Paris in the First Half of the Fourteenth Century." In *Practical Medicine from Salerno to the Black Death*, ed. Luis García-Ballester et al., 186–210. Cambridge: Cambridge University Press, 1994.

——. "Anatomy, Physiology, and Medical Theory." In *The Cambridge History of Science*, ed. David Lindberg and M. Shank, 590–610. Cambridge: Cambridge University Press, 2013.

Jacquart, Danielle and Claude Thomasset, *Sexuality and Medicine in the Middle Ages*. Trans. Matthew Adamsom. Oxford: Polity Press, 1988.

James, M. R. "The Bestiary in the University Library." *Aberdeen University Library Bulletin* 36:6 (1928): 529–31.

——. *The Bestiary: Being a Reproduction in Full of the Manuscript Ii. 4. 26 in the University Library, Cambridge, with Supplementary Plates from other Manuscripts of English Origin, and a Preliminary Study of the Latin* Bestiary *as Current in England*. Oxford: Oxford University Press, 1928.

Jones, Peter Murray. "The Medieval Encyclopedia: Science and Practice." In *The Cambridge Illuminations: Ten Centuries of Book Production in the Medieval West*, ed. Paul Binski and Stella Panayotova, 297–303. London: Harvey Miller, 2005.

Jordan, Mark D. *The Invention of Sodomy in Christian Theology*. Chicago: University of Chicago Press, 1997.

Jordan, William Chester. "Why 'Race'?" *Journal of Medieval and Early Modern Studies* 31:1 (Winter 2001): 165–73.

Jordan-Young, Rebecca M. and Katrina Karkazis. *Testosterone: An Unauthorized Biography*. Cambridge, MA: Harvard University Press, 2019.

Jung, C. G. *Jung on Alchemy*. Ed. Nathan Schwartz-Salant. Princeton, NJ: Princeton University Press, 1995.

Kane, Bronach. *Impotence and Virginity in the Late Medieval Ecclesiastical Court of York*. York: Borthwick Institute, University of York, 2008.

Kantorowicz, Ernst H. *The King's Two Bodies: A Study in Medieval Political Philosophy*. Princeton, NJ: Princeton University Press, 1997.

Karentzky, Patricia Eichenbaum. *The Life of the Buddha: Ancient Scriptural and Pictorial Traditions*. Lanham, MD: University Press of America, 1992.

Karkazis, Katrina. *Fixing Sex: Intersex, Medical Authority, and Lived Experience*. Durham, NC: Duke University Press, 2008.

Karkazis, Katrina and Rebecca M. Jordan-Young. "The Powers of Testosterone: Obscuring Race and Regional Bias in the Regulation of Women Athletes." *Feminist Formations* 30:2 (2018): 1–39.

Karras, Ruth Mazo. *From Boys to Men: Formations of Masculinity in Late Medieval Europe*. Philadelphia: University of Pennsylvania Press, 2003.

——. *Sexuality in Medieval Europe: Doing unto Others*. New York: Routledge, 2005.

Karras, Ruth Mazo and Thomas Linkinen. "John/Eleanor Rykener Revisited." In *Founding Feminisms in Medieval Studies: Essays in Honor of E. Jane Burns*, ed. Laine E. Doggett and Daniel E. O'Sullivan, 111–22. Woodbridge, UK: Boydell & Brewer, 2016.

Kay, Sarah. *Animal Skins and the Reading Self in Medieval Latin and French Bestiaries*. Chicago: University of Chicago Press, 2017.

Kaye, Joel. *A History of Balance, 1250–1375: The Emergence of a New Model of Equilibrium and Its Impact on Thought*. Cambridge: Cambridge University Press, 2014.

Keck, David. *Angels and Angelology in the Middle Ages*. New York: Oxford University Press, 1998.

Kelleher, Marie A. "The Fragility of the Female Sex: Women and the Law in the Fourteenth-Century Crown of Aragon." PhD diss., University of Kansas, 2003.

Kessler, Suzanne. *Lessons from the Intersexed*. New Brunswick, NJ: Rutgers University Press, 1998.

Kessler, Suzanne and Wendy McKenna. *Gender: An Ethnomethodological Approach*. New York: John Wiley, 1978.

Khanmohamadi, Shirin A. *In Light of Another's Word: European Ethnography in the Middle Ages*. Philadelphia: University of Pennsylvania Press, 2014.

Kilgour, Maggie. *From Communion to Cannibalism: An Anatomy of Metaphors of Incorporation*. Princeton, NJ: Princeton University Press, 1990.

Kim, Dorothy. "Introduction to *Literature Compass* Special Cluster: Critical Race and the Middle Ages." *Literature Compass* 16:9–10 (2019).

Kim, Susan. "Man-Eating Monsters and Ants as Big as Dogs: The Alienated Language of the Cotton Vitellius A. XV 'Wonders of the East.'" In *Animals and the Symbolic in Mediaeval Art and Literature*, ed. L. A. J. R. Houwen, 39–52. Groningen, The Netherlands: Egbert Forsten, 1997.

King, Helen. *The One-Sex Body on Trial: The Classical and Early Modern Evidence*. Farnham, UK: Ashgate, 2013.

King, Karen L. "Sophia and Christ in the *Apocryphon of John*." In *Images of the Feminine in Gnosticism*, ed. Karen L. King, 158–76. Philadelphia: Fortress Press, 1988.

Kinoshita, Sharon. *Medieval Boundaries: Rethinking Difference in Old French Literature*. Philadelphia: University of Pennsylvania Press, 2006.

Kirshner, Julius and Osvaldo Cavallar. "Da pudenda a prudentia: il consilium di Baldo degli Ubaldi sul caso di Giovanni Malaspina." *Diritto e processo* 6 (2010): 97–112.

Kitchell Jr., Kenneth F. and Irven Michael Resnick. "Introduction: The Life and Works of Albert the Great." In Albertus Magnus, *De animalibus*, translated as *On Animals: A Medieval Summa Zoologica*, trans. and ann. Kenneth F. Kitchell Jr. and Irven Michael Resnick, 2 vols., I: 1–42. Baltimore, MD: Johns Hopkins University Press, 1999.

Kline, Naomi Reed. *Maps of Medieval Thought: The Hereford Paradigm.* Woodbridge, UK: Boydell & Brewer, 2001.

Kłosowska, Anna. "Premodern Trans and Queer in French Manuscripts and Early Printed Texts." *postmedieval: a journal of medieval cultural studies* 9:3 (2018): 349–66.

Knight, Mary. "Curing Cut or Ritual Mutilation? Some Remarks on the Practice of Female and Male Circumcision in Graeco-Roman Egypt." *Isis* 92:2 (2001): 317–38.

Koch-Rein, Anson. "Monster." In *TSQ: Transgender Studies Quarterly* 1–2 (2014): 134–35.

Kodera, Sergius. *Disreputable Bodies: Magic, Medicine, and Gender in Renaissance Natural Philosophy.* Toronto: Centre for Renaissance and Reformation Studies, 2010.

Kolve, V. A. *Telling Images: Chaucer and the Imagery of Narrative II.* Stanford, CA: Stanford University Press, 2009.

Koyama, Emi. "Being Accountable to the Invisible Community" http://www.intersexinitiative.org/articles/invisible-community.html.

Kruger, Steven F. "Conversion and Medieval Sexual, Religious, and Racial Categories." In *Constructing Medieval Sexuality*, ed. Karma Lochrie, Peggy McCracken, and James A. Schultz, 158–79. Minneapolis: University of Minnesota Press, 1997.

——. *The Spectral Jew: Conversion and Embodiment in Medieval Europe.* Minneapolis: University of Minnesota Press, 2006.

Kudlien, Fridolf. "The Seven Cells of the Uterus: The Doctrine and Its Roots." *Bulletin of the History of Medicine* 39 (1965): 415–23.

Kuefler, Mathew. "Castration and Eunuchism in the Middle Ages." In *Handbook of Medieval Sexuality*, ed. Vern L. Bullough and James A. Brundage, 279–306. New York: Garland, 1996.

——. *The Manly Eunuch: Masculinity, Gender Ambiguity, and Christian Ideology in Late Antiquity.* Chicago: University of Chicago Press, 2001.

Kupfer, Marcia. *Art and Optics in the Hereford Map: An English Mappa Mundi c. 1300.* New Haven, CT: Yale University Press, 2016.

Kuzdale, Ann. "The Reception of Gregory in the Renaissance and Reformation." In *A Companion to Gregory the Great*, ed. Bronwen Neil and Matthew Dal Santo, 359–86. Leiden: Brill, 2013.

Ladin, Joy. "In the Image of God, God Created Them: Toward Trans Theology." *Journal of Feminist Studies in Religion* 34:1 (2018): 53–58.

Lampert-Weissig, Lisa. *Medieval Literature and Postcolonial Studies.* Edinburgh: Edinburgh University Press, 2000.

Langmuir, Gavin I. "The Knight's Tale of Young Hugh of Lincoln." *Speculum* 47:3 (1972): 459–82.

——. "Thomas of Monmouth: Detector of Ritual Murder." *Speculum* 59:4 (1984): 820–46.

Lapina, Elizabeth. "Anti-Jewish Rhetoric in Guibert of Nogent's *Dei gesta per Francos*." *Journal of Medieval History* 35 (2009): 239–53.

Laqueur, Thomas. *Making Sex: Body and Gender from the Greeks to Freud.* Cambridge, MA: Harvard University Press, 1990.

Lau, Jacob. "Between the Times: Trans-Temporality, and Historical Representation." PhD diss., University of California, 2016.

Laursen, John Christian and Cary J. Nederman, ed. *Beyond the Persecuting Society: Religious Toleration Before the Enlightenment.* Philadelphia: University of Pennsylvania Press, 1997.

Lavezzo, Kathy. *Angels on the Edge of the World: Geography, Literature, and English Community, 1000–1534.* Ithaca, NY: Cornell University Press, 2006.

——. *The Accommodated Jew: English Antisemitism from Bede to Milton.* Ithaca, NY: Cornell University Press, 2016.

Lawn, Brian. *The Salernitan Questions: An Introduction to the History of Medieval and Renaissance Problem Literature*. Oxford: Clarendon, 1963.

Le Goff, Jacques. "Head or Heart? The Political Use of Body Metaphors in the Middle Ages." In *Fragments for a History of the Human Body*, ed. Michel Feher, with Ramona Naddaff and Nadia Tazi, 3 vols., 3: 13–27. New York: Zone, 1989.

Lehr, Amanda. "Sexing the Cannibal in the *Wonders of the East* and Beowulf." *postmedieval: a journal of medieval cultural studies* 9:2 (Summer 2018): 179–95.

Lemay, Helen Rodnite. "Human Sexuality in Twelfth- through Fifteenth-Century Scientific Writings." In *Sexual Practices and the Medieval Church*, ed. Vern L. Bullough and James A. Brundage, 187–205. New York: Prometheus, 1982.

———. "The Stars and Human Sexuality: Some Medieval Scientific Views." *Isis* 71:1 (1980): 127–37.

———. "William of Saliceto on Human Sexuality." *Viator* 12 (1981): 165–81.

Lemos, T. M. "The Universal and the Particular: Mary Douglas and the Politics of Impurity." *The Journal of Religion* 89:2 (2009): 236–51.

Leupin, Alexandre. *Barbarolexis: Medieval Writing and Sexuality*. Trans. Kate M. Cooper. Cambridge, MA: Harvard University Press, 1989.

Lévi-Strauss, Claude. *The Raw and the Cooked*. Trans. John and Doreen Weightman. New York: Harper and Row, 1964.

Levin, Dan. "A Clash Across America Over Transgender Rights," *The New York Times*, March 12, 2020.

Lewis, Suzanne. "*Tractatus adversus Judaeos* in the Gulbenkian Apocalypse." *Art Bulletin* 68 (1986): 543–66.

Lifshitz, Felice. "The Persistence of Late Antiquity: Christ as Man and Woman in an Eighth-Century Miniature." *Medieval Feminist Forum* 38:1 (2004): 18–27.

———. *Religious Women in Early Carolingian Francia: A Study of Manuscript Transmission and Monastic Culture*. New York: Fordham University Press, 2014.

Lipton, Sara. *Images of Intolerance: The Representation of Jews and Judaism in the Bible moralisée*. Berkeley: University of California Press, 1999.

———. *Dark Mirror: The Medieval Origins of Anti-Jewish Iconography*. New York: Metropolitan, 2014.

Little, Lester K. *Religious Poverty and the Profit Economy in Medieval Europe*. Ithaca, NY: Cornell University Press, 1978.

Livingston, Julie and Jasbir Puar, ed. *Interspecies*. Special issue of *Social Text* 29:1 (2011).

Lloyd, G. E. R. "The Development of Aristotle's Theory of the Classification of Animals." *Phronesis* 6:1 (1961), 59–81.

———. *Polarity and Analogy: Two Types of Argumentation in Early Greek Thought*. Cambridge: Cambridge University Press, 1966.

Lochrie, Karma. *Covert Operations: The Medieval Uses of Secrecy*. Philadelphia: University of Pennsylvania Press, 1999.

———. "Presumptive Sodomy and Its Exclusions." *Textual Practice* 13:2 (1999): 295–310.

———. *Heterosyncrasies: Female Sexuality When Normal Wasn't*. Minneapolis: University of Minnesota Press, 2005.

Lomuto, Sierra. "The Mongol Princess of Tars: Global Relations and Racial Formation in *The King of Tars* (c. 1330)." *Exemplaria* 31:3 (2019): 171–92.

Long, Kathleen P. *Hermaphrodites in Renaissance Europe*. Aldershot, UK: Ashgate, 2006.

———, ed. *Gender and Scientific Discourse in Early Modern Culture*. Aldershot, UK: Ashgate, 2010.

———. "Illegible Bodies: Reading Intersex and Transgender in Early Modern France (The Case of Isaac de Benserade's *Iphis et Iante*)." In *Ovidian Transversions: 'Iphis and Ianthe,' 1300–1650*, ed. Patricia Badir, Peggy McCracken, and Valerie Traub, 213–40. Edinburgh: Edinburgh University Press, 2019.

———. "Intersex/ Transgender." In *The Bloomsbury Handbook of 21st-Century Feminist Theory*, ed. Robin Truth Goodman, 121–41. London: Bloomsbury, 2019.

Love, Heather. *Feeling Backward: Loss and the Politics of Queer History.* Cambridge, MA: Harvard University Press, 2007.
Luciano, Dana and Mel Y. Chen, ed. *Queer Inhumanisms.* Special issue of *GLQ* 21:2–3 (2015).
Lugones, María. "Heterosexualism and the Colonial/Modern Gender System." *Hypatia* 22:1 (Winter 2007): 186–209.
Luscombe, David. "Peter Comestor." In *The Bible in the Medieval World: Essays in Memory of Beryl Smalley*, ed. Katherine Walsh and Diana Wood, 109–29. Oxford: Blackwell, 1985.
MacDonald, Dennis Ronald. "Corinthian Veils and Gnostic Androgynes." In *Images of the Feminine in Gnosticism*, ed. Karen L. King, 276–92. Philadelphia: Fortress Press, 1988.
Malatino, Hilary. "Gone, Missing: Queering and Racializing Absence in Trans and Intersex Archives." In *Queer Feminist Science Studies Reader*, ed. Cyd Cipolla, Kristina Gupta, David A. Rubin, and Angela Willey, 157–71. Seattle: University of Washington Press, 2017.
Manion, Jen. *Female Husbands.* Cambridge: Cambridge University Press, 2020.
Markow, Deborah. "The Iconography of the Soul in Medieval Art." PhD diss., New York University, 1983.
Martin, Dale B. *Sex and the Single Savior: Gender and Sexuality in Biblical Interpretation.* Louisville, KY: Westminster John Knox Press, 2006.
Martin, Nell Gifford. "Reading the Huntingfield Psalter (Pierpont Morgan Library Manuscript M.43): Devotional Literacy and an English Psalter Preface." PhD diss., University of North Carolina, Chapel Hill, 1995.
Mathews, Thomas F. *The Clash of Gods: A Reinterpretation of Early Christian Art.* Princeton, NJ: Princeton University Press, 1999.
Matus, Zachary A. "Roger Bacon's Apocalypticism in Light of His Alchemical and Scientific Thought." *Harvard Theological Review* 105:2 (2012): 189–222.
———. "Alchemy and Christianity in the Middle Ages." *History Compass* 10:12 (2012): 934–45.
Mayr-Harting, Henry. *Perceptions of Angels in History: An Inaugural Lecture Delivered in the University of Oxford on 14 November 1997.* Oxford: Clarendon, 1998.
McAvoy, Liz Herbert and Teresa Walters, ed. *Consuming Narratives: Gender and Monstrous Appetite in the Middle Ages and the Renaissance.* Cardiff: University of Wales Press, 2002.
McCulloch, Florence. *Mediaeval Latin and French Bestiaries.* Chapel Hill: University of North Carolina Press, 1962.
McNamara, Jo Ann. "Canossa and the Ungendering of the Public Man." In *Render Unto Caesar: The Religious Sphere in World Politics*, ed. Sabrina Petra Ramet and Donald W. Treadgold, 131–49. Washington, DC: American University Press, 1995.
———. "An Unresolved Syllogism." In *Conflicted Identities and Multiple Masculinities: Men in the Medieval West*, ed. Jacqueline Murray, 1–24. New York: Garland, 1999.
———. "Chastity as a Third Gender in the History and Hagiography of Gregory of Tours." In *The World of Gregory of Tours*, ed. Kathleen Mitchell and Ian Wood, 199–209. Leiden: Brill, 2002.
McKinley, Kathryn L. *Reading the Ovidian Heroine: "Metamorphoses" Commentaries 1100–1618.* Leiden: Brill, 2001.
McVaugh, Michael R. *Medicine Before the Plague: Practitioners and the Patients in the Crown of Aragon, 1285–1345.* Cambridge: Cambridge University Press, 1993.
———. *The Rational Surgery of the Middle Ages.* Florence: SISMEL, 2006.
———. "The Writing of the *Speculum Medicine* and Its Place in Arnau de Vilanova's Last Years." *Arxiu de textos catalans antics* 30 (2011): 293–304.
———. "Surgical Education in the Middle Ages." *Dynamis* 20 (2000): 283–304.
Meeks, Wayne A. "The Image of the Androgyne: Some Uses of a Symbol in Earliest Christianity." *History of Religions* 13:3 (1974): 165–208.
Meinardus, Otto. "Mythological, Historical and Sociological Aspects of the Practice of Female Circumcision Among the Egyptians." *Acta Ethnographica Academiae Scientiarum Hungaricae* 16 (1967): 387–97.

Mellinkoff, Ruth. *Outcasts: Signs of Otherness in Northern European Art of the Late Middle Ages*, 2 vols. Berkeley: University of California Press, 1993.

Menache, Sophia. "Tartars, Jews, Saracens, and the Jewish-Mongol 'Plot' of 1241." *History* 81:263 (1996): 319–42.

Meredith, Jill. "The *Bifrons* Relief of Janus: The Implications of the Antique in the Court Art of Emperor Frederick II." In *The Brummer Collection of Medieval Art*, ed. Carol Bruzelius with Jill Meredith, 96–123. Durham, NC: Duke University Press, 1991.

Merisalo, Outi. "The Early Tradition of the Pseudo-Galenic *De spermate* (Twelfth-Thirteenth Centuries)." *SCRIPTA: An International Journal of Codicology and Paleography* 5 (2012): 99–109.

Metzler, Irina. *Disability in Medieval Europe: Thinking about Impairment During the High Middle Ages, c. 1100–1400*. London: Routledge, 2006.

——. "Hermaphroditism in the Western Middle Ages: Physicians, Lawyers and the Intersexed Person." In *Studies in Early Medicine I—Bodies of Knowledge: Cultural Interpretations of Illness and Medicine in Medieval Europe*, BAR International Series 2170, ed. Sally Crawford and Christina Lee, December 2010, 27–37.

Mews, Constant J. "The World as Text: The Bible and the Book of Nature in Twelfth-Century Theology." In *Scripture and Pluralism: Reading the Bible in the Religiously Plural Worlds of the Middle Ages and Renaissance*, ed. Thomas J. Heffernan and Thomas E. Burman, 95–122. Leiden: Brill, 2005.

Meyerowitz, Joanne. *How Sex Changed: A History of Transsexuality in the United States*. Cambridge, MA: Harvard University Press, 2002.

Milam, Erika Lorraine and Robert A. Nye. "An Introduction to Scientific Masculinities." In "Scientific Masculinities." Special issue of *Osiris* 30:1 (2015): 1–14.

Miller, Sarah Alison. *Medieval Monstrosity and the Female Body*. New York: Routledge, 2010.

——. "Monstrous Sexuality: Variations on the Vagina Dentata." In *The Ashgate Research Companion to Monsters and the Monstrous*, ed. Asa S. Mittman and Peter Dendle, 311–28. Aldershot, UK: Ashgate, 2013.

Miller, Timothy S. and John W. Nesbitt, ed. *Walking Corpses: Leprosy in Byzantium and the Medieval West*. Ithaca, NY: Cornell University Press, 2014.

Mills, Robert. "Seeing Sodomy in the *Bibles moralisées*." *Speculum* 87:2 (2012): 413–68.

——. *Seeing Sodomy in the Middle Ages*. Chicago: University of Chicago Press, 2015.

—— Mills, Robert. "The Birds and the Bees: Sexual Diversity and Animality in Medieval Art." Unpublished lecture, Rutgers University, April 2016.

——. "Visibly Trans? Picturing Saint Eugenia in Medieval Art." *TSQ: Transgender Studies Quarterly* 5:4 (2018): 540–64.

Minnis, A. J. "*De impedimento sexus*: Women's Bodies and Medieval Impediments to Female Ordination." In *Medieval Theology and the Natural Body*, ed. Peter Biller and A. J. Minnis, 109–39. York: University of York, York Medieval Press, 1997.

Mittman, Asa S. *Maps and Monsters in Medieval England*. New York: Routledge, 2006.

——. "Introduction: The Impact of Monsters and Monster Studies." In *The Ashgate Research Companion to Monsters and the Monstrous*, ed. Asa S. Mittman and Peter Dendle, 1–14. Aldershot, UK: Ashgate, 2013.

——. "Are the 'Monstrous Races' Races?" *postmedieval: a journal of medieval cultural studies* 6:1 (2015): 36–51.

Mittman, Asa S. and Peter Dendle, ed. *The Ashgate Research Companion to Monsters and the Monstrous*. Aldershot, UK: Ashgate, 2013.

Mittman, Asa S. and Susan M. Kim. "The Exposed Body and the Gendered *Blemmye*: Reading the *Wonders of the East*." In *Sexuality in the Middle Ages and Early Modern Times: New Approaches to a Fundamental Cultural-Historical and Literary-Anthropological Theme*, ed. Albrecht Classen, 171–215. Berlin: Walter de Gruyter, 2008.

——. "Monsters and the Exotic in Early Medieval England." *Literature Compass* 6:2 (March 2009): 332–48.

——. ed. *Inconceivable Beasts: The Wonders of the East in the Beowulf Manuscript*. Tempe, AZ: ACMRS, 2013.

Mittman, Asa S. and Sherry C. M. Lindquist. *Medieval Monsters: Terrors, Aliens, Wonders.* New York: Morgan Library and Museum, 2018.
Modersohn, Mechtild. *Natura als Göttin im Mittelalter: Ikonographische Studien zu Darstellungen der personifizierten Natur.* Berlin: Akademie Verlag, 1997.
Mogul, Joey L., Andrea J. Ritchie, and Kay Whitlock. *Queer (In)Justice: The Criminalization of LGBT People in the United States.* Boston: Beacon, 2011.
Morland, Iain. "Afterword: Genitals Are History." *postmedieval: a journal of medieval cultural studies* 9:2 (Summer 2018): 209–15.
———. "Intersex." *TSQ: Transgender Studies Quarterly* 1–2 (2014): 111–15.
———, ed. *Intersex and After.* Special issue, *GLQ: A Journal of Lesbian and Gay Studies* 15:2 (2009).
Moore, R. I. *The Formation of a Persecuting Society: Power and Deviance in Western Europe, 950–1250.* Oxford: Basil Blackwell, 1987.
———. *The War on Heresy.* Cambridge, MA: Belknap, 2012.
Morris, Sherri G. "Twisted Lies: My Journey in an Imperfect Body." In *Surgically Shaping Children: Technology, Ethics, and the Pursuit of Normality,* ed. Erik Parens, 3–12. Baltimore, MD: Johns Hopkins University Press, 2006.
Morrison, Elizabeth, ed. *Book of Beasts: The Bestiary in the Medieval World.* Los Angeles: J. Paul Getty Museum, 2019.
Morrison, Susan Signe. *Excrement in the Late Middle Ages: Sacred Filth and Chaucer's Fecopoetics.* New York: Palgrave Macmillan, 2008.
Muir, Carolyn Diskant. "Bride or Bridegroom? Masculine Identity in Mystic Marriages." In *Holiness and Masculinity in the Middle Ages,* ed. P. H. Cullum and Katherine J. Lewis, 58–78. Cardiff: University of Wales, 2005.
Muratova, Xenia. "The Bestiaries, an Aspect of Medieval Patronage." In *Art and Patronage in the English Romanesque,* ed. S. Macready and F. H. Thompson, 118–44. London: Society of Antiquaries of London, 1986.
———. "Workshop Methods in English Late Twelfth-Century Illumination and the Production of Luxury Bestiaries." In Willene B. Clark and Meradith T. McMunn, ed. *Beasts and Birds of the Middle Ages: The Bestiary and Its Legacy,* 53–63. Philadelphia: University of Pennsylvania Press, 1989.
Murray, Jacqueline. "Hiding Behind the Universal Man: Male Sexuality in the Middle Ages." In *Handbook of Medieval Sexuality,* ed. Vern L. Bullough and James A. Brundage, 123–52. New York: Garland, 1996.
———. "One Flesh, Two Sexes, Three Genders?" In *Gender and Christianity in Medieval Europe: New Perspectives,* ed. Lisa M. Bitel and Felice Lifshitz, 34–51. Philadelphia: University of Pennsylvania Press, 2008.
———. "Sexual Mutilation and Castration Anxiety: A Medieval Perspective." In *The Boswell Thesis: Essays on Christianity, Social Tolerance, and Homosexuality,* ed. Mathew Kuefler, 254–72. Chicago: University of Chicago Press, 2006.
Nagel, Alexander. "The Tenses of Drawing." Lecture presented at the Morgan Library and Museum, New York, May 9, 2017.
Namaste, Vivianne. *Invisible Lives: The Erasure of Transsexual and Transgendered People.* Chicago: University of Chicago Press, 2000.
Nash, Jennifer C. *Black Feminism Reimagined: After Intersectionality.* Durham, NC: Duke University Press, 2019.
Nay, Yv E. "The Atmosphere of Trans* Politics in the Global North and West." *TSQ: Transgender Studies Quarterly* 6:1 (February 2019): 64–79.
Neal, Derek G. *The Masculine Self in Late Medieval England.* Chicago: University of Chicago Press, 2008.
Nederman, Cary J. *Worlds of Difference: European Discourses of Toleration, c. 1100-c. 1550.* University Park: The Pennsylvania State University Press, 2000.
Nederman, Cary J. and Jacqui True. "The Third Sex: The Idea of the Hermaphrodite in Twelfth-Century Europe." *Journal of the History of Sexuality* 6 (1996): 497–517.

Needham, Rodney, ed. *Right and Left: Essays on Dual Symbolic Classification.* Chicago: University of Chicago Press, 1973.
Newman, Barbara. *Sister of Wisdom: St. Hildegard's Theology of the Feminine.* Berkeley: University of California Press, 1987.
———. *From Virile Woman to WomanChrist.* Philadelphia: University of Pennsylvania Press, 1995.
———. *God and the Goddesses: Vision, Poetry, and Belief in the Middle Ages.* Philadelphia: University of Pennsylvania Press, 2005.
Newman, William R. *Promethean Ambitions: Alchemy and the Quest to Perfect Nature.* Chicago: University of Chicago Press, 2004.
Nielson, Karen M. "The Private Parts of Animals: Aristotle on the Teleology of Sexual Difference." *Phronesis* 53:4/5 (2008): 373–405.
Nirenberg, David. *Communities of Violence: Persecution of Minorities in the Middle Ages.* Princeton, NJ: Princeton University Press, 1996.
———. "Love Between Muslim and Jew in Medieval Spain: A Triangular Affair." In *Jews, Muslims and Christians in and Around the Crown of Aragon: Essays in Honour of Professor Elena Lourie,* ed. Elena Laurie and Harvey J. Hames, 137–65. Leiden: Brill, 2004.
———. *Anti-Judaism: The Western Tradition.* New York: W.W. Norton, 2013.
———. *Neighboring Faiths: Christianity, Islam, and Judaism in the Middle Ages and Today.* Chicago: University of Chicago Press, 2014.
Noort, Edward. "The Creation of Man and Woman in Biblical and Ancient Near Eastern Traditions." In *The Creation of Man and Woman: Interpretations of the Biblical Narratives in Jewish and Christian Traditions,* ed. Gerard P. Luttikhuizen, 1–18. Leiden: Brill, 2000.
Nugent, Georgia. "This Sex Which Is Not One: De-constructing Ovid's Hermaphrodite." *differences* 2:1 (Spring 1990): 160–85.
Nummedal, Tara. "Alchemy and Religion in Christian Europe." *Ambix* 60:4 (November 2013): 311–22.
Obrist, Barbara. "Les deux visages du diable." In *Diables et diableries: La représentation du diable dans la gravure des XVe et XVIe siècles,* ed. Jean Wirth, 19–30. Geneva: Cabinet des Estampes, 1976.
———. *Les débuts de l'imagerie alchimique XIVe–XVe siècles.* Paris: Sycomore, 1982.
———. "Les rapports d'analogie entre philosophie et alchimie médiévales." In *Alchimie et philosophie à la renaissance,* ed. Jean-Claude Margolin and Sylvain Matton, 43–64. Paris: Vrin, 1993.
———. "Art et nature dans l'alchimie médiévale." *Revue d'histoire des sciences* 49:2–3 (1996): 215–86.
———. "Visualization in Medieval Alchemy." *Hyle* 9:2 (2003): 131–70.
O'Boyle, Cornelius. "Surgical Texts and Social Contexts: Physicians and Surgeons in Paris, c. 1270 to 1340." In *Practical Medicine from Salerno to the Black Death,* ed. Luis García-Ballester et al., 156–85. Cambridge: Cambridge University Press, 1994.
Olsen, Glenn W. *Of Sodomites, Effeminates, Hermaphrodites, and Androgynes: Sodomy in the Age of Peter Damian.* Toronto: Pontifical Institute of Mediaeval Studies, 2011.
Omi, Michael and Howard Winant. *Racial Formation in the United States: From the 1960s to the 1980s.* New York: Routledge, 1986.
Omont, Henri, ed. *Livre des merveilles: Reproduction des 265 miniatures du manuscrit français 2810 de la Bibliothèque Nationale.* 2 vols. Paris: Berthaud Frères, 1907.
Orchard, Andy. *Pride and Prodigies: Studies in the Monsters of the Beowulf-Manuscript.* Cambridge: Boydell & Brewer, 1995.
Oswald, Dana M. *Monsters, Gender and Sexuality in Medieval English Literature.* Cambridge: Boydell & Brewer, 2010.
———. "Monstrous Gender: Geographies of Ambiguity." In *The Ashgate Research Companion to Monsters and the Monstrous,* ed. Asa S. Mittman and Peter Dendle, 343–63. Aldershot, UK: Ashgate, 2013.
Otten, Willemien. "Reading Creation: Early Medieval Views of Genesis and Plato's *Timaeus.*" In *The Creation of Heaven and Earth: Re-Interpretation of Genesis I in the Context of Judaism, Ancient*

Philosophy, Christianity, and Modern Physics, ed. George H. van Kooten, 225–43. Leiden: Brill, 2005.

Ottosson, Per-Gunnar. *Scholastic Medicine and Philosophy: A Study of Commentaries on Galen's* Tegni *(ca. 1300–1450)*. Naples: Bibliopolis, 1984.

Pagels, Elaine. "The Gnostic Vision: Varieties of Androgyny Illustrated by Texts from the Nag Hammadi Library." *Parabola* 3/4 (1978): 6–9.

———. *Adam, Eve, and the Serpent: Sex and Politics in Early Christianity*. New York: Random House, 1988.

———. *The Gnostic Gospels*. New York: Vintage, 1989.

———. *The Origin of Satan*. New York: Random House, 1995.

Pahta, Päivi. *Medieval Embryology in the Vernacular: The Case of* De spermate. Helsinki: Société Néophilologique, 1998.

Painter, Nell. *The History of White People*. New York: W.W. Norton, 2010.

Palmer, Barbara D. "The Inhabitants of Hell: Devils." In *The Iconography of Hell*, ed. Clifford Davidson and Thomas H. Seller, 20–41. Kalamazoo, MI.: Medieval Institute Publications, 1992.

Panella, Vania Gasperoi and Maria Grazia Cittadini Fulvi. *Dal mondo antico al Cristianesimo sulle tracce di Giano: Il simbolismo della porta e del passaggio in relazione al Dio bifronte*. Perugia: Morlacchi, 2008.

Paravicini Bagliani, Agostino. "Storia della scienza e storia della mentalità: Ruggero Bacone, Bonifacio VIII e la teoria della 'prolongatio vitae.' " In *Aspetti della letteratura latina nel secolo XIII*, ed. Claudio Leonardi and Giovanni Orlandi, 243–80. Florence: La Nuova Italia, 1986.

———. *The Pope's Body*. Trans. David S. Peterson. Chicago: University of Chicago Press, 2000.

Park, Katharine. "Birth and Death." In *A Cultural History of the Human Body in the Medieval Age*. Vol. 2 of *A Cultural History of the Human Body*, ed. Linda Kalof and William Bynum, 17–38. Oxford: Berg, 2010.

———. "Cadden, Laqueur, and the 'One-Sex Body.' " *Medieval Feminist Forum* 46: 1 (2010): 96–100.

———. "Medicine and Natural Philosophy: Naturalistic Traditions." In *The Oxford Handbook of Women and Gender in Medieval Europe*, ed. Judith Bennett and Ruth Karras, 84–100. Oxford: Oxford University Press, 2013.

———. "Nature in Person: Medieval and Renaissance Allegories and Emblems." In *The Moral Authority of Nature*, ed. Lorraine Daston and Fernando Vidal, 50–73. Chicago: University of Chicago Press, 2004.

———. "The Rediscovery of the Clitoris: French Medicine and the Tribade, 1570–1620." In *The Body in Parts: Fantasies of Corporeality in Early Modern Europe*, ed. David Hillman and Carla Mazzio, 170–93. New York: Routledge, 1997.

———. *Secrets of Women: Gender: Generation, and the Origins of Human Dissection*. New York: Zone, 2006.

Park, Katharine and Robert A. Nye. "Destiny Is Anatomy." *New Republic* 204 (Feb. 18, 1991): 53–57.

Pasnau, Robert. "The Latin Aristotle." In *The Oxford Handbook of Aristotle*, ed.C. Shields, 665–89. Oxford: Oxford University Press, 2012.

Patton, Pamela A. *Art of Estrangement: Redefining Jews in Reconquest Spain*. University Park: Pennsylvania State University Press, 2012.

Peck, A. L. "Preface" to Aristotle, *On the Generation of Animals*, ed. A. L. Peck, v–lxxvi. London: Harvard University Press, 1963.

Pegg, Mark. *A Most Holy War: The Albigensian Crusade and the Battle for Christendom*. Oxford: Oxford University Press, 2008.

Pennington, Kenneth and Wolfgang P. Müller. "The Decretists: The Italian School." In *The History of Medieval Canon Law in the Classical Period, 1140–1234: From Gratian to the Decretals of Pope Gregory IX*, ed. Wilfried Hartmann and Kenneth Pennington, 142–60. Washington, DC: Catholic University of America Press, 2008.

Pereira, Michela. "Projecting Perfection: Remarks on the Origin of the 'Alchemy of the Elixir.' " *Micrologus* 24 (2016): 73–93.

Petrey, Taylor G. *Resurrecting Parts: Early Christians on Desire, Reproduction, and Sexual Difference*. London: Routledge, 2016.

Phillips, Kim M. *Before Orientalism: Asian Peoples and Cultures in European Travel Writing, 1245–1510*. Philadelphia: University of Pennsylvania Press, 2014.

Pormann, Peter E. and Emilie Savage-Smith. *Medieval Islamic Medicine*. Washington, DC: Georgetown University Press, 2007.

Postec, Amandine. "Un exemplaire singulier du *De animalibus* d'Albert le Grand et son illustration (Paris, Bibliothèque Nationale de France, Manuscrits, Latin 16169)." *Reinardus: Yearbook of the International Reynard Society* 26 (2014): 137–60.

Pouchelle, Marie-Christine. *The Body and Surgery in the Middle Ages*. Trans. Rosemary Morris. Cambridge: Polity, 1990.

Preciado, Paul B. *Countersexual Manifesto*. Trans. Kevin Gerry Dunn. New York: Columbia University Press, 2018.

Principe, Lawrence M. "Revealing Analogies: The Descriptive and Deceptive Roles of Sexuality and Gender in Latin Alchemy." In *Hidden Intercourse: Eros and Sexuality in the History of Western Esotericism*, ed. Wouter J. Hanegraaff and Jeffrey J. Kripal, 209–230. New York: Fordham University Press, 2011.

———. *The Secrets of Alchemy*. Chicago: University of Chicago Press, 2013.

Principe, Lawrence M., ed. *Chymists and Chymistry: Studies in the History of Alchemy and Early Modern Chemistry*. Sagamore Beach, MA: Science History Publications, 2007.

Puar, Jasbir K. *Terrorist Assemblages: Homonationalism in Queer Times*. Durham, NC: Duke University Press, 2007.

Ragab, Ahmed. "One, Two, or Many Sexes: Sex Differentiation in Islamicate Medical Thought." *Journal of the History of Sexuality* 24:3 (2015): 428–54.

Ragep, F. Jamil. "Islamic Culture and the Natural Sciences." In *The Cambridge History of Science*, ed. D. Lindberg and M. H. Shank, 27–61. Cambridge: Cambridge University Press, 2013.

Ramey, Lynn T. *Black Legacies: Race and the European Middle Ages*. Gainesville: University Press of Florida, 2014.

Reeds, Karen Meier. "Albert on the Natural Philosophy of Plant Life." In *Albertus Magnus and the Sciences: Commemorative Essays, 1980*, ed. James A. Weisheipl, 341–54. Toronto: Pontifical Institute of Mediaeval Studies, 1980.

———. *Botany in Medieval and Renaissance Universities*. New York: Garland, 1991.

Reis, Elizabeth. *Bodies in Doubt: An American History of Intersex*. Baltimore, MD: Johns Hopkins University Press, 2009.

Resl, Brigitte, ed. *A Cultural History of Animals in the Medieval Age*, vol. 2 of *A Cultural History of Animals*, ed. Linda Kalof and Brigitte Resl, 6 vols. Oxford: Berg, 2007.

Resnick, Irven M. "Albert the Great on Nature and the Production of Hermaphrodites: Theoretical and Practical Considerations." *Traditio* 74 (2019): 207–334.

———. "Conjoined Twins, Medieval Biology, and Evolving Reflection on Individual Identity." *Viator* 44:2 (2013): 343–68.

———. *Marks of Distinction: Christian Perceptions of Jews in the High Middle Ages*. Washington, DC: Catholic University of America Press, 2012.

———. "Medieval Roots of the Myth of Jewish Male Menses." *Harvard Theological Review* 93:3 (2000): 241-63.

Resnick, Irven M. and Kenneth F. Kitchell Jr. "The Sweepings of Lamia: Transformations of the Myths of Lilith and Lamia." In *Religion, Gender, and Culture in the Pre-modern World*, ed. Alexandra Cuffel and Brian Britt, 77–104. New York: Palgrave Macmillan, 2007.

Reynolds, Philip L. *How Marriage Became One of the Sacraments: The Sacramental Theology of Marriage from Its Medieval Origins to the Council of Trent*. Cambridge: Cambridge University Press, 2016.

Robbins, Frank E. *The Hexaemeral Literature: A Study of the Greek and Latin Commentaries on Genesis*. Chicago: Chicago University Press, 1912.

Roberts, Gareth. "The Bodies of Demons." in *The Body in Late Medieval and Early Modern Culture*, ed. Darryll Grantley and Nina Taunton, 131–42. Aldershot, UK: Ashgate, 2000.

Robinson, M. "Salmacis and Hermaphroditus: When Two Become One (Ovid, Met. 4.285-388)." *The Classical Quarterly*, New Series, 49 (1999): 212–23.
Roen, Katrina. "Clinical Intervention and Embodied Subjectivity: Atypically Sexed Children and Their Parents." In *Critical Intersex*, ed. Morgan Holmes, 15–40. Aldershot, UK: Ashgate, 2009.
Rolker, Christof. "Der Hermaphrodit und seine Frau: Körper, Sexualität und Geschlecht im Spätmittelalter." *Hist. Z.* 297 (2013): 593–620.
———. "The Two Laws and the Three Sexes: Ambiguous Bodies in Canon Law and Roman Law (12th to 16th Centuries)." *Zeitschrift der Savigny-Stiftung für Rechtsgeschichte kanonistische Abteilung* 100 (2014): 178–222.
———. "Off the Map? Hermaphrodites on the Hereford Map." *Männlich-weiblich-zwischen*, June 13, 2016. https://intersex.hypotheses.org/?p=3305.
Rollo, David. *Kiss My Relics: Hermaphroditic Fictions of the Middle Ages*. Chicago: University of Chicago Press, 2011.
Romero, Guadalupe Albi. *Lanfranco de Milán en España: Estudio y edición de la Magna Chirurgia en traducción castellana medieval*. Valladolid: Secretariado de Publicaciones, 1988.
Rosario, Vernon A. "Quantum Sex: Intersex and the Molecular Deconstruction of Sex." *GLQ: A Journal of Lesbian and Gay Studies* 15:2 (2009): 267–84.
Rosenfield, Kirstie Gulick. "Monstrous Generation: Witchcraft and Generation in *Othello*." In *Consuming Narratives: Gender and Monstrous Appetite in the Middle Ages and the Renaissance*, ed. Liz Herbert McAvoy and Teresa Walters, 222–34. Cardiff: University of Wales Press, 2002.
Roth, Cecil. "Portraits and Caricatures of Medieval English Jews." In *Essays and Portraits in Anglo-Jewish History*, 22–25. Philadelphia: Jewish Publication Society, 1962.
Rothstein, Marian. *The Androgyne in Early Modern France: Contextualizing the Power of Gender*. New York: Palgrave, 2015.
Rovinski, Jacques. "La cosmétologie de Guy de Chauliac." In *Les soins de beauté, Moyen Age; début des temps modernes. Actes du IIIe Colloque international, Grasse (26–28 avril 1985)*, ed. Denis Menjot, 171–82. Nice: Centre d'Études Médiévales, 1987.
Rowland, Beryl. *Animals with Human Faces: A Guide to Animal Symbolism*. Knoxville: University of Tennessee Press, 1973.
———. "The Art of Memory and the Bestiary." In *Beasts and Birds of the Middle Ages: The Bestiary and Its Legacy*, ed. Willene B. Clark and Meradith T. McMunn, 12–25. Philadelphia: University of Pennsylvania Press, 1989.
Rubin, David A. *Intersex Matters: Biomedical Embodiment, Gender Regulation, and Transnational Activism*. Albany: State University of New York Press, 2017.
Rubin, Miri. "The Person in the Form: Medieval Challenges to Bodily 'Order.'" In *Framing Medieval Bodies*, ed. Sarah Kay and Miri Rubin, 100–22. Manchester: Manchester University Press, 1994.
Rubenstein, Jay. *Guibert of Nogent: Portrait of a Medieval Mind*. New York: Routledge, 2002.
Runia, David T. *Philo in Early Christian Literature: A Survey*. Assen, The Netherlands: Van Gorcum, 1993.
Russell, Jeffrey Burton. *Lucifer: The Devil in the Middle Ages*. Ithaca, NY: Cornell University Press, 1984.
Salamon, Gayle. *Assuming a Body: Transgender and Rhetorics of Materiality*. New York: Columbia University Press, 2010.
Salisbury, Joyce E. "The Latin Doctors of the Church on Sexuality." *Journal of Medieval History* 12 (1986): 279–89.
———. *The Beast Within: Animals in the Middle Ages*. New York: Routledge, 2011.
Sanders, Paula. "Gendering the Ungendered Body: Hermaphrodites in Medieval Islamic Law." In *Women in Middle Eastern History: Shifting Boundaries in Sex and Gender*, ed. Nikki R. Keddie and Beth Baron, 74–95. New Haven, CT: Yale University Press, 1991.
Sandler, Lucy Freeman. *Omne Bonum: A Fourteenth-Century Encyclopedia of Universal Knowledge*, 2 vols. London: Harvey Miller, 1996.

Savage-Smith, Emilie. "The Exchange of Medical and Surgical Ideas Between Europe and Islam." In *The Diffusion of Greco-Roman Medicine in the Middle East and the Caucasus*, ed. John A. C. Greppin, Emilie Savage-Smith, and John L. Gueriguian, 27–55. Delmar, NY: Caravan, 1999.

———. "Medicine in Medieval Islam." In *The Cambridge History of Science*, ed. D. Lindberg and M. H. Shank, 139–67. Cambridge: Cambridge University Press, 2013.

———. "Zahrāwī, Abū 'l-Qāsim." In *Encyclopaedia of Islam*, 2nd ed., vol. 11, ed. P. Bearman et al. (Leiden: Brill, 1960–2004): 398–99.

Scafi, Alessandro. *Maps of Paradise*. Chicago: University of Chicago Press, 2013.

Scalenghe, Sara. "Being Different: Intersexuality, Blindness, Deafness, and Madness in Ottoman Syria." PhD diss, Georgetown University, 2006.

———. *Disability in the Ottoman Arab World, 1500–1800*. Cambridge: Cambridge University Press, 2014.

Scanlon, Larry. "Unspeakable Pleasures: Alain de Lille, Sexual Regulation and the Priesthood of Genius." *Romanic Review* 86:2 (1995): 213–42.

Schiebinger, Londa. *Nature's Body: Gender in the Making of Modern Science*. New York: Beacon, 1993.

Schleicher, Marianne. "Constructions of Sex and Gender: Attending to Androgynes and Tumtumim Through Jewish Scriptural Use." *Literature and Theology* 25:4 (2011): 422–35.

Schreckenberg, Heinz. *The Jews in Christian Art: An Illustrated History*. New York: Continuum Publishing Co., 1996.

Schweitzer, Jr., Edward C. "Chaucer's Pardoner and the Hare." *English Language Notes* 4 (1966–67): 247–50.

Schultz, James A. "Heterosexuality as a Threat to Medieval Studies." *Journal of the History of Sexuality* 15:1 (2006): 14–29.

Scott, Joan W. "Gender as a Useful Category of Historical Analysis." *American Historical Review* 91:5 (1986): 1053–75.

Sears, Clare. *Arresting Dress: Cross-Dressing, Law and Fascination in Nineteenth-Century San Francisco*. Chapel Hill, NC: Duke University Press, 2015.

Secunda, Shai. "The Construction, Composition, and Idealization of the Female Body in Rabbinic Literature and Parallel Iranian Texts: Three Excursuses." *Nashim: A Journal of Jewish Women's Studies & Gender Issues* 23 (Spring-Fall 2012): 60–86.

Shachar, Uri. "Pollution and Purity in Near Eastern Jewish, Christian, and Muslim Crusading Rhetoric." In *Entangled Histories: Knowledge, Authority, and Jewish Culture in the Thirteenth Century*, ed. Elisheva Baumgarten, Ruth Mazo Karras, and Katelyn Mesler, 229–47. Philadelphia: University of Pennsylvania Press, 2017.

Shyovitz, David I. " 'Unearthing the Children of Cain': Between Humans, Animals, and Demons in Medieval Jewish Culture." In *Monsters and Monstrosity in Jewish History: From the Middle Ages to Modernity*, ed. Iris Idelson-Shein and Christian Wiese, 157–86. London: Bloomsbury, 2019.

Silberman, Lauren. "Mythographic Transformations of Ovid's Hermaphrodite." *Sixteenth Century Journal* 19:4 (1988): 643–52.

Siraisi, Nancy G. "The Medical Learning of Albert the Great." In *Albertus Magnus and the Sciences: Commemorative Essays, 1980*, ed. James A. Weisheipl, 379–404. Toronto: Pontifical Institute of Mediaeval Studies, 1980.

———. *Medieval and Early Renaissance Medicine: An Introduction to Knowledge and Practice*. Chicago: University of Chicago Press, 1990.

Sissa, Giulia. "Philosophies of Sex in Plato and Aristotle." In *A History of Women in the West*, vol. 1, *From Ancient Goddesses to Christian Saints*, ed. Pauline Schmitt Pantel, 46–81. Cambridge, MA: Belknap, 1992.

———. *Sex and Sensuality in the Ancient World*. Trans. George Staunton. New Haven, CT: Yale University Press, 2008.

Skidmore, Emily. *True Sex: The Lives of Trans Men at the Turn of the Century*. New York: New York University Press, 2017.

Smith, Mark M. "Transcending, Othering, Detecting: Smell, Premodernity, Modernity." *postmedieval: a journal of medieval cultural studies* 3:4 (2012): 380–90.

Smith, Pamela H. *The Business of Alchemy: Science and Culture in the Holy Roman Empire*. Princeton, NJ: Princeton University Press, 1994.

Snorton, C. Riley. *Black on Both Sides: A Racial History of Trans Identity*. Minneapolis: University of Minnesota Press, 2017.

Snorton, C. Riley and Jin Haritaworn, "Trans Necropolitics: A Transnational Reflection on Violence, Death, and the Trans of Color Afterlife." In *The Transgender Studies Reader 2*, ed. Susan Stryker and Aren Z. Aizura, 66–76. New York: Routledge, 2013.

Soifer, Maya. "Beyond *Convivencia*: Critical Reflections on the Historiography of Interfaith relations in Christian Spain." *Journal of Medieval Iberian Studies* 1 (2009): 19–35.

Spade, Dean. *Normal Life: Administrative Violence, Critical Trans Politics, and the Limits of the Law*. Brooklyn: South End, 2011.

Spillers, Hortense J. "Mama's Baby, Papa's Maybe: An American Grammar Book." *Diacritics* 17:2 (1987): 64–81.

Stacey, Robert C. "The Conversion of Jews to Christianity in Thirteenth-Century England." *Speculum* 67:2 (1992): 263–83.

———. "Jewish Lending and the Medieval English Economy." In *A Commercialising Economy: England 1086 to c. 1300*, ed. Richard H. Britnell and Bruce M. S. Campbell, 78–101. Manchester: Manchester University Press, 1995.

———. "From Ritual Crucifixion to Host Desecration: Jews and the Body of Christ." *Jewish History* 12:1 (1998): 11–28.

Stallybrass, Peter and Allon White. *The Politics and Poetics of Transgression*. Ithaca, NY: Cornell University Press, 1986.

Stanley, Eric A. and Nat Smith, ed. *Captive Genders: Trans Embodiment and the Prison Industrial Complex*. Edinburgh: AK, 2011.

Steel, Karl. "How to Make a Human." *Exemplaria* 20:1 (2008): 3–27.

———. *How to Make a Human: Animals and Violence in the Middle Ages*. Columbus: Ohio State University Press, 2011.

———. "Centaurs, Satyrs, and Cynocephali: Medieval Scholarly Teratology and the Question of the Human." In *The Ashgate Research Companion to Monsters and the Monstrous*, ed. Asa S. Mittman and Peter Dendle, 257–74. Aldersot, UK: Ashgate, 2013.

Steel, Karl and Peggy McCracken, ed. *The Animal Turn*. Special issue of *postmedieval: a journal of medieval cultural studies* 2:1 (2011).

Steeves, H. Peter, ed. *Animal Others: On Ethics, Ontology and Animal Life*. Albany: State University of New York Press, 1999.

Stock, Brian. *Myth and Science in the Twelfth Century: A Study of Bernard Silvester*. Princeton, NJ: Princeton University Press, 1972.

Stoler, Ann Laura. *Race and the Education of Desire: Foucault's* History of Sexuality *and the Colonial Order of Things*. Durham, NC: Duke University Press, 1995.

Strassfeld, Max K. "Classically Queer: Eunuchs and Androgynes in Rabbinic Literature." PhD diss., Stanford University, 2013.

———. "Translating the Human: The *Androginos* in *Tosefta Bikurim*." *TSQ: Transgender Studies Quarterly* 3:3–4 (2016): 587–604.

———. "Transing Religious Studies." *Journal of Feminist Studies in Religion* 34:1 (2018): 37–53.

Strickland, Debra Higgs. "Sex in the Bestiaries." In *The Mark of the Beast: The Medieval Bestiary in Art, Life, and Literature*, ed. Debra Higgs Strickland, 71–97. New York: Garland, 1999.

———. *Saracens, Demons, and Jews: Making Monsters in Medieval Art*. Princeton, NJ: Princeton University Press, 2003.

——. "The Jews, Leviticus, and the Unclean in Medieval English Bestiaries." In *Beyond the Yellow Badge: Anti-Judaism and Antisemitism in Medieval and Early Modern Culture*, ed. Mitchell B. Merback, 203–32. Leiden: Brill, 2008.

——. "Monstrosity and Race in the Late Middle Ages." In *The Ashgate Research Companion to Monsters and the Monstrous*, ed. Asa S. Mittman and Peter Dendle, 365–86. Aldershot, UK: Ashgate, 2013.

——. "Meanings of Muhammad in Later Medieval Art." In *The Image of the Prophet Between Ideal and Ideology: A Scholarly Investigation*, ed. Christiane J. Gruber and Avinoam Shalem, 147–63. Berlin: De Gruyter, 2014.

——. "Edward I, Exodus, and England on the Hereford World Map." *Speculum* 93:2 (April 2018): 420–69.

Stroll, Mary. *The Jewish Pope: Ideology and Politics in the Papal Schism of 1130*. Leiden: Brill, 1987.

Stryker, Susan. "My Words to Victor Frankenstein above the Village of Chamounix: Performing Transgender Rage." *GLQ: A Journal of Lesbian and Gay Studies* 1:3 (1994): 237–54.

——. "Transgender Studies: Queer Theory's Evil Twin." *GLQ: A Journal of Lesbian and Gay Studies* 10:2 (2004): 212–15.

——. "(De)subjugated Knowledges: An Introduction to Transgender Studies." In *The Transgender Studies Reader 1*, ed. Susan Stryker and Stephen Whittle, 1–17. New York: Routledge, 2006.

——. *Transgender History*. Berkeley, CA: Seal, 2008.

——. "General Editor's Introduction." *TSQ: Transgender Studies Quarterly* 5:4 (2018): 515–17.

Stryker, Susan and Aren Z. Aizura. "Introduction: Transgender Studies 2.0." In *Transgender Studies Reader 2*, 1–12.

——, ed. *The Transgender Studies Reader 2*. New York: Routledge, 2013.

Stryker, Susan and Paisley Currah. "General Editors' Introduction." *TSQ: Transgender Studies Quarterly* 1:3 (May 2014): 303–7.

Stryker, Susan, Paisley Currah, and Lisa Jean Moore. "Trans-, Trans, or Transgender?" *Womens' Studies Quarterly* 36:3–4 (2008): 11–22.

Stryker, Susan and Stephen Whittle, ed. *The Transgender Studies Reader 1*. New York: Routledge, 2006.

Sullivan, Nikki. "The Somatechnics of Intersexuality." *GLQ: A Journal of Gay and Lesbian Studies* 15:2 (2009): 313–27.

Sullivan, Nikki and Samantha Murray, ed. *Somatechnics: Queering the Technologisation of Bodies*. Aldershot, UK: Ashgate, 2009.

Sytsma, Sharon E., ed. *Ethics and Intersex*. Dordrecht, The Netherlands: Springer, 2006.

Tartakoff, Paola. "Testing Boundaries: Jewish Conversion and Cultural Fluidity in Medieval Europe, c. 1200–1391." *Speculum* 90:3 (2015): 728–62.

——. "Segregatory Legislation and Jewish Religious Influence on Christians in the Thirteenth Century." In *Religious Minorities in Christian, Jewish, and Muslim Law (5th-15th Centuries)*, ed. Nora Berend et al., 264–76. Turnhout, Belgium: Brepols, 2017.

——. "From Conversion to Ritual Murder: Re-contextualizing the Circumcision Charge." *Medieval Encounters* 24 (2018): 368–76.

Taylor, Frank Sherwood. *The Alchemists: Founders of Modern Chemistry*. New York: Henry Schuman, 1949.

Taylor, Rabun. "Watching the Skies: Janus, Auspication, and the Shrine in the Roman Forum." *Memoirs of the American Academy in Rome* 45 (2000): 1–40.

Terkla, Dan and Nick Millea, ed. *A Critical Companion to the English Medieval Mappae Mundi of the Twelfth and Thirteenth Centuries*. Rochester, NY: Boydell & Brewer, 2019.

Theissen, Wilfred R. "John Dastin's Letter on the Philosophers' Stone." *Ambix* 33:2–3 (1986): 78–87.

Thijssen, J. M. M. H. "Twins as Monsters: Albertus Magnus's Theory of the Generation of Twins and its Philosophical Context." *Bulletin of the History of Medicine* 61:2 (1987): 237–46.

Thomas, Louis-Vincent. *Le cadavre: de la biologie à l'anthropologie*. Brussels: Éditions Complexe, 1980.

Tinsley, David F. "Mapping the Muslims: Images of Islam in Middle High German Literature of the Thirteenth Century." In *Contextualizing the Muslim Other in Medieval Christian Discourse*, ed. Jerold C. Frakes, 65–101. New York: Palgrave, 2011.

Tolan, John. *Saracens: Islam in the Medieval European Imagination*. New York: Columbia University Press, 2002.

Tompkins, Kyla Wazana. *Racial Indigestion: Eating Bodies in the Nineteenth Century*. New York: New York University Press, 2012.

Tougher, Shaun, ed. *Eunuchs in Antiquity and Beyond*. Swansea, UK: Classical Press of Wales and Duckworth, 2002.

Tracy, Larissa. "A History of Calamities: The Culture of Castration." In *Castration and Culture in the Middle Ages*, ed. Larissa Tracy, 1–28. Cambridge: Boydell & Brewer, 2013.

Trachtenberg, Joshua. *The Devil and the Jews: The Medieval Conception of the Jew and Its Relation to Modern Anti-Semitism*. New York: Harper, 1966.

Traub, Valerie. *The Renaissance of Lesbianism in Early Modern England*. Cambridge: Cambridge University Press, 2002.

———, "Introduction." In *Ovidian Transversions: 'Iphis and Ianthe,' 1300–1650*, ed. Patricia Badir, Peggy McCracken, and Valerie Traub, 1–41. Edinburgh: Edinburgh University Press, 2019.

Triea, Kiira. "Power, Orgasm, and the Psychohormonal Research Unit." In *Intersex in the Age of Ethics*, ed. Alice Domurat Dreger, 140–44. Hagerstown, MD: University Publishing Group, 1999.

Twomey, Michael W. "Inventing the Encyclopedia." In *Schooling and Society: The Ordering and Reordering of Knowledge in the Western Middle Ages*, ed. Alasdair A. MacDonald and Michael W. Twomey, 73–92. Leuven, Belgium: Peeters, 2004.

Tzanaki, Rosemary. *Mandeville's Medieval Audiences: Studies in the Reception of the Book of Sir John Mandeville (1371–1550)*. London: Ashgate, 2003.

Uebel, Michael. *Ecstatic Transformation: On the Uses of Alterity in the Middle Ages*. New York: Palgrave, 2005.

———. "Unthinking the Monster: Twelfth-Century Responses to Saracen Alterity." In *Monster Theory: Reading Culture*, ed. Jeffrey Jerome Cohen, 264–91. Minneapolis: University of Minnesota, 1996.

Valentine, David. *Imagining Transgender: An Ethnography of a Category*. Durham, NC: Duke University Press, 2007.

Van der Lugt, Maaike. "L'humanité des monstres et leur accès aux sacrements dans la pensée médiévale." Accessed on March 20, 2019, https://halshs.archives-ouvertes.fr/halshs-00175497/document. Published in *Monstres, humanité et sacrements dans la pensée médiévale*, ed. A. Caiozzo et A.-E. Demartini, 135–61. Paris : Créaphis, 2008.

———. "Pourquoi Dieu a-t-il créé la femme? Différence sexuelle et théologie médiévale." In *Ève et Pandora: la création de la femme*, ed. Jean-Claude Schmitt, 89–113 (notes on 262–67). Paris: Gallimard, 2001.

———. "Sex Difference in Medieval Theology and Canon Law: A Tribute to Joan Cadden." *Medieval Feminist Forum* 46:1 (2010): 101–21.

———. *Le ver, le démon et la vierge: les théories médiévales de la génération extraordinaire: une étude sur les rapports entre théologie, philosophie naturelle et médecine*. Paris: Les Belles Lettres, 2004.

Van Duzer, Chet. "A Neglected Type of Medieval *Mappamundi* and its Re-Imaging in the *Mare Historiarum* (BNF MS Lat. 4915, Fol. 26v)." *Viator* 43: 2 (2012): 277–301.

Van Oppenraaij, Aafke M. I. "Michael Scot's Arabic-Latin Translation of Aristotle's Books on Animals." In *Aristotle's Animals in the Middle Ages and Renaissance*, ed. Carlos Steel, Guy Guldentops, and Pieter Beullens, 31–43. Leuven, Belgium: Leuven University Press, 1992.

Ventura, Iolanda. "*Quaestiones* and Encyclopedias: Some Aspects of the Late Medieval Reception of Pseudo-Aristotelian *Problemata* in Encyclopedic and Scientific Culture." In *Schooling and Society: The Ordering and Reordering of Knowledge in the Western Middle Ages*, ed. by Alasdair A. MacDonald and Michael W. Twomey, 23–42. Leuven, Belgium: Peeters, 2004.

Verner, Lisa. *The Epistemology of the Monstrous in the Middle Ages*. New York: Routledge, 2005.

Vicinus, Martha. "Lesbian History: All Theory and No Facts or All Facts and No Theory?" *Radical History Review* 60 (1994): 57–75.
Vogt, Kari. " 'Becoming Male': A Gnostic and Early Christian Metaphor." In *The Image of God and Gender Models in Judaeo-Christian Tradition*, ed. Kari Elisabeth Børresen, 172–86. Minneapolis: Fortress Press, 1995.
Von Stackelberg, Katharine T. "Garden Hybrids: Hermaphrodite Images in the Roman House." *Classical Antiquity* 33:2 (April 2014): 395–426.
Wain, Gemma. "*Nec ancilla nec domina*: Representations of Eve in the Twelfth Century." PhD diss., Durham University, 2013.
Webster, James Carson. *The Labors of the Months in Antique and Mediaeval Art: To the End of the Twelfth Century*. Evanston, IL: Northwestern University, 1938.
Weheliye, Alexander G. *Habeas Viscus: Racializing Assemblages, Biopolitics, and Black Feminist Theories of the Human*. Durham, NC: Duke University Press, 2014.
Weisheipl, James A. ed. *Albertus Magnus and the Sciences: Commemorative Essays, 1980*. Toronto: Pontifical Institute of Mediaeval Studies, 1980.
West, M. L. *Early Greek Philosophy and the Orient*. Oxford: Clarendon, 1971.
Westrem, Scott. "Against Gog and Magog." In *Text and Territory: Geographical Imagination in the European Middle Ages*, ed. Sylvia Tomasch and Sealy Gilles, 54–75. Philadelphia: University of Pennsylvania Press, 1998.
———. *The Hereford Map: A Transcription and Translation of the Legends with Commentary*. Turnhout, Belgium: Brepols, 2001.
Whitaker, Cord. *Black Metaphors: How Modern Racism Emerged from Medieval Race-Thinking*. Philadelphia: University of Pennsylvania Press, 2019.
———, ed. *Making Race Matter in the Middle Ages*. Special issue of *postmedieval: a journal of medieval cultural studies* 6:1 (2015).
Whitney, Elspeth. "What's Wrong with the Pardoner? Complexion Theory, the Phlegmatic Man, and Effeminacy." *Chaucer Review* 45:4 (2011): 357–89.
Whittington, Karl. "Medieval." *TSQ: Transgender Studies Quarterly* 1:1–2 (2014): 125–29.
Williams, David. *Deformed Discourse: The Function of the Monster in Medieval Thought and Literature*. Montreal: McGill-Queen's University Press, 1996.
Wirth, Jean, ed. *Diables et diableries: La représentation du diable dans la gravure des XVe et XVIe siècles*. Geneva: Cabinet des Estampes, 1976.
Woodward, David. "Medieval *Mappaemundi*." In *The History of Cartography, I: Cartography in Prehistoric, Ancient, and Medieval Europe and the Mediterranean*, ed. J. B. Harley and David Woodward, 286–370. Chicago: University of Chicago Press, 1982.
Wolfe, Cary. *Animal Rites: American Culture, the Discourse of Species, and Posthumanist Theory* (Chicago: University of Chicago Press, 2003.
———, ed. *Zoontologies: The Question of the Animal*. Minneapolis: University of Minnesota Press, 2003.
Wolfson, Elliot R. "Bifurcating the Androgyne and Engendering Sin: A Zoharic Reading of Gen. 1–3." In *Hidden Truths from Eden: Esoteric Readings of Genesis 1–3*, ed. Caroline Vander Stichele and Susanne Scholz, 87–119. Atlanta: SBL, 2014.
World Health Organization. "Traditional Birth Attendants: A Joint WHO/UNFPA/UNICEF Statement." Geneva: WHO, 1992.
Yamamoto, Dorothy. *The Boundaries of the Human in Medieval English Literature*. Oxford: Oxford University Press, 2000.
Zajko, Vanda. " 'Listening With' Ovid: Intersexuality, Queer Theory, and the Myth of Hermaphroditus and Salmacis." *Helios* 36:2 (2009): 175–202.
Ziegler, Joseph. "Sexuality and the Sexual Organs in Latin Physiognomy 1200–1500." *Studies in Medieval and Renaissance History*, 3rd ser., 2 (2005): 83–109.

———. "Physiognomy, Science, and Proto-Racism, 1200–1500." In *The Origins of Racism in the West*, ed. Miriam Eliav-Feldon, Benjamin Isaac, and Joseph Ziegler, 181–99. Cambridge: Cambridge University Press, 2008.

Ziolkowski, Jan M. *Alain de Lille's Grammar of Sex: The Meaning of Grammar to a Twelfth-Century Intellectual*. Cambridge, MA: Medieval Academy of America, 1985.

———. "Put in No-Man's Land: Guibert of Nogent's Accusations Against a Judaizing and Jew-Supporting Christian." In *Jews and Christians in Twelfth-Century Europe*, ed. Michael A. Signer and John Van Engen, 110–22. Notre Dame, IN: University of Notre Dame Press, 2001.

Index

Page numbers in *italics* indicate figures or tables.

'Abbāsid caliphate, 105–6, 109–10
Abelard, Peter. *See* Peter Abelard
Aberdeen Bestiary, 93, 99; hyenas in, 70, *71*, 77, 87, 96–97, 101; Jews and, 70, 72–79, 96, 98; manticore, 74, *75*, 96; as second-family, 234n10
Abomination. *See* uncleanness
abortion, 44
Abramson, Henry, 94
Abstinence. *See* celibacy
Abū Bakr Muhammad ibn Zakarīyā al-Rāzī, 110, 167, 245n29
Acre, fall of, 64
Adam (biblical figure), 11, 18, 123, 166, 202; as androgyne, 21, 30; Augustine of Hippo on, 23, 24–25; as bicephalic figure, 16, *17*, 19, 20, 181; in Carolingian Bibles, 36; as double-faced, 38, 214n3; with dual sexes of creation, 22; Eriugena on, 26; Eve and, 177–80, *179*, 183, 188, 226n60; *Glossa ordinaria* on, 27; Guibert of Nogent on, 26; *Hexaemeron* and, 179–80, *182*; Hugh of Saint-Cher on, 29; monsters and, 43; mythic hermaphrodites with Eve and, 183; Peter the Chanter on, 28; primal androgyny and, 17; sexual heterogeneity and, 31
Admonitio generalis (789), 25
Adversus Iudaeos literature, 76
advowson, right of, 84
Aelred of Rievaulx, 191

Africa, 40, 46, 49, 58; with Africans, 34, 66–67. *See also* Ethiopia
afterlife, 32–35, 38, 39
Against Heretics (Contra haereticos) (Alan of Lille), 65
Against Jovinianus (Jerome), 31
Aizura, Aren Z., 9, 159–60
Ajootian, Aileen, 53
Akbari, Suzanne, 66, 236n30
Alan of Lille, 65, 66, 85, 87, 100, 193
Albert the Great (Albertus Magnus) (1200–1280), 30, 35, 45, 61, 236n30, 247n56; on Christ, 189; influence of, 131, 137, 168; influences on, 143; with natural philosophy and law, 117–21; on women, 129, 130, 175. *See also On Animals*
Albigensians (Cathars), 29–30
alchemical hermaphrodites, 168–75, *173*, *174*, 185–87, *187*
alchemical knowledge, in medieval Europe, 165–68
Alexander III (Pope), 145
Alexander of Hales, 121
Alī ibn al-'Abbās al-Majūsī, 110
Allegory of the Redemption, *93*
Amalric, 30
Amauricians, 30
Ambrose, 179–80, *182*
anasyromenos style, 53
anatomies, nonbinary sex, 131, 134, 138, 253n15
Andrew of St. Victor, 27

androgynes, 18, 20–21, 24, 28–31, 38, 47, 231n137. *See also* hermaphrodites; primal androgyne

androgyny: abstract thinking about, 4–5; angelic transcendence and, 31; Greek myths of, 20; hermaphroditism and, 27, 36–37; as unity in masculinity, 38; wisdom and, *192*

angels, 21, 26, 239n88; androgyny and transcendence of, 31; demons and, 87–88; without sexual boundaries, 88–89

animals, 26, 42, 44, 53, 101, 233n3, 238n75; with Aristotle, 106–9; with bestiaries, 70–79; copulation, 102, *103*; critical animal studies, 7, 42, 68, 222n8, 243n135; with dehumanizing depictions of Jews or Muslims, 65, 77. *See also* Albert the Great; *On Animals*; *On the Generation of Animals*; *On the Nature of Animals*; *Questions Concerning on Animals*

annulments, marriage, 144–45, 209n6

Anthony (saint), 88

anti-Judaism, 84, 96–98, 232n141

Aphrodite (deity), 6, 163, 173, 183

Apocryphal Acts of the Apostles, 25

Aquinas, Thomas. *See* Thomas Aquinas

Aristophanes, 20

Aristotle, 30, 102, 112, 130, 237n53; on androgynes, 47; influence of, 117, 118, 122, 142–43, 168; legacy, 106, 109; monsters and, 108; with natural philosophy and medicine, 244n11; "New Logic" of, 81, 106; theories, 106–9, 121; translations of, 81, 107, 115, 237n53. *See also On Animals*

Arnold of Villanova, 65–66

Arxiu Històric Provincial, 1

asexuals, 21, 37, 70, 118, 122, 168, 197

Ashmole bestiary, 79, 234n10

Asia, 40, 46, 49

assemblage theory, 222n7

Augustine of Hippo, 33, 121, 123, 129; creation and, 22–25, 216n29; influence of, 27; intersex infants and, 57; on monstrous races, 43; monstrous races and, 40

Aurora consurgens (*Rising Dawn*), 171–74, *173*, 264n37; hermaphrodite, 175–85

auto-fertilization, 119–20, 248n73. *See also* asexuals

Azo, 125–26

Bacon, Roger. *See* Roger Bacon

Bakhtin, Mikhail, 75

Baldassano, Alex, 9

Baldus de Ubaldis, 84, 128–29, 153

baptism, 57, 98, 130

Barbin, Herculine, 156

Barkan, Leonard, 262n6

Bartholomew the Englishman, 44, 45

Barton, William, 146

bathroom bills, 204

Baxter, Ron, 233n8, 236n37, 237n45

behavior: bestiaries as regulator of human, 80; marriage with standards of, 3; reversals, mythic hermaphrodites, 49

Bell, Margaret, 145, 146

Berengaria Castelló, 1–4, 134, 154–55, 209n1, 210n7

Bernard of Clairvaux, 80, 83, 99, 191, 242n130

Bernard of Cluny, 66, 85–87, 100

Berry, Duke of, 49

Bersuire, Pierre. *See* Pierre Bersuire

bestiality, demon-human sex and, 89, 92

Bestiaire (Guillaume le Clerc), 77, *78*, 93, *93*

bestiaries: 72–79, *75*; Ashmole, 79, 234n10; John of Salisbury and, 82–83; monstrous races and, 73; with naturalism and moralism, 233n6; Northumberland Bestiary, 79, *79*, 233n8, 236n43; as regulator of human behavior, 80; role of, 70; second-family, 234n10; societal influence of, 79; Westminster Abbey Bestiary, 59, *60*; worldliness, spirituality and, 80–81. *See also* Aberdeen Bestiary; *Bestiaire* (Guillaume le Clerc)

Bible moralisée, 36, 76

Bibles, Carolingian, 36

bicephalic bodies, 16, *17*, 19, 20, 181

binaries: defined, 6; scholasticism with, 81

binary sex, absence of, 21

biological sex, 33, 61, 204

births, monstrous, 56–59

blemmyes, 40, 45, 51, *51*

Boaistuau, Pierre, 94, *95*

bodies: anatomies, 131, 134, 138, 253n15; angelic, 29, 87–89, 239n88; at beginning, 19–22; bicephalic, 16, *17*, 19, 20, 181; Berengaria Castelló, 1–4, 210n7; with castration and impotence, 144–49; demonic, 87–94, 239n88; devil and, 29–30; hard, soft, active and passive, 151–56; human rights and, 9; of intersex people, 9–10; male and female, 111; as metaphor for community or kingdom, 96–97, 241n119; monsters and, 43; natural philosophy, laws and human, 121–24; perfect, 33–35; resurrected, 18, 32–35; rotting,

74; souls and, 44; surgeons correcting, 3, 134, 143; of transgender people, 9–10; of women, 100

Boethius, 81

Bonaventure of Bagnoregio, 190

Book of Marvels (*Livre des merveilles*), 49, 50, 51, 51–53, 183–84

Book of Monsters, 47, 228n87

Book of the Holy Trinity, The (*Das Buch der heiligen Dreifaltigkeit*), 172, 185–86, 195, 197

"Borghese hermaphrodite," 53

Boswell, John, 66

Bouchard, Constance Brittain, 27

boundaries: angels without, 88–89; eating dissolving, 87; hermaphrodites and, 6; monstrous races and, 45; sexual, 59–63, *60*

boundary stone (*herma*), 6

Boyarin, Daniel, 19, 216n25

Breviary in Catholic History (Rada), 27–28

Bruno Longobucco, 134, 139–40, 155, 254n33

Buch der heiligen Dreifaltigkeit, Das. See *Book of the Holy Trinity, The*

Burgundio of Pisa, 112

burning bush, 77, *78*

Butler, Judith, 61–62

Bychowski, M. W., 14, 55, 64

Bynum, Caroline Walker, 32, 34, 57, 99, 243n132

Cadden, Joan, 112

calendars, Roman, 54

calf, golden, 77, *78*

Camille, Michael, 55, 67, 100, 243n1

cannibalism, 74, 96, 235n21

canon law, Roman and, 106, 124–29

Canon of Medicine, The (Ibn Sīnā), 110, 115, 117, 120, 138

Carolingian Bibles, Adam and Eve in, 36

Carruthers, Mary, 80

castrates, 3, 10, 148, 158

castration, 70, 144–49, 152

Cathars (Albigensians), 29–30

Cavallar, Osvaldo, 250n110

celibacy, 29, 62, 148.

Chaucer, Geoffrey, 55

children, transgender, 204. *See also* infants

Christ, 190; church and, 123; crucifixion of, *189*; feminized, 191–94; philosophers' stone and, 162; Virgin Mary and, 185–86. *See also* Jesus hermaphrodite

Christianity: advocacy groups, 204–5; with androgynes, sodomy and heresy, 28–31; with bodies at beginning, 19–22; crusades in England and, 63–67; with dual sexes of creation, 22–25; Fourth Lateran Council and, 241n112; Genesis and, 16–20; Hereford *mappamundi* and, 12, 40, *41*, 58, 67; nonbinary sex and, 11–12, 32–37; primal androgyne and, 25–28; primal androgyny and, 17–18; resurrection and, 32; sexual duality and, 16; shift in, 95; subordination and, 18, 24, 37

Christianity, Social Tolerance, and Homosexuality (Boswell), 66

Christians: Jews and, 12, 63–64, 71–72, 95–97; Muslims and, 64–65, 97, 98, 99, 230n118, 242n124; sexual intercourse between Jews and, 241n119

Christine de Pizan, 183

Chronicle, or History of the Two Cities (Otto of Freising), 33–34

chronology, nonbinary sex, 11–15

Chu, Andrea Long, 206

Church, Christ and, 123

circumcision: 139; Jewish culture and, 255n58; medieval Jewish culture and, 254n26; surgical methods and goals in, 253n25

City of God (Augustine of Hippo), 16, 24, 57

Clark, Elizabeth, 38

Clark, Willene, 72, 234n10

Classen, Albrecht, 46, 65

classification, systems of, 5–6

Claudius Mamertinus, 148

Clavis physicae (Honorius of Autun), 26

climate: theories of, 49; race and monstrosity and, 226n54

Cohen, Jeffrey, 42–43, 45, 63

Colonna, Giovanni, 49, *50*, 176

Commentary on the Sentences (Peter of Palude), 123–24

communal integrity, 236n35

community, bodies as metaphor for, 96–97, 241n119

Complete Book of the Medical Art (*Pantegni*) (al-Majūsī), 112

complexion: 110, 119, 146. *See also* medicine

conjugal debt, 1, 3, 209n2

Conrad of Austria, 247n56

Constantine of Pisa, 167

Constantine the African, 112

Contra haereticos (*Against Heretics*) (Alan of Lille), 65
Coon, Lynda, 83
copulation, animals, 102, *103*
Corinthians, 23, 220n77
Corpus Iuris Civilis, 125
Council of Clermont, 63
Council of Toledo, 89
court life, 81–82
Cox, Laverne, 161
Crane, Susan, 101, 233n2
creation: Augustine of Hippo and, 22–25, 216n29; with bodies at beginning, 19–22; Eriugena and, 25–26; of Eve, *181*, *182*, *189*; Genesis and, 16–20, 205; hexaemeron and, 214n6; Honorius of Autun on, 26; nonbinary sex and biblical, 31; scenes of, *182*; of world, *180*
Crisciani, Chiara, 170
critical race studies, 38, 66, 68, 231n140
crossdressing, 158, 159, 229n110
crusades, in England, 63–67
cynocephali, 40, 43

Dante, 65
Daston, Lorraine, 58, 116
De corpore humano (*On the Human Body*), 121–23
Decretals of Pope Gregory IX, 256n65
De elementis (Marius), 242n130
Demaitre, Luke, 117
demon-human sex, 89, 92
demons: angelic bodies with, 239n88; angels and, 87–88; depictions of, 89–90, *92*; Jews depicted with, 93–94, *95*, 240n104; as policers of sexuality, 240n103; with *rouelle*, *94*; with uncleanness, 87–95. *See also* devil
De natura rerum (*On the Nature of Things*) (Thomas of Cantimpré), 43–44
De spermate (*On Sperm*), 113, 114–15
devil: body and, 29–30; burns Job's house, *92*; demons, 87–95, *94*, *95*, 239n88, 240n103, 240n104; hyenas and, 236n37; Satan, 89, *90*, *94*, *95*; as shape-shifter, 88; Temptation of Christ and, *91*
devotion, feminized Christ and, 191–94
Dialogue with Trypho (Martyr), 76
dietary distinctions, monsters and humans, 74
differences of sex development (DSD), 8, 211n20
Diodorus of Sicily, 248n79
Dioscorides, Pedanius, 245n32
disability, 35, 56, 127, 227n76

Dominican Order, 116
double-faced, 38, 49, 53, 214n3
Douglas, Mary, 73–74, 236n35
Drager, Emmett Harsin, 206
Dreger, Alice, 8, 157
DSD. *See* differences of sex development
dual sexes, of creation, 22–25

East: *Marvels of the East*, 47, 48, *48*; spatial differences between West and, 46–56. *See also* postcolonial studies
eating: boundaries dissolved by, 87; mouth, vagina and, 90; sexuality and, 74. *See also* food
Eden, 22, 31, 52–53, 166. *See also* paradise
effeminates: court life and, 81–82; Jewish men as, 76; sodomites with hermaphrodites, androgynes and, 231n137
Egerton Master, 51
Eliade, Mircea, 164
Elizabeth of Schönau, 192–93
Elliott, Dyan, 88–89, 100, 240n103
Elucidarium (Honorius of Autun), 239n85
Emerald Tablet, 167
Empedocles, 19
England: Aberdeen Bestiary and, 70, *71*, 72–79, 234n10; crusades and, 63–67; identity and, 66–67; Jewish and Christian relations in, 95–97; on the Hereford *mappamundi*, 58; taxation in, 76
Ephesians, 32
epiphagi, *51*
Epistle of Barnabus, 76
erasure, 13, 161, 268n5
Eriugena, John Scottus. *See* John Scottus Eriugena
ethical violations, 8
Ethiopia, 55, 67, 68. *See also* Africa
Etymologies (Isidore of Seville), 44, 47, 151–52, 236n34
Eugene III (Pope), 83, 238n64
eunuchs, 10, 127, 135, 147–48, 152, 158, 230n111
Evans, Ruth, 14
Eve (biblical figure), 11, 16, 18, 19, 21, 22, 38, 202; Adam and, 177–80, *179*, 183, 188, 226n60; Augustine of Hippo on, 23, 24–25; in Carolingian Bibles, 36; creation of, *181*, *182*, *189*; Eriugena on, 26; *Glossa ordinaria* on, 27; Hexaemeron and, 179–80, *182*; mythic hermaphrodites with Adam and, 183; Peter the Chanter on, 28; sexual heterogeneity and, 31

excrement, 74–75, 85, 235n25
Exemplar (Suso), 191
exemptions, Jews purchasing, 241n114
expulsion: of Jews, 72, 97, 202; of Muslims, 202

faces, Janus, 54, 176, 199, 201, 206
Fausto-Sterling, Anne, 61, 132
Feinberg, Leslie, 8–9
female circumcision (female genital cutting or female genital mutilation), 139
females: bodies, 111; as contrary to nature, 108; with male superiority, 107; as sexual category, 105, 233n3. *See also* women
fetus, and sexual differentiation, 61, 113–15, 117
Flower of Nature (Jacob van Maerlant), 44, 228n90
Fonrobert, Charlotte, 251n124
food, 74, 87. *See also* eating
Ford, A. J., 58
Formation of a Persecuting Society, The (Moore), 97
Foucault, Michel, 156, 260n135
Four Books of Sentences (Lombard), 188, 189
Fourth Lateran Council (1215), 241n112
Friedman, John Block, 42
Friedrich of Brandenberg, 185
Fuentes, Marisa J., 4

Gabriel Biel, 190–91
Galatians, 32, 198
Galen, 107, 110, 112–13, 116, 130, 134, 244n11; influence of, 139; on penis as tendon, 258n104; with sexual organs, "enlarged," 150
Gemini, 176, *177*, *178*, *179*
gender: defined, 61, 229n103; equality, 38; identity, 9, 127, 128, 153, 159, 203; medieval, 62; sex and, 38–39, 61, 134, 157, 205, 207. *See also* transgender
gender-crossing, 29, 59–63, *60*, 158
Gender Trouble (Butler), 61
Genesis, 19–31, 121–22; Augustine of Hippo and, 22; creation and, 16–20, 205; Guibert of Nogent on, 26; Middle Ages and, 26–27; Peter the Chanter on, 28; Priscillianist *tractates* and, 25; subordination in, 24
genitals: *anasyromenos* style, 53; exposed, 65; female genital cutting and, 139; hyena, 76; infants with atypical, 8, 255n58; lack of, 128; with "male" and "female" tissue, 245n29; of monstrous races, 59, *60*; mouth, vagina and, 90; nonbinary, 104–5, 142, 143, 186; surgeries, 8, 158, 255n45; uterus and, 114, *114*; women and "enlarged" sexual organs, 149–51. *See also* surgery
Gérard de Breuil, 248n73
Gerard of Cremona, 112, 115
gestation, and sexual differentiation. *See* fetus
Gilbert, Ruth, 197
Giovanni Malaspina, 128
Glossa ordinaria, 27
Gnostic texts, 20–21
Gratheus, 170
Gratian, 126
Great Mirror (Vincent of Beauvais), 44
Great Surgery (Lanfranc of Milan), 140–42
Great Surgery (Bruno Longobucco), 139–40
Greece, ancient, 19–20, 110
Green, Monica H., 125, 134, 252n139, 254n33
Greenstein, Jack, 179
Gregory IX (Pope), 256n65
Gregory of Nyssa, 21–22, 25, 32, 36
Gregory the Great, 83
Guibert of Nogent, 26, 84, 98
Guido da Vigevano, *114*
Guillem Castelló, 1
Guillaume le Clerc, 77, *78*, 93, *93*
Guy de Chauliac, 120, 134, 137, 139, 143–44, 146, 149, 252n13

Hadewijch of Brabant, 192
hagiography, feminized Christ and, 191–94
Hahn, Thomas, 66
hair, 127, 144
hares: Jews and, 238n75; Christ and, 175; nonbinary sex and, 70, 118
Harrowing of Hell, The, *88*
Hebrew law, 73
hell, 87, *88*
Heng, Geraldine, 66
Henri de Mondeville, 134, 143, 152
Henry II (King of England), 76
Henry Bate, 89
Henry of Brussels, 248n73
Henry of Germany, 248n73
Henry of Suso, 191, *192*
Hereford *mappamundi*, 12, 40, *41*, 55, 58, 63–67
heresy, 18, 25, 28–31
heretics, 29–30, 36, 65, 97, 236n30
herma (boundary stone), 6

hermaphrodites, 4; alchemical, *173*, *174*, *187*; androgynes, 47; Augustine of Hippo and, 24; *Aurora consurgens*, 175–85; "Borghese," 53; boundaries and, 6; connotations, 6, 7, 10, 18; defined, 6, 7, 38, 164; double-faced, 49; etymology, 6; with H, historiated initial, 16, *17*; Hereford *mappamundi* and, 12, 40, 58, 67; in Middle Ages, 6; monsters and, 41, 45–48, 117; sodomites with effeminates, androgynes and, 231n137. *See also* Jesus hermaphrodite; monstrous races; mythic hermaphrodites

hermaphroditism: abstract thinking about, 4–5; androgyny and, 27, 36–37; primal androgyny and, 30; sodomy and, 29

Hermaphroditus (deity), 6, 53, 55, 81, 163, *176*, 183, *184*

Hermes (deity), 6

Hexaemeron (Ambrose), 179–80, *182*

Hildesheim Cathedral, 36

Hillman, Thea, 8

himantopodes, *41*, 64

Hippocrates, 107, 113, 116, 139

Histoire ancienne universelle, 92, 92–93

Histoires prodigieuses (Boaistuau), 94

history: as usable past, 14, 203–5, 207; function in community creation, 9

History of the East, or Jerusalem (James of Vitry), 58

Holmes, Morgan, 8

homosexuality, 66, 219n56, 260n135. *See also* sodomy

Honorius of Autun, 26, 239n85

Hostiensis, 30, 128–29, 153, 258n113

Hugh of Saint-Cher (c. 1200–1263), 29, 66, 191

Huguccio, 126–29

Hulme, Peter, 74

human experience, transgender as, 210n18

human identity, 4, 5, 33, 42–43, 55, 68

human rights, bodies and, 9, 160

Human Rights Watch, 157

humans: behavior, bestiaries as regulator of, 80; bodies with natural philosophy and laws, 121–24; defined, 103–4; demon-human sex, 89, 92; dietary distinctions and, 74; monstrous races and definitions of, 42–45, 68–69; organisms and, 222n8; posthuman studies, 7, 42

husbands, conjugal debt and, 144–45, 209n2

hybridity: 7, 130, 194, 262n7.

hyenas: in Aberdeen Bestiary, 70, *71*, 77, 87, 96–97, 101; devil and, 236n37; genitals, 76; hell and,

87; Jews and, 72–73, 241n119; uncleanness of, 74, 86, 87

Iberian "Reconquista," 63

Ibn Sīnā, 106, 115, 117–18, 120, 134; with surgical traditions, 138–39; with Muslim traditions of sex, 109–12; with sexual organs, "enlarged," 149–50

identity: England and, 66–67; gender, 9, 127, 128, 153, 159, 203; human, 4, 5, 33, 42–43, 55, 68; intersex pride and, 8

Image on the Edge (Camille), 243n1

immortality, 21, 35, 107, 166

impotence, 144–49

incarceration, 204

infants: with atypical genitals, 8, 144, 255n58; with intersex variations, 8; monstrous births and, 56–59; prodigies and intersex, 124–25; with medieval definitions of humanity and intersex, 56–59

Inferno (Dante), 65

infertility, 245n29

intersectionality, 222n7

intersex, 1; afterlife and, 35; categories, 111; defined, 8, 10, 243n4; with identity, 8; infants, 8, 56–59, 124–25; LGBT communities and, 9; medieval marriage and, 210n7; variations, 8, 9, 157–58, 161, 204–5. *See also* laws; medicine; surgery

intersex people (people with intersex variations), 4, 5, 161, 202; activism and rights of, 8–10, 157, 204

intersex studies, 7, 8, 10, 160, 202, 212n32

Inventarium, or Great Surgery (Chauliac), 143–44, 149

Irenaeus, 20

Isagoge (Johannitius), 112

Isidore of Seville, 151–52, 236n34, 245n32; monstrous races and, 40, 44, 47, 48, 54, 57–58; sex and, 112

Islam, 30, 64, 110, 230n121, 231n131; and race and racism, 66–69. *See also* 'Abbāsid caliphate; Muslims

Jacob van Maerlant, 44, 228n90

Jacopo de Varagine, 54

James le Palmer, 16, *17*, 38, 49, 58

James of Venice, 81, 234n10

Janus (deity): double-faced, 49, 53, 214n3; faces, 54, *176*, 199, 201, 206; mythic hermaphrodites and, 53, 55; with single divine faculty, 226n66; temple of, 53–54; two doors and, *54*

Jean of Soissons (Count), 84
Jerome, 23, 31, 33, 239n87
Jerusalem, 64–65
Jesus hermaphrodite, 201; alchemical knowledge in medieval Europe, 165–68; *Aurora consurgens* and, 171–75; *Aurora consurgens* hermaphrodite, visual tradition of, 175–85; in context, 185–87; with feminized Christ, devotion and hagiography, 191–94; nonbinary sex, metamorphosis and, 194–99; rise of, 24; scholastic contributions, 168–71; scholastic theological approaches, 187–91
Jewish culture, 21, 27, 38; with androgyne, spiritual, 20; circumcision and, 255n58; circumcision and medieval, 254n26; Hebrew law and, 73; rabbinic law, 125, 251n124
Jews, 32; Aberdeen Bestiary and, 70, 72–79, 96, 98; Albert the Great on, 236n30; anti-Judaism, 84, 96–98, 232n141; with burning bush and golden calf, 77, 78; cannibalism, accused of, 96; Christians and, 12, 63–64, 71–72, 95–97; demons depicted with, 93–94, 95, 240n104; excrement and, 74–75; exemptions and, 241n114; expulsion of, 72, 97, 202; Fourth Lateran Council and, 241n112; hares and, 238n75; heretics, depicted as, 236n30; himantopodes and, 64; hyenas and, 72–73, 241n119; manticore and, 74; as moneylenders, 76, 98; Muslims and, 231n126; with race and racism, 76, 98, 236n30; sexual intercourse between Christians and, 241n119; sodomites, depicted as, 236n30; uncleanness and, 76; violence against, 12, 95, 97
Jiménez de Rada, Rodrigo, 27–28
Johannitius, 112
John Dastin, 167
John Mandeville, 43, 49, 50, 51, 51
John of Rupescissa, 170
John of Salisbury, 81–83, 84, 98, 238n64
John the Fearless, 49
Johns Scottus Eriugena, 36, 217n44, 220nn81–82; creation and, 25–26; influence of, 30; on resurrection, 32–33
Jordan-Young, Rebecca, 61
Juden Erbarkeit, Der, 94, 94
Julian of Norwich, 192
Jung, C. G., 164
Justin Martyr, 76

Kane, Bronach, 256n66
Karkazis, Katrina, 8, 61
Karras, Ruth Mazo, 62, 147, 154, 158
Katherine Paynell, 147, 148
Kay, Sarah, 79, 101
Kaye, Joel, 166
Kessler, Suzanne, 8, 156–57
Khanmohamadi, Shirin, 45
khuntha, 111, 125
Kim, Dorothy, 66
Kim, Susan, 45
kingdom, bodies as metaphor for, 96–97, 241n119
Kirshner, Julius, 250n110
Kline, Naomi, 65, 231n126
Koch-Rein, Anson, 223n10
Kuefler, Mathew, 125, 148, 230n111

Lanfranc of Milan, 120, 134, 148, 156, 248n79, 252n13, 254nn36–41; surgical traditions and, 140–42; with sexual organs, "enlarged," 149, 150–51
Laqueur, Thomas, 155–56, 248n79, 252n140
Latin Europe, sex differentiation in, 112–16
Laurent, Bo, 8
laws: canon, 126–29; Hebrew, 73; rabbinic, 125, 251n124; Roman, 57, 106, 124–29, 147. *See also* natural philosophy, laws and
Lectura ordinaria super sacram scripturam. *See Ordinary Reading on the Sacred Scripture*
Letter of a Good Man (John Dastin), 167
Leviticus, 70, 73, 74, 76, 77, 83, 86
LGBT community, 9, 204
licensing, physicians with training and, 135–37, 252n8
life chances, 204
Lifshitz, Felice, 25
Linkinen, Tom, 62, 158
Literal Meaning of Genesis, The (Augustine of Hippo), 22, 23–24
Little, Lester K., 99
Livre des merveilles. *See Book of Marvels*
Livy, 125
Lollards, 84–85
Lombard, Peter. *See* Peter Lombard
Long, Kathleen P., 197
Louis of Orléans, 183
Lucifer, 90. *See also* demons; devil

Macrobius, 54, 193
al-Majūsī, 112, 138–39, 140, 141

Making Sex (Laqueur), 155, 252n140
males: bodies, 111; with female inferiority, 62, 107; as sexual category, 105, 233n3. *See also* men
Mandeville, John. *See* John Mandeville
Mandeville's Travels (John Mandeville), 43, *50*, 51, *51*
manticore, 74, *75*, 96
mappamundi (map of the world), 47; church-commissioned, 67; defined, 41; fifteenth-century, 49; Hereford, 12, 40, *41*, 55, 58, 63–67; monsters of medieval, 55, 58; monstrous races and, 40
Marco Polo, 49
Mare historiarum (Giovanni Colonna), 49, *50*, 176
Marius, 242n130
Markow, Deborah, 35
marriage: annulment and, 144–45, 209n6; Augustine of Hippo on, 23; with behavior, standards, 3; impotence and, 144–47; intersex and medieval, 210n7
Marriage of Philology and Mercury, The (Remigius of Auxerre), 83–84
Martin, Dale B., 38, 214n5
Marvels of the East, 47, 48, *48*
masculinity: androgyny as unity in, 38; as superior to femininity, 129, 130
Mathews, Thomas, 191
Matthew of Paris, 96
Mayr-Harting, Henry, 89
McVaugh, Michael R., 209n1, 256n76
medical cosmetics, 136–37, 157
medicine, natural philosophy and, 244n11
medicine: Albert the Great and, 120–21; Muslim traditions of, 109–12; impotence and, 145–49; intersex and, 8, 146, 157; laws and, 128–29; licensing and training, 135–37; sex differentiation in Latin Europe and, 112–16; surgery and, 135–37; translations and, 112; types of practitioners of, 136, 252n4; women's and reproductive, 137. *See also* surgery
Medicine Before the Plague (McVaugh), 209n1, 252n4
medicus, 146–47
men, 32, 34, 47, 127; castration and, 148; impotence and, 144–49; Jews portrayed as effeminate, 76; nonbinary-sexed figures and wild, *52;* as sexual initiators, 258n100. *See also* males
Merchant's Tale, The (Chaucer), 55
Metalogicon (John of Salisbury), 238n63
Metamorphoses (Ovid), 6, 81, 163

metamorphosis: Barkan on, 262n6; hybridity and, 7; Jesus hermaphrodite, nonbinary sex and, 194–99; power of, 262n7
Metzler, Irina, 35, 144
Michael Scot, 30, 115
Midrash Rabbah, 214n3
Miller, Sara Alison, 100
Mills, Robert, 29, 158–59, 243n1, 261n144
minority groups, violence against, 97. *See also* Jews; Muslims
Mittman, Asa, 42, 45, 58
mixtures, purity and, 80
mollis, 152, 258n108
monastic women, 25
Mondeville, Henri de. *See* Henri de Mondeville
Money, John, 229n103
money: 99; as unclean, 76, 78; moneylenders, Jews as, 76, 98
Mongols, 64, 65, 235n21
monsters, 42–45, 228n87; Adam and, 43; Aristotle and, 108; bodies and, 43; defined, 42–43; dietary distinctions and, 74; etymology, 56; hermaphrodites and, 41, 45–48, 117; of medieval *mappaemundi*, 55, 58; in Middle Ages, 43; modern recasting of, 223n10
monstrous births, 56–59
monstrous races: 40, *50*; Augustine of Hippo on, 43; bestiaries and, 73; blemmyes, 40, 45, 51, *51*; boundaries and, 45; cynocephali, 40, 43; epiphagi, 51, *51*; without evolution-change, 230n112; genitals of, 59, *60*; Hereford Map, Muslims and crusades in England, 63–67; himantopodes, *41*, 64; with human, definitions of, 42–45, 68–69; intersex infants in medieval West and, 56–59; *mappaemundi* and, 40; mythic hermaphrodites and, 45–46, 62, 183; nonbinary sex, gender-crossing, sexual boundaries and, 59–63, *60*; Pliny the Elder and, 40; sex and, 62; with spatial differences between East and West, 46–56
Moore, R. I., 97
Moral Commentary on Genesis (Guibert of Nogent), 26
moralism, bestiaries with naturalism and, 233n6
Morland, Ian, 7, 8
mortality rates, of transgender people, 204
mortality: and fall from paradise, 21, 29–30; of organisms, 107. *See also* immortality
Moses (biblical figure), 77

mouth, vagina and, 90. *See also* eating
Muhammad, 65, 231n131
multiple-sexed, 20, 233n3
multispecies theory, 42, 222n8. *See also* animals, critical animal studies
Muratova, Xenia, 72, 234n10
Murray, Jacqueline, 146, 148
Muslims: cannibalism, accused of, 235n21; Christians and, 64–65, 97, 98, 99, 230n118, 242n124; expulsion of, 202; Fourth Lateran Council and, 241n112; Hereford Map, crusades in England and, 63–67; heresy, accused of, 65; influences of Greek antiquity and, 110; Jews and, 231n126; naturalist and medical traditions of, 109–12; racism and, 66–69; surgical traditions of, 137–39; with traditions of sex, 109–12. *See also* 'Abbāsid caliphate; Islam
mythic hermaphrodites, 41, 73, 98, 121; with Adam and Eve, 183; with behavioral reversals, 49; bipedal, 45; crossdressers and, 229n110; images, 47, 59, *60*, 61, 62, 66, 133, 181; Janus and, 53, 55; as against kind, 45; with lack of sexually divided labor, 53, 62, 63; as monstrous race, 45–46, 62, 183; split, 49, *50*

Natural History (Pliny the Elder), 40, 44, 47, 57
naturalism: defined, 106, 233n6, 243n7. *See also* medicine; natural philosophy
Naturalist, The. See *Physiologus*
nature, 53, 56–57, 66, 102; natural philosophy and, 108, 117–20, 122–23; as Nature/Natura (goddess), 86–87, 193; surgery and, 142–43. *See also* monsters; monstrous births; sodomy
naturalists, 12, 131, 161, 164, 243n7
natural philosophy: medicine and, 244n11; in premodern period, 243n7
natural philosophy, laws and: Albert the Great and, 117–21; Aristotelian theories and, 106–9; human body and, 121–24; Muslim traditions of sex and, 109–12; Roman and canon law and, 106, 124–29; sex differentiation in Latin Europe and, 112–16; *Summa "Omnes homines"* and, 130–31
natural questions, 130, 251n129
Neal, Derek, 147, 261n145
Nederman, Cary J., 250n110
Neo-Platonic tradition, 21
neuter, 36, 37, 190, 233n3
neutericum, 84

"New Logic," of Aristotle, 81, 106. *See also* Aristotle
Newman, Barbara, 193
New Pearl of Great Price, The (Petrus Bonus of Ferrara), 168–69
Nicholas of Lyra, 30, 33
Nicholas of Tournai, 29
Nicholas, Paynell, 147, 148
nonbinary: genitals, 104–5, 142, 143, 186; reduced to a binary, 126; transgressions, 83–85; unclean sex and, 85–87
nonbinary sex, 4–7, 10; anatomies, 131, 134, 137, 253n15; biblical creation and, 31; Christianity and, 11–12, 32–37; chronology, 11–15; defined, 10; at end of time, 32–36; figures, *41, 48, 50, 52*; gender-crossing, sexual boundaries and, 59–63, *60*; and human identity, 133, 160, 204–5; Jesus hermaphrodite, metamorphosis and, 194–99; in Middle Ages, 4; self and, 5, 202; transcendence and, 203
Norman consolidation of Sicily, 63
Northumberland Bestiary, 79, *79*, 233n8, 236n43

Obrist, Barbara, 170
Odo of Tournai, 75
Odoric of Pordenone, 49
Olsen, Glenn W., 231n137
Omne bonum (James le Palmer), 16, *17*, 38, 49, 58
Omont, Henri Auguste, 52
On Animals (Albert the Great), 120, 131, 143, 176; copulating, 102, *103*; marginal figures, 102, *104, 105*
On Animals (Aristotle), 102, 107, 115, 247n56
one-sex theory (Laqueur), 155–56, 248n79
On Minerals (Albert the Great), 117
On Plants (Aristotle), 117
On Sperm (*De spermate*), 113, 114–15
On Surgery and Instruments (Al-Zahrāwī), 138
On the Division of Nature. See *Periphyseon*
On the Generation of Animals (Aristotle), 30, 107, 108, 116, 117, 143, 168
On the Human Body (*De corpore humano*), 121–23
On the Literal Meaning of Genesis (Augustine of Hippo), 121
On the Nature of Animals (Ibn Sīnā), 117
On the Nature of Things. See *De natura rerum*
On the Properties of Things (Bartholomew the Englishman), 44, 45
On the Resurrection (Albert the Great), 35
On the Trinity (Augustine of Hippo), 23

Ordinary Reading on the Sacred Scripture (*Lectura ordinaria super sacram scripturam*), 31
ordination, and priesthood, 124, 127, 130
organisms: 107; humans and, 109, 222n8; mortal, 107; superiority of, 109
Orientalism. *See* Edward Said; postcolonial studies
Origen of Alexandria, 21, 22, 25, 36
Oswald, Dana, 42, 43, 59, 225n40
other, self and, 5, 46–47, 55, 68–69, 99
Otto of Freising, 33–34, 35, 133
Ovid, 6, 7, 54, 81, 163, 175, 183, 194, 195

Pantegni. See *Complete Book of the Medical Art*
paradise, 22, 31. *See also* Eden; afterlife
Paris synod (1210), 30
Park, Katharine, 58, 110, 116, 147
Pastoral Care (Gregory the Great), 83
Paul (biblical figure), 23, 32, 220n77
Paulus (jurist), 125
Penitentials of Theodore, 258n108
perfection: in alchemy, 166, 169; bodies and, 33–35, 198; with resurrection, 35; sexual division and, 215n10. *See also* immortality
performativity (theory), 61
Periphyseon (*On the Division of Nature*) (Eriugena), 25–26, 32, 217n44, 220n81
personhood, 35, 39, 57, 160
Peter Abelard, 43, 81
Peter Comestor, 27
Peter Lombard, 188, 189
Peter of Abano, 150
Peter of Auvergne, 45
Peter of Eboli, 152
Peter of Palude, 123–24
Peter of Poitiers, 66
Peter the Chanter, 28–29, 66
Peter the Venerable (1092–1156), 65, 77
Petrus Bonus of Ferrara, 165, 168–70, 172, 175, 186
Phillips, Kim, 46
Philo of Alexandria, 20
philosophers' stone, 162, 165, 166, 195–96
physicians: status and conflict with surgeons, 135–36, training and licensing of, 135–36, 252n8. *See also* medicine; surgeons
Physiologus (*The Naturalist*), 76, 236n34
Pierre Bersuire, 193
Pizan, Christine de. *See* Christine de Pizan
Plaint of Nature (Alan of Lille), 85, 87, 193
plants, 120, 122,124, 167, 169

Plato, 20, 21, 38, 199, 215n10
Pliny the Elder (23–79 CE), 40, 44, 47, 57, 248n79
Policraticus (John of Salisbury), 81, 83, 84
polygamy, sodomy and, 65
Posterior Analytics (Aristotle), 81
posthuman studies, 7, 42, 223n9
postcolonial studies, 46–7, 68, 232n154
Postilla (Nicholas of Lyra), 30
poverty, 99, 186, 204
Prester John (King), 66–67
pride, intersex with identity and, 8
primal androgyne, 201; embraced, 25–26; rejected, 26–28, 122; views on, 29–30
primal androgyny, 17–18, 21, 30, 53, 177
Prior Analytics (Aristotle), 81
Priscillian (bishop of Avila), 25
Priscillianist *tractates*, 25
Problemata Aristotelis ac philosophorum medicorumque complurium, 130
Prose Salernitan Questions, 113, 251n129
proto-humans, Zeus and, 20
purity (*puritas*): mixtures and, 80; systems and communal integrity, 236n35
pygmies, 45

queer of color critique, 222n7
queer temporality, 206–7, 212n30, 268n10
Questions Concerning on Animals (Albert the Great), 117, 119, 247n56
quodlibetal works, 89, 236n30, 248n73

rabbinic law, 125, 251n124
race and racism, 66–9, 76, 98, 231n140, 236n30
Ragab, Ahmed, 132
Ratramnus of Corbie, 43
Reims Cathedral, 89
Reis, Elizabeth, 8, 243n5
Religious Poverty and the Profit Economy in Medieval Europe (Little), 99
Remigius of Auxerre, 83–84
resurrection: of bodies, 18, 32–35; Christianity and, 32; disability and, 32, 35; perfection with, 35; women in, 34
Richard Anglicus, 167
Rising Dawn. See *Aurora consurgens*
Roger Bacon, 165, 166
Roland of Cremona, 189–90
Rolandus Passagerii, 126
Rolker, Christof, 129, 210n7, 250n110

Rome, ancient: calendars, 54; laws, 57, 106, 124–29, 147
Rosario, Vernon A., 157
Rubin, David A., 8
Rubin, Miri, 155
Rykener, John/Eleanor, 158, 260n133

sacraments. *See* baptism; marriage; ordination
Said, Edward, 46
Salamon, Gayle, 62, 161–62
Salisbury, Joyce, 79, 101
Salmacis (mythical character), 6, 81, 152, 163, *176*, 183, *184*
Sapientia (Wisdom), 172, *173*, 191, *192*
Satan: with attendants, 94, *95*; Council of Toledo and, 89; Lucifer with Christ in majesty, *90*. *See also* demons; devil
Scalenghe, Sara, 111
scatological language, 74–75, 85
scholarship, premodern perspectives and modern, 7–11
Scholastic History (Peter Comestor), 27
scholasticism: Albert the Great and, 117, 121; Aristotle and, 81, 116; definitions of the human and, 45; surgery and, 143; theology and, 27–28, 30–31, 34–35, 87; in universities, 115–16; with binaries, 81
Scorn for the World (Bernard of Cluny), 85–87
Scott, Joan W., 11, 61
Secrets of My Lady of Alchemy, The, 170–71, *171*
Secrets of Women ([Ps.]Albert the Great), 129, 130, 175
self: nonbinary sex and, 5, 202; other and, 5, 46–47, 55, 68–69, 99
sex (*sexus*): assignment, 109, 118–19, 124, 126–29, 141; biological, 33, 61, 204; with classification, systems of, 5–7; constructed nature of, 252n140; demon-human, 89, 92; differentiation in Latin Europe, 112–16; DSD, 8, 211n20; gender and, 38–39, 61, 134, 157, 205, 207; hair and, 127; monstrous races and, 62; Muslims and traditions of, 109–12; nonbinary and unclean, 85–87; one-sex theory, 155–56, 248n79; uncleanness and, 102; women as inferior, 82. *See also* nonbinary sex
sexual arousal: in impotence trials, 145–47, 256n66; law and, 125–26; surgery and, 141–42; women and, 149–51
sexual boundaries: 29, 149–51, 154; angels without, 88–89; gender-crossing, nonbinary sex and, 59–63, *60*; uncleanness and, 131. *See also* sodomy
sexual categories: as active and passive, 28–29, 61, 118–19, 141; animals with assigned, 233n3; male and female, 62, 105, 233n3
sexual division, perfection and, 109, 118–20, 122–23, 215n10
sexual duality, 16, 73
sexual heterogeneity, 31
sexual intercourse: between Jews and Christians, 241n119; in paradise, 22, 26; and sex assignment, 119, 141. *See also* sodomy; asexuals; impotence
sexuality: as active and passive, 28–29, 119, 141, 157; demons as policers of, 240n103; eating and, 74; gender-crossing, nonbinary sex and, 59–63. *See also* sexual arousal; sodomy
sexual organs: 70, 89–93, 108, 127; surgical interventions and, 137–44; women with "enlarged," 149–51. *See also* genitals
sexual reproduction (generation), 21, 26, 130, 166–69, 194
shape-shifting, 88, 262n7
Showings (Julian of Norwich), 192
Sic et non (*Yes and No*) (Abelard), 81
Sicily, Norman consolidation of, 63
Sidonian traditions, 20
Sigismund (Emperor), 185
sodomites, 10, 71, 76, 99, 159, 196, 218n55, 219n58, 219n62; with effeminates, hermaphrodites and androgynes, 231n137; heretics and Jews accused as, 236n30; Muslims accused as, 65; uncleanness with, 85–86
sodomy: androgynes, heresy and, 18, 28–31; hermaphroditism and, 29; polygamy and, 65; prohibitions of, 261n144; as sin against nature, 66, 86–87, 151
Solomon (biblical figure), 73
Sophistical Refutations (Aristotle), 81
Soranus, 112, 245n32
souls, bodies and, 44; as sexless, 35
Spade, Dean, 161
spatial differences, West and East, 46–56
Speculum Historiale (Vincent of Beauvais), 235n21
sperm, 113, 114–15, 120
spiritual androgyne, 20
Spiritual Franciscans, 186
spirituality: temporality and, 85; worldliness and, 80–81

Steel, Karl, 45, 248n75
Stephan of Antioch, 139
Stephen Langton, 29
Stock, Brian, 57
Strickland, Debra, 64, 66, 76, 232n141, 241n114, 241n119
Stryker, Susan, 9, 14, 159–60, 223n10
subaltern subjects, dealing with, 221n95
subordination, 18, 24, 37
Summa conservationis et curationis (William of Saliceto), 249n94, 256n69
Summa of Confession (Peter of Poitiers), 66
Summa of Theology (Alexander of Hales), 121
Summa "Omnes homines," 130–31
Summa on the Decretum (Huguccio), 126–27
Summa on the Notarial Art (Rolandus Passagerii), 126
Summa theologiae (Thomas Aquinas), 31
surgeons: bodies altered by, 3, 134, 143; with empirical observations, 254n36; expertise of, 135–37
surgery: medieval traditions of, 120–21, 137–44; with bodies, hard, soft, active, passive, 151–56; with bodies, impotent and castrated, 144–49; interventions on nonbinary bodies and, 137–44; modern perspective and medieval, 156–62; women with "enlarged" sexual organs and, 149–51
surgical instruction, institutionalizing of, 135–37, 252n6
Symposium (Plato), 20, 21, 199

Tartakoff, Paola, 97
taxation, in England, 76
Taylor, Rabun, 226n66
teleological thinking, 10, 161, 207, 244n11
teleologies, 107
telos, 107, 151, 258n102
temporality, spirituality and, 85; as queer, 206–7, 268n10
Temptation of Christ, *91*
tension, tenses and, 201–7
Teodorico Borgognoni, 252n12
Terkla, Dan, 222n1
Tertullian, 33
Testacea, 109
Thomas Aquinas, 30–31, 117, 152, 190, 239n88, 248n75
Thomas of Cantimpré, 43–45, 46, 58, 120

Thomas of Monmouth, 96
three-orders model, 221n98
Timaeus (Plato), 215n10
Time, as nonlinear, 199, 201, 206–7. *See also* queer temporality
Topics (Aristotle), 81
Tractatus de incarnatione contra Judaeos. See *Treatise on the Incarnation Against the Jews*
traditional birth attendants, 144
training: physicians with licensing and, 135–37, 252n8. *See also* medicine; surgeons
transcendence, 31, 37, 196, 203
transgender: defined, 9–10, 159–60; histories, 9, 158–60; as human experience, 210n18; studies, 7, 8, 10, 38, 160, 202, 212n32
transgender people: activism of, 8–9, 205–6; bodies of, 9–10; children, 204; erasure of, 161, 268n5; intersex and, 9; mortality rates, 204; violence against, 204
Transgender Studies Reader 2 (Stryker and Aizura), 9, 160
Transgender Warriors (Feinberg), 8–9
travel manuscripts, 49–50
travelogues, 40
Travill, Anthony, 117
Treatise on the Incarnation Against the Jews (*Tractatus de incarnatione contra Judaeos*) (Guibert of Nogent), 84
True, Jacqui, 250n110
tumtum, 125, 213n37
Twelve Conclusions of the Lollards, The, 84–85

Uebel, Michael, 46, 55
Ugo Borgognoni, 140, 150
Ulpian, 125
uncleanness: demonic, 87–95; of hyenas, 74, 86, 87; Jews accused of, 76; John of Salisbury and, 81–83; Leviticus and, 73; sex and, 85–87, 102, 131; with sodomites, 85–86. *See also* bestiaries
Urban II (Pope), 63
uterus, 113–14, *114*

vagina, mouth and, 90
Van der Lugt, Maaike, 120, 249n83
Venerabili (Teodorico), 252n12
Verbum adbreviatum (Peter the Chanter), 28–29
Verner, Lisa, 57
Vesianus Pelegrini, 1, 3, 134, 144, 154–55, 209n1
Vicinus, Martha, 221n95

Victorines, 27
Vincent of Beauvais, 44, 235n21
violence: against Jews, 12, 95, 97; against Muslims, 67, 98; against transgender people, 204
Virgin Mary, 172–74, 185–86
virginity, 62, 111, 229n110. *See also* celibacy; Virgin Mary
Visiones (Elizabeth of Schönau), 192–93
Vitry, Jacques de, 58

Walter of Mortagne, 145
Wenceslas of Prague, 185
West, spatial differences with East, 46–56
Westminster Abbey Bestiary, 59, *60*
Whitaker, Cord, 66
William of Saliceto, 134, 150, 249n94, 256n69
William of St. Thierry, 191
wisdom, androgynous, *192*

womanhood, 3, *127*, 149
women, 129, 130, 175; Azo on, 125–26; bodies of, 100; as failed males, 108, 130; as inferior sex, 62, 82; monastic, 25; polluting, depicted as, 100; in resurrection, 34; sexual arousal and, 149–51, 256n66; with sexual organs, "enlarged," 149–51; and sodomy, 151; subordination of, 18, 24, 37. *See also* Eve; females
worldliness, spirituality and, 80–81

Yes and No. See *Sic et non*

Zahlten, Johannes, 179
Al-Zahrāwī, 138–39, 141, 149, 155
Zentralbibliothek manuscript, *Aurora consurgens*, 173–75, *173*, *174*, 184
Zeus (deity), 20
Zoroastrian traditions, 20

GPSR Authorized Representative: Easy Access System Europe, Mustamäe tee
50, 10621 Tallinn, Estonia, gpsr.requests@easproject.com